Olivia's Story

First Edition 2010

Published in the United States by
Paragon House
1925 Oakcrest Avenue
St. Paul, MN 55113

Library of Congress Cataloging-in-Publication Data

Copeland, Jeffrey S. (Jeffrey Scott), 1953-
  Olivia's story : the conspiracy of heroes behind Shelley v. Kraemer / by Jeffrey S. Copeland. -- 1st ed.
    p. cm.
  Summary: "The story behind the landmark 1948 Supreme Court decision, Shelley vs. Kraemer, which struck down racially-based housing restrictions and opened the door to fair housing regulations in the United States "--Provided by publisher.
  ISBN 978-1-55778-884-9 (hardcover : alk. paper)
  1. Shelley, J. D.--Trials, litigation, etc. 2. Kraemer, Louis--Trials, litigation, etc. 3. Discrimination in housing--Law and legislation--United States--Cases. 4. Real covenants--United States.--Cases. 5. African Americans--Civil rights--Cases. 6. Discrimination in housing--Law and legislation--Missouri--St. Louis--Cases. I. Title.
  KF228.S53C67 2010
  344.73'0636351--dc22
                              2009038971

Cover photo credit: Special thanks to photographer Douglas Hartley for a current photo of the J. D. Shelley house at 4600 Labadie Avenue. The photo of Olivia and Inman Perkins is used courtesy of Paula Perkins-Taylor.

The paper used in this publication meets the minimum requirements of American National Standard for Information Sciences—Permanence of Paper for Printed Library Materials, ANSI Z39.48-1984.

Manufactured in the United States of America
10 9 8 7 6 5 4 3 2 1

For current information about all releases from Paragon House,
visit the web site at http://www.paragonhouse.com

Olivia's Story

The Conspiracy of Heroes Behind
Shelley v. Kraemer

by
Jeffrey S. Copeland

PARAGON HOUSE

Dedicated to the memory of J. D. Shelley, James T. Bush, and all those who came before us who gave so much of themselves for so many in the fight for justice and equality for all.

And for Margaret Bush Wilson and Dick Gregory, two true American treasures.

Contents

Author's Note

Many battles have been fought through the years to gain dignity, justice, and equality for all in America. Few of those battles have had the lasting significance and impact of the one described in the telling of Olivia's story. Olivia Merriweather Perkins joined a brave group of people in St. Louis, Missouri, who came together, without regard for their own personal safety and well-being, to fight for rights that had been denied to so many for so long. Their sacrifices eventually led to *Shelley v. Kraemer,* one of the most important legal battles of modern times, one that was felt in every corner of this country. It changed the face of a nation, not only in housing practices, but also in other areas taken for granted today. It is a story that shows the power of dreams and how these dreams can come true if people are willing to fight for them. This country still has much to do. I hope those who read this book will be inspired to take up this fight and continue to wage the war for equality and freedom.

All major events of *Olivia's Story* are true. The details of these events were gathered from archives, records centers, and legal documents of the period. However, as important as those materials were, they did not present enough of the humanity inside the story. This human side was collected through visits and interviews with many of the principal characters presented in these pages, as well as their children and other relatives, all of whom provided rich details of one of the alternately darkest and brightest periods in modern American history. It was through their actions, and especially their sacrifices, that seeds were planted, seeds that have produced a new era of equality and understanding. This change, this journey, still has far to go, but because of the actions of these brave individuals, our future is bright.

It should also be noted the time period involved was compressed to allow the story to unfold as presented. Also, for the obvious reasons, some of the names have been changed, and other characters are composites of several.

JSC

1

Emancipation
July 7, 1947

There were five goats in my kitchen.

Five.

Goats.

I guess I shouldn't have been all that surprised. When Elsie Dunsmore had her own "emancipation party," she came home to find a white horse in her living room. That poor thing looked like a fugitive from a glue factory, but it was still a full grown, sway-backed, hay-chomping, road-apple producing, living nightmare that wouldn't budge from the bale of hay next to her couch. It took five grown men to push it out of there and into her back-yard before guests arrived. To this day no one knows for sure, but rumor had it that "Thunderbolt" had just been retired from pull-ing a cart for the old scissors and knife sharpener in the neigh-borhood over by Fairgrounds Park. It was also rumored Charles Fredericks paid five dollars for the nag before somehow urging it all the way across town to Elsie's house. If he gave five dollars, he got taken. After the party, Thunderbolt lived in Elsie's yard for a whole week, until an elderly man with a floppy straw hat came by and offered to take it off her hands for five dollars. Elsie said the man looked suspiciously like the old scissors sharpener, but she gave him the five anyway.

I set down my box of groceries, put my hands on my hips, and just stared at the goats, who were now all staring back at me. I noticed each one had a letter painted on its side. There was T, R,

Y, A, and P roaming back and forth behind the table. I was trying to figure out the significance of the letters when the tallest of the lot wagged his head back and forth and charged toward me.

"Whoa!" I shouted as I quickly stepped around to the other side of the table. I kept going and propped opened the back screen door. My broom was on the porch, so I grabbed it and began ushering the goats outside. From the lilac bushes at the back corner of my lot I could hear muffled laughter.

"If that's you, Charles Fredericks, you're in big trouble, Buster!"

Swinging the broom wildly from side to side, I ran toward the bushes. I couldn't see their faces, but I saw the backsides of two men running as fast as they could down the alley. When I turned around to go back to the house, all five goats were standing right behind me. I started to swat them with the broom, but I stopped. I just stood there, sighed, and shook my head. I knew I'd been had. The goats were also now standing in perfect order: P A R T Y. I laughed until it felt like my appendix was going to explode.

These get-togethers were called emancipation parties with good reason. And at the party tonight, my best friend, Ella Jane Dunbar, was being emancipated—in more ways than one.

We lived in the section of St. Louis called "the Ville," just a short streetcar ride from the main downtown district. The Ville's borders were clearly defined: Taylor Avenue on the west, Sarah Street on the east, St. Louis Avenue on the north, and Easton Avenue at the southern rim. There were invisible fences along each one of those streets that kept families both in and out of the area, if not literally then symbolically, and we all knew it. There were precious few areas in the city where folks with dark faces could own their own property. The Ville was the best of these. Because of the real estate covenants in place in St. Louis, if we lived in most any other part of the city, we could only rent—not own—our own homes. The Ville had its own schools, stores, churches, and even a first-rate medical facility in Homer G. Phillips Hospital. In so many ways it was an island, but it was our island.

And we were proud of it. So proud.

Whenever a family bought a home in the Ville, it was cause for great celebration. Everyone knew that family had arrived, in every sense of the word. At least in part, they had also become emancipated from the legal covenants that said where people could, and could not, live in St. Louis. Now they were free to make their houses truly their homes, to plant roots that often grew from generation to generation as homes were passed down through families. The Ville itself also became an extended part of this home. We watched over each other on our island with care, devotion, and love. And tonight, we were welcoming a new member of our family.

Ella had just recently bought a small frame home two streets over from mine. The previous residents, the Edwards family, moved back to Mississippi, and they had no relatives interested in purchasing the home. Ella gave piano lessons to their youngest child every Wednesday afternoon and was there the day Mr. Edwards got word his uncle wanted him to come back to Jackson to work in his auto garage. Ella waited a respectable period of time—two days—before going back over there to express her interest in the home. No use waiting longer and risking someone else getting into the negotiations….

The emancipation parties were most often held in the newly purchased home, but Ella had decided to wallpaper the entire house, including the kitchen, and the place now looked, to put it charitably, like a tornado had swept through. The front porch, the bathroom, and a few other areas also needed work, so the renovation process was going to take some time. We had about two months before the school year would begin again, and it looked to me like Ella would need the entire time to make the place livable. I have no idea what possessed me, but when she asked if her party could instead be held at my home because hers wouldn't be ready by the date set for the event, I said yes. It was on my walk home from Ella's place that afternoon I suddenly realized what I had put myself in for. Emancipation parties were joyous celebrations, but they could also be exercises in the most extreme form of juvenile humor and behavior. I do have to admit, however, that this was part of the experience that no one would have changed for all the tea in Tortuga.

Tradition held that each guest had to bring a housewarming gift for the new owner. However, this gift had to be something completely useless, silly, or downright impractical. Typical gifts at past parties included electric lamps without cords, radios without control knobs, brooms with about a dozen bristles, pots and pans with holes drilled in the bottom of them, and, yes, even a horse in the living room. My favorite gift of all time, though, was a mattress given to Jack Enright when he moved into his new home just down the street from me. It had been given with such a straight face that at first he was really touched and thought it wasn't one of the silly gifts. That is, he thought that way until he tried to go to sleep that night and found out coat hangers had been sewn to the top of the mattress under the fitted sheet. Every time he rolled over he hit a spot more lumpy and painful than the last. When he finally discovered what was going on, it was already well after one in the morning. He immediately went outside and let out a yell that woke half the neighborhood. He also showed off marks and bruises on his back and legs for over a week—and did so with pride and a smile on his lips.

These "gifts" were, however, only part of the tradition. They were given the night of the party as a playful way of saying, "Welcome to the neighborhood." About two or three days after the party, the givers were then supposed to return to the home and present the new owner with a practical, and useful, gift. It was typical for playful debates to ensue over whether the givers should take home their original offerings. More often than not they refused, leaving the new homeowner to figure out what to do with the items. The day I agreed to have the party, I realized I had set my home up as a storehouse for these wonderful gifts.

Hence, five goats in my kitchen.

Ella was really going to owe me.

* * *

The rest of the afternoon passed uneventfully. Anderson's Restaurant, over on Taylor Avenue, was catering the main dishes, so all I really had to do was rearrange the furniture to make room for about fifty or so to mix and mingle, hopefully not all at one time. The forecast called for evening thunderstorms, and I was hoping and praying with all my might they would hold off so that the overflow, typically the single men, could hold court at the horseshoe pits over in the vacant lot across the street. If they were driven in by the rain, my house would be as packed as a sardine can.

I decided to take a quick nap before the onslaught of well-wishers hit my porch. It seemed like I had just barely closed my eyes when the doorbell rang, jolting me up from the couch. It was Ella, coming over early to help with last minute arrangements.

"Well, it's about time the queen showed up," I teased when I opened the door. "Thought you were going to get out of the hard part, did you?"

Ella sneered and stuck out her tongue. "Oh, I knew you'd have everything taken care of," she said, waving her arms back and forth like an orchestra conductor. "I just came over to make sure you didn't sleep away the whole afternoon. I know you, Olivia. You were asleep on that couch, weren't you? I swear, you'd better get some vitamin shots. If you were any more relaxed about life, you'd be dead."

"Very funny," I shot back. "If you'd have worked half as hard as I have to get this party off the ground, you'd be tired, too. And besides, my body is just slow and takes its own sweet time. I'm comfortable with that."

I then pointed toward the back of the house and said, "I'll show you what really riles my blood. Come take a look at this."

I took her hand and pulled her through the kitchen and out the back door. There, staring up at us, were P, A, Y, T, and R. "Here's your first gift—your new family," I said. "But I'd watch out for Mr. Y over there. He's a charger. I'm pretty sure you have Charles Fredericks to thank for this. If I were you, I'd corner him tonight and find out for sure."

"What in the…?" Ella replied, eyes wide, mouth open. "You mean these are for me? What am I supposed to do with them?"

"After tonight, that's your problem. All I know is I want them out of here by tomorrow afternoon. Look—they're already eating my yard!"

Ella laughed and patted me on the back. "I think they like it here, Liv. You sure you don't want to adopt them? I really wouldn't mind, you know. Not at all."

"You get these out of here tomorrow or you'll come home one day to find them in *your* kitchen!"

"Seriously. In the kitchen?" She laughed and continued, drawing the words out slowly, "I'd have given anything to see that."

"Oh yeah, very, very funny. Ha ha. You just get them out of here as fast as you can. They're your kids now—not mine. And I do mean *kids*."

Her grin told me she got the pun, but she pretended not to. Instead, she smirked and said, "Okay, okay. I'll put the arm on Charles tonight and get him back over here tomorrow."

Then, falling back into her thick Arkansas drawl, she added, "I'm sure he'll do it for little old me."

"Well, he better," was all I could think of to reply. "Now get yourself back in that kitchen and finish up those trays of snacks. They're all going to be here in a couple of hours you know."

"I'm going. I'm going," she said. Then, more sarcastically, she said, in that same drawl, "When you are finished playing with your kids here, why don't you come in and take another nap while I work?"

I picked up the broom I had left in the yard after chasing the goat givers and raised it to swat Ella on the behind. "March!" I said. "You've got work to do."

"You wouldn't dare," she replied.

"Oh no? Just watch me!"

I took a baseball stance and got ready to swing, but she had already taken off running for the house. After she had gone, the goats circled around me. "Well, what are y'all looking at?" I said in the best drawl I could muster. In unison, they shook their heads violently from side to side.

"I know," I said. "Me, too."

I turned and walked toward the house with my new friends in tow.

Ella had been my best friend from the very first day I met her. There was a chemistry between us that just clicked on like a light switch. She had been hired just over two years before to teach math at Sumner High School, where I taught the science classes. When I first met her, she was being cornered in the cafeteria by what seemed like every eligible bachelor in the school, including our one-eyed janitor, Elijah.

She had a natural beauty about her that radiated and attracted men like I had never seen happen before. She was just an inch or so short of six feet tall. Her body, slim and fit, was in perfect proportion to her height. She was also what my grandmother would have called "chesty," and that part of her anatomy was just about at eye level with most standing around her. That, no doubt, was a major point of attraction for the men. Her clothes were modest yet colorful and typically played off the hue of her brown eyes and light complexion quite well. If she had any physical flaws, and I couldn't detect any, they were more than covered up by her Arkansas drawl. Most of the time it was just there, like a light breeze. At other times, when it was to her advantage, especially around men, she could talk like she had a mouth full of maple syrup. The sweetness of her voice made her the Pied Piper of Sumner High School, and the bachelors followed her around like a pack of hungry dogs.

That aura lasted exactly three weeks, until The Rumor started. After The Rumor, the men fell away quickly, like a long string of dominoes.

One blistering hot afternoon, two deputy sheriffs from Blytheville, Arkansas, showed up to question her right in the middle of a school day. I was in the office using the typewriter to prepare student descriptions for the school yearbook when they arrived. The deputies took her into the small meeting room next to Principal Brantley's office. From where I was sitting, I could see them and hear most of their conversation.

It seemed Ella left Arkansas rather quickly after her stepfather came up missing. One of the deputies, a chubby man with bright red cheeks who never took off his sunglasses, asked Ella to confirm a report they had that the stepfather had taken off very early one Saturday morning to go fishing just outside Blytheville at a tributary of Mallard Lake called the Mallard Slough. The other deputy, who also looked like he hadn't missed many meals, made a point of mentioning that was a rough section of the countryside flanked on both sides by a thick canebrake, a place where many fishermen had become lost and confused as to how to get back to the main road. Eventually the deputies worked around to a pointed question. By the way they were squirming in their seats, I could tell this was really what they came over two hundred miles to ask about. They had just recently been told that Ella, on that same morning, also got up early and rode with her stepfather to the city of Blytheville, supposedly to see about a job there. The deputies asked Ella about where she had been dropped off, where she interviewed, how she got back home, and when she had last seen her stepfather.

At that point, it was Ella who got up and closed the door to the room. I couldn't see them or hear their words as clearly after that, but I could make out that the stepfather and the truck he drove that morning were never seen again. I could also hear the deputy with the sunglasses stating that several neighbors informed them the stepfather was an alcoholic who had abused both Ella and her mother regularly. He wanted to know if that was true. Right then several students rushed into the office and asked me some questions about the yearbook. In all the commotion, I couldn't make out Ella's reply.

The bell rang to signal the end of that period, so I had to

go back to my classroom. By the time school was over that day, the deputies were gone and Ella was back in her room getting ready for the next day. All seemed perfectly back to normal. However, our main secretary, Mrs. Gable, the biggest gossip in the entire school, had also overheard most of the conversation, and by evening the phone lines in the Ville were working over-time. Word spread so quick that no one would sit next to Ella in the lunch room the next day. I was appalled by how quickly people assigned guilt to her, but, at the same time, I could also understand the cloud of curiosity that now floated around her. From Pied Piper to potential murderer, all in the course of a few hours. Our principal, Mr. Brantley, called Ella into his office the next morning before school. Their conversation wasn't long and apparently satisfied him, at least for the time being. I didn't know what role, if any, Ella might have had in the disappearance of her stepfather, but I liked her and was going to give her the benefit of the doubt. I actually felt sorry for her. What a way to begin a new job.

And besides, Ella and I made quite a pair. My husband, Inman Perkins, had been killed in action in Italy during World War II when the Allies were cutting a path to Rome. It was later assumed, around school and in the neighborhood, by more than one caveman-thinking cretin, that as a married woman, I had learned from my husband enough knowledge in the area of love to be one of the Sabine women. On more than a few occasions I had to deflect fresh, and sometimes downright crude, behav-ior because of this new persona I had somehow been thrown into. As Ella and I became better friends and spent more time together, we made an imposing presence to the single men of the Ville. I'd ring his neck if I could ever find out who started it, but some lamebrain with obviously too much time on his hands nicknamed us the "Poison Sisters," a brand that stuck—and hurt.

Ella didn't like talking about her stepfather, so I usu-ally avoided the subject when we talked about her life back in Arkansas. But one night—and to this day I don't know what came over me—when we were playing cribbage at my house I cut loose. We were both tired after a long day at school and were on the verge of falling asleep when my curiosity ate a hole through my good sense. I actually meant it to be funny, but she sure didn't take it that way when I matter-of-factly asked, "So, did you kill that man?"

Ella scooted her chair back from my kitchen table, calmly folded her hands in her lap, looked me right in the eye, and softly replied, "Don't ever ask me that again. Ever."

I didn't.

In the days before her emancipation party, I played most of this over in my mind again, but as quickly as the thoughts came in, they evaporated. I had come to know Ella as well as anyone I had ever known, and I trusted her and wanted nothing to ruin our friendship. Ella had come a long way in two short years, from crime suspect to respected teacher at Sumner High School. She had also become my dearest friend and closest confidante.

Whatever had happened in the past, Ella now owned the present. Tonight she was officially becoming family.

And I was so proud to be a part of it.

2

Celebration

The party started off like a sweet, calm sea.

Too calm.

Too quiet.

I knew something was up right away when Jackson Taylor spilled punch on Trudy Baxter and immediately gave an exaggerated bow while politely saying, "Pardon me, Miss Baxter. I'm so very sorry."

This was the same Jackson Taylor, who a week before, just for grins, had purposely driven his car into a deep puddle along the road as Trudy and her sisters were coming out of Lorraine Irby's beauty parlor, drenching them and totally demolishing their new hairdos. If anything, I was expecting Trudy to throw a handful of bologna slices at Jackson or stab him with the cold-cut fork. At first it looked like Trudy had something similar in mind, but she quickly pulled her hand back before it got to the table.

Instead, she smiled insincerely, curtsied, and said, sharply, dragging out each word, "Don't mention it. Accidents happen."

Then, I turned around to see that Eddie Tucker and Johnny Edwards, mortal enemies since grammar school, were quietly playing checkers on the window seat in the living room.

I also noticed Ginny Thompson and Linda Watkins had shown up wearing nearly identical dresses. Ginny, on her best day, would never have been described as a happy person, and normally her claws would have been bared at the first sight of Linda's dress. Tonight, however, they were standing arm in arm, giggling softly.

And the coup de grace—Walter Chalmers, the same man who put goldfish from S. S. Kresge's five-and-dime store into the punch bowl at Elsie Dunsmore's party, was gliding around the room and politely inquiring whether anyone would like more hors d'oeuvres.

There was just too much polite behavior in the room, and it was making me nervous. And nauseous.

I'd had it with the courtly behavior. I decided I couldn't stand one more minute of it. These weren't my friends. They had to be from Mars or Jupiter or Pluto. I set down my cheese and cracker tray, stuck both index fingers in my mouth, and whistled so loudly all motion in the room instantly froze solid.

"Just what in the Sam Hill—" was all that came out of my mouth before my words were drowned out by the loudest rendition I'd ever heard of John Philip Sousa's "The Stars and Stripes Forever." As quickly as all had become still moments before, everyone, in unison, raced to peer out the living room windows.

There, in my front yard, in perfect formation, in full uniform, was the entire Sumner High School marching band under the watchful eye of Edgar Dale, chair of our music department. Everyone looked at me, then howled.

"Come on! Let's go!" Jackson Taylor said as he grabbed me by the waist and swung me around so that I was facing away from him.

One by one, all joined up ahead of us and behind us to create a conga line that stretched from the living room through the kitchen and back through the dining room.

For a moment I just stood there with my mouth open. "I give up," I said while falling into rhythm. "You people are absolutely positively nuts and should have your heads examined."

"Yeah, but you love us, and you know it," Paul Jacobs yelled over to me.

I just smiled back and blew him a kiss.

He was right.

Paul took my hand as the line swayed by him, and led me out the front door into the front yard. The entire conga line followed close behind. When we were all outside, the band stopped playing. Mr. Dale motioned for those playing the horns to move apart, leaving an aisle down the middle. From the back of the band, a figure started walking forward, a hat pulled firmly down over his face. When he was a few feet in front of me, he grabbed his hat and spun it to the side. Standing there, grinning from ear to ear, was Eddie "Tubby" Thompson. I took one look at him and didn't know whether to kiss him or sock him right in the eye.

Eddie, affectionately known as Tubby, even though he stayed skinny as a rail no matter how much or how often he ate, had his mind made up he was going to marry me come hail or high water. This was his third proposal to me in the last month. It was also certainly his loudest and most dramatic.

Tubby got down on one knee as the snare drummers began a loud drumroll. The bass drum then got into the action and started a series of slow, rhythmic beats. Between each beat, Tubby shouted, "Will…you…Marry…"

Then the musicians stopped. Tubby jumped up and walked toward me, arms outstretched, and shouted as loudly as he could, "Me!"

The crowd erupted, hooting and cheering. The snare drummers started rolling again, loud at first, then getting quieter and quieter until they could barely be heard. I looked around, and all eyes were focused on me. The people closest to me were leaning forward, straining to hear what my response would be. I also noticed Ella leaning against the porch, a wide smile appearing when our eyes met. I glared at her. I had a feeling she'd somehow been a part of this.

I knew I had to say something. I started to speak, but my mouth went completely dry. I reached over and pulled a punch glass out of Paul Jacob's hand, took a quick drink, and threw the cup over to Jackson, who caught it with one hand.

"Okay, okay," I said, raising my hands to quiet the buzz in

the crowd. "Look, I really do adore this man, but this is a personal matter, just between me and him."

"Go ahead," Jackson shot in. "We won't listen. Will we?"

The crowd broke into laughter and applause.

I turned to face Tubby, who was back on one knee. "Get up from there!" I scolded, wagging my finger at him. "Stand there. Don't say another word. Just you shut up and listen."

"Yes, dear," he meekly replied, smiling broadly.

There were "Oooh's" from the crowd, and some woman in the back added, "Yeah, you give it to him from the start, Sister! Show him who's boss!"

Loud enough so that even those in the back could hear, I started in, "If I'm ever going to accept a proposal, it's going to be someplace where there's candlelight, soft, romantic music, and a spectacular view—and where the two of us are *alone*."

"What do you call this?" Jackson chided. "You've got streetlights, a whole marching band, and just look at this view around here!" He pointed up and down West Belle Place. "What more could you ask for?"

Laughter ran through the crowd again, but only for a moment. All were still waiting to hear my response.

"And you, Jackson—you shut up, too," I said, smiling, but also giving him my best you-better-watch-out look.

The crowd let out a collective "Oooh" again.

"Look, it's just that I…I mean…Oh heck!" I paused a minute and looked over at Tubby, who was pretending to pout, his lower lip raised above his upper.

I had known Tubby since my college days at Lincoln University. He had been a guitar player back then in Cab Calloway's orchestra. One night when a group of my sorority sisters and I had gone to a dance down on the levee in the downtown area of Jefferson City, Cab's band was playing. I danced with several boys that night, but all night I had a nagging feeling I was being watched. As it turned out, I was. Tubby waited until the band's second break of the evening before getting enough nerve to come over to introduce himself. He tripped over a chair right before he got to me and crashed into a table full of glasses, sending them crashing to the floor. At first I thought he was one of the waiters and said, "There goes your salary for the night." He got up, straightened his jacket, and held out his hand to shake mine.

"I'm Tubby," he said. "I'm with the band. You know, up there." He pointed to the stage.

"Well, I hope you're a better musician than you are a waiter," I joked.

He smiled and said nervously, "I've been watching you all night, and I now know something."

He didn't continue. He just stood there, staring at me.

"Well, *what* do you know?" I asked.

He got down on one knee, took my left hand in his, and said, "You are the most beautiful thing I've ever seen in my life. Will you marry me?"

"You hit your head when you fell, didn't you?" I asked, jerking my hand from his. "We better see if there's a doctor around here somewhere."

"I'll give you a while to figure it out," he continued, "but I'm what you need. I'm your man, and I'm not going to give up until you say 'yes'."

"Then you are going to have a long wait," I replied. "A *really long* one."

When the band started playing again, it was late and time for us to leave because it was close to our eleven o'clock curfew. I thought I was rid of him, until a dozen roses showed up at the sorority house the next morning. Postcards then started showing up every week, sent from towns all over the country as the band traveled and gained popularity. I even read a small piece in the Columbia, Missouri, newspaper about the band when it played in St. Louis, and there, at the end of the article, was a picture of Tubby and his guitar, which, the article said, he had named "Olivia."

That was nearly a dozen years ago, and he still hadn't given up. Even when I married Inman, Tubby wasn't deterred. The postcards still came regularly. After he heard the news of Inman's passing, Tubby sent a letter with the words to a song he had written for me called "There Will Come a Day." It was a beautiful song, from a beautiful man. At the end of the letter he signed it, "With all my love, forever and ever." I knew he meant it. However, while I adored and loved Tubby, I wasn't in love with him then, and I still wasn't now. I considered him the best male friend I had, but that was all: a dear, wonderful friend.

The crowd inched closer. I stepped back from them and onto the porch, next to where Ella was standing.

"I know what all of you want me to say. And Tubby, I know…" My voice trailed off again. I felt the tears coming, but I wasn't exactly sure why. Maybe it was because I didn't want to hurt him again.

I finally got enough of my voice back to continue. "As I said, I adore this man—dearly. He's sweet, kind, and gentle. Goodness knows I don't deserve somebody like that."

I paused here and looked directly at Jackson. "If you say one word, I'm going to clobber you!"

I couldn't see who it was, but the woman standing behind Jackson reached around and clamped her hands over his mouth. That got a round of applause.

"I'm going to have to say no."

Before I could continue, boos rang out from every direction.

"Wait a minute!" I shouted. "Hear me out. I'm not saying 'no' for good. Not forever and ever. I'm just saying 'no' tonight. I've got to do some thinking. So you, Mr. Tubby, get your hiney into this house and help us celebrate. Tonight isn't my night—isn't our night. This is Ella's night. You should have known that. Shame on you."

I paused and pushed Ella in front of me. "We are here to celebrate a new member of our family. So, everybody, get inside. Don't forget, we've got food to eat." I paused, then added, "And *gifts* to give."

Then, pointing toward Edgar Dale, I shouted, "Maestro, how about some more march music to get these good folks moving!"

With that, he raised his hands, blew his whistle, and the band picked up right where they left off in "The Stars and Stripes Forever."

While music filled the air, I made my way back down the steps and motioned for Tubby to meet me over by my tulip tree.

"Oh, one more thing," I added to the crowd when I reached the sidewalk. "You'll have to excuse me. I've got a few words of my own to say to this man. Now get in the house and leave us be."

There were still a few groans from the crowd, but most headed immediately either up the steps and into the house or over to the horseshoe pits. When the crowd had cleared, I saw Charles Fredericks pull out his wallet, remove some bills, and hand them over to Jackson. I guess I was the odds-on favorite to cross the finish line this time—and Charles lost.

"That's what you get, jackass!" I said as I walked past and swatted him on the behind.

When Tubby and I were finally alone, I raised my right arm like I was going to slap him. "I ought to whip the tar out of you. What in the heck am I going to do with you?"

He shrugged and started to reply, but I cut him off by planting a kiss on him that made him stagger back and nearly fall.

"Just shut up and kiss me. Come here. The only thing I want to see those lips doing is dancing with mine."

He may have been just a dear friend, but he was also the best kisser I'd ever known. And, under these circumstances, I thought he owed me at least a sample of that.

"This is a *friendly* kiss," I teased. "And I *am* your friend. Just watch this."

I leaned over to kiss him again, but he stuck out a hand to stop me. "Hold your horses just one cotton-pickin' minute. I'm going back on the road tonight, but before I go I've got something else to say. Now *you* keep *your* mouth shut and listen."

He glanced at his watch before continuing, "One of these days you're going to say 'yes'. You still don't know it yet, but I *am* the man for you. In the meantime, while I'm away, I want you to think about *this*."

He pulled me toward him and gently brushed his lips against mine. Then, he brushed my cheek with his left hand, smiled weakly, and planted a kiss on me that took my breath away to the point I ended up gasping.

"That," he said, "is what you could have every day. *Every* day. You think about that while I'm away."

He walked over and picked up his hat from where he had spun it to the ground. He put it on his head and tapped it to the side. "See ya, Liv. I'll send a postcard as soon as we get to New Orleans."

With that, he turned and walked away. I waved, but he didn't look back.

"I'm not in love with him," I said to myself, over and over, as I watched him walk down West Belle Place into the falling darkness of the night.

"I can't be. I just can't."

It was getting harder and harder to convince myself.

* * *

When I came back into the house, the celebration was in full swing. The polite behavior that I had seen earlier had flown out the window. Eddie Tucker and Johnny Edwards were still playing checkers, but not like before. They were now using the checkers as projectiles and flinging them at unsuspecting people across the room. As I walked through the dining room, I also noticed about a dozen goldfish now in the punchbowl. I just shook my head. Yes, it looked like things were finally getting back to normal.

Ella was holding court in the kitchen. In her very best drawl, she was telling several of the single men about a time she lost part of her bathing suit when diving into the swimming hole back in her hometown. To say they were mesmerized wouldn't have even come close.

Even though she wasn't finished with her story, I walked over, took her by the hand, and dragged her out onto the back porch.

Almost in unison, the men shouted after us, "Oh, you can't leave now! Get back here—what happened next?"

"I ought to spank you," I said after closing the door behind us. "You knew about Tubby coming tonight, didn't you?"

"Oh, don't be mad, Liv. You know Tubby. How could I refuse? Besides, I think he did you an incredible favor. *I'm* the one stuck tonight with all these hormone cases. Tubby cleared the field for you. What man in his right mind is going to try making time with you tonight after a whole marching band was brought in by another suitor? I'm telling you what—I've had more hands on me already than you could shake a stick at. And you, well, you're getting a free pass."

I started to cut in, but she kept on rolling, "And you know who we really have to thank for all this attention, don't you? It's our old pal Reverend Danielson. I think he believes he won't get into heaven unless he first marries us off. He just can't stand the thought of the Poison Sisters having the run of the Ville. I guess he's afraid we're going to turn the place into some kind of Sodom and Gomorra, which, actually, might be kind of fun, don't you think?"

She paused and laughed.

"Why can't I ever get mad at you?" I said, shaking my head and glaring at her. "You drive me crazy sometimes. You really should have told me Tubby was going to do this. I'm so embarrassed now I could just crawl into a hole and die."

With her best syrupy voice, she said, "Oh, yeah. You're shy. That's right. I forgot. My mistake. You're the original Shrinking Violet. You always back away from tough situations, don't you, Sweetie?"

All I could do was laugh. I stepped forward and hugged her. At the same time, I gave her a swat on the behind as hard as I could. She jumped back and shot me a look of mock horror.

"Don't say it," I said. "Just get inside and enjoy your night. Now scoot."

Ella leaned over and kissed me on the cheek. "Thanks," she said.

"For what?" I asked.

She didn't answer. She took my hand, squeezed it gently, and we walked back into the house.

* * *

As soon as we opened the backdoor, Minnie Brown shouted, "They're back! Get ready!"

"Ready for what?" I asked.

"It's gift time, and we've got some doozies," she replied, rubbing her hands together. "Hurry up. Get in there. I think everything's ready."

Reverend Danielson had taken charge and crammed everyone into the living room and hallway so that they'd have a good view of the dining room, where the furniture had all now been moved to the side.

Reverend Danielson was pacing back and forth in front of the fireplace when he saw us. "About time you two showed back up," he said. "Ella, you sit over here by the window. Olivia, come over here and stand by me."

Smiling broadly, he added, "You're going to help me pass out these *wonderful* treasures to the newest member of our family."

Here he paused, straightened his tie, then continued, "But before we do, I want to say a few words on this momentous occasion…"

"Oh, no!" someone whispered a little too loudly from the back of the living room. Laughter spread through the room as everyone looked back to see if they could figure out who the culprit was.

"I heard that! Was that you, Jackson Taylor?"

Everyone laughed again as Jackson slowly squatted down behind the couch.

"Enough of that," Reverend Danielson said, sharply. "This is serious business. I promise I won't talk long, but there are a few things that need to be said."

More than a few responded with "That's right" and "Amen."

The shouts of "Amen" seemed to fortify Reverend Danielson because he raised the volume of his voice almost to sermon level.

"We've gathered together this evening to celebrate. We celebrate our many blessings. We celebrate this glorious life we have been given by the good Lord above. And, we celebrate our extended family, which tonight is growing again."

He paused and smiled at Ella.

He then continued, lowering his voice, "You all know we call these celebrations 'emancipation' parties. We therefore also pay homage to our past and celebrate the possibilities and dreams for the future. For so many of our families, the word *emancipation* conjures up a time when the bonds of slavery were finally cast aside. I could look around the room and make a list of those whose grandparents and great-grandparents were bound most of their lives by shackles and chains. Alice Townsend—your great-grandfather, a master blacksmith, was born and died in slavery. Jackson—your great-grandfather fled from his chains and joined the army of the North to help fight for our freedoms. Olivia's great-grandmother died after bearing her fourteenth child on the very plantation where she herself was born. I could tell a similar story for just about every face in this room."

He stopped a moment, pulled his handkerchief from his pocket, and wiped his brow. His words were now becoming louder and quicker.

"Many would say these shackles and chains are now just a part of history, but we know that's not completely true. The iron and steel may be gone, but there are restraints of a different kind with us today, and we also know that. The Good Book says we are all God's children, that we are all equal on this Earth. This may be true in the eyes of God, but, sadly, it isn't so right under our own feet. We still live in a world where many are told where they can work, eat, worship the Lord, and, yes, where they can live. It won't always be this way. At least I pray every day that it won't. I pray that in the same way the walls of Jericho came tumbling down, the walls of ignorance and prejudice that are still around us will crumble to dust. On the other side of that wall, I see freedom. I see a world that says the color of a man's skin or the faith he believes will not tie him down. I see a time when love and kindness and true affection for everyone will be the gentle rain that grows beauty and majesty everywhere around us. We've got a sloping, rocky road still ahead of us, but we can make that climb. We *will* make that climb, so help us God!"

Most in the room, including myself, shouted, "Amen!" A few added a crisp "Praise be!"

Everyone clapped loudly.

Reverend Danielson slowed his words again, emphasizing each one. "I began by saying tonight is an emancipation gathering, and it truly is. The St. Louis Real Estate Exchange sits in judgment of the housing needs of the citizens of this great city. There are many places where they say we can live, but there are only a handful of neighborhoods where they say we can purchase our own homes. When we do get a home, we gain a piece of freedom, freedom from the laws that are just still no more than shackles and chains. Are we totally free when we get this home? I won't lie to you. The answer is that we are not. However, at the same time, we *are* free to own the land under our feet. Today, that is the best place to start. It is from here we'll take that first step on the climb left before us."

Here he motioned for Ella to step over next to him. "I want to congratulate this young woman, Ella Dunbar. All of you know her as a skilled teacher at the high school and a ready volunteer whenever the call for help goes out at the church. I feel blessed to know her, and I'm proud to present her to you as the newest member of our family. I ask you to open your arms and hearts and welcome her and wish her well. As you all know, we couldn't have the gathering at her house this evening because more work needs to be done there. Therefore, I also want to thank Olivia for her hospitality tonight, for hosting this beautiful event. Let's have a round of applause for her."

I bowed slightly to the group and turned to thank Reverend Danielson.

Then, almost as an afterthought, Reverend Danielson slapped his head and added, "One more thing. What's wrong with me. I meant to give this announcement right at the start, but I completely forgot. Sorry, Ella. Sorry, Olivia. Please forgive me for adding this aside, but I think it's important. All of you—don't forget the church is sponsoring a trip to Sportsman's Park in just a few days. We're going to see the Cardinals play Brooklyn. That means we are going to see a man already making that climb up the steep and rocky road ahead of us all, Mr. Jackie Robinson. We should be there if we can to show our support. Please see me later tonight if you plan to go with us, and I'll arrange for your tickets. Again, I'm very sorry for the interruption, but we all know Mr. Robinson is also facing his own form of emancipation. I just thought I should mention that, too, on this night."

He paused one last time, wiped his forehead again, pushed Ella out in front of him, and said, "I now give you our newest family member, Ella Dunbar."

Shouts of "Here, here!" and "Congratulations!" rang out. Ella moved forward and hugged as many people as she could near the front of the group.

When the noise level finally lowered enough, Ella said, while wiping away tears, "I don't know what to say."

"Well, then, that would be the first time!" Jackson added quickly, producing a roar of laughter.

"Actually, I think he's right," Ella joked right back.

She paused again to wipe her eyes and continued, "I just want to thank all of you for your kindness and support. My family back in Arkansas was never that close. Being here has made me understand what family can do for a person. And you know what I've learned the most? That family isn't spelled f-a-m-i-l-y. *Family* is really spelled l-o-v-e. And if you have that, you are rich, just as I'm now richer than I ever have been in my life. I especially want to thank Olivia for all she has done for me. I love you, Liv. Thanks for everything. And to the rest of you, I love you, too. More than you will ever know."

Ella couldn't continue. The tears were now streaming down her cheeks. I put my arm around her while saying to the crowd, "Let's get this show on the road. I understand we have a few things to give our newest family member. Now remember—this is *my* house, not hers. If you have an especially interesting gift to present that might best be given at her place, consider saving it. I'm talking about things like the five goats I found in my kitchen this afternoon—Charles Fredericks!"

Charles threw up his hands and pleaded, "It wasn't me! I think I was framed!"

"Yeah, that's right," I shot back. "Framed. Charles Fredericks, you were *born* guilty!"

Reverend Danielson stepped in and said, "That's enough, you two. Back to neutral corners. Let's get on with the gifts, shall we? What do we have first for Ella?"

As if on cue, Ralph Cornelius came in through the front door. He was carrying a beautiful oak chair. It wasn't until he turned around next to the fireplace that we saw it had just three legs.

"I just know this will brighten your new home. Welcome to the neighborhood, Ella."

"Thanks a million," Ella said, leaning over to hug Ralph. "I'll make sure this is always reserved for you when you come visiting."

"It'll be perfect," yelled Charles Fredericks. "I hear Ralph is always on the floor on weekends anyway." He lifted his hand to make an exaggerated drinking motion. Everyone laughed, even Ralph.

"I'll be honored," Ralph replied as he bowed deeply.

Almarie Jordan stepped forward next. "This is in case the

roof leaks," she said in her squeaky, high-pitched voice.

From behind her dress she produced a large bucket. When she held it up to the ceiling light, we could see it had more holes in it than a Swiss cheese. The crowd cheered its approval.

Jackson was next. He handed Ella a wooden hammer with two handles attached to its head, each handle angling out slightly to the side.

"Thanks," Ella said, curiosity spreading across her face. "What is it?"

"It's the perfect hammer for a woman," Jackson replied. "You hold it with both hands so that you'll never hit your thumbs. I made it just for you."

Ella stepped forward and pretended like she was going to knock Jackson in the head with it. He quickly ran back to the group in the living room.

"This just may come in handy, Jackson. I'll keep this for when *you* come to call."

It was becoming more and more apparent to me Jackson was sweet on Ella. However, until recently, he was all bravado and no action. It was just in the past few weeks he started stopping by my house to ask me questions about her. Like a lovestruck seventh grader, he'd paw at the ground in my front yard, make small talk about the weather and the health of my parents, and only then would he worm in another question about Ella. I'd been teasing him unmercifully, but the look in his eyes tonight as he handed her his gift told me I better let up. Ella was still one of the Poison Sisters to most of the men in the Ville, but it appeared Jackson was willing to move a little closer to the fire.

Charles Fredericks then stepped into the dining room and turned to face the group. "I swear I don't know anything about those goats," he said, grinning broadly while raising and lowering his eyebrows quickly several times. "Really I don't."

"That sure looked like your behind I saw hightailing it down the street this afternoon," I said, pointing right at him.

That brought catcalls and whistles from the others.

"Oh, stop it, Olivia," he said. "You're making my heart flutter."

Turning toward Ella, he added, "And now I just might make your heart skip a beat or two. I got you something that will change your life. I just know you'll be thrilled. The only problem is it was too big to bring into the house. You'll all have to look out back to see it. Look way over in the very back corner of the yard."

"Stay where you are!" Reverend Danielson instructed the group. "I had a difficult enough time getting you in here in the first place. Ella, you go out through the kitchen and take a look. You can tell the rest of us what it is."

Ella squeezed through those standing in the hallway and made her way through the kitchen. A buzz swept through the group while she was gone. She returned directly, carrying my broom. She lifted the broom over her head and started chasing Charles around the dining room. Again, Reverend Danielson stepped in, laughing and reaching out to grab the broom.

"So, what did you see out back?" he asked.

"It's an outhouse!" Ella shrieked. "A two-holer!"

The room erupted in laughter. The curiosity of the group also boiled over as several tried to get into the kitchen to look out the window.

"Come back here!" Reverend Danielson implored. "You can all look later."

"I don't know where you got that," I said to Charles and loud enough for the group to hear, "but it better be out of my yard by tomorrow night. What will my neighbors think?"

"They'll think you're really lucky," Charles said. "One bathroom inside—and one out back. They'll think you're living high."

He then said, "Don't worry. I'll see that it's returned to its proper home. After all, those poor people will be shocked when they go out to use it tonight and all they find is a big hole in the ground. I sure hope they don't fall in!"

When the laughter finally stopped, Eddie Miller was next. He presented Ella with a beautiful oil painting a student had done of the faculty of Sumner High School. The only problem was each subject, including Ella, had several teeth that were now blacked out. I took one look at it and howled. Actually, I was jealous. I thought it would have made a great conversation piece for any living room in the Ville.

The gifts kept coming. Alva Singer brought a beautiful rose-colored blouse she said was to be worn while doing housework. However, the sleeves had been extended, making them about six feet long. Kenny Anderson gave her an electric kitchen clock that had only the hour and second hand. Marge Snyder brought a bowl of artificial fruit. Each piece had been repainted: an orange banana, pink pear, black apple, white grapes. Anne Mathews' gift received the most attention of all because it sent people scattering. She offered an electric fan with only one blade. When she plugged it in, it was so out of balance it immediately fell over and started bouncing and skipping across the floor.

Finally, Ella waived her hands and said, "Enough. Enough. I now officially feel welcomed to the neighborhood. I really do."

Everyone cheered and applauded.

"I know there are more of these magnificent gifts, but let's break for refreshments. I don't know about all of you, but if I don't sit down now, I'm going to fall down. Receiving gifts tires a body out, especially these! I'll be sure to look at all the other treasures later on."

Here her demeanor changed completely. "Before we break, I do want to thank all of you, from the bottom of my heart. I thank you for your gifts, but more than that, I thank you for your love and friendship. I had no family at all when I moved up here, and now look at me. I have the most beautiful family in the world, and I adore y'all. Even you, Jackson Taylor!"

Jackson smiled broadly and winked at her.

Ella then added, "My home will be finished before the start of school. At least I hope so. Each and every one of you are hereby notified you will always be welcome in my home. Thank you all. I'll never forget this night. Never."

We all applauded again and, one by one, moved in for a quick hug. I waited until last.

When I finally reached Ella, I hugged her and said, "I love you, too."

I then muttered, as I started making my way to the kitchen, "An outhouse. Where do you suppose he got that? Perfect gift, though."

Ella playfully whacked me on the behind with the broom.

When most had gone home, Reverend Danielson came into the kitchen and motioned for me to follow him back into the living room.

"I want you to meet someone," he said. "This is J. D. Shelley."

Mr. Shelley shook my hand gently and said, "I'm so pleased to meet you. I've heard so much about you."

To put it bluntly, Mr. Shelley was what my mother always called a "real sugar stop-and-looker." He was a slender man with a slightly receding hairline. His rich, brown eyes were bright and accentuated one of the most handsome faces I'd seen in a long time. He also had a thin, perfectly groomed mustache. As he stood there, I saw a man that radiated confidence. My next thought was, "Is this man married?"

Reverend Danielson seemed to sense my thoughts. He quickly added, "J.D. moved here from Mississippi with his wife and children a few months ago."

That ended those thoughts.

He continued, "J.D., I wanted you to meet Olivia because I think she can help us. As a matter of fact, I *know* she can help us. That is, if she will."

"Why, Reverend—you know I can never say no to you about anything. What can I do to help out?"

Reverend Danielson and J. D. Shelley just looked at each other and smiled.

As I looked at both of them, I had no idea what I'd just gotten myself in for, but I couldn't help but feel I'd really put my foot in it this time.

* * *

When everyone had finally gone home, I climbed up the stairs to my bedroom and sat in my rocking chair. I flipped quickly through the most recent *Life* magazine, just glancing over the stories. I didn't want to crawl into bed just yet. In the same way some animals could tell when it was going to rain, I could sense *the dream* was coming on again. I'd had the same dream from the time I was a little girl. Each time it happened, the dream got longer and more detailed. I hated the dream. It unsettled and frightened me to the point I'd usually end up with fits of insomnia for days after. I'd always had a vague feeling of something similar actually happening to me when I was small, back in Mississippi, but every time I got close to remembering anything for certain, my thoughts would go black and I'd suddenly catch my breath.

The events of the day had exhausted me, so I finally decided to close my eyes and rest, just for a minute.

* * *

We were hunched down behind a thick hedge of chinaberry trees. Through the crowded branches we could see the flames, which were already shooting higher than the barn.

The men inside the barn looked like angels sweeping from window to window. They pounded the glass with their fists. Their screams were muffled by the crackling of the timbers, the commanding roar of the fire.

"Get down!" Jimmy John screamed at me. "If they see us, we'll be in big trouble."

Suddenly an explosion rocked the barn. We covered our ears and spread ourselves out on the soft earth as ash filled the night sky. It looked like table pepper as it sprinkled over us.

3

Covenants

T hanks to my dream, I woke up the next morning drenched in sweat. The cool morning breeze sweeping in through the window gave me a chill that sent goose bumps running down my arms. I decided the best antidote would be a hot bath, so I sleepily shuffled my way to the bathroom to start the water. I stopped along the way to look at myself in the dressing mirror and was horrified by what I saw: My hair was so flat on the left side of my head I could have used it as an ironing board. A hair wash was definitely in the cards this morning or I'd be scaring away dogs and small children when I left the house.

When I finally eased into the bathtub, I leaned my head back against the porcelain and closed my eyes. Tubby's most recent proposal was the first thing that popped into my thoughts. He really was a sweet and kind man, and I adored him. "But I'm not in love with him," I said out loud, trying to convince myself again.

In so many ways, he reminded me of Inman. That, however, was the biggest problem of all, and I knew it all too well. Inman was the love of my life, and I didn't want to let go of the memories of our too short time together. Our whirlwind romance had been the most beautiful time of my whole life, overflowing with laughter, love, and a passion I hadn't known existed. We had so many plans for our life together after the war, and I had already started on the arrangements for most of them. The whole time he was overseas I worried about him constantly, but I never for once thought he wouldn't somehow make it back home. When the telegram came from the War Department, my whole world simply stopped moving. My heart went numb. I was lost in a fog of memories and broken dreams, and I didn't have a clue what I was going to do next.

If it hadn't been for my job at Sumner, I think I would have gone completely out of my mind. There was even a period of time when I thought I had not only lost Inman, but I had also lost my position at Sumner. They could have fired me. I had broken the rules, so they probably *should* have fired me. The St. Louis Board of Education had a rule that when women in the system got married, they had to resign immediately. It was an outdated rule and a bad rule, but it was, nevertheless, still on the books. That was why we had kept our marriage a secret from everyone but our immediate family and closest friends. To be perfectly honest, that element of secrecy about everything also heightened and magnified the excitement surrounding everything Inman and I did. We were like two kids who knew they were getting away with something—and were loving every minute of the flood of adrenaline the secrecy produced. What we were doing, in essence, was creating our own world, a world where we closed out everything and everyone else. And within this world our lives were glorious and full of so much promise. Then everything came crashing down in one blow, and our secret immediately exploded.

I was convinced I was going to be fired or forced to resign, but the circumstances caused the Board of Education to go slowly. They were caught between the proverbial rock and a hard spot. It was true I had broken the rules, but my husband, a man considered a hero to so many in the Ville, had lost his life while fighting to preserve our freedoms. How *could* they fire me? What message would that have sent at a time when so many were sacrificing so much? They eventually decided just to slap me on the wrist by sending a letter of reprimand, which was later read aloud for the record at one of the Board's public meetings so that other women would be sure to get the message, loudly and clearly.

I was jolted from my thoughts when the doorbell rang. "I'm

not getting out of this tub!" I thought to myself. "Whoever it is will just have to come back later."

The doorbell rang again. And again. And again. Then the person started banging insistently on the front door.

I started to worrying that there might be an emergency of some kind, so I quickly wrapped myself in a towel and ran down the steps, dripping all the way. I peeked through the curtains on the door and saw Ella standing there staring back at me.

"Geez, Liv. Do you always sleep the whole day away? What a lazybones! Let me in."

"Ella Jane, just what in the world are you doing here so early?" I said, in my best early morning crabby voice. "I think you beat the chickens up. I want you to know I got out of the bathtub because of you. What time is it anyway?"

I started to open the door, and Ella pushed it in on me. "Make way. I need coffee—and lots of it. You did start a pot, didn't you?"

"At this time of the morning? You've got to be kidding," I shouted at her.

"It's seven thirty. Shank of the day. Get your butt upstairs and get dressed. You're going to church with me. You *need* to go to church, especially after turning down Tubby's proposal last night. Can you imagine what people are thinking this morning?"

I blinked and let my mouth fall open. "Since when do you worry about what other people think? You're one to talk. If you want to worry about something, try this on for size. Everybody in the Ville knows Jackson is sweet on you—and that you're crazy about him."

"Go on! Who said that? Me, crazy about Jackson? This is a joke, right?"

Mocking her drawl, I responded, "Why Ella Jane, would I tease you? It's written all over your face, Sugar. You got it *bad* for that man."

With that, I started back up the stairs to the bathroom. Ella followed right behind me, stomping heavily on each step as if punctuating her words.

"I don't have it bad for *any* man, let alone Jackson Taylor."

At the top of the stairs she paused and added, "I do have to admit, though, he is kind of cute, don't you think?"

"Cute? I don't know that I'd go that far," I teased. "I guess he's kind of what my mom calls a 'medium'."

"A 'medium'? What's a 'medium'?"

"Exactly," I replied, drolly. "A 'medium' what? What do we really know about this man? He's always here for about two weeks. Then he's gone for about two weeks. No one ever knows where he goes or exactly when he's coming back. For all we know, he's on the lam from the police. I actually wouldn't doubt that. Marvin Duvall saw him carrying a gun one time."

"He's a traveling salesman of some kind. I'd bet on that," Ella said, defending him. "And besides, everyone knows Marvin Duvall wouldn't know the truth if it bit him on the rump."

"I don't know," I said, my tone full of question. "There's something fishy about this man. He once told me he goes on gambling trips. You know, plays the ponies and bets on sporting events. My dad practically brought me up over at the racetrack, so I'm not exactly stupid when it comes to the horses. I once asked him how often he bet the daily double, and he had no idea what I was talking about. I'm convinced he's not a gambler. A traveling salesman? Maybe, but if I were you, I'd do a little more digging before I planted anything in his garden."

"You worry too much," Ella responded. "And besides, I'm not going to be getting married any time soon. I love my job too much to give it up for some man. You were lucky."

Here she stopped in mid thought. I could tell by the way she quickly turned her head to the side and looked down she had caught herself getting ready to say something about Inman. I appreciated her thoughtfulness and hugged her and brushed her hair away from her forehead.

I said, softly, "Oh, hell. What men in their right minds are going to have anything serious to do with us anyway? After all, we're the Poison Sisters, right? We're just one step away from the flames of Hades itself. I don't think we have much to worry about, do you?"

"No," Ella replied. "Just Tubby and Jackson, that's all."

A smile of mischief spread across her face.

It spread across mine, too.

"Okay, Sleeping Beauty," Ella said. "Finish getting dressed. Hurry up now. We're going to be late. I'll go downstairs and make some coffee so we don't fall sound asleep in church. That Reverend Danielson can sure be an old windbag at times."

"And do something about that hair!" she yelled when she was about halfway down the steps. "You'd scare the straw out of a scarecrow."

"Gee, I'm so lucky to have a friend like you," I sarcastically called after her.

"Yes you are," she shot back. "You don't deserve me."

I probably didn't, but I was so grateful she was in my life. For a long time after Inman had passed, I kept thinking about that old expression: If a tree falls in a forest and no one is around, does it make a sound? My life had become pretty quiet. I wasn't even sure any trees were still falling at all. With Ella around, my forest soon had sound again. She could be a real pain in the posterior at times, but at least when a tree fell now, I had someone to share the moment with.

I *was* lucky, and I knew it.

* * *

Reverend Danielson's sermon was actually quite good—and appropriate. He told a story about a friend of his from Bible college who had inherited a sizable fortune from an uncle. This friend then quit his studies and went to live at the estate he had inherited. He was living the life of luxury until one day he realized he hadn't seen any of his old friends in months. He had been so busy taking care of his newly acquired estate and money that he hadn't had time to return any telephone calls or answer any letters from the people he knew the best and loved the most. He became very lonely and fell into a sadness that settled over him like a shroud. To top it off, he had fallen away from his religious beliefs, instead following the lure of the dollar and what it could purchase. He ended up surrounded by material goods but, as Reverend Danielson explained, he had lost what was most important in his life: his friends, his family, and his faith.

Reverend Danielson's story was just a variation of an old tale most of us had already heard many times before, but he had given new life to it by bringing it to the present. I don't think it was lost on anyone in church that, through the story of his friend, he was really trying to get us to think about the emancipation party held for Ella the evening before. Ella wasn't rich now because of the silly gifts she received or the real ones that were to follow shortly. She was rich because she had the love of those around her.

Reverend Danielson paused at this point. He walked several times silently back and forth in front of the first pew. Without saying a word, he then reached down and shook the hands of everyone in front, including the children, while smiling broadly. He finally looked up at the rest of us and summed up his story by saying, "This man, through all of his wealth, had become the poorest man in town. I want you to think about that as you leave this morning and walk out into this glorious day that has been given to us."

I was really surprised when I turned toward Ella and saw her dabbing her eyes with her handkerchief. She never really seemed to get all that emotional about anything. I reached over to squeeze her hand.

"I am rich," she whispered to me as she squeezed back.

"Me, too," I said. "Me, too."

Roxanne Endicott's eight-year-old daughter, Sarah, had obviously missed part of the moral and couldn't stand it any longer. Rising from her seat, she waved her hand until she had Reverend Danielson's attention.

"Yes, child," he said. "What is it?"

Sarah asked, with a seriousness only a child could muster, "I have to know. What happened to your friend?"

We all laughed. Sarah, confused and embarrassed by the laughter, sat back down and leaned close to her mother, as if trying to hide.

Reverend Danielson motioned for everyone to quiet down. He then continued, "Sarah, that's a very good question, and I'm going to tell you the answer. That man soon realized what he had lost and decided to do something about it."

Again, he paused and smiled at all of us before continuing. "That man," he said, "became your minister—and he is so glad he did. So glad... and so blessed."

I expected gasps and other sounds of disbelief from the congregation, but the church became very still. No one said a word. No one moved. Even those with fans stopped fanning themselves. I looked around, and while there were a few shocked expressions, most were just staring blankly ahead, as if not realizing the full import of what had just been revealed to them.

The silence became awkward. I knew someone had to say something. I stood up and said, "And we feel blessed, too, Reverend. I know I speak for all of us when I say we're grateful you chose to lead this flock. Goodness knows we could use some leading!"

I looked around the room and added, "Right?"

I started applauding. Soon, others followed, creating a beautiful eruption of sound. I motioned for everyone to stand up, and they did, still applauding.

Reverend Danielson quickly motioned everyone to sit down again. "Thank you," he said. "You all are being too kind, but I appreciate it. Thank you from my heart and soul."

Turning to the choir, he said, "If you please, let's try number 149 in our hymnal as we end our service this morning—"Keep Me Every Day." I heard Sister Mahalia Jackson singing this one on the radio the other night. Let's see what we can do with it."

As soon as the choir started, he joined in, his rich baritone voice louder than I had ever heard him before. He quickly walked to the back of the church and, while still singing, hugged all as they left.

He was rich again. And so were we.

* * *

Ella and I stuck around until everyone else had gone because we wanted to thank him for his help with the party the evening before. After hugging Ella, he said, "My dear, if you'll excuse us, I'd like a word with Olivia."

"Well, I know when I'm not wanted," Ella teased. "I'll wait outside."

"No, it's not that!" Reverend Danielson said, quickly.

Ella put her hand on his shoulder and said, "I know, I know. Just kidding. I swear, you're going to blow up one of these days if you don't lighten up some."

"You're probably right," he said. "I'll work on it. I promise."

When Ella had gone, Reverend Danielson pulled me aside and said, "You know that help I said I was going to want from you? Well, I'm going to need it sooner than I expected. Can you come back here about two this afternoon? We're going to have a meeting then, and I'd really appreciate it if you could come."

"Sure," I replied. "What's it all about? Why all the secrecy?"

"I'd rather not say anything just yet. You'll see why later," he added, smiling again.

"Ok, see you at two. Do I need to bring anything to this meeting?"

"Yes," he replied. "Bring every ounce of hope you can find."

Ella was waiting for me out by the street. "Well, what's it all about?" she asked.

I shrugged and said, "Honestly, I'd tell you if I could. I don't even know what's going on. Must be something good, though. I don't think there was this much secrecy surrounding the development of the atomic bomb. He just told me to come back to a meeting later on."

I then added, "I know I promised I'd come help with the

wallpaper work today, but I really should come back for the meeting this afternoon. You won't be too mad at me, will you? I'll try to get over later if this doesn't take too long."

"Oh, I guess you're excused. But you better call me tonight and let me know what this is all about. I can't stand secrets, you know. Deal?"

"Deal," I said, as we interlocked our pinkie fingers and shook, a ritual that we had picked up from our students the year before.

I went home and had a quick lunch of leftover cold cuts and crackers. I was also still pretty tired. I should have cleaned up the house a little more, but I decided to take a quick nap instead. Before I did that, I took the phone off the hook so that Ella wouldn't call and wake me up. For some reason, she couldn't stand me taking naps. I was going to have to talk to her about that.

At one thirty I started walking back to the church. Along the way, I was struck again by just how beautiful the Ville was this time of the year. Most of the front lawns had flower beds, and in early July they were rainbows of colors. The pride taken in maintenance of the homes was also evident here. I noticed many homes had fresh coats of paint, and trees were neatly trimmed. I was also pleased by the lack of litter along the sidewalks and gutters of the streets. As I walked along, I was reminded of one of my father's favorite sayings, one he used to scold my brother and me when our rooms would get messy: "A dog doesn't go to the bathroom where it sleeps." I didn't understand much of that at all when I was a child, but I did now. I could see the meaning of the expression in everything around me, and it made me smile.

When I entered the church, Reverend Danielson was right there waiting for me. He didn't even say so much as "hello." Instead, he took my hand and said, "Please follow me. We're going to meet in my study."

There were two men and a woman inside the study when we walked in. I knew the men. They both jumped up immediately when they saw me.

"Please, sit down," I said, smiling and nodding to each.

"Olivia," Reverend Danielson started, "I want to introduce you to Mrs. Josephine Fitzgerald. She is going to help us with a project we have in mind."

I wouldn't have a difficult time remembering her name. As far as I could recall, hers was the first white face I had ever seen in this church.

Mrs. Fitzgerald was a thin-waisted, attractive woman with hazel hair just starting to show touches of gray. I guessed her to be about forty-five years old. I also noticed quickly she had a nervous habit of playing with her left earring.

She reached out to shake my hand. I was still a little stunned and didn't raise my hand right away. She smiled warmly and said, "It's ok. I won't bite. I promise."

I was so embarrassed. "I'm sorry," I said. "I just wasn't expecting..."

I chose my next words carefully. "I mean, with all the hush-hush, I didn't think there'd be so many people here."

I quickly stepped forward and shook her hand vigorously.

My curiosity was moving to the boiling point when Reverend Danielson chimed in, "I believe you know these gentlemen. You met Mr. Shelley last night at the party."

He bowed slightly toward me, and I said, "Good to see you again, Mr. Shelley."

Reverend Danielson then turned to his right and said, "Although he doesn't come to church as often as he should..." Here he paused to clear his throat for emphasis. "I know you remember Mr. James Bush."

"Of course I do," I responded. "Mr. Bush and I are old pals from way back. We've had business dealings before. Didn't you even help me with some of the paperwork when I bought my house?"

"I most certainly did," he replied. "And I was honored to do so. The help was for a gracious and lovely lady."

I don't think it would have been exaggeration to say Mr.

James Bush, known as J.T. to his friends, was one of the—if not *the*—most highly respected men in the Ville. He had his finger on the pulse of everything that even remotely involved the world of business here on our island. He owned several apartment buildings, helped finance the purchase of so many homes in the Ville I had lost track of them all, and was now, by unanimous choice, the leader of a fledgling organization of real estate agents devoted to helping the Negro citizens of St. Louis find appropriate housing.

He was also one very handsome man. Every time I had seen J.T., he was impeccably dressed: dark suit, white shirt, colorful but tasteful tie. He wore glasses, but the lenses were thin and barely noticeable. Instead of being a distraction, the glasses seemed instead to accentuate the symmetry of his features and the smoothness of his skin. He was of medium build, but he carried himself with a confidence that lit up a room when he entered.

Reverend Danielson interrupted my thoughts by clearing his throat again and reaching for a glass of water on his desk. We all watched in amazement as he gulped every drop in the glass.

"Whoa!" I teased. "Better go easy on that. You'll drown yourself."

"I've got a dry throat today," he replied, hoarsely. "You better not make too much fun of me. You may be grabbing for water in a minute.

"I suppose I should be the one to start this meeting," he added, walking around his desk and sitting down to face the rest of us. "What we're going to do may get us all put into jail, and I want you to know this right up front. If anyone wants to back out, that will be fine. But, you'll have to back out today. Once we get started, there won't be any turning back. There *can't* be any turning back."

Here he paused again and refilled his water glass from the pitcher next to his Bible. He lowered his voice, glanced quickly at the windows of his study, and continued, even more serious than before, "I'm not going to mince any words here. The fact of the matter is, as you all know, adequate housing for us is getting harder and harder to find in this city."

He turned toward Mr. Shelley and said, "J.D. here is the perfect example of what I'm talking about. He and his family have been living for over a year in a run-down apartment down on 9th Street. His landlord could care less about fixing anything that breaks or quits working. If he weren't so handy with tools, the whole place would have fallen to pieces long ago. And do you think he gets anything off the rent he pays when he does the repairs? You know what happened this spring when he had to put in new pipes for the kitchen sink? His landlord actually raised his rent because he said the kitchen had been remodeled!"

Reverend Danielson paused to take a couple of quick sips from his glass before continuing. "As all of you know, the 9th Street area down by the manufacturing district isn't exactly the best place to raise children. There are too many clubs and bars, and there's too much crime. Why, J.D.'s youngest daughter was pulled into an alley last winter on her way home from school, and it was just lucky others came by before anything terrible happened."

"That was the last straw. That was it," Mr. Shelley interrupted, his voice rising quickly. "When I found out my children couldn't walk home from school safely, I knew we had to do something and fast. That's when I called Reverend Danielson."

Addressing the rest of us, he added, "The Reverend was one of the first people I met when we moved up from Starksville, Mississippi, and I knew he was a good man right from the start. When my daughter was hurt, I called him because I knew he'd know what to do."

James Bush turned to me and added, "That's where I come into this. Reverend Danielson called me and asked if I could help J.D.'s family find a home in a safe neighborhood. The problem is I get about fifty calls a week from families who want to purchase their own homes. Fifty."

He paused, looked down at the floor, and continued, almost

whispering, "And I can help, if I'm lucky, just one or two families a month."

Here his whole demeanor changed. He took a deep breath and quickly blew it out. Banging his hand on Reverend Danielson's desk, he practically shouted, "It's that damn Real Estate Exchange!

"I'm sorry," he said, directing his words to Josephine and me. "Forgive me. I'm just so frustrated. So frustrated."

He turned away from us, walked over to the window behind Reverend Danielson's desk, and just stared outside, obviously trying to give himself time to rein in his emotions.

Reverend Danielson got up from his desk chair and walked over next to me. "Olivia, stop me if I'm saying what you already know, but I want to make sure you hear everything about this before you decide whether or not you're going to join us."

He paused and looked deeply into my eyes, as if searching for a clue as to how I was feeling at the moment. "Most people say the Real Estate Exchange has more power and influence than any other organization in St. Louis. Goodness knows, we've lost every legal battle we've ever had with them. About fifteen years ago, dozens of white real estate companies got together and decided they would be the ones to determine where people could, and could not, live in this city. Every time they sold a home, they tried to get either a covenant or restriction added to the property deed. J.T., why don't you pick it up from here. You know more about this than anybody."

Mr. Bush turned from the window and faced us again. The pause had been good for him. He smiled and said, "Again, I'm sorry. This just gets to me right here, and so far there's been nothing I could do about it," he added, pointing to his heart, then his stomach.

"Reverend Danielson is right," he continued. "The Real Estate Exchange has had legal real estate covenants added to nearly every deed they could get their mitts on. These covenants all say basically the same thing, that the homes cannot be sold, under penalty of law, to anyone who is of Negro or Mongolian descent. You won't believe it—I didn't believe it until I saw it myself—but they've even gone so far as to have written into some of the deeds that persons buying the property cannot have more than 1/32 of their blood that is noncaucasian. Can you believe that? What's next? Blood tests before people can buy homes? This just makes me sick."

Here he stopped for a moment, again gathering his emotions. He then drew a folded piece of paper from the inside pocket of his suit.

"I almost had a home bought for a young couple about a month ago just across the Hodiamont streetcar tracks. However, right before the sale was completed, I received a special delivery letter from the Real Estate Exchange. Somehow, they had found out we were getting ready to close the sale. Their letter really caught me off guard. I honestly didn't know whether to laugh or cry when I read it. In their letter, they had underlined a new covenant statement they had just talked the seller into adding to the paperwork. There was also a handwritten note in the margin next to it. The note was just three words, all underlined, and written specifically for me and that young couple: 'Not for you'."

He carefully unfolded the paper and said, "I want you to hear this. This is what they added. This is what we're now up against.

"Reverend, do you mind?" he asked as he picked up the Reverend's glass and drank from it. He pushed his glasses up, straightened the letter, and read to us:

"'Be it known no part of said premises shall in any manner be owned or used or occupied directly or indirectly by any Negro or Negroes or any person commonly known as Colored, provided that this restriction shall not prevent the occupation, during the period of their employment as janitors or chauffeurs, of quarters in the basement or in a barn or garage in the rear or other servants' quarters, by said Negro employees when in the service of the rightful owner or occupant of said premises'."

When he finished reading, he slowly folded the letter and slipped it back into his pocket. He took off his glasses, rubbed his forehead, and again blew out a deep breath. He didn't say anything.

He didn't have to.

Josephine was the first to speak. She turned to me, put her hand on mine, and said, "This is where I come in."

She didn't mean it to be funny, but the way she said it, with such an air of confidence, broke the tension in the room. We all laughed, including Josephine.

She continued, "These covenants, obviously, were designed to keep you and me apart. In their infinite wisdom, the Exchange has decided the world is a box of crayolas, and only the colors that are the same are fit to be in the box. I'd say I'm sorry for people of my color, but I understand some Colored realtors have also signed on with the Exchange. I have no idea what they could be thinking. So, instead, I'm just going to say I'm sorry there is so much ignorance around here, apparently in multiple corners. I've never been one just to sit on my behind and watch this parade of stupidity go by. If I can, I want to help put a few holes in all this."

I looked at her carefully. By the look in her eyes, I had no doubt she was sincere. I wanted to say something, but at this point I didn't know what. Josephine seemed to sense this and smiled.

"I can see it on your face," she said. "You're asking yourself, 'So, what's *she* doing here?' I suppose you have a right to know, especially if you're going to join us. My story is really pretty simple."

Standing up to walk around the room as she spoke, she continued. "When I was in high school, I met a young man from Cuba who became the best friend I ever had. We had so much in common; we did everything together. We became inseparable. Still, I was afraid to bring him home to meet my parents because he was Cuban and his skin wasn't just dark; it was what they called down there 'rural Cuban black'. I finally invited Javier to supper, so my parents could meet him, and I was more than just a little surprised by their response. I never would have guessed it in a thousand years, but they welcomed him with open arms."

She paused, fumbled in her purse, and eventually pulled out a package of cigarettes. J.D. offered a light, and she leaned forward. After a deep draw on the cigarette, she exhaled and continued her story.

"However, even with my parents' blessing, the friendship wasn't always hearts and flowers. Most of the other kids at the high school were always on us because they thought we shouldn't be together—for any thing or any reason. To get away from all that, we started going to movies and restaurants farther and farther out of town. One night after we went for a long drive, we decided to stop at a small diner on the way back, and they wouldn't serve us. They had a whites-only policy, and they weren't about to budge from it. We didn't make a scene. We just left quietly and headed out to the car. Some of the locals who had seen us in the restaurant followed us outside and started yelling at us. As a couple, we had never faced anything quite like this before, so I think we were both too stunned to respond. Some of the men got in a car and followed us as we drove back to St. Louis. About halfway back they ran us off the road, and our car turned over. I was knocked unconscious. When I woke up in the hospital two days later, I found out Javier had been beaten to death. The police investigated, but they weren't much interested in finding the guilty parties. They finally closed the case and called it an 'accidental death'."

Josephine stubbed out her cigarette in the ashtray on the edge of the desk, looked right at me, and said, gently, "That's why I'm here."

"I'm sorry," I said, softly. "I'm so sorry."

She looked on the verge of crying, so I started to get up to hug her. She quickly motioned for me to sit back down.

"I'm alright," she said. "I'm fine. I just have my moments when I still get…"

Her voice trailed off, and she looked away from me.

"I understand," I said. "I really do."

When she regained her composure, she continued, "Truthfully, that's only partly why I'm here. Another part of my contribution here will be my skin color. How's that for irony? J.T., you want to tell Olivia the rest? I think I'm about talked out for now."

Mr. Bush, who was again staring blankly out the window, turned and said, "Yes. I suppose it's time to put all our cards on the table. Olivia, here's what we're going to do—and why *you're* here. J.D. and his wife have been blessed with five children, so they're about to burst at the seams in that apartment of theirs. They've also got to get out of that neighborhood, for the reasons you've already heard about. They need a place of their own. They've scrimped and saved, and now they're ready. Right now, though, nothing is up for sale in the Ville, which would have been my first choice for them. The schools would be ideal for their children, and they'd all be safe here, too. But, if we wait around for a house to come open, who knows how long that could take?"

Mr. Bush walked over to the window behind the desk and looked out again. This time he wasn't gathering his thoughts and emotions. This time he was checking to make sure no one was within hearing range of the building.

"I don't want to make this too dramatic," he continued. "However, Reverend Danielson was right when he said we could end up in jail. Actually, that's probably on the lighter end of the scale, especially for you women. The truth is, we might end up being targets for violence. I've seen it happen before—too many times. We need to be prepared as much as we can to make sure that doesn't happen. I'm not trying to scare anyone. I just want you to know what we're up against. Now that I've said that, let's get to business. Here's what we're going to do."

He motioned for us to move chairs together in front of Reverend Danielson's desk. Mr. Bush went to the corner of the study and picked up a large, rolled-up piece of paper. He came back over, unrolled it on the desk, and put books on the edges to keep the paper from rolling back up. It was a map of St. Louis, the type used by realtors to show an overview of the neighborhoods in the city.

"We're right here," he said, taking his pencil and drawing a square around the Ville. "Take a look here, just West of Taylor, in the neighborhood that borders the Ville. The street that runs over here parallel to the streetcar tracks is Labadie. There are several homes on that street that have been made into apartments, and I've been able to place some families in those. So far, so good. There haven't been any real problems to speak of—because they're all just renting."

He then drew a large X about halfway down the street. "Right here," he continued, "is 4600 Labadie. This house has just come up for sale."

Here he paused for emphasis and added, pounding his fist on the map, "And we're going to buy it! That is, the five of us are going to buy it—for Mr. Shelley and his family."

I looked up at Mr. Bush. His breath was coming in short, fast bursts. He was sweating profusely and was wiping his forehead almost constantly with the back of his right hand.

"However," he continued, "there's a problem. This house does have a covenant attached to it. The house was built way back in 1911, and they had covenants, believe it or not, even back then. The original deed says..."

He reached in his right trousers pocket and pulled out another piece of paper. Unfolding it, he read to us, "'In entering into this purchase agreement herewithin, purchasers of said property at 4600 Labadie Avenue agree that, in accordance with restrictions pursuant to said property, future sale will not be made to persons not of Caucasian race for a period of fifty (50) years from the date of undersignment of title'."

He continued, "This means that, legally, we couldn't purchase it until 1961. Think about that—1961."

Leaning forward and lowering his voice, he added, "Even though 4600 has that covenant, I think, with the right plan, we can buy this house now, and I'll tell you why. Now that I've placed families in rentals all up and down that street, it won't look suspicious to anybody if one more black face shows up. They'll assume, at least at first, that J.D. is just another renter. Only that won't be the case at all. He'll be the official and legal owner of the property."

"God bless you," Mr. Shelley said as he reached over to put his hand on Mr. Bush's shoulder. "This would be our dream come true."

"Let's don't get too excited yet," Mr. Bush added. "For all of this to work, we're going to have to be smart—and sneaky. *Very* sneaky."

"I suppose this is where I come in," I added, drolly.

"Only partly," Mr. Bush added, drawing out the words. "We'll all be sneaks before this is over. I'll get to you in a minute, Olivia. First, I want to go over a few more of the details. Here's the sequence of events we're going to have to follow."

Pointing to Josephine, he said, "Mrs. Fitzgerald here is going to be our *straw buyer.* Any of you know what that means?"

None of us had ever heard the term, so, in unison, we shook our heads that we didn't.

"A *straw buyer,*" Mr. Bush continued, "is a person who purchases a property for another individual. It's a person who goes ahead with the entire purchase process, gets the official deed in hand, and then transfers said deed to another party. This other party is, in reality, the party that wanted the property in the first place. A lot of big companies do this when they want to acquire property for expansion purposes. If a business, like say, Wagner Electric Company, wanted to buy a nice parcel of land for new buildings over on Page Avenue where there's all that open ground, the price of that land would suddenly really jump through the roof if the owners found out a rich enterprise like Wagner was interested. If, on the other hand, a person who has no apparent business ties shows an interest, the purchase price would be much, much lower. So, Wagner would hire a straw buyer to purchase the property. That person, for a fee of course, would then turn around and sell the parcel of land to Wagner—at the price they wanted in the first place. Smart, right? Sneaky, yes, but smart."

"That's great!" I shot in. "You mean that's legal?"

"Completely legal," Mr. Bush replied. "The *process* of using a straw buyer is legal. However, in our case, in terms of the Labadie property, we've got one fly in the ointment. We've got one piece that isn't so legal. That's why Mrs. Fitzgerald is here, and why I'm so pleased she has volunteered to help us with our mission. She's going to be our straw buyer."

Josephine stood and gave an exaggerated bow to each of us. We all applauded politely and nodded our heads.

Mr. Bush continued, "My company will handle the sale on behalf of Mrs. Fitzgerald. When we get the deed and title, we'll quietly sell the home to J.D. and rework all the paperwork. That's the part that's not so legal. We'll have to hope and pray no one is the wiser until all this goes through. With the covenant in place, we could lose everything if we get caught—or even worse than that—in a snap of our fingers. So, my friends, keep praying, with all your might."

"Amen!" Reverend Danielson added.

He beat me to the punch. I was about to say exactly the same thing.

Right at that moment, I suddenly saw the pieces falling together. We were each to be chess pieces, each with a specific purpose and mission on a very dangerous chessboard. The only thing I didn't yet know was which pieces would be involved and who would become them. Even though I didn't understand all of this yet, I was already feeling one thing for sure: This was one game I wanted to be part of, with all my heart.

"Olivia," Mr. Bush said, turning toward me, speaking sternly, "now we come to you. I think you've met my daughter, Margaret. She's an attorney, an officer of the court. As such, she can't be involved in anything that's even remotely illegal, even if it's known that *right* far outweighs everything else in a particular case. Oh, we'll need her and will use her services down the road, but for now she has to stay out of this. That's where you come into the picture. Reverend Danielson tells me, and I've heard it from countless other people as well, you're the best teacher we have at Sumner. Your skills in communicating are second to none, especially in the area of writing. That, more than anything, is why we need you. I know you're not a legal secretary, but before you're done with this, you'll be better than most of them out there. I'm going to need some property descriptions, abstracts, and other real estate documents written up—*to our advantage.*"

He then repeated, emphasizing each word, "*To our advantage.* I've checked, and it looks like not all the homes in that area have a covenant attached—yet. So, we just might be able to get away with this if we're good, and if we're also very lucky. In terms of the property at 4600, for us to have a chance, the sections of the documents displaying the covenant will somehow have to get lost in the shuffle. This isn't all we need to do by any means, but it's a major piece of the puzzle. There's more—much more, but we'll talk about that later. However, without this—without *your* part—the other pieces probably won't fit. You know what I'm implying, don't you?"

By the look on his face, his meaning was clear. Perfectly clear. Binding, legal documents would have to be rewritten for the transaction by me, and with an eye toward *accidentally losing* parts of them. Something else was also very clear: If I did this, my neck would be on the chopping block, right along with the others.

Before I could speak, he added, "There is also something else…"

His voice trailed off as he smiled and pointed to Reverend

Danielson, who cleared his throat again and said, "Well, yes, there *is* something else. Now I promise this will stay completely within this room because I know you don't like to talk about it. Olivia, I hear things from people. I happen to know you've helped, financially, three families when they purchased homes in the Ville. Most recently, you also loaned Ella most of her down payment."

I started to cut in, but I got only as far as, "How…"

He quickly continued, "As I said, I hear things."

Reverend Danielson paused again for a moment before continuing, his voice rising, "I've beat this bush long enough. I'm just going to say it. Young woman, the fact is you've got money. More than most. If worse comes to worse, we may need some of it, especially for legal help if things go bad. I hope and pray we won't need it, but we may. I know that's a lot to ask, but I have to ask it now—and you need to know about it now. We want and need your help, but we also want to be completely honest with you. I guess this is all my long-winded way of leading up to this. Knowing what you do now, I'm going to ask you a question. Will you join us in this endeavor? We'd be proud, and grateful, if you would."

He offered me a glass of water before continuing. "Please take a minute and think about all of this before you answer. And please know this—no one here would blame you or think less of you if you decide to walk out that door right now. I know it must seem like we're pressing you, but we don't have much time if we're going to try this. I'm terribly sorry, but that's the way it is. We really have to know your answer now.

I didn't answer right away. As I looked around at the others, the rest of the chess pieces fell into place.

Mr. Bush was to be our Bishop, the piece capable of playing the angles both literally—and figuratively.

J.D. would be our Knight, capable of patterned, although often seemingly unpredictable, movement—especially in comparison with the way other pieces moved; we'd need this unpredictability, this stealth, if we were to succeed.

Josephine, by virtue of her skin color, would be our Queen, capable of moving in all directions at any given time; her movements would have no restrictions, a characteristic we'd desperately need, but none of the rest of us had.

Reverend Danielson would be our center Pawn, sent out to be a pathfinder and gatherer of information for the rest of us; his work would help dictate the main strategy as we went along.

And I was to be the Rook, silent, yet powerful enough to strike suddenly and ruthlessly, although also often expendable; if I was going to play this game, I'd have to be willing to live with any and all consequences of my actions.

I didn't have to think long about this. Not at all. I knew what many of the consequences could be if we were caught, but, at the same time, I also knew what this could mean if we were successful. If everything fell as planned, we'd be able to put at least a small hole in the invisible fence surrounding the Ville. The Shelleys were just one family, but if we could stop, at least temporarily, the advance of the mission of the Real Estate Exchange, we might be able to open doors to possibilities none of us thought would ever be possible in our lifetimes. It would be risky. Very risky. But it was also a risk I felt worth taking—one that had to be taken. I looked at the others, and I saw it in their eyes as well. Suddenly, from deep in my heart, I knew there was only one thing to say.

"I'm in," I said to the group. "I know I should probably ask a million questions, but I'm not going to. I've heard enough for now. There's only one question I want answered before we leave. What's our first step?"

The others gathered around me. Each, in turn, without saying a word, hugged me. Tears were welling up in Josephine's eyes. J.D. and Mr. Bush avoided looking right at my face. If they had made eye contact with me, the floodgates would have opened. Reverend Danielson came closest to speaking to me, but his voice caught and he coughed instead.

When we had all finished blowing noses and rubbing eyes, Mr. Bush walked back over in front of me. He clicked his heels together, saluted me sharply, and said, "Welcome to the battle, Olivia. And I do mean battle."

"This is one battle we'll win," I said. "We have to."

"Yes, we do," Josephine said. "Yes, we do."

At this point, nothing else needed to be said.

The battle was on.

*   *   *

That night in bed, I tossed and turned, playing the events of the afternoon over and over in my mind. When I finally fell asleep, the dream swept over me again…

The angels were still screaming.

"Gimme them matches," Jimmy John said.

"Why?" I asked.

"Because we can't let nobody catch us with 'em."

I handed them over.

"We've got to run now. Hold my hand."

We started to run but Jimmy John stopped and pushed me to the ground.

"Somebody's comin'!" he said. "You keep down, low."

I could hear horses galloping fast.

Toward us.

4

Interlopers

The next morning it happened again.

I had just eased into the tub when the doorbell rang.

I was expecting it.

I had forgotten to call Ella the previous evening, as I promised I would. To top it off, I hadn't put the receiver back on the hook after my nap, so the phone line appeared busy all night.

I knew Ella was going to be hopping mad. I also knew she was the one at the door.

Wrapping myself in the towel I had placed next to the tub for just this circumstance, I hurried down the stairs, once again dripping all the way. I pulled the curtain to the side, and there she was, already wagging her index finger at me.

"Shame, shame on you," I could hear her saying over and over, each time louder than before.

I was half tempted not to open the door, but I knew that wouldn't do any good. Knowing Ella, she would have probably just climbed through a window somewhere.

"I know what you're going to say," I said, trying to calm her. "You've got to believe me. I'm sorry. Truly sorry. You're going to have to give me a Get-Out-of-Jail-Free card on this one. I messed up, and I know it. Come on in. The coffee is on, and it will just take me a couple of minutes to get cleaned up and dressed."

As soon as she walked in, I stopped her and kissed her on the cheek. "There, will that do it?" I asked.

"What? A lousy kiss on the cheek? Oh, you haven't even begun to pay for not giving me a jingle last night. Forget the

54

horrible curiosity attack I had. I was worried sick about you when you didn't call. I tried your line, but all I got was a buzz all night. If somebody hadn't stopped by to visit, I'd have been over here like a shot."

"So, *somebody* came over to visit?" I teased as best I could. "Now, who could that have been? Let's see. It must have been somebody pretty important to keep you from coming over here to see if your *best friend* was sprawled out on the floor somewhere. Let me think. Could that visitor have been, oh, say, Jackson Taylor?"

"Now wait a minute. We're not going to play that game. Forget about me. What happened with *you*? You're the one we were talking about, remember?"

Mimicking her Arkansas drawl, I replied, "Honey, I'd rather talk about…Jackson."

"Well, I wouldn't, so let's just close that book, shall we?"

"I'll close that one if you'll be quiet long enough for me to tell you what went on yesterday afternoon. Think you can manage that?"

"You've got me over a barrel. Do I have any other choice?"

Running her fingers across her lips, she added, "I'll zip it for now, but your story better be very good—and *very* detailed. I mean *very*."

She then asked, as she barged past me toward the kitchen, "But first, where's that coffee. If I don't get some, I'm going to faint."

"And when I'm done, *your* story better be very detailed," I called after her.

She turned on the kitchen faucet and said, "I can't hear you. What did you say? What did you say?"

I just laughed. There wasn't anything else I *could* say, so I just shook my head and went back upstairs to get dressed.

I finished putting myself together in what must have been record time for me, and the time could have been cut in half if I hadn't spent so much time poring over my scarf rack. For the past several years my main fashion weakness had been scarves I wore loosely around my neck. I loved the way they looked and felt, but I wore them probably more out of memory of and love for Inman than anything else. During our courtship he gave me scarves for what seemed like every occasion. He once even surprised me with one, of all things, on Arbor Day. I once asked him why scarves, as opposed to shoes or hats? He took me in his arms and whispered, "Scarves are colorful, full of life and joy—just like you. Just like our love." My knees nearly buckled as he drew me close and gently kissed me. After that, I was hooked. I vowed to wear one every chance I got, even during the summer months.

I was still lost in thoughts of Inman, finishing my hair, when I heard a plate crash as it hit the floor down in the kitchen.

"Sorry, Liv," Ella called up to me. "Just slipped. Had a crack in it anyway. Wasn't any good."

Somehow, Ella could always make any mishap seem like a just or divine intervention.

She was just that kind of friend, and I loved her for it.

I was at the bottom of the stairs when she called out, "Liv, get in here. You've got to see this. Hurry up now."

She motioned for me to get behind her so we could both peek through the back curtains. There in the backyard was Charles Fredericks, running in circles, trying his best to round up the goats. He was wearing overalls and a floppy straw hat that had a gaping hole on top. The more he ran, the more his thick, black hair seemed to rise up through that hole. Ella noticed it first and said, "If we wait long enough, we'll probably see eyes on top of that hat. Ever see anything like that?"

I had to admit I hadn't. It was so ridiculous it was actually cute.

"You know what this is?" I asked. "It's just one more example of how downright stupid men can look when they try to impress women. You can bet your bottom dollar Charles knows we're watching him. This is all for our benefit, you know. Just look at him. I bet he's also figuring we're going to feel sorry for him and go out there to help—and then invite him in for breakfast."

"Well, aren't we?" Ella asked, wryly.

"Not on your tintype, Sister. As far as I'm concerned, he's on his own. He brought those mangy looking yard eaters over here, so he can just chase them around all day if that's what it takes."

"You talk tough, but your eyes say something else. Are you falling for this man?"

"Charles Fredericks? Are you nuts? I wouldn't have anything to do with him if we were trapped in a well together."

"But look at those arms. Look at that chest. Look at those muscles."

"Yeah," I said, "but I'm betting the biggest muscle of all is right between his ears."

"Maybe," Ella said, "but how come you're smiling right now?"

I didn't answer. We sat down, poured some coffee, and watched the rodeo continue. Charles was on the ground as much as he was on his feet. I had no idea goats were so fast and nimble. Every time he fell, he'd get up and shake his fist at the goats and lunge after them again. If anything, he was persistent. He'd also stop every once in a while and look up at the window, and we'd quickly duck down. I didn't need any more men in my kitchen, literally and figuratively.

When Charles finally had all the goats roped together, he led them through the back gate and down the alley. He paused one last time, looked back, shrugged his shoulders, and was gone.

When he was out of sight, Ella said, "You're a mean old witch. You know that, right? You could have at least cooked him some eggs."

"Men are also like dogs," I replied. "You feed one once, and it will keep coming back. There will be no food for this dog."

"Keep saying that. Rather, keep telling *yourself* that," Ella said, smiling broadly. "You better. I have the feeling this dog will be back, and sooner than you think."

"Maybe," I said. "Maybe. We'll see."

I drew back the curtains and looked outside one last time. I was half hoping I'd see him walking back, but the alley was now empty.

"Just one more dog," I said. "Just one more."

I cooked up some eggs and grits, and while we ate we exchanged tales of our adventures the previous afternoon. Jackson had stopped by Ella's house, and the two of them spent the better part of the afternoon and early evening in her porch swing. Ella said he was good company, very gentle and kind. She repeated several times that in private he wasn't nearly the loud-mouth he typically appeared to be. The way she talked about him I could tell she was definitely developing feelings for him. Her tone was still casual and somewhat clipped, but I had known her long enough that I could read between the lines. I had more than ample opportunity to tease her about his visit, but I bit my lip more than once. Just as it was for me, it had been a long time since Ella had let down her guard when it came to matters of the heart. I did get one shot off, though. I couldn't resist. When she said she was surprised by how much common sense he had and what a good head he seemed to have on his shoulders, I couldn't take it any more.

I held up my hand and said, "Stop! Good head on his shoulders? I've seen a better head on a glass of beer!"

I went back to eating my eggs. When I looked up, Ella flung her napkin right in my face.

I then told her as much as I dared about my meeting at the church. I had promised to keep everything secret, but Ella was my dearest friend in the world and I wanted to talk to someone I trusted about all of this. I also knew if I didn't tell her about it, she'd bug me to death until I finally caved in. I decided to save us both the wear and tear, so I shared with her the general plan of attack.

"You just be careful," she said, finally. "You could end up in a shallow grave somewhere if the wrong people find out about this. I'm not kidding."

"That's not going to happen," I replied. "You worry too much."

I then added, "Besides, I'm tougher than you think. I can take care of myself, you know."

"I know that. I'm just worried about you. That's all. This isn't a game, Liv. If you're caught, you could lose everything—for real. You can't afford that, and I can't afford to lose you. I'm going to be keeping a closer eye on you. If you need me for anything, you just let me know. Promise?"

"Promise," I said, leaning over to hug her tightly.

We sat there in silence a few minutes, silence that only best friends can share.

Ella finally split the silence when she stood up, slapped her forehead, and shouted, "I can't believe I almost forgot this! Sweet Moses—this is why I came over here in the first place this morning. I brought something for you."

She opened her purse and began digging through it, placing its contents in a row out on the table as she continued her search. She finally drew out a small envelope, held it high in the air, and said, "You won't believe what this is. If you guessed until you were a thousand you'd never come up with it. Liv, this is for you. This is a small way of me saying thanks for everything you've done for me lately. This is...well, just take a look."

She handed me the envelope. I quickly tore it open and a ticket fell out. I looked at it, jumped up, and screamed, "Where did you get this! Where'd you get this! I can't believe it!"

I stepped forward, took her hands in mine, and we both jumped up and down like a couple of school girls jumping rope.

"We're really going? This isn't a joke, right?" I asked.

As I held the ticket tightly, my hands were shaking. The ticket was for the new flower show at the Jewel Box in Forest Park. I had been praying that somehow a ticket would become available, but I had just about given up all hope.

"Well, one of us is going," she replied. "It took some doing, but I got a ticket. *One* ticket. That's all I could get. I know how

for the event, but at the same time I didn't want to come so casual I'd look out of place.

As I looked around me, however, I realized I could not have been more out of place, that I could not have stuck out more if I had come with a revolving searchlight attached to the top of my hat.

All the women around me were wearing enormous hoop skirts and had their hair coiled in long ringlets that swished and swayed as they shuffled by.

I also noticed something else: There were no dark faces attached to those skirts.

None.

A line about fifty feet long stretched back from the entrance to where I was standing. The women were clustered in small groups all around me, as the line inched slowly forward. I was my own group of one, encircled by skirts that kept brushing against my legs as we continued our forward progress. There were occasional glances in my direction, but no one made eye contact.

At the door, the woman taking tickets, an older woman who looked like a character right out of *Gone With the Wind*, said to the group in front of me, "I'm so glad y'all could make it. Sit yourselves over in the corner by the fountain. That will give you the best view of our speaker."

Her voice was very much like Ella's. It was very slow, drawn out, full of vowels of the South. I stepped forward and handed her my ticket. She was gloved—white gloves up to her elbows. With her right index finger and thumb, she slowly and deliberately pulled up my ticket and looked at it.

"What do we have here? I don't think you need this. The refreshments are being prepared out back. You cooks and waitresses don't go through this way. Go around back, child."

Inman had always accused me of having the shortest fuse he had ever known. I never denied it. And at this moment, the fuse was already burning.

In an instant, I felt my breath catch. I reached out, yanked

On normal days, the meandering paths between the rows of
~ers and plants appeared like pictures I had seen in *Life* maga-
~ of the mazes people in England added to their gardens. The
~nts and trees growing along the paths were tall enough that
~ could not see the view through to the other side, which made
anticipation and surprise at every twist and turn. For tonight,
~rything near the entrance to the main path had all been dug
~ and moved so that a small stage could be erected. The ticket
~ker had been right; the area near the fountain had a direct view
~ the stage, so I walked over and put my purse on the chair on
~e far outside, to reserve my spot.

I was just about to take a quick walk through the special
~isplay of Hibiscus when I noticed it. There, hanging on the wall
~ehind the stage, was a long banner. On it, in large, bright red
~etters, was the name of the local group hosting the event.

The Daughters of Dixie.

That explained the hoop skirts. That explained the jockey
holding open the door. That explained why, as I looked more
intently around the room, I may have seemed lost to some of the
curious gazes I noticed coming my direction.

I knew of "White's Only" events, but I had never actually
been to one.

Until now.

And now, thanks to me, this one was going up in smoke.

I was staying. If these Daughters wanted me out of here,
they'd have to use dynamite.

I was halfway around the first turn when someone started
pounding a gavel. Startled, we all immediately headed back
toward the lecture area. When I got to my chair, I found the
ticket taker seated in it, staring daggers at me. My purse was now
propped against a large urn a few feet away. Without a word, I
picked up my purse, turned, and stepped right on the bottom of
her flowing skirt. I pivoted to move away, and when I did the distinct sound of a tear could be heard by all around us.

"Oh my heavens!" I exclaimed in my best Ella drawl. "I'm so

the ticket from her hand, and stuck it right u1

"First of all," I said, putting my hands on

your child, a fact which should be obvious to y

I reached over and rubbed my hand on he

backed away from me, slowly, wide-eyed.

"And furthermore, I'm not a cook or a ser

Merriweather Perkins, and I grow the best dar

the city of St. Louis."

And then I got mad.

"I'm a guest here. This is my ticket, bought an

I'm going in right here. I'll sit over there by the four

sure to have a good view of the speaker. Don't wor

I'll have a grand time."

I tore my own ticket in half, handed her the botto

headed in. An elderly Colored man wearing a jockey

the door open for me and smiled broadly as he ushered

"You look like an idiot," I said to him out of the

my mouth as I strolled past. "Take that ridiculous hat

get rid of that vest. We're not Darkies anymore, and

forget it."

I paused one last time and turned to face the tick

She was beet red, and her mouth was gaping open.

I just couldn't resist adding, "I'd also close that m

yours if I were you. You're going to catch flies."

No one around her said a word. It looked like they wei

ing to catch flies, too.

I then stepped into the most beautiful room I had ever

in my life. The interior of the Jewel Box was about the same

as the interior of our church. It wasn't huge by any means, but

a greenhouse, it seemed like a cathedral. Spotlights were plac

behind the flowers so that their shadows were lifted up and pr

jected on the cantilevered glass walls. Those were the images

had seen coming up the sidewalk. The images were beautifu

from the outside, but they were absolutely magnificent from the

inside.

clumsy and so sorry."

The ticket taker was speechless. She looked down at her skirt, but because of the way the material was arched she couldn't see near the floor. She looked at me with a blank stare, as if saying, "What did you just do?"

I didn't give her a chance to say anything. I quickly walked behind the chairs in that section and stood against the side wall. The jockey, now minus his hat, had apparently seen everything. He walked quickly toward me, carrying a small folding chair. He opened it for me and motioned me to sit down. As I did, he winked at me.

I winked back.

When the commotion in the room finally settled, the woman pounding the gavel, a chalky-looking woman about mid-forties with the biggest head of hair I had ever seen on a human being, welcomed everyone. She made a point of looking right at me just long enough to indicate her displeasure.

I smiled and nodded back to her.

She then addressed the group. "I want to welcome y'all to this year's most excitin' event—the Hibiscus show."

She started clapping, her eyes widening and darting around the room. The crowd enthusiastically added their applause.

She continued, "As most of you know, I'm Mrs. Beauregard Johnson, President of the St. Louis chapter of the Daughters of Dixie, an organization dedicated to preserving beauty wherever and whenever we can. To this end, we'll be sponsoring several events here at the Jewel Box this fall. Our next will be our annual Rebel Cotillion, which will be held here for the very first time."

More applause followed. The ticket taker turned in her chair and craned her neck to see where I was sitting. Our eyes met, and I nodded smartly and smiled, doing my best to indicate to her, "Yes, I'll see you at the Cotillion!" My expression must have worked because she looked like a woman ready to launch her dinner.

Mrs. Beauregard Johnson looked at her watch and continued,

"Oh my—time is running late. One more thing before we begin. This is also our recruitment and pledge season. If you know a deserving individual to join our ranks, please complete one of our nomination forms and deliver it to our membership chair, Mrs. Dotty Endicott, who is seated right over there."

She pointed to the ticket taker. She stood, waved, and everyone applauded politely. When she turned to acknowledge those behind her, our eyes locked again. I know I shouldn't have done it, but my fuse was still smoldering. I pointed to her, then moved my hand as if I were writing something across the air, and finally pointed back to myself. I narrowed my eyebrows and flashed her the OK sign, trying to indicate to her that I'd be honored if she'd sponsor little old me.

I could hear her say quite loudly and to no one in particular, "Well, I never in all my days!"

She snapped her head back around and clamped her hands on the belt around the middle of her skirt. Her fuse was, clearly, now also lit.

Mrs. Beauregard Johnson then continued, "Tonight we've been blessed by the presence of the gentleman with the greenest thumb around, Mr. Thomas A. Sullivan, chief architect and groundskeeper for the now nationally famous Missouri Botanical Gardens. He is going to share with us his secrets for the care and nurturing of the Hibiscus. From those delicate beauties he brought with him and added to the display here, it's clear as the air we breathe that Mr. Sullivan has magical powers."

Here she paused, looking around as if to make sure there were no Yankee spies in the bushes, and added, "One more thing, ladies. He is not just a handsome man. He's also an unmarried man!"

This got the loudest applause yet. Several of the older women near the front vigorously plied their hand fans back and forth near their blushed faces.

I had to admit he was a fine looking man. He was tall, muscular, and had a rugged look about him, like he had just come from chopping down trees, which he probably really had. He stepped forward to the podium and motioned for quiet.

A few women were still giggling when he said, "Thank you, Mrs. Beauregard, but you are too kind. It's true I'm not married in the traditional sense, but I guess you've never seen me with all the delicate ladies I have growing over at the Garden. Right now, they keep me plenty busy, and I sure feel married to them! They're all delicate and beautiful, like the Daughters of Dixie."

Someone in the back shouted out, drawling the words slowly, "I'm sure we can also arrange a traditional marriage for you, too!"

The room erupted in laughter and nods of heads. Mr. Sullivan smiled and bowed deeply. "You honor me. I'd be lucky indeed if that were true."

As he reached for a glass of water on the podium, he found the gavel and started banging it loudly on the lectern. "The time *is* running late, so with your permission, I'll begin. I don't speak to groups very often, so I'm just going to visit with all of you like you're my helpers at the Garden. If you get lost or confused as I go along, just raise a hand and ask questions."

His voice was firm, yet friendly, with an even cadence that carried one piece of information smoothly into the next. When he came to the point of the importance of weed control, he reached in his pocket and pulled out what looked like a small clump of grass.

"Who can tell me what this is?" he asked. "Anyone?"

He waved it back and forth for all to see.

"I'm going to tell you what it is. It's death to all Hibiscus everywhere. It's the common weed. Now tell me, what is the best way to prevent an invasion of weeds around Hibiscus roots? Come on, ladies. Show me what you know."

The room became still. A few of the women near the front looked back and forth at each other and then shrugged shoulders.

"Oh, come on. Somebody here has to know."

He was right. *Somebody* here did know.

I knew.

I raised my hand and waved it slowly back and forth. It was then I think he noticed me for the first time.

With a startled expression on his face he pointed at me and said, "I see we have a brave soul over here. Tell us: How do we keep those deadly weeds at bay?"

All eyes turned my direction. Many, who had also apparently just noticed me, let out a collective gasp.

No, I wasn't exactly a Daughter of Dixie….

The spotlight was clearly on me, and I was never one to shy away from the light. I barged right ahead.

"Pecan shells," I said. "Crushed pecan shells. You spread them around the base of each plant."

Mr. Sullivan's eyes widened and he leaned forward. "And why would that be?" he asked, clearly wanting me to continue.

"There are many schools of thought on this," I said. "Some say it's because of an acid that leeches out of the shells and gets into the soil when they get wet. The acid destroys the climate for the weeds but doesn't hurt the plant. Others say the shells just block sunlight better than, say, grass clippings. Me? I use a combination of both."

Mr. Sullivan didn't respond for what seemed like an eternity. The room was also more quiet than before. He finally said, "You are exactly right. I'd have bet a week's pay no one here would have known the secret of pecan shells. Let's give this gardener a round of applause. She deserves it."

He started clapping, but only a few others followed his lead, and even those just struck their hands together softly. He seemed to sense what was going on, quickly thanked me again, and moved to the next point in his lecture, but not before looking back at me and smiling.

His talk was fascinating, especially when he told us about the year he developed a new method of preventing root rot. Well, *I* was fascinated. Most in the room looked half asleep or lost in dreams of ways to end his unmarried status. When he gave his closing remarks, it was obvious some weren't following what he was saying at all and had to be nudged from their inattention.

"I'll stay around a few minutes in case there are questions," he said, "but I really must get back to the Garden tonight to take care of a sprinkler problem. With the heat we've been having, we have to get that done quickly. I hope you understand. Thank you again for having me tonight. Ladies, it has been a pleasure. I look forward to seeing all of you again soon—at the Garden!"

We all applauded again as Mrs. Beauregard Johnson stepped back up to the podium.

"Thank you, Mr. Sullivan. Your talk was most instructive. If you'd be so kind, we'd like to have you remain while refreshments are served. I think there are some girls here who'd like to get to know you better."

Nervous laughter and giggles rang out again. A final round of applause was given, and all stood as servers carried silver trays of food and beverages up the path and into the lecture area.

The servers didn't look like Daughters of Dixie either....

All around me it started to look like a revival of plantation life in the old South, and I'd had enough of it. I decided to walk around the crowd and slip down the path to get a few pictures of the Hibiscus before leaving. I wasn't half a dozen steps into the path when a hand gently grabbed my arm. I turned to see Mr. Sullivan raising his other hand to offer me a glass of punch. I thanked him for his kindness.

"Pecan shells," he said, laughing loudly but not meanly. "I never heard of that in all my life. Pecan shells? Does it really work?"

"But you said…"

"I know what I said," he interrupted, gently. "Let's walk a minute. You're probably the only one here who can tell a Hibiscus from a pineapple, and I'd like to hear what you think of this year's bounty."

"Yes," I said, smiling back sincerely as we began our walk.

"Yes, what?" he asked.

"Yes, the pecan shells really do work. You should try them."

"I will," he said. "But, you can imagine what an awful pile of shells it would take to cover what we'd need at the Garden."

We both stopped in our tracks and laughed.

"I get your point," I said. "I guess that wouldn't be all that practical, would it?"

"Probably not, but just think of all the pecan pies we'd have. Wow!"

I just shook my head. "Is food all you men think of?" I asked.

"Not me," he said. "Trust me on that."

He motioned me to follow him again. When we came to the exhibit, he went down the row and explained the differences between each type of Hibiscus. I asked a few questions, and he eagerly and enthusiastically gave more information. Several times he also stepped in front of my camera when I paused to take pictures of the flowers, each time making a silly face as he entered the frame.

"Now, how am I going to display these pictures?" I asked, in mock disgust.

"I know—I know. Too much beauty in each picture now, right? Too much for your audience to handle, right?"

"Well, they do say beauty is in the eye of the beholder, don't they?" I said, in my best teacher tone. "I think my audience will be able to handle these."

He clutched his chest and replied, "You've stabbed me in the heart. Want me to get on the floor so you can stomp on it, too?"

"No, I might trip and then miss all the rest of the flowers. Just stand to the side and let me through."

"Are you always this mean?" he asked.

"Not me," I said, mocking his earlier words. "Trust me on that."

"I'm not sure I do," he said, laughing. "Time will tell."

We continued along, each remarking excitedly about the change in colors of the petals from variety to variety, from pink to lavender to red to autumn yellow. At one point he took my hand and gently brushed it against the tip of one of the flowers.

"Feel that?" he said. "That texture is how you can really tell if a Hibiscus is healthy or starting to fade. The tip will be soft as angel hair, soft as a baby's breath."

He didn't let go of my hand. He squeezed it gently and looked deeply into my eyes. His hand was warm, and I could feel his heartbeat in his fingers.

I didn't pull my hand away. I stood there studying his face, noticing his deep, brown eyes. His outward demeanor was confident, but his eyes were sad, those of a man whose emotions had traveled far.

I started to ask him to tell me more about himself, about his life away from his flowers, when a tall, bucktoothed Daughter of the South came up behind him, put her arm around his waist, and without a word started ushering him back up the path.

He dug his feet into the soft gravel and said to his escort, "I'll be right with you. Give me a moment."

She still didn't speak. She looked first at him, then at me, turned, and stomped off.

He started to say something, but I stopped him. "Your public awaits. Better get going."

He looked at his watch. "I guess I better. I've got to get out of here—and soon."

"Odds are you'll never make it past those matchmakers up front," I teased. "They've really got it for you, you know."

"That's very funny," he replied. "That's just what I need. If only there was another way out of here."

"Well, maybe I can repay you for all you've taught me tonight. I just happen to know there is another way out. I've seen people bringing plants and small trees in through a door behind the waterwheel back over here. If you're serious, I'll show you."

"I'll show you just how serious I am," he said. "Just you lead the way."

We walked quickly to the waterwheel and climbed over the rope fence in front of it. The door was nearly hidden from view because of some giant ferns growing there. He turned the handle and the door popped right open. The cool evening air rushed into our faces, and it felt so good.

"They are positively going to kill me for doing this," he said as he started stepping outside.

"I can top that," I said. "I think I saw them making a noose for me."

"I wouldn't doubt it," he said. "You be careful getting out of here. Say, I have an idea. You want to sneak out with me? You can come back to the Garden with me if you want."

He smiled and added, "I'll show you my Hibiscus."

"Mr. Sullivan!" I shouted in mock horror. "Is that something like coming up to see your paintings?"

He was flirting, and my heart was pounding.

"Probably something like that."

We both stood a moment in silence. I finally reached out to shake his hand. "I better not go," I said. "I better not."

"I'm sorry," he said. "For both of us. My Hibiscus really do look incredible at night, and they're best when shared."

"I'm sure they do," I said. "Maybe another time."

He took my hand in his and said, "I'll look forward to it."

Reaching into his shirt pocket, he drew out a business card and handed it to me. "This has my number. Call me when you're ready."

"I'll do that," I said.

"Promise?"

"You better get going. Somebody is going to see you back here and wonder what the heck's going on."

"Tell them I ducked out with one of their Daughters. That should keep them buzzing and fainting all night."

"Then I'll definitely make a point of telling them exactly that," I said, laughing nervously.

He then looked at me curiously and asked, "Hey, what's your name? I don't even know your name."

"I'm Olivia. Olivia Hibiscus."

"I'd really like to see you again, Olivia Hibiscus. Please, do make it soon."

"And maybe you shall, but you better get out of here. Now!"

"See you soon?" he asked one more time.

"I'll bring pecan shells," I said, dryly.

"I have no doubt you will."

He waved, winked, and stepped through the door, closing it firmly behind him. My heart was still racing. I more or less floated back up the path and headed straight for the front entrance. The ticket taker stepped in front of me and asked, "Where's Mr. Sullivan? We saw you two back there."

"Why, I just saw him kissing a lady who was sitting way over yonder earlier tonight. Way over there on the other side of the stage. The two of them were back by the ferns. I had to cover my eyes. Go back and look for yourself if you don't believe me. I thought I was going to faint dead away."

Her face turned mean. "You leaving so soon?" she commanded more than asked.

"Not soon enough, apparently."

"We won't be seeing you again, will we?" she added, her message quite clear.

"You never know," I responded. "I may just show up when you least expect it."

"I wouldn't try it," she said coldly.

"I do so love a challenge," I said. "I really do."

With that, I turned and walked out into the night. The shadowy reflections of the flowers inside were still bright against the upper glass walls of the Jewel Box. I stood and looked at them one last time. I then looked at Mr. Sullivan's card. Tears welled up in my eyes, and I started to cry. I didn't want anyone to see me, so I hurried down the sidewalk, quickening my pace as I heard the sound of the streetcar bell off in the distance.

I made it to the Oakland Avenue stop just in time to jump aboard. The conductor rang his bell several times and announced to all aboard, "Jewel Box to your left. Quite a sight at night, isn't it?"

I didn't look back. I couldn't.

* * *

The ride back home took over an hour because the car's power pole slipped off the overhead electric wire four times. The conductor apologized profusely each time he had to climb out and correct the problem, but no one really seemed to mind. It gave us all a chance to sit quietly with our thoughts under the beautiful constellations of a late summer sky. My thoughts were jumbled, still back at the Jewel Box. There was so much I still didn't understand, not just about what I had experienced there, but about myself as well. When the rhythmic clang-clang of the streetcar bell signaled my stop at the Ville, it didn't register completely. If it hadn't been for a member of my church leaning over and nudging me, I probably would have just stayed aboard and ridden all the way to the streetcar barn.

When I reached my house, I walked up the sidewalk, carefully avoiding the cracks. While fumbling in my purse for my keys, I noticed the house was pitch dark. I usually left a light on inside next to the stairs, but it appeared I had forgotten it this time. I turned my key in the lock, but it met with no resistance. The door pushed open easily, with only a small squeak. I entered slowly, kicked the door closed behind me, and felt my way in the darkness toward the light switch.

It happened so quickly I had no time to react.

I felt a thick, sweaty arm slide smoothly around my neck while from the other side a hand clamped tightly over my my mouth. I was lifted slightly off the floor, just the tips of my shoes still touching. Instinctively, I swung my arms back as forcefully as I could, trying to free myself.

The grip on my neck only tightened, nearly closing off my breath.

"Shhhhh," a voice whispered behind my left ear. "I'm not going to hurt you. You have to believe me. You have to trust me."

I struggled again, this time kicking and rocking my legs

forward, hoping to upset our balance. Just as I thought we were going to topple, I looked down and saw his shoes. The breeze fluttering through the living room curtains allowed for only a moment a flash of the streetlight outside. In that instant, I could tell they were wing-tips, splotched with what appeared to be light colored paint.

I relaxed, letting my full weight fall gently forward. When I felt the grip around my neck loosen slightly, I swung my right arm over my head, catching something solidly. I heard a low moan, like a child's moan. Then his grip tightened sharply. The curtains fluttered again. This time the streetlight went red, then black. A wave of dizziness swept over me. I couldn't catch my breath. I was falling, falling, falling… down into a deep silence.

I came to on my bed. I had no idea how long I had been there, but I could tell I still had my clothes on and had been wrapped tightly in the sheet. Blankets had been rolled up and placed along my sides. I wriggled from side to side but couldn't free myself. I was cocooned. My mouth was too dry for me to scream. I started to cry.

From the darkness of the corner of the room I heard a voice, soft, gentle, "You blacked out. I'm sorry. Don't you scream."

Here he paused and then drew out each word again, slowly, emphatically, "Don't. You. Scream."

I didn't reply. The tone of his voice, even as a whisper, made me realize he meant his words. I tried to focus my eyes in the darkness but could still make out only a shadow.

"You're strong," the voice continued. "I wish…"

His voice trailed off. I waited for him to speak again, but he fell silent, as did the room, save for his labored breathing. I could tell he was breathing mostly through his mouth. Huffs of air were being expelled, like from a man lifting a heavy piece of furniture.

My tongue felt huge as I was finally able to speak. I tried to stay calm, but my voice cracked as I asked, "What do you want with me? Is it money?"

The voice responded immediately, "Yes, but not yours.

Where are all the gifts? The presents? I want those."

"The gifts?" I said.

At first it didn't register. I still felt so weak, so scared. Then it came to me. "You don't mean Miss Dunbar's gifts?"

"Yes, where are they? I know you have them. Tell me where they are and I'll take them and go. I won't hurt you. I promise."

I knew I had to be careful. I didn't want to make him angry. Ella's gifts? He was either really stupid or really misinformed. In either case, the news had to be broken just right. I took my time putting my words together.

"You're welcome to her gifts, but there is something you should know. I take it you're not too familiar with this neighborhood. Am I right?"

I paused, but he didn't respond.

"You can't be. Otherwise, you'd know Miss Dunbar received joke gifts the other night. They weren't appliances, furniture, or regular housewarming gifts."

I waited a moment before adding, "Now you are going to have to trust me. We just had fun with her at her party. The real gifts never come until up to a week later. I'm sorry, but you're early. That's the truth."

Then, bolder, but evenly, I said, "Actually I'm not sorry. You should be ashamed of yourself, trying to take away presents from someone new to the Ville. You're welcome to whatever you can carry away, but you'll make no money from anything brought here the other night. Not a red cent."

"You're lying," he said, almost in a normal voice. "I know you have them. You better tell me where they are. I have to have them. I can't leave without them."

"I've told you the truth. Look, I'm trapped and can't get up, and I won't scream. Search the house from top to bottom if you want, but you won't find a single thing of cash value given to her. If you have to take something, my purse fell when you grabbed me in the hall. I've got about five dollars in there. Take it and go. That's all you're going to get."

The room became very silent again. I could hear him cracking his knuckles, first on one hand, then the other.

"I need money," he said, "but not yours. I'm not taking
yours."

I could hear him stand up and push back my dressing chair.
"I know I should just shut up and be grateful," I said, "but why?"

"You weren't supposed to be home yet," he said, whispering
again. "I didn't want you to be part of this. You're ..."

He walked to the window while carefully shielding his face,
pulled back the curtains, and appeared to be looking up and
down the street below. He then lifted a scarf from the rack and
placed it over his head and face, tying it loosely around his neck.
When he turned around and faced the bed, the scarf hid his
features.

"I'm leaving," he said. "After I'm gone, move slow and you'll
be out of there quick enough. Don't struggle—It'll only make it
worse. I hope I didn't hurt you. Wasn't my plan. I'm sorry for
that."

He loosened the blankets slightly and stepped back. "I owe
you because of this, and I always pay back my debts. Always.
Someday you'll need help, and I'll be there. You'll never see me,
but I'll be there."

With that, he turned and walked quickly from the room. He
paused for a few seconds, then rushed down the stairs. The front
door opened quickly and was closed quietly. I didn't hear him on
the sidewalk, but I knew he was already gone. I did what he said
and moved slowly and deliberately. It took less than a minute for
me to free myself.

I turned on the lamp next to the bed and the light nearly
blinded me. When my eyes finally focused, I got up and walked
down the stairs and stood by the front door. I wasn't sure what
to do. Call the police? The St. Louis City Police seemed like they
cared little about crimes committed in the Ville. More often than
not, it seemed like the individuals reporting the crimes ended
up being treated more like criminals than victims. Very little

follow-up ever took place, even when a report was taken seriously, unless the crime somehow involved someone with skin a lot lighter than what was usually seen in our community. There was White Law, and there was Colored Law—and, sadly, everyone knew it.

I picked up the phone and started to dial for the operator. Then I stopped and put the receiver back in the cradle. I sat down in my rocking chair, covered my eyes, and tears began streaming down my cheeks.

It was then I noticed I had wet myself.

I didn't get up. I pulled a coverlet off the couch and pulled it tightly around my shoulders. I closed my eyes and rocked myself to sleep.

This night, there were no dreams.

5

Conspiracy

The bright early morning sun reflecting off the mirror on the wall next to the front door woke me with a start. I hadn't moved all night. It all seemed like just a bad dream, like I hadn't really been there at all. I ran the events over and over again in my mind, each time trying to remember something, but I couldn't quite put my finger on what I was searching for. Maybe I was searching for a reason, some logic in the madness of the darkness. The sanctity of my own home had been violated, along with a sense of pride and dignity I had come to know only through rebuilding my life after Inman's passing. I didn't just feel vulnerable now. I felt lost, emotionally drained, frightened of what would come next. What does one do when a life has been so invaded? What are the next steps, the next answers to be sought?

I started crying again, not out of fear this time, but out of confusion. I knew I shouldn't call the city police. They'd come, ask perfunctory questions, and finally end up telling me it was, in the end, somehow all my fault. I couldn't tell Ella. He was after her presents; she'd be so upset, she'd never forgive herself for not having the party at her place, no matter its state of repair. I could change my locks, but deep down I knew that wouldn't keep the intruder out if he wanted back inside. The intruder…. When I finally focused on him again, a sliver of what was just on the edge of my thoughts snapped in front of me.

I had seen his shoes before.

But where?

Try as I might, the memory just wouldn't open for me. Church? School? In the neighborhood? Or was it even in the Ville at all? A dull ache started at my temples and ran toward my eyes, and the more I thought about the shoes, the worse the pain became.

My clothes were clammy and sticky, a result of my wetting myself. I rose slowly from the rocker and walked to the window. It was going to be a beautiful day outside, bright and clear skies. Through the glass I could feel the beginning of the day's warmth. Looking at the sidewalk, I could see my flowers had already opened fully.

I sat down on the couch, covered my face with my hands, and wept.

* * *

Ella called just after nine to ask if I was still going in the afternoon with the church group headed to Sportsman's Park to see the St. Louis Cardinals play the Brooklyn Dodgers. I did want to go. Badly. This wasn't going to be the hometown Cards against the Bums, as the Dodgers were called. It was going to be the continuation of a war between the segregation of St. Louis and a lone member of the Dodger team: Jackie Roosevelt Robinson.

Seemingly against all odds, Jackie was the first Negro allowed to play in the Major Leagues. He had been with the team now for over three months and had proved, through his skills, he belonged on the field of play. It seemed such a sad commentary that he was the solitary soldier on one side of this war. Yet, through a quiet grace and determined perseverance, he seemed to be if not winning the war, at least trying to sue for peace, not an easy task for a man standing alone. Our church group was going today to show him he wasn't really alone, that there were, indeed, plenty of troops behind him.

The *Argus*, the newspaper favored by those in the Ville, had followed his exploits daily and in great detail as the season had moved along. There were stories of his ill treatment, in just about every way imaginable, everywhere he came to play. Most frightening of all were reports of death threats made to him in nearly every city he visited. At one point earlier in the season, we seriously doubted he'd be able to continue. Also, in a deeply grisly form of gallows humor, betting pools started popping up in the Ville related to how long it would take before someone shot him. I admired him greatly for his valor, for the pride that was evident. I never wondered why he was doing what he was doing. That was obvious. What I wondered was how he was able to *keep doing* what he was doing.

Yes, I wanted to see Mr. Jackie Roosevelt Robinson continue his fight, but not today. When Ella called, I told her I had been inspired by the Hibiscus show and wanted to work in my flower garden instead.

"Liv, you're getting to be an old woman," she said. "You really do need to get out more."

She was right. I did need to get out of the house more often. However, today just wasn't the day. I needed to be alone, to try to sort through an avalanche of emotions.

"Well, then I'm coming over before I go to the game. There's something I'm dying to ask you. Before I get there, I want you to be thinking about it so you'll have your answer ready. So, tell me, Liv, what was it like last night? Did you sign up for the Daughters of Dixie?"

She then started laughing as she hung up the phone. It took me a minute before it dawned on me what she had said.

"Daughters of Dixie!" I shouted back into the phone, even though the line was already dead.

"Ella Jane!" I screamed. "Just wait until I get my hands on you!"

I stewed all morning, alternately laughing and screaming her name. I'd been had. Royally.

Ella was a practical joker, plain and simple. It wasn't a month after I met her that she got me for the first time. She had been teasing me about how much time I spent on the telephone in the evenings. That afternoon, just before she left my house, she taped down the buttons on the phone so that when the receiver was lifted, the phone could not be answered. It just kept ringing and ringing and ringing all night long. I found out later most of the calls had come from Ella, who, no doubt, was howling over at her house. I didn't discover the tape until the next morning when I tried to make a call for a repairman.

A few weeks later, Ella wrote a short love note to the milkman, snuck over to my porch early one morning, and left it in one of my milk bottles. After that, poor Mr. Daws, our neighborhood milkman, flirted with me unmercifully for a week before we finally figured out we'd both been had. At least I received a week's worth of free butter and eggs along with my milk that week.

After that, I knew the battle lines had been clearly drawn. My first salvo back was an old trick Inman witnessed and then wrote me about while he was in the service. Ella was incredibly proud of her new car. She bought it secondhand from a man who worked at the barbershop over on Sarah Street, but if you believed her, it had the smoothest ride ever put on four wheels. One moonless night I took a baking potato and shoved it as far as I could into the tailpipe of her beloved chariot. I knew she was driving down to the city early the next morning, so I dressed early, hid behind her neighbor's garage, and waited for her to start the car. When she did, the explosion that followed could be felt in the wall of the garage I was leaning upon. Her screams were loud and clear all the way to my hiding spot. The potato had also taken flight across the alley and just missed her neighbor's collie, who took off like a shot. Ella jumped out of the car as if it were on fire, and I ran down the alley past her, laughing and shouting, "Smoothest car I ever heard! Smooooooooooth!"

It was then the war intensified. Shortly thereafter, I started receiving a subscription to *Man's World* magazine, the rag with the risqué photos of scantily clad young women. One can only imagine what my postman must have thought. I followed by putting a "Free Pumpkins" advertisement in the *Argus* newspaper close to Halloween and listed Ella's phone number; she received so many calls, she finally just had to take her phone off the hook. Ella followed that up by advertising my car in the *Argus* at such a ridiculously low price I had eager buyers almost instantly showing up to look at it. I finally had to put a big sign up on my porch that said "Car Sold!" to keep them out of my hair.

The situation was getting out of control, but neither of us would blink, would back down. When word got around the Ville about our juvenile behavior, Reverend Danielson made the mistake of trying to step in to make the peace. Ella's response to him was to place an ad stating that rooms were for rent in his home. With the housing shortage in the area, she might just as well have placed an ad for free pots of gold at his home: potential boarders showed up in droves. Reverend Danielson quickly learned his lesson and said he'd stay away from both of us until we came back to our senses.

And now, the Daughters of Dixie....

"Ella Jane!" I shouted over and over while trying to gobble down my breakfast.

I knew I would have my revenge.

It would come soon.

It would be sweet.

* * *

When Ella marched up my sidewalk, her shoulders back, her head held high, her disposition that of rank confidence, I was waiting for her. Squatting in my front bushes, I had one hand on the outside faucet and the other on my hose. I had intended to give her a good dousing, but I noticed she was wearing her brand new dress. Not even I could be that mean. Instead of turning on the faucet, I quickly jumped out, pointed the hose right at her face and said, "Look out!"

Caught completely off guard, she stumbled back, the heels of her shoes catching along the ridge of the sidewalk. Down she went right on her behind. Some early morning dew was still on the grass, and as she stood up, cursing a blue-streak at me, I nearly fell down myself from the laughter that poured out when I took one look at the back of her dress. She looked very much as if she missed a very important bathroom stop.

"Oh, you've had it now!" she screamed as she rushed forward.

"Stop!" I said. "It's loaded, and I'm not afraid to use it."

I held out the hose once again. This time, it suddenly arched downward as the weight of the nozzle sent it sliding toward the ground. We both doubled over in laughter.

"Truce?" I asked.

"Well, for now at least," Ella responded. "But I owe you one, Liv. Look at this dress! Just look at it!"

"You're not going to get much sympathy from me this morning. Daughters of Dixie, indeed! You knew all about that before you gave me that ticket, didn't you!"

"You always told me nothing could keep you away from a good flower show. I didn't think a nice, quiet, cultured group like the Daughters of Dixie would pose a problem for you. They didn't, did they?"

"Ella Jane, I could wring your neck, and I probably should. You have no idea what those people were like. No idea at all."

"Well, take me inside and give me some coffee. Then you can tell me all about it. I'll listen. I guess I do owe you that much."

"Oh, you won't get off that easy. I promise you that. You'll get your coffee, but one of these days, when you least expect it, you'll also get your just deserts. Of that, I have no doubt. None."

"See," Ella said, motioning for me to lead the way up the porch, "this is what friends do for each other. Ever felt so alive this early in the morning? Tell me the truth. You may be mad at me a little right now, but we do have a chemistry, Liv. Tell me you don't feel that. Tell me your heart isn't racing right this minute."

I stopped at the top step and turned to face her. I said, softly, "I've never had a friend like you before. I'm not sure what that chemistry is that you mentioned—and I'm a science teacher and should know. All I do know is my life is blessed because of our friendship. It's true you drive me crazy half the time, but you're now such a part of my life, and I'm glad. So glad."

Ella looked away from me and shielded her eyes from the bright sunlight. "It's going to be a beautiful day, Liv. And even more beautiful for me because you'll be in it. I thank you for that. Before I came to St. Louis, I hadn't had any beautiful days in a long time. A very long time. I…"

Here she paused, turned even farther away from me, and let her voice trail off.

"Let's get that coffee," I said. "I need it."

"Me, too," she said. "Me, too."

* * *

The phone rang about fifteen minutes after Ella left. I figured she was calling to tease me again about my evening with the Daughters of Dixie, so I picked up the receiver and said, "Joe's Bar and Grill. Who you lookin' for, Mac?"

Dead silence on the other end of the line suddenly turned into the Reverend Danielson's voice.

"Olivia, is that you?"

"Sorry," I said, sheepishly. "Thought you were somebody else."

"Obviously," he replied, sternly. "Look, Olivia, I need you to drop whatever you're doing and get right over to the church. Can you do that?"

"What's it all about?" I asked. "Sounds serious."

"It is. Can't go into it now. Remember, we both have party lines, so no telling how many sets of ears are listening. How soon can you get there?"

"I wasn't going out today. Is this really that important?"

"Very. I need you there, okay?"

"I'll be there in half an hour. Will that do?"

"Just come on in and come right back to my study. We'll be waiting for you."

"I'll hurry," I said.

"Please do," he said, dragging out each word. "Please do."

When I arrived at the church, Mrs. Fitzgerald was just finishing a cigarette on the front steps. What a curiosity she must have been to those in the Ville who were passing by. When white people showed up, it was usually bad news. Very bad. Little did those strolling by know just how important she might be for the future of us all. Or, it also occurred to me, she could end up being just one more ring in the noose. On this subject, my own thoughts were still more than a little divided.

I walked right up the steps and shook her hand, warmly this time. "This may sound funny to you," I said, "but I wish you wouldn't stand out here. What will people think has happened to the neighborhood?"

She first looked taken aback. Then, my smile betraying me, she realized I was teasing her.

"You got me," she said. "I mean but good. Shame on you!"

"Couldn't resist," I replied. "Just wanted to see what you were made of today."

"I'm made up of nerves," she said, holding a hand out and shaking it in front of her.

"Me, too," I replied. "Know what this meeting is all about? Why are we here?"

She turned serious. "Something about you, I think. Reverend Danielson mentioned something about your past. Something that will probably keep you from helping with all of this."

"But I don't…" That was as far as I got before I saw her bite her bottom lip.

"Touché," I said, curtseying. "My hat's off to you. I don't fall too often."

"Just seeing what you're made of today. No hard feelings, okay?"

"Pax?" I said.

"Pax," she replied.

I took her hand, and we walked into the church.

Reverend Danielson, Mr. Shelley, and Mr. Bush were all seated around the study table.

"Close the door and make sure it's tight," Reverend Danielson said as we entered. He then stood and paced back and forth behind the table, hands behind his back, a long minute before he spoke.

"It's started," he said, matter of factly. "This morning about ten thirty our journey officially began. I'm not going to lie to you. I'm scared—and not afraid to admit it. Heaven truly only knows what will happen next. Mr. Bush, would you please take it from here. I can't talk any more. I don't have any saliva left."

Mr. Bush said, "Before we begin, let's get all these names straight. If we're going to be working closely together, let's settle this once and for all. Most folks call me J.T. And, most folks call Mr. Shelley by J.D. That's just too many initials and too confusing any way you slice it. Just call me James. Mr. Shelley, if you don't mind, you'll be J.D. from now on. Mrs. Fitzgerald, are you called Josephine, Jo, or something else? What's your preference? Olivia, I've heard your friends call you Liv. Which do you prefer? Let's get this taken care of now if you all don't mind. Each of you take a turn and fill us in. "

"Good idea," I said. "I'll answer to both, but Liv is what many of my close friends call me. Either will be just fine."

"I've been called many things in my day, but most just call me Josie, so that'll be fine."

"Everyone calls me J.D., so that makes sense here."

"Nice to meet all of you," James said, pretending to tip a hat to us. "Now, let's get serious. Josie and I met last night with the owners of the Labadie property. I posed as her agent. They didn't seem all that thrilled to see me there in their living room, but it soon became obvious they are anxious to sell because they have their eyes on another home a little farther out from the city. Frankly, I think they would have let in the Devil himself if they thought he had cash in his pocket. We haggled back and forth a little, but we finally got them to agree to our price. I also asked that the transaction be completed as quickly as possible because of Josie's upcoming travel plans. That was a downright lie, but it was necessary. They said that was fine with them. The sooner the better. We left there with everyone appearing to be as happy as clams. Then, this morning they came to my office, and we completed most of the paperwork we needed for their end of the sale. There were no hitches. As soon as they left, I went over to the Bank of Wellston to work with a friend there to start getting the financial side in order. That's one of the few places around here where a whole real estate transaction can be done under one roof. For a fee, of course. They make good money at this. In any event, if all goes well, we'll be able to close the whole transaction in not much more than a week. I'm sure that probably seems fast, but I know people who can speed up the process dramatically. This will end phase one of our plan."

"I'll take over from here," Josie cut in. "As soon as the papers are transferred to me, we're going to try an end run—and a pretty risky one at that. It will take careful timing. Precision timing. The very same day the papers are all in my name, we're going to start the process of selling the property to J.D. At least we'll start doing all the paperwork. Once we get the ball rolling, everything will happen very fast. The Friday of the week we have all the new paperwork in hand, whatever week that turns out to be, will be our D-Day. We'll take all the papers, both mine and the ones with J.D.'s name on them, to the bank about half an hour before closing time. This is where it will get really tricky. We'll pick the newest and least experienced clerk to help us out. We'll say we need to get the new transaction completed by the end of the working day because I'm leaving for that extended trip James mentioned. There's no way we can do everything in half an hour, so we'll offer the clerk twenty dollars to stay until we're finished."

James interrupted, and added, "The bank employees are not supposed to do this, but I've seen it done many times before on Friday afternoons. Those young clerks get barely twenty-five dollars a week in salary. For that extra money, they'd probably stay until midnight if necessary. We should have no trouble at all finding one to help."

Josie then continued, "The clerk, hopefully, won't have time to do much checking, especially about the old covenant that was attached to the property. If all goes well, we'll be in and out before anyone knows what's happened—and J.D. will be the official new owner. At least that's the plan."

It was such a simple plan, yet it was brilliant. However, there were still a lot of ifs and buts to cover.

As if sensing an uneasiness in our group, James spoke up again. "For this to work, we'll all have to be a perfect team. We'll all have to be willing to finish this at all costs once we get in the bank that day. I feel we can do it. No, I *know* we can do it. I want to go over now what each of us will do. Please pay close attention and speak up if you have any questions at all."

Standing so that he could face us all at once, he started laying out the plan.

"J.D., we'll have to have all the legal papers and your loan papers ready to go so that they can be signed quickly. You and I will talk about this more tomorrow when I come to your place. Right now, you need to make sure you have the down payment in cash. The rest of the financing will be taken care of by one of my colleagues with a connection to the bank. We'll have all that ready for you. And one other thing. On the day of the sale, you actually won't be there with the rest of us."

Before we could all ask how the sale could go through without J.D. being present at the bank, James anticipated our curiosity and quickly continued. "We'll simply say J.D. is too ill to come to the bank. Josie is a Notary Public, so J.D. will sign the papers beforehand, and Josie will notarize everything. This is actually legal. Josie is well known to everyone at the bank, so this won't come as a surprise to anyone. If anything, if we lay it on thick enough, they'll be worried about J.D.'s health and be thinking about sending him cards and flowers before we're finished with this."

Laughing, James added, "So, J.D., think about what illness you want to have, but don't make it too contagious."

Then, turning to me, he said, "Liv, before the big day we'll need quite a few papers prepared. I'll drop off some samples at your house in a day or so. You'll need to study them so you'll know how our new ones should look. I'll also bring a stack of my stationary and some blank forms. You'll be working as my secretary, so you'll also put my seal on everything. That will make your work legal. Well, sort of. At least legal enough I hope you don't have to go to jail one of these days."

"Me, too!" I piped in. "I wouldn't look good in city jail!"

"You'd look good anywhere," he shot back. "But I admit jail clothing wouldn't be the most attractive option for you."

To Josie, he said, "As much as anything, you'll need to keep the clerk distracted that day. I don't care how you do it. Keep his mind on everything but what he's supposed to be doing. For instance, I'm sure you know there are ways women can dress to draw a man's eyes. Women also have other skills in this area. You're a very good-looking woman, and I'm sure you'll figure something out. That's all I'll say. I'll leave this area entirely up to you."

Reverend Danielson covered his eyes and shook his head. I hoped he was being playful.

James then turned to Reverend Danielson. "We joked before about your main job being that of offering prayer. Yes, we'll need plenty of that, but you'll have one other job, and it may turn out to be the most important of all. You're going to be our main decoy during all this. Everyone around here, white or colored, knows you. You're going to come into the bank that afternoon and strike up conversations with as many people as you can. Hey, with a man of the cloth hovering around, this will create a diversion that should keep everyone else away from Josie and our clerk."

He turned to me again and said, "Okay, diversion number two. Olivia, you'll also need to be in the bank that afternoon. Make a late appointment with Mr. Stivesant, the bank manager.

I know you two are friends. Didn't he provide the equipment and funds to start your photography club at Sumner?"

James didn't wait for my reply. He continued, teasing me this time, "And besides, everyone seems to think you two are sweet on each other because you're always showing each other your photography. I hear he's also a pretty good shutterbug, right?"

This time I did get my two cents in. "Now wait just a minute," I said. "It's true he helped me start the photography club. It's also true we share a passion for cameras. But, that's all. That's all. We just know each other through taking photos at exhibits and such."

"Now don't get your dander up," James teased again. "I meant no offense. If you can do it, we need to play on your friend-ship with him. If you can find some reason to keep him occupied and away from Josie and the clerk that afternoon, I think he's the last link in the chain we have to worry about. He's probably the only other person who would think to check for a covenant on the property. Think you can come up with something?"

I thought for a minute, and it suddenly came to me. "I've got it!" I said. "I'll take the pictures I just took of the Hibiscus show at the Jewel Box. I think he'd actually be interested in seeing those. I'll take a few extras and give them to him. He'll like that."

The minute I said it, the irony struck me. A whites-only flower show might provide a shield for our journey into the world of segregated housing regulations. The thought made me smile.

James said, sharply, "Perfect. That should do the trick. Good thinking, Liv."

He paused before adding, "Okay, that's about it for now. Anybody have any questions?"

There were no questions, but I still had something to say. "You know what? After hearing all of this, I'm pretty sure we're all really going to hell. Even you, Reverend Danielson. Probably especially you. Are we really all up to this?"

"I always expected I'd go to hell anyway, "J.D. said.

"Me, too," James added. "I'm sure there's a chair there with my name on it."

Josie just nodded.

"Well, if I do end up there," Reverend Danielson said, "I guess I'll be in pretty good company."

We sat in silence for a long time. It was a lot to digest so quickly. So much was at stake, for all of us.

And we all knew it.

James finally broke the silence. "We won't meet again as a full group until it's time to act, until our D-Day. It would be too risky to be seen together again. Reverend Danielson and I will keep in touch daily, and he'll make the necessary calls to keep the rest of you informed in the days ahead. He'll be our quarterback. This doesn't mean we won't be able to see each other at all. I'll need to visit separately with J.D. and Liv, and Josie will need to meet with most of us at some point to give updates. Let's just try to keep these meetings as low key as possible. Our secrecy, and surprise, will be our best weapons. Everyone still feel good about this?"

One by one, we each nodded to him.

J.D. then said, "Good grief. With all this secrecy and all these plans, you'd think we were robbing the place."

"Well, aren't we, really?" I asked.

"Now that I think about it," Josie said, "I guess you're right. In a way, this really is a robbery, isn't it?"

Her meaning wasn't lost on anyone. Yes, some might call us thieves, but what we were stealing really belonged to us in the first place, didn't it? So, could it really be considered stealing?

That's what we all were about to find out.

James, who had been doodling with a pencil on a piece of paper, looked up and said, "You can call this anything you want. To me, the only thing that matters is this: What we are doing is *right*. As long as I feel that, I'll sleep fine at night, and I hope the rest of you will, too."

He paused before adding, "As far as I'm concerned, we have just one more thing to do today. Reverend Danielson, would you please lead us in prayer. I think we could use that."

"Heavenly Father," he began, "please watch over us and guide us as we begin this journey. Though we be unworthy servants, we ask you to give us the strength to continue forth, to each be pure in our hearts and diligent in our thoughts. We pray that through your guidance we will find the light of day, the power of peace, the fulfillment of our dreams, with dignity and grace. We thank you, oh Lord, for being with us in this hour of our need. Amen."

"Amen," we each, in turn, added.

As I picked up my purse and prepared to leave, I could see it in the faces of my friends.

From this day forward, our lives would never be the same.

* * *

Just before leaving the church, Reverend Danielson pulled me aside and invited me to supper.

"Please come over this evening and dine with us," he said. "I have a surprise for you, and I have the feeling you'll enjoy it. Be there promptly at six. Don't let me down. I'll be expecting you."

Reverend Danielson was a hard man to turn down for anything, so I just nodded and said I'd be there. I went home, freshened up a little, and took a quick catnap on the couch. It wasn't until I woke up that my thoughts traveled back to the intruder. Thankfully, the day had been full, so I hadn't had much time to dwell on the events of the previous night. But now, in the quiet of my own home, I felt a sadness and helplessness I had never known before. Suddenly I couldn't wait to get to the Danielson's and to be with others.

Tonight wasn't a night to be alone.

I arrived at the Danielson home about ten minutes late because I stopped along the way to enjoy the flowers growing in our neighborhood park. The recent heavy rains had brought them all back to their full attention, especially the Rose of Sharon, and they easily swished and swayed in the early evening breeze. I could have stayed there all night long and been perfectly happy, but I knew Reverend Danielson had more he wanted to discuss with me.

Mrs. Danielson answered the front door and welcomed me with a hug that just about took my breath away.

"Please come on in, Olivia," she said, tugging insistently on my arm. "You've got to rescue me from all this talk about baseball. If I hear one more thing about batting averages, whatever they are, I'm going to start yanking my hair out."

"What are you talking about?" I asked. "What's this about baseball?"

I hadn't finished my question when I saw him. There, at the far end of the dining room table, sat Jackie Roosevelt Robinson.

It didn't happen very often, but I can say I was totally and completely speechless.

Reverend Danielson stood up and motioned for me to enter the dining room. "Somebody here I want you to meet," he said. "This is—"

I cut him off. "Yes, I know this man," I said. "I'd be a pretty poor baseball fan if I didn't."

I held out my hand to shake his and continued, "I'm so pleased and proud to meet you, Mr. Robinson. I haven't had all that many heroes in my life, but I'd put you right near the top of that list."

I should just have kept my mouth shut, but I couldn't resist adding, "Well, you're either one of my all-time heroes—or you're a complete idiot."

"Olivia!" Reverend Danielson bellowed. "What a thing to say. You apologize to Mr. Robinson right this minute!"

Jackie turned his head to the side and studied me. "No. No," he said, smiling slightly. "No apology is needed. She's right. I mean, about the idiot part. I've heard that from every corner of the world, so it must be true."

I quickly jumped in, "Believe it or not, that was supposed to come off as a type of left-handed compliment. I am truly sorry. I shouldn't have said it. What I meant was that it takes a person of the strongest will and determination to do what you've been doing. Either that, or the person is, well, you know what I mean. I really didn't actually mean to imply *I* thought you were. Please forgive me."

Turning to Reverend Danielson, Jackie whispered, but loud enough for me to hear, "Is she dangerous? Is she, you know, touched?"

He pointed to his head and made a circular motion with his finger.

Reverend Danielson looked at me, squinted, and we all ended up laughing. "Yes, I'd definitely say she was dangerous," he said. "Oh, you just have no idea."

"Stop it now," I said, slapping him playfully on the shoulder. "I said I was sorry. Let's move on, shall we?"

"Let's sit down," Jackie said, motioning for me to sit in the chair next to him.

I sat down and turned my chair toward him. He was tall, much taller than his pictures in the papers seemed to suggest. His shoulders were broad, and his hair was tinged with just a smattering of gray around the temples. His nose and cheekbones were strong, prominent. He appeared every inch the athlete, but there was also something about him that made him seem gentle and kind. It may have been the way he held his hands upright in his lap or the way his lip curled slightly when he smiled. Whatever it was, I felt instantly at ease with him.

That didn't mean I felt he was off limits to barbs.

"So," I continued, "Let's talk about that ground ball you booted this afternoon. What did it let in? Was it two runs?"

Jackie had just started sipping his iced tea when I posed my questions, and he spit some of it back in the glass.

I had listened to part of the game on the radio as I drifted off for my afternoon nap. I later found out the Dodgers had won the wild, back-and-forth game by the score of 11 to 10. Our hometown radio announcers said Jackie had mishandled a short hop and the ball got by him, allowing two runs to score. However, he more than made up for it later in the game by driving in three runs himself.

"Olivia!" Reverend Danielson shouted again. "What is the matter with you?"

He shook his head in feigned disgust and fell heavily back into his chair, exhaling deeply in the process.

"Wait just a minute," Jackie interrupted, laughing softly. "That play wasn't ruled an error. You can't pin that one on me. That ball hit a rock or something and shot off my glove. And what about those hits I had later in the game?"

"Well, I guess I could forgive you for booting that one, but the Dodgers did end up beating my Cardinals. We'll never catch you in the standings if we don't pull some of these games out in the late innings."

Mrs. Danielson shouted out from the kitchen, "Just great. I ask another woman to come over to rescue me from this kind of talk, and what do I get? Another expert. I might as well have asked everyone to come over from the pool hall."

"Sorry, Mrs. Danielson," I shouted back. "We'll change the subject."

"Yes, let's do that," Reverend Danielson added, exasperation filling his words.

"Fine with me," Jackie added, tilting his head again as he stared sharply at me.

Reverend Danielson started to speak, but I quickly cut him off. "Mr. Robinson, I do have to ask one more question."

"Just one more? I doubt that."

"Why, Mr. Robinson. What you must think of me by now!"

"I won't tell you what I'm thinking," he said. "Not just yet. I'm still waiting to hear your question. Then I'll let you know. By the way, I think you can just call me Jackie, okay?"

"Fair enough," I replied. "And I think my question is justified."

I stood back up, put my hands on my hips, stepped forward so that I was right over him, and asked, "Just what in the name of Babe Ruth are you doing here in Reverend Danielson's home?"

He laughed again, loudly, and clapped his hands together. However, the laughter didn't last long. His smile soon disappeared and a frown replaced it. Reverend Danielson looked down at the floor.

Speaking softly, he began, "It seems there was some confusion at the Chase Hotel downtown. You know that's where the team stays. For some reason—the hotel people say it's a mystery to them—the room they reserved for me was no longer available. They also said there wasn't another empty room in the whole building. Funny thing, though. The same thing happened to my reservation there when we visited St. Louis earlier in the season."

"That's not funny," I interrupted.

"No, it's not," he said, matter-of-factly. "But that's the way it is."

He shrugged his shoulders and added, "And that's why I'm here. Well, in part, anyway. I'm really here for the best cooking in this city."

He made sure his words were loud enough to reach the kitchen.

Mrs. Danielson called back, "You don't have to say that, Jackie. You'll get plenty of this roast beef anyway."

"Just making sure," he shouted back, smiling again.

"It just makes me sick," I said. "Someone should set fire to that hotel."

Before Reverend Danielson could chastise me again, I motioned for him to keep his mouth closed.

"The good Reverend has invited me to stay the night here, and I'm truly grateful. This is so much better than the Chase Hotel in every way."

He then added, "And on top of everything, I get you to talk to tonight. I'm used to the sportswriters being after my hide, but you—I can tell you're not finished with your questions. Not by a long shot."

"I'll be good from now on," I said. "I promise. I do have to ask, though. Is it this way in all the cities where you play?"

"Pretty much," he said. "The reception is a little hotter in some cities than in others, but the end result is usually the same. My reservations are lost or canceled, and the hotel helps me find a place to stay with what they always refer to as a 'Negro host family.' I've known Reverend Danielson and his beautiful wife for a long time now, so I called them when my reservation was lost. That's the short version of all this."

"Let's go back to one of my initial questions," I said. "I'm sorry, but I have to ask it again, even though I've already apologized for this once. Are you an idiot? How can you keep doing this? How?"

"I noticed you didn't ask why I'm doing this, and I'm glad. I can tell you the why and the how can't really be separated. Playing baseball is all I have ever wanted to do. I'm sure you know I played a long time in the Negro Leagues. I probably would have stayed my whole career there and would have been perfectly happy. However, Mr. Rickey, the President and General Manager of the Dodgers, came to see me one day back in the summer of 1945 and asked if I'd like to play in the Big Leagues someday. I thought *he* was the one who was an idiot."

Mrs. Danielson was carrying serving bowls out of the kitchen and setting them around the table as Jackie spoke. When the table was set, Reverend Danielson stopped the conversation and offered the blessing. As soon as the Amen's were given, Jackie continued, first passing the meat to his right.

"Mr. Rickey said he'd been looking for a player to help break through the segregation in professional baseball. We talked for a long time about what this would mean, not just for me, but for everyone else, especially those I played with and heard about in the Negro Leagues. Men like Josh Gibson, Satchel Paige, Cool Papa Bell, Judy Johnson. There are so many great players who are still trapped where they are. Don't get me wrong. I'm proud of my time in the Negro Leagues, but I always felt that playing well there was like saying I was the smartest dumb kid in class, if you know what I mean. We all know this separation is wrong. No, it's not just wrong—it's disgusting. Somebody had to jump up so that Josh and Satch and the rest would at least have a fighting chance someday to play where they should be playing."

He looked out the window and drummed his fingers rapidly on the table. He then continued, "I had myself talked out of being part of Mr. Rickey's plan until I started thinking about the exhibition games we used to play against white teams. I'll never forget two things about those games. I remember thinking we were just as good as they were—and usually better. I also remember how sick I felt after we won some of those contests. Sick to my stomach. Were we, as I thought, really better than they were? How could I say that with any honesty, any conviction at all, when the white teams climbed aboard new buses afterward and drove to their beautiful home ballparks while we stayed behind on our dirt fields.

"Eventually, I just realized it had to be somebody," he continued. "I just happened to be handy, and I couldn't say no to Mr. Rickey. So, am I an idiot? Probably yes, but I guess the answer to that won't be known until we see what happens down the road a ways. At least, that's what I think."

As he spoke now, there was a darkness in his eyes, a sadness in his voice. He seemed like a man watching a house burn who wanted to help extinguish the flames but knew getting too close to the fire might consume him. It was also clear he felt in his heart it was important to move forward, even as the wind blew the fire steadily toward him.

I reached over and squeezed his hand. "I'm sorry I teased you. I now realize I'm the true idiot here. Please forgive me, will you?"

"On two conditions," he said. "First, you have to promise to come see me play the next chance you get. Second, pass me more of those green beans over there."

"Done on both accounts," I replied. "Consider them done."

"And, please, no more talk about baseball," Mrs. Danielson added, scolding all of us.

We all politely nodded to her.

The rest of our time passed quickly. Too quickly. We talked

at length about music, one of Jackie's great passions away from the diamond. I'm sure it was more than somewhat embarrassing for the Danielsons, but I gave a detailed account of the local nightclubs Jackie might want to visit the next time the Dodgers came to town. Jackie shared that he secretly always wanted to play the saxophone in a jazz band. Listening to his enthusiasm about this, I was convinced he could have the same excellence with a sax as with a baseball bat if he put his mind to it.

At one point, Mrs. Danielson bragged about my flower garden. That opened the door to my experience the previous evening with the Daughters of Dixie. I did my best to recreate my experiences with the ticket taker, and Jackie laughed so hard I thought he was going to start crying.

I finished my story by saying, "So, Mr. Robinson, you aren't the only person in this room to crash a whites-only party. And I've got to tell you—it felt good. Deep down, it felt so good."

"Maybe it will for me, too, one of these days," he said. "Right now, I just want to stay one step ahead of the death threats. For me, that's enough."

His words struck us all. We just sat there and didn't say anything for a long time.

Finally, Mrs. Danielson said, "Liv, why don't you come in the kitchen and help me with the dishes. We need to give these old friends time to get reacquainted."

My heart sank. Washing dishes was the last thing I wanted to do, but I couldn't refuse. Grudgingly, I started gathering up plates and bowls and marched to the kitchen.

Jackie and Reverend Danielson moved out to the backyard. Through the kitchen window I could see them playing a game of catch. That was it for me. I couldn't take it any longer. With soap suds all the way up to my elbows, I turned to Mrs. Danielson and said, "Look, I can stay here and wash dishes, or I can go out there and play catch with Jackie Robinson. What do you think I ought to do?"

Mrs. Danielson rolled up a dish towel and swatted me with

it. "I should have known better," she said. "Go ahead. Get on out of here. You're not getting the dishes clean anyway."

"Thanks," I said, not really to her but in her direction. Without uttering another word, I was gone.

I was going to play catch with Jackie Roosevelt Robinson.

6

Rage

For a change, Ella didn't call or show up at my door while I was taking my morning bath. It had become such a ritual I was almost disappointed.

I was just finishing my breakfast dishes when there was a soft knock at the front door. I looked through the curtains, and there stood Ella, wearing sunglasses and with a bright blue scarf draped over most of her face.

I opened the door and said, "My, don't we look like a woman of mystery this morning. Either that, or awfully hungover."

She stepped inside and quickly closed the door behind her. In one sweeping motion, she removed the glasses and the scarf. Her upper lip was twice normal size, and her right eye was almost swollen shut.

"No!" I screamed, my breath catching. "What happened to you?"

I reached over to touch her lips.

"Oh, Liv," she said, her voice cracking.

She hugged me and started sobbing hard against my shoulder. I had never seen her like this before, and it scared me.

"Who did this?" I asked, rage building inside me. I led her to the couch and we sat down.

"Tell me about this," I demanded. "Right now."

"I don't know if I can. I've never been through anything like this before. Ever. I—I just can't believe it. I don't know where to begin."

"At the beginning," I said. "I want it all. Go."

She blew her nose and then began, her voice barely above a whisper at first, her thoughts running together quickly. "It all started at the ballpark yesterday afternoon. Our tickets were for the Pavilion area way out behind right field. Jackson told me until a couple of years ago we had no choice, that we had to sit there. Now mixed seating is supposed to be allowed everywhere. Oh, Liv, this was all my fault. I thought it was too hard to see what was going on from where we were sitting, so I told everybody we should move closer to a section that had plenty of empty rows. I figured what could it hurt? Jackson and the others didn't want to move, but I practically shamed them into it. It didn't help that when Jackson balked, I called him a chicken. We made our way to the new seats, but it wasn't ten minutes later that some asses behind us started throwing popcorn and wrappers at us. Everybody told me to ignore them, but I couldn't. They really got to me when they started calling us names. I finally stood up and said something like, 'Real tough men. Throwing garbage at women. Bet that makes you feel real brave.' That shut them up for a while, but one of them started spitting beer at the backs of our heads. Jackson had had enough and ushered us over to the next section of seats. I thought that was going to be the end of it. We all did."

At this point, she started to cry again, harder this time, her shoulders heaving with each breath. I put my arm around her and pulled her close. She needed a good cry, and I told her to let it out.

When she was finally ready to continue, her demeanor changed. The tears dried up almost instantly and a look of pure hatred filled her face.

"After the game, they followed us outside the ballpark," she continued. "Six, maybe seven of them. All big men. Tall. Looked strong as oxes. I was the first one to notice them behind us. Jackson told us just to keep ignoring them as we walked. We did, at least for a while. Several blocks down Grand Avenue, we decided to cut through an alley to the streetcar stop. I thought that would shake them, but it didn't. About halfway down that alley they jumped us. They got to Jackson first and pulled him into an open garage. Everyone else started scattering, but they also grabbed Merl Dickson, Oddie Sutherland, and Alice Reynolds' son, Jimmy. Jackson and Oddie really fought back, really lit into them, but there were just too many. The goons piled on and got them to the ground. They were kicking them and beating them with everything they could get their hands on in the garage. When one of them went after Jackson with a shovel, I jumped on him and clawed his face."

Ella held out her right hand to show all the nails were now jagged, their irregular shapes indicating they had found their target.

She then continued, "He punched me in the face, Liv, and I got so dizzy I felt like I was passing out. Funny thing, though. Now that I think about it, I don't remember feeling any pain. The next thing I knew, the goons were running down the alley. Jackson and Jimmy were cut up bad and needed help. Jimmy's neck was also hurting him. Merl was curled up on the ground. He had been kicked over and over, but he was finally able to get back to his feet. Oddie was having a hard time breathing and thought his ribs were broken."

She started crying again, softly this time. I tried to comfort her, but she knocked my hand away.

"No," she said, "please don't. I don't want your sympathy. All I want is revenge. I want those men to suffer."

"You better forget it," I said. "They're long gone. You'll never see them again."

"I wouldn't bet on that. As soon as I got my balance back, I ran toward the streetcar stop to look for help. Jimmy followed close behind me. Right before the stop, we saw a plumbing truck drive by. The sign on the side said 'Compton's Plumbing.' I'll see those big red letters the rest of my life because two of those men were riding in that truck. The one who hit me was driving. I saw him plain as day."

"Did you call the police?" I asked, deep down already knowing the answer.

Ella took in a long breath and said, "I've been up here long enough to know this is just like Arkansas. The police won't do any good, won't be any help. No, we know who these men are, and that's enough."

Here she stared blankly at me and spoke slowly, deliberately. "You forget I'm a southerner. We don't get mad. We get *even*."

"Whoa, my dear. Wait just a minute. You're right that this is like Arkansas, which means if you do anything to them and get caught, nothing on heaven or earth will save you. They'll be made heroes—and you'll get buried. Never forget that. Never."

"Believe me, I know that. I'm not stupid. But I'm also not going to let this go. I know where some of them work. Compton's Plumbing."

She then stood up and said, "Thanks, Liv, for listening. I needed to see you. Needed to tell someone. I'm okay now. Please forgive me, but I've got to run. We all finally made it to Homer G. Phillips Hospital yesterday to get checked over. They did x-rays on Jimmy because his neck still hurt and decided to keep him for the night. He was in traction by the time the rest of us got to go, and he seemed pretty scared. I want to go see him and let him know we're all praying for him."

"Would you mind if I tagged along?" I asked. "Right now, I want to be with *you*."

Ella started to protest, but I cut her off. "And besides," I added, quickly, "when I was at school the other day, I saw the new class lists, and Jimmy is going to be in my homeroom class this fall. I also know his mom, so I think I *should* go with you. Okay?"

"If you really want to go, get your purse right now," she said, sternly. "My car is out front. I'll meet you there."

With that, she was out the door and taking two steps at a time down the porch. I followed close behind.

Homer G. Phillips Hospital was the Negro hospital in St.

Louis. It took five years to build, finally opening its doors in 1937, and it quickly became the one true place we could go for quality medical care. Before the hospital opened, Negroes were provided only limited and irregular medical care at one of the two city hospitals, both a long way from the Ville. Homer G. Phillips was grossly understaffed from the start and didn't have near enough beds in the wards, but local committees and organizations from the community worked constantly and tirelessly to try to correct this.

Homer G., as it was called, wasn't just a hospital. It represented hope and inspiration for all, young and old. It was also a monument to Mr. Homer Gilliam Phillips, a brave and visionary man who helped establish the initial funding for the facility. Mr. Phillips was a well known attorney and politician who fought the injustices of racial segregation all of his life. Everyone knew he was the driving force behind a bond issue in the early 1920s that provided the funding for the hospital, and after the bond issue passed, he attended every important planning meeting that led to the hospital's construction. The quest to achieve this goal became a driving force in his life.

Then, suddenly, in 1931, nearly one year to the day before the groundbreaking ceremony for the construction, he was standing at the streetcar stop, reading his newspaper and waiting for the car to take him to work. Two men ran up to him and fired five bullets into his chest. He died before he hit the ground. The men who fired the shots were later arrested, but they were never brought to trial. It was ruled there wasn't enough hard evidence to make a case against them. To this day, his murder is still listed as "under investigation" in the official police records. Years later, when preparations were being made for the dedication ceremony, there was no doubt in anyone's mind what the facility should be called. None at all. It was simply called, in his honor and memory, Homer G. Phillips Hospital.

As Ella and I entered the large, arched doors, I stopped her and pointed to Mr. Phillip's picture, which was displayed proudly and prominently behind the Information Desk.

"He was a great man," I said. "One of the greatest."

"I've heard," she replied. "Wish I could have known him."

"Look around you," I said, "and you'll know him. This was his dream. This *is* the man. He'll always be here."

The receptionist at the Information Desk interrupted our thoughts. "Can I help you?" she asked.

"Jimmy Reynolds—which room is he in?" Ella asked. "We'd like to see him."

The receptionist slowly scanned a clipboard on the counter in front of her, finally stopping near the bottom. "He's in 206, and it says he can have visitors. Take the stairs over there."

"Do you know how he's doing?" I asked.

"No, you'll need to stop at the Nurses' Station at the top of the stairs. They'll visit with you."

"Thanks," I said. "We will."

At the nurses' station, I was surprised to find one of my former students, Opal Brown, in charge.

"Mrs. Perkins!" she screamed, much too loud for the setting. "It's so good to see you. What are you doing here?"

"The question is what are *you* doing here? I haven't seen you in a dog's age, since you went away to college. I completely lost track of you. Now look at you. You're all grown up. A nurse!"

Ella nudged me. "I'm sorry," I said to her. "Opal and I will catch up later. I know you're in a hurry."

Turning back to Opal, I said, "We're here to see Jimmy Reynolds in 206. What can you tell us? How's he doing?"

"A lot better than last night, I think. He'll be sore for a long time, but he'll live. Doctor Winslow said we're to keep him in traction at least for today. After that, it looks like he'll get a brace for his neck and be sent home to rest some more. Are you two going to be here when he's released? He might need help getting home."

"I'll be here," Ella said. "Count on it. I'll be glad to help. Can we see him now?"

"Of course. Go right on in. Try to stand right over him so he doesn't need to move his head when he talks to you."

"Got it," I said. "And after our visit, I'll look around for you so we can catch up with each other. I want to hear all about your family and your college days."

"I'll look forward to it," she replied. "Look for me down the hall, down there by the lounge area."

When we entered room 206, the first thing I noticed were the sandbags weighing down ropes that were attached to a harness over Jimmy's shoulders. There were so many ropes he looked like a bug caught in a spider's web. His eyes were closed, and he appeared to be sleeping. Ella started to sit on the edge of the bed, and I immediately yanked her back up. The slight ripple she made on the bed shot right through Jimmy's body. His eyes snapped open.

"Sorry!" Ella said. "I forgot."

"It's okay," Jimmy replied, weakly.

"How are you doing this morning?" Ella asked. "Feeling any better?"

"I guess a little better, but my neck's still plenty sore."

I stepped forward and squeezed his hand. "I'm Mrs. Perkins. You don't know it yet, but I'm going to be your home-room teacher this fall. Room 128, next to the cafeteria door. I just wanted to make sure you were doing okay and to see if you needed anything."

He tried to move his head so he could face me. As he did, I noticed tears slipping down his cheeks, one tear catching the corner of his mouth. He wasn't exactly crying, although his breaths started coming in short bursts. More than anything, I thought he appeared distraught.

"Thank you, Mrs. Perkins," he said as his hand squeezed tightly back. "Thank you for coming to see me. You're very kind. Too kind."

"Don't be silly," I said. "Just let me know if there's anything—and I mean anything—I can do."

"Same here," Ella added. "Is there anything you'd like right now? Anything at all?"

"Yes," he said. "Tell me about the others. They ok? And how about you, Miss Dunbar? I can't see, but your eye…"

"We'll all make it. Don't you worry about us. Why, Jackson and Oddie are probably even at work this morning. Merl's fine, too. You just concentrate on getting better, alright?"

He swept the back of his right hand slowly and carefully across his cheeks and closed his eyes as he inhaled deeply. "The truck," he said. "Did you find out anything yet?"

Ella leaned forward and whispered, "Forget about that now. This isn't the time. We'll talk about it later. You just get well. That's the important thing right now."

"I feel so helpless," he said, his voice again breaking.

"You sure weren't yesterday," Ella said, laughing softly. "I saw you knocking the tar out of the biggest one in the group before the rest jumped you. I'd like to see *his* neck this morning. It's probably stretched two feet long!"

Jimmy laughed, then grimaced. "Thanks, Miss Dunbar, but no more jokes, okay? That hurt!"

"Sorry," she said. "I forgot again."

"We better go," I said. "He needs to get some good rest, and we're definitely not helping the situation. Jimmy, if you need help when they let you out of here, I want you to know you can call us. Please don't forget that."

"Thanks for coming," he said. "I really do appreciate it. I really do."

Ella leaned down and gently kissed him on the cheek. He made no sound, but tears streamed from his eyes again.

We turned to leave the room, when, out of the corner of my eye, I saw them.

The shoes.

Covered with splotches of white paint.

My breath caught, and I stopped so suddenly I fell forward, my head crashing to the door frame.

"Liv, what in the world? You okay? What happened?"

My heart was pounding. I felt a sudden rush of sweat on my forehead.

I looked back at Jimmy, but he was now a blur, fading to black. Everything spun so quickly in my head I couldn't figure out what to do. I wanted to grab something, anything, and hit him. Hit him hard. Hit him until I couldn't swing my arms any more. Then I wanted to pull him out of the bed, to drag him down the hallway, to announce to everyone what he had done. I wanted to scream in his face, for him to see the hurt in my eyes, in my heart.

But I didn't do any of those things. I wanted to, but I couldn't. I couldn't. I just wanted to get out of there. I ran down the hall to the stairs. I saw Opal walking up the corridor toward me, but I didn't stop when she tried to grab my arm. I kept running, running, gasping for air. As I descended the outer steps, I heard Ella calling to me from inside.

I didn't stop. I ran all the way home and locked myself in. When I did, I looked down and noticed I had lost my shoes. I stood there, shaking, in the entryway and looked at myself in the mirror.

The reflection looked so far away.

So far away.

7

Friendship

I didn't move from where I was seated in the entryway when Ella started pounding on the door and insistently ringing the bell. I didn't want her in the house. I didn't want anyone in the house. I wanted to be completely alone with my thoughts, as disjointed and jumbled as they were. I had seen the shoes. The shoes were Jimmy's. Jimmy had been in my home. My home had been violated. The safety and security of my world had been stomped on, had been torn to shreds. What had been my one safe haven in a world of constant change was now just a set of walls, and those walls were spinning out of control, as if lifted up by a massive storm. I suddenly felt so lost, so alone.

"Liv, you better open this door or I'm going to knock it down. I'm not kidding. I'm not. You let me in. Now! You hear me?"

I knew she wasn't going to go away. I stood up and moved over by the door.

"I'm not going to let you in," I said, softly, evenly. "Go sit in the swing. I'll go in the dining room and open the window so we can talk."

"This is stupid," she said, her voice rising. "What did I do? Why won't you let me in?"

"It has nothing to do with you," I replied. "I just don't want to be with anyone or look at anyone right now. And I don't want anyone to see me. Please, Ella. Please. Just go to the swing and sit down. Do this for me."

I walked into the dining room, cracked open the window,

pulled a chair over, and sat down. A light breeze outside moved the bottom of the curtains slowly into the room and then back to the sill. I could see Ella's outline in the swing, and I knew she could see me at the side of the window.

"What's going on? Did I do something to upset you? You have to tell me. I can't stand this. Oh please, Liv. What's going on?"

"I told you it isn't you. It's not. Really, it's not. It's something in me that…"

I paused, feeling nauseous, the room spinning upward. I leaned over and, with both hands, squeezed the rim of the sill, steadying myself.

I started to cry, and Ella heard me.

"That's it," she said, emphatically. "I'm coming in. You open that door this minute."

"Please sit down," I implored. "Please."

She stopped by the window and put her hands on the screen. Softly, gently, she said, "I've got to know why you are suffering so. You have to tell me. Please tell me."

I spoke slowly, deliberately, "You remember the day I asked about your father and you told me never to ask you about that again? This is something like that, only it has to do with me."

"If you're in trouble, Liv…"

"No, that's not what I mean. I mean it's something that shouldn't be talked about, even between dearest friends. Not now, anyway. Some things are better just left alone. That's what's going on. I might want to talk about this sometime, and if I do, it'll be with you. I promise you that. But right now…"

Ella moved closer to the window and leaned forward so that her lips were right at the screen. "I love you, Liv. I'm worried about you. *I'm* the one, as you saw this morning, who can really let the tears roll. But not you. Never. That's why I'm so worried. I just want to help any way I can. I'll do anything. Anything."

I put my hand on the screen and pressed it against hers.

We didn't speak again for several minutes. I wanted time

to decide what to do about Jimmy, and I didn't want to talk to anyone else about that, not even Ella. I wanted time for my head to clear, my heart to heal. I wanted options, at least some plan of attack, to come to me, but nothing did. Nothing. My thoughts were still spinning too fast.

Ella finally broke the silence. "What do you suppose the odds are of us both falling apart on the same morning? Answer me that."

She was trying to calm me down. She was also fishing, and I knew it. The bait was now dangling right out in between us, and I wanted nothing to do with it. I knew she'd be mad, but instead of biting, I decided to stall and steer the subject as far from the present as I could.

"I want to talk about something else," I said. "I had a letter from Tubby yesterday. What am I to do with him?"

Ella then took *my* bait. She immediately blurted out, "Don't you talk to me about men. I've had it with 'em. I'm telling you, that Jackson is driving me crazy. I've never had a shadow like this before, and it's really starting to get to me. He's turning up everywhere I go. I mean everywhere! On top of that, Reverend Danielson stopped me on the street yesterday and did everything but demand you and I come to the church dance and fundraiser this weekend. By the way he talked, I got the distinct impression he has already been lining up dance partners and potential suitors for us. He's still bound and determined to marry us off. We're going to have to talk to him, you know, before this gets completely out of control. Who does he think he is? Cupid's cousin?"

"Oh, I have no doubt he has our dance cards full," I said, wiping my eyes. "We better be prepared. Wear your toughest shoes so the clods don't break our toes. Pick out a brooch or necklace that's sharp as nails so the mashers won't be able to pull us close. If you can think of any other precautions, let me know. Sing out before Saturday."

We both fell quiet again. I walked to the dining room table, picked up the letter, and returned to the window.

"Want to hear Tubby's letter?" I asked.

"Would it do any good for me to say I didn't? I've known you too long. Go ahead and read it."

"Good. This will save time. You know good and well you'd pester me to death until you heard this anyway. So just sit back and relax. Tell me how you'd reply to this."

I raised the window a little higher, propped the first page of the letter against the screen, and started reading.

My Dearest Olivia—My Love,

I take pen in hand to send my most sincere thoughts from my heart to yours. I'm writing this from the Charlton Hotel in Atlanta. I've been in some real dives before, but this takes the cake. When the lights are off at night, I can hear rustling around the room. When I flip the lights back on, silverfish and roaches do their rustling even faster as they run for cover. Okay, so this isn't the most romantic way to begin a letter to the woman I love most in this whole world. I mention the bugs because even as I sit here and complain about them, I'm thinking about you—about us. No, I'm not comparing us to bugs. I'm telling you that no matter where I am or what I am doing, you are always in my thoughts. You are the first person I think of when I wake in the morning, and you remain in my head and my heart all through the day. You're always there with me. Always.

We played a new song last night for the first time. I think you'll remember Artie, our sax player. He's one of the quietest men I've ever known. That's funny because when he gets fired up on stage, he's the person everyone in the audience will watch because of his wild gyrations. Then, when he's off stage, he's as quiet as a fog. Well, Artie wrote a love song, which is really quite something for a guy who blows the sax. He said he was inspired to write it because of the way I talk about you, because of the way my eyes look when I'm describing our time together. He said that's the type of love he wants someday—the type he has always prayed for but has never found. So, his song is really, in a way, our song. It's so beautiful, Liv. We'll play it for you the next time we hit St. Louis.

His song also reminded me of just how beautiful you are and how deep you are in my heart. I know you've suffered greatly in your life, and I know some of the reasons why. I'll never be like anyone else, and I also know that is part of the problem—that I'm not like someone else you've known. I'm not dumb. I know that. I also know that each leaf of a tree is different, yet they are all equally important to the health of the tree. In other words, you need me, Liv. You just don't realize it yet. I'm different and I'm my own person, and I always will be. Someday I hope that is enough for you. Someday I hope our lives will join in a way that both of us will hold in our hands such a love that will be everything for both of us. I pray that happens, for both our sakes. In the meantime, I'll set pen aside and think of you until sleep takes over. I know, without a doubt, you'll be in my dreams tonight, as you always are.

With all my love,

Tubby

P.S. The song Artie wrote is called "Brown Eyes in St. Louis." It's dedicated to you.

After I finished reading the letter, I started crying again. Ella leaned closer to the window and said, gently, "He adores you, Liv. But I've always known that, and so have you. I think you're upset because you know he may never be enough, and you don't want to hurt him. I'd be sad, too. How often does a man fall that hard for a woman? Nobody ever has for me. But one-sided love is a cruel thing. If that spark isn't there on both sides, it never works out. Never. I mean, one person's dreams are never fulfilled, and when that happens, the cracks finally show up. They always do. I don't know what to tell you about Tubby. You may be able to keep him as just a friend, but he's going to have something to say about that, and soon. You better be prepared for him to tell you to take a hike if you keep putting him off. You know that, right?"

Ella was right, in everything she said, and deep down I knew it. But I really didn't want to talk about Tubby. It was true I'd been stewing over his letter, but I had used it now simply as a stall tactic, a way to lead Ella away from what was really bothering me. Jimmy. I could still feel his grip on me, smell this sweat, hear his voice. I suddenly felt so dirty. So ashamed.

I knew she was still waiting for me to say something, but all I could think of to say was, "I know. You're right. So right."

We sat there in silence for several more minutes. Ella lit a cigarette, and the smoke blew in the window. The swirling smoke connected us soundlessly.

She deserved at least a partial explanation, so I chose my words carefully before beginning. "I'm still not ready to talk about this, but there's something I want you to know. I'm scared. I've never been so scared in all my life. I always thought I was safe, that this place, this neighborhood, was everything I'd ever want and need. Something has happened that has made me question that. I don't know if I'll ever feel safe again. I don't know if the Ville will ever be enough again. I may not be making much sense to you, and I'm sorry if I'm not. This is a difficult thing for me to put into words.

"Until recently, I guess I was just content living from day to day and assuming that my life would always be the same. But something happened that broke all that to pieces, and I feel like I don't know what to do next. I bet you have a million questions you'd like to ask now, but please don't. I just want you to be close to me, to be there for me. I know that's incredibly selfish because you don't know what I'm talking about. It's like you jumping on a train that you don't know where it's going. Right now, I don't either. All I know is the one constant in my life right now is you, and I need you now more than ever. I wish I could tell you more. I want to tell you more. I just can't now. I just can't."

When I stopped talking, Ella pressed her hand more firmly on the screen and said, "I'll always be here, Liv. Always. You don't ever have to worry about that. All you need to do is let me know how I can help. That's it. I'll do everything I can. You should know that by now. I wish you could tell me more about this, but I won't press you. I'll wait. When you're ready to talk about it, you just let me know."

She then sat in the swing and pushed it so it rocked freely back and forth. I sat there and watched her for what seemed like a long time. She finally stood up and, without a word, walked slowly down the steps and out to the street.

I leaned against the sill, closed my eyes, and wept.

*   *   *

The rest of the afternoon was a blur. I cleaned the house, washed some clothes, hung them out to dry, and took a long nap. By the time I woke up, it was almost time to start cooking supper. I was feeling a little better, but I wasn't all that hungry. Not wanting to cook, I decided just to walk the four blocks to the diner to grab a sandwich and a cup of the soup of the day. I also thought the walk would do me good. On the way there, I passed one block south of the hospital. My steps quickened until I was sure I couldn't be seen from any of the hospital windows.

Just before I entered the diner, I saw Reverend Danielson getting a newspaper at the stand across the street. I waved to him, and he motioned for me to stop. He quickly crossed the street, took my arm, and ushered me several feet back down the sidewalk.

"I've got news," he said, out of breath, panting. "Big news."

He leaned closer and continued, his words coming in short bursts, "I just heard. J.D. got the rest of his money lined up. Now that this has been taken care of, James is going to be contacting you to start on some of the real estate paperwork. This is all going to be taking off really fast from now on."

Here he paused and studied my face before continuing, "You sure you're still ready for this?"

"You don't know how ready. Just tell him I'll be there, night or day, whenever he needs me. This is something I want to be part of now more than ever."

"Good," he said, taking my hands and squeezing them. "I'm still scared, but I'm with you. The more I study on this, the more I feel good about everything. This is right, Liv. It is."

"I know," I replied. "I know it in my heart. I really do."

"We better get going," he said, still breathing hard. "I've got to get back to the church. Where you headed?"

"A quick bite to eat. Want to join me?"

"Better not. Mrs. Danielson would skin me alive if she knew I was still sneaking back here to the diner for some of that incredible cherry pie they always have. She's had me on a diet now for two months, and I'm supposed to be avoiding all sweets. I think she's starting to get suspicious, though, because I've actually gained four pounds."

"So, we've been sneaking some pies, have we?" I teased.

"I'm not saying," he said, mocking my tone of voice. "Let's just say I'm not eating any more pie today and leave it at that."

"Don't worry. Your secret will be safe with me."

"I'm counting on that," he said while crossing the street again. "And one more thing. Don't you eat that last piece of cherry pie—just in case."

For a minister, he could be a great sneak. And I adored him all the more for it.

I entered the diner, sat in a booth in the back, and ordered a bacon, lettuce, and tomato sandwich and the soup of the day, which turned out to be potato. Elston's Diner always had good food, but it couldn't be proved by me on this visit. I was still so upset I wolfed down my food while staring out the side windows of the diner. I could see a steady stream of people stopping by the newsstand to get the evening editions of the papers or the latest magazines. They all looked so happy, so carefree, so full of the joy of the day.

All I could feel was anger.

As I sat there, I stirred my coffee over and over again and stared into its darkness. In that cup, I saw the reflection of the waitress as she came over to see if I wanted my coffee topped off. Without saying anything, I pushed the cup toward her and nodded. I poured in some sugar, added milk, and started stirring again. My thoughts were spinning as fast as the spoon. I kept thinking about the night before, about how I was now suddenly afraid to go back home. Home. I wasn't sure what that meant anymore. That was to be our home, mine and Inman's. Only he was never coming back. He died helping end the war, helping make the country free, helping so many come back to homes of their own. He was now resting in Nettuno, Italy, and he was never coming back. Home? Without Inman, it would never be a home. It was now my *house*, and it would never be anything more. Still, so many of my dreams and hopes were born there. Inman may have been gone, but I couldn't let go of them. I couldn't. If I let go of them, then I'd have to let go of Inman, and that was unthinkable. He was the one true love of my life, and I still felt him with me.

And he always would be.

Always.

The waitress asked one more time if I wanted a topper while placing the check on the table. Again, I didn't reply. I took the money from my purse and handed it to her, waving for her to keep the change for her tip.

She thanked me, started to walk away, then stopped. "Honey, are you okay?" she asked.

"I really don't know," I said, smiling weakly. "I hope to be. But it's going to be hard. So hard."

"Then you take care of yourself. Tomorrow will be better.

Just you wait and see."

I'd been telling myself the same thing for a long time.

I quickly walked home, climbed into bed with my clothes on, pulled up the covers, and tried to lose myself in sleep. I prayed the dream wouldn't come, but when I closed my eyes…

* * *

We didn't know the men on the horses, but their faces were like ours. They didn't get close to the barn. The horses were fighting them, backing away from the heat and the flames. An angel called to them through a window. They didn't answer, didn't move. The men watched the barn for a minute, whispered something to each other, turned, and rode off, kicking their horses over and over. Soon they were out of sight.

"They didn't see you, did they?" Jimmy John asked.

"I don't think so," I said.

"You better pray they didn't. Pray with all your might."

8

Explanations

The next morning I woke early, jolted from a sound sleep by the oddest dream. I was driving my car on a deserted, winding gravel road out in the middle of nowhere. I was driving so fast rocks and dust flew up behind me. I finally came to a traffic light next to a large barn. As I skidded to a stop, I saw what at first appeared to be all my colleagues and students from Sumner running from the barn toward me. They were all shouting, "Go back! Go back!" Then, as they came closer, I saw none of them had faces, just featureless heads without hair. At that moment, I sat right up, my eyes snapped open, and the dream slowly fell away as I realized I was actually in bed and not in my car.

I tried to get back to sleep, but I kept hearing the group shouting, "Go back!" I finally just decided to slip into my housecoat and head downstairs to start a pot of coffee. The sun was just starting to rise, but it was still dark enough in the house I needed to turn on some lights. While turning on the front hall switch, my breath caught as I noticed a figure sitting on the front porch. The sudden light caused the figure to bolt upright and turn toward me.

Unlike the featureless people in my dream, this figure had a face, and it was now staring right at me.

It was Jimmy.

I didn't scream. I didn't move. I couldn't. I suddenly felt woozy, faint.

"Please, wait!" he shouted. "I'm not coming in. Please, just listen. Please!"

Before I could reply he added, "Call the police if you want. I won't run. Get a gun and shoot me if you want. I won't move. Do whatever, but I'm not leaving until I say something."

My first thought was to run for the phone, but the remaining darkness of the early morning couldn't hide the tears streaming down his cheeks or the shaking of his shoulders. As I stood there staring through the glass, I couldn't feel sorry for him. I felt only fear, only disgust. Then I noticed the large brace on his neck. That calmed me enough that I was able to shout back, "Leave! Now! I don't want you here. Ever. Leave me alone."

"I'm not going," he said, determination filling his voice. "Not until you hear me out."

Neither of us moved. I couldn't—and he wouldn't.

"Please," he begged again. "Just listen to me. I never meant to hurt you. I never meant to see you at all. You weren't supposed to be home yet. All I wanted was to get the presents and go. That's all."

I could see him wiping tears from his eyes. His breaths were coming in short bursts as he spoke.

"I needed the money. I don't know if you want to hear why— maybe it doesn't matter to you now—but I hope you'll listen to me. I've been doing everything I can to get money. I've done all the odd jobs I can find. I've run out of them. I'm not proud of it, but I've also taken a few things and sold them. I need this for my father."

He moved closer to the door and continued, "He was a trader on the floor of the Chicago Stock Exchange until about six months ago. He was *passing*. About six months ago he drove to Champaign, Illinois, to visit my grandmother. While he was there, one of the men he worked with saw him with Grandmother and put two and two together. He's been blackmailing him every since."

He paused, looked at me to see if I was listening, and continued, "When my father was a young man he worked as a chauffeur for a rich family in Washington, D.C. Their oldest son was a trader there. He was drunk so much of the time he couldn't work most days, and Father ended up doing everything for him except the actual work at the Exchange. The son died in a car accident one night when he was drunk. After that, Father felt he'd learned enough about trading stocks that he could do it himself, so he left Washington and moved to Chicago. He figured the odds would be pretty slim that anyone there would have known the son, so he took his identity, his diplomas, and all his legal paperwork with him. That got him a job in an investment company."

Jimmy inched still closer and took a deep breath before continuing, "Mrs. Perkins, please, please listen to the rest of this. Please. I've got to make you understand. He worked his way up to being a trader and was doing fine—until he got caught. This is where the real problem comes in. He just can't walk away from this. He had to be bonded to be a trader. In getting that, he signed some papers that would get him locked up for fraud if it came to court. The man also threatened to hurt Mom if the payments didn't keep coming, so that's why Mom and I moved here so quickly. I didn't want to leave, but I couldn't let her come alone. To top everything off, my father got sick last month and hasn't been able to work since. The man, and I'd give anything to know who he is, still wants his money. That's why I came after the presents. I thought if I could sell them, I'd have enough to keep my father out of court—and jail. I swear this is the truth. I swear it."

I studied him for a minute before responding. I was still so angry I was shaking. "Why didn't you just tell me this in the first place. I would have helped you."

"Pride, I guess," he said. "Plus, I didn't know you that well. I also figured the fewer people who knew about this the better. I know it doesn't excuse what I did, but this is why I did it. Please, I'm asking you to forgive me. Please."

As I listened to his explanation, it made me suddenly think of the secrecy surrounding our plans for helping Mr. Shelley. That, in turn, helped me understand at least part of his reasoning.

He was right—the fewer involved with this, the better it would be. Getting caught passing would be bad enough, but to combine that with breaking the law would probably get his father thrown in jail for years.

"This still doesn't excuse what you did," I said. "I understand this better now, I think, but do you have any idea what this did to me?"

"I know it isn't enough—never will be—but I'm sorry. So sorry."

"Sorry doesn't cut it, Jimmy. It just doesn't."

"I know," he said. "But I don't know what else to say."

I wasn't sure what to say or do next, but I knew we couldn't keep talking through the door, especially not at this time of the morning. Something in the back of my mind said not to do it, but the words were out of my mouth before I could stop them.

"Come inside. We'll talk more. We'll see if we can figure out what to do next."

Jimmy sighed and his shoulders finally relaxed. "Thank you, Mrs. Perkins. Thank you."

"Don't thank me just yet. You haven't heard what I'm going to say."

"It won't matter," he replied. "I'll do whatever you want me to do. I promise."

Opening the door, I said, "Then come on in. Let's go into the kitchen. I'll get some coffee going."

"I'm surprised you're letting me in," he said, stepping inside.

"So am I, so don't dawdle. Get in here—before I change my mind."

After I put the coffee on, I sat in the chair across the table from him. He was nervous. Very nervous. He was rubbing the palms of his hands together and was avoiding my eyes.

"Would you like something to eat?" I asked.

"Not hungry. Just coffee will be fine."

"Look," I said, "you can relax. I'm not going to call the police. I should, but I'm not. But I want you to know the reason

I'm not doesn't have anything to do with you. I'm thinking of my mother now. Like your father, she had to pass in order to get the job she always wanted. She worked in the garment district downtown. That is, she passed until she'd get caught, which always happened. No one blackmailed her because the men who owned the businesses didn't want anyone to find out they had actually hired a Negro. That would have hurt their pride and their reputations after all. The last time she got caught they threatened her with violence, so she had to quit. She had no choice. That's why I'm not going to turn you in. It isn't because of you. It's because of my mother and your father—and what he's going through. Do you understand that?"

"Yes, I think so. I think I do. I feel terrible, Mrs. Perkins, but I just don't know what else to try. I've tried everything legal I can think of to raise the money, but when that didn't work, I jumped over the line. I know it was wrong. I do. I just don't know..."

"The first thing we have to do is figure out how to stall for time. We can do that if we raise the next blackmail payment. How much is that man asking for? How much do you need?"

"He makes my father pay him twenty-five dollars a month. Right now, that might as well be twenty-five thousand. After everything I've been able to raise, I'm still almost ten dollars short, and there's only a week left before he says he'll go to the police."

"First of all," I said, "he won't go to the police. At least not this soon. He'll wait and see what happens because he doesn't want to kill the Golden Goose. As long as we're close to twenty-five dollars, he won't do anything but some screaming and threatening. You can count on that."

I got up and walked into the living room to get my purse. I had a ten dollar bill tucked in the side pocket that I was saving to put toward a new camera. I plucked it out and headed back to the kitchen. Placing the bill on the table in front of Jimmy, I continued, "Add this to what you have and get it to your father. Don't tell him where you got it. Don't! I mean it. I don't want anyone to know I'm involved in this. We'll just keep this between the two of us. Understand?"

He was speechless, but his eyes told me everything I wanted to hear. He stood up and started to lean over to hug me, but when he realized what he was doing, he quickly sat back down.

He then said, "I'll never forget this. Never. Not as long as I live."

"No, you won't, but it won't be for the reasons you're thinking right now. For that ten dollars, I want something in return."

"Name it," he said, strongly.

"Don't be so fast. I want you to listen to me all the way through before you respond. Things are changing here in the Ville. You haven't been here very long, but you'll soon find out we're all very proud of this neighborhood. However, it used to be that young families had a real chance to buy a house or some land where they could build something here. Now all that land is gone. The Ville is full. That is a wonderful thing because we now all have a place we can really call home. It's also a very bad thing because there aren't many opportunities for others to move in. All those young couples who moved here thirty, forty years ago when housing wasn't as tight are now getting up in years. Some are sick and frail and can't take care of their property like they used to. They need help. This is where you come in. You're going to help them."

Jimmy interrupted, "I'm going to do what? Help them how?"

"I'm putting you on probation. My probation. You're not going to get off with just an 'I'm sorry' for all this. What you did was wrong, any way you slice it. To make up for it, you're going to have to balance the scales, and I figure a good way to do that is help out here in the Ville—and especially help out our older neighbors. Just for example, Mrs. Ferguson right down the street has holes in her screens on her front porch. She can't get around well enough to fix them herself, so you're going to patch them for her. Next to her is Mr. Anson. His garage is falling down. I'm not sure it can be saved, but if it can, you'll be the one to fix it. Get the idea?"

Jimmy smiled at me and blew out a deep breath. "So, you're my jailer now, right?"

"I wouldn't call it that," I said. "Let's call it your 'contractor.' That sounds better. And don't you think this all sounds better than you going to jail?"

"You'll get no argument there. Not from me. I'll do it. Everything you want. Just don't get mad at me if I'm a little slow getting some things done, especially with school starting up pretty soon."

"Oh, I'm not saying you won't be busy. But maybe some of this work will help keep you out of trouble. It better. And, I don't want to hear about you stealing anything else in the Ville. Got that?"

"Then it's okay to steal outside of the Ville?" he replied, playfully.

"You shouldn't steal at all. But, if you have to, yes, it better be outside the Ville."

We both smiled. Looking at him now, I saw not the thief who turned my world upside down but a boy struggling to juggle too many balls in the air at one time. And the burden of doing that was heavy, heavier than he could manage by himself. Maybe I could help. I didn't know if he would let me completely in his circle, but I had to try. I just had to.

"Then we understand each other, right?" I asked.

"We do. I'll get started on Mrs. Ferguson's screens tomorrow. I do have one question, though. How am I going to explain being at these places when I do the work?"

"Don't worry. I'll take care of that part. We'll plan your work schedule, and then I'll call them and tell them you are helping out as part of one of our community projects we put together at school. They'll never know the difference. But we will."

"Mrs. Perkins, I'm the crook here, but I'll be darned if you aren't more sneaky than I ever could be. Please don't take that the wrong way. I mean it as a compliment."

"Just don't you think I'm being a pushover here. You're

being punished. Make no mistake about that. You'll probably work harder doing this than you would have on a chain gang. As a matter of fact, you may end up wishing you had chosen a chain gang. Time will tell."

"I'll take my chances with you," he said.

The way he looked up at me made me feel I wasn't taking much of a chance at all.

*   *   *

By Friday afternoon, Jimmy had repaired Mrs. Ferguson's porch screens, fixed Mr. Anson's garage, and painted the entire south wing of the church.

Probation suited him.

I spent the rest of the week studying the documents James dropped off for me so I'd know how to create new ones for our plan. I had no idea real estate transactions involved so much behind-the-scenes paperwork. I most enjoyed the title opinions and abstracts I read through. Basically, these were narrative histories of the property and descriptions of the geography involved. They also contained any covenants that were attached to the property. These documents were most often prepared by attorneys, but James said he routinely wrote them himself and had a notary attach a seal to his work. This seal didn't really testify to their accuracy, but it did give everything enough of an official look that the papers weren't scrutinized closely. In our case, this would play into our hands nicely because our team had its own notary, Mrs. Fitzgerald. It would be like the fox watching the hen house, which was perfectly fine, and fortunate, for us.

I had already started preparing my notes for the title opinion and abstract for the Labadie property. The geography— dimensions of the lot, specific plot location—and ownership history would all be fairly easy to prepare because I could lift most of that from existing documents. However, my brain froze every time I came to the covenant stating the property could not be owned by those of noncaucasian backgrounds. This section would, of course, have to disappear, but the question in my mind was whether I should just leave it out or replace the slot in the paperwork with one of a dozen other common covenants, like whether the structure could be used as rental property or host a commercial enterprise—to offer a diversion when the bank clerk read through it. After giving it a lot of thought, I finally made up my mind. I'd insert a covenant restriction that said the new owner could not raise livestock on the property. Considering the yard there was little bigger than a postage stamp, I thought this would be a nice touch.

The more I worked on the documents, the more I felt what we were doing was right. Not that I had any big reservations initially, but seeing the current covenant over and over reminded me of the injustices that were still all around us. If anything, I was feeling ever more grateful and proud I'd been asked to help out with this.

Very proud.

9

Suitors

The rest of the week passed quickly, especially because Reverend Danielson roped Ella and me into helping with the decorations and plans for refreshments for the church dance. We also had to figure out what to wear and discussed this almost constantly. I wasn't kidding, not one bit, about us needing to wear some type of "man-repellant" clothing. Otherwise, I knew the slowest of dances would be sheer torture as the gropers tried to establish beachheads. Soft and inviting clothing would simply not be appropriate given these circumstances. Scratchy and conservative attire would be the order of the day. Ella wanted us to meet in the middle on this, but I held my ground firmly.

"I've been through this before—last year at the spring party," I said. "When I finally got home that night, I felt like a football that had been passed around and fumbled more than a few times. Just you wait and see. You'll have bruises in spots you didn't think could have them. I'm telling you—you best protect yourself as much as you can before you go."

Ella just laughed and shrugged off my comments. She'd just have to learn—the hard way. After much discussion, mostly with herself in front of her dressing mirror, she decided upon a light green dress with a fairly low neckline. I scolded her for that, but she waved me off again as she pointed to the large, very stiff, crocheted borders around the waist, neckline, and hem. When she first showed it to me, she said, "Five bucks says somebody ends up with bloody hands after tangling with this thing. They may try to touch, but if they do…"

Even though it was out of season and I knew I'd end up roasting, I chose tan wool slacks with a matching jacket, and my thickest and widest crocheted scarf to wear around my neck. "I'll be like a cactus," I told Ella. "Those crumbs won't stand a chance."

Ella added, "And let's wear our shoes with the tallest heels. Those will do some real damage if we need to step on some toes when they move in for the kill."

We ended up giggling like fifth graders and nodded knowingly. I was glad for the laughter because I really did not want to go to the dance. Since Inman's passing, I had tried my best to avoid events like this. They reminded me of him so much because he loved to dance and listen to music. I always ended up feeling so lost and lonely. But, as much as I was dreading everything, I knew there were two important and practical reasons why I had to go. The first was a portion of the money raised was going to help with our projects at Sumner, and I knew some of those funds were to be earmarked specifically for the photography club. That meant I had no choice; I had to be there.

The second reason was, I felt, absolutely crucial. Mr. Stivesant, manager of the Bank of Wellston, had long been a great supporter of our initiatives in the Ville. It was an open secret he was going to bring a sizable check and donate it to our drive to obtain a new vehicle for our Driver's Training course at Sumner. While he was there, I could use the opportunity to tell him about the Hibiscus show and offer to bring my pictures to show him at the bank. He had been so kind to us all I hated to trick him so, but this was war, and I had decided all was fair.

Ella, on the other hand, could easily have ducked out of the event. She moaned and complained at just the right pitch, but she was a lousy actress when it came to the subject of Jackson. She wanted to be there at the dance to keep an eye on him, yet she refused his invitation to take her on a formal date that evening. Instead, she told him she'd see him there and, if he was lucky, she might save a dance or two for him. If I'd been Jackson, I'd have been very upset. However he was clearly smitten and probably felt he had no choice but to accept the terms. I didn't understand why she turned him down because if she had agreed, she would have been able to avoid the potential stampede of suitors lined up by Reverend Danielson. No, I didn't understand her thinking at all, but she didn't want to talk about it, and I didn't press the issue.

Late on Saturday afternoon, after my nap, I started getting ready when the doorbell rang. I just knew it had to be Ella, so I stormed to the door, flung it open, and without looking shouted out, "Get your skinny hiney in here. You can help with my hair."

"Love to," a masculine voice replied. "Let's get started. I'm game."

It was Tubby.

I had on nothing but my ratty housecoat—not even any makeup. I was mortified.

"What are you doing here!" I screamed. "You're supposed to be in Memphis this weekend."

"Plans got changed. Part of the Orpheum burned down last Monday, so that job literally went up in smoke. Our train connection brought us back through St. Louis on our way to Wichita, so I thought I'd chance a quick stop to see you. I'm impressed how you dressed to receive me."

"Very funny," I replied, pulling my housecoat closer around my neck. "You should have called. I don't like surprises, and you should know that by now."

"Just wanted to see you, Liv. Even if it was just for a minute. And besides, I didn't want to call and give you time to think of a way to say no to my coming here."

He looked good, downright handsome, what with his fresh haircut and pressed suit. I should have been mad at him, but I just couldn't be. I hated to admit it, but I had missed him. For all his outward bravado, he was one of the kindest and most gentle men I had ever known. In private, with me at least, he was thoughtful, considerate, and soft spoken, all almost to a fault. On top of that, the way he would take me into his arms and kiss me, with a softness that spoke of his true feelings for me, touched my heart so deeply. I should have been proud and happy that any man would want me so. But, instead of my heart opening to accept the fullness of his, my mind always ended up taking center stage. The fact was, while I loved Tubby, I wasn't *in* love with him, no matter how hard I tried to be. I told myself a thousand times I'd be a complete idiot to push him away. An equal number of times, I also told myself it would be cruel, on so many levels, to live my life with a man who couldn't give me what I wanted most of all. I wanted a man who made my heart skip when he entered the room. I wanted someone I'd miss the minute he left that room. I wanted kisses that I felt in the deepest reaches of my heart. I wanted someone to share the most private and intimate moments with without having to speak—to be able to say everything with our expressions and caresses. I wanted a man who made me feel the world was ours and that our journey would be full of laughter, passion, and adventure.

In short, I wanted Inman back.

But only his memory remained, burned so deeply into my soul. As long as this was the case, no other relationship would be possible, and I knew it. I had no idea if I'd ever find this magical happiness again, but I also knew I had to give it a try. I just had to. There was always the possibility of lightning striking twice. My heart told me that every day.

"Well, don't just stand there," I said. "Get your sorry self in here before someone sees you. You can sit at the top of the stairs while I get dressed—if you promise to be good. I have to be to the church in an hour. I *have* to be there, so don't try talking me into anything. This is our big fundraiser. Sorry I can't spend more time with you, but I can't. If you'd have called, I'd have been able to tell you this and that would have saved you a trip."

"I'll take what time I can get," he said, entering the house and taking me in his arms. "This is what I've been thinking about for days."

He kissed me so softly, so gently. Then, pulling me closer, he cupped his hand at the small of my back and kissed me with an intensity that he had never shown before. His kisses were beautiful, but they left me hungry, starved even more for the lightning to strike again. It didn't. I hoped my eyes would tell him this, but he was lost in the moment, oblivious. When I realized this, I pulled back and started to tell him what I was feeling.

"Tubby, I—"

He pressed a finger to my lips. "No talking," he said. "Not now. All I want is for you to feel this, to remember this while I'm away."

He kissed me again, this time pecking around my lips as his hands gently brushed my cheeks. When his hands became more bold, I stopped him in his tracks by stepping back quickly.

"I have to get dressed now. I'm sorry—we have to stop. We really do. Tubby, I just don't know what to say. I know what you want me to say, and I wish I could say it. I do."

"Then just don't say anything," he interrupted. "Just let me be with you a few more minutes. Okay? That's all I ask."

He suddenly looked so sad, so down, I felt an odd sort of guilt well up in me.

"Come upstairs with me. You can sit there and tell me all about your trip. I want to hear everything. Everything."

"Then you shall. Lead on. Just show me where to park this old carcass."

While I dressed, he went over, in great detail, what must have been every event on the trip. I listened, but I heard very little of it. What I heard instead was the sound of my heart, and it was still alone.

* * *

Tubby walked me to church, but he refused to go inside. "Here's where I get off," he said. "I'll hop the Hodiamont streetcar and be at Union Station before you get your first glass of punch."

Then, putting his arms around me, he said, "I'll write, if that's still okay with you."

"You better. I don't know what I'd do if you stopped. You're such an important part of my life. I just don't know how to say it the right way."

"I know I'm not enough right now," he said, looking down at the ground. "But someday I may be. I think I'll stick around a little longer and see what happens."

"You do know you're a fool to do that," I said, as gently and heartfelt as I could.

"I know," he said, "but I can't let you go. I can't walk away. I love you, Liv. With all my heart. I always will."

"And I love you. I do. But—"

He cut me off, "I'll be late for the train. See you in a couple of weeks. In the meantime, keep me in your heart. You'll be in mine. Constantly."

He turned away quickly and headed up the street. Ella came up behind me and asked, "Tubby?"

"Yes," I said. "Tubby."

I could tell by the look on her face she wanted to ask some questions, but she didn't. She instead squeezed my hand and said, "Let's go inside. The Poison Sisters have work to do."

I just shook my head and laughed.

"We do at that," I said. "Follow me, Sister."

The dance started off so smoothly we were both quickly nervous wrecks. Ella and I kept busy helping serve refreshments and picking up empty plates and glasses from the tables. However, this didn't last long. As soon as Reverend Danielson saw us, I could see him wave his arms wildly to a group of men lined up in chairs in the stag section along the wall.

Ella saw this too and whispered to me, "Uh oh. Here it comes. Brace yourself."

Over the next hour, we were both inundated with Reverend Danielson's flock of single men assembled this night just for us. I didn't know what he saw in each potential suitor, but I could sure tell what Ella and I were thinking—and our thoughts were not pretty.

The first to ask me for a dance was "Outhouse" Jones. I'm sure he had a real first name, but he had been known as Outhouse for so long no one could remember it. He earned the name because this man didn't just smell, he was positively rank. As he pulled me close, I could smell what seemed like rotting prunes radiating from his pores. The music had a lively tempo, and thank goodness for that. The welcome distance that grew between us during faster movements still left something like a fog trailing behind him that I'd step into. I held my breath as best I could, but it wasn't enough. I still had this odor in my nose when the song ended. He bowed politely and asked if I'd save him another dance later on. I didn't reply. I couldn't. I was still holding my breath as I backed away from him.

The next brave soul to run up was Steven "Smoky" Fulton. This man always had a lit cigar in his mouth, as if it were surgically attached. He was called Smoky because two years before, he had fallen asleep while smoking in bed. He escaped serious injury, but the resulting fire nearly burned his house to the ground. However, that wasn't the complete story of his name. Three weeks after that, while driving on Highway 21, he threw a lit cigar out his car window and the wind blew it back into the back seat, which promptly caused the interior to catch fire. The car was already so full of cigar smoke he didn't realize what was going on until a car passing him on the highway slowed down and its passengers motioned wildly for him to pull over. By the time the fire department got there, his car was nothing but a burned-out shell. This was the man now before me, trying to pull me close while puffing on the most acrid, putrid stogie I had ever had a whiff of. I had put a small amount of straightener on my hair while getting dressed, and I was scared to death it would catch fire if the tip of his cigar got anywhere in the area. I must have looked like a chicken trying to avoid the hatchet while he rocked me back and forth to the beat of the song.

I looked over at Ella, and she was faring no better. Her first partner was the man all the women in the Ville knew as

"Little Caesar," and that had nothing to do with actor Edward G. Robinson either. His real name was Theodore MacMillan, but the name Little Caesar was planted on him because he had "Roamin' hands," which were constantly trying to find a soft spot to land. Being around him was like trying to fight off a giant spider because his hands seemed to be everywhere all at once. The look on Ella's face was priceless when he reached around and patted her repeatedly on the fanny. She patted him back, too, only her pats were harder and were on his forehead. However, instead of getting the message, this seemed to cause him to pick up steam. He next pretended to be brushing something from the front of her dress, and his hand might as well have had a spotlight on it because everyone in the room seemed to notice he brushed right across her breasts in the process. That was enough for Ella. Immediately, those big heels of hers found their mark, and Little Caesar was forced to retreat, hobbling back to a seat along the stag line where he sat down, took off his shoes, and inspected his mashed toes. Everyone howled as this unfolded. Everyone, that is, but Ella.

As soon as he departed, and before Ella had a chance to catch her breath, up shot Billy "Butter Knife" Phillips. This was a cruel nickname, but it was, unfortunately, an apt one. I had known Billy for years, and I had to admit he truly wasn't the sharpest shovel in the shed. People were always playing tricks on him because they believed he lacked the mental acuity of a gnat. It wasn't six months earlier that Oscar Travis talked Butter Knife into buying, for twenty dollars, half interest in an invisible dog that Oscar told him they could eventually sell for a small fortune to a circus. Oscar was a pretty fair ventriloquist and was able to convince Butter Knife the dog had taken up residence on his porch. That was a cruel thing to do. What was more cruel was everyone looking the other way for a whole week while Butter Knife put out food and water for the dog. Oscar finally told him the dog had run away, and because he was invisible, they'd probably never find him; Oscar also kept the twenty dollars. I always thought Billy was, deep down, a very nice man. He just wasn't a fast thinker. As I was being swept near where Ella was dancing, I could hear her asking him, "So, did you know I used to be the Queen of Arkansas?" I glared at her for being so mean. She sneered back.

My next hoofer was Preston "Pigpen" Taft. He didn't smell like Outhouse Jones, but by the look of him it was a shock he didn't. If the man had taken a bath within the last month, it was not readily apparent. His hands were so dirty and sweaty they left prints on my jacket everywhere he touched me. I started looking like a sidewalk where kids had left their handprints in wet cement. His clothes were just as filthy as his hands. One stain, right near the collar of his shirt, was bright orange. "Popsicle drippings?" ran through my head, but it was too orange even for that. Actually, at this point, I didn't want to know. I just wanted to stay away from the cleft in his chin when he tried to press his cheek to mine as the music slowed. That cleft in his chin was so deep and so dirty he might have been able to grow a crop of strawberries in there.

And they just kept coming, without letup, one after the other. Ella was also graced by the physical stylings of George "Stubby" Hill. Even with lifts in his shoes, he couldn't have broken five feet tall, which put his head, during a long, dreamy waltz, right in the middle of Ella's breasts. As hard as she tried, and she tried mightily, she couldn't dislodge him.

I next suffered through a rhumba with Clarence "Cotton" Caruthers. Clarence was just a shade over thirty years old, but his hair was already snow white. He was also a mama's boy who took his frail, elderly mother everywhere he went. As we danced, I could see her constantly waving to us from where she was seated by the refreshments. I couldn't tell whether her wave was to get our attention so we'd stop and get her a cup of punch or if she needed to be rushed to the hospital. Clarence also had a tendency to cry, for reasons no one ever understood, at the drop of a hat. I once heard Jackson say that Clarence had to be the one who taught weeping willows to cry, and that didn't seem all that far-fetched when he started crying right in the middle of our dance. He wasn't just whimpering, he was bawling, which made every-one in the room stare at me. They didn't stare for long, though. After all, I was one of the Poison Sisters, so it was expected I'd make men cry. Just not right in the middle of a dance.

With Reverend Danielson flagging them on, they kept com-ing, trying to establish toeholds. Ella also drew Henry "Ducky" Smithton, a man with feet so big he left shadows when he lifted his shoes while dancing. They also ended up on Ella's feet often enough that she started to hop around like a kangaroo. At first I thought she was teaching him a new dance, but the grimace on her face quickly changed my mind. Ducky was also the person who spiked the punch at every event in the Ville. Tonight had been no different, except he had obviously dipped into the bottle more than a little before pouring the rest into the punch bowl. Now he wasn't just mashing Ella's feet. He was staggering far and wide, while trying to hold on to Ella and, in the process, was stepping on everyone, men and women alike, within his range. At least Reverend Danielson had the decency to come over and rescue Ella—and everyone else—and haul Ducky over to the cof-fee pot to try to sober him up.

The last straw for me was Arthur Rhodes, affectionately known to everyone as "Arthur Ritis." Arthur was so old he still sported on the lapel of his suit both a campaign button for Teddy Roosevelt and a workman's pass for the 1904 St. Louis World's Fair. This man wasn't old; he was three days short of being older than dirt. For a standard box-step waltz that was fired up when it was his turn to drag me around the room, a dance tradition-ally consisting of four related movements, the best Arthur could muster was one long, circular, sweeping motion of his right leg while his left leg remained planted in one spot. If he'd have moved any more than that, I'm guessing he would have collapsed in a heap and his old bones would have crumbled like a week-old sugar cookie.

I'd had enough. When the band mercifully decided to take a break, I ran over and grabbed Ella's hand and marched us off the dance floor, out the side door of the church, and into the safety of the parking lot.

"That's it!" I screamed, raising my hands up to the stars. "No more! If I have to be mauled by any more of these cretins, I'm liable just to kill somebody. Seriously!"

Ella laughed and pulled me close to hug me. Then, in one motion, she started pushing and pulling on me roughly while stepping on my toes.

"Ouch! What are you doing?" I asked.

"Just getting you ready for your next dance partner. Right before the break I saw Reverend Danielson shoving "Jerky" Jennings your direction. I can't wait to see you cut the rug with that!"

"No!" I said, over her laughter. "Not going to happen. No!"

"What's going on here?" two voices said in unison behind us.

It was Jackson and Charles, climbing out of Jackson's car. Until now, we hadn't seen them all night. Earlier in the evening, when she wasn't being pawed on the dance floor, I saw Ella scanning the room and knew she was looking for Jackson.

"You're just in time," I said, sternly. "Come over here. I've just this instant decided something, and I need you both."

They both looked at each other and shrugged their shoulders as if to be saying, "Uh, oh! What's she want now?"

"Jackson—you walk right over there and put your arm around Ella. While you're at it, why don't you kiss her, too."

Before either of them could respond, I turned to Charles and said, "And you. You're mine. Get over here and put your arms around my waist. If you do a good job, I may even let you kiss me once or twice. That is, if you're a really good boy and do what I tell you to do."

"Liv, you okay?" Ella asked.

"I'd like to know that as well," Jackson added.

Charles stood there a moment, stunned. Then, his face lit

up and he rubbed his hands together as he came over to put his arms around me.

"This is what we're going to do," I said. "I'm tired of being groped and chased by every one-eyed dog in the Ville. You two are going to be our boyfriends, from now on."

"Sounds good to me," Charles practically shouted.

Jackson responded by turning quickly and kissing Ella right on the mouth.

"Wait a minute now, boys," I said, coldly. "You better understand something first. I'd like to think you're going to benefit from this arrangement, but make no mistake about it, this is going to be for Ella and me."

"What do you mean?" Ella asked.

"Just this. When my father took me duck hunting for the first time, I was shocked he didn't shoot the ducks that were in the water right in front of us. 'Those aren't real ducks,' he said. 'Those are decoys.' I didn't know the difference back then, and neither will anyone else back in that church. You two are going to be our decoys so we don't have to put up with all that—ever again. You're going to take us back inside, dance every dance with us, and hold us close like you mean it. You can take liberties, within reason, as long as everyone else sees you do it. We're going to be putting on a show, after all. You are going to have to be the best decoys in the world, and if you are, we'll make it worth your effort. Right, Ella?"

"You've flipped your lid this time," Ella said, matter-of-factly. Turning to Jackson, she added, "She's crazy, right?"

"Maybe crazy like a fox," he replied, smiling. "I get it. I really do. You want to *use* us to scare off the wolves, right? That's okay. I can live with that. For now. But, our services will cost you both dearly. *Dearly.*"

"What do you mean by that?" I asked.

"Well, if we're to be great decoys, we'll need you to go with us on dates so people can see us together more than at just events like this. I'm thinking we should go to movies. Nightclubs, too.

Maybe even a drive to Art Hill to park and steam up the car windows a time or two just for good measure. I think I can also speak for Charles here. We'll do this for you, but we want just as much on our end of the bargain. What do you say to that?"

Ella jumped in, "*We* get to decide on the rewards, if you get my meaning. Let's make that clear up front."

I added, smiling, drawing out each word, "Rewards will be meager at first, boys. We'll start with holding hands and maybe a friendly kiss or two tonight. We'll see how it goes from there."

Charles, who had been quiet during this whole exchange, finally got into the conversation. "Wait just a minute. It's my turn to say something, and you're all going to shut up and listen."

Turning to Jackson he said, "And, no, you can't speak for me. I'll speak for myself. Liv, this is a harebrained idea. It's true I like you. I think you know that. But I don't want to be chewed up like a piece of meat and then spit out. Rewards? Don't insult me like that. I'll be with you if I want to—and I'll drop you like a hot potato if I want to. Nobody is going to tell me what to do."

I had hurt his feelings, badly. He did like me, more than just a little, and I did know it. I should have thought of something better than the decoy story to explain what I wanted to happen. As it often did, my mouth had run faster than my brain.

"I'm sorry, Charles," I said as sincerely as I could. "I meant no disrespect. To the contrary, I wouldn't have asked anyone else on this planet to be with me in this scheme. I mean that. I like you, too, and I think you also know that. I'm not promising anything will ever come of us, but I think we can have a good time together in the meantime. That won't kill us, and we might even enjoy each other's company. And it will certainly help us out and make our lives easier."

Then, to Ella and Jackson, I added, "And you two. You're pathetic. Even a blind man could see the wheels moving in your heads. I don't think you'll have to do much pretending, will you?"

"Liv!" Ella shouted. "That'll be enough of that!"

"She's right, though," Jackson said. "I don't think I'll suffer too much during our *pretend* time together."

"Well, how about you?" I asked Charles. "What have you decided? Are you willing to be in on this?"

"I'll stick around for the first round or two and see what happens."

He walked over to me, and added, "We might as well start the show right now. I see a lot of faces looking out the window and right toward us. Let's see what they think about this."

With that, he leaned down and gently kissed me. I started to pull back, but he held me close. It had happened so quickly it startled me. What really shocked me, however, was what a good kisser he was, and how, once our lips touched, I didn't want it to end. Then, just as quickly as he had moved in, he pushed me back away from him.

"Those will be your rewards, if you play your cards right," he said, boldly.

Ella's mouth dropped open and she started to laugh again—until Jackson, following Charles' lead, quickly wrapped her up in a kiss, a kiss that went on and on and on….

I could see a lot of movement and fingers pointing at us from the well-lit windows of the church. The plan was already working, and I tried to get the attention of all to let them know. Ella and Jackson were still lip locked and paid no attention whatsoever to me. I turned to Charles and said, "Look at those nosey people. You'd think they'd never seen anyone kiss before."

Charles said, "They haven't seen anyone kiss like this before."

He took me in his arms again, and I'll be darned if he wasn't right.

* * *

Word of our parking-lot passion quickly washed its way to Reverend Danielson—and spread like a typhoon through the rest of the church. "Why didn't you tell me you two had boy-friends?" he asked. "Would have saved me a whale of a lot of time and trouble."

"Ella and I like our privacy," I said. "Besides, these are recent developments. You couldn't have known."

That was true. I didn't even know myself until a few minutes before.

"You shouldn't be displaying that much affection in public, though," he scolded, wagging a finger at me. "You should know better. You're a teacher, after all."

"Yes, sir," I said. "I agree. I'm very sorry."

Well, I actually wasn't sorry. I had found a perfect decoy— one whose kisses were incredible. Maybe the only thing I was really sorry about was not finding this out sooner.

I looked over at Ella and Jackson holding each other close during the first dance after the band's break. The way they were looking at each other kept any other potential suitors at bay. Ella lifted her head off Jackson's shoulder long enough to look my direction and wink.

At that moment, Charles came up and swept me into his arms right in beat with the rhythm of the song. "This dance is mine," he said. "As a matter of fact, all the rest of them tonight are, too."

I didn't say a thing. I leaned closer and put my cheek against his, losing myself in the music and the gentleness of his touch.

We never left the dance floor the rest of the night. One song flowed into the next, and our movements became more fluid and natural. By the time the trumpet player announced they had just one more tune to offer, I felt like Charles and I had been dancing with each other for years.

Jackson, holding Ella's hand, walked over and tapped me on the shoulder just before the song ended. "We better take you two home now, don't you think? It'd be good for everyone else to see that."

I wanted Charles to walk me home. I wanted his kisses again. But, I also knew this was unfolding too fast. Way too fast. Brakes would have to be applied, and right now, or this train would quickly become a runaway. From the way Ella was looking at me, I had the feeling she was thinking the same thing.

"Not tonight. We better not. Look at Reverend Danielson over there. His sermon tomorrow will probably be about the four of us. No, I think we better just go our separate ways right now. We've started a brushfire tonight, but we don't want to it rage into a forest fire. Okay?"

Charles and Jackson looked dejectedly at us a long time, studying our faces to see if we were serious about this. Charles finally spoke, "I hate to admit it, but you're probably right. I don't like it one bit, but... We'll say our goodbyes now, but I think we should get together again soon—just for the sake of showing everyone we're couples now. Under those conditions, I'm fine with leaving without you. Jackson, you fine with this?"

"I'll have to be," he said. "Do I have any other choice?"

"I'll save you a *reward*," Ella drawled, deliberately.

"I'll save one for you, too, " I said to Charles. "Thanks for everything tonight. You two have been wonderful."

"You're welcome," he replied. "Any time. Us decoys always aim to please."

Motioning to Jackson, he said, "Let's get out of here." Then, mimicking Ella's drawl, he added, "Our services are no longer required."

After they had gone, Ella whispered to me, "I'm getting out of here before anything else happens tonight.

"Goodnight, old maid," I teased.

"Goodnight, old crow," she replied, sticking her tongue out at me.

We joined hands and exited the church. When we reached the sidewalk and headed home in opposite directions, Ella called back after me, "Old crow!"

I yelled back, "Old maid!"

I walked home under an August sky full of the most beautiful stars I had ever seen.

10

Decoys

One of my early morning rituals was reading through the newspaper headlines while sipping my first cup of coffee. I'd note the headlines of interest and mark them with a pencil so they'd be easy to find again when I had more time to read the articles later in the day. The *Argus* was my favorite paper, but it wasn't a daily. I supplemented it with a subscription to the *St. Louis Globe Democrat,* one of the citywide newspapers, which I'd usually find flung, by my scatter-armed delivery boy, somewhere in my front yard every morning.

I was stirring the sugar into my coffee when the headline on page two jumped out at me: "Compton's Plumbing Burns, Arson Suspected." Startled, I snapped upright in my chair and started reading the article:

> *City fire officials say a three-alarm fire late last night that burned longtime St. Louis business Compton's Plumbing of 4110 Delmar Blvd. may have been arson. The building was a total loss. Fire Chief Frank Scarpetta refused to confirm arson was the cause, but investigators on the scene reported finding evidence of a suspicious nature, although they would not provide details. Chief Scarpetta said a full investigation would begin immediately. City police have also been brought in and are encouraging anyone with information that might be helpful to step forward.*

"No, she couldn't be involved," I thought to myself immediately. "She wouldn't do something like that. She was furious, but she wouldn't…"

Then it dawned on me. Jimmy was just as upset about what had happened during their walk home from Sportsman's Park as Ella was. He was also now on my probation, as a "doer of good deeds." Would he have considered this a good deed in his own mind?

With the newspaper in my hand, I started to head for the phone to call Ella, stopped, turned around, and sat down again.

I just couldn't believe either one of them could be involved in arson. They just couldn't be.

I kept telling myself that over and over as I started stirring my coffee again.

The phone rang about nine thirty. I immediately recognized Reverend Danielson's voice on the line. I could also immediately tell it was important because he didn't even say hello.

"Olivia, can you meet me at Elston's Diner in about fifteen minutes?"

"What's going on?" I asked.

"Can't say right now. I imagine we have 'party-line ears' listening."

"I'll be there in ten. I'll order us each a piece of pie."

He stuttered a minute and said, "Yes, yes, please do. And make mine cherry. You know, I think I can get there in ten now."

We both laughed and, without another word, hung up.

The thought of the pie must have really lit a fire under him because he beat me there.

"Let's go inside—to a booth in the back. We'll be able to talk better there," he said, opening the door for me.

After we were seated, the waitress brought us glasses of water and offered menus. "Just pie," I said. "I'll have cherry. Reverend, what'll you have?"

"I'll also take cherry, with a sidecar of vanilla ice cream. And some coffee."

"Coffee for me, too," I added.

As soon as the waitress walked away, he began, "I have a message from James. If you can finish your work and get it to him to be checked over by this weekend, we think everything will be ready for next Friday."

I was stunned.

"Next Friday? That quick? How so?"

"James has connections everywhere. He was able to get Mrs. Fitzgerald's paperwork processed in what must have been record time. He said everything's just about ready. So, if you can be finished, next Friday it will be. Can you do it?"

"I'll stay up tonight as long as I have to to get it done. I'm close already. I just need to add some finishing touches and type up everything. Tell him I'll drop the papers off after supper tomorrow night if that's okay with him."

"Good. That's what I was hoping to hear," he said, flatly, looking down at the table.

I could tell something was wrong. "What is it?" I asked. "What's the matter?"

"I was just thinking," he said. "I was thinking about what will happen when all of this finally comes out—and I have no doubt it will come out. Are we strong enough to do this? Are we opening Pandora's Box and we just don't know it?"

"I've been thinking about that, too," I replied. "You're right. It is like Pandora's Box. I have no idea what we'll find inside, but I can tell you this much. It's a box that has to be opened, and I, for one, am proud to be opening the lid. We have to do this. We just have to."

"I know it," he said. "But I'm still worried."

"I'd be worried if you weren't worried," I said, patting his hand gently. I then added, "Yes, we *can* do this. Have a little faith, will you?"

That brought a little smile to his lips. "Faith. Yes, that's what I need. Thanks for reminding me."

"My pleasure," I said as the waitress brought our pie and coffee.

We ate in silence, but that pie suddenly tasted so incredibly good.

* * *

Ella and Charles were rocking in my porch swing when I got back home.

"What in the world are you two doing here?" I asked as I headed up my walk.

"We have a proposition for you," Ella said.

"Well, this is the morning for it," I replied. "Go ahead and let me have it."

Charles jumped out of the swing and landed before me.

"Great dismount, Charles," I said, teasing him. "Very graceful. Like a cross-eyed acrobat, but still graceful."

"I always try to be," he said. "But I'm not always completely successful. Let's see how graceful I can be with this. Liv, we're going on a date tonight. Did I ask that gracefully enough?"

"What?" I asked. "What are you talking about?"

"Ella and I figured this all out. We need to start showing up together in public as soon as we can. All four of us."

"Okay, I get that. You're our decoys. But just what did you two have in mind? What did you two cook up?" I asked, looking from one to the other. Both were smiling. Too much.

"Just this," Charles continued. "Tonight there's a great group playing at the Club Riviera. Dud Bascomb and his Dynamic Deluxe Recording Orchestra will be there with that songbird Spizzie Canfield. And the best part is they're also having a dance contest, and I thought we'd get out there and 'cut the rug' a little."

He stuck out his arms as if holding a partner and stepped back and forth quickly, ending with a deep dip.

"I'll be happy to dance with you," I said, "but you can forget about us cutting any rug. You're not going to haul me around any dance floor like that! I like my dancing to be slow and sweet. If we're going to dance, it'll be my way. That sound okay to you?"

"Oh, be still my jumping heart," he said, pretending to faint and falling back against the porch railing. "You're just teasing me, right? I'd slow dance with you from now until dawn. Lead me to that dance floor, quick!"

"Down, boy," I commanded. "And I expect you to be a perfect gentleman. Don't you forget that when you have your hands on me."

Charles pouted, stuck out his lower lip, and playfully pulled out his handkerchief to dab at his eyes.

"Come on, Liv," Ella chimed in, drawling her words even more than usual, for emphasis. "He's going to be helping us out. The least you can do is give him a little sugar once in a while or hug him close while he's decoying. You do owe him that much, you know."

He nodded his head up and down quickly and smiled at me.

"We'll see," I said. "Treats will be awarded based upon how good you act tonight. That's all I'm going to say about this now. You'll just have to wait and see."

"I can wait," Charles said, quickly. "At the same time, I can't wait to get to the club. This is going to be so great!"

Ella then said, "If she doesn't suit you tonight, we can always switch partners, you know. You're a little skinny for me, but I think you'd do alright. Keep that in mind."

"I will," he said, walking forward to put his arms around Ella to dance right there on the porch. She clubbed him gently with her purse and pushed him back. He first looked stunned, then started laughing.

"I get it," he said. "No treats from you either until I show what I can do, right?"

"You better believe it, mister," Ella replied. "And you better be good!"

"Don't worry," he said. "I will be."

"You two are both sick," I said, shaking my head. "Pretend dates. Dancing. Treats. The whole thing sounds crazy to me."

"Well, then just think of what the good Reverend has in mind for us—and then tell me again if you want to go to the club tonight. What do you say to that?"

"Now that you mention it, I'd say I'm ready to dance. Charles,

I'm your partner! Pick us up here at eight. We'll be ready."

"And so will I," he said, rubbing his hands together.

"Now remember," I said, "you still have to be good. I'm not kidding about that."

He nodded his head, danced down the porch steps, and started singing the new popular song "Peg O' My Heart," while heading down the sidewalk.

"Great. There goes my new dance partner," I said, dryly.

"Aren't you lucky," Ella said, dragging out the words, teasing me.

I just shook my finger at her and laughed.

* * *

The boys showed up right on time, just as we finished primping and getting our wraps on. They were, to put it mildly, a sight to behold.

"Have you ever seen anything like it?" I asked Ella, as we watched them dancing up the sidewalk toward the porch.

"Never," she said. "Not even close. Look at those screwballs. Just look at them!"

"Maybe it's just the fading light," I said, hopefully.

"I don't think so," Ella said. "I don't think we're seeing things."

She pinched my arm, and I quickly knocked her hand away.

"Yes, we're both awake," I said, rubbing my arm.

Jackson and Charles were dressed exactly alike. Both had on what could only be described as the most mismatched blend of colors ever witnessed in one place. I'd never even seen a rainbow that could compete with them.

Both had on black trousers and jackets, but those were the only two articles of clothing that seemed close to normal, civilized dress. Their shirts were both bright red. Their socks, clearly visible below their too short trousers, were yellow. In my wildest imagination I couldn't imagine how they managed to find them, but each had on a purple vest over their red shirts. To top it all off, they had tilted on the side of their heads white fedoras with extra-wide brims. Their shoes, also white, matched the hats.

When they got to the foot of the porch, they both bowed deeply and said, in unison, as if practiced, "Good evening, ladies." Then, pointing to Charles's car, they added, "This way to pleasure."

"This is a joke, right?" Ella said, placing her hands on her hips. "You two look like fugitives from a circus fashion show."

I added, "Either that or peacocks that have run through fans! Just what the heck are you two supposed to be?"

"Why, what do you mean?" Jackson said. "We look great! You have any idea how long it took us to look this good for you? Why, this is the latest style."

"Style, my foot!" Ella practically shouted, stomping on the porch. "You two are out of your minds if you think we're going anywhere with you looking like that. I wouldn't go to a dance at the circus with you—they'd keep us all with the rest of the clowns."

"You've hurt our feelings," Charles said, pouting and looking down at his white shoes. "We thought you'd be thrilled."

"We're thrilled, alright," Ella said, crossing her arms and tapping her foot on the porch. "Thrilled to see you two march right back down that sidewalk and out of our sight!"

Standing there, sad looks on their faces, they looked so pitiful. I really had never seen anything—man or beast—that looked anything like them, but it seemed they genuinely had tried to please us. Being seen with them in public would be like being seen with cartoon characters right out of *Gasoline Alley*, but their hearts seemed pure. I had to give them that much. And besides, in spite of their clothing, they were, in an odd sort of way, cute. Horribly attired—but cute.

"Wait a minute, Ella," I said, grabbing her arm to try to settle her down. "I agree their sense of fashion isn't up to…well, it isn't quite up to anything I can think of. But I'd have to say they're trying. And, after all, won't people really expect this type of escort around town for the Poison Sisters? I say we go and have a good time. Why not?"

"Now you're kidding, right?" Ella asked, tapping her foot now on the top of mine. "You'd really be seen in public with these—these clothes clods."

"Yes, I think I would," I said, walking down the steps and taking Charles by the hand. "I'm ready. Lead the way, Romeo."

Ella stood on the porch, her arms still folded. "Oh, good grief. You're out of your mind too, Liv. But I'm not staying here by myself. Okay, I'll go, too. But you boys have to promise to walk five feet behind us when we get there. And you have to promise to sit in the stag area until they lower the lights. Then you can come over and ask us to dance. Maybe the darkness will lessen the glare of those vests. Purple? Where in the Sam Hill did you both find purple?"

Jackson, who had been very quiet for him, started laughing and said, "Girls, we've got a surprise for you. Give us a minute, okay?"

Before either Ella or I could respond, they both walked to Charles's car, reached inside, and pulled out small suitcases. They walked back to us, setting the suitcases down at our feet.

"What's in the suitcases?" I asked. "Better not be matching clothes for us."

"No," Jackson said, smiling. "We better fess up before you two run off. Our real clothes are in here, and I hope the jackets aren't too wrinkled by now. We might need your iron, if you don't mind."

The realization hit Ella and me at the exact same time, and we started playfully slapping at and kicking both of them. They had not only pulled the wool over our eyes—they had brought along the whole sheep. And we fell for it, hook, line, and sinker.

"You boys are horrible!" Ella screamed. "How'd we ever get hooked up with you?"

"I second that," I said. "And horrible isn't the word I'd use, but I don't want to shock your ears this early in the evening!"

Jackson and Charles started laughing so hard I saw tears in

their eyes. Then, suddenly, they started dancing with each other right there in the middle of my front yard.

"You two get in the house before someone calls for the people with those big nets," I demanded, shooing them up the steps.

"Don't worry," Charles said, "it won't take us long to get dressed. I think you'll see quite a difference—and soon."

"But you'll still have the same faces," Ella said, needling them.

"Ah, but what fine faces they are," Jackson shot back. "You girls are really lucky. You just don't realize it yet."

"Get in there and get dressed!" I ordered.

"Now, no peeking," Charles said. "I don't want to see your faces pressed against the window."

"You are so, so funny," Ella said, rolling her eyes. "Why would we want to do that? Now get in there. We're going to be late!"

Both entered the house and closed the door loudly behind them. As soon as the door closed, Ella took my hand and pulled me to the window. "Won't hurt to check out the merchandise, will it?"

"Why, Ella Jane," I said, "I believe you are full of the Devil tonight."

"Just watch out you don't run into my horns," she said, inching closer to the glass.

"Move over," I said. "I'll take my chances."

* * *

The Club Riviera was, by far, the most popular nightclub in the area. It had achieved, and deservedly so, the reputation of having the best music of any of the clubs hosting orchestras and jazz groups. It was now also the most difficult place to get into because of the tremendous crowds that always showed up. Adding to this was the fact that many whites in the city started coming there as well because, for them, it was the thing to do, especially for those who were seeking a thrill by walking on the thin edge of social acceptability. Nightclubbing wasn't a two-way street in St. Louis. Those with dark faces had their own places to go, and those with lighter skin could go anywhere they pleased. Fair? No. Fact of life? Yes. And it also made the crowds even larger, making it even more difficult for everyone to get inside.

When we arrived and as Charles pulled the car in a large lot across the street, we could see a line running from the front entrance of the club well back out onto the sidewalk.

"Looks like we better find a different place tonight," Ella said, sadly. "What a crowd. Just look at that."

"Not to worry," Jackson said, reaching over to pat her on the hand. "We'll get in. Don't you worry."

I didn't see how we could get in, but the glint in Jackson's eye was enough for me to get out of the car and take a chance.

Jackson led us to the front of the line, then motioned for us to wait there while he stepped inside. He returned a minute later and waved us to come in. Once inside, a waiter immediately showed us to a table right on the dance floor.

"How'd you do this?" Ella demanded to know. "This is the best table in the house."

"Don't ask," Jackson said. "Just sit and enjoy."

"How did he do it?" I leaned over and whispered to Charles.

The minute they sat down, Jackson and Ella immediately got back up and headed to the dance floor. After they had gone, Charles leaned even closer to me and whispered, seriously, in my ear, "You better watch out what you want to know about Jackson. We've become pretty good friends because of all this, but I've got to tell you there's something dark about him. He may seem like all laughs and fun when he's at parties and such, but when he's away from our crowd he has a side that scares me. When his car broke down the other day, he called me and asked if I'd come give him a ride home from Brown's garage. When I pulled up, I saw him taking a pistol from Old Man Brown, who everybody knows is the biggest fence in St. Louis. I asked him about it on the way to his place, and he said, kind of like he was mad, 'You didn't see anything. I'm telling you that. Don't you dare ask me again'."

"A pistol?" I asked. "You sure?"

"And not only that, he's never let me come up to his flat. Not once. I'm starting to think he's hiding something up there. You don't suppose he really works for Old Man Brown, do you?"

"Who knows? Nobody really seems to know anything about him. You really don't have to hang around with him, you know, so why are you doing it if you're so worried?"

"It's hard to put into words. He seems like such a nice person at times—and then in the next minute like someone who'd shoot you for a dime."

He then shrugged his shoulders and added, "But being around him has me here with you tonight, so I think I'll take my chances."

Charles moved his chair closer and put his arm around me. I didn't move away. It felt nice, made me feel pretty on an otherwise fairly ugly day. He was a good man, a kind man. He was both a gentle man—and a gentleman. For all the mystery surrounding Jackson, Charles was so much the opposite. He was a good churchgoing man and someone who was always helping out those in need in the Ville. He'd make a fine catch for any woman lucky enough to land him. He already looked like he wanted to be hanging from my fishing pole, but I honestly didn't know whether I wanted keep fishing. My heart still hurt so much, and Inman was still so deep in it. Sitting there and looking at Charles, I decided I'd just wait and see what might happen. When he offered me a cigarette, I declined. Instead, I leaned over and softly kissed him on the lips.

"Please ask me to dance," I said. "I could use it."

He stood up and pulled back my chair. Once on the dance floor, he guided me gently around the floor to the easy rhythms of Dud Bascomb's Dynamic Deluxe Recording Orchestra. In Charles's arms, I felt safe, alive. I pressed my cheek to his as he held me close. My world, for the first time in years, felt at peace.

We remained on the dance floor for three or four songs until the orchestra took its first break. Jackson and Ella were back at the table waiting for us.

"I thought we were going to have to call the fire department to get you two pried apart," Ella teased us as we sat down.

"She's a great dancer," Charles said, taking my hand again.

"You're not chopped liver yourself," I replied.

"If you want to see a dancer," Ella said, pointing to Jackson, "you should get a load of this man. I'm out of breath from trying to keep up with him."

"No," Jackson said. "You're out of breath because I'm so handsome, and it's just about too much for you."

"And he's modest, too," Ella added, laughing softly.

Jackson reached over and brushed a curl away from Ella's cheek. Like Charles, I still didn't know what to make of him, but it was clear to me he had fallen for Ella. Right now, that was enough for me.

"Here comes Jordan Chambers," Jackson suddenly said, motioning all of us to look up on the stage.

"Who's he?" I asked.

Jackson replied, "The owner of the club. He's a fine man. Knows his business. Also owes me some…"

His voice trailed off. He didn't finish his thought, but I could guess what he left out. Charles must have as well because he squeezed my hand under the table and smiled at me.

Mr. Chambers stepped to the microphone and greeted everyone by saying, "Is it a good night?"

Nearly everyone in the place shouted back in unison, "Yes!"

Mr. Chambers then asked, louder, "Is it also a *great* night?"

Everyone again shouted back, "Yes!"

He then asked, his voice becoming still louder, "Is it going to be a night to remember?"

The room erupted, "Yes!"

Jackson quickly turned to all of us and said, "Get ready— here it comes."

Mr. Chambers paused, lit a cigarette, then practically

screamed into the microphone, "Then what are you doing here?"

Everyone in the room howled. I'd never heard so much laughter in all my life.

Jackson did his best to shout over the laughter, "He does this every night. People would be really mad if he didn't. It has become his trademark."

When the laughter subsided enough, Mr. Chambers added, "If you're going to waste your time here, then you might as well drink up and get to dancing. And then drink some more. Remember—if you drink enough, your dates are going to look awful pretty later on!"

The laughter erupted again. He then motioned for all of his waitresses to get busy and hustle around the room to take drink orders. And they did.

"I don't need a drink tonight to know I'm with the most beautiful woman here," Charles said, taking my hand again. "I can tell that right now."

"Stop it," I said. "You're just supposed to be a decoy, remember?"

"I think it's too late," Ella said.

"He's already gone," Jackson added. "Pitiful. Just pitiful."

"Now you two stop it," I said. "Leave him alone. I can handle this."

"That's what you think," Ella said.

Jackson reached into the pocket inside his jacket and pulled out a black ball a little larger than a baseball. He sat it on the table and said, "This will tell you your future—and what you really want to know about Charles."

"What is it?" I asked.

"I'll tell you what it is," Ella groaned. "It's what's been sticking me in the side on the dance floor all night."

Jackson said, "If you'll all be quiet for a minute, I'll tell you. I picked this up in Memphis last time I was there. These are really *the* thing to have down there. It's called a Magic 8-Ball."

When he rotated it around so we could see the other side of

it, it looked like a much larger version of the billiard ball of the same number, complete with the black number against a round white background.

"Watch this," he said. "Oh, Magic 8-Ball, answer me this. Will Ella give me a kiss tonight?"

He then shook the ball and quickly flipped it over. The bottom of the ball had a small flat area with a clear window across it. Jackson held the ball over close to me so I could see what happened next. A small cube of some kind was floating in water inside the ball. It was spinning slowly until it finally came to a stop as it floated up and rested against the small window. I couldn't believe my eyes. On the cube were these words: "Definitely yes!"

I read the cube out loud, and Charles and Ella leaned forward and grabbed for the ball at the same time.

"Let me see that!" Ella shouted. "How'd you do that!"

"Easy!" Jackson said. "You'll all get your turn to ask the 8-Ball. Don't crowd."

"Hand that to me," I said in my best teacher voice, like I was asking a student to turn over a note being passed in class.

Jackson gently placed it in my hands. "Be careful. Don't drop it," he cautioned.

While I cradled it, he said, "Go ahead. You can be first. Ask a question. Anything you wish. It won't bite."

"Okay," I said. "Here goes. Is Charles going to ask me to dance again tonight?"

"Go ahead and shake it up," Jackson said, motioning with his own hands. "Now turn it over and read what it says."

I turned the 8-Ball over and read the cube, which said, "Our sources say Yes!"

We all laughed and shook our heads in amazement.

"Where'd you get this?" Charles asked again. "I want one of these!"

"I told you. Memphis. I imagine they'll be up here to St. Louis before long."

"Give it to me," Ella commanded. "I want to ask it something."

She shook the ball, while asking, "I made a wish last night before I went to bed. Is it going to come true?"

"Hey, no fair," Jackson said. "You have to say it aloud. All of it."

"Sorry—not this one," she said, turning the ball over to see what message would appear. She read aloud for all of us to hear, "Ask again later."

"Ask again later? What gives? What's that mean?"

Jackson said, "It means the spirit of the 8-Ball wants you to kiss me first before he will answer. He leaned toward Ella and puckered up. Ella shocked him by kissing him so hard he nearly fell to the floor.

"You may not have gotten your answer," he said to her, "but I think I just got mine!"

We kept asking the 8-Ball questions, each one getting more silly than the last. Jackson asked if he was going to be rich someday, and the response was, "You can count on it." When that came up, we all clapped. Charles asked if he and I would get married, and it responded, "Doubtful."

"I don't think I like this 8-Ball," he said, passing it to Ella. Ella then asked, "Will Jackson propose to me one of these days?" He playfully tried to grab the ball away from her, but she leaned away from him, turned the ball over, and said, without looking at the ball, "Of course he will—he's mad about you—he can't live without you—he adores you—he loves you—" Charles and I laughed until our sides hurt. Jackson, in mock horror, said, "Sounds like that 8-Ball has got my number!"

The ball was then passed to me. "I don't have anything else to ask," I said as I tried to hand it back to Ella.

"Go ahead, Liv. Do one more question."

"Okay," I said. "One more. Let's see…I've got it. Magic 8-Ball, answer me this: I have something dangerous coming up. Will everything go okay?"

When I turned the ball over, there were the words: "Don't know for now."

"Well, then, that makes two of us," I said. "And it's probably better I don't know now. I'm actually glad it said that."

I passed the ball to Charles, but he set it down without looking at it. Instead, he stood up and pulled my chair back so I could do the same.

"We don't want to make a liar out of the 8-Ball," he said as the orchestra started playing again. "It said I was going to ask you to dance again tonight, so I will. Olivia, may I have this dance?"

"Yes, sir," I said, standing and saluting him. "And all the other dances tonight as well. They're all yours."

The minute we entered the dance floor and he took me in his arms, I didn't need any sort of magic to tell me if I wanted to be with him.

I held him close, as close as I could. I clung to him, feeling his warmth and strength pressing against me.

Charles suddenly pushed me slightly away and looked deeply into my eyes. We stopped dancing, amid the sea of bodies swirling around us. He drew me to him and kissed me, softly at first and then with a passion I had all but forgotten. I leaned back to catch my breath and studied his face. He took my hand and held it to his chest.

"Feel my heart," he said.

"Probably the same as mine."

He pulled me close again and we danced some more, continuing even after the music had stopped. Ella finally came over and pulled us back to the table, through the laughter of those sitting at the other tables along the rim of the floor.

"What's the matter with you? What were you two thinking?" she asked, shaking her head.

I didn't know what Charles was thinking, but I knew what I was.

I was thinking it was wonderful to be alive.

* * *

That night, as I drifted toward sleep, I felt the dream coming again...

The flames were burning the moon. They were shooting higher and higher, first just barely touching its chin, then turning its whole face orange. The stars around it blinked white, then red, over and over again. The angels in the barn were still screaming, still flying from window to window. One angel's white robe was suddenly blue, and smoke curled up from its pointed hat. I saw the angel's eyes, wide, staring right at me. I covered my face with my hands and fell to the soft dirt behind the hedge. The screams grew softer, more distant...

11

Secrets

Ella and I were hanging her new living room curtains and teasing each other about our date with our decoys the previous evening when we noticed the police car ease to a stop at the curb in front of her lilac bushes. I could tell by his uniform that the driver was a member of the St. Louis City Police. The other two who exited the car were the same officers who had come from Arkansas to question Ella at Sumner. All three were furiously puffing cigars as they chugged up the sidewalk.

"Here we go again," Ella said, exhaling loudly. "Liv, no matter what they tell you to do, I'd like you to stay here. Please. I don't want to be left alone with them."

I nodded that I would. Ella added, her tone even more serious, "You may be shocked by what you hear. I don't know. We'll talk after they leave, okay?"

I nodded again.

The knock on the door was loud, insistent.

When Ella answered the door she immediately commanded, "The cigars have to go, gentlemen. Not in my house."

The St. Louis officer brushed her aside and led the other men in. They kept their cigars.

"I'm Sergeant McDougald," the one from St. Louis said. "I believe you remember officers Ryan and Lawson. They have some more questions for you, and you better be straight with them. You better tell the truth if you know what's good for you."

Turning to me, he added, "Time for you to go. Right now."

Ella looked at me, her expression begging. "I'm staying," I

163

said, firmly. "I'm her sister. Her half sister. I have a right to stay."

"I don't remember hearing about you," the larger of the two, Officer Ryan, said disgustedly. "Where'd you come from?"

"Same as you did," I said. "The stork brought me."

"You shut your mouth," McDougald erupted, getting right in my face. "This isn't funny. I'll run your ass in if you get in the way. If you're staying, sit over there and keep your big trap shut."

I moved over to the rocker and sat down. Ella quickly jumped in, deflecting McDougald's anger, "Please sit on the couch. There's room for all of you. I'll pull up a chair from the dining room. How about some coffee?"

Her tone was calm, unemotional.

"No coffee," McDougald said, his voice softening some. "Let's get down to brass tacks. These officers have driven a long way. Again."

At that point, Officer Ryan didn't mince any words, didn't offer an ounce of sympathy. Rather, he barked gruffly at Ella, "We found your pappy's body. At the Mallard Slew, just outside Blytheville. Some fishermen found him. Back of his head was bashed in."

Here he paused, appearing to study Ella's face, before continuing, "No doubt it was murder. None at all. What do you have to say about that?"

Ella got up and walked over to the window. She stared outside and calmly asked, "You sure it was my father? You sure it wasn't someone else?"

"It was him alright," Ryan replied. "Body was a real mess, but his wallet was still in his pocket and he still had his watch. No doubt about it."

I couldn't take it anymore. I stood up and let Officer Ryan have it. "Don't you have any decency, any common courtesy? You come charging in here and without so much as a how-do-you-do you tell her her father passed on. What kind of man are you?"

"He didn't pass on," Officer Ryan said, sneering at me.

"Don't you get it? Someone bashed his skull in. He was murdered, plain and simple."

"I don't care how he died," I said. "You should be more understanding. That kind of news isn't the type you blurt out. What's the matter with you?"

McDougald jumped in, "Well, if you're her sister, was that your father, too?"

Thinking quickly, I added, "I'm her half sister. Different fathers. He wasn't mine, but even with me you should have been... more gentle at least."

McDougald didn't apologize. Instead, he said, "Well, we might have been except for one thing. Your sister there..."

Ryan interrupted him. "I'll take over," he said. He paused and lit his cigar again, exhaling a large puff of smoke. Turning to face Ella he said, "You told us you were in Blytheville interviewing for a job at a store there the last morning anyone saw him. We tried to confirm that, but the owner of that store just passed on, so now he can't vouch for your story. Funny, no one else at the store remembers you that day. Right now, it looks to me like you were the last one to see him alive. Looks to me like you better come up with a better alibi."

He rolled his cigar back and forth along his full lips, still studying Ella, who had turned back to face him.

"There was someone else who saw him that morning," she said matter-of-factly.

"And who would that be?" Officer Ryan asked.

"Obviously, the person who killed him. Father dropped me off in town. I told you that before. That's the last I saw of him."

Her face was expressionless. She turned quickly back toward the window and said, "My father is dead. I need some time alone. I'm going to have to ask you to leave."

"Not by a long shot," Officer Ryan added, his tone almost bitter. "Not 'til we get to the bottom of this."

"You won't get to the bottom of anything here," Ella said, quietly. "I don't know anything more to tell you. And it doesn't matter how many times you ask me, my story will be the same, just as I told you before. I can't tell you anything more if I don't know anything more."

The three were staring at her intently. I said to them, "Look. She's obviously in shock. Look at her. I'm going to take her into the bedroom and put her to bed. If you have any more questions, please at least wait until I can get a doctor here."

When they didn't respond, I added, "Haven't any of you lost a loved one before? For the love of Pete, get out of here and leave her alone. That's the right thing to do, and you all know it."

The officer who hadn't spoken, Officer Lawson, finally said something. He said, evenly, "She's right. We should go. But this isn't finished. There are plenty of other questions we need to ask, but I guess they can wait. We'll be back tomorrow. And you better be ready to answer them or you're coming with us—back to Arkansas. Understand?"

"That's more like it," I said, smiling weakly at Officer Lawson. "Let her get some rest and think about this some. This is quite a shock. Thank you for understanding."

I immediately took Ella's arm and walked her to the bedroom. I could hear the men opening the front door. A few seconds later I saw them through the window heading back down the sidewalk toward the car.

Ella was standing before me, staring blankly ahead. "There, there," I said, urging her to climb into bed.

I was shocked when she instead walked briskly to the window and watched the car pull away from the curb. She exhaled deeply and said, "Good job, Liv. I didn't think they'd leave that easily. You're pretty good with people, you know that? Even with crackers like that."

"You okay?" I asked. "You really looked out of it just a minute ago."

"The only thing I'm upset about is that they came back. And now, they'll be back again. They won't get anything else out of me, though. Not a thing."

She added, nonchalantly, "Ready for some coffee? How about some toast and that new blackberry jam? I'm starved."

She walked past me and down the hallway toward the kitchen. I didn't know what else to do, so I followed her.

As I sat down to the table, I asked, "I know I said I wouldn't ask any more about this..."

"Then don't," Ella interrupted, as she continued setting the table. "Please don't."

I stared into my coffee while I stirred it. Ella finally stopped moving and sat back against the sink. She chose her words slowly, carefully. "I'm going to tell you a story," she began. "Please, just listen. Don't say anything. Not a single word. This is the only time I'll ever tell you this story, and I want it to be the last time we mention it."

I looked up and nodded that I understood.

She continued, "When I was almost eight, my mother died one day while picking okra. That day she just collapsed and fell right in the field. I found her when I was walking home from school. She looked so calm, so peaceful, I thought she was taking a nap. When she didn't answer my calls, I ran to her. She was gone. I hugged her and sat there with her until my father came home. The first thing he did was whip me, while my mother was still lying there. He made me feel that somehow it was all my fault."

"Ella, I—"

"No. Let me finish. After the funeral, my Aunt Lillian wanted to take me to live with her, but Father wouldn't let her. He wanted to keep me around, to punish me for what had happened. He beat me almost every night. He didn't even have to be drunk to reach for the weeping willow branch he kept in the kitchen just for use on me. I'd just be sitting there and he'd pick it up and start in. If I ran, I'd get it worse when he finally caught me, so I finally just learned to take it."

She paused here, lit a cigarette, and then continued, slowly drawing out the words. "I tried one time to hit back. I picked up a beer bottle and caught him on the side of the head. All that did was make him even more furious."

"See this?" she said, untucking her blouse and pulling it up from her waist. There, on the left side of her stomach, was a long, jagged scar. "When he got the bottle away from me, he broke it on the table and cut me with the part that was left in his hand. It was a quick swipe. I didn't even feel it. I finally saw the blood dripping on the floor, and I remember just staring at it, like it wasn't even a part of me. Like it was from someone else. We had just one doctor in the whole county who would look at Negro patients, and he was gone somewhere. Father finally carried me to his truck and drove me to a neighbor's house. The wife sewed my skin back together with a quilt needle. Can you imagine? A quilt needle."

Ella sat back in her chair and sipped her coffee, her expression blank again. I started to speak, but she again motioned me to stay quiet.

"It wasn't long after that he started drinking even more. The bottle became his home. I tried to stay away from him as much as I could, especially at night. The beatings got worse. It wasn't until I started high school that anyone else figured out what was going on. It was my first boyfriend who came by one evening and heard me screaming. He knocked the door off the hinges, rushed in, and ripped him off of me. They wrestled around some until my boyfriend finally put a knife to his throat and told him he'd kill him if he ever touched me again. It was fine for a while after that, but he kept drinking and drinking and drinking."

She lit another cigarette and continued, "He got to the point where he couldn't pay the bills, so we had to move. Over and over again. We ended up in a tiny sharecropper shack because the man who owned that farm felt sorry for us, I guess. When I was finally old enough, I got a job as a custodian at the local college. It took some doing on my boyfriend's part, but he finally convinced me to take classes at night to get my teaching certificate. I didn't know if I really wanted to teach, but I knew I wanted away from that shack, so I started the classes. After a semester I got a provisional certificate and worked as a substitute teacher in the local schools. At the same time, my father stopped drinking for a while, and I actually started feeling sorry for him. He was my father, after all, and I thought I could help him. Instead—"

She stopped abruptly, standing and walking over to the sink. While still facing away from me, she said, "Deep down he was probably a good man. I prayed for it, but I just never saw that part of him. I never did."

Part of me so badly wanted her to continue the story. The rest of me knew it would probably be better if she didn't. By her actions and expressions, I could tell she knew something about her father's death. But, whether she had anything to do with it or just knew something about it was still hanging there in the air between us, and I wasn't sure that should be touched. As I studied her face, her emotions were still hidden from me. She didn't look like she wanted to provide more information, so I didn't press the issue. It certainly wasn't my usual character and it was difficult for me to do, but I just sat there, silent, waiting for her to continue.

"Liv, I may have to leave St. Louis one of these days. If I do, I want you to know how much you mean to me—how much you'll always mean to me. I've never had anyone like you in my life before. You can make me laugh and cry in the same breath. You make me feel like I'm important, like I belong here. More than anything, though, you've made me understand that life can be beautiful, that it doesn't have to be dark all the time. Since becoming close to you, I can sleep at night with the lights off for the first time in my life. I love you, Liv, and I always will."

I walked to the sink and hugged her tightly. Tears were streaming down my cheeks, but I wasn't really crying. They dripped on her dress, forming little circles on her shoulder. She started sobbing and her arms tightened around my waist.

We held each other close, not wanting to let go.

12

Justification

Two days went by and, much to our surprise, the police did not return as they said they would. Ella didn't want to talk any more about the subject, and I didn't press the issue. We spoke only by phone for those two days. Ella said she didn't want me coming over, didn't want to get me any more involved than I already was. I told her she was being silly—that we should just go about our business—but she said she wanted a buffer of time to place over everything.

I didn't agree with her, but, deep down, I understood.

I spent most of that time finishing the rest of the paperwork James had given me. It was a great deal of work, but I enjoyed the challenge. Before doing this, I had absolutely no idea so many forms and documents were present behind the scenes for what I always assumed was a simple transaction. It all was, in so many ways, like putting together a jigsaw puzzle, especially because I was making sure a couple of the pieces would come up missing....

I didn't understand at all one of the forms that also tied into the financing of the property, so I called James at his office to ask him about it. I was aware that party-line ears might have been listening, so I chose my words carefully. Apparently, I chose them too carefully because not even James could tell what I was asking about.

Out of frustration, James finally interrupted me and said, "Olivia, I'm getting ready for my lunch break. How would you like to join me for a quick sandwich? We could also talk about your work."

"I think that would be wonderful," I replied, relieved. "Great idea. Where should I meet you?"

"I'll drive by your place and pick you up in, say, fifteen minutes. Would that work for you?"

"I'll be ready. I'll wait out on the porch so you don't have to get out of the car."

"See you then," he said as he hung up.

I put the papers in my school briefcase and headed out to the porch. The day was overcast and muggy. I sat in the swing, and the second I touched the wooden slats I noticed sweat was already causing my dress to cling to my back. I pulled the material away from my skin and leaned forward as I rocked.

James must have missed every red light because he pulled up in less than ten minutes. As soon as he stopped the car I headed down the sidewalk and waved to him. Always the gentleman, he got out and opened the door for me.

"Thank you, kind sir," I said, sitting and swinging my legs into the car.

"And how are you today?" he asked, closing the door and walking back to his side before I could answer. However, I knew he wasn't being rude. He just seemed very preoccupied, which I could certainly understand given the events that were to unfold shortly.

When he was seated and had started the motor, he said, "Would you mind taking a little drive with me first—before we go to the diner? Do you have time?"

"Sure," I said. "Where to?"

"I want to show you something. It won't take long."

"What is it?" I asked, my curiosity starting to get to me.

He didn't answer me. Instead, he said, more to himself than to me, "We'll be there in a minute. It's not far."

He stared intently ahead and kept his hands gripped tightly on the wheel at ten-and-two. I had never seen him like this before, and it unsettled me more than a little.

We finally turned onto Labadie Avenue. About halfway

down the block he slowed down, eased to the curb, and stopped, turning off the motor.

"There it is," he said. "4600. I wanted you to see what we're working toward."

It was a plain, two-story brick home very much like those all around it up and down the street. It was a nice home, in a fine area, and I immediately could see why the Shelleys fell in love with it and wanted it so badly. All the neighboring yards were well manicured, and I didn't see a single piece of trash anywhere along the gutters of both sides of the street. Compared to where they were living on 9th Street in the city, this had to look like heaven itself to them.

"So this is it," I said. "I've been down this street before, but I guess I never really paid much attention to the homes because, well, because they really weren't a possibility for us."

"They are now—at least one of them," James said, softly. "I never thought in my lifetime I'd see any of our neighbors owning property across Taylor Avenue. This is just a stone's throw away from the Ville, but for as long as I can remember it might as well have been a thousand miles."

He paused, his tone becoming more serious, and said, almost whispering, "Maybe I'm just dreaming. Maybe it still is a thousand miles. I don't know.... There's so much to come that has to fall completely our way for us to pull this off. So much. But every time I start to worry, my thoughts always come back to one thing. Now's the time to try. We have to. Not just for the Shelleys, but for every one of those families on the other side of Taylor. We may not make it, but we'll go down swinging. I guess we'll just have to do the best we can and trust for luck."

"And pray," I added. "Lots of praying."

Mimicking Reverend Danielson, he added, "Aaaaaaamen to that! We need all the help we can get."

He looked at me, and we both burst into laughter.

We then sat quietly for a few minutes and watched an older man two doors west of 4600 water his flowers and bushes. His movements were slow, deliberate, like he had all the time in the world. As he sprinkled them, he gently brushed the tips of the flowers, making sure the water soaked into them. It was clear, from watching the care he was taking, that he was proud of his corner of the world.

"Wonder what he'll think when he finds out who his new neighbors will be?" I asked, pointing at him.

James also pointed toward him, wiggled his finger, and said, "I'm going to go out on a limb and guess he won't like the Shelleys as much as he does those flowers. Want to bet?"

"I'm a gambler by nature," I said, "but I won't take that bet because I think you're probably right. I'd say he'll think the Shelleys will be thorns in his flower garden. I'd like to believe otherwise, but I can't."

"Let's get some lunch," James said. "Frankly, I don't care what that man thinks."

"Me neither. Get this car going. I'm starving."

As we drove past, we both waved to the man when he looked our direction.

He didn't wave back.

* * *

Our lunch was delicious—tuna salad sandwiches on rye served with a cup of steaming vegetable soup. While we ate, James was able to answer all my remaining questions about the documents so that I fully understood what still needed to be done. His explanations were detailed, but clear and precise. Listening to him, I thought about what a fine teacher he would have made.

As we each took a last sip of coffee and stood to leave, he told me he had one more stop to make in preparation for the transfer of the deed. I knew he was terribly busy and still had other work to do before we all met at the bank the next day, so I offered to walk home to save him some time. He tried to talk me out of it, but I needed the exercise, needed to get outside and clear my head a little more and get myself in the right frame of mind for what was to come. I thanked him for lunch and suggested we do it again sometime. He said he'd be glad to—that is, if we didn't both end up eating off metal trays in the city jail. I squinted and shook my finger at him. He may have intended it as gallows humor, but I still didn't need to hear it. Not at this point anyway.

"Olivia," he said, taking my hand, "good luck tomorrow. Be strong. Be proud of what we're doing."

"You, too," I said. "Best of luck."

Without another word, we each turned and left.

The walk home took me past King Aldridge's Bakery, Bentley's Dress Shop, the Fritz Radio Company, Dr. Massey's office—known as the "King of Skin Whitener Treatments," Henry Boyd's Laundry, and my favorite establishment, Goldye's Ladies Ready-to-Wear store. I had been so busy of late I'd forgotten just how beautiful the Ville was and how much it had to offer. It truly was a magical place to live.

As I continued my walk, I also remembered one of my teachers at Lincoln University repeating to us a famous expression: "An island is only an island if you are looking at it from the shore." Sadly, to many, the Ville was, indeed, still an island, one surrounded by a wall of fear and misunderstanding. I hoped and prayed we could help the Shelleys enough to knock down some of this, which would in turn help get some of those in the Ville to the shore where their perspectives would change and their lives would have possibilities never dreamed of before.

Time would tell.

That time was coming fast.

13

D-Day

The dog days of August were refusing to die. By Friday morning, the temperature was hovering right at one hundred degrees. The only thing positive I could say about the heat was I hoped it would keep people home in front of their fans and not at the bank while we were there.

When the phone rang, I was already so edgy I nearly jumped out of my skin. It was Reverend Danielson.

"Olivia, it's time for you to get going. You ready for this?"

Fully conscious of the party line clicking I heard in the background, I said, "Absolutely. I'll get my purse and be out the door before you can hang up."

"See you soon. Lord be with you—with us all."

"Thank you," I said, also repeating, evenly, "And with us all."

I had, thankfully, been right about the heat keeping people indoors. Easton Avenue was nearly deserted as I walked the two blocks from the streetcar stop to the bank. For an odd minute, the only movement I saw was a mangy hound walking down the street right in the middle of the streetcar tracks. By the way it was jerking up its paws as it walked, I could tell it, too, was feeling the heat.

F. W. Woolworth's department store was right across the street from the bank, and I was supposed to wait there until ten minutes after seeing Josie go in. Woolworth's had the best lunch counter and soda fountain in the area. Although there were no signs posted anywhere and I'd never actually heard of any conflict there, it was clearly understood by all that Negroes were allowed to sit only in the private booths to the right of the main counter section. For this reason, I hated coming into Woolworth's, but on this day, prejudice would play right into our hands. I chose the table closest to the corner, the table with the best unobstructed view of the bank through the front window. I couldn't have asked for a better spot, and I smiled as that thought came to me.

The counter waitress yelled over to me, "Hey, you. You'll have to order up here if you want anything. Not doing tables right now."

By the look in her eyes, it was clear she really meant, "I'm not doing your table right now."

"Just waiting for a friend," I said, smiling weakly. "I'd like a glass of cool ice water for the time being."

The waitress grunted and turned away. She soon returned with the water, placed it on the counter, and said, without looking at me, "Water. Come and get it."

"Thank you," I said as insincerely as I could.

She did turn toward me, but I didn't make eye contact. I quickly grabbed the glass, spun back around, and sat back down. I wanted to say more, but this wasn't the time. There'd be another day for conversation with my Woolworth's waitress.

And, oh how I would be looking forward to it.

The time passed so slowly as I sat there sipping my water. With so little movement out on the street, I didn't have much to distract me from the almost constant glaring of the waitress. I checked my watch several times against the clock behind the counter and the large one on the side of the bank building. I was starting to wonder if something had gone wrong when I saw Josie walking briskly around the corner and to the door of the bank. Just as she grabbed for the door handle she paused, turned slowly around, and appeared to bow slightly in my direction.

That was my cue. Ten more minutes.

Even though it was nice and cool in Woolworth's, I felt sweat forming at the collar of my dress. I was nervous, but it also didn't help that I could see waves of heat dancing on the pavement outside. The contrast of temperatures made me shiver. I was also thinking about something else. I knew it was silly to be concerned about her, but I didn't like the way the waitress was staring at me—as if she knew I had a secret I was protecting. Reaching into my purse, I withdrew a penny. I scooted my chair a little more to the side so she couldn't see what I was doing. I then licked Lincoln's face and dropped the coin into the water glass. That would be her tip.

Tip for tat.

When I exited, the heat rushed into my face, nearly taking my breath away. I decided I'd kill a little more time by walking down to the corner newsstand to see if there were any new movie magazines. Halfway there I saw a late-model sedan pull to the curb and stop in front of the bank. It was James. The first thing I noticed was his blue three-piece suit. In this heat he must have been roasting. He reached back into his car and pulled out his briefcase.

As if on cue, Reverend Danielson approached up the sidewalk from the left. They greeted each other as if they hadn't met in a long time. Reverend Danielson slapped him on the back, and they entered the bank together.

I looked at my watch. Three more minutes. I quickly scanned the racks of magazines and chose one with a picture of Clark Gable on the cover. I paid for it, rolled it up, and stuck it in my purse next to the photographs I was going to show to Mr. Stivesant. I figured if I walked slowly enough, I'd make it to the bank right on time.

I couldn't have been more than ten feet from the door when I heard someone yelling from behind me.

"You! Hey, you! What are you doing here?"

I wasn't sure the words were being directed to me—that is, until I turned and found myself face to face with Sergeant McDougald.

Before I could say anything, he added, curtly, "Out of your

neighborhood a little bit, aren't you? Your sister with you?"

"No!" I said a little too quickly, a little too nervously. "Just me today."

"What are you doing here?" he asked, first looking at me, then at the bank.

I could think of nothing better to say than the truth. At least, part of it.

"Mr. Stivesant is a good friend of mine. I've come to show him my new photographs."

I moved forward and looked him right in the eye while continuing, "I don't suppose you're also a lover of flowers. Want to see them?"

I opened the envelope and started pulling out the top picture when he said, gruffly, "How do you know Mr. Stivesant?"

"He's one of our biggest supporters at Sumner. I thought everyone knew that. I also hear he's a great supporter of the City Police, too. That right?"

I took a gamble. "Want to come in with me to say hi?"

The veins on his neck bulged out as he moved even closer to me, getting right in my face. "Don't you get uppity with me. I know your kind. You go ahead and go in the bank. You see your good friend. But that won't change anything. By dark you'll be back where you belong. You'll be back in your Ville. Every day at the end of the day, you always will be. And I'll be out here…"

Then, backing up slightly and flashing a sick smile, he added, "I think you know what you can do with those pictures."

I stood there and stared right back, unblinking.

As he started backing away, he said, sharply, "I'll be seeing you. I do mean *seeing* you. You can bet on it. And that sister of yours, too. We're not finished. I think you know it."

Sweat trickled down my forehead and into my eyes. I brushed it away and continued to stare at him. My heart was pounding. I knew I should keep my mouth shut, but I couldn't let him have the last word. I extended my hand to shake his. He recoiled in horror as I said, "I'll look forward to it. Stop by for coffee when you're in the neighborhood. Anytime. I have a special kind just for people like you. Until then… you be sure to take care."

He walked over and opened the door for me, first getting right in my way, then stepping to the side, as if punctuating his next words. "I'll be watching you," he said.

"Why thank you—for holding the door. That's most kind of you. But isn't it kind of dangerous? I mean, won't people see this and think we're, well, you know…"

Before he could reply I stepped inside, pulling the door shut tightly behind me—and blew him a kiss. Sergeant McDougald's face was beet red and pressed against the glass. I could see sweat from his cheek sliding down the door. He was speaking rapidly, but I couldn't make out the words.

Didn't matter. I had a pretty good idea what those words were…

I walked straight to the receptionist near the main office and told her I had an appointment with Mr. Stivesant. She glanced at me only briefly and said, "I'll see if he's ready."

Out of the corner of my eye I saw Josie laughing with a very handsome young clerk while patting him on the back of the hand. She was bent forward and leaning slightly over a stack of papers on his desk. Her ample cleavage was overflowing. Her dress didn't just have what Ella would have called a "plunging" neckline. It had already plunged. This was not lost at all on the clerk. Josie was smoking a cigarette, and every time she turned her head to the side to exhale smoke, the clerk's eyes darted immediately to the target. She was good. Very good. And she knew it. But then again, Josie had natural attributes most of us could only dream of having. As a result, that poor clerk didn't stand a chance.

James was seated to her left at the far end of the desk. He was signing papers, stamping them, and placing them in a pile before the clerk. He might as well have been invisible. The clerk never once looked in his direction.

Josie and the clerk laughed loudly again as she leaned

completely across his desk and began straightening his tie. With that, the clerk stopped any gentlemanly pretense of averting his eyes; his gaze was now bold and focused.

At that exact instant, James calmly placed an ink pen in the clerk's hand and directed him to sign a document unfolded before him. The clerk barely looked down as his hand moved across the paper. James's eyes followed closely, his face stone cold.

The secretary returned and told me I could come inside. I stifled a smile and stepped through the hinged gate separating inner and outer office. Mr. Stivesant walked briskly out of his office to meet me.

"So good to see you, Olivia, and especially today. *Today* has been a zoo around here. I haven't had a moment's peace. So, come on into the office and visit a while. Rescue me from this madness."

Little did he know the madness he had already experienced this day would be child's play compared to what we had in store for him.

"Good to see you, too," I said. "And I'll do my best to distract you. I promise."

And that, ironically, was exactly the truth.

When we were seated in his office, I immediately pulled the pictures from my purse. "I've got something here you might be interested in," I said, removing several of the pictures from the envelope. "I know you couldn't make the recent Hibiscus show, so I took these for you. I want you to have them. These are yours to keep. I know it isn't the same as being there, but beauty like this comes along so seldom. Here, take a look for yourself."

I handed him the pictures, stood up, and walked around to his side of the desk so I could provide details about each. While I did, he said, "Oh, my, these are absolutely beautiful! What kind of lens did you use? How did you get the lighting just right? Just look at this one. It's magnificent!"

"In good time," I said, tapping my finger on the first picture. "But we need to talk about something first. I'll share my little secrets of nighttime shooting with you if you'll consider sharing with me how your full sunlight shots never have the glare I always get. That sound like a fair deal to you?"

"More than fair," he said, still staring at the picture in front of him. "Olivia, I've never seen anything like this. Look at the contrast here. How'd you do it?"

I laughed and said, "To be honest, it was mostly luck, and I better admit it right up front. But, there are a few things that can be done to make sure we can take advantage of that luck when it shows up. Here, look at the next few pictures. I'll show you what I mean."

For the next fifteen minutes we went through each one of the pictures in the envelope. For each, I explained everything from camera distance from the object to the photographic angle used in relation to the direction of the available light. To add some time to our discussion, I also added in the effects of different variations of shutter speed, film type, and lenses. The last on the list, the use of different lenses, was nearly an obsession with Mr. Stivesant. He admitted owning twelve different types of lenses, all used for different light conditions and subjects. I had three lenses of my own, and one was a little foggy because of how long it had sat in bright sunlight in a pawnshop window before I rescued it. Still, I knew enough about lenses, and about his desire for knowledge of them, to keep him entertained several minutes longer.

There was a large window in the wall of his office that faced the main lobby. Through this window I could see Josie and the clerk still laughing and flirting with each other. I could also see James was still furiously stamping papers and placing them in another pile in front of the clerk.

Through this window I could also see the front door of the bank opening.

I immediately felt sweat forming on my forehead again.

In stepped Sergeant McDougald.

I gasped lightly. Mr. Stivesant looked up at me and asked,

"You okay? What's the matter?"

Caught off guard, I stammered, finally saying, "I—I just thought of something. I left my lens box open on the kitchen table. They'll be dusty when I get back home. And I sure hope this heat and humidity doesn't fog any of them."

"You should be more careful," he scolded me. "Lenses are delicate, like the flowers in these magnificent pictures. You sure I can keep these copies?"

"I'll be upset if you don't keep them," I said. "I've got more copies, and I'm going to use them this fall to help me teach my students in the photography club at Sumner. I'm still the faculty sponsor of the club. And don't you forget you promised to come teach them a thing or two when you can. I know you're a busy man, but I'm going to take you up on that promise."

I looked again through the window and saw Sergeant McDougald peering intently around the lobby. It was clear he was looking for me, but that didn't bother me. What did bother me was how his stare froze when he spotted James. He started walking across the lobby toward James, and my heart started pounding. He couldn't have known anything about our plan, but James had the skin color that made McDougald see red—and black. Red and black and hate. Especially hate. And now, it appeared he was on a mission to find out why two of us were in this bank at the same time.

"Look! There's a friend of yours!" I shouted, pointing through the window. "Why, it's Sergeant McDougald. Let's get him in here."

Mr. Stivesant looked as if he had no clue what I was rambling on about. Before he could stop me, I walked to the doorway and yelled, "Yoo-hoo! Sergeant McDougald! Please come in here a minute. We want to see you."

Sergeant McDougald was only steps away from James when I caught his attention. He stopped in his tracks, turned, and stared curiously at me as I motioned him toward the door. I felt Mr. Stivesant bump into me from behind. "Whatever are you doing, Olivia? Who did you see out there?"

"Why, it's your good friend, Sergeant McDougald. I was visiting with him earlier today, and he said you two were old friends. I thought he also might like to see the pictures I brought today."

McDougald looked right past me to Mr. Stivesant.

"John," Mr. Stivesant said, "good to see you, but what are you doing here?"

Sergeant McDougald looked back and forth from Mr. Stivesant to me and said, "Nothing really. Just doing a security check. That's all."

"Security check? Are there any problems? What's going on?"

"Not to worry. Everything's fine." Here Sergeant McDougald paused, stared intently at me, and continued, "She a friend of yours?"

"Yes, Olivia and I go way back. She said you two know each other. You interested in photography, John? I didn't know that."

"My interest in pictures goes more along the lines of mug shots at the station," he said, looking directly at me so his point wouldn't be lost.

We stood a few seconds in uncomfortable silence, each waiting for someone else to speak. Finally, I jumped in, purposely using McDougald's first name, "John, I'm sorry to interrupt you while you're working. When we spoke earlier you mentioned you hadn't seen Mr. Stivesant in a while. I just thought you might like to come in and take a load off—and look at my new pictures. But, I can see you're busy. I'm sorry—shouldn't have bothered you."

Not really paying attention to my words, Sergeant McDougald pointed toward James and asked Mr. Stivesant, "What's he—"

He never got a chance to complete his thought. The front door of the bank flew open, and Ella and Jimmy charged in, both yelling and screaming at each other. Ella was shouting, "It was *your* fault. Not *mine*!" Jimmy was right in her face, yelling back, "Where'd you learn to drive, lady? On a demolition derby course? You should be kept off the street. You're dangerous! I bet you were the one driving the Hindenburg, right?"

Ella started lightly slapping at Jimmy with her purse until a clerk ran over to stop her. Jimmy just put up his arms to deflect the blows and repeated over and over, "Not my fault! Not my fault!"

Ella glanced quickly at me but made no indication of any kind that she knew me. Rather, she walked over, stood right in front of Sergeant McDougald, and said, "Well, of all the luck— I guess you'll have to do. I never thought I'd be asking *you* for help. See this idiot here? He backed his car right into mine right out front. It was his fault. All his fault. I think our bumpers are locked. What am I going to do—I'm late for the beauty parlor and this *idiot* runs into me!"

Jimmy jumped into the fray. "Idiot? Idiot? Who's an idiot? It was not my fault. You ran into me. I was already in the space! You're out of your mind, Lady. Mr. Policeman—please help me. Not only is this all her fault, I think our cars really are stuck together, and now the road is blocked on this side. This might even block the streetcar. Come outside and look. Please!"

Jimmy grabbed for Sergeant McDougald's arm, but he pulled it back, sharply. "Wait a cotton-pickin' minute," he said. "I didn't hear any crash. Where'd you say this happened? And why'd you come in here? What's going on? You both better have some quick answers."

Ella spoke right up, "I saw your car out front and figured an officer must be in here. That's why I came in—to look for you. You've got to help me. You've got to save me from this—this fiend of the road!"

"Fiend of the road?" Jimmy shouted. "Lady, you're nuts. This is all your fault!"

Everyone in the bank was now focused on our little group. Mr. Stivesant, clearly uncomfortable this was unfolding right in the middle of his bank and was upsetting the regular customers, strongly urged Sergeant McDougald to take the conversation outside to get everything cleared up. Sergeant McDougald nodded, took both Ella and Jimmy by the arm, and ushered them outside. Both were still screaming "Idiot!" at each other as the door closed behind them.

As soon as they were outside, Mr. Stivesant turned to me and asked, "What in the heck was that? Some people!"

"Yes," I said, "*Some* people!"

"We really should go outside and see what's going on," Mr. Stivesant said. "This is going to be good. McDougald hates car accidents. With a passion."

"Then I'm sure he'll hate this one," I said. "Sounds like neither one of those drivers will give an inch of ground. Wouldn't you love to be a little fly on the outside wall of the bank right now!"

"Maybe we can crack open the door a little and do some spying."

"Why Mr. Stivesant," I said in mock horror. "I didn't know you could be such a snoop."

"I love my gossip as much as the next person. This job can get pretty boring from time to time. Anything that can liven it up—except robbery mind you—is always very welcome. What do you think? Should we go out there?"

"Better not," I said. "Believe me, I'd love to, but the police are usually funny about people getting in the way. And I have the feeling McDougald would never forgive us if he caught us."

I really did want to know what was going on. Ella and Jimmy just didn't show up because of a little fender-bender. The timing was too grand to be coincidence. They had put on their little act on purpose, but why? What were they really doing here? Ella also never once so much as smiled at me. As a matter of fact, she completely ignored me. Something was up. I was sure of that much.

With sad eyes, Mr. Stivesant finally shrugged his shoulders and said, "I know you're right. It's really none of our affair. Oh well…"

We started walking slowly back to his office when, as if he

had suddenly remembered something, he snapped his fingers and started walking over toward the clerk helping Josie and James. "Excuse me a minute, Olivia. I'll be right back," he called to me over his shoulder.

I started to grab his sleeve to stop him, but Reverend Danielson, who had also been watching from a chair in the foyer, saw the desperate look on my face and quickly stepped forward to intercept him.

"Mr. Stivesant," he said, strategically placing himself between Mr. Stivesant and the clerk "Glad I caught you. If you're not too busy just now, I've been wanting to talk to you about something. It's very private—and very important. Can we go into your office?"

Then, turning to me and acting as if he were just seeing me for the first time, he added, "Olivia! I'm sorry—you must think me so rude! What's the matter with me? Are you visiting with Mr. Stivesant? I didn't—Please forgive me."

"Good afternoon, Reverend Danielson. Nice to see you. Yes, Mr. Stivesant and I have been having a wonderful visit. I've been showing him the pictures I took at the Hibiscus show. Hey—I just thought of something. I know you also love flowers. Why don't we all go look at the rest of them."

I bit my lip to keep from laughing. Mr. Stivesant, Sergeant McDougald, Reverend Danielson—I was running out of people to invite to see those pictures.

Mr. Stivesant looked at me, then Reverend Danielson, then at the young clerk. Josie turned and winked at Mr. Stivesant and seductively mouthed the words "Hi there"—which made him immediately blush crimson.

I had heard Josie and Mr. Stivesant had a history, but I had no clue how much of one until that blush. The expression now on his face spoke volumes that I couldn't wait to quiz Josie about.

Reverend Danielson's diversion worked perfectly because it appeared Mr. Stivesant forgot all about the clerk. He started walking toward his office, and we marched close behind. Then he stopped again, turned around, and just stood there, staring toward Josie. He started to say something but stopped, obviously flustered. It was obvious his thoughts were spinning a mile a minute, and I almost felt sorry for him. However, any sympathy I might have been mustering didn't last long. It was replaced by my own bolt of amazement. I was absolutely taken aback by what I saw next.

One of the counter clerks noticed him first and shouted, excitement rising in his voice, "It's him! It's really him! It's Vern Stephens!"

And it was. Vern Stephens was the All-Star second baseman for the St. Louis Browns baseball team. He was by far the best player on the team, and, by all accounts, one of the best loved and most popular people in all of St. Louis. He wasn't just a celebrity—he was a person everyone seemed to genuinely admire. He was a champion for those down on their luck, and he appeared at so many charity events people were starting to call him, respectfully, "Charity Stephens," a name that made him cringe every time he heard it.

Those of us in the Ville loved Vern Stephens because he was just the same with his Negro fans as he was with everyone else. The Browns weren't nearly as good as the Cardinals, with whom they shared the stadium, but we felt much more welcome and safer at their games, and Mr. Stephens was one of the biggest reasons that was the case. One other thing endeared him especially to those of us in the Ville. The St. Louis Cardinals might have had a pretty fair player in Stan Musial, but Mr. Musial was a very quiet, private man, one who shied away from the limelight. On the other hand, Mr. Stephens was outgoing and loved meeting his fans. That was partly why the previous year he had agreed to come help with one of our major fundraisers at Sumner. His presence helped us raise enough money to buy equipment for every team in our athletic program. I had worked with him on that, and I found him to be charming and genuine, characteristics that most athletes seemed to be missing. He was also one of the most handsome men I'd ever seen, always clean-shaven and with a boyish grin. His picture was plastered all over the St. Louis papers so much he couldn't go anywhere without immediately drawing a crowd, and he was doing just that now right before my eyes.

"Holy Jumpin' Jonah!" Mr. Stivesant exclaimed. "It is him! Pinch me—it's him!"

As I studied Mr. Stivesant's face, for some reason I suddenly remembered what I'd heard so many times before. The color of a person's skin did not matter to him. Not one iota. The only color he ever saw was the color green—the color of the money in his vault. When it came to people, he was blind to everything else, and for good or bad, that was why we all respected and admired him. So, it could have been the Reverend Danielson or Vern Stephens in front of him—he would always treat them both with the same dignity and respect.

When Vern stopped right in the center of the entry foyer and looked around as if lost, Mr. Stivesant practically ran toward him.

"Mr. Stephens," he said, "I'm Mr. Stivesant, manager of the Bank of Wellston, and I'd like to personally welcome you."

They shook hands warmly. Vern said, "I'm very pleased to meet you, sir. Very pleased."

"What brings you here?" Mr. Stivesant asked.

Vern started to respond, then stopped. He spotted Reverend Danielson and called loudly over to him, "Reverend, how in the world are you doing? Get over here and let me look at you."

Then, catching sight of me, he said, "And Olivia—this is like old home week. It's so good to see you two. I was just thinking about both of you on the way over here. I'm not kidding. I was wondering how you think your sports teams will do this year. See any championships coming your direction?"

Then, to Mr. Stivesant, he said, "Pardon me—do you know my good friends here?"

"Of course I do," Mr. Stivesant replied. "They're both also dear friends of mine."

Vern immediately replied, "In that case, then I have the answer to the question I had when I came into this bank. That's good enough for me—this bank is the one I'm looking for. You're probably wondering why I'm here. Well, first off, the Brownies are in town, and I had some time on my hands. Second—and this is really why I'm here—I'd like to open an account here in St. Louis. You may know—everyone seems to—that I don't live here in the off season. Because of that, I sometimes have a tough time cashing a check around here. It finally dawned on me if I kept some money in a local bank, it would be a lot easier and more practical for me."

He looked at his watch and continued, "Yes, this is the right bank. However, and I'm really sorry about this, I'm in something of a hurry. I have to get back to the ballpark for a meeting pretty soon. Think we can get this taken care of quickly?"

Mr. Stivesant's excited look had everything except saliva drooling down his chin. "Of course we can do this quickly. Don't you worry about a thing. I'll take care of this personally. Olivia, Reverend, if you'll excuse us…"

I was still too stunned to reply. Reverend Danielson spoke for both of us. "Of course we will. You go ahead. We can see you anytime, right Olivia?"

All I could do was nod. I just stood there, staring at Vern, still not believing he was really there. I was the one who was supposed to be providing a distraction, but now I was distracted to the point of not having a clue what else was going on around me. Some help I was.

From our right, the clerk helping Josie and James walked over, his eyes wide. "Mr. Stephens," he said, "could I please have your autograph?"

"Be glad to," Vern said, reaching for the paper in the clerk's hand.

"No, not that," the clerk said, quickly pulling the paper back. He then handed the paper to Mr. Stivesant and, without taking his eyes off Vern, said, "Please sign this, sir. It's the approval for the loan I've been working on with Mrs. Fitzgerald and Mr. Bush."

"Then good thing I didn't sign it," Vern joked loudly, getting a laugh from us all.

Vern handed Mr. Stivesant a pen and said, "You go ahead and sign your autograph—then I'll sign mine for everyone here. How's that?"

Reaching into his trouser pocket, he produced a baseball. Holding it high, he said, "And I think I'll sign this for you, Mr. Stivesant. That be okay?"

Mr. Stivesant's eyes lit up. "That would be wonderful! I'll display it over in the window where everyone can see it."

Without looking at the paper in his hand, he scribbled his signature near the bottom of it and handed it back to the clerk. He gave the pen back to Vern.

"How would you like this signed?" Vern asked. "To you? To the bank? I'll be happy to do whatever you wish."

"How about to my little boy, Lars."

The clerk piped up while still staring at Vern, "Mr. Stivesant, I didn't know you had any children."

"Don't you have something to do? If you don't, I'll find something for you."

Turning back toward us, Mr. Stivesant blushed brightly. Vern laughed and clapped his hands softly. "Your son, Lars, right?"

"Okay," Mr. Stivesant said, "so you caught me. I'm guilty. I admit it."

Reverend Danielson stopped laughing long enough to say, "You needn't be so embarrassed. Earlier in the summer, I tried to get him to do the same thing for me. I guess we've all got a lot of little boy left in us."

Vern said, "If we didn't, life would be so dull—and I'd be out of a job. So, thank goodness for that."

He then signed the ball, quietly saying the words out loud as he did, "To my good friend, Lars. Best wishes. Vern Stephens."

Vern handed the ball to Mr. Stivesant, who clutched it as if it were a bag of gold. "Sir, I was serious about needing to get back to the ballpark soon. Is it okay if we get started on my account now?"

Finally finding my voice I said, "You two go right ahead. Mr. Stephens, you better hurry or they'll skin you alive if you don't get back on time. I've read about the fines players get for breaking the rules. Mr. Stivesant, I'll come back another time so we can go through the rest of the pictures. You two get going. Scoot!"

"My business will wait, too," Reverend Danielson said. "Don't give it another thought."

Mr. Stivesant then said, "Well, Mr. Stephens—"

"Call me Vern," he interrupted. "All my friends do, and I can tell we're going to be great friends."

"Okay, Vern. Let's go to work. Please follow me. This way."

Vern turned one last time to me and Reverend Danielson and said, "I'll see you both soon. You take care of yourselves."

Reverend Danielson hugged him and whispered something in his ear. I hugged him, too, but I was speechless again.

When they left, I looked at Reverend Danielson, who was smiling broadly.

"Okay," I said, "Let's have it. Spill the beans. You did that, didn't you?"

"Well, well," Reverend Danielson stuttered.

We both laughed, softly.

"I knew he was going to be in town, and well, a little insurance never hurt anyone, right?"

Shaking my head I said, "I'm just glad you are on our side. You really *are* a sneak—and a darn good one at that."

He cleared his throat and said, "If that's a compliment, it sure is left-handed. I don't like the word *sneak* all that much. I prefer *prepared*, if that's fine with you."

"Whatever," I said. "Call it what you want to. You're amazing. And that's the truth."

I then added, "How much does he know? What did you tell him?"

"Oh, nothing, really. He stopped by the church early this morning to drop off some old baseballs and bats, and when I found out he was going to stop by a bank today anyway, I suggested he come here—and do his best to do so at a certain time. I told him his celebrity would help us in a great cause. He didn't ask for details, so I didn't offer any. He's a good man. A very good man."

"And so are you, even if you do seem to be *prepared* at times much more than the average person, and especially the average minister. All things considered, I'd say much more *prepared*.

He was now looking intently past me toward James and Josie. I turned to look as well. Josie, leaning over the desk so far she was practically in the clerk's lap, was writing something on a small piece of paper. By the way she held her left hand in front of the paper to block anyone else from seeing what she was scribbling, I guessed she was writing down her phone number or a quick, personal note to the clerk. She, too, was playing her role to perfection to the very end. It was also clear she needn't have shielded her writing. The clerk's gaze was nowhere near the piece of paper.

She folded the paper four or five times, into a small square, and passed it to the clerk while standing up to shake his hand. She moved close to him, whispered something in his ear, ran her right index finger gently down his cheek, turned, and started walking away. After she had moved a few steps, and almost as an afterthought, she called back to James, "And thank you for your help, too. I really appreciate it. Good job!"

She completely ignored us as she waked briskly to the front door, opened it, and stepped outside, the door banging loudly behind her.

I looked back at the clerk, who had stopped smiling and was now looking intently at his watch. James reached into his jacket pocket and withdrew something that he placed slowly and gently in front of the clerk. Even from where I was standing I could see it was money. The clerk quickly covered it with a piece of paper and smiled at James. In this case, it appeared the old expression was true: "Time is money"—and in this case, more particularly, our money bought us valuable time.

"Nothing else for us to do now," I said to Reverend Danielson. "What do you say we get out of here?"

"Lead the way, child," he said. "I'm right behind you."

I winked at James as we made our way to the door. He winked back and saluted with his index finger. I could hear him say to the clerk, "One last piece of business…"

At the door, Reverend Danielson and I stopped one last time, looked back at Mr. Stivesant's office, and saw him and Vern laughing it up.

We stepped outside and the late afternoon heat was oppressive. "Ouch!" I said. "Out of the frying pan and into the fire!"

"I'd say certainly into the fire," he replied, wiping his forehead with his handkerchief. "But I'll take this over the frying pan any old day. And while we're on that subject, do you see that policeman anywhere?"

"No," I said, "and I don't see Ella and Jimmy either. Wonder where they all went. I hope not to the police station."

Reverend Danielson didn't respond. When we were about halfway down the street, he stopped suddenly, looked up toward the sky, and said, "Thank you, thank you, thank you."

I wrapped my arm through his, and we strolled the rest of the way to the streetcar stop in silence. No words were needed.

None at all.

* * *

Josie was waiting on the steps when we got to the church.

"Didn't I once tell you that you shouldn't sit out here—that it'd look like the neighborhood was going downhill?"

"Funny," she said, sneering at me. "Very funny."

Reverend Danielson frowned at me.

"Private joke," I said, patting him on the back. "Never you mind."

"Let's go inside," he said. "James will probably be here in a couple of minutes—and we shouldn't be seen together just yet."

We had barely eased into our chairs in the study when James barged in, threw down his briefcase, and shouted, "Yahoo! We did it! We really did it!"

"Well, we had some help from those," I said, dryly, pointing to Josie's chest.

We all howled, even Reverend Danielson.

Reverend Danielson cleared his throat, then said, "Yes, well, beauty really can often bring out the beast. And I'd say that poor clerk became a monster this afternoon, and I guess I don't mind that one bit."

"Reverend Danielson!" all of us said at once.

He continued, "I may be going down below now when my time comes, but if I do, I'll still do it with a clear conscience. Think for just a minute about what we just did. I fully realize it is only the first step, and maybe a wobbly one at that, but it feels mighty good, doesn't it?"

"Yes it does," James said. "Even better than I thought it would. I feel so—clean. Does that make any sense?"

Josie spoke up. "It isn't often a chance comes by to do something that feels good right here, right in the heart. This was one of those times, and I wouldn't have missed it for anything. Not a thing. And, while I'm at it, I'd also like to say my conscience won't lose any sleep over this either. If anything, my dreams tonight will be sweet. I'm sure of that."

They all then looked at me as if to ask, "And what are you thinking now?" I wasn't really sure what to say, so I chose my words carefully. "I look at it this way," I said. "We've all been living like rats crammed into a shoebox for too long. We've been told where we can live and, in many cases, how we can live. We've been told how big the world is—and where terra firma ends for us. Basically, we've been told how life is to be—and we've had very little say in the matter. We haven't even been invited to the table to take part in the discussions. Is that fair? Not in the least, but we haven't had any recourse. We'll get to that table now, one way or the other. Either this will go down smoothly, which I pray it does, or we'll all end up in court or in the pokey. Frankly, at this point I say one is just as good as the other as long as someone, somewhere hears what we have to say. If that happens, then this will all have been worth it. I won't lose a second of sleep over what we've done. Not one. None of you should either."

When I finished, I sat down in one of the desk chairs and just sat there, not knowing what to do or say next. I was exhausted, physically and emotionally. I looked around the room, and it appeared everyone else was feeling the same way.

After a minute or so, James broke the silence. "I hate to bring up the practical at a time like this, but I'm afraid I really have to. Just so we all stick to the same plan, I'd like to go through the next steps one more time. I may not need to do this, but please humor me. The good Reverend was right—this was just a first step. These are the ones that will follow, at least the ones I can think of now. Look at my hands—they're shaking! Please forgive me. I still feel like I'm in that bank."

He opened his briefcase and pulled out a clipboard. He quickly scanned it, turned again to us, and said, "I'll call J. T. tonight. We need to get him into the house as quickly as we can. It is said that possession is nine-tenths of the law, and we may need every one of those tenths before this is over with. Olivia, you've arranged movers to help J. T. You and I will work together to schedule the actual move. We'll talk later tonight. We'll keep the Shelleys away from the home until all the furniture is moved in. That way, any nosey neighbors will just figure the movers are taking the furniture in for white folks. Next, now that the papers are signed, I'll see they get moved down the line and become completely official. Well, as official and legal as they can be under the circumstances. That will be my top priority. Finally, we need to decide what to say when the cat's out of the bag, and I'm guessing that will be soon enough. I'd say we agree not to say a word— nothing. If this goes to court, and odds are it will, the less we say now, the better it will be for all of us. So, no matter who comes to us with questions, let's just keep quiet. If you get pestered, just send them to me, okay?"

We all agreed this was a good plan. We prayed it was a good plan. We all shook hands with and hugged each other. This was done without a word being said. Our eyes told each other everything.

It was also clear to all it was time to disband. However, something was still eating at me, and I just couldn't stand it any longer.

"Josie, I'm not going to let you out of here until you tell me something. I saw you pass that note to that poor clerk. What did it say? I have to know. I can't stand the suspense any longer. If you don't tell me, I'm going to burst."

Josie sat on the desk, crossed her legs, raised her skirt slightly and said, "For a good time, call Harrison 9-3789."

"Josie!" Reverend Danielson scolded.

"Wait a minute," I said. "That's not your number."

"You're right. It's the number for my eye doctor."

We all howled.

"My turn," James said. "This was driving me crazy all the way over here. Just what in the world was Vern Stephens doing there? It about killed me not to run over to ask for his autograph, but when he got there I was able to get us through the paperwork twice as fast because nobody was looking at anything but him. Reverend, look me right in the eye: It sure looked like you had something to do with that. Did you?"

"Yes, he had something to do with that," I said. "All he did was get him to be there right at that exact time. I'm telling you what—I never want to be on the good Reverend's bad side! He may not be able to part the Red Sea, but I wouldn't bet against him on anything else."

"Red Sea!" Reverend Danielson responded, laughing. "All I did was ask a friend to stop by. That's all. Wasn't a big deal. And, don't worry—he doesn't know why he was there. He just knew he was doing me a favor."

"Our Reverend is certainly always *prepared*," I added. "And I, for one, am grateful. So very grateful."

"So are we all," Josie added.

And we were.

* * *

Ella and Jimmy were sitting in my porch swing when I finally got home. Both were grinning like idiots.

Before either could say anything, I jumped in, "Miss Ella Jane—you've got some serious explaining to do. And you, too, young man. Just what was that at the bank? I want some answers. Now!"

I didn't know how much they knew about today's events, but their smiles told me they at least had an inkling. But how could they?

Ella pointed to Jimmy and said, "He's on probation for me, too. He does what I tell him."

Jimmy rolled his eyes and shrugged his shoulders.

"That doesn't explain anything," I said. "Not a thing. Let's have it. You better start talking. And I mean right this minute."

Ella stood up and put her hands on her hips. "Don't you be getting all huffy. There sure as heck is a lot you didn't say. Not even to your best friend."

I didn't know what to say. I didn't know what I *should* say. So, I went fishing.

"You talk first," I asked quietly. "How much do you know about today?"

Then, turning to Jimmy, I said, "For the time being, you just keep quiet. I'll get to you in a minute."

Ella replied, "Enough. Enough to know there just might be a jail cell somewhere with your name on the door. What were you thinking getting involved in a harebrained scheme like this?"

"Like what?" I replied, innocently.

"Oh, that's good. Almost sounded sincere. Not quite, but almost. You're going to have to do a better job than that, though, to fool anyone else. You're not good at this, Liv. Never have been—never will."

I stood there a minute in silence. "And him?" I asked, pointing to Jimmy.

"Don't you worry about him. He knows. I told him enough. But he won't say anything, will you?"

"No, ma'am," he said, sharply and definitely.

"Because he knows if he does…" Ella's voice trailed off.

She continued, "I knew what you were up to all along, but I didn't say anything. I thought there might be a time when you'd need help, and I knew you wouldn't just come out and ask me for it. So, I stayed in the background and got Jimmy sworn in just in case. We were sitting on the steps of the library, catty-corner from the bank. When we saw that cop show up, we figured it wouldn't hurt to put on a little show. Pretty convincing, wasn't it? I bet he's still writing up his report."

After pausing to study my face, she added, "So, how'd you think we did? I'd say we were great. We should be in the movies, don't you think?"

I shook my finger in her face and tried to look mad. But it was Ella, and I just couldn't. My frown turned into a smile, and I said, "Absolutely magnificent. But you still haven't said what I most want to know. How'd you find out about this? You have to tell me. You just have to."

"No I don't," she said, curtly. "Now it's my turn for a little secret. Serves you right for keeping me in the dark. How could you! We don't keep things like this from each other. We never have."

"Then at least tell me who else knows. I deserve to know that much."

"Nobody," she said. "We're the last link in the chain—for now. You do realize this is all going to come out, and when it does…"

"I'm not worried. Well, that's not exactly true. Maybe I am just a little. But I'm ready. I know what could come of this—and I'm ready."

"I'm not sure you really do. At least not completely. Before this is said and done, I have the sneaking suspicion you'll need me and Jimmy again. Only next time it won't be for a show like we did today."

"That's entirely possible," I admitted. "But you two shouldn't be sticking your necks out. You shouldn't."

"That may be so," she said, "but I love you, and, well, he owes you. Yes, we'll both be here. That you can count on."

"Goes for me, too," Jimmy said. "You can take it to the bank."

The pun was horrible, even more because it was intentional. We laughed the laughter of a friendship forged by fire.

That is, we did so until we all saw it—all at the same time.

Sergeant McDougald drove slowly past my house, waving three times. Once for each of us. He then held up his right hand, aiming his index finger as if it were the barrel of a revolver, and dropped his thumb as if firing at us.

"Well," Ella said, her voice rising. "Don't just stand there. Wave to the jerk. And whatever you do, don't forget to smile. Show lots of teeth. Lots."

We did, until long after the squad car was out of sight.

I could tell we were all thinking the same thing.

We'd be seeing McDougald again.

* * *

I was so exhausted I thought I'd be able to drift right off to sleep. However, I ended up tossing and turning—until the dream came again...

Jimmy John grabbed my hand and we ran to the door of the barn. A crooked piece of firewood was jammed through the handles so tight it wouldn't budge.

"Help me," he said. "Push on it. Hard as you can."

We both pushed, but our feet slid backward as we pressed forward. I lost my balance and fell. I could see under the bottom of the door, and the feet of the angels were rushing back and forth.

Some pounded on the door, but still it didn't open. Heat and smoke blew into my face. I couldn't catch my breath. I started coughing and couldn't stop.

Jimmy John pulled me up. "Let's get out of here. Nothing we can do."

Then we were running again… toward the flaming moon.

14

Invasion

The calm that followed our work at the bank scared me to the point I couldn't sleep through the nights. I'd wake up at all hours, but two thirty in the morning became a constant. I'd crawl out of bed, sit in my dressing chair by the front window, and stare out at the street below until I'd get drowsy and crawl back in bed again. Then I'd soon get back up and go back to the window. The streetlight at the corner threw shadows that reached all the way to my front yard. Anything that walked past that light, human or animal, was magnified to the point it appeared giants were strolling past. One night, a cat ran back and forth several times across the street, its back arched high. The resulting shadow stretched the full width of the street in front of my house. I was already spooked enough, but the image of this monstrous cat drove me deep under the covers many nights after that.

My nights at the window also taught me something I never knew before. A whole new world comes alive after the stroke of midnight. In a stretch of one week, I saw a car sideswipe another near the intersection; heard a man yelling obscenities at what I guessed was his wife as he pulled her down the sidewalk; saw a group of kids running up the street, followed a few minutes later by a speeding police car; and witnessed an obviously inebriated man down on his hands and knees, throwing up the good cheer he swallowed earlier in the evening.

This new world after midnight turned me into a voyeur. This new world was fascinating on one level. However, on another level it reminded me of just how vulnerable we were while we slept at night—and that thought kept me awake even more.

During the daylight hours, I also fell into a regular routine. James thought it best we all keep low profiles for a few more weeks, and we had agreed to try. However, I didn't have a chance to feel lonely. Ella, worried about my safety, showed up for breakfast every morning and stayed with me until about lunchtime, when we'd both head to school to get our rooms and materials ready for the start of the coming new year. It was such an honor to teach at Sumner that none of us wanted to give anything but our very best to our students. Charles Sumner High School was known by most as the first high school west of the Mississippi River built for Negroes, but it was so much more than that. The school was the hub of the community. It was also a place where dreams were born and skills to achieve them were taught. It was a place of hope, pride, and strength. And we were all proud to be part of it.

I was firmly into my new routine when it happened. Three weeks before school was to start, the calm suddenly came crashing down around us. I couldn't say it was unexpected. I was actually surprised something like it didn't happen sooner.

On a muggy Tuesday afternoon, J.D. had finished work early and had taken the bus to the stop two blocks from his new home. When he stepped off the bus, three city police officers were waiting for him. They asked if he was the new owner of the home at 4600 Labadie Avenue. When he said that he was, he was immediately put into a squad car and taken to the station, where he was grilled for several hours without being able to make a phone call. They tried to get him to talk about how he came to own the home, but he refused to say anything, which made them grow angrier by the minute. J.D. later said one officer got right in his face and asked, sarcastically, "Don't you know Negroes aren't allowed to buy a home there on Labadie? What's the matter with you, boy?" When J.D. didn't respond, the officer struck him on the back of the head with a long-handled wooden paddle. No telling what would have happened that night if a member of our church, Ronald Sallis, hadn't been at the station to deliver an order of sandwiches and coffee to the detectives. While there, Ronald saw J.D. being taken to a holding cell and immediately called Reverend Danielson, who went to the station to see if he could help. It took some doing, but when he suggested maybe the chief of police should be notified of the goings on, he was finally able to get J.D. released.

The cat was out of the bag.

The next day, a letter was delivered to the Shelleys just as they sat down to supper. In it was notice a suit had been brought against them by Fern and Louis Kraemer, who lived in the 4500 block of Labadie Avenue. The suit, and attached injunction order, claimed the Shelleys had no legal right to own their new home because a restrictive covenant was in place in the area that allowed for only white ownership of property. Either we hadn't buried the covenant well enough or the Kraemers were the nosiest neighbors in all of St. Louis. Either way, we had a fight on our hands.

The Shelleys were devastated. Our worst nightmares had come true. However, while we hoped this would not happen, we had already made some contingency plans just in case it did. We weren't going to roll over. Not by a long shot. We were ready to fight, just as long and as hard as we needed to.

Late the next afternoon Reverend Danielson called us all together to talk strategy. When I arrived at the church, all were waiting for me in the study.

"Olivia, thank goodness you're here," Reverend Danielson greeted me as I entered the room. "We've got trouble."

"I half expected we would," James said, somberly. "But not this soon."

Josie tried to calm him. "Now, now. Take it easy. Now's not the time to worry. We can fight this thing. We're going to fight this thing."

J.D. was pacing slowly back and forth behind Reverend Danielson's desk. He finally stopped and addressed us all.

"Look," he said. "I'm not moving again. That house is ours now. They're going to have to kill me to get me out of there."

Reverend Danielson went over and put his arm around him. "We'll have none of that talk, J.D. Nobody is going to get hurt. We'll take care of all this legally."

"What chance do we really have?" J.D. asked, his voice rising. "How can we fight them? How can we?"

"I've already thought of that," I said, moving over next to James. "I have an idea, a plan."

"Good. Let's hear it," James and Josie said almost at the exact same time.

I continued, "There's only one man in St. Louis who can win this fight, and all of you know who I'm talking about."

"George Vaughn?" James asked.

"Yes," I said, "George Vaughn. Not only is he the best attorney in town, but he has more experience in real estate disputes than anyone in the whole Midwest. Plus, he knows other attorneys, both Negro and white. He knows their styles, so he always has an edge. That's something we're going to need. An edge."

"But isn't he expensive?" J.D. asked. "I can't afford him."

James smiled and said, "Don't worry. Money is going to be the least of our problems. I'll put up as much as I can, and I'm sure we'll be able to get others to help out."

"You're right that money won't be one of our big problems," I said. "James, I think you and I can cover his fee. I'm pretty sure of that."

"And you two would do this for me?" J.D. asked, emotion filling his words.

"Yes, J.D.," I said. "We'd do it for you, but it won't be just for you. We'll do it for us. For all of us. Your home's going to be the front line, but there's a battle back here, too. There always has been. This is the time we have to take a stand. We've been shoved around and boxed in long enough. Now we fight. We can't back down."

"I agree with Olivia," Reverend Danielson said. "This is the time. And if you two can't get enough funds together, the church will help. I promise you that."

Here he paused, before continuing, speaking softly now, "I wasn't going to mention it unless absolutely necessary, but we also have an ace in the hole here that I want all of you to know about. A dear friend of mine, a professional athlete, promised me if we got to the point where we needed him, he'd be proud to cover any expenses we couldn't. So, I'm not worried about the money. Not at all."

"Jackie?" I whispered excitedly to Reverend Danielson. "Did he say he'd help?"

Reverend Danielson nodded his head, but, at the same time, motioned for me not to press the point in front of the others. I knew Jackie was a very private man, so I immediately understood what Reverend Danielson was trying to tell me. Still, just the thought of Jackie helping out made me feel better. *So* much better.

Josie added, "And so will I. I've got money put away, and I can think of nothing more important to use it for."

"Sounds like we're all in agreement," I said. "I'll get in touch with Mr. Vaughn as quick as I can. The sooner he can get started, the better. Let's just hope he'll take the case."

We then all sat quietly, deep into our own thoughts, until J.D. broke the silence. "I'm not ashamed to admit I'm scared, through and through. I also want you to know just how much I appreciate everything all of you are doing for me—for my family. Most folks would have run off by now—and I certainly couldn't blame any of you if you still did. I just want you to know no matter what happens from here on out, I'll never forget..."

His voice trailed off, choked again by emotion. We were all close to the edge. Josie walked over, put her arm around his shoulders, and said, "We've already shown we're a pretty darn good team. Think of how far we've come already. Most wouldn't have given us a snowball's chance in Hades that we would have gotten this far. We're not done yet. Far from it. Am I right?"

When no one spoke up, she repeated it again, shouting it this time, "Am I right?"

That got our attention, brought us back together.

"She's right," James said. We're a darn good team. Darn good. Let's go to work."

"And if we ever need reinforcements," Josie added, glancing downward, "we can always count on my ample beauty."

At first we were all stunned. Then we howled. Even Reverend Danielson.

The laughter felt good. So good. When the room fell quiet again, we all looked at each other and could tell—we were now officially a team again.

And ready for the fight.

* * *

When I got back home I was tired, so I sat on the couch and took a late nap—but not for long. The growling of my stomach woke me up. I suddenly remembered I hadn't eaten any lunch.

I went to the kitchen and reheated the morning's pot of coffee. I decided I wasn't hungry enough for a full supper, so I thought I'd fry up a couple of eggs, toast some bread, and make egg sandwiches. Egg sandwiches and coffee sounded pretty darn good to me.

It was then I heard a gentle, rhythmic knocking on my back door.

Few people ever came to the back door. It was usually kids in the neighborhood looking for small jobs to do to earn some candy money, or Ella, trying to pull off some practical joke. The last time she came to the back door, she knocked and then hid in the bushes next to the porch as I opened the door. She did that three times before she caught her dress on the bottom part of the railing and was trapped there until I could swat her several times with my broom.

I halfway expected to see her when I walked to the door. The window panes were covered by blue lace curtains, thick enough to keep people passing in the alley from being able to see in, but thin enough to let in a generous amount of sunlight in the early morning. I set down my coffee cup, walked to the door, and pulled one side of the curtain back. I jumped back and dropped the spoon in my other hand.

There, smiling, staring through the window, stood Sergeant McDougald.

"Open the door!" he commanded.

I didn't reply. I was still stunned, confused. Several questions raced through my mind, but one question finally surfaced: "Why is *he* here?"

"If you don't open up—" he said, tapping a finger on the glass.

I still didn't move, still couldn't speak.

Then his face softened, and he said, more gently, "It's about your sister. It's important. Open up."

About Ella? Was she hurt? Had she been arrested? Without thinking more, I quickly unlocked the door and pulled it open.

"That's better," McDougald said, stepping heavily into the kitchen.

I backed up, slowly, as he kept walking toward me, until my back was right against my sink counter.

"What's the matter with Ella?" I asked. "What do you want here?"

"What do you think I want?" he said, slowly, deliberately. "You need to be taught a lesson. And I'm here to give it."

He reached over and brushed his hand slowly down the front of my dress. I slapped at his hand. He laughed, softly at first, then loudly. His face then turned dark, serious. He was breathing loudly and rapidly.

His voice turned low and harsh as he said, "It's high time you were put in your place."

I tried to scoot to the side to be able to run toward the living room, but he must have sensed it and stepped in front of me. His eyes were menacing and his intentions were clear. I wanted to scream but no words would come. He lunged at me and his dirty hands were on me as I felt my dress ripping at my left shoulder.

Using both hands and legs, I starting slapping and kicking him. He laughed and roughly pulled me to him.

"I know you are going to like this," he snarled. "Relax...." Old Sarge is going to take care of you. Let's go upstairs and get to know each other better."

He leaned forward and tried to kiss me. I turned my head to the side as quickly as I could, but his lips still caught the corner of my mouth. His breath was foul, tinged by whiskey and cigarettes. I struggled as hard as I could, kicking his legs with my feet and my knees. He held both my wrists in one massive hand as his other started sliding my dress away from my shoulder.

Every time I blinked the overhead kitchen light seemed to turn off, and on, and off again. I felt dizzy, weak, like I was falling. Then his lips were crushed against mine, and the stubble of his chin cut across my cheek. His grip on my wrists tightened as he pulled me even closer. I shut my eyes, tight, as tight as I could.

When I opened my eyes and the kitchen light slowly came on again, out of the fading darkness grew a figure, coming from the door, moving rapidly toward us. Like a sudden bolt of lightning, a shadow crossed in front of the light before striking the back of McDougald's head. At once, I felt McDougald's full weight fall forward against my chest. His grip on my wrists loosened as his limp body started sliding toward the floor. As he fell, I saw his face. He looked asleep.

I followed his body until it hit the floor, then looked up.

Jimmy.

"I'm so sorry, but I really have to do this," he said, his face expressionless. "It's the only way."

I saw him raise his right fist and felt the blow against my chin. And then, darkness... darkness everywhere.

The kitchen light went off and didn't came back on.

* * *

A nurse was taking my pulse when I woke up.

"Where am I?" I asked, trying to sit up in the bed.

"Take it easy," the nurse said, pushing me back down. "You're going to be fine."

"But where am I?" I asked, becoming more panicked as I looked at the dark curtains surrounding us.

"You're in Homer G.," the nurse said, calmly. "You took a nasty blow to the head and were out a long time. The doctor wants you to be kept for observation tonight, but you'll be all right. You will."

"How'd I get here? What happened? Who—?"

"Do you remember anything?" the nurse asked. "Anything at all? The police have been here twice to see if you were awake. They're going to ask you the same thing."

"The police?" I said. "What for? What happened?"

"Near as we can tell, a robber must have been hiding in the bushes and jumped you in your backyard when you were taking out your trash. Some white police officer was driving through the alley and saw it—and actually stopped to help you. Just when I thought I'd heard everything. Goes to show, I guess we really can't tell a book by its cover. Imagine, a white cop stopping to help a Negro. Next thing you know Niagara Falls will stop flowing."

After checking my pulse, she leaned forward and listened to my heart with her stethoscope.

My thoughts were still jumbled, still fuzzy. I remembered Sergeant McDougald, and I had a faint memory of seeing Jimmy. But what happened? My head began to throb. I reached up to rub my temples.

"What white cop?" I asked. "What are you talking about?"

She pulled the ends of the stethoscope from her ears and asked, "You really don't remember anything? Well, I guess I'm not really surprised. You took a pretty good blow. You may never remember everything, and I'm guessing that would probably be a good thing. You just rest now. The doctor will be back to see you pretty soon."

I reached over and grabbed her arm so she couldn't leave. "Please, don't go yet. I want to ask you something else. How'd I get here?"

"One of your students brought both of you here. Good thing he did. The cop might have died if he hadn't. He was walking through the alley when he saw the fight."

"Fight?" I asked. "What fight?"

"Well, some of the details aren't clear yet, but I guess the cop and the crook were really going at it. You were already unconscious. The crook must have had something like a two by four because the cop's face is a real mess. Busted some of his teeth and broke about five ribs, too. Not sure yet, but he might even lose an eye. Yup, if I hadn't heard this with my own ears, I'd never have believed it. You really owe this cop. You could have been killed or, well, you know, if he hadn't stopped to help."

"Where is he? Where's the policeman?" I interrupted, now more confused than ever.

"He's here, just down the hall. He was too critical to move to City Hospital. I've been working here now for almost three years, and he's the first white man I've ever treated. He's a first all right in so many ways."

"And who did you say brought me here?"

"One of your students. I started to tell you, he was going by and saw the big fight going on. It must have really been something. I guess the crook was just about to kill the cop when your student ran into the yard. Once a witness showed up, the crook lit out. They've been looking for him, but they'll never find him. He's probably long gone by now. I know if I nearly killed a white cop I'd sure be gone in a flash, wouldn't you?"

"But how did I get here?" I repeated. "How?"

"Your student. I told you that. After he chased the crook off, he carried both of you to your car and drove you here. If he hadn't happened by, no telling what would have happened—to both of you."

"What was his name? My student's name?"

"I think it was Jimmy. Yes, that's what it was. Jimmy something or other. Know who I'm talking about?"

It was now becoming more clear to me, at least in bits and pieces. I remembered Jimmy coming into the kitchen. I remembered him saying he was sorry, but I still couldn't remember much after that. I just remembered the kitchen turning dark again.

The nurse tucked the sheet up around my neck and said, "They're saying the cop is a real hero. He might even get a medal for what he did."

"A medal?" I thought to myself. If they only knew the truth. And what exactly *was* the truth? It sure wasn't the story the nurse told me. The only one who could tell the whole story was Jimmy.

"Where's Jimmy now?" I asked.

"The police questioned him about the crook for a long time. He gave them a description and everything. I heard one of the other cops say they were going to put out a dragnet and an all-points bulletin. If you ask me, that Jimmy deserves a medal, too. After all, he not only helped you, he helped that white man as well. Yup, tonight is a night for a lot of firsts for me."

"So, where is he?" I asked again.

"I think he's down in the waiting area. He said he was going to hang around until he knew for sure you'd be okay. Want me to see if he's still there? If he is, he can only stay for a minute. You need your rest now more than anything."

"Please," I said. "Go see if he's here. I'd like to see him."

"I have to go down and check on the cop again anyway, so I'll stop by on my way and see. Remember, if he's here, only for a few minutes. I'm serious about that."

After the nurse left, I tried running the events over in my mind again. I remembered Sergeant McDougald hurting me. I remembered his lips against mine. I remembered Jimmy. And then again, nothing. After that, it was all still blank.

A few minutes later, Jimmy opened the curtains and walked slowly in and moved quietly to the bed.

"Please listen before you say anything," he said, sternly, looking back to make sure no one had followed him. "We don't have much time."

"Jimmy, I don't remember—"

He cut me off. "Please, Mrs. Perkins, just listen. This is important. We have to have our stories straight. Down to the last detail."

"What happened?" I pressed on.

Jimmy glared at me. "Shut up!"

Then softly, gently, apologetically, he leaned forward and almost whispered, "I'm sorry. I didn't mean to yell at you. But I'm serious—we don't have much time. Just listen, okay?"

I nodded my head.

"Good. I'm going to quickly tell you what really happened—then I'm going to tell you what you and I are going to say happened, got it?"

I nodded again.

He then continued, "I was down by the park when I saw McDougald driving past. I knew that meant trouble. He was going real slow, like he was looking for something. I got up and followed him and saw him pull over to the curb in front of your house. He didn't get out of the car. He sat there a couple of minutes and then pulled to the middle of the street and down the alley. I ran between some houses so I could see where he was going. He stopped behind your garage and turned off his engine. Then he got out of the car and walked to your back door. I didn't know what was going on, but I know cops don't go to the back door that late at night. I hid in the bushes down by the gate and watched. Your curtains were closed on the door, but you forgot to close them on the side window. I saw everything. When he went for you..."

His voice cracked and tears filled his eyes. I reached over and took his hand and squeezed it.

"When he went for you," he continued, "I came in and hit him on the back of the head as hard as I could. He went down. Then—"

Jimmy paused, wiped the tears from his left cheek, and continued, "I had a white cop on the floor in front of me. I knew what that would mean. No one would believe a word I said. No one would believe he was trying to hurt you. I don't know how it did, but it just came to me. I knew I had to make it look like *both* of you had been jumped. I knew that was the only way out of this. So I hit you. I'm so sorry about that. Please—you have to forgive me."

I squeezed his hand again, and he added, even more quietly than before, "I carried both of you outside and put you next to the side of your garage. You were still out cold, but he started coming around. I started kicking and punching him, over and over. I was so mad I could have killed him. I finally stopped—I didn't want to—and put both of you in your car because I knew you always leave your keys in it. I drove here and started yelling for doctors to help. I told everybody I was walking by when I saw a man sitting on McDougald's chest and beating him. I said I chased the guy off. I also told them you said to me before you blacked out that the guy was trying to rob you when McDougald came to your rescue."

"But why did you hit me?" I asked.

"Because I had to make it look like there really was a robber there. You had to have marks, too."

"I think I see now," I said, pulling him down to kiss his cheek. As I did so, my lips throbbed. "Ouch!" I said, rubbing my bottom lip. "I think I understand. But you could have hit me softer, couldn't you?"

"Sorry about that," said. "I tried to get a clean chin shot, but I think I got your lips at the same time."

He grew deadly serious again before continuing, "Here's where our stories really have to match. I gave them a full description of the robber. You have to tell them you don't remember anything. Tell them you were knocked out too fast to see his face clearly."

"What did you tell them he looked like?"

"I told them what they wanted to hear. I said it was a Negro about twenty-five years old. I said he had on old clothes and dirty shoes—and had a hat with a hole in it. I said he was big, tall, with a really black face, big lips, and white eyes that glowed in the night. I said he looked shifty—and mean."

I started to laugh. My lip throbbed again.

"You should have seen the cops who talked to me. They wrote down everything I said so seriously. Even asked me if I'd sit down with one of those artists who draws pictures of crooks they're chasing."

Jimmy smiled and brushed his hand gently across my cheek. "I am really sorry. It was the only thing I could think of to do."

It then suddenly dawned on me. "McDougald!" I shouted. "What about him? What's he going to say?"

"What can he say? He sure can't say he was going after you in your kitchen. And, besides, we've now made him a hero. A really big hero. One of the other cops told me he was going to recommend him for some type of medal the mayor gives out. I'm not worried about him. He's trapped. He also has no idea what really happened to him. He was out like a light before he knew what was going on. Who knows—he might even think all this actually happened. No, you don't worry about McDougald. I'm going to talk to some reporters who are on their way over here. By the time I get done telling them the story, he'll be the greatest hero in the history of St. Louis."

"You really are something," I said. "First you try to rob me. Then you punch me in the face. And now I'm thanking you. Thank you, Jimmy. Thank you."

"For what?" he asked. "Why, I didn't do anything. It's Sergeant McDougald you really have to thank. I'll make sure the reporters stop by to see you so you can also thank him in the papers. I know you'll want to do that."

"Jimmy, you're a—I can't come up with the word right now, but I'm sure I'll think of it later. What am I going to do with you?"

"Just go along with my story," he said. "That's all I want. Besides, I still owe you, remember? I'm on probation."

"Not any more, you're not," I said, pulling him back down to me again. I kissed him on both cheeks and hugged him.

"Now get out of here," I ordered. "Go see those reporters. Let's make sure this gets in the morning editions."

"Yes, ma'am," he said, standing back up.

He smiled at me, shook his head, turned, and left.

I closed my eyes and fell back to sleep.

* * *

Ella and Reverend Danielson were sitting at the foot of my bed when I woke the next morning. When I smiled at Ella, she turned to Reverend Danielson and said, "Well, I owe you a dollar. Looks like she's going to live. That's another bet I lost."

"You're too funny," I said, propping myself up. Sorry to disappoint you, but I think I really am going to live. Hello, Reverend. How are you doing?"

"Me? How am I doing?" he replied. "The question of the day is how are you doing. You gave us an awful fright. Oh, and what you must have gone through. My poor child…"

"You okay, Liv?" Ella asked, taking my hand.

"I'm going to be fine. Really. I just got punched a little. That's all. I must look a mess."

Ella teased, "Well, now that you mention it…"

"Ella!" Reverend Danielson scolded. "You stop that. She looks just fine. Just fine."

"Thank you, Reverend. At least I know one of you cares about me."

Ella leaned closer and whispered, "Is it true? Did that idiot cop really rescue you? Please say it isn't so. That would wreck my whole opinion of police everywhere."

I didn't want to keep anything from her, but I felt I shouldn't say too much in front of Reverend Danielson. The fewer people who knew about this the better it would be—for me and especially for Jimmy. I decided I could always tell her later, in private.

"I still can't believe it myself," I said. "Just when I was convinced he was an animal, he saves me from who knows what."

"What happened?" Ella pressed.

"I don't remember much."

I so hated to lie to her, but I saw the look in Reverend Danielson's eyes and knew the party lines would be clicking at full speed all around the neighborhood the minute he got home. The Reverend was a fine man, but, at times, he was also one of the worst gossips in the Ville.

I continued, looking right at him, "I remember taking some trash out to the burn pit. The next thing I knew, I was being knocked to the ground. It wasn't long before McDougald was there, fighting with the other man. That's when I blacked out I guess. The next thing I knew, I was here."

Ella sat up straight and said, "I'll be darned. I still can't believe it. I can't."

Reverend Danielson unfolded a piece of paper he had been holding in his left hand. "I wrote this down this morning," he said. "I started writing it down the second time I heard it on the radio. It was the main story every half hour when they stopped for news. Listen to this. 'Last night a story right out of the movies unfolded in our fair city when Sergeant McDougald of the St. Louis City Police rescued a damsel in distress. Details are still sketchy, but it appears McDougald, risking his own life and limb, held off an armed attacker as he came to the aid of Mrs. Olivia Perkins of 4341 West Belle Place. Off duty at the time of the incident....' And it went on and on from there. Everyone in the Ville is buzzing about it this morning, and I do mean everyone. That's quite a story, Olivia. This is all going into my sermon this Sunday. There's a message here—and a moral—for all to hear."

Ella rolled her eyes and grumbled, "Oh, great. Is this going to be another one of those 'We're all the Lord's children' sermons?"

"It wouldn't hurt you one bit, wouldn't hurt all of us, to hear that message over and over. The world sure would be a better place if we all understood that."

"Yes, Reverend," Ella said, dryly.

"You two stop it now," I said. "You're giving me another headache."

"Sorry," they both said at the same time.

"You must be tired, Child," Reverend Danielson said, standing.

"I am, a little."

"Then we better go," he said. "Anything we can get for you? Do for you?"

"No, I don't think so. I just want to thank you both for stopping by. That means a lot to me."

"You go ahead, Reverend," Ella said. "I want to talk a minute with Liv about a, well, you know, some *female* things."

"Oh, of course!" he said, hurrying for the curtains. "I'll be running along. Time for me to go."

As soon as he left, Ella shook her head and said, "Ever notice how men shoot from the room the minute *female* things are mentioned?"

"You're awful!" I said.

"You don't know the half of it," she shot back.

I started laughing, which made my temples throb again. "Don't make me laugh. Please don't. I still hurt too much."

"Okay, I won't," she said. Here she moved her chair right next to the side of the bed and whispered to me, "No one else is around now. You can cut the baloney. I want the truth. What really happened last night? I can see it in your face. You just lied to the good Reverend. You're a terrible liar, Liv. Come clean with me. I want all the details."

Just then the curtain opened and two police officers walked in. Ella and I both jumped.

"Good morning, ladies," the older of the two said, politely. "How are we today?"

"I'm doing fine," I answered. Ella didn't say anything.

"Are you up to a few questions now?" he asked.

"Sure. Fine. Go ahead."

The younger officer opened a notepad and started jotting notes as I answered the older officer's questions. I recounted the same story Jimmy and I had gone over the night before. The last question the officer asked me was, "What do you think about Sergeant McDougald?"

He was smiling as he asked this. I answered immediately, "I think he's a hero. He's certainly my hero now. If he hadn't come along, I'd surely have been killed. Or violated. I'll never be able to repay him. Never."

I paused, then added, "Please, Officer, tell me. Is he going to be all right? I'm worried about him. After all he's done for me…"

"He's pretty banged up, but he'll be fine after a couple of weeks off to rest up. Don't you worry about him. He's a pretty tough character."

I nodded and said, "He must be tough. Good thing he's on our side."

The officers thanked me. The younger one was shaking his head as they walked through the curtains.

He must have known Sergeant McDougald.

The nurse came in right after they left and made Ella leave. She was hopping mad. She said, while being ushered out, "I'll be back later. I want the whole story, Liv."

I just smiled and waved to her, which made her even more upset.

"How are you feeling now?" the nurse asked. "Any more headache?"

"Just a little," I said. "It isn't too bad."

"Good. In that case, I think the doctor is going to let you go home this afternoon."

Here she paused and looked at me as if she had something else she wanted to say.

"What is it?" I asked. "Tell me."

"There are some reporters down the hall with that cop who

helped you. They want to take your pictures together. I can get a wheelchair and push you down there if you feel up to it. That's up to you."

"But you wouldn't do it?" I asked.

"It isn't my place to say," she said.

"Go on," I insisted. "What's on your mind?"

"Well," she said, "You're the prize donkey now, you know. They want to show you two together to show everybody what a big hero he is. I think they could care less about you. Do you want to be a part of that?"

I didn't want to explain myself to her, so I said, curtly, "I want to. I really do. Take me down there, please."

What I really wanted was to have him look into my eyes and see the anger and disgust. I wanted him to know I had something on him, and I never wanted him to forget it. I wanted those pictures because they would free me from him. With all that publicity, with us being tied together forevermore, he'd never be able to hurt me again. But, more than anything, I wanted him to see that I was fine, that I was stronger than he was.

"Fine, I'll get the chair," the nurse said, almost sadly. "Be right back."

Sergeant McDougald was in the very corner area of the floor, and he was also surrounded by curtains. He was, in effect, segregated from the rest of the patients. That seemed terribly funny, and fitting, to me.

I could hear laughter as I entered the curtains. Two reporters immediately stood up. Both also immediately reached into their pockets and pulled out flashbulbs.

The one on the far left said, "Mrs. Perkins—look this way, please. Let me get a shot."

The flash was bright and hurt my eyes. I raised my hands to cover them.

"Only two more, boys," the nurse said. "Better make them count. This isn't good for her eyes right now, you know. She took a nasty blow to the head."

The other reporter, a short man with his hat still cocked sideways on his head, said, "Then how about if you wheel her over here, next to the Sergeant. I'd like a couple of shots of you two together. You know, the rescuer and the—"

"Donkey," the nurse whispered to me. No one else heard her. I looked up at her, expressionless.

It was then I noticed McDougald's head was bandaged tightly all the way down to his eyes, with his right eye partially covered. His left arm was in a sling, and his left leg was elevated on some pillows. When he coughed, he winced in pain and drew his right arm to his side. He was coughing with his mouth open, and I could see one of his top front teeth was missing. I wanted to jump on the bed, onto his chest, and stomp on every inch of his body. I wanted to knock the rest of his teeth out—knock them down his throat. I didn't care that he was obviously in a great deal of pain. I knew it wasn't the Christian thing to be thinking, but I wanted revenge. I couldn't jump on him, but I knew—oh, how I knew—how to get that revenge.

"Gentlemen," I said. "You're looking at a real American hero here. This man saved my life. If he hadn't come along when he did, I'd be six feet under right now. Or, I'd have been violated. I'm sure of that."

I was gathering steam. Both sat down their cameras and started writing on small pads as I continued.

"Yes, what we have here in this lonely hospital bed is a man who put his personal safety on the line to save a life. There aren't too many people like this in the world. I'd say he's the greatest hero since... General Patton."

The reporters liked that comparison. Both wrote it down and underlined it heavily.

"And one more thing," I said, reaching over and putting my hand on Sergeant McDougald's. He tried to pull his away, but I held firm. "This man deserves a medal. He deserves the highest honor that can be given to an officer of the law. He really is something. Yes, something."

McDougald had not said a word the entire time. He looked to me to be completely stunned.

The nurse looked down and shook her head. The reporters flashed away, getting shots of me holding McDougald's hand.

I knew that would please him.

"Time to go," the nurse interrupted. "Time for both of them to get their rest. Now get going. I mean it."

The reporters thanked me, thanked Sergeant McDougald, and left quickly, no doubt mindful of their deadlines. After they had gone, I asked the nurse, "Could you please give us a minute. I'd like to thank this man."

"Okay," she said. "But I'm serious. I want you to get your rest. I'll be back in one minute."

She swept her way through the curtains. When I heard her shoes heading down the hallway, I wheeled myself closer to McDougald and said, unblinking, "I was hoping you'd die, but I see you're not going to."

With his mouth so swollen and his tooth missing, all he could do was wheeze out his words. He glared at me and said, "Just what the hell is going on? What happened?"

I was relieved. He really didn't know. At that moment, I knew I had him.

"I'll never tell, so you'll never know. The rest of your natural life you'll always wonder, won't you?"

"You go to hell!" he said, starting to raise up but then wincing in pain and falling back.

"Nice way for a hero to talk," I said as sarcastically as I could. "By the way, I heard you probably will be getting that medal I was talking about. For saving a Negro. Imagine that. A Negro."

He coughed and some blood shot out onto his gown. "Maybe I know something, too," he said, hoarsely. "I know you had something to do with that Shelley thing, didn't you?"

Before I could respond, the nurse suddenly walked in and said, "That's all. Time for both of you to rest. Let's go, Mrs. Perkins."

"You take care, now," I said to McDougald. "People need heroes."

He started to say something but stopped and again clutched his side. The nurse wheeled me out into the hallway and said, "So, how does it feel to be the donkey?"

"Like a million dollars," I said, smiling broadly.

The nurse just looked at me and shook her head.

15

Retaliation

In my naive mind, I thought the publicity surrounding Sergeant McDougald's *heroic* rescue of me would ease at least a little of the tension between those in the Ville and those outside of its boundaries. I thought it might create something of a bridge of understanding and, possibly, compassion.

It had exactly the opposite effect.

The radio and the papers gave the story quite a bit of play. Sergeant McDougald's picture was in the paper three days in a row, but the picture of the two of us never made it to print. I imagined he was very sorry about that. However, in spite of all the publicity, a sudden backlash soon came roaring in. Many wanted to know why Sergeant McDougald was in the Ville in the first place, and most could come up with only bad reasons. Speculation soon ran high, from him being there to purchase illegal goods to him looking for a certain type of female companionship and while there he just happened to stumble into the event. Apparently, his reputation followed him closely and wasn't going to be washed clean by one good deed. Others wanted to know why he would even attempt such a rescue. Those people believed crime in the Ville should be handled by those who lived in the Ville and that the St. Louis City Police should stay out of it as much as possible.

If anything, the publicity ended up providing fuel to the argument that there was a place for Negroes and a place for whites, and the twain should never meet. It may have been coincidence, but the local newspapers also started running more stories about Negroes being lynched in the South and emphasizing every criminal event in St. Louis involving those with darker skin. It soon appeared the whole Negro community, all across the city, was being put under the microscope, and the purpose of this examination was clear: to provide fodder for those who believed "separate" was better.

The atmosphere in St. Louis might have settled down some if one last piece of coal hadn't been thrown onto the fire. None of us had any idea how news of the Shelleys' home purchase— and impending suit against them by the Kraemers—had leaked out, but it spread faster than a windswept firestorm. No one in the Ville, other than our little group, seemed to know very many details, but everyone was buzzing about how the invisible line across Taylor Avenue, the street forming the westernmost border of the Ville proper, had been breached. While Sergeant McDougald's celebrity faded quickly, the Shelleys' notoriety grew exponentially with each passing day. For many, they were the new heroes in the Ville, especially after news of J.D.'s grilling at the police station became public knowledge.

However, with that new celebrity came floods of gossip, gossip which found its way quickly to every corner of the city. Hot debates soon filled every meeting place, from barber and beauty shops to restaurants and churches. People, Whites and Negroes alike, had differing views of it. Some thought what the Shelleys had done was terribly wrong. In the other camp, a much smaller number thought this type of "coming together" was long, long overdue. Newspaper editorials in the *Argus* and in the city papers started picking up this social and political hot potato and served it often—a little too often for my tastes. Naturally, there were also groups, on both sides, that threatened action, even violence, if this all didn't just go away—and quickly.

I tried not to pay too much attention to what those groups were saying until one afternoon when Jimmy stopped by to see how I was getting along. I had been letting him borrow my car so he could haul his tools and supplies to jobs he had picked up in the neighborhood. He had done such a fine job during his probation with me that his reputation as a superb handyman got him so much work he was busy every day practically from morning to night. He was also now making good money, which he used to help out his family, and especially his father. I was so proud of him.

Even if he had just punched me in the face.

On this particular afternoon he pulled up to the curb out front just as I was just about to sit in the porch swing.

"Mrs. Perkins!" he shouted. "Can I please have a word with you?"

"Of course, Jimmy," I replied, sensing the urgency in his voice. "Come on up here. Swing with me and we'll talk."

He ran up the porch steps, but he didn't sit down, even after I motioned twice for him to do so. He was breathing hard as he said, excitedly, "We're in trouble. We're *all* in trouble."

"What do you mean?" I asked, motioning again for him to sit down. "What kind of trouble?"

He was starting to catch his breath and quickly added, "You know Cootie Williams, don't you? He's in my grade at school."

"Yes," I said. "I know Cootie."

"He got sauced last night and ran his car into a fire hydrant down on Pine Street. The police arrested him and took him to jail. After he slept it off and got up this morning, his dad went down to bail him out. But before he got sprung, he overheard two cops talking about what was going to happen to the Ville— to us. They thought he was still asleep, but he fooled them. He heard everything they said."

"What did he hear?" I asked, dragging my feet to stop the swing.

"Cootie said the cops were talking about a group of guys they knew who were going to get Mr. Shelley. They knew all about him buying the house. They also said they were going to show the rest of us our place, and especially us in the Ville."

I interrupted him. "You sure he heard it exactly this way?

I've heard things like this all my life. Maybe they were just talking big."

"Cootie's a lot of things, but he's not a liar. I'd stake my life on that. He said that's what he heard."

Here he paused before adding, "And there's one more thing, Mrs. Perkins. Cootie said they were going to pay a visit here tonight. Tonight!"

"Now don't get excited just yet. We don't know for sure they actually said that. Cootie is no liar, but he does get confused a lot. And we certainly don't know if they were being serious or just stupid. We need to know more before we put everyone in a panic."

"But I've got to tell everyone!" he said louder, his voice shaking. "What if it's true? What if any part of it's true? We have to let people know!"

I waved again for him to sit in the swing with me, and this time he did. "Push your feet," I said. "Let's think about this a minute."

"What's there to think about?" he asked. "We have to warn people. We have to."

"Jimmy, you're not listening to me. Look at me. Until we know more about this, we better not get everyone riled up. Right now, that would do more harm than good."

Just as I started to push the swing, he jumped up. "I'm sorry, Mrs. Perkins, but I know I'm right."

He started walking quickly down the stairs. I called after him, "Please, think about going to see Reverend Danielson. He'll know what to do. If he thinks something should be done now, he can get the word out."

"That'll be too late," he said, not looking back and continuing down the sidewalk. "I just know it."

When he got to the car he stopped, turned back toward me, and said, "Please get out of the Ville tonight. Please. I don't want anything to happen to you. I couldn't stand it if…"

"I'll be alright," I said. "Don't worry about me. And please calm down. I still think you are making too much out of this. And one more thing—how do you know Cootie wasn't still up to his gills?"

"I'm right, Mrs. Perkins," he said, grimly, getting in the car and slamming the door. He started the motor and sped off down the street.

I'd been hearing threats of one type or another involving the Ville ever since I was a little girl. That was why, from the very beginning, I had no doubt more than a few people would be furious when they found out about the Shelleys, but I couldn't imagine that anger being directed to everyone in the neighborhood. The Shelleys, maybe. The rest of us, no—absolutely not. Still, if the police had talked about this so openly and freely, as Cootie reported, then just maybe there was at least a little something to it.

It was then I realized I wasn't going to be home tonight anyway. Ella and I, and our "decoys," were going to see *Thunder at Dawn* at the Tivoli movie theater on Delmar Avenue, several miles west of the Ville. I still wasn't worried, but I started thinking about whether I should stay close to home, just in case something did happen.

"No," I said to myself. "Silly to give it another thought. Couldn't happen. Won't happen."

I repeated that over and over, trying to convince myself.

Doubt finally caught hold of me. I walked into the house to get dressed for the movies—and locked the door behind me.

And drew the curtains shut—tight.

*   *   *

It turned out *Thunder at Dawn*, should have been titled something like *Quiet at Dusk* because it was so dull all four of us, at different times, fell sound asleep. Each time one of us nodded off, the others would quickly and playfully start making snoring noises, which would wake up the sleepyhead. At one point, Jackson reached into his coat pocket, pulled out the Magic

8-Ball, and asked loudly, "Oh, Spirit of the Ball, will this movie ever end?"

A chorus of "Shhhhhhh!" rang out all around us.

"Stop that!" Ella said, reaching over and grabbing the ball. However, I noticed she was soon playing with it herself.

Charles, when he wasn't asleep, seemed to be enjoying himself, especially when he had his arm around me. I put my head on his shoulder and was soon asleep myself.

When the movie was mercifully over, and we walked out of the theater, Ella said, "I don't know why we wasted our money like this. We all could have just stayed home and taken a nap!"

Jackson yawned and added, "That was the best sleep I've had in a long time. I feel like I got my money's worth."

"Me, too," I said, also yawning.

"We're a bunch of live wires tonight," Charles said, taking my hand and pulling me close. "So what should we do now? Anyone up for a late bite to eat or some music?"

"I don't know about the rest of you," Ella replied, "but I'm in favor of a short night tonight. I haven't been sleeping too good lately."

We all started to tease her about falling asleep during the movie when she quickly cut in, "I mean other than in there. No, I'm serious. I'm really tired. If you don't mind, can we just go back to my place, maybe listen to the radio a little bit, and then just call it a night? I think we could all use the rest."

"Sounds good to me," I said. Then, turning to Charles, I asked, "Okay with you?"

He said, pulling me even closer, "I'll go along with it, but it will cost you a kiss."

He closed his eyes and puckered his lips.

"Here it comes," I said. "Keep your eyes closed tight."

I motioned for Jackson to quietly walk over and stand next to me. I quickly kissed Charles and stepped to the side, pulling Jackson to where I had been standing. When Charles opened his eyes, there stood Jackson, making kissing noises.

"You didn't!" Charles shouted so loudly everyone on our side of the sidewalk stopped and turned to look at us. Charles then started chasing Jackson down the sidewalk. "When I get my hands on you...!" Charles shouted.

"Come on," Ella said. "We better catch them before Jackson knocks the tar out of him."

"They can be such little boys," I added, laughing.

"I don't know about yours," she said, "but mine can also be quite a man. *Quite* a man."

Just then they started running back by us again, Jackson still in the lead. Ella stepped in front of him, which caused Charles to run into both of them. I quickly ran over to help keep them all from tumbling down.

"Truce!" I yelled. "That's enough. He didn't kiss you, Charles. It was really me. So, you just stop it. I want you to know if anyone should be upset here, it should be me. Me! After all, after I planted one on you, you thought he did it. What does that say about my kisses! Yes, I'm the one who should be mad here. If you don't watch it, I'm going to chase *you* down the street."

Charles was still winded but found enough voice to say, "You must be slipping, Olivia. We better practice some more tonight."

Ella and I both shook our heads and headed for the car. "Little boys," I said. "What are we going to do with them?"

"I've got some ideas," Ella said. "Let's get back home."

"Let's," I said. "I've also got some ideas of my own."

* * *

I started seeing billows of smoke rising up toward the sky when we were still a couple of miles from the Ville.

Ella noticed it too and asked, "What do you suppose is on fire up ahead? Suppose Old Man Brown is burning tires again. Somebody is going to club him if he doesn't stop that. The smell gets into the house and stays for days. Even gets in your hair."

"Probably just some firebugs burning their trash," Jackson said, leaning forward to get a better look out the window.

When we reached the corner of Sarah Street and Easton Avenue, we turned left onto Easton and then right onto Whittier to get to Ella's house. We weren't but four or five houses down the street when Charles slammed on the brakes, and we skidded to a stop.

On the left side of the street, the front yards were on fire. People with hoses and buckets of water were frantically trying to douse the flames.

"Wait here. I'll go see what's going on," Charles said, opening his door and stepping out.

"Doesn't make any sense," I said. "What would cause this?"

It didn't take long to get an answer. Charles came back to the car, poked his head in the window, and said, grimly, "Gas fires. Some men in cars threw gas cocktails in the yards. Looks like we just missed them."

Charles pounded his fist on the roof of the car, anger spreading across his face.

"Can we do anything to help?" Jackson leaned forward and asked.

"No," Charles said, "the gas will just have to burn itself out. They're just making sure it doesn't spread until it does. Looks like their houses will be safe."

From behind us we could hear a fire truck's siren getting closer and closer. We all turned to look. The truck roared past on Easton without turning onto Whittier. Instead, it sounded like it went on for a few blocks before stopping.

"Let's take a look," Jackson said to Charles. "I have a bad feeling about this."

Charles climbed back in the car and drove to the next intersection. Just as he was about to turn left, we saw a large group of people running down Cote Brilliante Avenue. Charles quickly changed directions and drove toward the crowd. As we drove down the street, we saw the reason. From what we could tell, it appeared the front windows had been broken out of most of the homes on the street. Those who lived there were standing in their yards, surveying the damage. Neighbors were rushing to see if they could help. Ella shouted out the window to a young man running down the sidewalk, "What's going on here?"

He replied, without breaking stride, "We've been attacked! The whole Ville has!" He cut through a yard and ran up to where several others were studying a broken picture window.

"Attacked?" Ella said. "What's he talking about?"

I suddenly felt sick to my stomach. I recalled Jimmy's warning earlier in the day. "It just can't be," I said aloud but softly.

"What do you mean, Liv?" Ella asked.

"Jimmy came to see me today. He told me about some men who found out about the Shelleys buying their home. He said they were going to teach somebody a lesson."

"Oh, Liv, I just can't believe that," she said. "That's ridiculous, isn't it?"

"What are you two talking about?" Charles asked. "What's going on?"

"Revenge—and stupidity. That's what we're talking about. I'll explain more later. Please, let's drive over by Ella's house. This may not be all that's been done."

Charles started driving again and turned down Billups Avenue. Crowds were formed every fifth house or so. All the yards there were covered with trash—old tires, fruit crates, empty cans, and pile after pile of what looked and smelled like rotting food. None of us said anything as we continued to Ella's house.

We didn't have to.

When we turned down St. Ferdinand, we discovered why we had seen so much smoke earlier. It wasn't because of the grass fires on Whittier. Three cars parked on the left up ahead were blazing. It wasn't until some of the smoke drifted away that we saw the fire truck we had heard roar past before. Firemen were standing in the street spraying the cars, but the fires were not going out. The two outside tires on the middle car were ringed with flames that danced, making it appear the car was moving.

"Get to my house, quick," Ella implored. "Please don't let it be..."

Her voice stopped as she lowered her head. Jackson put his arm around her and gently hugged her.

People were running everywhere as we drove around more trash that had been thrown in the street.

"Now I see why the kid said we've been attacked," Jackson said angrily. "We've got to find out who did this!"

"First things first," Charles said, stopping the car in front of Ella's house. It looked fine—the yard, front porch, the—

"Oh no!" Ella shouted, climbing over Jackson to get out of the car. "My beautiful door!"

Ella's front door had three large triangular panels of prism glass that made it stand out from any other door in the neighborhood. She was so proud of that door she cleaned the glass every day, polishing the panels until I thought she would rub right through them. The front door appeared to be fine, but the panels were now gone. Someone had carefully, without harming the rest of the door, shattered them and knocked them inside the house. Not a shard of glass could be seen on her porch. The person who did this took his time.

While I stood on the porch with Ella, Charles and Jackson quickly hurried around the house to check for other damage. They soon came back, both shrugging their shoulders.

"Looks like that's all," Jackson said.

"It's enough," Ella said, her tone growing angrier by the second. "If I find out who did this..."

Jackson interrupted her, "You two go in the house and lock the door. You'll be okay there. We're going to drive around and see if we can help."

"Not on your life!" Ella barked at him. "We're going, too. This is personal now."

Ella didn't give Jackson a chance to respond. She charged back down her steps and headed for the car. "You coming?" she said. "Or do I have to go alone?"

"You should really stay here," Charles said to me.

"Ella's right," I said. "I'm going, too."

We piled in the car and drove up and down the streets of the Ville. We didn't say much to each other as we did. I, for one, said nothing because I was shocked, stunned, by what we were seeing. On Kennerly, the fronts of homes all up and down the street were splattered with what looked like black paint. Most of the homes on Billups had crosses stuck in their front yards. As we drove down Lambdin, front fences had been driven over and splinters of wood were everywhere.

On Cottage Avenue, where Sumner was located, a car had been overturned in the middle of the road. As we drove past the school, we noticed a long line of people streaming into the side entrance of the auditorium.

"Let's stop," I said, tapping Charles on the shoulder. "This is where everyone is supposed to come for shelter in an emergency. We better see what's going on in there. Maybe we can find out why this is happening."

"Might as well," Charles replied. "Doesn't look like we can do much out here."

When we entered the auditorium, Reverend Danielson was up on the main platform. He was pacing back and forth, occasionally stopping to look out at those gathering before him.

"I'll be right back," I said as I left the group and headed for the platform.

I walked right up to the Reverend, but he didn't seem to see me right away. The look in his eyes was so far away.

"Reverend Danielson—are you alright?" I asked, rubbing his arm.

He quickly jerked his arm away. When he finally did notice me, he looked up and said, "I'm so sorry. I was just trying to think of what to do, what to say to everyone."

I wasn't sure I wanted to ask the question—wasn't sure I wanted to know the answer—so I stalled a minute and just stood there, smiling weakly. When I could finally speak, I asked, quietly, "Reverend, did we do this?"

"No, Child. We did not. It was done by ignorance and hate. Those two were here long before us and will be here long after we're gone."

"What do we do now?" I asked.

"We pray, we wait, we do the best we can."

"Reverend, I'm so sorry. So, so sorry."

"I know," he said, nodding slowly. "Me, too."

Then, pointing to those crying and sitting on the floor of the auditorium, he added, "We can feel for them, but we can't be sorry for what we've done."

"But what do we do?" I asked again. "We have to do something."

"Yes, there is something we can do. And I'm going tell everyone exactly that. Now is the time to put our faith to the test. That's what we do."

He stepped forward and hugged me. We held each other close, both on the verge of tears, but we didn't cry. This wasn't the time for tears. This was the time for strength, for coming together.

We had to. We had no other choice.

* * *

Charles and Jackson wanted to go with some of the other men who had decided to set up roadblocks at all entrances to the Ville in case the attackers decided to come back. They asked if we wanted them to drive us home first, but we urged them to go right away with the others. After they had gone, Ella insisted on walking me home, and I didn't protest. I was worried about what we might find, but when we got there, it appeared my house had been spared. My yard was fine, and I didn't find a board or shingle out of place. We also did a quick walk-through on the inside just to make sure. When we didn't find anything missing, I asked Ella to stay a while and offered to make a pot of coffee, but she said all she wanted to do was get home to cover the broken windows in her door.

I offered to go with her and help, but she said, "No, Liv, we're all tired. You stay here and get some rest. I'll call you first thing in the morning."

She kissed me on the cheek and walked out the door.

Ella was right. I was tired. Bone tired. My mind was racing but I decided just to go to bed. After making sure the front door was locked, I went upstairs and slipped on my nightgown. I took off my watch, combed down my hair, and pulled back the covers.

And there it was.

I picked up the greasy piece of paper from the pillow and read it.

It said, simply, "We know."

I dropped the paper to the floor, walked to my chair by the window, and sat down. People were still rushing in both directions up and down the street. I leaned against the sill and closed my eyes.

I didn't remember going to sleep.

* * *

The next morning the papers didn't have a single story, not a single word, about what had happened in the Ville.

Not a single one. If one believed the headlines on the front page, all was fine in the city of St. Louis.

Only it wasn't.

It also seemed a miracle, but, somehow no one had been hurt seriously. There were minor cuts, mostly from broken glass, and a few burns on those helping with fire control. But this attack wasn't about inflicting physical violence.

It was intended as a message.

As it turned out, some people of the Ville heard a message, but it wasn't the one that was intended. And it definitely wasn't the one Reverend Danielson had given in the auditorium, about turning the other cheek.

The retaliation came swiftly.

The next night, in the small hours after midnight, fires sprung up in a wide, circular pattern in the neighborhoods surrounding the Ville. Several garages burned completely to the ground north of the Ville in both the North Grand area and the Pemrose Park community; no cars were in any of the garages at the time. East of the Ville, a Roebuck's shoe store in the Fairgrounds Park area burned all through the night as the rubber soles refused to be extinguished; the thick, acrid smoke caused people to shut their windows tight all the way back to the Ville. In South City, in the neighborhood below the Easton Avenue border, explosions continued for hours in a large liquor store; no employees were there at the time. On the east, two whites-only diners, one in Pine Lawn and the other in Hyde Park, were both reduced to a pile of ash.

It seemed the only nearby area not included was Wellston, where Mr. Stivesant's bank was located.

No one was hurt in any of the fires, but the damage, from a financial standpoint, was considerable. One newspaper on the following afternoon posted a large headline: "Mysterious Fires Plague City." The lead article below it went on to say officials were still unsure if the fires were a result of arson—or merely "coincidence."

The only "coincidence" I could find in the whole affair was Jackson and Jimmy hadn't been seen by anyone since the night of destruction in the Ville.

Tensions were running high on both sides of the fence. The city was turning into a battlefield, and the lines were clearly drawn.

16

Rumors

I was just finishing my breakfast when there was a knock at the front door. After my visit from Sergeant McDougald, I jumped every time I heard anyone at either door, and this time was no different. I dropped my last piece of bacon on the floor.

The knock sounded like Ella's, but I didn't want to take any chances. When I got to the door, I pulled the curtain back slowly and peered out. J.D. was looking right back at me. He smiled and waved.

I flung open the door and said, "J.D.—it's good to see you, but what in the world are you doing here at this time of the morning?"

"Couldn't sleep," he said, rubbing his eyes and yawning. "I've just been walking around for a couple of hours. You wouldn't have a cup of coffee you could spare for this weary traveler, would you?"

"I do," I said, motioning him to step in. "Go ahead and have a seat here in the living room and I'll be right back. Cream? Sugar?"

"Just a squirt of cream," he said. "That'll do it for me."

When I returned with the coffee he was sitting on the couch, his eyes closed.

"Are you sure you're okay?" I asked, handing him his cup.

"To be perfectly honest, I don't know anymore," he said. "Everything I saw the other night and this morning—I can't get it out of my head that none of this would have happened if I hadn't bought the house. I feel like it's all my fault."

He shook his head and closed his eyes again.

"I felt the same way the other day," I said. "I'll tell you the same thing that Reverend Danielson said to me. We didn't do this. Ignorance and hate did this. We have to believe that."

"Thanks, but it's hard to do when your neighbors are suffering like this," he said, pulling back the curtain and looking outside. "What do I say to them? What *can* I say to them?"

"You don't have to tell them anything," I said. "They're not expecting you to. They're not stupid. You've got to give them more credit. They understand what's going on. They know what's at stake here. You're acting like they're going to be mad at you or hate you. They're not—and they won't. You're just doing what every one of them has thought of doing dozens of times. Only they didn't—and you did. No, you don't have to worry about what they're thinking. You worry about yourself and your family. That's your first responsibility now. By the way, how are they holding up? Everyone okay?"

"Ethel's fine, and the kids are, well, kids. So far, we've tried to keep most of this from them. I don't know how good of a job we've been doing, though. The other night our whole yard was trashed, and real brave souls threw a stink bomb through our living room window. It was kind of hard explaining that to them without scaring them to death."

"I'm so sorry they're having to see any of this. They probably know more than you realize. Do they at least like their new home?" I asked.

"You can't believe how happy they are," he said, pausing to take a gulp of coffee. "Where we lived on 9th Street was beyond terrible. Bugs everywhere, no hot water, we had to share a bathroom with two other families in the building. It seemed like the electricity worked only when the moon was full, and the windows leaked so bad the street noises sounded like they were right in the bedroom with us. The last straw was when our youngest daughter got a black eye one day on her way home from school. I just couldn't take it anymore. I knew they all deserved better than that, and I vowed to get it for them."

He took a long drink of his coffee and set the cup firmly on the table.

"And you are going to get it for them," I said. "I have no doubt about it. None."

I stood up and gently patted his shoulder. "Now, I'm going to get us some more coffee. Be right back."

I returned with the pot and, after filling our cups again, I set the pot on a towel on the end table. As I sipped my coffee, I studied J.D.'s face. He was a very striking man. He wasn't terribly tall—probably about five foot ten inches, but he was solid and carried himself proudly. I noticed the corners of his eyes and his cheeks were starting to show crow's feet, probably from worry, I guessed. The past few days certainly had been rough enough to cause most of them. However, I'd also heard something of the hard times he had before coming to St. Louis. From all accounts, his life had not been easy, not by any stretch of the imagination. I didn't know if I should ask him about his past but decided to take a chance.

"J.D., I've heard different versions of what happened to you down in Mississippi. As I'm sure you know, the grapevine is very short here in the Ville. If you don't want to talk about it, I'll certainly understand, but I've been curious about what really went on."

He set down his cup and leaned back, exhaling heavily.

"That's okay. I'm sorry I asked," I said, quickly.

"It's not that. It's just that with all this going on, I guess I forgot about all that. That seems like such a long, long time ago now."

He reached for the cream and added a dash to his cup. He shook his head and continued, "I've also heard several of those versions making the rounds. One of them has me killing two white men who tried to lynch me, and another has me stealing a car from a sheriff's deputy and hightailing it up here to St. Louis."

"So which was it?" I asked, laughing.

"Neither of them. The truth is we were walking home from church one Sunday afternoon and found a young girl beaten half to death in a ditch by the side of the road. She was in bad shape. Hanging on by a thread. Never seen so many bruises and welts on a human being in my life. We carried her home and did the best we could to take care of her. By the grace of the Lord we were able to keep her alive. But the men who beat her found out about what we did and came looking for me. They wanted to show the others what would happen if we interfered with their doings. Word got to me they had an idea about a necktie party, so I sent Ethel and the children to relatives. I got out of there as fast as I could and came up here to say with my uncle until I could send for them."

"Is that it?" I asked. "All that just from helping a young girl?"

He continued, "Well, that's not exactly the whole story. I don't think anybody knows this part. Ethel had been working as a cook for a rich white family there in Starksville. She wanted more time to stay at home and be with the children, so she told the woman she was going to quit. The woman, Mrs. Simmons, asked Ethel to find someone to take her place before she quit. Ethel found this young girl, Opal Jean, who needed the money bad, so she got her the job. One day, some of Mrs. Simmons' jewelry came up missing, and she accused Opal Jean of stealing it. That's when the men—there were about six of them—beat her within an inch of her life. Because Ethel had brought her to the house, and because we had helped her out, the Simmons got the idea we must have had something to do with the missing jewelry. That's the other reason they were after me. I found out later they probably would have done me in if I hadn't gotten out of there so fast. You want to know the really sad part of this? It wasn't a week after the jewelry came up missing that Mrs. Simmons found it all exactly where she had put it—behind a large picture on her dressing table. Can you believe that? All of that happened because that woman couldn't remember where she put her jewelry."

J.D. shook his head, and we both fell silent. Without

speaking, I held the coffee pot up, and he motioned he'd like just a little more.

"The truth isn't nearly as good as the rumors I've been hearing. I won't tell anybody what you just said. We'll just let them believe you went on a rampage down there."

"Thanks," he said, insincerely. "Just what I need at a time like this."

At the same time, we both laughed again. J.D. looked out the curtain before turning back to face me.

"Olivia, I've heard some stories about you, too, you know. What's this I hear about you being one of the 'Poison Sisters'? What's that all about?"

His question caught me off guard. "Poison Sisters," I repeated, drumming my fingers on the table. "Hmm. Let me see if I can explain that one, but I'm afraid the truth, as in your case, isn't going to be nearly as interesting as what you've probably heard. Well, you know my friend Ella—you've met her. She is, to put it mildly, a person who speaks her mind—at all times, even when she should probably keep her trap shut. Truth be known, I think she's loud at times because she's actually afraid of getting close to people. At least that's what I think. She has a heart of gold and would do anything to help out if someone needed help, but she doesn't want people to know that. She'd rather be seen as a selfish loner, but that really isn't her at all. She's my best friend, and I just adore her."

I stopped there because I didn't want to tell him any more about Ella. I trusted J.D., but I still thought I should avoid anything related to her background in Arkansas. When J.D. didn't ask me to continue, I immediately shifted the conversation.

"And me, well, that's another story. I'm the bad widow— the *black widow*—which I'm sure you've heard. I haven't talked about this with many people because there are some who are still very upset with me. So, I'd appreciate it if you kept most of this to yourself, okay?"

He nodded, and I continued, "My husband taught with me

at Sumner before he went off to the Army. When he came home on leave, we snuck over to Illinois to get married so we could keep it a secret from everyone back here. I don't know if you've heard, but women who teach have to quit their jobs once they get married. It's an old Board of Education rule that goes way back. It's a terrible rule, but it's still a rule—one we're expected to follow. I love my students and I love teaching, so I didn't want to lose all that. That's why we kept it a secret. What we did came out later, and it almost did cost me my position. If my husband hadn't died in the war, I think they would have forced me to resign. The fact that I was so sneaky about everything is part of the reason I have the reputation I do. But that's only part of my story. The other part is because as a widow it's assumed that I have knowledge of, well, let's just say knowledge of marriage bliss that I might use to ruin some marriages around here, or heaven forbid, that same knowledge might even rub off on some of my students. I guess they believe that just being around me is dangerous."

I then continued with my best sarcastic voice, "On top of that, we all know that widows are hungry for male companionship and, supposedly, we can't live without that bliss any more once we've experienced it. Naturally, that makes me someone right out of the flames of Hades itself. Some of the unmarried women around here actually seem to be scared of me because of that."

J.D. laughed and said, "My, my—if I'd have known that, I don't think I'd have come into your house this morning without a chaperone!"

"You better not let anyone see you leave here this early in the morning," I said. "You think there are rumors about you now? And now that I think about it, it wouldn't do my reputation any good either!"

We both laughed again and reached for the coffee at the same time.

"After you," he said, politely. After filling my cup, I reached over and topped off his.

J.D. then said, "I forget how you worded it, but earlier you were so kind when you said you didn't want me to talk about my past if I didn't feel comfortable doing it. I'm now going to say the same thing to you. If you don't want to talk about this, I'll understand. But if it's okay, I'd like to ask about your husband. I've also heard a few things about him. Everyone seems to think he was a wonderful man. Was he—"

Before he could finish his question, I cut in, "I don't mind talking about him. I'll just say it to you bluntly: Inman was the love of my life. I've never known a kinder, more gentle man. He was naive in some ways because of how and where he grew up, but his heart was gold. He also loved his job at Sumner, and his students adored him. When he went to the Army, they wisely had him use his teaching abilities, and he ended up basically being in charge of a whole battalion of very special men. He did a wonderful job, just like he had done in his classroom back here. While he was away, he wrote me about it almost every day, and I've kept those letters. I reread them all the time. He was so proud of what he was doing. So proud. Then, one day when he was out repairing communication lines near Rome, he was lost. There aren't too many days that go by he isn't my first thought when I wake up in the morning, and it will probably always be that way."

"I'm so sorry for your loss," he said gently. "What you just said confirmed everything I've ever heard about him. I wish I could have known him."

We sat quietly again, each sipping our coffee and staring out the window. Even at this early hour, we could see neighbors gathering to help each other clean up their yards and houses.

J.D. finally broke the silence when he asked, out of the blue, "Olivia, why did you help me? You've really stuck your neck out."

I didn't hesitate in responding, "Because it was the right thing to do."

"There's more than that," he said, interrupting me. "I can see it in your eyes. What is it? I'd really like to know."

I was now afraid the tears were going to come, so I looked

away from him before answering. "I knew Inman wouldn't have turned his back on you. That's why I did it."

"He truly was a great man, wasn't he?" he said, putting down his cup and standing to leave.

I could tell he sensed it was time to close the conversation, and I was grateful for that. I also understood now, more than ever, that J.D., too, was a very special man, and I was proud I was able to call him my friend.

I didn't respond to his question. I didn't think I needed to. I walked J.D. to the door and opened it for him.

"Before I go," he said, "I just remembered something else I wanted to tell you. Maybe you've already heard—you were so right that the grapevine really is short around here—but I wanted to make sure you knew the court case is now scheduled to start in a few days. Ethel will be there, but I'm going to stay away if I can avoid the paper server. It's better if I'm not there. Believe me—*much* better. Will you be there?"

"I'll be there. Wouldn't miss it. Please let me know if there is anything I can do. Anything. And please tell Ethel that, too."

"Thanks, Olivia. I can't say enough about how much I appreciate all you've done."

He started out the door and stopped, suddenly, and backed into the house again.

"Do you think I should duck out the backdoor?" he said laughing. "Now you've got me worried what people will think if they see me leaving."

"Do you think it would be better if they saw you going out the backdoor?" I asked, handing him his hat, which he had forgotten earlier.

"You've got a point there," he said. "I'll just run like mad and hope for the best."

"You do that. And pull your hat down over your face as much as you can."

"Bye, Olivia. You take care of yourself, okay?"

"Always do," I said. "Don't you worry about me."

J.D. then pulled up the collar of his shirt, pulled down the brim of his hat, and ran sideways down the sidewalk.

I stood there and howled with laughter.

*   *   *

After J.D. left, I put on my old house-cleaning clothes and walked down the street to see if I could help Mr. and Mrs. Williams clean up their yard. Their fence had been smashed and splintered to the ground by one of the cars that drove through the yards on West Belle. Either those same idiots or a following car had also dumped enough garbage and old tires to cover the entire lawn. To top it off, their side drive was one of those that received a paint bomb.

"Just look at this!" Mr. Williams said as I walked up. "Looks like the city dump. I'd give anything for five minutes with the trash that dumped this trash."

"They're not worth thinking about," I said. "Let's just get this cleaned up and wash our hands of them."

"But look at my driveway! That'll never come off," he said, pointing to the large, black circle that spread across it and into his grass.

"Kerosene," I said. "We'll get some kerosene and scrub it off. Don't you worry about that. By the time we get finished here, you'll never know the difference."

I knew what I was saying wasn't completely true, but I could tell he needed hope, needed to know his world would have some order again. And if a small fib would help, so be it.

It wasn't long before a large group of students from Sumner came over with rakes, shovels, and boxes. The show of support was wonderful, but there were now too many bodies crammed into the yard for practical work to be done. So, after using my best teacher voice to direct traffic and give out work assignments, I decided to head back home.

I spent the rest of the morning doing laundry, cleaning and dusting the house, and rearranging the furniture in the living room. I wanted the couch moved so that it was easier for me to see out the front window. The world outside had become quite active in recent days, and I didn't want to miss any of it.

At straight up noon I was just setting up my ironing board when the telephone rang. The operator said, "Long Distance calling. Please hold the line for a call from Topeka."

Long Distance calls were seldom good news, so when I heard the voice on the other end, I was relieved.

It was Tubby.

"Olivia, I just called to see how you were doing. I've been so worried about you I can't sleep."

"Worried? How come?"

"How come! We've been doing one-nighters for over two weeks, so I've been pretty out of touch. I called my sister last night to see how she was, and she told me about you being in the hospital and about what happened to the Ville. And you wonder how come I'm calling! Are you sure you're okay?"

When I assured him I was, he asked, "Liv, what's going on there? What's it all about?"

"There's so much happening I just don't know where to begin. It's true I spent a night at Homer G., but I wasn't as bad off as they first thought. I just had a bad bump on the head. That's all."

Tubby's voice was cracking as he interrupted me, "Is it true somebody tried to rob you—in your own yard?"

I knew there were others listening on the line—I had heard the clicks—so I said, "Yes, and I still can't believe it. I was just lucky a policeman came along when he did. If he hadn't, no telling what would have happened."

"Thank goodness you're okay. I don't know what I'd do if..."

Tubby fell silent, showing me his concern. I heard still more clicks on the line, so I knew I shouldn't say any more about it.

Tubby finally asked, "And what about the Ville? What about your house? Is it okay?"

"Fine—just fine. My place wasn't touched."

I didn't want to tell him about the note on my pillow. I knew there was nothing he could do and knew he'd just worry himself sick about it. Plus, it never left my thoughts that there were others listening to our conversation.

Fully aware of the party-line ears, I said, loudly, "Tubby, you should have seen the neighborhood that night. It would have broken your heart. And there's still so much to do. I went down to the Williams' place this morning to help them clean up the damage. You can't believe the mess they've got, but they're not as bad off as some. It'll be weeks before we're halfway back to normal around here."

"Liv, why'd it happen?" he said, quietly, sadly.

"We're not completely sure yet, but it looks like it was done by a bunch of hoodlums who wanted to let us know they don't want us to leave the Ville. Same old story. Only this time, their message was even uglier than it has ever been before."

For the benefit of those listening, I added, "That's why we have to stand up and fight, now more than ever. Did your sister tell you about the Shelleys? They're going to be in court soon to keep the house they just bought over on Labadie. A suit was brought against them to get them thrown out. Mr. Vaughn—you remember him—he's going to be their lawyer. He won't go down without a fight, and everyone I've talked to in the neighborhood is behind him. Completely. I'm hoping that people all over the Ville will fill that courtroom to the rafters. We've got to show up, especially because of what just happened. This is the time for all of us to stand tall and together. It's just time!"

I pretended I didn't hear it, but one of the party-line ears let slip, "That's right!"

"Liv, I know I've got only a minute or so left and I'm out of quarters, so please listen to me. I'll make this fast."

His voice was nervous, hoarse.

He continued, "You know how I feel about you. I've done everything I could to show you that I'll always love you and be good to you, Liv. I want you to give me your answer—and you know what answer I want—the next time I'm back in town. I need you, and I know you need me, more than you know. We should be together. I just know it and, deep down, I think you know it too."

The operator came on and asked if he wanted to deposit more money for additional time, but he didn't respond to her. Instead, he said one more thing to me.

"I love you, Liv. With all my heart. I promise you—"

The line went dead. Before I placed the receiver in the cradle, I heard a sob and a series of clicks.

I then sat on the couch, now facing the window, and let his words swirl through my mind again. He did love me. I knew that. And he was an adorable man: smart, kind, generous. He would make the perfect husband.

Just not for me.

I also knew life with Tubby would be fun, full of laughter and good times. He'd be a wonderful partner to have while growing older.

Just not for me.

But as a friend—a dear, dear friend—I could take him that way. I just didn't know if that would ever be enough for him. The way he had been of late, I doubted it.

And what about Charles?

Charles brought out in me a hunger, a passion, a lust for living that I hadn't felt in a long, long time. But I also knew that wouldn't be enough—and Charles wouldn't be enough—in the long run.

"What should I do? What do I want?" I asked myself, pounding my fist on my knee.

I didn't need to ask the questions. I already knew the answer. I wanted Inman. I'd never forget him, and he'd never leave my heart. I knew I should try to make room for someone else, but this just wasn't the time. Maybe someday, but not now.

For now, my teaching would be my life, would fill my days. Teaching also filled half of my heart, and I'd just have to hope and pray the other half would find fulfillment somehow along the way. If a special love came to me again, I'd be twice lucky, twice blessed. My experience was that didn't happen to too many people, but it was possible. I'd hang on to that hope, with all my might.

*   *   *

That night the minute my head touched the pillow I knew it was coming. I got back up and read for a while, hoping to become so exhausted my mind would go blank. It didn't work…

We were running and running….

Behind us we could hear the roof of the barn crackling and popping. Flames were shooting up through holes on the side nearest the road, and smoke slid out the edges of the windows.

"There it goes!" Jimmy John suddenly screamed, pulling me close.

The roof shook—and then it was gone, stars dancing and twinkling where it had been before. Ash fell into our eyes. The angels screamed louder and louder.

Then, they were quiet….

The angels were gone.

17

Prosecution

When Ella and I entered the courtroom, we immediately stopped right in our tracks.

Courtroom 2A was absolutely packed.

I had expected nothing like this. After all, this wasn't the Lindbergh Kidnapping or one of the trials we read about nearly every day in the newspapers involving some famous war criminal. This was, in so many ways, a very simple matter. It was a fight for a piece of property owned now by a man with dark skin. These sorts of fights had been taking place since the end of the Civil War, so I didn't expect this one would shock too many people. However, judging by the attendance in the courtroom, word of J.D.'s case had spread like wildfire, to those of all races. And maybe, just maybe, the room was so full in part because of the violence that had taken place in recent weeks, both within and outside the Ville. Because of that violence, maybe it was now also a fight that people were taking personally. It sure looked like it as I scanned the deadly serious faces filling the room.

The seats on the left side of the room, behind Mr. Vaughn's table, were filled with dark faces, and I knew nearly every one of them. Most were members of our church, but the others were a Who's Who of ministers, politicians, and civic leaders from the broader Negro community in St. Louis. The lone exception on this side of the room was Josie, who was seated in the very back corner of the room opposite the door.

The other side of the room, behind Mr. Seegers' table, the attorney representing the Kraemers, was a sea of white faces, all attired in what appeared to be their Sunday best clothing. The lone exception on that side of the room was one of dress, not of skin color. In the last row, opposite the door on that side of the room, sat Sergeant McDougald, in his dress uniform, bandage still over one eye. They were all taking this seriously and, judging by the looks on their faces, appeared ready for the fight.

And so were we.

Much more than they knew.

Ella and I sat on the aisle about halfway toward the front because those were the only seats available. We offered polite greetings to those around us, but the atmosphere was serious, almost somber.

Just after we sat down the bailiff stood and announced, "These court proceedings assigned herewithin to Division Number Three of the St. Louis Circuit Court, Cause Number 19283, are hereby now in order. All please rise for the Honorable Judge William K. Koerner."

Judge Koerner was an older man and very tall, easily well over six feet. The top of his head was shiny bald, but he had shocks of white hair that stuck out over his ears. He wore small, gold-framed reading glasses that were perched at the end of his nose. As soon as he sat down, he flipped quickly through some papers, wrote something in a book sitting on his right, and then addressed the attorneys.

"Good morning Mr. Seegers and Mr. Vaughn. Nice to see both of you again in my courtroom. I see this case involves a piece of property at 4600 Labadie Avenue, which is within the jurisdiction of this court, so all seems in order. Any motions or other declarations from either of you before we begin?"

"No, Your Honor," they each said in turn.

"Good," he replied, nodding toward each. Then, he raised his gaze and scanned the room. When he got to our side of the room, his eyes widened and, though it was only for a matter of seconds, he appeared to smile. He took his glasses off, tapped them boldly on his bench, and said loudly and firmly to everyone, "Ladies and gentlemen, you are welcome to observe the proceedings of the court, but it must be understood there will be no outpourings of support or negativity to either side. To do so will be considered contempt of court and will be dealt with severely. Is my meaning here understood?"

A very light chorus of "Yes, Sir" seemed to swell forward from the back of the room.

"Good," he repeated. "With that said, I'll allow opening remarks. Mr. Seegers—you're up."

Mr. Seegers was dressed in a snappy, tight-fitting tan suit. As he moved from behind the table and walked slowly toward the center of the empty space between his chair and the Judge's bench, I could see his tie and shoes were blue and didn't match his suit. I started to point that out to Ella, but before I could he bellowed, "Covenant!"—taking us all by surprise.

Then he grew silent, looked down at the floor, turned, stared at us on the left side of the room, walked back to his chair, and slowly sat back down. He exhaled loudly and started drumming his fingers on the table.

After an uncomfortable silence, Judge Koerner asked, incredulity filling his voice, "That's it? That's all you have to say?"

Mr. Seegers then stood again, faced the Judge, and said, "It should be, Your Honor. It really and truly should be. It *should* be enough, but I'm afraid it won't be."

His voice was even but tinged by a slight lisp. He continued, "In the world of real estate, covenants are a matter of course. Some are designed to limit the type of commerce that can be held in a specific area. Others are put into force to allow the construction of multiple-family dwellings, to help ease the current housing crunch. Others are there to protect the health of our families, our children, by keeping heavy industry from building plants next to our parks and other recreational facilities. And still others, like the covenant present in this case, are instituted to protect the housing rights of the citizens involved. These covenants, which are nothing new and, as a matter of fact, have been around for almost half a century in St. Louis, must be maintained for the good of not just the individuals involved, but for the entire city around us. Mr. and Mrs. Kraemer want nothing more than what is rightfully theirs—the enforcement of a covenant specific to their neighborhood. So, Your Honor, it really is that simple. They are owed a protection of their rights as citizens of this great city of St. Louis. Nothing more. That's all they are requesting. I don't think that is too much to ask. Not at all."

He sat back down and added, "That's all for now, Your Honor."

Judge Koerner then turned to Mr. Vaughn and said, "Counsel, you may now address the Court."

"Thank you, Your Honor. Like Mr. Seegers, I intend my opening remarks to be brief."

Then, standing and walking to the same spot where Mr. Seegers first spoke, he shouted, catching us all completely off guard, "Covenant!" He next turned, walked back to his chair, and sat down, drumming his fingers on the table the exact way Mr. Seegers had done.

It started as a very quiet chuckle, but it soon grew into a chorus of loud, ringing belly laughs.

At least on our side of the room.

Judge Koerner slammed his gavel on the bench several times and said, sternly, "That will be enough of that, Mr. Vaughn. We're not going to have that in my courtroom. Not by a long shot."

He paused, then continued, "I'll ask you the same thing. Is that all you have to say?"

Mr. Vaughn stood again and replied, "It should be, Your Honor. That *should* be enough. But, sadly, it won't be. At least not right now."

Whirling in place to face those seated behind him, on both sides of the room, he continued, "Do any of us really know what a *covenant* is, what it represents? Learned counsel there offered us some examples. And he was right about those—up to a point. He presented one side of the picture, but he sure as the day is long left out the other side of this. He never once mentioned that the same rights are to be afforded to all citizens of this city, not just to those of one particular group of individuals. The Fourteenth Amendment to the U.S. Constitution—"

"I object—most strongly—Your Honor!" Mr. Seegers interjected. "The U.S. Constitution is not the issue here. This is a State, civil matter, first and foremost and completely. I knew Mr. Vaughn was going to bring this up and, frankly, I'm surprised he didn't open with it, instead of mocking me. Your Honor, l respectfully request that you remind Mr. Vaughn of the parameters of this case."

Judge Koerner said, quite sternly to Mr. Seegers, "Counsel, I don't need any directions from you about the parameters of this case. That will be enough of that. Don't do it again. And you, Mr. Vaughn, just where are you going with this? This *is* a civil matter, and you know that. I'm going to sustain Mr. Seegers' objection. Let's get on with this, shall we?"

"I apologize, Your Honor. I was attempting to add definition and clarification to the information offered by Mr. Seegers. That's all—for now. So, again, I apologize, most sincerely."

Here he paused, took a drink of water, and continued, this time facing the Judge, "Mr. and Mrs. Shelley lived on 9th Street down in the city before purchasing the property and moving to 4600 Labadie Avenue. On 9th Street they lived in a run-down apartment that wasn't fit for rats to live in. They wanted to better themselves, as we all do, and they wanted to provide a better living environment and life for their children. Can any of us honestly blame them for that? They were following a dream—a beautiful dream shared by so many. They wanted out of that rattrap. Your Honor, the fact is that Negroes are still not allowed to live where they want in many parts of this city—and it's the same way in too many other places in this great country of ours. We all know this is the case. They can't own their own property, which causes a multitude of problems. Landlords who don't live in the buildings they rent to Negroes let the structures fall into such pitiful conditions that I wouldn't have my dog live in most of them. Sanitation is also poor in those places. The amount of rent they are forced to pay because they don't have other housing choices is disgraceful. The crowding gets so bad that sickness becomes a way of life to many. That is what Mr. and Mrs. Shelley wanted to get away from, and they found a way to achieve their dream at 4600 Labadie."

Here he turned slightly so that he was also facing Mr. Seegers, then added, "Mr. Seegers seems to think the crux of this case centers on a real estate covenant. I don't think that's the issue at all. That's nothing more than a red herring, an attempt to get us away from the real issue. Mr. Seegers mentioned rights. That's the one thing we agree upon, and I think that is really the core of this. We're talking about a simple human right—the right to own property where we are able to purchase it. Covenant? I've looked through all the paperwork presented to me, and I don't see a covenant that pertains to this case. I really don't. Not a single one. I sure don't see one attached to this particular piece of property. Therefore, Your Honor, I intend to demonstrate that the Shelleys are the legal and rightful owners of said property. Covenant? Personally, I abhor the very word. I believe covenants, in cases like this, to be unfair, and, more importantly, completely illegal. However, my own personal opinion here doesn't matter. What does matter is that any covenant that might be exhibited here will have no bearing on the ownership of the home at 4600 Labadie—and I intend to prove that, beyond a shadow of a doubt."

Mr. Vaughn started to sit down, then paused. Standing up straight again, he said, "And one more thing, Mr. Seegers. I won't mention the Thirteenth Amendment, which abolished slavery, even though covenants reek of trying to bring that practice back. And I won't mention the Fourteenth Amendment until later, even though that goes to the heart of equal protection under the law for all our citizens."

"I object!" Mr. Seegers shouted as he stood and stomped his right foot on the floor. "Your Honor, this is ridiculous—and unprofessional."

Banging his gavel again, Judge Koerner interrupted him, "Yes, I have to agree with you. Objection sustained. Mr. Vaughn, we'll have no more of that. You know better."

"Sorry, Your Honor," he said, smiling, sitting down. "That's all I have to say for now."

"That's fine," Judge Koerner said. "Let's continue. Mr. Seegers, now that opening remarks have been given, are you ready to call your first witness to the stand?"

"Yes, Your Honor. I call Mr. Martin Seegers."

The bailiff called out, "Mr. Martin Seegers. Please come forward and take the stand."

Martin Seegers stated his name for the record, was sworn in, and sat down to the left of the Judge.

"Before we begin," Mr. Seegers said, "we better make something clear." He laughed before continuing, "Mr. Martin Seegers, are you related to anyone present in this courtroom?"

"Yes, Sir, I am," he replied, smiling.

"And you would then be related to whom?"

"Well, there's my wife, sitting over there. That's Mrs. Seegers. My son is next to her. His name is James. And, well, there's one more here."

"And who would that be?"

"Well, you. I'm your uncle."

His response produced laughter from both sides of the room. The Judge let it go. He, too, was laughing.

After the laughter died down, he continued, "Okay, with that now out of the way, I'd like to ask you a couple of questions. First, I want to ask you this: Are you a member of what is known as the Marcus Avenue Improvement Association?"

"Yes, I am," he replied.

"Do you hold any particular station or office in this association?"

"I was one of the founders of the association, and I'm now one of the recruitment officers."

"In your own words, would you please tell the court the purpose of this association."

"I'd be glad to. The Marcus Avenue Improvement Association was started to help keep up neighborhoods the way they should be. We want to keep them clean and safe—and places we can all be proud of. And I want to say something else right up front, something that most just don't understand. This isn't just for whites. No, Sir, it's not. There are black neighborhoods and white neighborhoods. We feel both should have protection, and both should have standards to be kept up. If we keep our neighborhoods clean, then we can set a good example for those people. That's why we promote the use of covenants—so that everyone will know what they need to do in their own neighborhoods."

He paused, then continued, his voice loud and full of passion, "We have another purpose, too. We want to keep out things like slaughterhouses and junk shops. We want to keep the neighborhoods places for families."

Here Mr. Seegers interrupted him. "Mr. Seegers, that's fine, but please stop for just a minute. I'd like to ask you another question that may provide a context for what you have just said—and make this more clear for Judge Koerner and everyone else in the room. How did this group come about? Did the members just come together and decide to form the association?"

"The Association was actually founded back in 1910. We were all homeowners and businessmen, and we all wanted to keep our neighborhood clean and free of nuisances and to keep up our standards. Between our founding and about 1930 or so, we worked together to see that a covenant covered as many parcels of property as we could influence, either for their present owners or for new owners when places were sold. I'm proud of the members who worked on this. They did a fine job."

Attorney Seegers interrupted and said, "Let me get this straight. You said that one of the major goals of the association was to get a covenant on all pieces of property in that area. Is that right?

"Yes."

"Then please state for the record what type of covenant you're talking about here."

"It was a covenant to restrict sales of the homes in the area to whites. This isn't illegal. We're not trying to deny anyone their liberties. We just prefer to live separately, which is our right under the law."

At this point, Mr. Vaughn stood and said, "Your Honor, I object to this last statement. The witness is not an officer of the court and is in no position to render judgment as to the legality of anything."

Judge Koerner said, "Objection sustained. Now please continue."

Attorney Seegers then asked, "And today? Does your group have support from other groups, and if so, which ones?"

"We do have support, and help for our cause, from a number of groups. Most would say our largest supporter would be the St. Louis Real Estate Exchange. As a matter of fact, some of their members are also members of our association."

"And, to the best of your knowledge, what is the Real Estate Exchange?" Mr. Seegers asked, turning to look at our side of the room.

"Why, that's the biggest organization of realtors in St. Louis. They work with us to keep the city clean and safe. We both work together on that. We both want St. Louis to be the greatest city in the Midwest."

"Thank you. One other question, and I think that will be all. You mentioned earlier part of your mission is to establish appropriate covenants for different neighborhoods. Based upon your work with the Association, can you tell us if there is a covenant of any type that would pertain to the home at 4600 Labadie Avenue?"

"I object, Your Honor," Mr. Vaughn said, remaining seated.

"Mr. Martin Seegers cannot possibly speak to the issues surrounding 4600 Labadie Avenue. He wasn't part of the recent real estate transaction or the recording of the deed. Any response he would give would be hearsay, irrelevant, and immaterial."

Judge Koerner tapped his glasses on the bench again and appeared deep in thought. He finally looked up and said, "I'm going to allow this for now. Objection overruled."

"Thank you, Your Honor," Mr. Seegers said. "Now, let's continue. Are there any covenants in the immediate area that would involve the property at 4600 Labadie Avenue?"

"Yes, there is. It has always been understood that the homes in this area are for whites only. We first established this way back in 1910 when the first covenants were added to property deeds. The Negroes have their own area across Taylor Avenue. This area west of Taylor Avenue is another story. West of Taylor Avenue, the homes are for sale to whites only."

"Thank you, Mr. Seegers. I think that will be all for now."

Ella leaned over and whispered to me, too loudly, "That man's an idiot!"

"Which one?" I whispered back.

"Both of them," she replied, shaking her head.

Judge Koerner then asked Mr. Vaughn if he had any questions for the witness.

"Yes, Your Honor. I do have a few."

He walked up close to Mr. Martin Seegers and said, "Good morning, Sir. How are you today?"

"Fine, thank you. I'm fine. And you?"

His question brought muffled laughter from everyone. Mr. Vaughn smiled broadly. Then, almost instantly, his face turned deadly serious. He replied to the question, "I'd be a lot better if I understood why organizations like yours even exist today. My grandfather told me there were groups like this during Reconstruction, but I thought they were all gone now. Guess I was wrong."

Mr. Vaughn walked back to his table, picked up a piece of

paper, and slowly made his way back near Mr. Seegers. "Now, Mr. Seegers, I'd like to ask you a couple of things. First, you mentioned there were neighborhoods for whites and for Negroes. Why is that?"

"I object, Your Honor," Mr. Seegers said, loudly and sharply.

"I'm going to let this one go. I'm going to give both of you some latitude in this early stage. Overruled. Proceed, Mr. Vaughn."

"Again, Sir, I ask you why is that? Why are there separate neighborhoods?"

Mr. Martin Seegers shifted nervously in his chair before responding, "Because that's the way it should be. Because that's the way it's best for both whites and Negroes. Everyone knows when we mix, neighborhoods go downhill. And property values go down. For whites and for Negroes. Everyone knows that."

Mr. Vaughn frowned and said, "You mean that's when the slaughterhouses and junk shops you mentioned show up. After the races mix. That right?"

"Something like that," Mr. Seegers replied.

"I see," Mr. Vaughn said, stroking his chin. "When a neighborhood goes downhill, it's always the fault of the Negro. Is that what you are saying?"

"Objection!" Mr. Seegers shouted.

"Overruled," the Judge replied.

"It does happen," Mr. Martin Seegers added. "More often than not."

"Is that why your association promotes the covenants involving race?"

"That's part of it. But only part. We want to keep the neighborhoods clean—and safe."

Mr. Vaughn repeated, "Clean—and safe. I see. Okay, let's talk about one more thing. You mentioned earlier that there was a covenant involving this section of Labadie, and specifically at 4600. What exactly is that covenant? Please share that with the court."

"Well, I don't have the exact wording with me, but it says that people of Negro blood cannot own property there."

"And you can swear under oath that you've seen such a covenant on the property deed at 4600 Labadie Avenue. Is that right, Sir?"

Mr. Martin Seegers paused and shifted in his chair again. "Well, no, not exactly. I haven't seen the deed to 4600, but that doesn't matter. When we started the association and started getting the property owners to add the covenants, the understanding was that all property in the area would be covered as each was sold. Everyone agreed to that. Everyone."

"Everyone," Mr. Vaughn repeated. "You say everyone agreed to it. That's interesting, Mr. Seegers. Very interesting. Thank you, Mr. Seegers. I think that will be all."

The left side of the room let out a collective gasp. A low rumble of voices spread through the aisles. That was all? No one could believe that Mr. Vaughn didn't press Martin Seegers for more information about the racial inequality of these covenants. Why did he stop his questioning when he obviously had him on the ropes?

Ella was beside herself. "And this man is supposed to be the best attorney around? No wonder we've been put in our place all these years. *He's* the idiot in this courtroom. I could have done a better job than that!"

"Just wait. Give him a chance. He knows what he's doing," I said, confidently. However, my outward confidence didn't match my inner feelings. Even I was upset he didn't press the issue with Martin Seegers. I just hoped he really did know what he was doing.

"Your Honor," Mr. Seegers then stood and said, "I'd like to call Mr. George Anderson to the stand."

The bailiff announced him, and Mr. Anderson came forward. After stating his name and being sworn in, he sat down. Mr. Anderson was a short, plump man with a pencil-thin mustache that looked like the one Clark Gable usually wore in the movies. He was dressed in plain, brown trousers and a white cotton short-sleeved shirt. He also had a terrible summer cold and kept coughing into his hand.

Mr. Seegers began, "Mr. Anderson, do you own a business at the eastern corner of the 4600 block of Labadie Avenue?"

"Yes, Sir, I do. I'm the owner of Anderson's Bakery."

"And how long have you owned the bakery?"

"The family has owned it now for over thirty-five years. My dad started it, and I took over when his eyes starting going. It's a family business. We make all types of breads, cakes, and pies."

"Do you also live there on the property?"

"Yes, we do. We live on the floor above the bakery."

"And you are the rightful and legal owner of this property?"

"Yes, Sir, I am."

"Do you have your property deed here with you today?"

"Yes, Sir, I do. It's right here in my hand."

"Would you then please read from Section Twenty-Nine of that officially recorded document?"

Mr. Anderson reached into his shirt pocket and withdrew his glasses. After putting them on, he started reading: " 'Section Twenty-Nine: Restrictions. Ownership of this property shall not be transferred to anyone commonly known as Colored, or having one thirty-second part or more of Negro blood.' That's all it says, Mr. Seegers."

"Thank you. Based on that section, would you ever attempt to sell your property to a Negro family?"

"No, Sir, I would not. It wouldn't be right."

"And it wouldn't be legal, would it?"

Mr. Vaughn started to object, but Mr. Seegers interrupted him and quickly added, "I withdraw the question. That will be all, Mr. Anderson. Your witness, Mr. Vaughn."

Mr. Vaughn then stood slowly, stared at Mr. Anderson, and said, "I have no questions of this witness, Your Honor."

Another rumble of voices filled the room, now on both sides. What was Mr. Vaughn up to? Why was he avoiding the fight? It was obvious from the shocked looks on the left side of the room and the smiles and nods on the right side of the room that something had to happen—and soon.

Mr. Seegers then called Mr. Anthony Sullivan to the stand. Mr. Sullivan was the chairman of the St. Louis Real Estate Exchange. He was also a man most on the left side of the room put in the same league with the Devil himself. Mr. Seegers asked Mr. Sullivan to go through the different types of real estate covenants that were found in different parts of the city. Then, finally, he asked him to give his opinion as to the covenants that were attached to many of the pieces of property on Labadie Avenue. Mr. Sullivan said, quite clearly and forcefully, that Negroes were simply not to own property on that stretch of Labadie and for them to do so would be considered illegal by the Real Estate Exchange and, he hoped, by the courts of the City of St. Louis. This seemed to me to be a perfect time for Mr. Vaughn to make an objection. It didn't take a lawyer to know he was letting information be presented that wasn't fact or that was open to speculation and, therefore, should not be allowed on the record. Instead, Mr. Vaughn took notes while the information was being presented, but he said nothing. Absolutely nothing.

When Mr. Seegers had completed his questioning of Mr. Sullivan, Mr. Vaughn stood and again said, without looking at Judge Koerner, "I have no questions of this witness."

The low rumble around me then became louder and could actually be felt in the courtroom floor, like the vibration of distant thunder at the start of a sudden summer storm. Now I was getting worried. Very worried.

Mr. Vaughn, appearing quite calm, simply continued jotting notes, finally looking up when Mr. Seegers called Mrs. Kraemer to the stand. Then, his whole demeanor changed. He dropped his pencil, straightened his posture, and stared intently at Mrs. Kraemer when Mr. Seegers started his questions.

"Mrs. Kraemer, I hope you are well today. Are you?"

"Yes, sir. Just a little nervous, that's all."

"No need to be. You just relax. I have just a couple of questions for you. Take your time and answer them as best you can, okay?"

Mrs. Kraemer nodded her head. She then reached into her purse and pulled out a handkerchief, which she used to wipe perspiration from her forehead and the backs of her hands. Mrs. Kraemer was a slightly-built woman I guessed to be in her mid forties. Her auburn hair was starting to gray at her forehead. When she turned to the side, I noticed her nose was large and out of proportion to the rest of her features. Her eyes were small and dark, and she dabbed at them over and over with her handkerchief.

"Mrs. Kraemer, my first question is this. Why did you bring suit against the Shelleys? Please explain that for the court."

Mrs. Kraemer was now visibly nervous, shifting her weight back and forth in her chair. She wiped her eyes, cleared her throat, and in a husky whisper began, "They shouldn't be allowed to own that property. They're right down the street from us. As you know, we live at 4532 Labadie. We've lived there a long time, and my parents lived there before us. Everyone knows this is a white neighborhood, and Negroes shouldn't be allowed to buy any of the property."

"Why is that, Mrs. Kraemer? Why do you say that?"

"Because it's all written down here."

She opened her purse again and removed a large piece of paper that had been folded in half to fit in there. She unfolded it and began reading.

"Wait a minute, please," Mr. Seegers interrupted. "Please tell us from what you are reading before you begin."

"Sorry, Mr. Seegers. I'm so nervous I forgot. This is the deed to our property. I'm reading from the 'Restriction' section near the end. It goes like this: 'No people of Negro or Mongolian races may purchase or occupy property on said section of Labadie Avenue for a period of fifty years'."

"Fifty years?" Mr. Seegers interrupted. "When was that document first recorded?"

Mrs. Kraemer replied, "1911. That is when my parents bought the house, and this same restriction was on the deed when it was transferred to us."

Mr. Seegers continued, "It says, 'on said section of Labadie'—correct?"

"Yes, sir. That means the whole block."

At that moment, Mr. Vaughn started to rise, but didn't. This was noticed by everyone around him. Again, a low moan filled the left side of the room. Why was he making no objections? Why was he allowing this?

Mr. Seegers continued, "Mrs. Kraemer, did you bring any other supporting documents related to this restriction?"

"Yes, sir, I did. I have on my chair back over there a copy of the papers from the Recorder of Deeds in City Hall. I'm sorry. I left them back there. Those City Hall papers show the exact same restriction on the deed to our property.

"Your Honor, I'd like to enter both of these documents into the record."

"Any objections?" the Judge asked Mr. Vaughn.

"No objections, Your Honor."

"Then, bailiff, please retrieve those papers on Mrs. Kraemer's chair and bring them up here."

While the bailiff was getting the papers, Mrs. Kraemer said something to Judge Koerner that I couldn't hear. She then suddenly stood from her chair and bolted for the back door on the other side of the courtroom. When she had gone, the Judge said, "We'll take a short recess at this time to allow the witness to, well, to take care of some physical needs."

Physical needs? It looked to me like she was about to throw up. If that's what it was, *physical needs* was certainly a polite way of saying that. As I scanned those sitting on the left side of the room, it looked to me like if things didn't improve, and quickly, many would also need a break for their own "physical needs."

Ella elbowed me in the ribs. "This isn't going well," she said.

"You think?" I replied, sarcastically. "But let's still give Mr.

Vaughn the benefit of the doubt. We have to. He's the only hope the Shelleys have. Heck, he's the only hope all of us have."

I studied the faces of those around us. I could tell I wasn't the only one thinking this right now.

A few minutes later Mrs. Kraemer reentered the courtroom and walked slowly back to her seat beside the judge and sat down. She was still dabbing her eyes with her handkerchief. Mr. Seegers then said, "I hope you're better now. Are you ready to begin again?"

"Yes, Sir, I'll try."

"Good. One last thing I'd like you to tell the court. You brought up some legal restrictions, and I thank you for doing that. Are there other reasons you feel the Shelleys should not be allowed to live at 4600 Labadie Avenue?"

"Because it will ruin our property value. Everyone knows that when those people move in, you might as well just rip up your deed. And I'm not going to do that. They're not going to wreck my property value. I'm not going to let them."

There it was. The gauntlet had finally been thrown down. The real motivation for the suit was there in front of us all, as if on a silver platter. No doubt now. None at all. Both sides of the courtroom went silent. Completely silent. It was as if Mrs. Kraemer's words had sucked the breath out of every single person present. Even Judge Koerner was staring straight ahead, unblinking. Mr. Vaughn was looking down at the floor. Mr. Seegers appeared to be looking at a ceiling fan over Mrs. Kraemer's head. At that moment, the whirring of the fan blades was the only sound that could be heard.

That is, until someone, I couldn't tell who it was, about halfway back on the right side of the room said loudly enough for everyone to hear. "Black sons a'bitches. Want to ruin the world for everybody."

Judge Koerner slammed his gavel on his bench and barked, "Who said that? Bailiff, can you tell? Who said that? Bring that person up here."

The bailiff peered intently around that side of the room but ended up shrugging his shoulders. No one on that side of the room moved, as if not wanting to indicate where the voice had come from. The words might have come from one person, but it was clear it could have come from just about anyone on that side. Seeing that the person would not be found, the judge ordered Mr. Seegers to continue.

"I have no further questions of Mrs. Kraemer, Your Honor."

Mrs. Kraemer stood up and started to leave. After his recent lack of action, I fully expected Mr. Vaughn to let her go without questioning.

However, he proved me, and everyone else, wrong when he said, loudly and forcefully, "Not so fast, Mrs. Kraemer. You may not want me to live on your street, but in this courtroom, you're on *my* street now. Sit back down. I have a few questions of my own."

This brought the left side of the room to life. Feet were shuffling, excited whispers could be heard, a few even clapped softly, as if all were anticipating Mr. Vaughn going on the attack.

He didn't disappoint us.

"Mrs. Kraemer," he began, "you don't much like Negroes, do you?"

She paused before saying, "I just don't want to live next to them. That's my right."

"Your right?" Mr. Vaughn asked. "Let me get this straight. You say that it is your *right*, under the law, to decide, all by yourself, where the Shelleys can live. Is that correct?"

"I have a copy of the restriction right here—"

Mr. Vaughn cut her off. "I'm not talking about any so-called restriction. I'm talking about you, Mrs. Kraemer. What gives you the right to bring about a suit like this, against these good people?

Mrs. Kraemer repeated again, "I have a copy of the restriction—"

Mr. Vaughn interrupted again, "Mrs. Kraemer, I think you

know what I think you can do with that restriction."

The cheers on the left side of the room nearly drowned out the objections Mr. Seegers was now shouting. Judge Koerner pounded his gavel again and demanded order in the court. Before he could say anything else, Mr. Vaughn continued.

"Mrs. Kraemer, I want to ask you something. Since you are so bent on sharing that so-called restriction with us, tell me this one thing. Was that restriction written for the property at 4532 Labadie Avenue?"

"It was."

Mr. Vaughn started pacing back and forth in front of Mrs. Kraemer's chair. He walked faster and faster, turning military-style each time he changed directions. He finally stopped right in front of Mrs. Kraemer and shouted, "Then how in the hell can one restriction written for one particular parcel of property tell everyone else in the neighborhood what to do? Just because your property is described one way does not mean that your property can determine the fate of everyone else around you!"

Here loud cheers rang out from the left side of the room. Judge Koerner then warned everyone that if there were any more displays like that, he'd clear the courtroom.

Mr. Vaughn didn't even look at the judge before continuing, "Mrs. Kraemer, now it's my turn. I want to read something to you. I have in my hand here a copy of something I'd like for you to explain. Listen to this. I'm going to read off some names. Ready? Hicks, King, James, Shackelford, Williams, and Boxley. I particularly want you to remember the name of Grace Boxley. Do you recognize any of these names, Mrs. Kraemer?"

Mrs. Kraemer didn't respond.

"I didn't think so," Mr. Vaughn said, disgust filling his words. Mrs. Kraemer, these are all people who have owned property on Labadie Avenue through the years, both before and since 1911, the year we heard some so-called restrictions were written. And do you know what they all have in common? Mrs. Kraemer, they are all Negroes. All of them. I have the list right here, right from the records at the Recorder of Deeds. Your Honor, I'd like this document entered into the record."

Mr. Seegers did not object.

Mr. Vaughn was now on a roll. He continued, "Let me repeat the name Grace Boxley to you. Mrs. Kraemer, Grace Boxley was granted deed to property on Labadie, at 4628 to be exact, way back in 1882. That's right—1882! She was willed the property from the people she worked for. And, yes, they were white. Grace Boxley passed the property along to her children when she passed, and they still live there, although I'm sure you've never stopped by to say hello or to break bread with them, have you?"

Mr. Vaughn walked back to his table, took a long drink of water, and turned again to face Mrs. Kraemer. This time, almost gently, he asked, "So how, Mrs. Kraemer, can you say your property value would suffer—when Negroes have already owned property, since the year 1882, on Labadie—right down the street from where you live? No, property values haven't gone down there. Not at all. As a matter of fact, I'm sure the Real Estate Exchange would tell you that property values have shot up in your neighborhood and elsewhere because of the housing shortage all around town. Therefore, your logic makes no sense at all. None... at... all... None at all!"

Mrs. Kraemer looked like she was going to have "physical needs" again, but Mr. Vaughn didn't give her a chance to get up and run out of the room. He moved to her left, right in the middle of the path she had taken before.

"One more thing, Mrs. Kraemer. I want to go back one more time to what you say is your 'right'—your right to determine where people can live and not live. You have no right to do that, and I think, deep down, you know it. No one has that right. No one."

Cheers rang out again from the left side. Judge Koerner used his gavel again, but this time he didn't say anything.

Mr. Vaughn turned to face Mr. Seegers and the right side of the room. "I have no more questions for Mrs. Kraemer at this time, but I'm going to reserve the right to recall her if I have other questions later on."

"In that case," Judge Koerner said, "Mrs. Kraemer, you may step down."

The second the words were out of his mouth, Mrs. Kraemer again ran out of the room, covering her mouth with her hand. *Physical needs* were calling. And I, for one, was glad.

"Maybe she'll choke on her own vomit," Ella said, loudly, staring over toward the middle of the right side of the room. Her words were heard, but no eyes turned in her direction. They were all looking either down at the floor or straight ahead.

At this point, Mr. Seegers rose slowly and said, "Your Honor, I know we've been here a long time already, but if you please, I'd like to call one more person to the stand today. I'd like to call Mrs. Josephine Fitzgerald."

The bailiff announced, "Mrs. Josephine Fitzgerald, please come forward."

"Here we go," I said to Ella. "Hold your breath."

Ella reached over, took my hand, and squeezed it tightly. I squeezed back.

Josie stood and shuffled sideways out of her row until she reached the aisle. She was dressed nothing like she was that after-noon at the bank. She had on a conservative blue skirt, white blouse, and a small string of white pearls around her neck. Her hair was pulled back and tied with a ribbon matching the color of her skirt. To me, she looked like she worked in a bank, and the irony made me smile.

As soon as she had been sworn in and sat down, Mr. Seegers didn't waste any time launching his attack.

"Mrs. Fitzgerald, do you know what fraud is?"

"Your Honor!" Mr. Vaughn practically screamed.

Judge Koerner stopped jotting notes and quickly looked up. "Never mind, Mr. Vaughn. I'll take this one. Mr. Seegers, you're on thin ice here."

"I think it's a fair question, Your Honor, but I'll withdraw it.

I'll rephrase my question. Mrs. Fitzgerald, did you once own the property in question at 4600 Labadie Avenue?"

"Yes, Sir. I did."

"And Mrs. Fitzgerald, how long did you own that property?"

"I'd have to check my records. I don't think I could say exactly right now."

Josie appeared cool, confident, as she responded to his questions.

"You don't have to be exact," Mr. Seegers continued. "Estimate for us. A year? Six months? How long, approximately?"

Josie, still quite calm, replied, "A few weeks, I think."

This time a low rumble of voices grew steadily from the right side of the room.

"You think? You think? Can you be more specific?"

"You said to estimate, and I did. I'd say for a few weeks."

"Mrs. Fitzgerald, did you ever live in the home on that property during the time you owned it?"

"No, Sir."

"Then why did you purchase the property?"

"It was an investment."

"An investment? Are you sure, Mrs. Fitzgerald?"

Josie crossed her legs, leaned forward, and said, "I don't know what you are asking."

Here Mr. Seegers paused before continuing, moving closer to Josie. "Mrs. Fitzgerald, do you know what a *straw buyer* is?"

"Why of course," she replied quickly. "That's a farmer who needs straw for his livestock. I guess you're not a country boy, right?"

The courtroom, on both sides, erupted in nervous laughter. Judge Koerner picked up his gavel, but gently put it back down. He quietly reminded Josie that the proceedings were serious and that she should make her responses accordingly.

"Sorry, Your Honor," she replied. "I promise to be good."

More laughter followed, but not from Mr. Seegers.

"I'm glad you have a sense of humor," he said. "You may

need it before this is all said and done. Now, let's continue again. Do you know the term *straw buyer* when it is used in the context of a real estate transaction?"

"I don't know if my definition would be the same as yours, but, yes, I've heard that term used before."

"Would you give us your definition, please?"

"I believe it's someone who helps another person purchase property."

Mr. Seegers moved closer to her and said, "Helps? How? Please continue. I'm quite interested in this."

"By making the process easier. That is how I would describe it."

"Mrs. Fitzgerald, then let me ask you this. To whom did you sell the property at 4600 Labadie? Whom did you *help out*?"

Here Josie paused and looked at Mr. Vaughn. I noticed he nodded his head slowly as if to indicate she should continue.

"Mr. Shelley."

A low buzz swept through the right side of the room. Judge Koerner looked up, but he did not ask for quiet.

Mr. Seegers continued, "So you didn't really buy the house for an investment, did you? Isn't it true you were really trying to hide the real purchase, and your real purpose, which was to serve as a straw buyer for the Shelleys? And now, I ask you once again. Do you know what fraud is?"

"I object, Your Honor!" Mr. Vaughn shouted, rising from his chair. "This is way out of line. Mrs. Fitzgerald is not on trial here. Any motivations she might have had are irrelevant to this case."

Judge Koerner replied, "I agree with the first part of what you said. Mrs. Fitzgerald is not on trial here. Mr. Seegers, be careful how you tread here. You're close to the line."

"I'm sorry, Your Honor, but this is a point vital to my case. I respectfully request I be allowed to continue this line of questioning."

"I'll overrule the objection, but, please, let's get back on track here. And I mean right now. Understand?"

"Thank you, Your Honor." Then, turning back to Josie, he continued, "Now, Mrs. Fitzgerald, I'll ask a simple question. Please answer the question by replying *yes* or *no*. That's all. Did you buy the property at 4600 Labadie with the intention of reselling it specifically to the Shelleys?"

Here Josie looked first at Mr. Vaughn, then at Judge Koerner. Then, very calmly, as if she had been asked if she would like some tea, she replied: "Yes."

A loud gasp erupted from the right side of the room. Mr. Seegers smiled broadly, walked over to Mr. Vaughn's table, and without turning back to face Josie, addressed her once again. "Thank you, Mrs. Fitzgerald. Based on that response, I'm not going to ask you if you know what fraud is. I'm not going to do that."

Then, with sarcasm dripping from his words, he added, "I don't think I need to, do I?"

"Your Honor!" Mr. Vaughn bellowed. The buzzing in the room became so loud Judge Koerner used his gavel liberally. Before he could say anything, Mr. Seegers said, "That's all, Your Honor. I'm finished with this witness."

The second he sat down, Mr. Vaughn jumped up and walked quickly over to Josie.

"Mrs. Fitzgerald," he said, calmly, "I have a few questions of my own, but I want to go down a different path than the one taken by Mr. Seegers. This is what I want to know. First of all, when you purchased the property at 4600 Labadie, did the Marcus Avenue Improvement Association approach you about signing a covenant of any type related to that property?"

"No, Sir."

"Did any other group ask you to sign any type of covenant or restriction?"

"No, Sir."

"Did you add any restriction, or covenant, yourself while you owned the property?"

"No, Sir."

"Then that's all, Mrs. Fitzgerald. I have no further questions. I think you've just covered everything that's important and relevant here. Thank you."

Josie started to get up, but Mr. Seegers said, "Your Honor, if I may, I have something to ask on redirect. Mrs. Fitzgerald, take a minute and think carefully before you answer this question. And before you object, Mr. Vaughn, I want to remind you that you opened the door here. Mrs. Fitzgerald, to your knowledge, was there a covenant or restriction on the property at 4600 Labadie when you purchased it?"

This was the moment I was fearing and I knew all of us involved in the sale were fearing it, too. If the cat was going to come roaring out of the bag and around the courtroom, this was the moment. I was shocked Mr. Vaughn opened this door. I thought he would have wanted to avoid this discussion at all costs. I saw no way Josie could answer this question without committing perjury. I also knew something else. If she told the truth, I'd probably be the next person called to the stand.

I squeezed Ella's hand, a little too much. She said, "Ouch! What the—" Then, as if realizing why I was on pins and needles, she leaned over and hugged me, firmly.

The courtroom became absolutely quiet, and all eyes focused on Josie, who, much to my surprise, reached into her purse, pulled out a fingernail file, and stared working on her nails.

"Did you hear me?" Mr. Seegers asked, clearly irritated by Josie's calm demeanor.

Josie looked up and said, "I'd like to see the original sale papers—the ones that were used when I bought the property—before I respond. Do you have a copy of them, and can I see them?"

"I don't have those papers, Mrs. Fitzgerald. It seems they have been *misplaced*."

"That's too bad," Josie said, evenly. "If I could take a look at them again, I could answer your question."

Growing angrier by the second, Mr. Seegers continued,

again moving closer to Josie, "You mean to tell me you don't know whether there was a covenant? Is that what you are saying? Is it?"

"What? Do you think there was a covenant?" Josie responded. "Did you see those papers?"

"Your Honor!" Mr. Seegers called out, facing the judge. "She's evading the question."

"And doing it rather nicely, I'd say," the judge replied. "Mrs. Fitzgerald, you've been asked a direct question. Please do your best to answer it. And remember you are under oath."

"Yes, Your Honor. I understand that. It's just that I've seen so many papers that I honestly can't remember everything I've seen. I'm not a realtor or lawyer, and my memory isn't all that good. All I can say is that when I sold the property to Mr. Shelley, I did not see any covenant on the sale papers that were assigned from me to Mr. Shelley. No one asked me to add one. And I didn't add one myself. That much I can say."

"But the original papers you signed when you purchased the property yourself—" Mr. Seegers cut in.

"I don't know where they are. I don't know where they go. I just assumed the bank or someone else would keep them. What happens to all that paperwork, anyway?"

"That's what I'm trying to find out!" Mr. Seegers shouted, getting right into Josie's face.

"Your Honor, this is getting ridiculous," Mr. Vaughn said. "Can we put a stop to this?"

Judge Koerner said, "Mr. Seegers, if you are through with this witness, I suggest you move back so she can get down."

"I can see I'm not going to get an answer to my question, so I'll stop here. Still, Mrs. Fitzgerald, not giving an answer tells us a lot, doesn't it?"

"Objection, Your Honor!" Mr. Vaughn shouted.

"Sustained," the judge replied quickly.

Mr. Seegers then stepped back, staring intently at Josie as she walked past him. Instead of returning to her seat, she walked slowly down the center aisle and out the door on the right. All eyes followed her.

She had done it.

Ella and I hugged each other. I felt a tear slide down my cheek, and I didn't bother to wipe it away. Ella just smiled at me and nodded.

I had no idea how Josie dodged those questions under these conditions. I couldn't have done it, and I didn't know many people who could have. Josie was amazing.

Truly amazing.

Josie's testimony had also taken the wind out of Mr. Seegers' sails. He looked like a prizefighter who had just gone ten rounds with a tough opponent. He walked slowly and deliberately back to his chair and sat down heavily. Then turning to the Judge, he said, "My roster of witnesses is now complete, Your Honor."

"Thank you, Mr. Seegers. We'll now turn our attention to Mr. Vaughn. I see you have a fairly long list of those you wish to offer testimony, and the time is getting late. Unless either of you has any objections, court will adjourn until nine tomorrow morning."

There were no objections, so the judge slammed his gavel one last time on his bench and said, "Court is adjourned." The bailiff then instructed everyone to rise as the judge left the room. As soon as the door shut behind him, the courtroom became what could only be described as "tense."

Very tense.

The right side of the room stared daggers at the left, and their looks were matched and returned. Individuals from both sides started to leave at the same time, entering the center aisle. All suddenly stopped, refusing to allow those in front of them to go first, refusing to give any ground. No words were exchanged, but the meaning was quite clear—to everyone. Finally, those who had entered the center aisle, from both sides, retreated. They motioned the people in their rows to go the opposite direction so that they could leave by using the narrow strip of floor next to the walls. This also created an interesting sight at the back of the room. All were then able to leave from the door on their own side of the room.

Separate but equal?

Or, separate but unequal?

At this point, both sides, no doubt, had definite opinions on this.

As Ella and I left the room, we saw small pockets of people forming all down the corridor leading to the main entrance to the courthouse. Groups of whites were on the right, groups of Negroes were on the left, just as it had been in the courtroom. As we walked past, each group fell into animated discussion.

"Want to stop and visit with any of these people?" I asked.

"Not on your life!" Ella said. "I just want to get out of here. My legs are killing me after all that sitting. I need a smoke, and I could certainly use a drink. Why don't we go to my house and kick off our shoes. You up for that?"

"Definitely," I said, "You just lead the way."

I put my arm through hers, and she steered us out of the courthouse. When we reached the sidewalk outside, I turned and said, "I have just one question for you. Just one. I'm not saying Josie lied or anything like that, but I have a hypothetical question for you. If you were trying to cover up something, would you ever lie on the stand? Do you think you could?"

"Depends upon what it was all about, I guess. But, yes, I think I could. I think I would. Until there is one truth for everyone, I don't think we can say what a lie really is."

"That's profound," I said, squeezing her arm tighter. "You know, I don't care what anyone says. You're not dumb at all."

Stopping short, Ella jerked her arm away from mine, whirled and said, "Oh, you're as funny as a crutch. Ha ha! Very, very funny. Dumb am I? We'll see about that."

"Just kidding," I said, leaning over to hug her. She tried to pull away, but I held her close. "Let's get out of here—before anyone asks me any questions. This place gives me the willies."

"Then off we go," she said, hooking my arm again. "And don't look back."

I should have taken her advice. Instead, I looked back one last time, and there he was, leaning against the last pillar on the left.

Sergeant McDougald. Staring right at us. Our eyes locked.

I didn't say anything to Ella. I pulled her closer and said, "Let's hurry. I'm ready for that drink. As a matter of fact, several of them."

"Now you're talking, Girl," Ella drawled. "It'll do us good to let our hair down."

I quickened our pace—and this time didn't look back.

18
Defense

W hen Ella and I reached her front door, we could hear the phone ringing. She fumbled with her keys, quickly unlocked the door, and ran inside, letting the screen door slam into my shoulder.

Before I came inside, I looked back toward the street, half expecting to see Sergeant McDougald lurking there. He wasn't, at least not where I could see him, so I stepped quickly inside.

Ella picked up the phone, listened for a few seconds, and started to squeal and stomp her feet on the living room floor.

"Wasn't it great!" she practically shouted into the phone. "I wasn't sure what Vaughn was up to at first, but now I think he's sly like a fox. He's got Seegers on the run. I can't wait to see what he's going to do tomorrow!"

She paused to let the person on the other end say a few words, then interrupted, "Okay, I have to go. Say a few extra prayers tonight. We all should. Bye."

"Who was that?" I asked.

"Wendy. You know—from the beauty parlor. She did my hair last time."

"Wendy? I didn't know you were such good friends."

"Oh, we're not. She said she's calling everyone. She was there today and is so excited she can't sit still."

"Well, she better," I said, "or she's going to get awful tired. This looks like it's going to be a long battle."

"Stop it, Liv. Don't be such a stick in the mud. Let her be excited. I'm excited. You should be excited. Everyone else sure seems to be."

Ella got up and walked back to the front door. She opened it and said, "Just listen to that. Come see this."

A steady stream of cars poured down the street, many horns honking steadily and sharply.

Ella said, "Looks like everyone at the courthouse must have driven there. Ever see so many cars at one time here in the Ville? I sure haven't."

"It's too early for any celebrating. This is ridiculous," I said, shaking my head.

"They're not celebrating, Liv. You're missing the point. They're just showing that we're all sticking together through this, no matter what. That's the sound of belonging, of caring for each other."

Before I could respond, the phone rang again. Ella picked up the receiver and said, "Why, hello, Mrs. Thomas. Yes, I saw you there today. What did you think?"

Ella looked over at me, mimicking Mrs. Thomas's fast-paced voice. I laughed until a knock on the front door made me jump. Ella motioned for me to go see who it was.

It was Jackson, holding a bouquet of yellow daisies.

"Come on in," I said. "Welcome to Grand Central Station. If she ever gets that phone out of her ear, you better move in quick."

"Good to see you, too, Liv. How've you been?"

Smiling slyly, I said, "You know, I haven't seen much of you lately. Why is that? Funny, but now that I think about it, I haven't seen you since all those buildings were set on fire. Very strange."

It was already rumored Jackson was part of what was now being called *The Great Retaliation*. By the look on his face, it appeared I struck a nerve.

He replied, "Just been away on business. That's all. Just been busy. Really."

"I bet you have," I said, dryly.

"Whatever are you implying?" he said with a faint smile.

I smiled back and said, "Nothing. Nothing at all."

With Jackson's arrival I could tell I was going to be a third wheel, so when Ella hung up the phone I said, "All that sitting today made me really tired. I think I'll just head on home. I'll take a rain check on that drink if that's okay with you."

Ella looked first at me, then at Jackson. "Where'd you come from?" she said to Jackson. "I haven't seen you since—"

"Leave him alone," I said, smiling again. "We just went all through that territory. This man just brought you flowers. Take them, give him a kiss, and then give him my drink. He looks like he needs it more than I do."

"You're a peach," Jackson said to me. "If Ella kicks me out, I think I'll come over to your place. Would that be okay with you?"

"Hold your horses, Buddy," Ella said, hurrying over and planting a hard kiss right on his lips.

"Never mind, Olivia," he said. "I'll be staying here."

"And I think I'll be leaving now," I said. "Ella Jane, I'll see you tomorrow. Want to go together again?"

They kissed again, completely oblivious to me. I didn't wait for an answer to my question. I locked the door behind me as I left.

Truth be told, I was dog tired. When I got home, I took a nice, long nap, had a light supper, listened to the radio for an hour or so, and then went to bed about ten o'clock.

I was tired. And scared. I still wasn't on the official witness list, but that didn't mean I couldn't still be added. I couldn't get rid of that thought as I tossed and turned. I also kept thinking about what I had asked Ella, about whether she thought she could lie under oath. I still didn't know if I could—still didn't know if I would have to. And that possibility was still very much out there.

* * *

Morning came way too early.

I had forgotten to set my alarm, so I was up almost forty-five minutes later than I had intended. I quickly dressed, gulped down a cup of reheated coffee, and was just putting on my hat when Ella knocked on the front door.

"My car's out front," she said. "We're driving today. If that parade of cars starts up again this afternoon, we're going to be a part of it."

I just shook my head, grabbed her hand, and without a word led her down the sidewalk to the car.

When we entered the courtroom, we were much earlier than we had been the day before. We could have found seats practically anywhere we wanted, but we returned to our places from the day before. Looking around the room, it seemed to me that most people had also done the same thing. It was just like in church, where people always sat in "their" seats. Only this wasn't church. Far from it.

About ten minutes later the room had filled up with people and sound. The bailiff announced Judge Koerner, and we all stood while he made his way to his chair. I looked around the room, and while I couldn't exactly put my finger on it, something was different today. I finally decided it was the atmosphere. At the end of the previous day, the mood in the room was intense, angry. Today, however, the mood seemed to be reflecting the uncertainty, the nervousness in the room. No one on either side knew what Mr. Vaughn was going to do today—or how he would be doing it. Would he fight, or would he run? Or would he work for a draw? He had the reputation as a fighter, so he should have been given the benefit of the doubt, but some of his moves—or lack of moves—from the day before were still fresh in our minds.

However, it didn't take long to learn what his strategy would be on this day.

He was going to attack.

Quiet clapping and cheers spread through the left side of the room when he stood and said, "Your Honor, I'd now like to call my first witness, Mr. James T. Bush."

The bailiff called James forward and, after the identification and swearing in, he took his seat. Mr. Vaughn didn't waste any time setting the tone.

"Mr. Bush, would you please state your occupation for the record."

"Yes, sir, I'm a real estate broker. I have been for almost fifteen years."

James appeared calm, collected, almost too relaxed.

"Mr. Bush, I'm going to ask you a very pointed question, because I know Mr. Seegers' would most certainly ask it, and I'd like to get this on the record right now. Did you help Mr. J. D. Shelley with the purchase of his home at 4600 Labadie Avenue?"

"Yes, Sir, I did."

"Why did you do that, Mr. Bush? Why did you get involved in this transaction?"

"That's an easy question to answer," James replied, leaning forward in his chair.

Mr. Vaughn then said, "Please, go ahead and tell us why."

"As I said, I'm a real estate broker. I buy and sell all types of property, both commercial and residential. And, like Mr. Anderson, I'm also a member of a real estate association. Only mine has a different purpose. My association is a small group of Negro realtors who work to find adequate housing for Negroes in St. Louis and its surrounding areas."

"Is finding adequate housing a problem these days?" Mr. Vaughn asked, evenly.

"More than most people understand. I'll give you some facts and some examples. Before the war, the Negro population in St. Louis was just over a hundred thousand. When the war started, several thousand more came here to work in the defense plants. After the war, many liked it here and decided to stay. And by the way, J. D. Shelley worked in one of those plants. Many don't know that. Anyway, after the war the Negro population ballooned to over one hundred and sixteen thousand."

"A hundred and sixteen thousand?" Mr. Vaughn interrupted. "Are you sure of those numbers?"

"Yes, sir, I am. One hundred and sixteen thousand. We had a serious housing shortage before the war, so you can imagine what has now happened. Most of those who remained in St. Louis have been forced to live in one small area of the city, the area east of Grand Boulevard, toward the city proper, and in the area known as the Ville. To put it bluntly, these individuals are not just crowded, they're trapped."

"Trapped?" Mr. Vaughn asked. "Sir, what do you mean by that?"

"I receive well over fifty requests for housing from our Negro citizens every month. These requests are from both those wanting to rent and those wanting to purchase their own homes. Right now, I'm able to help about one or two of these families a month who want to purchase homes—and not all that many more who want to rent. If you do the math, you'll see the others aren't just crowded. They are truly trapped, in every sense of that word. There just isn't enough available housing."

"Your Honor," Mr. Seegers interrupted. "I'm sure this is all very interesting information, but I don't see the relevance to the case at hand. Everyone knows there is a shortage of housing all across the city since the close of the war. That shortage is there for people of all races, not just the Negroes. I'm afraid I'm going to have to object that this whole testimony is irrelevant and immaterial."

"Irrelevant and immaterial?" Mr. Vaughn shouted. "You've got to be kidding, right?"

Then, turning to Judge Koerner, he continued, "Your Honor, I think it is important, for the record, to show the full context in which these so-called covenants reside, not just from a legal standpoint, but also from a moral one. I'd like your permission to continue with this."

The Judge studied Mr. Vaughn's face, then looked briefly at Mr. Seegers. "I think I'll allow this, Mr. Seegers. In my judgment, I don't think it is any different from you presenting information about the Marcus Avenue Improvement Association. I'll allow it as foundation. Mr. Vaughn, please continue."

"Thank you, Your Honor. Now, Mr. Bush, one more

question. What happens to all those families who can't find adequate housing?"

"Right now, they live in apartments just like the one the Shelleys moved out of before they purchased the home on Labadie Avenue. God bless them all."

"Yes," Mr. Vaughn said, "God bless them all. I have no more questions for this witness at this time. I pass to you, Mr. Seegers."

Mr. Seegers was already on his feet by the time Mr. Vaughn had taken a step back toward his chair. "Now, Mr. Bush, you have testified you are a realtor. In good standing?"

"I beg your pardon," James replied. "I'm not sure what you mean."

"I mean, are you a member of the Real Estate Exchange or the larger St. Louis Board of Realtors?"

"No, sir, I am not."

"Why not, Mr. Bush?"

"I'm afraid you'd have to ask them," James replied, dryly. "Although I think we can guess why, can't we?"

Mr. Seegers spun around and said, angrily, sarcastically, "Everything is always because of color, isn't it?"

The right side of the room buzzed. Several people clapped, loudly.

"I object to that, Your Honor!" Mr. Vaughn stood up and shouted.

"And so do I, Mr. Vaughn. Sit down. Mr. Seegers, I'm not going to warn you again. Do you understand me?"

"Yes, Your Honor. I'm sorry. Please forgive me."

Then, turning again to James, he continued, "You've also testified you helped with the sale of the property at 4600 Labadie Avenue. Did you help the same way Mrs. Fitzgerald helped?"

"Your Honor!" Mr. Vaughn shouted again.

Before the judge could speak, Mr. Seegers said, "I withdraw the question. Now, Mr. Bush, I have one very important question for you, and I want to remind you that you are under oath: Was there a covenant or restriction on this property when it was sold to either Mrs. Fitzgerald or Mr. Shelley? Think carefully before you answer."

"I always think carefully," James responded, cooly. "Yes, I distinctly recall there was a covenant on the paperwork presented to Mr. Shelley."

A collective gasp erupted from both sides of the room. I felt like I was going to faint. Actually, I soon felt like I was going to throw up. Ella again squeezed my hand and said, "Hang on."

"Now we're getting somewhere," Mr. Seegers said, smiling broadly. "Please continue, Mr. Bush. Tell us about this covenant."

"I'd be glad to. It was a covenant that stated, very plainly, that no livestock could be kept on the property at 4600. I've got a copy of it here if you'd like to see it."

The left side of the room exploded in nervous laughter. The right side of the room was silent, grim.

"I'm aware of that covenant," Mr. Seegers said, seething. "I've seen the new deed. I'm talking about any type of covenant related to racial restrictions."

"Then I'm sorry," James continued. "I didn't see anything like that on the paperwork I presented to the Shelleys."

When I heard him say the word "I," my blood pressure went down incredibly. If he had slipped and said "we," I might have been the next person called to the stand. The thought made me shiver.

"One more time," Mr. Seegers began, "Were there any racially restrictive covenants in any of the paperwork related to either sale?"

James leaned back in his chair, looked up, and appeared to be studying the matter. Finally, he leaned forward and said, "Mrs. Fitzgerald was right. If I could see the original paperwork—but that has all been, as you said, 'misplaced'. I'm sorry about that. If you could produce it for me to examine, I'd be glad to give you my professional opinion. I know I'm not a member of the Real Estate Exchange, but I *can* read."

James was baiting Mr. Seegers, quite successfully. Mr. Seegers turned and shouted at James, "Why you little—"

He didn't finish his sentence. Judge Koerner was already banging his gavel. Mr. Seegers started to ask another question but suddenly stopped. Saying more to himself than to anyone else, he said, "Funny how those original papers just simply disappeared, isn't it?"

Judge Koerner asked, "Mr. Seegers, any more questions for this witness?"

"No, Your Honor. I don't think it would do any good. I'm finished with him. And thank goodness."

James grinned from ear to ear as he left the stand. As he made his way to the back of the courtroom, he spotted me and winked. I winked back.

I also leaned back and exhaled sharply. James had managed to get through the entire questioning without lying, which I didn't think would be possible. He did it by carefully avoiding pieces of the questions, and in doing so, he never once said anything specifically about the original paperwork. Instead, every time he responded, he had made sure he prefaced his comments by saying "On the paperwork presented to Mr. Shelley." In each of those instances, he was right—he was telling the truth. On *those* papers, there were no restrictions other than those having to do with livestock. That was the truth. As I turned and watched James take his seat, I realized just how much I had come to admire him.

After James stepped down, Mr. Seegers whole demeanor changed. Not being able to break James down had a dramatic visual effect on him. He started slouching when he stood, and his lisp grew more pronounced. His voice also started trailing off at the ends of his sentences. His heart just wasn't into the fight any longer. Mr. Vaughn brought in a long parade of witnesses, and Mr. Seegers objected to nearly all their testimony on one ground or another. However, even when he was objecting, his voice sounded mechanical, distant. He appeared like a fighter who knew he had already lost on points and was just waiting for the final bell to put him out of his misery.

After the lunch recess, Mr. Vaughn called Mr. Robert Watts to the stand.

"Mr. Watts," he began, "Please tell us where you live."

"I live at 4592 Labadie."

"Sir, who is the owner of that property?"

"I am."

"You are? Didn't you hear about the so-called racially restrictive covenants we've been talking about the last two days? And, Sir, you are a Negro, correct?"

Mr. Vaughn didn't give him a chance to answer the questions. He continued, "Mr. Watts, is there a racially restrictive covenant on the deed to your property?"

"No, Sir, there is not."

"You mean there isn't one that says that only Negroes can own the property at your address?"

Mr. Seegers should have objected to Mr. Vaughn's sarcasm, but he didn't. He just sat there, doodling on a piece of paper in front of him. Seeing Mr. Seegers' lack of interest, Mr. Vaughn went for the jugular.

"Mr. Watts, then if there isn't a covenant on your house, that must mean there isn't one covenant that covers the whole block, the whole area, there on Labadie, right?"

Mr. Seegers did object, but his voice was calm, seeming almost disinterested. He said, "Your Honor, Mr. Watts is not a real estate expert or an attorney, so he cannot say one way or the other whether there is a covenant covering that area."

"You have a point there, Mr. Seegers. Mr. Vaughn, would you like to rephrase your question?"

"Yes, thank you, Your Honor. Mr. Watts, let me put this another way. To the best of your knowledge, have you ever been approached by any member of the Marcus Avenue Improvement Association or any other group about adding a restrictive covenant to your property?"

"No, Sir, I have not."

"And, again, please repeat this for me. You said there is not a racially restrictive covenant on the deed to your property, is that correct?"

"Yes, Sir. That is correct."

"Then, Mr. Watts, you can say with confidence that not everyone living on this section of Labadie Avenue has a racially restrictive covenant on their property, correct?"

"Yes, that is correct."

Mr. Vaughn, looking dead serious, turned and faced Mr. Seegers. At the same time, he said, "That will be all, Mr. Watts. Thank you for your testimony. He's all yours, Mr. Seegers."

"No questions," Mr. Seegers said, weakly.

This time the buzz was on the right side of the room. Several people could be heard saying quietly, but emphatically—and imploringly, "Mr. Seegers! Mr. Seegers!" He did not acknowledge them. Instead, he continued doodling.

Mr. Vaughn then called to the stand, in order, Francie Cook, a member of the St. Louis Race Relations Committee; John Clark, Executive Director of the Urban League; and Toliver Brown, owner of one of the largest Negro real estate firms in the city. All presented stories of the overcrowding and unsanitary living conditions facing the vast majority of Negro citizens of St. Louis. Mr. Seegers halfheartedly objected that their testimony was irrelevant, mostly on the grounds that what they had to say had nothing to do directly with the property at 4600 Labadie. Mr. Seegers, obviously, could find no connection at all, and it was obvious many others saw no connection either, as indicated by the ever-increasing restlessness growing on the right side of the room.

On the left side of the room, however, their testimony could not be separated from the property on Labadie Avenue. I couldn't tell from Judge Koerner's face whether he was just being impartial, as he was sworn to be in all matters before him, or if he felt anything similar to what I was feeling in my heart, but he let all of their testimony stand.

Mr. Vaughn finally rose and said, "Your Honor, I have one more witness, Mrs. J. D. Shelley."

As she stepped forward, jeers and boos rang out from the right. Over toward the wall, some brave soul called out, "Go back to where you belong!" It appeared Judge Koerner didn't hear it, but the rest of us did, and we weren't going to let it go. The left side of the room immediately started clapping for Mrs. Shelley as she walked up the aisle and took her seat. The judge, not under-standing what was happening, admonished us again.

When the bailiff asked Mrs. Shelley if she would swear to tell the truth, she said, plainly, that she would not. The swear-ing-in process was the same from person to person, so most of us weren't really paying attention when she declined. The judge, however, heard her and asked why she was refusing.

"Because, Your Honor, my religious beliefs make it a sin to swear, so I'd rather not do it."

Both Mr. Vaughn and Mr. Seegers stood at the same time, unsure of what to say. Judge Koerner saw this and said to Mrs. Shelley, "I can respect your religious beliefs, Mrs. Shelley, but you are going to have to make us believe you are going to tell the truth. In lieu of swearing, would you promise to tell the truth, so help you?"

"Yes, Judge. I'll do that." She then took her seat.

Mr. Vaughn spoke gently and respectfully to her. "Mrs. Shelley, I'll try to make this as brief as I can. I'd like to ask you a few things if you don't mind."

He then went back to his table, filled a glass with water, and brought it to her. At the same time, he said, "Okay, Your Honor?"

Judge Koerner nodded his approval.

Mr. Vaughn then asked, "Mrs. Shelley, it seems like a heck of a lot of people don't want you to live at 4600 Labadie Avenue. So, tell me—Why do you want to live there with white people?"

Mrs. Shelley was nervous, slightly shaking as she first sipped from the glass of water before responding, "Mr. Vaughn, I don't want to live with white people."

Another gasp spread quietly around the room—on both sides of the aisle.

Mr. Vaughn then said, "I beg your pardon, Mrs. Shelley. What did you say? You don't want to live with white people?"

"That's right. In the eyes of our Lord, we're all his children. All of us. I think it's wrong to judge a person by his color. I was brought up to believe it was what's in here—in the heart—that matters most of all. So, when I say I don't want to live with white people, I mean I don't care what color they are. And I pray that some day, at least for the sake of my children, others will not notice the color of my skin first thing when they meet me. I don't know if it will happen on this earth, but I pray it becomes so."

There were a few shouts of "Amen!" from the left and more than a few icy stares from the right.

"Please continue, Mrs. Shelley. You were saying?"

"I was saying all I want at our new home is to give my children a safe and comfortable place to lay their heads at night. That's all. I'm not going to cause any trouble there. I'm not going to bother anybody. I just want my family to be together—to be safe and happy. You see, I've got five children, and I'm also raising my little sister. We're a large family. We needed the house on Labadie. We needed it bad. We couldn't live anymore in that tiny apartment on 9th Street. We just couldn't."

Mr. Vaughn walked close to her and said, "I'd take you for a neighbor, Mrs. Shelley. In a heartbeat."

Then turning to Mr. Seegers, he said, "I pass to you."

Mr. Seegers stood and walked slowly toward Mrs. Shelley. Before he could ask her a question, she burped loudly, so much so that she could be heard in the back of the room. Those on the left, myself included, laughed loudly. That wasn't the reaction on the right; that side of the room groaned in unison, as loud as the burp had been.

"I'm so sorry!" she exclaimed. "Oh, please forgive me! I'm sorry. Your Honor, my stomach is hurting me so bad, it just slipped out. I'm so, so sorry."

Judge Koerner was kind. "That's okay, Mrs. Shelley. Happens to the best of us at times. Would you like more water?"

"No, I'll be fine. Just give me a minute."

She then opened her purse and took out a small medicine bottle. Unscrewing the cap, she shook a pill into the palm of her hand, threw it into her mouth, and quickly gulped some of her water.

Mr. Seegers had been patient. He even offered to get her more water. She politely thanked him but said she didn't wish to have any more.

When she seemed more composed, Mr. Seegers said to her, his voice even, "Mrs. Shelley, I'm not going to make this long. I have just one or two questions. First, when you and your husband purchased the house, were you made aware of any covenants or restrictions on the property?"

"No, Sir, I was not. I didn't even know about the rule on livestock."

Her response produced a low laugh from Mr. Vaughn. Mr. Seegers turned to look at him but didn't say anything.

Mr. Seegers continued, "Then, Mrs. Shelley, you didn't know that Negroes were not supposed to purchase property on this street?"

"Objection, Your Honor," Mr. Vaughn said, standing.

"Sustained," was all Judge Koerner said in response.

Mr. Seegers then said, "I'll rephrase the question. Mrs. Shelley, were you aware of the fact a covenant existed that covered houses in the area?"

"No, Sir, I was not. We're just right across the street from the Ville. I just thought it wouldn't bother anybody. I had no idea we'd end up here, in court. I'm sorry this all happened and that so many people are obviously suffering. Before we bought the house, I saw so many children playing in the street there. They were white children and Negro children—and they were playing together. When I saw that, I knew it was a place I wanted my family to live. I also remember thinking at the time that—"

Her voice trailed off. She paused and looked down at the floor.

"Go ahead, Mrs. Shelley. What were you going to say?"

Mrs. Shelley took another drink from her glass, and continued, "I was thinking that children are pretty smart, that most don't yet see colors. Who makes them see colors, Mr. Seegers? Can you answer that for me? Who makes them see colors?"

Mr. Seegers didn't answer her. Instead, he said, "One more thing, Mrs. Shelley. Your husband, J.D., was given a subpoena to appear in this court. He isn't here. Where is he?"

Mrs. Shelley sat up straight in her chair and looked sternly at Mr. Seegers. "He didn't accept the paper. He never got it. Wouldn't matter because I doubt he would have come anyway. You can't take any more of his dignity away. They tried to lynch him in Mississippi before we came here. He was an hour away from the rope when he had to leave and come to St. Louis. Then, after we moved in on Labadie, he was hauled off to jail—all for trying to make things better for us. He didn't want any of this. He's a good man. A very good man. He just didn't want to have any part in this because he didn't want to have to fight for something that was already rightfully his. That may not make any sense to you, but you haven't had to live like we have. That's all I'm going to say. That's all."

Mr. Seegers next spoke slowly, apparently choosing his words carefully. "Mrs. Shelley, you seem like a very nice person. I have no doubt of that. However, I also think you've been given some very bad advice. You and your family don't belong on Labadie. You don't."

"Then where would we go, Mr. Seegers? You tell me that. Where would we go?"

Mr. Seegers didn't answer. He turned quickly, walked to his chair, and sat down. "That's all, Your Honor. I have no more questions."

There were rumblings from the right. It appeared many wanted their pound of flesh, and they weren't satisfied with what they had just seen. There were a few boos, but this time they were not directed at Mrs. Shelley.

This time they were directed at Mr. Seegers.

Judge Koerner then addressed both attorneys. "It's late, counselors. Let's call it a day. We'll convene tomorrow morning at nine for closing statements. That will be all for today. Court is adjourned."

He tapped his gavel twice on the bench, stood, and quickly walked out. As soon as he was gone, the same scenario as the day before played out. This time, instead of the initial charge to the middle aisle, both sides walked slowly to the outer aisles and headed out the doors there. There were no words exchanged, no glares or glances across the aisle. The room emptied without incident.

Once outside, I said to Ella, "What's Vaughn going to say tomorrow? It better be good. He had a fine day today, but he hasn't won anything yet. I think the judge can still be influenced. What do you think?"

Ella lit a cigarette. After inhaling deeply, she said, exhaling, "I don't know what he should say. What else can he say? I bet the judge has already made up his mind."

"You think he has?" I asked.

"I don't know, but did you see how fast he moved out of the room? Unless he had 'physical needs' like Mrs. Kraemer, he's already made up his mind. I'm sure of that. I just don't know which way his gavel will fall."

"I'm worried," I said. "I know what this could mean for all of us."

"I know, too, but there isn't anything either you or I can do about it right now."

After dropping her cigarette and stepping on it, she added, "I'm sorry about yesterday, about Jackson showing up. I still owe you payment on your rain check for that drink. How about it right now? I promise I'll throw Jackson on his ear if he shows up today. What do you say? Please?"

"I will," I said. "I don't want to be alone just now. Let's go park ourselves and not talk about this, okay? Let's just have a drink and try to relax. I need that."

"So do I," she said, gently. "So do I."

On the way home we noticed there was no stream of cars zooming through the Ville. No car horns were honking. No groups of people clustered on street corners. As a matter of fact, we saw very few people at all on the way home. It appeared everyone else in the Ville was feeling the same way we were.

"Looks like it's going to be a quiet night," Ella finally said.

"I sure hope so," I said. "With all my heart."

19

Summations

The next morning came too early.

I had spent most of the previous evening at Ella's house. We fully intended to have a few drinks and unwind, but when we got to Ella's, she remembered Jackson had taken all of her alcohol for a poker party he had gone to the week before. That was probably just as well. We were so tired and hungry we just wanted to collapse and rest. Ella cooked us breakfast for supper—eggs, toast, and bacon—and we washed it all down with steaming cups of the strongest coffee I had ever put into my mouth. I complained about the coffee, but Ella just laughed and said, "My mother always said if you can't stand your spoon up in it, it isn't fit to drink." I also complained about small brown chunks that kept floating to the top of the cup. "Egg shells," Ella said, matter-of-factly. "It isn't coffee without them in there. I thought everyone knew that." All I knew was I kept having to spit the chunks out between sips.

After our breakfast-supper, we went out to the porch swing and rocked back and forth for almost two hours. A few neighbors strolled past, but the greetings were short and almost too polite.

"What's going on?" Ella asked. "You'd think we were lepers or something."

"It isn't us," I said. "It has nothing to do with us. I think everyone is just scared. Scared of what could happen tomorrow."

I kicked my legs so that we rocked even higher and continued, "Have you forgotten already the emancipation party we had for you at my house? That was so special, so wonderful. But think of the hundreds—maybe thousands—of others who are waiting to have their own parties, and they can't have them because they can't find homes to buy. That's what people are thinking about tonight. If Mr. and Mrs. Shelley lose this case, guess what happens? It won't be long before there will be no more emancipation parties. We won't be able to have any because there won't be any more homes people can get. If that happens, heaven help us all."

Ella swung her legs and made us go even higher. "Tell me something, Liv. What will happen to the Shelleys if they lose?"

"I guess they'll be forced to move out of their home. They'll be put out."

"Well, if that happens, I'm taking them in here with me. I'm serious. I have room. I'll take them all in."

"Ella Jane, they have five children and a sister living with them. There's eight of them. You can't take them in here."

"Then you take half of them, and I'll keep the other half."

"We can't do that," I said, softly, dragging my feet to slow down the swing.

"And why not?" Ella asked, turning to face me.

"Because if we do, then the Marcus Avenue Improvement Association has really won, and not just a battle, but the whole war."

"Sometimes I don't understand you, Liv. Whatever are you talking about?"

"Don't you see? If the Shelleys lose and we take them in, it will be another way of saying to everyone that Negroes don't need or deserve normal homes—that it would be perfectly fine for us if we all just crowded and crammed ourselves together. That's what many people think we deserve anyway. No, I wouldn't take them in. Before I did that, I'd comb the city to find somewhere else they could live, on their own, until those ridiculous covenants can be ripped from the books."

"I know you're right," Ella said. "You're always right when it comes to things like this. But I can't stand the thought of them being thrown out of their home."

"Let's not lose hope yet," I said. "Tomorrow will be a big day. Bigger than any of us ever dreamed. Tomorrow will tell us so much. So much."

"You're right again, Liv. We'll just have to wait and see. But if that association wins—"

I knew what she was thinking. I was thinking the same thing.

By the looks on the faces of those walking by, so did we all.

* * *

The courtroom wasn't nearly as crowded as it had been on the previous days. We walked to what had become our seats and sat down. I immediately noticed there were whole rows empty on the right, and there were plenty of spaces in most rows on the left.

"Where is everybody?" Ella asked. "I thought this place would be packed to the rafters."

"I think what you are seeing," I said, "is what happens when fear settles in. And I'm talking about on both sides. Look over there. You could shoot a canon down that aisle and not hit anyone today and yesterday they were pressed in like sardines. Same can be said for over here. Notice that our entire church choir is absent today. They were all jammed into the second row before, and now none of them are here. Fear caused this. I can feel it, and I can smell it."

Ella looked at me like I was out of my mind. "You can *smell* it? Liv, you ok?"

"I'm trying to be serious," I said. "Notice what you don't smell today? Remember that heavy perfume we made fun of yesterday? It's gone. Remember how hot it was in here and the stuffy air we moaned about? That's gone, too. What's left? I'll tell you what: fear. Fear is left, and that's why the room smells like this."

"If you say so, Liv. All I smell is that man sitting over there. I swear, he stinks worse than Smoky Fulton!"

Ella pointed to Tommy Henderson, a member of our church and a heavy smoker. Tommy was never hard to find. He always reeked of cigars.

"Believe me," I said, "I'd rather smell Tommy than what's in this room right now. Tommy will be gone soon. He'll go outside to puff on a two-for-a-nickel cigar, and we'll be done with him. But the smell of fear, that's another thing."

I suddenly thought of my dreams, of the fear that was constantly just on the edge of my life. I closed my eyes and tried to think of something beautiful, something to distract me—anything. Ella put her arm around me and pulled me close, and I clung to her, burying my face in her shoulder.

We were all soon ordered to rise when Judge Koerner entered the room. He looked tired, as tired as we all probably looked to him. He sat down heavily and immediately said, "Counselors, are you ready for closing statements?"

Both replied they were.

"Good. Mr. Seegers, you may begin."

Mr. Seegers was no longer in his tan suit. Today, all but his shirt was black, even his shoes. He walked out to the center area before the Judge, turned and nodded to Mr. Vaughn, then began.

"I don't think I really need to make this long. This is all pretty simple to me. Everyone has tried to make this an issue of color. It isn't. It also isn't an issue of overcrowding or disease or safety, which others have tried to make it. It isn't. It may be all of these things to some people, and those people are probably not going to change their minds—ever. I'm not going to worry about them right now. I'm not even going to think about them right now because this isn't an issue of color or race. It really isn't. This is, plain and simple, an issue of law. Of the law!"

He paused here and moved closer to Mr. Vaughn's table. "Do you mind?" he said, picking up one of Mr. Vaughn's water glasses.

Mr. Vaughn said, "Help yourself. Here, I'll get that for you."

Mr. Vaughn picked up the water pitcher and poured the glass full. Mr. Seegers thanked him and then drank deeply. It didn't take a genius to tell he had asked for some of Mr. Vaughn's water on purpose: a Negro filling up a white man's water glass, for all to see. Was he thinking this would demonstrate racial harmony, that it would show everyone in court, symbolically, that Negroes and whites could work together? If this is what he was thinking, it didn't work. Another low rumble spread through the left side of the room. Mr. Seegers' efforts were as transparent to many as the water in that glass. This case truly might not have been about color to him, but it was to so many others.

He finally set down the water glass and continued, "Again, this truly is an issue of law. At the heart of our proceedings we have had the issue of covenants. Covenants are legal, and the enforcement of covenants is legal. They have been upheld time after time in court cases all across the land. Therefore, the covenant at hand, specifically in reference to limited ownership of property on Labadie Avenue, is legal and in force. The original covenant encompassing that area was first written in 1911. The homeowners belonging at that time to the Marcus Avenue Improvement Association all agreed to it. That's a fact. "

He paused again, walked back near Judge Koerner's bench, and continued, "Now, the Shelleys are good people. I believe that. They want what's best for their children. I don't blame them for that. As a matter of fact, I admire them for that. However, they are Negroes, and the covenant on Labadie is quite clear: They can't own property there. It's that simple. Really that simple. The Kraemers are also good people. I really believe that. All they want is to have their rights protected and upheld, and those rights are tied, inseparably, to the covenant on their own property and over the whole of Labadie Avenue. The covenant established in 1911 gives them the right to live in the type of neighborhood they want. And they want the covenant enforced. Again, that's their right."

Turning to Judge Koerner, he said, raising his voice slightly, "Your Honor, I ask the court to find for the Kraemers, to have the law protect their rights and privileges as citizens of this great city. Thank you, Your Honor. I have nothing else to say."

Judge Koerner then turned to Mr. Vaughn and used his

gavel to motion that he now had the floor. Mr. Vaughn picked up a stack of papers, walked to the central spot in front of the judge, and began.

"Thank you, Your Honor. Like Mr. Seegers, I don't think I need to be long-winded here, but there are a few things I feel need to be said. First of all, I take issue with Mr. Seegers' belief that this case is not about color. It insults my intelligence to hear that said out loud. Not about color? What if we were to turn the tables and have a covenant that said that whites could not live on Labadie Avenue? What do you think the reaction of the Kraemers would have been if this were turned around? Would that not be an issue of color? Of course it would. But I will admit, Your Honor, that this is not *just* about color. If it were, the Shelleys probably wouldn't stand a chance, wouldn't have gotten this far, because race relations in the country have a long way to climb. No, it isn't just about color. Where I do agree with Mr. Seegers is that this is an issue of law."

Mr. Vaughn paused here. He walked over to Mr. Seegers' table and picked up one of his water glasses. Mr. Seegers picked up his water pitcher and started to pour its contents into the glass, but Mr. Vaughn pulled the glass back. He then sat the glass back down on the table, smiled, and headed back to his original spot in front of the judge. Mr. Seegers sat down the pitcher and glared at Mr. Vaughn. The left side of the room was full of smiles. I saw no smiles on the right.

Mr. Vaughn continued, his voice rising, "Let's talk about that law. Restrictive covenants are not new. They have been around a long time. I wish they'd all just go away, but it looks like that isn't going to happen, at least not anytime soon. So, since we're stuck with them, and legally in some cases, let's examine this one under the microscope of the law, shall we? Let's see, the covenant on the Kraemer's deed says, and I quote, 'No people of Negro or Mongolian races may purchase or occupy property on said section of Labadie Avenue for a period of fifty years.' Okay, I'll buy that. They have a covenant. It is very specific. They want it enforced. Fine. Let them have it enforced under protection of law."

Mr. Vaughn paused long enough to let the gasps from the left and the low buzz from the right die down. He looked from one side of the room to the other, as if gauging their reactions before continuing.

"However, let it be enforced only for their own property, and not for anyone else on that street. Why? I'll tell you why. Let's go back to the law again."

He was on a roll now, pacing back and forth in front of the judge as he spoke. His voice became even more forceful, more powerful with each sentence.

"When a covenant is established, it must be signed by all residents of a specific area for it to be in effect for that *entire* area. The fact is, it doesn't matter how many people signed the covenant born by the Marcus Avenue Improvement Association back in 1911—whether that was one person, or fifty. The most important and salient fact here is that it is not on the property deeds of all parcels in this area, and it has not been signed by all current owners in this area. Your Honor, I have the figures right here. I can show that nine current property owners on Labadie have not signed the covenant and, more importantly, do not have the covenant attached to the deeds for their property. If that isn't enough, I have one more statistic for you. In checking the records, I see that two people on Labadie, both members of the Marcus Avenue Improvement Association, and who signed covenant documents, weren't even the rightful owners of the property for which they signed. They were just renting the property and had no ownership rights whatsoever. And one more statistic: Negroes have been living on Labadie since 1882 when Grace Boxley was deeded property there. Many have lived there for as long as twenty to thirty years. Now you tell me, if there have been Negroes living there for all that time, then how can it be said that *all* the owners in the area signed the covenant? Plain and simple, it is not true that *everyone* signed the covenant. And, therefore, because not all parties involved signed it, the covenant cannot be legal. That's the law. I repeat, for a covenant to be legal, every affected party must sign on. In this case, that has not been done, so we cannot blanket the whole of Labadie Avenue with a covenant that is specific only to specific parcels of land. Again, that's the spirit of the law."

Loud applause started at the rear of the left side of the room and moved its way forward. Judge Koerner used his gavel again, but this time he tapped it on the bench and waited for the applause to die down. He then asked, "Mr. Vaughn, are you finished?"

"One more thing, Your Honor, before I wrap this up. I'm not asking this for the Shelleys. I'm not asking this for myself. I'm asking this for the city of St. Louis—for all its residents, for both whites and Negroes alike. I'm asking you not just to follow the law, but to look deep within your own heart when you rule on this case. For all the citizens of St. Louis, I respectfully ask you to do just that. Thank you, Your Honor. Thank you."

The left side of the room applauded politely. The judge let it go without comment. The right side was silent as a tomb.

Judge Koerner then said, "Counselors, I have heard the testimony and have received numerous documents from both of you. It is now time for me to review the testimony and study the documents before rendering my decision. Because some of the documents are quite lengthy and contain maps and statistical features, this may take some time."

Here he paused and studied what appeared to be a calendar before continuing. "We'll tentatively set judgment for—let's see—nine a.m. this Friday. That's two days from now. That should be enough time."

Then, looking up, he asked, "Anything else, counselors?"

When neither spoke, he added, "Then we will stand adjourned until nine a.m. on Friday."

He slammed his gavel on the bench one last time, stood, and quickly left the room, so quickly that the bailiff didn't have time to tell us to stand. Those on the left stood anyway.

Those on the right did not.

The room emptied the same way it had the day before, those on each side entering the aisle closest to the wall on their side of the room.

As we started to leave, Ella looked at her watch and said, "I thought it would take longer today. It's still early. Want to walk to Woolworth's for lunch? I'll treat."

I thought of my last visit to Woolworth's, the day of our work at the bank. The day the waitress at Woolworth's received my one-cent tip—the day in so many ways all of this had started. Yes, Woolworth's would be a fitting location for lunch. For me, it would also bring the events closer to full circle, and I needed that.

"That would be grand," I said. "We can eat first, and then there's someone there I'd like to talk to. Oh, how I've been looking forward to talking to her. You simply have no idea."

Ella, confused, asked, "What are you talking about?"

"Just you wait and see," I said. "Just you wait."

I grabbed Ella's hand and practically pulled her out of the building. I couldn't wait to get to Woolworth's. I had a closing speech of my own to give.

And, if I did it well, the waitress would never forget it.

20
Verdict

The two days seemed like two years.

We tried everything we could think of to keep busy, but the hands of the clock moved slower than either of us could ever remember. Ella would say, "Liv, what time is it now?" I'd generally reply, "Oh, about fifteen minutes later than the last time you asked." Then, a few minutes later, I'd ask the time, and she'd respond, "Half past a donkey's ear." I had no idea what that meant, but we'd both giggle like little kids.

The slow passage of time offered plenty of opportunities to talk: about school, about travel, about fashion, about the neighborhood, about men—especially about men. It was becoming more and more clear that Ella and Jackson had sparks that were seldom found in relationships. I thought this was both a good— and a not-so-good thing. Good because Ella had actually softened somewhat from being around Jackson; not so good because there was so much mystery surrounding Jackson, and I worried more than a little about what Ella might be getting herself into. Still, I was happy for her, happy she was experiencing something other than the ugliness she left behind in Arkansas.

While we waited, even our talks about Jackson became a game. We'd be sitting at the table and playing cards, and I'd blurt out a question, like, "So, how does Jackson kiss?" Ella would always raise the back of her hand to her forehead and give some silly reply like, "Just like Cupid himself." Each time I asked a question, her response would grow more ridiculous. Late that first night, while we were relaxing and reading the afternoon paper, I blurted out, "So, how does Jackson drive a car?" Ella responded, "Like Curly of the Three Stooges." I'd pretend the answer was reasonable—and then we'd both burst out laughing.

I enjoyed the "boyfriend question game." That is, I enjoyed it until Ella turned the tables and asked me questions about Charles and Tubby. "My, my," she'd say. "I don't know how you can tell the players without a scorecard. Why, you've got a whole team of boyfriends, don't you? People are going to start talking about you—more than they do now! And by the way, what do you suppose your children would look like if you married that Tubby?"

I'd respond formally, seriously, to her questions, then we'd roll with laughter again.

Silly? Definitely. But we weren't just killing time. We were waiting for a court ruling that could change the very face of the landscape around us. We also discussed the various ramifications at length. On the one hand, if the decision went against the Shelleys, property in the Ville and the other sections of the city populated by Negroes would become even more valued—and desirable. On the other hand, if the Shelleys landed on the winning side and covenants started to be abolished, we decided many of our friends and neighbors would move out of the Ville to other parts of the city—just because they could. They'd finally have more housing choices, and maybe, just maybe, they'd find homes more appropriate for the number of children they had and for other family needs. I told Ella this discussion reminded me of a cafeteria downtown on Washington Street called Mrs. Huntington's. It was a whites-only restaurant. When we'd go by the front window there, we could see the long line of tables that held dozens of types of foods, all of which were choices for the patrons. I reminded Ella that one day when we passed by, she had said, "If I ever get to eat in there, I'm going to have some of that roast beef. That looks so good." I had said in response, "If I ever get to eat in there, I'm going to have a bite of everything they have!" Ella and I decided that, given more housing opportunities, many in the Ville would go out and take a look at everything available, in the same way we'd dine at Mrs. Huntington's if we ever got the chance. Therefore, many would find something they felt more appropriate for their needs and would move away. We decided if that happened, we'd be happy for them—but we'd also be sad for us that the tightly knit community we'd both come to know and love would find itself in a state of great change. We felt silly even to be worried about something like this, but, still, we couldn't get it out of our minds.

While we waited for Friday to come around, we also went through each other's closets—twice—to see if we could do any trading of clothes. Ella was much taller than I, but we had the same shoe size. She was also just about as fond of scarves as I was. We both had a love of earrings that bordered on an illness. Whenever either of us had a birthday or when anyone asked what present could be bought for us, we both always responded, "Earrings!" So like youngsters trading marbles or baseball cards or small toys, we spent the better part of the second day trading our wares. The going rate seemed to be two pair of earrings for one nice scarf—or two scarves for a pair of shoes, depending upon the condition of the heels—or a pair of shoes for four pairs of earrings. Actually, it got so confusing at times we fell into laughter and just started grabbing as much as we could before the other person caught on and demanded fair trade.

Late in the evening of the second night, as we sat in my living room and listened on my new Philco radio to a horrible violinist perform on the local *Ted Wilks Amateur Hour*, Ella suddenly got up, walked into the kitchen, and started sobbing. I immediately jumped up and ran to see what was wrong. When I entered the kitchen, Ella hugged me and said, "Liv, I don't know what to do." I held her close as the sobs grew louder.

"Shhhhhh," I said softly, patting her on the back, trying to comfort her. "What is all this? Tell me all about it. Please. I'll help any way I can."

"I'm so scared," she said, her whole body shaking against

mine. "I—I may have to leave here. I may have to—"

Her words came in short bursts, drowned in tears.

"Leave here?" I said. "Whatever are you talking about? Why would you want to leave? Is it Jackson?"

When she gained enough composure to continue, she said, avoiding my eyes, "No, it's not Jackson. That's not it at all. It's just that—I may not have any choice in the matter. I may *have* to leave."

"Why?" I asked again.

"I had a long distance call from one of my cousins the other night. The police—the police down in Blytheville may be coming up here to get me. They may take me back. If they do, I know I won't stand a chance. They don't care who killed my father. They just want somebody to hang so they can close their books. I've seen this time and again, especially when Negroes are involved. Justice? That's a laugh. If they come take me away, I'll never see the light of day again—and I can't let that happen. I can't."

"I won't let them hurt you," I said, stepping to the side so she could look into my eyes. "I promise you that. I'll get you the best lawyers. I'll stick by you. No matter what they try to do, I'll be there at every step to make sure you'd be alright. Don't you worry about that. Ever."

I hugged her again and smoothed her hair with my right hand. "Now, let's stop this crying. No need for it. They're not here yet. They may not even come at all. Even if they do, we'll be ready for them. So you dry your eyes. You hear me?"

She smiled and blew her nose one more time. After delicately folding her handkerchief, she said, "I know I can count on you. Hell, I've always known that, from the first time I met you. But I don't want to drag you into this. It could get ugly. Just knowing you are here is enough for me. That alone will help keep me going. I've said this before, but I'll say it again. Liv, I've never felt such a connection with anyone before. You've made my life so wonderful, so different from what I ran from down in Arkansas. You've shown me how beautiful life can be, and I'll always be grateful. And I'll always love you for it. Always."

My cheeks were now wet. Ella leaned forward and gently kissed me on the forehead. Then she hugged me and said, "After that first time we talked about it, you've never asked me again if I killed my father."

I put a finger to her lips. "And I never intend to ask again," I said. "Never."

We hugged each other tighter and cried together.

The volume on the radio suddenly shot way up as the horrible violinist finished his tune. We both stepped back, our eyes widened, and we burst out laughing.

The timing was perfect.

* * *

Friday morning dawned bright and cool, a refreshing change from the torrid Indian Summer we had been having. As a matter of fact, it was so cool I had to keep my robe tightly shut and tucked under my chin as I put on my makeup.

After a quick breakfast of a hard boiled egg and two pieces of toast smothered in grape preserves, I headed out the door to my garage. Ella and I had decided it was my turn to drive, plus her car was now in the shop, so I said I'd stop and pick her up on my way. The cool air must have also been bothering my old Ford because it barely started.

Ella was waiting, hands on hips, on the top step of her porch when I pulled up to the curb. "About time you showed up," she shouted. "You'd be late to a fire sale!"

"Just shut up and get in the car," I scolded, trying at the same time to hide my smile.

Ella was halfway down her sidewalk when she heard me, and she stopped short, stumbling and almost falling down.

"And another thing," I said, "who wears heels that high to a courthouse? Ladies of the night are the only ones I know of, and they do because they are under arrest. Those heels are part of their uniform, you know."

"Anything else, Sugar?" Ella said in her most insincere drawl. "I'm shocked you'll let little old me in that fancy car of yours. What is it, Sugar? Isn't this what they called a Model A? And that A stands for—"

"Stop right there. Don't you finish that sentence," I commanded. "Not if you want a ride today. At least my car runs, which is more than I can say for your fine vehicle."

Then, with all trace of the drawl gone, she said sternly, "Let's get a move on. We're going to be late, and I don't want anyone else to get our seats."

"Then let's go," I said. "Quit holding us up!"

She slapped me gently with her purse as I pulled away from the curb.

Just as it had been the first morning, the courtroom was nearly at standing-room-only capacity. Our seats were still there when we entered the room, but Ella had to ask the people next to us to squeeze together to get us some breathing room.

Mr. Vaughn was already seated at his table, but Mr. Seegers was nowhere to be seen. I looked around the room, and when I turned around, my eyes met Sergeant McDougald's. He smiled, nodded his head, and stuck out his tongue at me.

"Well, I never." I said to Ella. "That idiot cop just stuck out his tongue at me. I can't believe it!"

"Then you really won't believe this," she said, turning, catching Sergeant McDougald's gaze and, using her little fingers, pulled her mouth wide open and clicked her tongue back and forth. Then she stopped and blew him a kiss.

He was furious, to the point he stood up and started making his way toward us through the crowd. However, he had taken just a few steps when Mr. Seegers entered from the door right behind him. The Kraemers were with him. Mr. Seegers said something to Sergeant McDougald, and this broke the Sergeant's train of thought. The two men shook hands, and Sergeant McDougald shuffled back to his seat and sat down.

As soon as Mr. Seegers and the Kraemers reached the table

and took their seats, the bailiff walked to the door behind the bench, opened it, and said something to a guard standing right there. It couldn't have been more than a minute later Judge Koerner walked quickly into the room.

"All rise for the Honorable Judge Koerner," the bailiff shouted.

"Please be seated," he said to everyone when he had settled into his chair.

He didn't waste any time.

"Mr. Vaughn, Mr. Seegers, I'm now ready to pass judgment on this case. I'm first going to preface my ruling with a few remarks."

He paused, then said, "Mr. Vaughn…"

As soon as he said Mr. Vaughn's name, a collective, sorrowful moan spread through the left side of the room. Ella had told me on the way over a rumor was spreading through the Ville that the judgment in the case could be told instantly by seeing which lawyer was addressed first by the Judge. Supposedly, the first one addressed was on the losing end of the case. Judge Koerner appeared quite shocked by the moans and hit his gavel several times on his bench. When order was restored, he began again. Still, as I looked around us, I saw many faces already appeared full of sorrow.

"Let's try this again. Mr. Vaughn, in this matter before the court, you brought forth a number of witnesses who testified to the terrible living conditions and lack of housing options facing many Negroes in the city of St. Louis. If a person is a humanitarian, if a person has any feelings at all, he couldn't help but be moved by this information. I know conditions are poor, and I know something must be done about it. But, Mr. Vaughn, that information, I'm sorry to say, has no immediate, direct bearing on the issue at hand, which is, first and foremost, the legal occupancy of the property at 4600 Labadie Avenue."

Then, turning to Mr. Seegers, he said, "And Mr. Seegers, you provided information about an organization I previously did not know existed, the Marcus Avenue Improvement Association. You also presented a great amount of detail related to the work of that association and the history of real estate transactions in our city. That was all useful information for me as I studied the documents entered in evidence."

Judge Koerner then spread out some papers before him before continuing, "In making my ruling, I also considered the following. First, of all the documents brought before the court, not a single one of them listed lot numbers or legal property descriptions that would help the court determine the legal ownership of each parcel—to allow the matching of ownership with each parcel. In other words, from the material given to me, I can't tell who owns what on Labadie Avenue, especially at the time the suit was drawn."

He turned over a piece of paper and added, "Second, real estate covenants and restrictions are not in violation of the Constitution of Missouri. Therefore, a legal covenant can cover property in a designated area, if it is created properly. In this case, the intent of the covenant was to have all legal owners of property in the area sign said covenant. However, while this was the intent, this did not happen. It has been shown that Negro homeowners in the area did not sign the covenant. On top of that, there is no indication that the covenant in question was part of the deed to the property at 4600 Labadie Avenue, and there is certainly no evidence that any previous owner of said parcel signed such a covenant. Therefore, for such a covenant to be in force now in this area, it would have to be signed by all homeowners on the block. Until that is the case, the covenant cannot be enforced."

We all leaned forward, on both sides of the courtroom, anxiously waiting for the Judge's ruling. After turning over one last piece of paper, Judge Koerner continued.

"Therefore, my judgment is that the case brought before the court is without merit. I'm ruling in favor of the Shelleys."

At that exact moment, those on the left side of the room

stood and shouted. I couldn't tell what they were shouting. Everyone seemed to be saying something different. What was the same was the look on the faces, a look of sheer and utter joy. People hugged each other, stomped their feet, kissed their neighbors. Ella and I held hands and jumped up and down, screaming our delight. Our church choir was back today, and they immediately started singing "Praise Be to the Lord," the Reverend Danielson's favorite song of inspiration. Mr. Vaughn was mobbed by well-wishers, each hugging and trying to hold on to him. Judge Koerner let the celebration continue for only a minute. He then struck his gavel over and over until the voice of the bailiff could finally be heard.

We quieted down long enough to hear the Judge say one more thing.

"And I hereby order the Kraemers to pay court costs of seven hundred one dollars and one cent."

The room erupted, and not just the left side. Across the aisle, many were crying uncontrollably. Others were screaming at both Mr. Seegers and at Judge Koerner. Their words were also not clear, but their meanings sure were. Their world had just come tumbling down around them, and it would never be the same again.

I felt sorry for none of them.

Mr. Seegers sat hunched over his table, a rolled-up piece of paper still in his hand. Someone threw a large, wadded-up piece of paper that struck him on the back of the head. He didn't turn around.

Mr. and Mrs. Kraemer, still seated to Mr. Seegers' right, held each other close. Mrs. Kraemer's face was toward me, and our eyes met for an instant. The look in her eyes could only be described as one of terror.

"Let's get out of here," I said to Ella over the roar of jubilant voices.

"I'm with you. Let's try to get out of here."

We did our best to inch through the crowd—the left side

of the room had now filled the center aisle. We were stopped by total strangers who shook our hands and hugged us as we went by. When we were finally out the door, we both exhaled sharply.

"Ever see anything like that?" I asked Ella.

"No. And, apparently, neither have they." Ella then directed my attention to those from the right side of the room, all of whom were now quietly exiting, most with their heads held low, through the side door.

"They better get used to it," Ella said.

"I have the feeling they never will," I said.

"Now they have to," Ella added, pointing at Sergeant McDougald, who looked our direction but didn't acknowledge us. "Just look at him. Look at him!"

"I don't see anything," I said. "Nothing at all."

"You've got that right," Ella said, taking my hand. "That's nothing at all."

We hurriedly exited the building and ran to my car.

"We're going to join that parade today," Ella commanded.

"Wouldn't miss it," I replied. "Not for all the world."

When we were seated, Ella reached over and started honking the horn. Ours was soon followed by the blast of horns all across the parking lot.

"Beautiful music, isn't it?" she asked.

"Best I ever heard," I said. "The very best."

We pulled in behind a long stream of cars heading back toward the Ville.

We all honked the whole way home.

Home.

That word suddenly took on new meaning.

Our worlds would never be the same.

It was time.

Time long overdue.

For us all.

* * *

The celebration that unfolded almost immediately after we got back to the Ville was unlike anything I had ever experienced. The hub of the celebration, fittingly I thought, was Sumner High School. Tables from the cafeteria were brought out to the street, where they were set up on a long row that reached well down Cottage Avenue. Then, in a matter of just over an hour, all the restaurants in the Ville sent a steady stream of free food to be enjoyed by all who gathered there—chicken, chops, sandwiches, and a wide assortment of vegetables and baked goods. When word of free eats spread throughout the neighborhood, people swarmed in like ants. At one point, Cottage Avenue was so crowded the overflow had to fill plates and move to the athletic field to find a place to sit and eat.

The Sumner marching band also gathered and struck up one lively song after another: The Ink Spots' "To Each His Own," Count Basie's "Open the Door, Richard!," Hoagy Carmichael's "Huggin' and Chalkin'," Duke Ellington's "Don't Get Around Much Anymore." Then, after taking a short break, they started playing one of my favorite tunes, Nat King Cole's "I Love You for Sentimental Reasons." When they did, nearly everyone put down their plates and started singing the lyrics, loudly and passionately, their voices filling the night.

Away from Sumner, down the side streets of the Ville, families gathered at intersections and held impromptu picnics. As cars drove past, they urged those inside to stop and join them. Most of them did.

When night had fallen completely and stars began to appear, the event that brought everyone together, that punctuated the celebration, that highlighted the events of the day, unfolded in magnificence before us. From the steep hill behind Sumner, a steady stream of fireworks suddenly shot toward the sky. One rocket after another streaked upward and exploded, each one seeming more colorful than the last.

After one particularly colorful burst of green and red lit up the sky, I turned to Ella and said, "Take a good look. We'll probably never see anything like this again. Ever see anything so beautiful?"

"Never," she replied, moving closer and placing her arm around my shoulders. "Never."

When the fireworks stopped, a sudden quiet spread through the assembled crowd. For a moment, no one moved, no one spoke. Then someone started clapping. Others followed until we were all clapping. This was soon followed by a thunderous cheer, one of pure bliss and joy.

Ella and I cheered right along with them.

* * *

The jubilant celebration in the Ville continued all through the night. I sat in my chair by the window and watched revelers go by until my eyes grew heavy. I was emotionally drained from the days' events and finally decided to crawl into bed. When I pulled up the covers I closed my eyes and started drifting...

"Let me see your hands," Jimmy John said.

He pulled them near his face and pried open my fingers. "Do you have any more of my matches? Don't lie to me now."

I shook my head that I didn't.

Jimmy John said, "We can never talk about this. Never. You understand? You listen to me. You tell me you understand. Now!"

I couldn't speak. I tried to, but I couldn't. Jimmy John hugged me tight. As he did, the walls of the barn all caved in, one after the other. He turned me away so I couldn't see it any more, but I still felt the heat on my back.

"I had to start that fire," he said. "They killed my parents. They killed my brothers. I'm sorry you came along and saw me, sorry you saw this. You're little, and you might not understand now. I had to do it. I just had to."

"We'll wash off at the river," Jimmy John said. "We'll wash it all off."

I looked at my hands. Jimmy John looked at his.

Jimmy John said, "But, some things can never be washed all the way off. Never."

Tears fell from his cheeks, and I caught them in my hands.

"Let's go," he said. "And remember, you never saw me here tonight. And I never saw you. We weren't here. You can never forget that. Not as long as you live. If you ever tell, you'll end up in a fire just like that. You don't want that, do you? You don't want to burn up in a fire."

One last flame rose from the ashes and lit up Jimmy John's face.

My heart pounded all the way home.

21

Dreams

It was three thirty in the morning when, wringing wet, I bolted straight up in bed. I was still breathing hard, gasping for breath. When the curtains fluttered, allowing the streetlight to shine directly into my eyes, I thought I was still next to the barn, close to the flames. As I slowly realized I was in the safety of my own bed, I shivered, my shoulders shaking almost uncontrollably.

I threw back the covers and stood up. I felt I should do something, but I didn't know what. Still confused, I sat down and watched the shadows of tree limbs dancing on the wall close to the bedroom door. The cool breeze sweeping in through the window toppled the picture of Inman and me to the floor, glass shards scattering everywhere around me. The shards caught the streetlight, and dozens of tiny reflections suddenly shot up toward the ceiling. Then I felt myself falling back on the bed, and I just kept falling.

I woke again at five. This time, I got up and immediately walked toward my chair by the window. I had forgotten about the glass and stepped roughly onto one of the larger pieces, cutting the heel of my left foot. I reached down and pulled out the glass before continuing carefully ahead to the chair. It was still dark, the only light coming from the streetlight, which was now flickering. As I sat there, the fog in my thoughts lifted and the dream came back to me again.

For the first time in my life, it had an ending.

Suddenly, bits and pieces of my past, of my childhood, started fitting into place. I had lost almost all memory of my early life in Mississippi, before my parents moved north; what few memories I did have had grown more cloudy and distant with each passing year. As I grew older, my parents seldom spoke about that time, most often changing the subject entirely when I asked questions about it. I could now recall that Jimmy John was the older brother of my very best playmate, Marta. They lived with their grandparents because their parents and older brothers had perished when their house had been torched by night riders. Jimmy John and Marta escaped, barely, climbing down through a hole in their bedroom floor and running quickly into the nearby woods. The next morning, my father found them huddled there behind a large oak tree and took them to their grandparents. I also had a vague memory of Jimmy John and Marta staying for a short period of time with us after that while the burials took place. Then their grandparents came back to get them and take them home.

As I sat in my chair, the cool morning air rushing into my face, still more pieces came together. On Saturday afternoons I was allowed to go visit Marta at her grandparents' home. Jimmy John would walk me back home after supper. One night supper was later than usual because we had waited a long time for Jimmy John to get there. He never did show up, so we finally ate without him. When it was time for me to leave, I said I was old enough to walk by myself. I could remember it was already dark when I started out. About halfway along I saw a bright, orange light flickering off in the distance, up a nearby logging trail. I walked toward the light, and the closer I came to it, the more curious I became. I finally saw the barn, engulfed in flames. I remembered a hand clamping around my arm and pulling me behind a row of chinaberry trees. The hand was Jimmy John's.

All my life I had tried to remember why I was there—and why the angels were there. I could see them now, clearly. They were night riders. In my young eyes, their robes had made them seem like the pictures of angels in our church hymnals. The images of them running from window to window as they tried to get out of the barn had haunted me all my life.

Through the years, matches were in my hands in so many parts of the dream, but I realized now for the first time, I had not started that fire. Jimmy John had—to avenge his parents and brothers. His admonition that I'd "burn like the angels" if I every told anyone what had happened pushed the memories, the images, so deep I could not pull them back again.

Until now.

As I watched the sun slowly rising in the east, I felt a calm, a peacefulness I'd never experienced before.

I placed my face in my hands and cried the tears of freedom. I knew the dream would never return again.

*   *   *

I dressed quickly and went downstairs to fry up some eggs and bacon. Suddenly, I was starved. My thoughts were also still more than a little jumbled, but I already knew one thing for sure. A lifetime of uncertainty, of gut-wrenching guilt, had been washed away, and for the very first time, I felt a relief of spirit that I didn't think I'd ever be allowed to know. A heavy shadow had been lifted from me, and I was now sure each day ahead would be just a little more bright.

The image of the angels came to me again as the bacon grease sputtered and splattered in the skillet. I knew I'd probably never be able to forget what I had seen that night, but now at least, I understood why I had been there and what my actions had been. And, more importantly, I finally knew what they had not been. The events of that night should never have happened, for any reason. Jimmy John had been wrong to seek that revenge, but I now could feel what must have been in his heart. That, too, I could now understand.

I had shared bits and pieces of the dream with Ella from time to time, but I never told her that I felt I might have actually been part of something like that as a child. Still, the look on her face, when I talked about it, let me know she, too, must have had her doubts. After finishing my breakfast I decided to call Ella. I needed to tell someone about this, and I knew she would understand and keep it all locked in secrecy. I dialed her number but got no answer. I guessed she was probably in the tub at this early hour, so I decided to head over there and, for a change, pester *her* while *she* got ready for the day. I left the breakfast dishes to soak in the sink, put my favorite blue scarf around my shoulders, and headed out the door.

The walk to Ella's house soon filled my eyes with tears of joy and hope. It was hard to put a finger on, but something in the neighborhood was different. Very different. It might have been the remnants of the previous evening's celebration that I was strolling past and what they represented. It might have been the fact that even in the daylight all the porch lights were still burning bright, a symbol to all that the Shelleys had won and, therefore, we had all won. It might have been the friendly bantering of neighbors, an incredibly large number of which were already out mowing and watering lawns and getting rid of the last reminders of that horrible night a few weeks back. On this morning, the Ville was putting on its best face, one that had not been seen this clearly since the day World War II had ended. As I turned down Ella's street, an older gentleman I didn't recognize called out to me, "Keep your eyes up. It's a beautiful day!" I shouted back, "I will. It is. And you, too!" We waved to each other and smiled.

When I got to Ella's house, Jimmy was sitting in her porch swing, his head down. I startled him, and he jumped up when I asked, "What are you doing here? Where's Ella?"

"She's gone," he said, softly.

"Gone? Where to? Where could she be at this time of the morning?"

Jimmy didn't reply. He raised a hand and motioned for me to sit next to him in the swing.

"What's going on?" I asked, now concerned. Jimmy's eyes were red. He'd been crying.

His shoulders were hunched forward and he continued to

stare at the floor when he finally responded. "She's not coming back. Ever. I'm sorry I didn't tell you about this before. I knew about it, but she made me promise I wouldn't say anything until she was gone. She wanted it that way, and I—"

I jerked his arm hard so that he turned toward me. "What are you talking about? What do you mean she's not coming back? For how long?"

My heart was racing, and I felt sick at heart.

He wiped his left eye before adding, "She somehow made arrangements to pay the mortgage payment for six months so that my mom and I could move in here and not have to pay any rent. Here—this is also about the house. She left this for you."

He handed me a large envelope. I quickly opened it and saw she had prepared the paperwork to sell me the house for the sum of one dollar.

While I scanned through the papers, Jimmy continued, his voice even more quiet than before, "She also signed over her car to me. I tried to pay her something, but she wouldn't take it."

He stopped talking, his voice choked with emotion. He looked up at me and said, "Oh, Mrs. Perkins…"

I leaned over and hugged him tightly. Taking my handkerchief from my purse, I gently wiped his eyes and cheeks.

I felt my own tears welling up, but I was still too worried, too concerned, to cry. "Jimmy, I want you to tell me everything. Please. Take your time, but I want to hear it all. Tell me everything you can."

When his breathing slowed, he said, "She wouldn't tell me everything, but she said she had to leave now because of something in her past. I could tell she was in trouble—bad trouble—and I told her I'd help any way I could. She said the best way I could help would be to help her get ready to leave. I did everything she asked, and I kept my promise not to tell. I wanted to tell you. I really did. But she said if you found out, you'd also be in trouble. She was so serious about it I believed her. That's why I didn't say anything to you. I didn't want you in trouble, too."

Here he paused, wiped his eyes again, and continued, "She made me promise something else. She asked me to keep an eye on you and help keep you safe. I told her she didn't need to ask me to do that—that I'd do that anyway. She said she just wanted to make sure."

He reached into his back pocket and withdrew another envelope. "The last thing she said to me was she wanted me to give this to you after she was gone. I know I shouldn't have, but I opened it and read it. I was just so worried about her, I wanted to see if there was anything else I could do."

I took the envelope from his hand and removed the letter. It said,

My Dearest Liv,

I know you're going to be terribly mad at me, and for that I am truly sorry. I didn't want to tell you anything about this because I knew you'd try to stop me. And don't be mad at Jimmy. He was just following orders. After all, he's still on my probation, too. I have to go, and maybe someday you'll understand that I'm right. As I told you, a cousin called me and let me know they might be coming soon to take me back. I just found out they're coming for sure, and I decided I just couldn't go with them. Arkansas still hangs Negroes at the drop of a hat, and I don't have much faith in their justice system down there. Unlike you, I'm not much of a gambler. So, I'm going to try to take control of my own destiny. Jackson said he'll make an honest woman out of me, but I don't think he knows what he's getting himself in for. He may be still a little rough around the edges, but give me two months with him and I'll have him whipped into shape.

By the time you read this, we'll be far enough away that I doubt anyone will ever be able to find us. The only thing I'm really sad about is that I won't be able to come over

and bother you in the mornings anymore. How many times did I get you out of the tub? Actually, what I'm going to miss most is just being with you. You will always be so deep in my heart, Liv. I've never known anyone like you before, and I've never cared for anyone the way I do about you. Thank you for all you have done for me. Thank you for being you.

I'm not going to tell you where we're going so you don't have to lie when the police show up. Maybe sometime down the line I'll be able to drop you a note and let you know how we're doing. In the meantime, you take good care of yourself, you hear? And think about giving Tubby a real chance. That man really does love you. Just be happy, Liv. That's what I want more than anything.

With all my love,

Ella

P.S. Please burn this after you read it, if not for your sake, then for Jimmy's. I don't want them to find out he helped me.

I crumpled the letter in my hands, and the tears finally came. Jimmy moved closer and held me.

"What do we do now?" he asked, holding me even closer.

"I don't know," I finally said, pulling back from him enough to see his eyes. "I guess for now we pray for her."

I thought for a minute, then added, "And always keep her in our hearts. Always."

"I will," Jimmy said, turning away from me.

"And so will I," I said. "Forever."

* * *

I went home, sat on the couch, and just stared out the front window for what must have been over an hour. I was thinking about all that had taken place in the past couple of months: Ella's emancipation party, my trip to the Jewel Box, getting decoys, Sergeant McDougald, the attack on the Ville, helping J.D. purchase his home—and now, losing my best friend. Reverend Danielson had been right in a recent sermon: It isn't what one has in life, it truly is what one does that makes a difference, that makes life so worth living and so glorious. We had all done so much of late, for ourselves and for each other. And for that, we were all rich.

So rich.

As I sat there, I tried to be mad at Ella, but I just couldn't. Deep down, I knew she was right, but that still didn't make it any easier to accept. I thought about how much we had been through together and how much I was going to miss her. I actually laughed as I thought of something else—I didn't mind being one of the "Poison Sisters" as long as I had her to march beside me. What was I going to do now? Friendships like ours were like bolts of lightning, seldom striking twice in the same place. At the same time, I thought about how blessed I had been to have her in my life for as long as I did. I was just going to have to cling to the hope she'd somehow eventually be able to return. I had to hope for that.

I started for the kitchen when the phone rang. It was J.D.

"Olivia, how are you this morning? Did you make it through the celebration last night?"

"Wasn't that wonderful?" I said. "I've lived here a long time, and I've never seen anything like that before. Did you see all the food over at Sumner? And wasn't that fireworks display really something! You should be proud, J.D. This happened because of you, you know."

"That's why I'm calling. I didn't get a chance to see you at the courthouse after the ruling. I just want to thank you again for everything you've done for me, for my family. I know we never could have—"

His voice cut off. I could tell he was struggling.

"Just glad to help," I said. "And besides, I really didn't do all that much. We all made a pretty darn good team, didn't we?"

Finding his voice again, he replied, "Yes we did. A darn good one. I'll never be able to repay the kindness and support. Never."

"You don't ever need to try," I said. "We're the ones who should be repaying you. Do you really have any idea what this could mean for everyone? With a court ruling now under our belts, things have to change. They have to. Groups like the Marcus Avenue Improvement Association don't stand a chance anymore. They'll never be able to tell anyone where they can and can't live ever again. Just think of that. No, it's you we should be thanking. This took guts. I don't know too many people who would have even tried this. I want to thank you, from the bottom of my heart. Thank you—and bless you—J.D."

He paused for a minute before saying, "Stop it, Liv. You're being too kind. Really. I hope this also helps others. To be perfectly honest, I'm not going to be able to celebrate too much myself until I see what happens next. Last night Mr. Vaughn pulled me aside and said they'd be fools not to appeal. He's betting it will happen pretty fast, too."

"Don't you worry about that now. What will come, will come. What's important is we got farther up the road than anyone has ever been before, and I don't think anyone can make us go back. I'm usually right about these things."

"I hope so, Liv. I really do."

He cleared his throat and continued, "Ethel and I would like you to come over to *our* home—that sounds so wonderful—next Wednesday for supper. We'd be honored if you'd come. We're going to have you and James and Josie and Reverend Danielson over as a way of saying thank you to everyone. Please do come. It would mean a lot to us. And bring Ella with you."

"I wouldn't miss it for the world," I said. "Wild horses couldn't keep me away."

I thought about telling him that Ella wouldn't be able to make it, but I heard enough clicks on the line to know our conversation would be all over the neighborhood by the time we hung up. Instead, I added, "Tell Ethel I'll be calling to see what I can bring. Tell her I'd also be glad to bring a couple of cherry pies. I know Reverend Danielson would really like that."

"I'll pass it along," he said, "but you really don't have to bring anything but yourself. See you then. You take care of yourself."

"You, too," I said.

* * *

I had just drifted off into a deep sleep on the couch when someone started knocking insistently on the front door. My first thought was of Ella, but when the cobwebs started clearing, I knew it couldn't be her. I walked to the door, peeked through the curtains, and there was Tubby staring back at me.

I opened the door, and before I could ask what he was doing here, he said, "Geez, Liv—let me guess. You were taking a nap, right? I swear, you're going to sleep half your life away."

"Great," I said to myself. "Just what I need, another Ella ..."

"What?" he asked, stepping inside.

"Oh, nothing. Nothing at all. But I do have a question for you." Raising my voice, I playfully shouted at him, "Just what in blue blazes are you doing here? And during the day. I thought you musicians only came out at night, like vampires."

"I'm glad to see you, too," he said, pouting.

"Oh, come here," I said, pulling him close. Just shut up and kiss me a minute."

And he did—until I could barely breathe.

"Now, that's more like it," he said. "You may have even missed me a little, unless I miss my guess."

"You stop it, Tubby," I scolded him. "You know darn good and well I missed you, but heaven only knows why. You musicians are bad news. Everyone knows that. Well, apparently everyone except me. I keep opening the door when you show up, so I guess I'm getting what I deserve."

He smiled and said, "I'll tell you what you deserve. You

deserve an afternoon on the town. I've got the whole day and all of the night free. I say we go to a movie, go out to eat, take a nice walk—anything but listening to music. Other than that, your every wish is my command."

Tubby reached inside his jacket pocket and pulled out a small envelope. He removed what looked like tickets and handed them to me, saying, "And by the way, we might even want to take a look at this. That is, if we can make the time."

They were tickets to the just opened "Fall Flowers of Missouri" exhibition at the Missouri Botanical Gardens.

"Tubby!" I screamed, stomping my feet and accidentally catching one of his in the process. He winced as I continued, "How in the world did you get these? I heard the exhibition was sold out two hours after tickets went on sale."

"We musicians may be—how'd you put it?—bad news, but we also know a lot of people. I just lucked into these. That's all. I thought you might like to go to this, but if you're too busy today..."

"Too busy! Are you out of your mind? Just you wait here a minute. I have to get my camera. And check your watch—what time is it? The bus schedule is next to the phone. See if we have time to catch the next one or whether we'd be better off to take the streetcar. Let's don't waste any time. I want to be there before dark so I can see the blooms. I still can't believe you got tickets!"

I was headed upstairs to get my camera when it hit me. I stopped short and turned to face Tubby. "Look again at those tickets," I said. "Look near the top. What group does it say is hosting the exhibition?"

Tubby looked closely at them but just shrugged his shoulders. "I don't know what you mean. What am I supposed to be looking for?"

"Hand me the tickets," I said, stepping back down the stairs.

Instantly I saw what I had suspected. There, in a small banner an inch or so down from the top, were the words: "Exhibition sponsored by the Daughters of Dixie."

I stood there, shaking my head, until Tubby asked, "What is it? What's the matter?"

"Nothing, really. I just think we're probably going to surprise one heck of a lot of people when we show up."

"What do you mean? How so?"

I thought of the Hibiscus Show at the Jewel Box, of the warning I had been given by the ticket taker as I left there. I thought of the looks on the faces all around the room that night. I thought of the hoop skirts, the doorman in his ridiculous costume, the dark faces that served the refreshments. I had cried that night, but I didn't fully understand why at the time.

Now, after sitting in a courtroom for the better part of a week, I did. I saw it all now, more clearly than ever before.

Today was a new day, the beginning of a new world, one full of new hope and new dreams. The invisible fences were coming down, finally, and our lives would never be the same. There was still much to do, but now we didn't have to look constantly over our shoulders.

It was time for change long, long overdue. The future was now, and it opened up before us like so many beautiful flowers.

"Get your hat," I ordered. "It's time for us to go."

Tubby started to speak, but I put my finger to his lips. He quietly followed me outside.

We walked down the sidewalk, arm in arm, into our new world.

It felt so beautiful.

So incredibly beautiful.

Epilogue

As it turned out, the St. Louis Circuit Court ruling was just the end of round one of a three-round fight, a fight that would stretch out for nearly three years. It is argued by many that the initial ruling was one of the most important legal decisions in the history of America. It may have been just the first stage of battle, but without that battle, the larger war never could have been fought.

After that initial ruling, the jubilation felt by those in the Ville didn't last long. The Kraemers immediately appealed the decision to the Missouri Supreme Court. The Missouri Supreme Court overturned the ruling, stating that not all parties in a given area had to sign a restrictive covenant in order for the covenant to be considered valid. Therefore, they ruled the covenant for Labadie Avenue should be enforced. In addition, they ruled that covenants of this type did not violate either the Thirteenth or Fourteenth Amendment of the U.S. Constitution, stating that neither Amendment prohibited private groups from establishing restrictions governing their own homes and property.

The Shelleys, while dismayed and discouraged by this reversal, chose not to give up the fight. Again with the help of Mr. Vaughn, they decided to appeal to the United States Supreme Court. The timing was very much in their favor as a similar case, *McGhee vs. Sipes,* was also to come before the Court. (The McGhees had purchased a home in Detroit, Michigan, in a neighborhood where a restrictive covenant was in place; the Michigan Supreme Court had ruled against them.) The Supreme Court, however, decided the two cases had enough in common that they could be taken together. Therefore, while *Shelley vs. Kraemer* was considered to be the central case, the Court heard oral arguments for both. Several months later, in a landmark 6-0 decision handed down on May 3, 1948, the U.S. Supreme Court ruled that racially biased real estate covenants violated the Shelley's and the McGhee's rights under the Fourteenth Amendment of the United States Constitution, in that the covenant violated their right to equal protection under the law. Their ruling was based, in part, upon the following section of the Fourteenth Amendment:

> No State shall make or enforce any law which shall abridge the privileges or immunities of citizens of the United States; nor shall any State deprive any person of life, liberty, or property, without due process of law; nor deny to any person within its jurisdiction the equal protection of the laws.

In an odd twist, the Court also ruled that while restrictive covenants could, indeed, be created, they could not be enforced by state or federal courts, thus, essentially ending the practice. Their ruling had immediate and far-reaching effects. No longer would it be legal for people to be denied housing based upon issues of race. This would change the face of America forever.

For those in the Ville, the ruling turned out to be both a blessing and, in an ironic way, also something of a curse. Because the invisible fences had been knocked down, many in the Ville chose to leave the neighborhood *because they could*. Before the ruling, the Ville was, of necessity, a self-contained and self-sufficient community, with its own businesses, schools, and medical facilities. Once families started moving out, the atmosphere there changed almost immediately. In many ways, the community spirit, which had served as a common bond for all, slowly started to erode as a population shift became dramatic. After the United States Supreme Court ruling, in the period from 1948 through the late 1960s, the number of those living in the Ville dropped by almost forty percent. As the families moved out, many businesses followed. Even the main streetcar line down Easton Avenue, the Ville's most important link to the rest of the city of St. Louis, shut down, a victim of reduced use. Homer G. Phillips Hospital also closed its doors in 1979.

While a strong sense of pride still filled those who remained in the Ville, the neighborhood would never be the same again. Along with many other cities across the country, St. Louis began experiencing, in the early 1960s, a cycle of urban decay and, eventually, renewal. The Ville experienced these same pains, only more because of its declining population. Today, that original spirit in the Ville is returning, helping to make it a vital community, one experiencing a new dawn of growth and hope.

* * *

J.D. and Ethel Shelley settled into their new home at 4600 Labadie Avenue and enjoyed many years there while raising their family. In a great irony, to supplement their family income, they rented their second floor apartment to a Caucasian woman. To the end of his life, J.D. was so proud of what he had accomplished. He was a loving husband, father, and a kind and considerate neighbor to all around him. He passed away on March 2, 1997, at the age of 91.

In April of 1988, the home at 4600 Labadie Avenue was added to the *National Register of Historic Places.* Then, on October 23, 1990, the United States Department of the Interior designated the home a National Historic Landmark. Today, a handsome marker rests prominently on the front lawn, a reminder to all who pass by that one of the most important battles in American history was fought right there.

* * *

James T. Bush lived a long and fruitful life, one devoted in so many ways to bettering the lives of others. Through the years, he was able to expand his real estate business and helped hundreds of families find and purchase their dream homes—in every section of the city. Almost immediately after the reversal of the Circuit Court decision by the Missouri Supreme Court, Mr. Bush founded the Real Estate Brokers Association of St. Louis, a network of Negro real estate dealers who fought to end racial discrimination in housing practices in St. Louis. They also helped finance the Shelleys' appeal to the U.S. Supreme Court.

* * *

Reverend Danielson remained always a source of inspiration and hope for those in the Ville. In August of 1963 he organized a "Freedom Bus" trip from St. Louis to Washington, D.C., so that members of his congregation could hear Dr. Martin Luther King, Jr., deliver his "I Have A Dream" speech and participate in the now famous "March on Washington." On the way back to St. Louis, he fell asleep in the back of the bus and never woke up. His heart, which had been so full of love and kindness, had finally given out. His legacy lives on in the Ville to this day.

* * *

George Vaughn, already highly respected for his legal expertise before the court ruling, soon thereafter was in such demand as an inspirational speaker that he could barely keep up with the invitations. He also expanded his legal practice and tirelessly continued to fight for equality and justice. His legal briefs related to *Shelley v Kraemer* also became so popular he eventually had them printed and started selling them, with all proceeds going into a fund he established to help those fighting discrimination. He died on August 17, 1949, a little over a year after the landmark Supreme Court ruling. At the time of his death, he was in his favorite chair and reading through his original notes related to the case.

* * *

Mrs. Josephine Fitzgerald's role in the purchase of the Shelley home was not popular with many. After her court appearance, she received threats of all manner and variety. No one knows for sure, but it was rumored that rather than live her life in fear of reprisals, she moved away from St. Louis and changed her name, never to be heard from again.

* * *

Sergeant McDougald, while off duty on September 13, 1949, was found face down in a pool of his own blood at the foot of the Eads Bridge. He had been shot twice in the back of the head. A full investigation ensued, but his killer was never found.

* * *

Charles Fredericks remained one of Olivia's dearest friends and confidants the remainder of his life. He moved to Birmingham, Alabama, in 1960 to work in a cousin's insurance company. Two years later, he was attending church one Sunday morning when a bomb was thrown into a side window, killing Charles and three young children. Members of a white supremacist group were later questioned by the local authorities, but no arrests were ever made.

* * *

Jimmy Reynolds, a year after his graduation from Sumner, moved to Cleveland, Ohio, where he attended a technical school for Negroes. He eventually owned and operated a chain of handyman service companies there. He married, had four children, and became a pillar of the African-American community of greater Cleveland. He never forgot he was still on "probation" and helped those less fortunate every chance he could.

* * *

Eddie "Tubby" Thompson proposed to Olivia, by her count, sixty-seven times throughout the years. He continued traveling and playing in bands until arthritis slowed his fingers. He then opened a music store in the North Grand area of St. Louis. Although he and Olivia were nearly inseparable, they never married. At his funeral service in 1973, Olivia told those gathered, "Tubby was the kindest and most gentle soul I've ever known. He was my friend, and I loved him dearly." In his will, he left his entire estate to Olivia. Attached to the will was a small greeting card addressed to her. When she opened it, she found this message: "Will you marry me? Love, Tubby." If nothing else, he was persistent.

*   *   *

Ella and Jackson disappeared the day after the circuit court ruling and were never heard from again. At least that's what Olivia said every time the police questioned her about Ella, which they continued to do quite often through the years. However, Olivia did receive a card every Valentine's Day, each year from a different city, from a Mr. and Mrs. Arkin Saw. The handwriting was unmistakable. The cards continued until 1967. Olivia received a small box that year from Arkin. He wanted Olivia to know his wife had recently succumbed to cancer. Her last request had been that her favorite scarf, one that Olivia had given to her so many years before, would be returned to her. Pinned to the scarf was a note that read, "For the other love of my life."

The investigation into Ella's father's death remains officially open.

*   *   *

And finally, Olivia Perkins continued to teach at Charles Sumner High School in a career that spanned nearly forty years. Her dedication to her students helped build a climate there that filled each one with a pride and dignity that carried them into their adult lives. Some of the students at Sumner were Tina

Turner, Chuck Berry, Arthur Ashe, and her favorite student of all, Richard "Dick" Gregory, who became one of the most important voices of the Civil Rights Movement of the 1960s and beyond. When Olivia retired, she was honored by being added to Sumner's centennial list of "The 100 Most Outstanding Teachers" in the school's history.

Olivia never remarried. Her heart remained devoted to Inman. On July 6, 1995, she passed peacefully. She is buried in Oak Grove Cemetery in north St. Louis, just a few miles from her beloved Ville. Just a week before she died, Olivia had reread every letter Inman had written to her during WWII. On the day she died, she had just framed a picture of the two of them sitting on the steps of the Soldier's Memorial in downtown St. Louis. When she was found that day, the picture was still in her hands.

So many friends and former students attended her memorial service it had to be held twice so that all had an opportunity to pay their respects.

In the lives of the students and all others whose lives she touched, her legacy will never die.

Acknowledgments

This book could not have been written without the generous assistance of many wonderful people:

Sharon A. Dolan, Records Center Supervisor/Archivist for the St. Louis Public Schools, provided detailed educational records, especially those related to Charles Sumner High School and other St. Louis city schools.

Jason Stratman of the Missouri History Museum Library and Research Center offered invaluable help in sourcing historical information and court documents.

Stan Lyle, Research Librarian, University of Northern Iowa, provided information related to St. Louis history of the era.

Douglas and Judy Hartley assisted me with St. Louis geographical information of the period.

For providing photographs and background information related to the family histories involved in the story, I would like to thank Mrs. Paula Taylor (Inman Perkins' niece); Chloe Williams (cousin to Olivia); Alvan Williams (cousin to Olivia); Mrs. Debra Davis (J. D. Shelley's granddaughter); Mrs. Chatlee Williams (J. D. Shelley's daughter); Margaret Bush Wilson (James T. Bush's daughter); Mrs. Roslyn Moore Blair (cousin to Olivia); Mrs. Francis Stiph Washington (Olivia's college friend and classmate at Lincoln University, Jefferson City, Missouri); Azim Aziz, St. Louis Argus Newspaper; and Grant Hartley, genealogy consultant.

Dana Peiffer, Technology Support Specialist, University of Northern Iowa, provided the full range of technology support services.

I'd also like to thank Amanda Miller and Zachary Umsted for photo technology and restoration, and T. Matteson Toenjes and Elizabeth Dvorak for help with manuscript proofing, editing, and preparation.

Crystal Copeland, and my parents, Jack and Donna Copeland, were always there for me with support, love, and inspiration.

I'd also like to give a special thanks and recognition to my wife and partner, Linda Copeland.

I'd also like to recognize and pay tribute to "Shelley v. Kraemer: A Celebration," a special monograph prepared from 1986-1988 by the St. Louis Chapter of Girl Friends, Inc. to commemorate the fortieth anniversary of the U.S. Supreme Court ruling. This monograph, created under the direction of then Chair Margaret Bush Wilson, has been a source of inspiration to so many, including this author, through the years.

And finally, I'd like to thank Rosemary Yokoi of Paragon House for believing in this project, this second path on this incredible journey.

Thank you, and bless you all!

Pictures

Olivia on the front steps of Charles Sumner High School.
(Copeland collection)

Olivia and Inman on the steps of Soldiers Memorial in St. Louis.
(Photo Courtesy of Paula Perkins-Taylor)

Olivia and the Sumner Photography Club, 1941.
(Photo Courtesy of the St. Louis Public Schools Archives)

Charles Sumner High School Faculty, 1943.
Olivia is on the third row up from bottom, far left.
(Photo Courtesy of the St. Louis Public Schools Archives)

Sergeant Inman Perkins.
(*Photo Courtesy of Paula Perkins-Taylor*)

The Ville entrance marker,
corner of Easton Avenue (Martin Luther King Dr.) and Sarah Street.
(Copeland collection)

Charles Sumner High School.
(Photo Courtesy of the St. Louis Public Schools Archives)

A Victory For Democracy

Atty. George L. Vaughn, chief ents, Mr. and Mrs. J. D. Shelley, counselor in the Shelley restric- exchange congratulations over tive covenant case, and his cli- their victory.

Left to right: Mr. George Vaughn, Ethel Shelley, J. D. Shelley.
Photo taken the day of the U.S. Supreme Court ruling, May 3, 1948.
(Photo Courtesy of the St. Louis Argus*)*

Mr. J. D. Shelley.
(Photo Courtesy of Debra Davis)

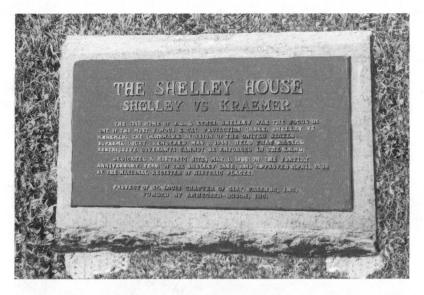

"The Shelley House" was placed on the National Register of Historic Places in 1990. This is the marker. *(Douglas Hartley photo)*

J. D. Shelley at the National Register of Historic Places dedication ceremony. *(Photo Courtesy of Debra Davis)*

Mr. James T. Bush.
(Photo Courtesy of Margaret Bush Wilson)

THIS IS A CALL TO ACTION
THE MENACE--RESTRICTIVE COVENANTS!!
Present and future home ownership and residential expansion threatened

THE NEED FOR ADEQUATE AND DECENT HOUSING is the gravest problem facing all groups in every city in America.   There are not enough places in which to live. Yet, in spite of this grave situation, which is a menace to good citizenship and health, there are a few, a very few Americans, who persist in using un-American methods to deny 13,-000,000 citizens of our country the right to decent housing.

ONE OF THE METHODS USED IS THE ADOPTION OF RESTRICTIVE COVENANTS, neighborhood agreements among property owners which provide that their property shall not be sold to, or occupied by, persons not of the Caucasian race. The real object, of course, is to prevent Negroes from buying or renting property in the neighborhood covered by the agreement. After careful survey, we find that these agreements would never be entered into except for the activity of a few individuals in these neighborhoods who are steeped in racial prejudice or have selfish motives behind their activities. These individuals make a house to house canvass, spread vicious propaganda and picture a calamity that will occur if Negroes move into the block. They have even threatened violence to those who hesitated to sign the agreements.

RECENTLY, THE SUPREME COURT OF MISSOURI, in the case of KRAEMER vs. SHELLEY, ruled that restriction agreements based on race were valid, reversing the decision of our local Circuit Court to the contrary. If this ruling is allowed to stand it means the Shelleys will lose their home and with it their life savings. More serious than the Shelley's loss is the fact that FURTHER EXPANSION OF NEGRO NEIGHBORHOODS IS AT AN END!

THE REAL ESTATE BROKERS ASSOCIATION OF ST. LOUIS REGARDS THE COURT'S DECISION AS A CHALLENGE NOT ONLY TO THE NEGRO BUT TO ALL PEOPLE WHO BELIEVE IN TRUE CHRISTIAN AND DEMOCRATIC IDEALS. WE, THEREFORE, ACCEPT THE CHALLENGE AND ARE APPEALING THE CASE TO THE UNITED STATES SUPREME COURT. WE HAVE 100 CITIZENS SUPPORTING OUR MOVEMENT AND WE WELCOME SUPPORT AND SUGGESTIONS FROM ANYONE WHO BELIEVES WE ARE JUSTIFIED IN THE ACTION THAT WE HAVE UNDERTAKEN.

REAL ESTATE BROKERS ASSOCIATION OF ST. LOUIS

Real Estate Brokers Assn., 3912 Finney Ave: I believe the validity of restrictive covenants based on race should be settled for all times and am enclosing $———to be used to help pay the costs of an appeal to the United States Supreme Court.

Name_____

Address_____

"Restrictive Covenants Flier" printed after the Missouri Supreme Court overturned the initial ruling. Funds gathered through these campaigns were used to help finance the appeal to the U.S. Supreme Court.
(Photo Courtesy of the St. Louis Argus)

Judicial Circuit Court of St. Louis,
where the initial court battle took place.
(Copeland collection)

Part I

Mick

My luve is like a red, red rose. . . .

Robert Burns, stanza 1 of "A Red, Red Rose"
JOHNSON'S MUSICAL MUSEUM, 1796

Chapter 1

The most highborn lady Mick had ever been with — the wife of a sitting member of the House of Lords, as it turned out — told him that the French had a name for what she felt for him, a name that put words to her wanting his "lion-hearted virility" — he liked the phrase and remembered it.

" 'A yearning for the mud,' " she told him. "That's what the French call it."

Mud. He hadn't much liked the comparison. Still, from the moment he heard it, he hadn't doubted the phrase's clear sight or wisdom. Posh ladies who took a fancy to him had to make some sort of excuse to themselves, and this was as good as any. He was a novelty at best. At worst, a bit of mud to play in for ladies whose lives'd been scrubbed clean of good, earthy fun.

He lay now on the floor, dirtier than usual, truth be told, his palms and belly flat to the floorboards of a dress shop in Kensington. Three silky ladies stood over him — they stood very far over him, one on a chair seat, one on a countertop, and one on the last inch or so left of a shelf taken up mostly by bolts of fabric. These three

9

watched him, breathless, while Mick, his ear turned to the floor, listened.

He was a big man — he took up a long length of floor. He had wide shoulders, a hard, muscular chest, long, weighty limbs. Handsomely made, he didn't doubt it. Vigorous. Five minutes ago, he'd been out back, using this very fact to flirt with the seamstress's assistant. He'd made her laugh, his first triumph, and had just stepped a little closer, when the seamstress and her customer inside the shop had begun screaming, "Mouse! Mouse!" The only man nearby, he'd been pressed into service.

Now, when scared, mice had a nasty habit. They'd run up anything, including a person's leg. The nightmare for a lady was that a mouse'd scamper into the understructure of her dress — her petticoats, dress-improvers, and half-hoops — where it could run around indefinitely in a maze of horsehair and steel wires.

Hoping to avoid a mouse circus inside their dresses, the seamstress, a patron, and now her assistant had climbed as high as they could in the room, pressing their dresses to themselves, frightened out of their wits. Mick could've told them it wouldn't do them no good. Mice could get onto tables and chairs easy. But he didn't mention it. He didn't want to frighten them more.

He lay quiet, scanning the floorboards, palms flat, elbows up, toes curled to support some of his weight, ready to spring up if a mouse came

into sight. Then he spied it, and it was sort of a letdown. A little thing, it was more scared than the ladies, shaking over in a corner at the base of a sewing machine in the shadow of a press-iron. Barely more than a baby. He could catch it in his hand. There were no others, no noise under the floor, no activity.

"Is there a nest?" whispered the seamstress, her voice hushed with worry. "Are there more?"

Now, right here, Mick should've said no and stood up. But he didn't. He got distracted.

He turned his head to use the other ear, to listen again and make sure. And there, through a doorway into a back room, under a painted screen, in a mirror he saw a pair of legs, a second customer. There were four women, not three. This one'd been trying on dresses, he guessed, when the commotion broke out. She was trapped in the dressing room. In the mirror he could see she'd leaped on top of something, maybe a trunk. Anyway, with his position, her having moved up and out of the protection of the screen, and what with the angle of the mirror, he was looking right at a pair of devilish long legs. Bloody gorgeous, they were.

He lay there, caught in his own admiration. She was on her toes, dancing a little, nervous, the long muscles of her legs flexing beneath pink stockings with a hole at the knee. Long. Hell, *long* wasn't the word for these legs. They went for yards and yards — she had to be a tall one, this one. And shapely — her legs were poetry. Bal-

11

ance, muscle, motion. They gave new meaning to *fine*.

Now, normally, Mick was a polite man. He would've protected a woman caught off guard by turning his head. Or at least he thought maybe he would've. But these were the damnedest legs. "Sh-h-h," he said in answer to the seamstress's fears.

In unison, the ladies above him drew in their breaths, trying to calm themselves, to allow him to hear any skittering or chewing or other nasty mouse sounds. One of them murmured, "This is so heroic of you, Mr. —" She was asking for a name.

"Tremore. Sh-h-h."

Oh, yes, heroic. The hero lay on his belly, getting his eyes as low as he could so as to stare across the floor into a mirror at the prettiest legs he'd yet seen in thirty years of living. If he'd been standing up, he'd've seen to maybe just above the ankles — the screen in front of her came within a foot of the ground. That alone would've been an eyeful, since her ankles were narrow, her foot pretty with a high arch and instep, the anklebone showing against the soft leather of her shoe.

But when he got his head just right, he could see in the mirror: from the toes of high-buttoned shoes up long, neat shins, plenty of curvy calf, past the knee-ribbons of silk knickers to halfway up willowy thighs that went forever. Dream legs.

In his dreams, Mick *did* see legs like these. He loved long legs on a woman. In his sleep he got to

12

put his mouth on them. It took a dream-eternity to get his tongue from the back of the knee, up the thigh, to the indentation under the buttocks. Strong legs. In his dreams they gripped him with athletic urgency. They could squeeze him till he was nearly unconscious with lust.

"Mr. Tremore, Mr. Tremore!" one of the ladies behind him called. "Over here! It's here."

No, it wasn't. The ladies were jumpy, imagining mice everywhere. They began to make noise, thinking the mouse active again. Little shrieks, ladylike huffs, nervous giggles as they shifted around on their perches.

Mick held up his finger. "Sh-h-h," he said again.

He hated to get up and take care of a mouse, when there were legs like these to look at. Legs and knickers, a blessed sight if ever there was one. Above him on the counter, though, the seamstress was gulping air so hard that, if he didn't do something, she was going to lose her tea biscuits.

Softly, Mick said, "Wait. I see him. Don't move."

Mouse time. He shoved against the floor, pushing up, getting a knee and toe under him, and sprang, quick and quiet. He went after the mouse from the side of the pressing iron, so when he scooted the iron a fraction, the mouse fled forward. With a sideways lunge, Mick snapped him up by the tail, then, straightening, dangled a mouse in front of him, out for inspection.

13

The seamstress shrieked. He thought she was going to faint. "Easy," he said.

The customer, nearest him, climbed down bravely from her chair. "O-o-oh," she breathed.

As they all clambered down, he stood a head or more taller than any of them. He looked down on three women who tittered and made a fuss now that the danger was past. Mick was "so brave." He was "so agile." "Lionhearted," one of them said, and he laughed. Then: "With such a deep, rich laugh."

He turned. Now, even when covered in floor grit, Mick was fairly used to sending a stir through the ladies. The younger ones were generally at a loss, but the older ones he had to watch out for.

The customer who liked his laugh came right up to him, looking at the mouse. She was decked out in a lot of velvet and beads, her thin face sort of lost under a big hat decorated with a large feather and a stuffed bird.

She stretched her arm out toward him, her gloved hand dropped at the wrist. "Lady Whitting," she said. "The Baroness of Whitting."

He stared at her hand. She expected him to kiss it, he guessed, but he didn't do that sort of thing, even when he wasn't holding a mouse. "Nice to meet you." He turned around. "Nell?" He looked for the seamstress's assistant. "You got something to put this fellow into?"

The baroness walked around him to put herself in his way again. Lowering her hand, folding

14

it into her other, she eyed him then smiled. "That was quite a feat, sir. The way you leaped and captured that mouse. Quite impressive."

Mick glanced at her, knowing she wasn't impressed with mice or heroism or anything very noble.

She said, "You should have a prize. A hero's prize."

He stopped. He was a workingman with a lot of family back home who counted on him, so a prize interested him, especially a monetary one.

The way her smile sort of softened when she got his attention, though, told him they weren't talking about money.

"I don't need nothing, duck," he said. "My pleasure to help you."

The other ladies were watching, keeping their distance. Mick turned away from the baroness, remembering his coat on the floor. As he bent to get it, he happened to glance into the back room. He caught a glimpse of a dress floating into the air. Purple. The most beautiful shade of purple. The dark color of lavender in August. Behind the screen, narrow sleeves raised overhead, long fingers wiggling their way out, up and into the open. The dress shushed loud enough that he heard its rustle as it dropped down, ending all hope of ever seeing again the finest legs he could imagine.

He straightened up, gently dusting his coat, then pushed back his hair — his hand came away with soot. He frowned down at his dirty palm. Oh, lovely, he thought, just lovely. This must

have happened when he looked up the flue for the mouse.

The baroness continued, "So what is the payment due a hero?"

"A jar for the mouse would be nice." He looked past her to the seamstress.

As if she wasn't listening, as if it had been her plan all along, the seamstress quickly reached under the counter and handed him a button tin, empty. He unscrewed the lid.

"How about these?" the baroness said. Beside him, she tapped her gloved finger on top of a glass case. A soft, dull click.

Mick dropped the mouse into the tin as he glanced over at what she pointed to. The case held a lot of intimate feminine things. Knickers and stockings and garters. He paused, staring at what was inside the case more from curiosity than anything else. There were some pretty things on the glass shelves. Amazing things. Lacy, thin, feminine. Not a speck of it practical.

The baroness didn't ask so much as she commanded, "Miss?" She spoke to the seamstress, a woman at least ten years older than her. "Can we please see these?"

The seamstress brought out a pair of dark pink garters ruffled with lace, heaped with bows, and weighted down with a lot of pearls the size of tomato pips. "These would make a nice prize for a hero," said the baroness, turning to dangle one off her finger.

The garter was one of gaudiest things he'd ever

set eyes on. She thought they'd appeal to him though, which said what she thought of his taste.

When he didn't immediately light up at the sight, she explained, "They're expensive."

So maybe it was her taste that was on the flashy side, he thought. He shrugged. He pointed to garters still in the case that sat next to where the others had been. "These be nicer." It was more a matter of trying to straighten her out than anything else. He pointed to white ones, the color of cream. Narrower. Satin, with one creamy-pink flower on each, two tiny leaves the color of moss. Nothing more. Simple. Elegant.

She raised one eyebrow. At first he thought it was his taste that struck her. But no, it was his accent. She said, "What an amusing way you have of pronouncing things."

His sound came from a country dialect. He could actually speak a little Cornish, a lost language.

The baroness smiled at the tall, handsome mud she was keen to welter in. "These then," she said. She indicated the garters he'd chosen. The seamstress handed them to her.

On the end of her crooked, gloved finger, the baroness offered Mick a prettier garter. "Here," she said. "You take this one. I'll take the other. Then we'll meet somewhere" — her eyes lit — "and unite them."

He laughed. The rich got up to the damnedest games.

Games he'd played more than once. He

thought about this new offer. The baroness here was on the pretty side. Making a rich lady happy had its moments. He couldn't complain that it'd ever been terrible.

Mick stroked his mustache a moment. It was soft and sleek, his mustache. Thick, dark, his pride. His "lionhearted virility" on display. His thumb to his cheekbone, arms across his chest, he dragged his finger down the mustache till the inside of his knuckle rested in the indentation of lips. There, he thought. The gesture did something to his head. It made his mind clear.

Against his finger, he murmured, "A yearning for mud."

"What?" The baroness in the bird hat got a puzzled look.

He took his finger away, straightening. "It be from French," he said.

Now he'd really confused her. A country man like him wasn't supposed to know beggar-all about French. He shrugged, trying to make little of it. "What it means is, I guess not, love."

He stepped away, slipping his arms into his coat, thinking that was the end of it. He smoothed his hand down the front of him and absently weighed his pocket, checking its contents. Good, still there.

"Ah," the baroness said. She added in a cynical tone, "How unusual. A faithful man."

Faithful to himself.

She continued, "So there's a lucky lady elsewhere?"

He let her think so.

She lightly hit his shoulder, a rap with her folded fan, then laughed. "Add them to my bill, will you, miss? A pair of garters for our hero here to give to his lady fair."

He looked over his shoulder, thinking to tell her not to bother, but she was out the door, just like that, with him the proud owner of a pair of fine lady's garters — and way too many lady-fairs to start trying to pick which one.

Well, hell. What was he going to do with those? he wondered. But then he thought, Well, of course. He went into the back.

The only person there was Nell, the seam-stress's assistant. She sat with her blonde head bent close to the sewing machine. She was trying to thread its needle, but stopped when he entered, smiling up at him.

"Where be the lady who was trying on clothes back here?" he asked.

"She left." Nell tipped her head in the direction of a back door. When he dropped the garters onto her sewing table, her smile got bigger. "Coo, these are plush, aren't they?" She laughed, picking them up. "And about ten times nicer than those horrid things Lady Whitting wanted."

"The other lady," he said. "The tall one what was trying on dresses. She buy anything?"

"We altered some dresses for her."

"She take 'em?"

"We're sending them."

"Then put those in her package, will you?"

She held up the garters looped round her hand. They were fine. Not scratchy like the lace ones. Soft. Simple. Right diabolical in their appeal. Like the long legs he imagined wearing them.

Nell said, "I don't think she'd accept garters from you, Mr. Tremore. She's a proper lady, Miss —"

He bent, putting his finger against the girl's lips, leaning his weight, his palm down, on her sewing table. He didn't want to know a name. He didn't want to know nothing about the lady behind the screen. He already knew enough. "Tell her they're from you then."

"From me?"

"From the shop. For being a good customer, you see. No need for her to know where they come from."

There now. Perfect. Tomorrow, somewhere in London a long-legged lady would be walking around in a sweet pair of garters that were just right for her pretty legs. The idea was a little on the indecent side, but Mick felt heroic anyway for making it happen.

Then Nell blindsided him. She stood up from her chair, her face coming right up to his, and whispered, "No one would know if, well —" She murmured in a rush, "My father's asleep upstairs. He works the night shift. So does my brother. My uncle and cousins are out, and Aunt Milly is busy in front. No one would know if, say —" She paused, like she wasn't sure

20

where to go from here. "If, say, I fixed your shirt for you."

"My shirt?" Mick looked down. "What's wrong with my shirt?"

She reached out, casually resting her hand on his chest. "It has a hole."

"No, it —"

Yes, it did: He looked down and watched her put her fingernail through a smooth place where the linen was worn. His shirt had a fingernail-sized hole before he had the presence of mind to grab her hand and hold it.

She let out a soft sound, more satisfaction than distress. He watched her lower her eyelids as a little smile spread on her face.

Oh, fine. He laughed, a single burst. Well. Nellie girl here was surely unexpected. He'd been wooing her all week with little success — till he'd caught a mouse then been propositioned by a baroness.

And at least *she* knew the difference between pretty garters and gewgawed ones that were only costly. But . . . what was wrong? She was . . . too short, he decided. He wanted longer legs all of a sudden.

He was shaking his head no, pushing her back, when Nell got hold of his trouser button. She was going to pull the damn thing off, if he wasn't careful. He took hold of her hands again. She resisted, and damn if she didn't like resisting. She wanted to fight him, but in that way women sometimes wanted to. She wanted to lose.

So how did he win without winning? This wasn't going well.

Then it complicated. "Nellie?" Her aunt wasn't nearly as busy as Nell had thought. "Nell? What are you doing —"

Old Nellie here was making fast work of what buttons were left on his shirt, was what she was doing — she'd popped two off, the clumsy girl.

And, from here, the whole situation went to bloody effing hell.

Chapter 2

Edwina Henrietta Bollash was sitting in Abernathy and Freigh's main tearoom, quietly eating the best scones and cream in London, when a very undignified racket rose up outside in the street — like the caterwauling of a dozen cats and dogs fighting over butcher scrap. Inside the room, a little chorus of teacups clinked on saucers. Heads lifted, faces turning, as the noise grew louder, closer. Then quite suddenly — chairs scraping back in alarm — the ruckus burst through the tearoom doors.

A tall, half-naked man — his frock coat open, his shirt partly out and mostly undone, his trousers unbuttoned at the top — careened into the room. "Blimey!" he shouted as a furled umbrella behind him whooshed through the air, narrowly missing his head.

The weapon was wielded by a woman who chased in after him. She yelled, "You blighter! You — you — you ratcatcher!" as she attempted to thrash him with her umbrella.

Another man, then two more charged in behind the woman, a parade of ranting people all of whom seemed intent on catching the fellow for

reasons that did not sound for a minute friendly.

"When I get me 'ands on you . . . !"

"We'll be makin' meat pies out a' ya!"

"Yer dirty ferrets can pick yer bones when we're through . . ."

Edwina laughed at first, at the surprise, the unlikely spectacle that had claimed the crowded, dignified tea parlor.

A young woman charged in behind the others. She wept and called to the rest — something about nothing having happened like they thought. Ah, Edwina concluded, young lovers caught *en flagrante delicto.*

More people entered. Another man raced in behind the crying girl. After him, two well-dressed gentlemen trotted in, though once inside they immediately stepped back against the wall as if to watch — the wild goings-on apparently bringing in the curious from the street.

Edwina herself came to her feet. Other patrons of the teahouse rose, tried to move back, yet it was hard to tell which way to turn in order to stay out of the fray. She was stranded in the midst of clamor that grew around her. Over the sound of ladies' shrieking and men's "Now see here!" carried the righteous exclamations and bitter complaint of the fleeing fellow. His pursuers shouted after him, promising mayhem, while he narrowly avoided it, cursing them and dashing round one table then the next. He left behind him a trail of quickly vacated chairs and tables and clanking, shimmying china.

His adversaries, less spry and more worked up, whipped against people and objects he avoided, rather like the tail of a cyclone. They knocked chairs sideways, overturned a table, then sent one man sprawling. When they grabbed for the frisky fellow over another table, they ended up pulling off the table linen. They sloshed over countless teapots and tossed clotted cream onto the floor by the bowlful.

At this point, an apron-fronted waiter joined in, then another waiter. Mr. Abernathy himself materialized from the back offices, his glasses on his forehead. The stout little owner frowned, then waved, trying to organize his staff; he gave chase, too.

Thus pursuers multiplied. Then divided — Mr. Abernathy and the waiters split up, darting round a table from two directions in an effort to corner a fellow who couldn't be cornered: His frock coat and shirt flapping open on his bare chest, the man vaulted the dessert trolley (with nary a cream puff disturbed). Everyone in pursuit, from both sides and behind, collided at the cart — catching their prey only insofar as to spatter the backs of his leaping boots and trousers with crème anglaise. Every last pursuer went down, their limbs floundering like spatulas in a concoction of mixed pastries. As they rose, they were covered in berries, cake, cream-puff cream, and biscuit bits.

Edwina laughed outright. Even though it wasn't funny, of course. No, no. It was awful that

Abernathy and Freigh's famous Saturday afternoon cream tea should become a free-for-all. She put her hand to her mouth, stifling the laughter that wanted to break out.

The leader of the parade headed for the front door in the lull, and would have made his exit, but a bobby came in just as the fellow was about to run out. "Dia-*bol*-ical!" he said emphatically as the bobby spread his arms, blocking the doorway.

The fellow swerved back into the room. The umbrella-flourishing woman — who now looked familiar somehow, as if Edwina would know her in a different context — landed a good swipe as he sailed past. "Ai! That 'urts, loov," he said.

The vaguely familiar woman led the pack again and, for a brief moment, was close enough to deliver several more thwacks on the man's forearm as he protected his head.

"Stop! This be blewdy insane, ye silly old cow."

Edwina tilted her head, her interest shifting. The man had the oddest speech pattern. Beneath a strong dose of East Side London lay a country idiom that rarely left the southwest tip of England. A mishmash of Cornish and Cockney. Remarkable.

"Beggar me," he protested. "Nothin' 'appened!" After which his feet hit some of the cream that had spilled on the floor. His arms flew out as he slipped in it, his reflexes agile enough to keep him upright — though not sufficient to keep

26

him from pure, blind swearing. "Aw-w, blewdy 'ell fokin' mawther a' Gawd. . . ."

His words gave Edwina only momentary pause. She quickly ducked down under her table to dig a notebook and pen from her drawstring purse. What luck. Why, she could have traveled miles and never heard the Queen's English so marvelously slaughtered.

"What's he saying?" someone asked behind her as she took a step back.

She interrupted her rapid scribbles, thinking the question addressed to her. But no, she realized it was one of the two curiosity-seekers who had followed the commotion in; they were talking together.

"Who cares?" answered the second. "I'll give you five-to-one odds they brain him here."

"Here in the tearoom?" asked the other. Both men were well-dressed: dark frock coats, striped trousers, gray gloves, gray top hats, as if they had come from a garden party or wedding. Then she blinked and looked again: The men were twins, all but identical. One was perhaps ever so slightly taller and thinner.

"No, no," the taller one said, "they'll get hold of him by the scruff here, drag him into the street, and brain him outside. My fifty against your ten pound note."

"You're on. He's bigger than any of them. And faster — they aren't even going to catch him; they've been trying for more than a city block. . . ."

She dismissed their silly conversation; neither the syntax nor inflection was interesting. Both born near Brighton. Upper-class. The taller one had been to Eton; neither had seen university.

Inflections and syntax, yes. She made notes: The crying girl was from the London district of Whitechapel; so were her relatives — the pursuers were all related, same household, though the girl and the woman with the umbrella had veneers of refined diction, the sort learned if trained in a nice London shop.

It occurred to Edwina: the seamstress and her assistant from the dress shop off Queen's Gate. That's who the two women were. Not that it mattered. Any interesting facts buried in their speech were tidbits, mere crumbs of richness, when compared to the treasure trove of linguistic atrocities coming from the mouth of the elusive, bare-chested man.

As an extra bonus, his voice rang, distinctive, deep; it carried with an athletic vocal clarity. Which made for a nice, clean study of the aberrations he put into English speech. His attack of initial H's, some dropped, some added where they didn't belong, was unequivocal. His short vowels were prolonged so clearly they almost made for an extra syllable.

Rarely had she heard anyone who could so completely distinguish himself, by simply opening his mouth, as coming from the bottommost rung of the lowest order of society.

His speech put him from the mining districts

of Cornwall, come to London now no doubt to make his fortune as a — well, he could have been anything from a dustman to a pickpocket. Or a ratcatcher, wasn't that what someone had called him? Perfect.

His resounding voice all at once let out a roar. "Na-a-w! Bugger me!"

Edwina looked up from her notebook just in time to see her study-subject dive after something, something that seemed to have come from his coat pocket. A *live* something. A brown bit of fur scampered into the debris on the floor.

With more guttural sounds of exasperation, the fellow rose onto his hands and knees. Several of his assailants tripped over him as he scooted toward the thing, making small smacking sounds with his lips. " 'Ere, loov. Now, now. Come to yer Mick, loovey."

His importuning made the thing halt. It looked to be no more than a wiggly tail of an animal, a tail come alive on tiny paws. With it momentarily stopped, the man snatched it up and dropped it back into his pocket. Before he could get to his feet, though, a waiter had hold of his coattail. The seamstress and her umbrella got another clear shot. She landed a blow on the kneeling fellow's back. He flinched, raising an arm in defense, and grabbed, knocking the umbrella flying. But the two older men got hold of his arm, and he was down — protecting whatever was in his coat by putting his cheek to the floor, tenting himself over his swinging pockets.

At this point, confusion broke out in earnest as everyone converged on him.

Those who had chased him in wanted his hide.

Mr. Abernathy pounded his fist on his palm, demanding recompense for untold damages.

Patrons spoke loudly in umbrage at the mess of their clothes.

The bobby called for order, but didn't get it.

Everyone talked at once, while the poor fellow on his knees and cheek, one arm pinned back, cursed the air blue as he absorbed blows from any enemy who could reach him.

The police officer yelled louder. Edwina stopped writing when, over her spectacles, she saw the man on his knees take — she blinked, her chest tightening in spasm — a blow from the policeman's billy truncheon.

No. Perhaps he deserved trouble. Yet he had stayed so swashbucklingly ahead of it until he'd decided to save the tail-thing that had leaped from his pocket: He didn't deserve to be on his knees taking a clubbing — or at least he didn't deserve it more than anyone else who'd participated in the chase. No, no —

"Excuse me," she said. She began to push her way into the little pack of arguing people. "Excuse me, please," she repeated, this time louder in her no-nonsense tone. She felt less confident than she sounded, but the crowd opened up for her anyway. She marched forth, a tall woman with a businesslike walk.

At the front of the group, the bobby was saying

to the captured man, "I'm asking you again, Do you live here in London?"

"Ace, ye bug-brine," said the man below him, his slander, happily, skewed by the fact that his mouth was pressed to the floorboards. "Ace, ace, ace."

The policeman raised his billy again. "If you answer 'Ace' one more time —"

"*Yes,*" Edwina interrupted. "He means *yes*. If you'll let him up, you'll be able to understand him better."

"Do you know this man, miss?"

"No."

"Why are you speaking up for him then?"

"I'm not —"

"Then mind your own business. He's bein' smart —"

"With regard to that particular word, he's being Cornish — in a way one hardly hears in London. He was raised somewhere near St. Just, I'd say." The man below them made a sound of satisfactory startlement, an indication that she was on the mark. More confidently, she added, "Though heaven knows his accent has more than Cornwall in it. Let him up, would you please."

One thing she could say for herself: Her own accent — through little or no effort of her own — was as genteel as ever came from a lady's lips. The diction of the Queen herself did not imply more quiet authority. It always struck her as a marvelous contradiction that she could sound so

31

sure of herself for no more reason than the open-ness of her vowels and the briefness of her final R's.

The little group straightened themselves, looking from one to the other as they stepped back and let the bobby and a waiter bring the fellow up by his arms.

The man they brought to his feet was huge, much taller than she'd thought, wild-looking, and utterly furious. If his good nature were put upon by being chased, it did not survive at all being pinned to the ground and beaten. He stared narrowly down at her.

A novel experience. A man had to be over six feet to look down at Edwina Bollash. This man was easily. Long-limbed, wide-shouldered, he stood at least six and a quarter feet tall. He was also more robust than she had imagined. Not heavy so much as well-built, filled-out — with his arms held back, his frock coat and shirt gaped open onto chest muscles that looked akin to the tanned, tooled breastplate of an old Roman cui-rass, if such armor had had —

Edwina blinked, widened her eyes, then glanced down. (While her mind continued on its own: *Hair. If such armor had hair that flowed into a wedge of black that narrowed downward into a neat line.* She had never seen a man's naked chest, ex-cept of course on statues, which never had hair. She felt a pinch of betrayal — what else, she won-dered, was inaccurate on the stone men she had so carefully and curiously studied?)

32

"Could someone get him a proper shirt?" she asked. She might have requested instead that he button his own or his coat, except his shirt had exactly two buttons on it, both at the bottom, and was ripped down the front as if it had caught on something. His coat had no buttons at all, not a one down its long placket.

After a small to-do, a tablecloth was draped over the fellow's shoulders. As it fell over the front of him, he spoke to her. "Ye'll be excusin' me, duck," he said. "Idden me choice to stand 'ere without me shirt done up."

"I'm sure," she said. She let herself take in the more modest sight of him, tilting her head till the flowers on her hat shifted, taking her head sideways another degree.

The hair on his head was long, wild, and dark. He wore a positively feral mustache — walrus-like and jet black. It went with the dense stubble on his cheeks. Beyond this, he had a faintly alarming face: a broad, square jaw, its sharp right angles below his ears made more severe by knots of muscle that flexed, an angry man trying to regain control of himself. Dark coloring. A deep, jutting brow. It was a dramatic face, strong. The word *villainous* immediately leaped to mind, though, in fairness, it was a handsome face — handsome enough at least for a seamstress's assistant to risk her reputation.

Edwina couldn't help but ask, "So you were born in St. Just, but how long have you lived in Whitechapel?"

33

He frowned at her. "Do I know ye?"

"No. I'm a philologist. I study people's speech. And yours is most interesting."

The bobby interrupted. "Excuse me, miss, but we have things to settle: I'll be arresting this fellow now."

"Arresting me? What'd I do 'cept keep meself from bein' kilt? In fact, I be reporting these bug-brines here fer . . ."

Bug-brains. Diabolical a few minutes ago. He was verbal in the way some Cockneys were: a love of words and colorful talk. Neither won him any ground here, however.

Mr. Abernathy drowned him out, calling for everyone's arrest. Others joined in, the chaos rising again in waves of defense and accusation. The apparent father of the weepy shop assistant said something that made her begin to cry again. The seamstress, the girl's aunt apparently, stiff-armed the father with the heel of her hand, telling him to button his lip. And so it would have begun all over.

Except, surprisingly, one of the gentlemen twins who had followed the fracas in stepped from behind Edwina and held up his hand. "Stop! Stop!" he called.

The group quieted reluctantly — as they watched him remove a notecase from his coat pocket.

"Most of this is just mess," he said, then added cavalierly, "that the waiters can clean up. Other than mess, I see one broken chair, which I am

34

happy to pay for." He slid a ten-pound note from the notecase's billfold, enough to buy half a dozen chairs, offering it to Mr. Abernathy. "Call it the cost of a morning's good sport." He beamed at the fellow wearing the tablecloth. "You led one jolly good chase, old chap. And earned me fifty quid for it."

The mustachioed fellow laughed as if they were suddenly mates. "Which we'd be 'appy to take 'alf of." *Tike 'arf of.* Edwina was mesmerized by the muddled syntax and thickness of his self-invented dialect.

The other brother, standing beside her, concurred. "Amazing," he said, "I can barely understand a word he says. It's English though, isn't it?" He shook his head, a condescending smirk on his lips. "Honestly, don't prolong his agony by helping him, Jeremy. If you had any mercy, you'd just shoot him for being so poor and stupid."

The Cornish-Cockney turned around sharply. "I ain't *stupid*," he said. *Styoo-pid.* He mimicked the other man's pronunciation quite well. "And I ain't a blewdy poncey-arsed nob whot thinks his buttocks don't smell when he shites."

Happily, the smug twin didn't understand what the man had said. He turned his back as his brother with the open notecase withdrew another bill. When Mr. Abernathy still didn't take the money, the mediating twin swung his arm like a boom around toward the whimpering girl and her family. "She's your daughter, yes? It

seems you could do the lady the honor of believing her. When a lady says nothing happened, then nothing happened."

The idea of the girl's being a lady made her whole family scratch their heads — and stare at the money. As encouragement, he added, "The truth is, I'd pay a good bit to beat my brother here in a bet. Take this money for the young lady's trousseau or dowry, then let her be." He nodded, a small bow toward her as he offered the money to her father. "To your future, mademoiselle."

The father snatched it up.

To Abernathy, the gentleman opened his billfold, showing a wad of bills inside. "How much? What is the price of a new chair, a good mopping, of asking your baker to come in early and turn out some more of those delicious scones? Why, sir, by tomorrow, you could be as good as new. In fact, better than before. Everyone will want to come see the scene of today's adventure. You will be the talk of London."

It took three more bills to appease Mr. Abernathy, along with the assurance from first one brother then the other that they were very willing to take tea presently at a small side table while the mess was being cleared away.

And that was that. As if by magic, the angry group dispersed. Mr. Abernathy ordered his waiters to get mops. The bobby followed the family out. Edwina was left at the side of a demolished tearoom standing with a tall ratcatcher

wearing a tablecloth.

"I thank ye kindly," he said, "fer speakin' up fer me." He ran his hand down the front of his threadbare frock coat, as if straightening an elegant garment. Then he bent forward slightly, adjusting himself into his trousers before his grimy fingers rather indiscreetly fastened the top button.

His trousers had faded to a shade so colorless it was impossible to say if they'd been brown, black, or gray. These were tucked into a pair of hobnail jackboots, the waxy pitch on them cracking from age.

He was in scruffy shape. His thick, dark hair looked to be cut in hanks by an axe. It dangled onto his collar, touched his shoulders here and there; it stayed back from his face in a gravity-defying way that suggested pomade, though, if so, the predominant ingredient in his pomade seemed to be soot. He had a high forehead, or possibly a slightly receding hairline. In either event, the feature lent him an air of intelligence: cunning. His mouth, up against the mustache, was wide, with plump, rather perfectly shaped lips for a man. Chiseled. A pretty mouth on a shrewd piece of riffraff.

This mouth pulled up on one side in what was half a smile, a crooked sense of humor. "And I bain't Coornish, loov. Though Feyther and Mawther was." He wiggled his eyebrows. He was making a joke. Then he smiled more crookedly still — one side of his mouth simply and natu-

rally went up higher than the other, cutting a deep dimple into one cheek. "I be a Londoner now," he explained. "The best ratcatcher from Hyde Park to the borough of Bethnal Green. If ye got rats, I'd do ye fer free."

"Um, no, thank you. So this *is* your profession, catching rats?"

"Indeed. I be the pride of me family, a great success at it, ye see." He laughed softly, perhaps even ironically, then tipped his head, a man blatantly trying to see into the shadows under the brim of her hat.

She bowed her head enough to be a hindrance. In the face of a directness she rarely saw: He showed no fear in revealing himself. As if he had not a thing in the world to hide.

A little foolish of him, she thought, but useful in speech studies. He wouldn't be self-conscious about his pronunciation. On impulse, she said, "I'll give you five bob if you'll come by my house in Knightsbridge tomorrow afternoon and do some speaking exercises for me."

"Yer 'ouse?" he said. His lopsided grin broke slyly back onto his face. He cocked his head to the side. "Alone?"

Boldly, he glanced down the length of her. Edwina cranked her head back. The look he passed over her was purely obnoxious — almost too trite to be insulting. Honest to goodness, what could he possibly think?

Then she felt her cheeks infuse with heat.

She knew what he thought: Gangly. Over-tall.

Overeducated. A myopic spinster for whom there was no brim in the world wide enough to hide all that was wrong with her. Edwina was accustomed to people thinking her unfeminine, unattractive. She was, however, unaccustomed to anyone leaping from that judgment to the notion that she was so desperate for the company of a man that she would hire one off the street.

She drew herself up, showing the scallywag her most righteous demeanor. There was a flicker of something, a teasing in his lopsided smile — though, if so, it was the wrong subject on which to tease her.

She scowled. "My house is not empty. I do not live alone, Mr. —" She paused for a name.

He supplied, "Mick."

"You have a family name?"

"Yes, love" — *Ace, loov* — "Tremore. But everyone calls me Mick."

"Well, Mr. Tremore, I'm not your love. My name is Bollash, Miss Edwina Bollash. And I merely want to study your speech, do a palatographic, perhaps make a gramophone recording. So if you are interested in —"

"Excuse me," said a voice to the side. "I have to ask: Are you *the* Miss Edwina Bollash?"

She turned to find that the two gentleman brothers had not dispersed with the rest. The slightly shorter one, the one who was generous with his billfold, was addressing her.

"I know of no other," she answered.

He shot his near-duplicate a smug look, then

held out his hand by way of introduction. "My brother, Emile Lamont. I am Jeremy Lamont of Sir Leopold Lamont's family, of Brighton and lately of London." He offered his card as he nodded toward Mr. Tremore. "So you speak this chap's language?"

She nodded.

The thinner, and somehow more snide, brother asked, "You are the same Miss Edwina Bollash who is renowned for her skill in teaching" — he left a pause — "shall we say, less than graceful young ladies how to enter gracefully into society? The one who did the Earl of Darnworth's daughter?"

"*Did* her?"

"Turned her from that — that *thing* she used to be into the elegant creature who married the Duke of Wychwood last month."

Edwina was rather proud of this particular feat, but she never, never took public credit for her work. It demeaned the accomplishments of the young ladies themselves. "I can't imagine where you heard such a thing, though it is true that I tutor private students in elocution and deportment, if that is what you are asking." She opened her reticule, offering her own card in exchange. *Miss Edwina Bollash. Instructor of Elocution and Deportment. Philologist, Phonetician, Linguist. Expert in Social Graces and Polite Behavior.*

"You groom the ugly ducklings of society into swans of the upper class. All the rich mamas

were whispering about it in Brighton this summer," said Jeremy as he shot a look of significance, a raised brow, at his thinner, more skeptical version.

Emile Lamont laughed. "Come now. You can't be serious," he said to him.

His brother protested, "I am. And you are absolutely wrong. Why, she could take this very fellow here and make him into a gentleman in a fortnight. I would bet it." Turning to her, "Couldn't you?"

"Make him into a gentleman?" The idea startled a laugh out of her.

"Yes. Change the way he speaks — being a gentleman is hardly more than talking properly, wearing decent clothes, and a few polite manners."

"It's a good deal more than that, I'd say —" She glanced at the beggarly-looking fellow, who now watched her with the same interest he might have given to a houseful of rats.

"Yes, but you could do whatever it took," Jeremy insisted. "I know. I've spoken with Lady Wychwood. She confided that you helped her, that you picked her clothes, had someone come in for her hair, taught her how to move, even how to intone her voice."

Emile Lamont let out a derisive snort. "Lady Wychwood *was* a lady," he said. "That was no trick. I still say there is no science that can make — well, a silk purse out of a sow's ear. And I still say" — he poked the air in front of his brother's

face for emphasis — "that anyone who can't speak the Queen's English properly may as well be shot, for there is no hope for their ever living a decent life. They are nothing but a drain on society."

"You see? You see?" his brother exclaimed. His face reddened. "I have to live with this arrogant fellow! Have you ever heard such a thing?"

In Jeremy's defense, she said to his brother, "You're quite wrong. You can change the way a person speaks. Heavens, you can teach a parrot to talk."

"But not well."

"Well enough."

"She could do it well enough," Jeremy said. "You see? It can be done."

There was a pregnant moment, in which his brother seemed to contemplate their discussion — after which he raised one eyebrow and smiled. "Let me buy you each a cup of tea." He smirked then added, "You, too, Mr. Tremore. For I have an idea. I can see a way here for me to win back my money from my brother and then some."

Edwina allowed herself to be sat at a table to the side of the cleanup, facing the strangest trio of men she could remember in a while. Two rich, idle young gentlemen who had little to do beyond bicker. And a robust-looking ratcatcher wearing a tablecloth.

As a waiter walked away with their orders, Jeremy said, "Emile, I know what you were thinking —"

"You like to think you do —"

"You were thinking that this man was born poor and will die poor, that his poverty is in his blood. But I say it's in his speech. And I'm willing to back my opinion with a wager you will be hard-pressed to refuse." He took a breath, then leaned intently toward his brother. "I'll bet you a hundred pounds that she" — he pointed at Edwina — "can turn him" — he jabbed a finger in Mr. Tremore's direction — "into a gentleman by simply fixing the way he talks and teaching him some manners."

Oh, my. She had to interrupt. "No, no. I appreciate your faith, but I can hardly take on such a large project —"

"How long would it take?"

She blinked. "I don't know. More than a fortnight, certainly. And it would be expensive —"

"What if we covered your fees and costs?" Throwing a nasty grin at his brother, he added, "The loser, of course, would have to reimburse the winner."

She blinked again. "I don't know." She glanced at Mr. Tremore. He was listening carefully, wary but curious.

He was certainly an interesting case. Perfect in any number of ways. The clear pronunciation, or mispronunciation actually. He loved words. He could mimic accents. Moreover, a man who simply said what he had to say would make faster progress than one who hesitated or hedged.

Emile Lamont tapped his long, thin fingers,

43

then after a moment lifted an eyebrow speculatively. "We'd have to find a way to determine who had won the bet," he said.

His brother pulled his mouth tight, till his lips whitened. "I win if he becomes a gentleman."

"Yes, but who will decide if he is a gentleman or not? You? Her? No, no. You'd simply clean him up, dress him up, then *call* him a gentleman."

"Well, we're not going to let *you* be the judge, if that's what you're suggesting."

Emile Lamont shrugged, as if he had won the bet already because his brother could not find a way to validate the end result.

"We will find an arbitrary judge, an objective third party," Jeremy protested.

"Who? One of your friends?"

"Well, not one of yours."

"Mine would be more impartial, but never mind. It can't be done, and you'd cheat anyway." Emile shrugged again, losing interest.

The bet was off.

Then on again: "Wait —" He sat back, smiling as he tented his fingers. "I have an idea." It was a wicked idea, she could tell by the way he narrowed his eyes. "The Duke of Arles's annual ball," he announced. "It's in six weeks. If you can pass him off there as — oh, say, a viscount." He laughed. "Yes, a viscount. If you can bring him, have him stay the entire evening with everyone thinking he is a titled English lord, if no one catches on, then you have won." He laughed heartily.

44

Edwina almost laughed herself. She felt light-headed all at once. The Duke of Arles was her distant cousin — though there was no love lost between them. Arles had inherited her father's estates twelve years ago, leaving her with whatever she could eke out on her own.

Passing an imposter off at his annual ball would infuriate her cousin.

She stared down into her teacup. Yes, it most certainly would. Why, it would make the old goat apoplectic.

The notion took on a strange, unexpected appeal. Arles's annual ball was a hurdle she always enjoyed surmounting, though in the past she had always done so legitimately: seen girls made comfortable there who deserved to be comfortable in the presence of the duke and his friends. But passing off an imposter. Well, it was absurd, of course. And if people found out, it could be damaging. She was allowed her little life on the fringe of society partly because she had been born to society, but partly too because she didn't challenge it.

But, oh, to fool the duke and know she had fooled him for the rest of her days. Yes —

No. No, no, it was a dangerous idea. But in imagination, it was amusing to consider. In fantasy, the idea made something inside her give a joyous jump. A small, vindictive lurch in her chest that was surprising for its liveliness. What a thought: Old Milford Xavier Bollash, the fifth Duke of Arles, mocked by his plain cousin for

whom he had no use.

She looked at the mustachioed man in front of her. He swilled tea like a pint of lager, grasping the teacup whole in the palm of his hand. He drained his cup, then raised his hand, clicking his tongue and snapping his fingers to get the waiter's attention. When the waiter looked over in alarm, Mr. Tremore pointed, a downward poking gesture with his finger, and called, "We'd 'ave s'more, Cap'n."

Dear Lord. His manners were a nightmare. He was unwashed, threadbare, and coming apart at his buttons.

Yet there was something about him. His posture was straight. His teeth were good. Excellent, actually. A shave, a haircut, some good, clean clothes. And a trim, at the very least, of that feral-looking mustache. Why, there was no telling. He would probably clean up rather well, which, with the girls at least, was always half the battle.

When the second cup of tea came, he wouldn't let the waiter take the old cup. Then Mr. Tremore reached under the table and withdrew a surprise — the animal from his pocket, the one he'd saved at his own expense.

It was a small, weasly-looking thing. A ferret. It had to be, though Edwina had never seen one. But that was what ratcatchers used, wasn't it? Ferrets and terriers? What a vocation.

It had a shiny brown coat and a long, supple body, which it folded in half to "kiss" Mr.

46

Tremore on his dark-stubbled cheek. The animal's shape was strange but good, she supposed, for wiggling through rat mazes and rabbit burrows. One of nature's better adaptions.

When Mr. Tremore lowered it out of sight, he also took the teacup. A moment later, the cup returned to the table, missing tea — or rather tea was in different places, in little sprinkles all around the inside of it.

She frowned. While the two brothers continued to argue, she argued with herself, staring at a ferret's teacup. A ratcatcher. Don't be preposterous, Edwina. An illiterate, crude ratcatcher —

Yet Mr. Tremore's eyes, as they remained intent upon his animal, his livelihood, were alert. Astute. He was a sharp one, there was little doubt. Not well-educated, but not unintelligent.

He glanced up suddenly, from re-pocketing the ferret, then caught her staring. He winked at her.

She jerked, blinked, then picked up her own teacup, pouring her attention into it. Goodness. Certainly, if he were willing to tone down his swagger to mere arrogance, he would have enough of it to fit in with Arles and his lot. A little help with his diction, a few rules and manners. . . .

Besides, he only had to get through one evening, not a lifetime. And he seemed able to wind his impromptu way through any number of scrapes.

A ratcatcher. Oh, yes. It was delicious. To pass

a London ratcatcher off on the duke as a . . . a viscount.

Not so dangerous, she told herself. She could do it. No one would know. Just herself, a thirsty Cockneyfied Cornishman, and two quarrelsome brothers — none of whom would want the truth to come out.

Meanwhile, what a gift that knowledge would be: I outdid him, outfoxed him. Made a mockery of what deserves to be mocked. It would be her triumph, her little joke for the sake of her own amusement. At the expense of her old cousin, the Duke of Arles, also known as the Marquess of Sissingley — once her own father's title — and other lesser titles, who, by any and all his names and titles, deserved to be made fun of. Most surely he did.

The brothers must have sensed her willingness, for Emile Lamont suddenly began to discuss expenses, how much she would need to begin. As if the bet were laid, her part agreed.

It was only at the end that Mr. Tremore folded his thick-muscled arms over his broad, table-clothed chest and leaned back in a lordly manner. He said, "Well, I be a very important bloke here, seems to me. But I ask ye: Whot's in it for ol' Mick?"

All three of them went quiet. Edwina herself had assumed the man understood. "A better way of speaking, for one," she said. "Without question, I can give that to you, provided you cooperate."

He eyed her suspiciously. "Ye'd be in charge?"

"Yes, in matters related to your learning how to speak and conduct yourself."

"Yer a woman," he observed.

Well, yes. She thought about shoving away from the table then, withdrawing from the whole farce. Here she sat, thinking to tutor a big oaf, who, though theoretically clever, was apparently not smart enough to appreciate that a woman — heavens, anyone — in matters of speech and genteel behavior might know more than he did. She stared at him, her gaze dropping to the brutish, thick mustache that took up most of his upper lip —

His chest has hair on it. The idea popped into her mind, just like that.

She jolted, scowled, and looked down into her teacup. What a strange leap of thought. Chest hair. No, no, don't think about such things, she told herself.

A good trick, though, how not to think about something.

Any glimpse of his mustache seemed now to proclaim the fact to her: Beneath that tablecloth was the strangest sight. A naked chest with dark, smooth-patterned hair — black, shiny hair, a thick line of it down the center of his chest between heavy pectoral muscles. Why, who would have thought —

No, *don't* think — dear, oh, dear. The mustache. Oh, she wished she didn't have to look at that wicked thing — wait, that was it! The mus-

49

tache should go. He should shave it off. It was wiry, rough, like a broom on his lip. Not gentlemanly in the least.

Yes, oh, yes! Edwina thought as she stared at Mr. Tremore's mustache. The knowledge that she could tell him to clean himself up, smooth himself out, starting with his upper lip, made her feel jubilant all at once, eager for the whole business.

Meanwhile, Emile Lamont sneered at Mr. Tremore across the table. "You brawling, ungrateful swine," he said, "what you get out of this is you won't be hauled to the gaol for all the damage you wreaked today. I have a good mind to go demand our money back and call the constable again."

"No, no, no," his brother broke in quickly. "Mr. Tremore. Think of it this way: You'll have a cushy place to live for a few weeks. You'll get a regular gentleman's wardrobe, which you can take with you when you go. And" — he raised his finger dramatically — "you will be given a new manner of speech that will be yours forever, taught by an expert. Why, there is no telling what a man with your resources can do with such an advantage."

Mr. Tremore eyed them, a man suspicious of so much good fortune.

Then he drained his own teacup again, wiped the wet from his mustache with his arm, and smiled across the table at the three of them. He said, "I need twenty pounds today. It be fer me

family who won't be getting anything from me while I do this. Then I want fifty pounds when I be through —"

"Why, you —" Emile Lamont came up out of his chair.

"Be quiet," Jeremy said. "Of course, Mr. Tremore. You'll want to have something to start yourself out in whatever new direction you take. It's only fair." He withdrew his ever-open note-case again, took out a bill, then with a flourish of his wrist he offered a twenty-pound note between two fingers.

His brother, however, quickly cupped his hand over the money, holding it back. "All right," he said. "But fifty at the end only if you manage it." He smiled condescendingly. "Not a ha'penny if you're too stupid to carry it off."

Mr. Tremore contemplated him stonily for several seconds. Then he said, "A hundred if I do it."

Emile laughed, a dry burst of reluctant amusement: disbelief. "You have some gall," he said, then shrugged, giving in. "Done." Taking his hand off the money, he glanced at his brother. "The loser pays."

The twenty-pound note sat there now between Jeremy's fingers, available, while Mr. Tremore stared at it for an uncomfortably long minute, as though it had turned to dung in the meantime. In the end though, he reached across and took it. "Yes," he said — *Ace* — "done." He stood, scraping back his chair as he pocketed the bill.

51

"Now, where be the loo? I gotta shake 'ands with an ol' friend, if ye know what I mean. Blimey, but tea runs through a bloke. I don't know 'ow ye nobs do it."

Chapter 3

The Lamonts took Mick to a tailor's on a street called Savile Row. Bloody hell, it was a dandy place. And so long as Mick held out his arms or let them measure him up his leg, everyone let him crank his head and have a good look. The carpets on the floor were so thick and soft, the tailor kept having to haul him up by the arms — he wanted to touch them. The wood floor was polished up so shiny it looked wet. Old velvety chairs reflected like they stood on a lake. Tea tables floated on the floor's shine. The place had mirrors, gold vases with armloads of flowers that took up half a wall, and show-offy glass boxes as tall as a man's waist, with things inside he could buy, like buckles and buttons to sew onto the clothes they made him or neckties out of silk as colorful as peacock feathers. Who would've thought a place for blokes could get so fancy? He liked to think he'd seen some of the world, but he was impressed, he couldn't help it.

In the end, though, the Lamonts only wanted Mick to have dull things. Pah. Some brown trousers, some gray ones, a couple shirts, all white, a coat and waistcoat — Mick was allowed to pick

the lining when he made surly over the whole ordeal. He picked a fine purple with gold cloverish things on it, like some draperies he remembered from a first-rate bordello he'd ratted.

When the bell over the tailor's door rang and Edwina Bollash stepped through the doorway, he was delighted to see her. His new partner, come to fetch him, in what was turning out to be a choice adventure.

He wanted to tell her all the good done them today. "We ordered some right fine clothes, then had some fixed up they be sending later."

She only froze in the doorway, though. Like he was bald and naked. "I thought they were going to see to a bath," she said.

"Naw. I don't need one."

He looked at the Lamonts who, in turn, looked at the tailor. They'd all had a little to-do over the bath idea.

He said right away, "You should feel some of the stuff we got, like God's own miracle under your fingers. And *hoo,* the rare, sweet smell what come off a bolt of new fabric." He laughed just remembering. "The whole shop smells new, don't you think? Like beeswax and varnish. No" — it was so true that it made him grin for having thought of it — "like fresh-printed money, etched and watermarked." It was a smell he knew from helping his friend Rezzo print near-perfect fivers in the cellar of the Bull and Tun. Not that he spent any of the false money himself, but Rezzo had fifteen children, and there was no

other way for a dustman to feed them all.

Miss Bollash's voice, though, was a little unsteady when she repeated, "Etched and watermarked?" She let out a fainthearted laugh before asking, "What do you know about fresh-printed money?"

Didn't take him a second to know he wasn't answering that. He turned and said good-bye to the tailor and thank-you-very-kindly to the Lamonts.

He and Miss Bollash stepped out into the street, with her eyeing him and him ignoring her. Begger me, he thought. There they were, starting out off-kilter. Magic, his terrier, picked up and followed them as they walked shoulder to shoulder. He kept thinking, If he could see her face, he'd know better where he stood. But he could only see the lower half of it — the brim of her hat was that big.

She was sure a puzzle, Edwina Bollash. He thought she could be pretty. It was possible. She dressed nice. Quality. Her clothes sounded pretty, like reedy grass rubbing together in the wind — a noise that always sent him into heaven, silk on silk. He loved, too, the way she smelt like sunshine or clover or something. Not all flowery and perfumey, but a little cloud of smell around her. He wanted to get closer to it, sniff it in, but even he knew it wasn't polite. Anyway, she could be pretty under that hat. Or not.

She was a long girl, that was certain. In her shoes here, she must've pushed six feet. Almost

as tall as him. A lot of woman, lengthwise speaking. Width-wise, though, the top of her was on the skinny side. Long bones, small bristols — sweet though, little dumplings on her chest. The bottom of her wasn't so skimpy maybe. Her backside looked pretty full, though it was hard to tell what with the way fancy ladies padded out their bums these days.

She didn't have a pretty woman's way about her. He couldn't say why he thought so, except maybe how her hat tilted down when she walked. Like she was looking at the pavement, keeping track of it to make sure it didn't leap away from her. Smart steps, no doubts or dithers, but there was something nervy in her quick movement. Like a jill who been down the rat hole once too often, he thought: knew the job, knew her part in it, but knew, too, what it was like to be bit and just couldn't get over it. He wondered what bit her.

At the carriage, Mick could tell he surprised her when he held out his hand. He'd seen gents do it, so he tried it out.

He helped her into a carriage that had all its windows open, then got a bonus as he followed her in: a chance to look close up at her bum, no one to tell him not to. And yessir, it was all her own, he was pretty sure. A bottom as round as a pear. It made him smile. Her jacket fanned out into a little ruffle over her backside. It pinched in at her waist. Pretty. My, oh, my, he thought, weren't the gentry's clothes full of details plain

folk didn't dream of — gold buttons, velvet ribbon sewed around the edges, skirts the color of lavender —

Wait one minute.

Tall.

A purple skirt. And Miss Bollash's legs here'd be long.

Did they go forever?

Would there have been time for his leggy lady to put on her dress, walk over, and order tea? As he reasoned this out, though, another woman walked past them — in a skirt with a lot of dark purple in it — and Mick laughed at himself. After what he saw in that mirror this morning, he must have legs on his brain, hoping they were walking under every skirt he glanced.

Still, as he sat down opposite Miss Bollash, he couldn't help but stare at where her knees made her skirt bend. Yessir, her legs'd be right long. Slender, too. There was no telling, though, how pretty a woman's legs were till you actually got her undressed. He folded his arms, sat back, and stared, smiling. He wondered if the woman under that hat fancied mud in any form.

Besides a lot of hat, she was a lot of skirts. Her legs were buried under folds and folds of that thin sort of stuff a man could almost see through, except there was enough of it he couldn't see through nothing. Edwina Bollash was like that herself. Lots of her, none of it coming to much. Hard to see through.

Being a long, thin thing lost in a pile of skirts

didn't keep her from complaining though — as hardy as the Queen with her toes on fire — when Magic jumped into the carriage.

"May as well let him ride," Mick said. "He be the damnedest dog. He'll only run alongside till he drops, then find us a day later from the smell of the wheels or something."

She didn't like *damnedest* any more than she liked the dog in the coach, but she settled back and let both ride. Magic, Mick could tell, was grateful. It'd been a hell of a day.

As the coach pulled away, he realized it was finer than fine. All leather and soft cushions and springs in the ride. Funny thing, it wasn't near as strange as he might've thought to trot off in such a handsome bit of conveyance. Felt good. Felt right. All-bloody-right. Well, Mick thought, who would've predicted? A nice coach. Him sitting in it across from a long piece of fluff who was willing to squawk over a man getting his head bashed in. He liked Edwina Bollash. Good girl, this one.

The two blokes he did not like at all. He didn't know their game, but he knew their kind a mile off. Not that he could say — a ratcatcher didn't call gentlemen humbugs. Especially, Mick smiled to himself, if the humbugs were going to pay for him having gentleman lessons from a sweet little teacher in a fancy dress that made sliding *jsh-jsh* sounds just sitting there fidgeting.

He made her nervous. He should've tried to put her at ease, said something, but he sort of

liked that she was nervous.

He decided to mention, "They be puppies, you know."

"Puppies?"

"Confidence men," he explained.

"Who?"

"Them two Mr. Lamonts."

"Don't be ridiculous. They're rich gentlemen."

He shook his head. "They be setting us up for something."

She clicked her tongue in a sort of high-minded way. "Granted, they aren't too nice to each other, but they were perfectly nice to us. Besides, they have money. They don't need to set up anyone."

He shrugged. It was all one to him, nothing he had to prove. It would prove itself.

After a while, though, in a very quiet voice, she asked, "Why don't you like them?"

He shrugged again. "They be arseholes." While you, me darling, be a lovely long bit. He really liked the look of her. Though he wished for goodness sake she'd take off the blooming hat.

At *arseholes*, the only part of her face that he could see under the hat squinched up like she had a drawstring in her lips, a drawstring she pulled tight. Ha, he could've predicted. She made another one of those little clicks, teeth and tongue, that he was sort of coming to like. Then said, "*Are*."

She was correcting him.

It made him blink, frown. Well, hell. He knew fixing how he talked was what they were both going to do, but here it was, and he didn't like it. "Right. They *are* arseholes," he said.

The hat tilted. Her mouth pinched tighter.

He laughed and leaned back, stretching his arms out along the top of a leather seat, stretching his legs in front of him across fancy wood floorboards. Yes indeed, a fine day. A pretty ride.

When Miss Bollash's front door swung open, a fellow was standing behind it like he been waiting on the other side of it the whole time she was gone: ready to open it the moment he spied her come up the walk. He held it wide so Mick and her could enter, then closed it silent-like behind them — it made Mick turn around there in the entry hall just to see what happened.

Her house wasn't what Mick expected. Not like her clothes. It was plain. Better than anything he could claim, but not as big or fancy as he would've guessed.

She owned lots of books. *Hoo,* if the woman read all the books she had, she never did nothing but read. He'd been in lots of fancy houses for his job. Some had flowers for decoration. Some had carpets and fancy drapes or pictures all over the wall. Miss Bollash's house had books. Lines of them. Rows of them. Stacks of them. All neat. No mess or nothing. Just everywhere. They lined walls and filled tables.

"Thank you, Milton," said the lady as she pulled at the fingers of her glove. "Is Mrs. Reed still here? I'd like her to make up the east bed-sitter. This is Mr. Tremore. He's going to be our houseguest for a few weeks."

A few weeks. Mick frowned to hear the length of time. It seemed long all at once. He had regulars. He hadn't thought about that till now. Some might wait, but some for sure would take their problem to someone else when they couldn't find him.

As he walked down a hallway — with small marble statues in the niches of walls covered in faded green silk — a crawly feeling tickled up his spine. The way it did sometimes when he started to smell more under the planks of a job than he'd counted on.

Milton, the bloke who opened the door and looked old as Eden, was saying to Miss Bollash, "Mrs. Reed just left, your ladyship, but I can make up the rooms. And Lady Katherine is in the solarium. She's arrived early for her lesson."

"Thank you. I'll get to her in a few minutes." Miss Bollash slid her glove off as she said to Mick, "Milton will take your, um . . . tablecloth. Then, if you'll follow me, I'll show you upstairs."

Rooms. She meant it. Two of 'em. In Cornwall, Mick'd shared one room, smaller than the bedroom here, with his five brothers. His bed in London was in a cellar. In this house though, if he understood right, he got a big room with a four-poster in it to himself — he asked if he

61

shared it with Milton, but the answer was no — *and* a room connected to the bedroom that had a desk, paper, pens, ink, lots of stuff. And of course more books.

It made him stop and think. Looking at an actual bed, rooms, thinking of the clothes, all so different than what he knew . . . well, the crazy, fool bet, what it really meant, all at once seemed to matter in a different way. No one else had the same investment as him. A bit of money. Some pride. And Miss Bollash was keen for bookish reasons, too. But him . . . why, they were all talking about changing how he was.

What kind of man, he wondered, slept on a bed that had curtains on it and a skirt around its legs?

A man, he figured, who better get by to feed the other dogs and ferrets, then see if Rezzo would watch over them till . . . till whatever it was he was doing here came to whatever end it did. A man with a case of nerves, he guessed, and a few arrangements to make.

Sometimes Mick dreamed of a fancy life. (Money and legs. He would have been embarrassed to tell anyone how common-minded his ambitions were.) He always felt guilty doing it. Disloyal or something. He was a workingman. A good, solid man of the working class. He didn't think fancy fellows were happier than him. Didn't think they were nicer to their families or that God gave them a easier time of it. They still got sick or lame or died, just like everyone else.

So why was he here?

Aside from a hundred and twenty pounds, twenty of which he already had in his pocket — the total being more than he made in a year?

He laughed at himself. That was why. Hell, he sure didn't have dreams that turning himself into a gentleman for a few weeks was going to make him a better man somehow. No, sir, it wouldn't.

But the life nobs led seemed easier, he admitted. It smelled better maybe. They had time to think about things. Is that what he wanted? Was that the reason he dreamed of a rich life some nights? Time to think?

Meanwhile, all he seemed to have here was time to be surprised. Another door, one that he thought opened into the hall, opened into a loo, and not just a hole in the floor neither. There was a flush-toilet with a chain to pull on. And bloody hell, there was another pull overhead that made light come on. Electricity. He'd seen that once in a building he ratted over near Parliament. Miss Bollash's whole house had it, not a candle or gas lamp anywhere to be found.

She showed him all this in the time it took for her to pull off her other glove as she walked her quick walk and pointed at rooms. Then, in his new sitting room, she said, "Do you need anything I haven't thought of? Will it do then?" She was in the doorway, about to leave him here.

He tried to sound chipper. "Not a thing, love.

Cozy as a mouse in a churn." But he wasn't chipper.

"Love," she said.

He smiled, looking at a tall, thin woman in a big hat. Right friendly of her. About time.

But then she ruined it. She explained, "You said *loov*. It's *love*."

He frowned, feeling addled by a lot of correcting without much understanding doled out.

She stood there. She wasn't being nasty, he didn't think. Hard to tell. More like she was sizing him up. It was a nervy feeling, being sized up by a hat that looked right at him, being spoke to by a mouth with no eyes. What was wrong with her? he wondered. Were her eyes crossed? Was she bug-eyed?

She was ugly, he decided. Had to be a fright to wear her hat all the time.

"We'll work on it, though," she said. "We'll start in the morning. I have students this evening." Then she turned again and called over her shoulder, "Milton? Mr. Tremore will have a bath now. Will you please draw it. And see to a shave for him. Take off the mustache."

Mick blinked, then snorted. He went as far as the doorway, looking at the back of her. She was at the stairs in a second, on her way down. Hell, what was this? Even he knew gents wore mustaches. And he wasn't having no bath. He might've said, but she was going at her fast clip, a woman with the devil on her tail, not looking back. Her hat disappeared into the stairwell.

Hell. All right then, he'd settle with old Milton.

As it turned out, though, the fellow was as stubborn as Magic.

"If Miss Bollash says you're to take a bath," old Milton said with a poke, poke — Mick took hold of his finger to stop it — "then you'll have a bath, sir." With a big, stirred-up show of disgust, he added, "Just look at yourself!"

Now, Mick wouldn't mind cleaning up. He'd sort of had that in mind. It'd been a hard day. But he wasn't doing his private toilette the way Milton wanted him to, and not how Miss Fancy-Skirts wanted neither, for that matter. Too personal. Being a reasonable fellow, though, and just to be nice, he let Milton pull him into the room to show him the tub — the bloke was so bloody proud of it. A big, white, claw-foot thing that was just for bathing a body. The damnedest waste. Mick could've washed a month's laundry in it.

"Right nice," he told Milton with real wonder in his voice.

Things degenerated from here, though. *No, sir* didn't slow the old fellow down. *Not on your life, Cap'n* didn't give him the hint. *Not me. Not Mick.* And still that Milton ran a lot of hot water in the tub, talking like Mick was going to hop in any moment. When he started pulling on Mick's clothes, though, well — Mick was not the sort to let another bloke undress him for any reason. It pretty much sent him over the top.

"Since you like bathing so much," he said,

"you try it." He picked the fellow up — he was light enough Mick could've done it by a fistful of coat, but he gathered the old bloke up real polite — and dumped him into the water. Clothes and all, a big swooshing *ka-plosh*.

Mick was gentle with him. Didn't want to hurt him, just sort of showed him he wasn't getting in any tub of hot water, which was fine for carrots but not the likes of Mick Tremore.

No sooner did the water slop to a standstill than he heard Miss Bollash, feet pounding up the staircase, all those skirts churning. When she burst through the doorway, though, he was struck dumb, nothing to say for himself.

Well, well, well. His new teacher certainly wasn't ugly. No, sir. She wasn't pretty neither exactly, but with her hat off, God bless her, she was something to look at.

Her hair was red-gold, thick and shining. It lit her face — the way light coming through a window could make a ordinary room glow like a church. Her skin, white as milk, was dusted with pale freckles, like she been powdered with gold dust. Freckles so close and so many of 'em, he couldn't see between some. She had big, round eyes — or, no, maybe they were just startled. They blinked behind eyeglasses. But the best thing about her face was her nose. It was long and thin and curved like a blade, a strong nose — and a good-sized one, too, for such a thin woman. If she'd held her head up a bit and showed it off, he'd've said it give her real character.

Though, given the caution in the eyes behind Miss Bollash's eyeglasses, he was bound to say she didn't cherish her looks.

Still, with her hat off she was a sight. Bright-colored, funny-looking in a pretty way: like coming upon a fairy in the woods.

A tetchy fairy. She said, "Oh — Oh — Milton! Are you all right? What have you done, Mr. Tremore! I could hear your swearing downstairs!"

Milton and Mick talked at once.

"All I done was protect meself from his slimy fingers —"

"Yes, I'm wet, but fine —"

"I ain't swimming in no bloody tub. No one mentioned no tub of water today —"

"If I may say so, your ladyship, the man belongs in a zoo, not a bathtub —"

"Not for no hundred quid do I let some ol' sod —"

"Enough!" she said. "Enough of your oaths and fulminations, Mr. Tremore."

Ungrateful woman. Mick sucked himself up, squared his shoulders, and, trying to hold back from yelling, told her, "I'll have you know, duck, if it wasn't for me 'fulminations,' as you call 'em" — he mimicked the word, tone for tone, though he could only guess what it meant — "I'd be standing here in the rude with me widge hanging out."

That caught her back. Her big eyes grew. They got as wide and round as blue saucers.

67

Good. While he had her quiet, he drove home his point. "You can't tell me no gent soaks in water like a plucked chicken, like he was dinner —"

"Mr. Tremore, gentlemen most certainly do take a bath —"

"And how do you know? You ever seen one take a bath?"

She blinked, scrunched up her freckled brow, then swung her eyes onto the dripping fellow who was climbing over the edge of the tub. She asked, "You — you take a bath, don't you, Milton?"

"Indeed, madam. Though usually I remove my clothes first."

"Which explains," Mick pointed out, "why he's so wrinkled and stiff-looking. Too much water —"

The over-washed servant continued to mutter complaints, but she ignored him. She only shook her head at Mick with her lips pressed together. "You must take a bath." She didn't know how to make him do it, he thought, and it mattered to her. His refusal made her right upset. So upset that for a minute he wanted to do it. Almost. Just for her. For the sake of her worried expression and shy sort of pluck.

For his own sake, though, he had to tell her the truth. "I don't have to do nothing. And I gotta tell you, too, that the mustache stays where it be: on the lip."

She wrinkled her brow again, deeper, puck-

ered her mouth, which in turn puckered her long chin. It was pathetic, her look. She stared at his mustache like it wanted to bite her, focusing on it. She was fighting looking lower, he realized — at his chest. He folded his arms over it, not to cover it but because he knew it flexed chest muscle. It made it look better, stronger. The hell with her. "The mustache stays," he repeated.

She squinched up her mouth some more, then said, "Well, a trim then. We'll trim your mustache for now. But you have to wash in the tub."

"I won't."

Oh, she wanted him in that tub. Her mouth pressed into a strained, fretful line — while her eyes shifted nervously to stay above his neck. She told him, "I can't make you into a gentleman, sir, if you insist on the toilette habits of a beggar."

He let out an insulted snort. "Listen, duck. There be an important understanding to get to here. I know them blokes asked you to change me, but, thing is, I'll take charge of me, all right? You say. I'll listen. But I'll decide what be right for Mick Tremore. And a swim in soup water ain't right."

She put her fists on her waist, her long, thin elbows poking out into the doorway. Her face was getting pink. She was really working herself up. "Then it's over, because you're filthy. Which reminds me" — she pointed a finger at his pocket — "you have to get rid of that as well."

She meant Freddie. And she meant the bet was off, if Mick didn't get in the bathtub. He

69

straightened, gently brushed his coat down the front, and tried to gather some dignity. Bad enough he stood here missing buttons and pieces of his shirt, bad enough he had to hold his manliness together against some fellow who wanted his clothes. Now some bossy woman expected him to put Freddie out.

Then she pointed at Magic. "And your dog has to have a bath, too."

Ha. Mick began reasonably, "Well, if you can get Maj in your tub, feel free to wash him. But Miss Bollash, if this cockeyed bet goes sour, Freddie here be me livelihood. Freddie be the best damn ferret what ever was. I gotta have her with me."

"I can't have some rodent —"

"Ain't a rodent. The opposite. She hates rodents. She hunts them."

"He can't hunt them in my house."

"She. Freddie be a jill, and she's gotta be with me. A good ferret is like gold, you see."

She waffled. He thought he was going to win for a second, when she asked, "How do you keep her where you live?"

"She has a cage she sleeps in sometimes."

"Can we get it?"

"I'd guess."

"All right. Can we put the cage out back in the carriage house?"

"No, gotta have her with me, I'm saying."

"Not in the house."

He thought about it. He wanted the bet to go,

he guessed. It was going to be harder, more than he first thought, but he wasn't ready to give it up. He didn't lose a hundred pounds easy. Besides, the idea of talking posh and living nice, more for fun than anything, had grown on him. "Well, if the carriage house is close. And has light and lots of air, and I can go see her plenty. But no bath, all right? I'll wash up in a sink."

"And a bath, Mr. Tremore. For you. A bath and a haircut and a shave." She frowned at his upper lip again. "A shave every day," she continued. "And clean clothes. This is not going to be a lark, sir." She took a breath, pink-faced. For a skittish thing she sure could get her knickers in a knot. "You will be struggling with a lot of new ideas, a bath being your first, I suppose. You will have more than mere difficult sounds and constructions of the English language to learn. If you intend to be a gentleman in six weeks, you'd best begin by listening to me."

"I ain't the one who ain't listening," he said. "I'll learn all what makes sense to me, but nothing else. How can I? Things got to make sense or I'll just be mimicking what I don't see, what I gotta see from the inside, you know? And a bath I don't see at all. It be unhealthy for one. I'll catch me death. I could drown — I can't swim. I'll wash up in a basin. I always do. I'm a clean bloke —"

"Not clean enough —"

"Bloody clean enough for some." Damn her anyway. He told her, "You ain't the first fine lady,

71

you know, to take me upstairs, Miss Bollash —"

He watched her face turn white. Oh, hell, he thought. He ran his hand into his hair — and got a palmful of soot. He'd forgotten. Bloody hell, he didn't doubt he looked like a cat caught all night in a coal bin. He'd been up a flue, crawled around on a floor, then been chased partway through London only to end up beat on by a dozen people.

All right, he was dirty. All right, he wished he could call that last back. The fact that ratting rich ladies' houses had occasionally landed him upstairs in rich ladies' beds — ladies a lot less particular than this one — was most surely something *not* to discuss with Miss Edwina Bollash.

As brittle as ice, she told him, "You'll have a bath or leave immediately." She wasn't joking. Once she had a bite-hold of something, there was no getting it away from her.

But he meant what he said, too, and would damn well see she give him respect for his part in what they were planning to do. "Not unless you and Milton here be strong enough to put me in it."

Her bottom lip came up, covering a piece of her top lip as she pressed her mouth tight. She looked pained for a moment. Then she said softly, "Leave."

"Pardon?"

Louder, "Leave."

He scowled, staring at her. Relentless, she was.

"Fine then," he said. "Suit yourself."

He pushed past the two of 'em: the prudey Miss Know-It-All, wasting her time trying to wash life clean, and her manservant, soaking wet from trying to help her do it.

Didn't need this. Stupid idea. No, made no sense whanking around with a bloody-arse bet that wasn't good for nothing but entertaining a bunch a' rich folks. Sod them. Sod them all to Hades and back. Let them play with their money, not him.

Halfway down the block, though, he was already regretting his decision. Dream or not, what if she *could* show him how to be a proper gentleman? What if he could change himself into a . . . a bloody valet or . . . whatever that fellow Milton was now, a butler, wasn't it? Then, Mick, ol' chum, you could live in a fine, clean house all the time, too. And send a lot more money to Cornwall and the brood. Everyone could live better. Even Freddie here might just appreciate a carriage house, if it was dry and clean and got sunlight into it. And you like the way she talks, you know. Not to mention the way she smells.

Besides, a gentleman almost certain got to get a lot closer than any ratcatcher to the tall, timid-fierce girl who'd thrown him out over bathwater.

Chapter 4

Mr. Tremore's foot treads diminished without a pause, his and the soft-click trot of his dog's. Down the stairs they went, through the front hallway, then the front door opened and slammed. Edwina stood there in her modern bathroom, listening to silence. It was a funny moment, the house achingly quiet where only a moment ago it had rung with the most colorful talk, and lots of it.

She listened, waiting to hear his knock downstairs on her front door. He'd return, because he was smart and because it was in his best interest to reconsider. And because he was wrong.

When hushed stillness, however, only attested to his intention to remain wrong, she was surprised by the steep descent of her disappointment.

"My lady?"

She startled. It was Milton. "Yes?"

"Shall I clean up the bathroom then? Do you wish anything further?"

She had to think a moment to make sense of his questions. "Oh. No." She shook her head. "I mean, yes. Please clean up. But I won't need any-

thing further from you. Not till tea at ten." She always had a cup of chamomile before bed.

She left the room, thinking, So. That was that.

A shame, she consoled herself. Mr. Tremore was perfect in any number of ways. She didn't very often hear a linguistic pattern as distinctive as his. And she would have guessed by his alert attention, not to mention the way he mimicked sounds, that he would have made a good student. An excellent study. Ah, well.

What a plummet though. She felt utterly depressed as she came down the stairs.

She went about her business. The house was calm and orderly. She spent the afternoon tutoring: first a lawyer's daughter with a lisp, then a Hungarian countess who wanted to pronounce English better, then the daughter of country gentry who had "picked up an accent" in her native Devon. The last girl left. Edwina went to dinner, which was punctual, elegant, and delicious, thanks to a French–schooled cook.

Very late that night, however — with her in her flannel nightgown, padding around in the dark, looking for the key so she could wind her father's old clock — she heard a faint knock at the door below stairs, then voices at the kitchen entrance.

She went to the top of the stairwell to be sure, then smiled: There was no doubt. The sound of Mick Tremore's unmistakable, deep voice filled her with a kind of joy. It was so delightful to hear his dropped H's, his *wadden*'s for *wasn't*'s, his ruined diphthongs and flat vowels.

"I come to a decision," he said. "And it wasn't" — *wadden* — "that chronic to get to."

"Chronic, sir?"

"Long and painful. Was easy, once't I saw it."

Edwina's smile widened as she heard Mr. Tremore ask quite clearly, "So would you help me" — *'elp me* — "what's your name again?" *Whot's yer nime?*

Clearly or not, Milton didn't understand him. They grappled with Mr. Tremore's pronunciation for a few moments, until Milton finally said, "Oh, you want my name?"

"Yes." *Ace.*

"Milton, sir."

"Milton, I be wantin' a bath and shave, since the lady says I got to."

Edwina felt her senses come alive. Elation. As she heard Milton admit Mr. Tremore into the house, she did a little dance in her slippers there on the landing. But she stopped still as a lamppost to hear, "She be a smart woman, ain't she?"

"Yes, sir."

"I shouldn't've made such a fuss. I can get in some water."

Just like that, he admitted he was wrong. What an amazing conversation.

He continued graciously, "See, I be pigheaded sometimes." He laughed, a deep, rich vibration that made something move in her chest, *thudda-thud*, the way a bass drum did in a parade. "It come from bein' mostly right, 'course. But she knows a thing or two about the gentry, I guess."

"Yes, sir." She could tell Milton had little or no idea what the first part had been about. He responded graciously to the last though, saying, "She's gentry, sir."

"That's what I thought. Will you help me then?" *'Elp me thun?*

"Yes, sir. My pleasure, sir."

Edwina turned and all but floated up the main staircase to her bedroom. Why, she wouldn't be surprised if he shaved the mustache as well. He was being so reasonable.

In the morning, she would pretend nothing had happened, that Mr. Tremore had done just as he should have in due course, no argument, no embarrassment. She envisioned saying good morning to him at breakfast (his face clean-shaven), inviting him nonchalantly into her lab — *When you're finished with your meal, you can find me down the hall, last door on the right.*

Once in bed, though, she didn't go to sleep. She wasn't sleepy, she decided, so she picked up a book instead. She opened it, then never read a word. Instead, she listened to the water cut off, the pipes clanking as the flow stopped. She jolted slightly against her pillow as she heard a *ka-plosh*, then, "Ai, that be hot!" — Mr. Tremore entering a tubful of water. She lay there listening to the substantial splashes and sloshes of his large body moving through the business of a bath.

She thought about his naked chest again. Her memory of it both fascinated and repelled her. Hair. It had been there again as they had argued

in the bathroom. She shuddered. Who would have thought? Yet she had studied it with surreptitious care: a pattern of dark hair, two perfect swirls over muscles that bunched when he folded his arms, swirls that converged to become a dense pattern in the crevice between chest muscles, then (when he pulled his arms away to push back his hair) ran in a dark, ever-narrowing line, like an arrow pointing downward. Mick Tremore in the rude, as it were. This way to the widge.

Edwina started. Heavens! Up till now, she realized, she had carefully avoided forming in her mind any word for that part of a man. Even the scientific word made her vaguely uneasy; her sensibilities veered away from it. Still, she'd known immediately what Mr. Tremore referred to when he'd said *that*. His word seemed friendlier. A fond name. Were men fond of that part of themselves? It was certainly not the best part of statues; she made a point not to look there. And it changed, it grew. She'd read that astounding piece of information in a book. That was the worst part, the horror — or it had been the worst until this very moment, when it occurred to her that, goodness, a man might have hair there, too. She did. Oh, something that grew larger, up and out of a tangle of hair. How disgusting.

No, no, she mustn't think of it anymore. Enough. She must think of something else.

The mustache. From down the hallway came *ka-plosh, ka-plosh.* Mr. Tremore getting clean. Truly clean — taking off all the thick, wiry hair

that grew on his lip. Good. With that satisfying thought, punctuated by the pleasant, occasional lap of bathwater down the hall, she fell into a doze. There was no telling for how long, but she came to herself with a start, her reading light still on, the house quiet.

Then no: She rose up onto her arms, for a different sound reached her. The noise of movement, someone walking in the dead of night. Edwina sat all the way up, thinking, What the blazes. It seemed to come from the direction of her father's study.

She hopped off her bed, putting her arms through the sleeves of her faded blue dressing gown. She walked quickly out into the hall, lifting her heavy braid from where it was caught with one hand as she pushed her spectacles up from where they'd slid down her nose with the other.

At the far end, the door to her father's study indeed stood partly open. The light was on. She walked toward it, continuing to hear the soft shuffle of someone moving about. She thought irritably, It must be Mr. Tremore prowling around. But when she pushed the door open further, she could only step back.

It was a stranger, standing in quarter profile and holding her father's crystal decanter of cognac up to the light.

The room's wall lamp made the brandy, as it tipped gently back and forth in the decanter, cast amber prisms across the side of his face, his shirt.

Gold light. It made him look like an apparition. She might have said the intruder was a handsome, genteel burglar, for he was elegantly proportioned and certainly well-dressed, but he was in no rush — too much at his ease to be robbing the house. His shirttail was out, his shirt cuffs turned back. He wore a vest, but it hung unbuttoned. Less like a burglar, more like a ghost, one of her father's old friends come as a houseguest.

Mr. Tremore, she thought again, trying out the idea. Who else? It had to be him. Yet the man standing before her seemed so unlike her new student. Yet similar: He had the same dark hair, dark as night, but it was slicked close to his head and combed away from his face. Was Mr. Tremore this tall, so square-shouldered, so straightly built? This man looked leaner, neater. Handsomer. His clothes were simple, but nice. His white shirt was neatly pressed, open at the neck; it was missing its collar. The vest —

She frowned. His vest was oddly familiar. As were the trousers somehow, or what she could see of them. He stood behind the edge of her father's desk.

He turned toward her, lowering the decanter in front of him, as if suddenly aware of her. Their eyes met. His face changed, drawing up into a crooked smile, showing a deep dimple to one side of a thick, well-trimmed mustache that rose up on a lot of even, white teeth. A remarkable contrast. Edwina was halted for an instant in the warmth of his smile, the way a small animal is

stopped foolishly in the road sometimes when the beam of a carriage lamp swings, too bright, suddenly onto it. Lord, the man was good-looking. A sharp good looks, the sort that absorbed a woman's good sense and turned it to mush in her head. Refined, cultured somehow, with a subtle air of competence.

Not Mr. Tremore, who certainly was vigorous-looking and masculine, but —

He held out his arms, the bottle in one hand, the other palm up, and said, "Well, whaddaya think?"

Edwina quite nearly fell over as he offered himself for inspection, turning slowly. It was, of course, none other. "Mis-Mister Tremore," she said, though almost as a question, looking for confirmation. "I — um — ah — you —" she stammered.

Even staring right at him, she couldn't quite believe it was the same man. To say he cleaned up well was so much an understatement, it stood reality on its head.

"How do I look?" he asked.

"Unbelievable." His mustache. Someone had trimmed it, made an attempt — not all that successful a one — to tame it.

"Diabolical," he suggested, wiggling his eyebrows, then laughed. He loved the word; he must, he used it enough. "I look like a bloody lord, don't I?"

Edwina cleared her throat. Well, yes. And here stood another unwelcome bit of truth: The

81

handsomest "bloody lord" she had ever seen was a ratcatcher wearing her father's outdated trousers, shirt, and vest — and wandering her house in the middle of the night so as to steal brandy or whatever else he could find, no doubt.

She drew herself up, then demanded, "Put that down."

He looked at the decanter, seemingly surprised to find his fingers around its neck. "Ah," he said, as if now understanding. He made a knowing cluck with his tongue, then grinned gleefully, a man smiling at a good joke. "Wasn't pinchin' none, if that was what you be thinkin'. It just shook me, see, a little —"

"Put it down."

He put it on the desk, though he frowned, doing a very good imitation of a man unfairly called to account. He repeated, "Wasn't pinchin' none. See, I have this dream sometimes —"

"I'm not interested in your dreams of easy liquor, Mr. Tremore. You may not enter this room, unless you do so in my company."

He grinned again. "Well," he said. "Then come in, Miss Bollash."

When she only stood there scowling at him from the hallway, he came toward her.

Lord, with his mouth shut, he even moved right. Lithe, graceful, a male who was physically confident of himself, in the full flush of bold health — and probably used to smiling at women who stood in a dim hall in the middle of the night.

"You be a right fine sight in that, Miss Bollash."

She looked down. Her dressing gown was unsashed on her night-shift. She quickly pulled the gown around her. Not because there was anything here to make a man misbehave, but for pride's sake, so neither one of them had to admit there wasn't.

He stopped at the doorway, her in the hall, him in the room. "Do your mates call you Edwina?" he asked. "Ain't you got a sweet name?"

She stiffened, frightened somehow. "I don't have any 'mates,' Mr. Tremore, and *Miss Bollash* sounds respectful — sweet enough to my ears."

He screwed up his mouth, making his mustache slant sideways — it looked more fashionable for its coiffing but no less rough, bristly.

"Winnie," he said suddenly.

She jumped.

He put his hands on either side of the doorjamb, arms spread, elbows bent, and contemplated her for a few moments. Then he repeated, "Winnie. That be it. That be what you call an Edwina, right?" He smiled because she admitted, either by her frown or her jump the moment before, that she identified with the name, a name she hadn't heard in ages. "Ah." He nodded. "Much nicer. Soft. Dear-like, you know?"

The way he said it . . . His tone gave rise to a kind of confusion. Embarrassment somehow. Fright again. His expression invited her to smile

83

back at him, but she couldn't have if she'd wanted to. And she didn't; she certainly didn't want to, she thought. He was playing her for a fool, trying to distract her from the fact that he'd been stealing liquor, which, of course, she had to put a stop to.

She said, "No, *Winnie* is not nice. When I was little, my cousins used to neigh like a horse when they said it. They used to call me Wi-i-i-n-n-ie." She whinnied for him as she said her name. Then she wished she hadn't.

Because he winced, reacting to the pain of it. His concern made her look away. She heard him say, "Well, you bloody well fooled 'em, Miss Bollash. 'Cause you be a beaut, if ever I seen one."

She glanced at him — as harsh a glare as she could muster — then contradicted his malarkey. "Mr. Tremore, I am a gangly, plain woman with speckled skin, who wears glasses on a nose that looks like an eagle's. I'm taller than any man I know." In a moment of confusion, she had to re-think that statement. "Except you." She went on with forced patience, "But I'm an honest woman, a smart woman. And I don't hold truck with a lot of lying falderal from some Cockney-Cornish womanizer who thinks he can talk his way out of being caught red-handed in the liquor shelf. If you wish to drink, you may go to the public house on the corner of the next block. Sit in the pub, drink till your heart's content, then come back when you are sober."

Goodness, she couldn't remember telling anyone off like that. Of course, she couldn't remember anyone trying to flatter her so dishonestly. The injustice of it made her angry. Surely there was something else she did right, something he could praise, without dragging her odd looks into the matter.

His face remained focused on her, furrowed with curiosity and consternation. He shook his head. "I didn't take a drop," he said. He smiled his crooked smile that, despite herself, was somehow appealing. A charming villain, this one. "Want to smell me breath?" he offered.

God, no. She took a step back.

He took a step closer, letting go of the doorjamb, coming through the doorway into the dim hall. He smelled of soap and something else, barber's talcum perhaps. Milton had taken some scissors to his hair. It was shorter, neater. Up close, with her standing there in her bare feet, he was tall enough that she had to bend her neck back to look up at him. She wanted to laugh: She felt short next to him. "I'm not pretty," she murmured.

His shadow, a silhouette with the room's light behind him, shook its head. As if speaking to a dim child with whom he was having difficulty communicating, he said, "Miss Bollash, we already know you be better with words than me. So all what I can tell you be this —"

His head bent toward her. No, he wouldn't, she thought, almost giddy now from the absurdi-

ties that ran through her head. He certainly wouldn't . . . well, no — Men had to know women well to do that, didn't they? So, no —

But, yes. Much to her dismay, her new student's moustache brushed her lip, then his mouth pressed to hers. The feel of his lips, the warmth that radiated off his face were such a surprise — a disarming surprise — it didn't leave her with the presence of mind to do anything. She just stood there befuddled. Being kissed.

Strange, what her first kiss, at the ripe old age of twenty-nine, brought to mind. Her first reaction was to cry. To just plain weep and wail. Damn you, she thought. Damn you. Don't play like this.

Her second thought, though, was to simply blank out the first thought. She said nothing, did nothing — half-waiting for him to laugh, to announce his funny joke on her, half-praying he would be kind about it: while one of the most elegant-looking men she had ever seen pressed his mustache, warm and dry, against her mouth.

It wasn't prickly at all. Not bristly. Not broomlike. It was soft. Cushiony. It moved gently with his mouth.

She backed away a little; he followed. She drew in a breath, though it sounded more like a hiccup of air than breathing. He caught her arm, pulling her toward him a little, his hand strong, warm, sure. The skin of her lips was more sensitive than she would have dreamed. His mouth was smooth against hers, and so soft — she would never have

thought a man's mouth was so soft to touch, when the rest of him looked so hard and rough. As his mouth skimmed hers, she knew a tiny place on the curve of his lip where it was chapped. She could feel so much with her own mouth. Who could have imagined it was so . . . alive with feeling like this?

His thumb touched her cheek. She made a small jerk to realize his hand was at her face. Jumpy. Nervous. While pleasure materialized in the pit of her belly like smoke, wisps of it that became soft billows. The feeling was so keen and foreign, she didn't know what to do with it. His mouth stayed on hers till the clock downstairs suddenly began to chime. *One, two, three* . . . It awakened good sense. She jumped at *four*, shoved away at *five*. It continued chiming, counting off the moments till midnight, while her palm lay flat against the chest she'd seen. Its predominant feeling was hardness, as solid as a cliffside under the shirt. And warm. His chest was several degrees warmer where it provided resistance against her hand.

His face was close. "Ah," he said. "Yes." *Ace,* his ridiculous *ace.* He nodded, as if he were agreeing with something. "I was fair enough sure I'd like kissin' you, and I do. You, Miss Winnie Bollash, are better than pretty —"

Oh, the insult of his game. The hurt of it. Tears rose up. She wanted to knock him down, to laugh, to cry. Outwardly, though, she moderated herself, only pushing him back more firmly. She

was, after all, the sophisticated one here, the one who was supposed to teach him rules he didn't know to play by.

Her throat tightened around the words even as she said them. "I want you to know" — she paused, gathering herself — "that I am not angry with you." Just the bare bones, Edwina. Just make him stop. "Um, you caught me off guard, Mr. Tremore. You can't do, well — do what you just did. Don't ever do that again." There. Hold to the rules, she thought, and all will be fine. "It's not right. You can't do what you normally do." Something made her add, "I'm not a shop girl who can be flattered into believing nonsense, just because it suits your cheeky sense of fun."

He laughed. "Fun," he repeated, saying that particular word exactly right. "Miss Bollash, life be rich. Why don't you bite yourself off a piece?"

She had no answer. Speaking to him in the middle of the night in a dim hallway — about whether or not he could kiss her — was like walking into an unfamiliar, pitch-dark room. She wasn't sure which way to turn without running into something, without hurting herself. Every direction was potentially unsafe.

His head bent. He was looking at her night-clothes. As if her simply standing there in them was somehow provocative. Now *that* was an unusual feeling. It made her spine shiver. It made her heart beat in a panicky rhythm. The shadows of his shirt rose and fell, his chest making it move, a deep rising, falling. The sight sent such a

shot of apprehension through her, her knees turned liquid.

She'd already told him once, and he wasn't stepping back. She burst out with, "I wouldn't be standing here in my nightclothes, Mr. Tremore, if you weren't prowling my house in the wee hours like a piece of Bow Bells riffraff, taking stock of what he can steal."

He cranked his head back. Light from the study cut across his shoulder, revealing a plane of his face: the look of insult. She regretted having said those precise words, yet couldn't think of different ones, better ones.

He tilted his head to look at her, then said quietly, "You can rest easy, lovey." *Loovey,* he said. "I ain't no thief. I work hard, and I be good at what I do."

She continued to be up in arms. "Not so good that you can keep yourself clean and in decent clothes."

His insulted expression softened into a kind of disappointment. He folded his arms over his chest, letting his weight fall against the edge of the door frame. "You be a snooty thing, ain't ya? Think you know everything there be to know about a bloke, because he don't talk like you, because he catches rats for a livin' —"

"I know a man too lazy to sew the buttons onto his coat. And who ends up being chased —"

He let out a single snort of laughter, loud enough to silence her. "First," he said, "who I be chasin' or who be chasin' me ain't none of your

business." His face took on the shadows of his crooked smile before he added, "At least not yet. Second, the coats what I can afford don't right off have many buttons, and what buttons they do, I sell. See, I got ten younger brothers and sisters in Cornwall what depend on me to support them. I send most of me money home. And third — you will notice, I can count, by the way, all the way to *third,* and I can read, too, Public Education Act, you see. And third, loov, you ain't so funny to look at as you think. You be right nice to look at. True, you ain't pretty exactly, but you be —" He struggled for the right word, frowned, looked down, then said, "I can't explain it. I like lookin' at you." The dim light seemed to show him grinning again; it was hard to be sure. But there was wryness in his voice when he offered, "Different. A long pretty thing with the face of a moppet. You be loovly, Miss Bollash." He repeated softly with satisfaction, "Loovly."

Lovely, he meant, of course, but the softness and rhythm in the way he said it struck her.

"Loovly," she repeated, saying it his way. Then laughed. She meant her laughter to be ironic, a hollow humor full of disdain. Her usual kind of laugh when confronted with her own looks. But despite herself, she felt genuine amusement. "More on the long side though than the loovly side," she added.

"Well, long *and* loovly, yes." He laughed, too, possibly at her attempt at his word, at her saying it less naturally than he did.

He stood there, his chest reverberating with that low, base-drum sound again. While Edwina released herself into her own laughter, letting it out softly, letting it go till it ended of its own accord. The two of them slowly calmed till they were just looking at each other.

And there it was: For an instant, reality permutated. For an instant — villainous black mustache and all — a handsome gentleman smiled on her. It seemed suddenly plausible that a man could find her appealing. In a loovly sort of way. Mind-boggling, but plausible.

Then a moment later she truly *did* want to burst out laughing. For here in the half-lit corridor, of course, was only mousy, lanky Winnie Bollash — being flattered by a ratcatcher who didn't know any better.

She sighed, both her smile and the nice feeling dissipating into that sure piece of truth. She stepped back, pulling her dressing gown up tight, wrapping her arms around herself. "Please don't go into the study. It was my father's."

"Your father's?"

"He's gone now. Dead."

"Sympathies, loov."

"Thank you." She nodded. "It was a while ago."

He hesitated a moment, only a moment, then said, "You should have the room then. Your father don't need it now."

Edwina looked away, as if around them she might see something besides the dark landing.

"The whole house was his," she said. "I've taken over all the rest, made it my own, but I've left his study as it was." She murmured, "I use it as the masculine place to take my ladies, to show them how to be comfortable in a man's world." She laughed without humor. "A good joke, don't you think? I'm not very comfortable in such a world myself. Except in that room. My carefully preserved upper-class male habitat." Like a museum, she thought.

She'd said too much already. "Good night." She walked past him, into the study, ostensibly to put out the light. Then she thought to ask, "You have everything, yes?"

He nodded. The question, she realized, was just an excuse to look at him in better light. He stood just beyond the doorway in the corridor, partly in light, partly in shadow. The study's electric bulb threw sharp definition up the front of him: Her father's trousers were too short; they came to the top of his boots. Chances were, under the long shirttail, the trousers weren't buttoned. The vest without doubt couldn't be. No cravat, no collar.

None of this stopped Mick Tremore from being handsome, however. His jaw was square, chiseled. He had a straight, high-bridged nose — a Roman nose that, with his deep brow, shadowed his eyes like a ledge. He was striking, there was no doubt about it. Elegant, she thought again. Not just good-looking. Handsome in a polished way that defied explanation. The luck

of heritage, an accident of features. Whatever made him so, it was a stroke of good fortune for her — and for Jeremy Lamont. It was much easier to pass a man off as a gentleman when he lined up with preconceptions of what a splendid one looked like.

Which, she realized, in another sense was not a stroke of luck for her at all.

"Good night," she said again.

She went into the study, but delayed pulling the chain on the light. She made herself dawdle, reshelving a book, realigning a vase. She didn't let herself look back at him, not once. Even though she knew he watched her, waiting. It was at least a full minute before she heard his foot-falls turn then walk the short distance to his room at this end of the hall.

Good. Once he was gone, she put the light out, then went back to bed.

Edwina gave herself a good talking-to as she lay back down into her sheets.

He was lying. Don't believe him. Long and loovly, indeed. He was romanticizing, at the very least.

She herself was no romantic. She knew her own narrow face, the thin blade of her nose with its bony bump on the bridge that was fine for holding up her spectacles but did nothing for her womanly charms. She'd long ago given up on the freckles that covered her skin, from her face down her neck, right down her body over the

tops of her toes. She had no breasts to speak of, while she had too much bottom to be symmetrical. And her height, well, it went without saying it was as far from feminine as was Gargantua.

Homely. Hopeless. How could any man look at her and even think to — She grew warm lying there in her bed, staring into the dark. To what?

Kiss her. He'd kissed her. Goodness, it was a night for saying things to herself she had never voiced before. *Kiss.* She sighed.

Why had he done that? Had she misinterpreted? Maybe it wasn't a kiss. Had her mouth looked dirty? Had she looked as if she needed air? Was he trying to figure out how to say something by feeling the movement of her lips? Was there any reasonable explanation for Mr. Tremore to have touched her like that, put his mouth — his mustache — on her?

Lying there, she grew faintly frightened again — a state, it was safe to say, in which she lived almost perpetually. The only place Edwina felt utterly safe was downstairs in her laboratory, where she wasn't so much safe as lost to herself, unaware of anything else but her work. It didn't matter though. Tomorrow, like yesterday and the day before, she'd simply cover her fear by working hard, holding to the rules: immersing herself in the day and what ought to be done. All the while trying to quell worries like, What had she done to make him act like that? Would he ignore tonight tomorrow? Should she? Would he

make fun of her now? Was he angry at her? She could have said things better. . . .

And if Mr. Tremore, or anyone at all, did any one of these things — ignored her or became angry or made fun — she felt responsible. She might spend weeks trying to figure out what she had done to deserve it. As if the next time, she could avoid the roughness of life by doing something differently herself.

Often, as now, she chastised herself — how spinsterish to agonize over what couldn't be controlled anyway — yet she couldn't stop her thinking. It was too old a habit. A superstition pounded into her from her youth: the belief that if she were just a good enough, smart enough girl, if she could just think about it long enough, she'd figure out the "right" thing to do, and then life would be kind to her.

No, a woman who looked like she did — who thought as she did — could not afford to be romantic. That was why Edwina was practical. And responsible. And hardworking.

And up all night thinking about what Mr. Tremore had said and done and how sincere he had seemed when he said it and did it. And what could it possibly mean? And would he do it again? And did she want him to?

Chapter 5

Mick stretched. He lay on a feather mattress. Sweet. Slowly, he lifted his eyelids, opening his eyes on shadows from bed curtains, a glow coming through their edges. It was a finer room than usual, but the light was the same as when he always woke up. Same time every day. Daybreak. No matter where he was, the sun found him and nudged him awake.

He swung his legs off the high bed, then had to step over Magic to walk to the window. He pushed open the shutters. The day's light poured in. It brought with it a lot of quiet. London at dawn was about as still as she ever got. Hardly a sound. A dog somewhere, not so lazy as Magic, barked far off. Nearby, a cart rolled on cobbles. Nothing else. Mick rested his palms on the wood sill, leaning straight-armed to look out.

Miss Bollash's back garden was damp with dew. Pretty. Her neighbors' houses were silent and still. No one. He loved this time of day — like he had the world to himself. Being alive felt good. Life was in order. It made sense.

Of course, he knew an hour from now he probably wouldn't feel the same. Most days usually

fell apart, one way or another. But he knew, too, if he was alive at sunrise tomorrow the new morning'd feel like a gift. No noise in the day yet, no noise in his head.

Magic came over and bumped against Mick's leg. The dog got his first scratch, while Mick rubbed the back of one knuckle down his mustache. It felt different on his face the way Milton trimmed it. Different, but all right. Miss Bollash sure wanted it off. Wasn't happening. It wouldn't earn him a shilling more to shave it. It wouldn't make him talk better, give him a better profession, wouldn't give him or his a better life in any way. So it stayed, because he liked it — he wasn't even certain he'd know himself without it. He'd had a mustache of one kind or another for a dozen years.

And taking it off would not make him more a gent, that was sure. Bloody hell, the Prince of Wales had one. Miss Bollash didn't want it off for that.

Standing there at the window, scratching Magic, it came to him: She wanted it off for herself.

He couldn't think why. But, well, well, well, he thought. It made him smile. She still couldn't have it off. But wasn't that just the most interesting thing now?

Down the hall, Edwina awakened with a lurch, her mind filling with consciousness and the day's worries simultaneously, like water down a slough.

Before the day was even in focus before her eyes, she already had a pounding sense of everything to do and no time to do it. A normal morning. It was her habit, to gain control of her daily panic, to lay in bed and make lists, organize her concerns, tame them if she could with a plan — often an overambitious, overwhelming plan but nonetheless something to go by.

This morning, though, she lay there trying to dredge up the worry that had disturbed her sleep. What was it? Something new, something she hadn't thought of until her sleeping mind had hit upon it. What? What? She racked her brain.

Mr. Tremore. All her worst fears revolved around him, surely. What about him? She reviewed the worst that lay ahead. (Ignoring staunchly what worry of him that lay behind in a dim midnight hallway.) Changing his sound, his accent itself, was going to be the hardest work, though it could be changed; in time he could do it. His grammar and diction would be easier, though only slightly. Beyond these, he required regular coaching in acceptable upper-class social behavior, and they had to come up with a plausible background for him: enough detail to be convincing if anyone asked, to make him fit in, yet without filling in enough that people could verify specifics.

The new problem suddenly came to her. "O-o-oh," she groaned, throwing her arm up over her eyes. "Crumbs, crumbs, crumbs."

No matter what she did, no matter how well she coached him, after dinner on the night of the ball, the ladies would retire to the drawing room while the men had their port and cigars. She could offer him no help when it came to how gentlemen behaved on their own: She didn't know. He was going to have to invent his way along himself for as long as forty-five minutes.

Edwina was at the top of the upstairs landing when she first heard the laughter. It was faint but coming from below her in her own house. A laugh she had never heard before, though the voice in it sounded somehow familiar.

By the bottom of the stairs, she knew who it was. Her day-help who came to cook and clean, Monday through Friday: Mrs. Reed. The woman was laughing herself silly. The sound was coming from the serving kitchen off the dining room, a little half-kitchen where breakfast was prepared and served and where, years ago, banquets had been kept hot, course at a time. The laughter now was infectious, so round and rippling and from-the-belly it made Edwina's own mouth draw up as she imagined what might be the cause.

When she opened the door, though, she expected anything but what she saw: Mr. Tremore stealing a sausage over Mrs. Reed's head from her skillet. He complained it was hot, *yike*, as he popped it into his mouth, while the woman did battle for her sausages with a spatula. Mrs. Reed

was wiping her eyes from laughing so hard. Mr. Tremore took another, letting out a triumphant crow, then bent, swooping the woman up, taking her into his arms.

"Oh, sir," the cook said in reprimand, though it was a reprimand that relished itself. He danced Mrs. Reed away from the stove, his cheek pressed to hers — which was saying something, since he had to bend down a good foot and a half to get it there. The cook was enjoying herself as Edwina had never imagined the woman could — Mrs. Reed was always so quiet with her.

Edwina stood there in the doorway, watching an alien merriment — nothing like she'd ever seen in her father's house, nothing that had ever existed in her own. While the source of it — an unexpectedly good dancer, if a person liked a two-step jig — led a woman around the kitchen to the rhythm of his own humming. Mr. Tremore's deep voice carried a clear tune. He moved well, guiding Mrs. Reed confidently, round and round, with her fussing with him to stop, as she laughed and rushed her feet after his to keep up.

Edwina frowned. The game seemed to be an ongoing invention of Mr. Tremore's. Part of her wanted to stop it; part of her was oh-so-curious to watch.

To stop it, of course, would make her the spoiler, and she already felt dour enough standing on the fringe. So the part of her that was curious watched and listened to laughter as it filled

the close room. It made the little serving kitchen alive in a way she'd never have predicted. Its warming ovens, closed and dark, its bare shelves empty of the huge serving dishes they had once held — neither looked the worse today for disuse. The room's double window was thrown open, the flower box outside bursting with color, red and pink and yellow and coral coming over the sill. And there was Mr. Tremore dancing in the window's wide beam of sunlight.

The back of his vest, a silvery green, was bowed so he could wrap his long, white-shirted arm around the waist of a woman who was head-and-shoulders shorter and several feet wider, not to mention more than twice his age. His black hair shone silky and soft in the light, sharp against the white of his collar.

His clothes from Henley's had arrived apparently. Everything fit. All was new and better in quality than what her butler had found for him last night. And all quite suited Mr. Tremore. She could have believed, standing here watching him, that he was perhaps an easygoing country gentleman — there were such things. Men who remained in their native counties, landowners who talked like the locals — she knew because she occasionally trained their daughters to speak more like the *ton* if they wished to go a Season in London.

Mr. Tremore saw Edwina and slowed.

Mrs. Reed caught on and looked over her shoulder. In the end, Edwina didn't have to say a

thing. Her presence alone was enough to end the amusement. Her cook and houseguest let go of each other, parting, straightening. Mrs. Reed began to make apologies, clearing her throat. She set the spatula down and adjusted her apron.

"It's all right," Edwina said, though she couldn't decide how she felt about what she'd witnessed. It was silliness, foolish enough that they were both embarrassed to be caught at it. It was nothing. It accomplished nothing. Yet she envied their lighthearted good time.

She wished she could think of anything to say but what she felt she must: "Mr. Tremore should have his meals in the dining room, all the proper silver set out. We'll do full service, at least until he catches on and is comfortable with it. Could you ask Milton to serve, please, Mrs. Reed?"

"Yes, miss."

A positively stupid thought came to mind as Mrs. Reed waddled out to get Milton: Mr. Tremore had kissed the woman. Not out of passion or lust, God forbid. No, but a bussed cheek, a peck; either was possible. Even likely. And both were aggravating somehow to envision. This overly curious, probably dishonest Cockney-Cornish ratcatcher certainly liked the ladies. Inside of twenty-four hours, with only two women under the same roof, the odds were he'd kissed them both. The skinny spinster and the heavyset cook.

He wasn't very particular, Edwina thought.

Mr. Tremore said nothing as she led him out

into the dining room. "You sit here," she said, touching the high-backed chair opposite hers. When he went to sit in it though, she added, "After you hold my chair for me."

He came around. As she sat, he murmured from behind, "We was just havin' fun."

"I know."

He went back around a table more than twenty feet long. Once it had held a line of elaborate candelabra, bowls of flowers, platters of food. Once the dozen chairs on his side, the other dozen on hers, had been filled regularly with guests. Mr. Tremore sat opposite her, into one of the empty chairs, and eyed her.

He explained further, "She don't understand what I say every time. You be the only one here who does."

"So you had to dance with her?"

"She knew stealing sausages. I was telling her I liked the smell of her cooking."

"I see." She tried to. Yet there seemed any number of other ways to convey one's appreciation. She didn't dance with people over sausage, no matter how delicious it was.

They said nothing more till the porridge arrived, then he picked up the wrong spoon.

"The larger one," she said.

He frowned down at the mass of silverware surrounding the plate, as if it were a riddle of metal and shape. Good, she thought, for no explicable reason. He found the porridge spoon, picked it up.

"No," she said. He held it wrong. She got up from the table, came around, and took it out of his fist.

Frowning, he gave his fingers up to her, relaxing them completely into her ministration. She found herself in sudden, disconcerting possession of a man's willing hand. Large, warm, heavy. Smooth-fingered. A strong hand with neat joints. That hadn't the first idea how to balance a spoon. She quickly put the instrument into his correct grasp.

As she sat down again, she pressed her palms once — they'd grown damp — onto the starchy-dry linen of her napkin in her lap, then she looked across the table.

He was still holding the spoon out, staring at how she'd wrapped his fingers around it, a look of distress on his face.

After this, breakfast was silent.

Mr. Tremore picked up a corner of leftover toast from his plate. Porridge had been followed by eggs, tomatoes, and sausages with fried bread. He'd eaten a good bit, though Edwina had the feeling he'd have eaten more if getting the food into his mouth hadn't been such an ordeal. The utensils had proved frustrating.

By the end, Edwina had let him be. Better he had half a lesson and ate something.

She only wished she could make him more realistic. When she mentioned her fear regarding his being alone with the gentlemen after dinner

on the night of the ball, he said, "Won't be a problem." With the toast he mopped up the remnants of eggs and tomato as efficiently as if no one would wash the plate between here and dinner. "I'll listen," he said, "and see what all the other blokes get 'emselves into."

"Nothing," she said. "Gentlemen don't get themselves into anything. That's what makes them gentlemen."

He was going to argue, but, as if he thought better of it, he picked up his knife from his plate. He reached for the jam —

"No, the spoon."

He exchanged the knife for the spoon, then used it to scoop out jam, after which he flipped the spoon over to spread jam with the back. "Then I won't say anything either."

"Well, they talk about *something*. Put the spoon down — you use the knife to spread it."

He shot her a contrary frown, as if she were inventing all this just to confound him. He answered, "Whatever they do, I'll do."

"They may ask you questions."

"I'll answer 'em."

"No, no." She shook her head. He didn't take her concern as seriously as he should, acting as if it were little more than a few details he'd pull together when the time came. "It's a time when men relax," she tried to explain. "They drink brandy and smoke cigars and, oh —" What did they do exactly? She didn't know. They behaved like men. With frustration, she said, "You're li-

able to answer like a — a ratcatcher —"

He laughed. "It be fact that I will. But I'll talk pretty, as pretty as you show me, and no one'll know the difference. Gents ain't as smart as all that, truth be known. And you got rats."

"Excuse me?" Edwina frowned at him.

"You got rats," he repeated. "In your house or nearby."

"I do not."

"Yes, you do. Not many, not a problem yet — not so you see them unless you know what to look for. But you got a hole in a corner baseboard over there, and you got sounds under the floorboards. I be tellin' you: There be a nest of them somewhere."

"Oh, fine," she said, tossing her napkin onto her plate. The gentlemen she knew were all easily smart enough to pick out a ratcatcher among them if he started talking about noises under the floorboards. "You have to stop thinking — talking — like a ratcatcher, Mr. Tremore."

She felt unappreciated — keen to improve him, while he seemed to dispute her changes were even improvements. She told him, "This is more than an adventure: more than a month of sporting about in fine clothes. It could change your life forever, make it better."

"It could make it different," he contradicted. "Maybe better, maybe not." He lifted his chin enough that his eyes came out of the shadow of his brow.

Fair, level eyes. It made her nervous to meet them. She glanced down, focusing on the table as he reached for the jam again. He mounded more on his last corner of toast — he did it just right, the spoon, then the knife.

His hands were surprisingly graceful. They weren't calloused as one might have expected, though his left was scarred, the marks of a bite. They were aesthetic hands, attractive, with long, straight fingers. Unlike her own funny digits that thickened at the joints and turned slightly up at the tips. She stared at her hands in her lap.

"You want that I do somethin' about it?"

She jerked, looked. "About what?"

"The rats," he said brightly. "For free. No charge."

"No." She pressed her lips between her teeth, then remembered to say, "Thank you. No, thank you." She took a breath. "You have to begin to think like a viscount, Mr. Tremore. What would a viscount see if he were sitting here? Not a hole in the floorboard."

He snorted. "I hate to tell you, loovey, but from where I be sittin', unless he be blind, he'd see a hole, a hole what, if it didn't make him think of rats, he'd be stupid." He shrugged genially, as if the next were an earnest concession. " 'Course," he said, "I think a good many gents be as bloody stupid as blocks, so you could be right."

She frowned, shaking her head. It was the bath all over again. She wanted to pick him up and

107

dunk him, headfirst, in English upper-class manners and vocabulary and sounds. While he sat there, his mind heavily entrenched in his own ways; rough, uncouth, unmovable.

She pushed back from the table. "Fine," she said. She sighed as she stood up. "Meet me in my lab, if you will. Please hurry. I have a student at noon, and you and I have a lot to do."

She felt as if they had a mountain to level, with only a porridge spoon held correctly to do it.

Chapter 6

Mr. Tremore failed all morning. Then he failed all afternoon till tea. Failure, of course, was a difficult thing for anyone. Edwina tried to tell him that to get very little right at first was quite normal, yet it seemed particularly hard on him.

He balked at recording his vowels and consonants on a gramophone-recorder. Why record them until they were right? She explained the need for a record of progress. While he maintained that saying things into a machine — wrong, he emphasized — only made him feel like "a blewdy ahrss."

The best that could be said for the day was that he got to where he could *hear* himself being wrong.

"This is real progress, Mr. Tremore."

He didn't believe it. He'd expected perhaps to speak like a "gent" by the end of the afternoon. When, instead, by the end of the afternoon he spoke like a man becoming — necessarily — self-conscious about each sound he uttered.

That evening after dinner, Jeremy Lamont paid a call, no doubt to inspect how the odds on

his bet were shaping up. He asked a few pointed questions, asked to see the furnishings he and his brother had provided Mr. Tremore, then wanted to observe the lessons themselves, hear Mr. Tremore speak. Edwina and Mr. Tremore accommodated him, of course, but she could have told him that in one day no miracles would happen.

"And when might his progress be noticeable?" Mr. Lamont asked.

"It's noticeable now, but not to you," she told him. "There is little you can do. Why don't you visit, say, during the fifth week, the week before the ball. You will get a very good idea then whether Mr. Tremore is able to learn a sufficient amount for your purposes."

Mr. Lamont asked a few more questions, mostly about "tricks" to make Mr. Tremore "seem more genteel," then left.

Not so unusual really. A client paying attention. To be expected. Yet his visit left Edwina uneasy.

Then again, she told herself, she was always uneasy about something. Perhaps she just had a lot on her mind. She was still finagling her finances to pay for a new coal furnace. A carriage horse had a tendon problem that was taking money and time. Her bank's balance on her account was different from hers, and she hadn't been able to figure out why. So what was so different about today's uneasiness? She would have thought she'd be used to the state of mind by now.

At the end of the day, Edwina had a habit she used sometimes to calm herself. Perhaps once or twice a week, it was her secret that she carried a pitcher of water to her evening primroses that grew wild at the back of her garden behind her house. The plants bloomed at night, so, if anyone asked, she was outside to see them, to smell them, and of course to nurture them. But in fact she nurtured them in a way she would have been hard pressed to explain to anyone.

She liked to go out and sing to them. Oh, it wasn't really even singing. She couldn't carry a tune very well. She hummed in rhythm to words she whispered as she confided her worries to the primroses and the night.

"The Misters Lamont, la, la, even the nicer one, are so strange," she sang. "But they pay their way, and I shouldn't complain." She sang some more, about the bill for the coal furnace and the horse with the limp, then moved on to Mr. Tremore's retroflexed R's. She was just working up the courage to sing on a more personal theme regarding Mr. Tremore, when from the dark another voice off to her right suddenly, quietly joined in.

She jumped, drew back. It was Mr. Tremore himself. He was on the bench under the wisteria, sitting in the shadows.

She didn't hear what he sang at first; she was too busy cringing, trying to figure out an explanation. There was none. She withdrew to the shadows, silent, utterly silent, the only safety she

knew while she waited for him to berate her.

He stood up more into the light, and his voice became clearer. "I hope, la, la, he's taking good care of my dogs, la, la . . ."

He was imitating her, making fun of her, she thought. Inside, Edwina died a little. Her throat tightened and her stomach grew hot, as if it were trying to digest something thick and burning.

Never had anyone caught her in this childish consolation. She couldn't even rally enough defense to demand why he was out here in the dark himself. What was he doing roaming her house — and now the grounds to her house — in the dead of night?

She wanted to hide when he stepped fully from the shadows, his handsomeness itself assailing her. So innocently, he came into the moonlight of her back garden, his white shirt brighter than the moon itself, his face shadowed and planed.

"I did drills today, la, la, that was too hard and my tongue wouldn't do right," he said.

She frowned. He wasn't smiling. He didn't seem to be taunting her. Yet . . . no, it couldn't be. She didn't trust her own judgment.

Yet he appeared to be trying her plant-singing out.

He sang his own song to the plant and the stars and the dark, his tune echoing hers, though his voice carried the rhythm into more of a melody. With his hand, he rustled the leaves of the hedge

that shaded the primroses, as she had. Then, stranger still, he looked at her and sang the words to her.

To her.

"I hope tomorrow is easier, and I get something right," he sang, his words so soft that she had to strain to hear them.

Edwina didn't know how to react to his appropriating of her foolishness. She said nothing.

He stopped. They stared at each other. He opened his mouth as if to speak.

But all she could do was turn quickly and walk toward her back door.

She didn't want him to explain or make excuses, if he was being kind. If he was being something else, she didn't want to know.

Mick watched as the tall woman with delicate-like feelings marched away. The moon was just behind the house, so he saw her only for a few seconds before she fell into the house's shadow. She was movement in the dark, then the latch of her back door clicked, and she was gone.

Begger me, he thought, but she was an easy girl to chase away. What an odd one Win was.

She sang to the moon. Or to plants or to something out here. She wouldn't sing to him, even though he'd invited her to. He didn't think he would ever see anything more tender or sad than the way she told her problems to no one: to leaves. And he couldn't think of anything more brave than carrying on anyway with a such a

113

load. She was strong, Winnie Bollash. As strong a woman as he knew. Capable-like.

And the most vulnerable creature he'd ever met.

Chapter 7

They spent all the next day doing tests. It was late in the evening when they began the last of these, with Edwina striking a tuning fork into vibration. "Tell me when the sound stops for you."

She went to touch it behind Mr. Tremore's ear, but he pulled back sharply. "What you be doin'?"

"It's a hearing test. Though let's fix some of your grammar while we do it. Two birds with one stone. I'd like you to stop using *be* with every pronoun —"

"Every what?"

"It doesn't matter. It's not *What you be doing.* It's *What are you doing.* You *are*, we *are*, I *am*, he or she *is*."

He wasn't listening. He tilted his head, watching her, frowning as she bounced the tuning fork again in her palm.

She reached toward him. "Say when you stop hearing it —"

He drew back again the moment the fork touched his mastoid. "What you got there?"

She paused, looked across the table at him.

"It's a way of testing your hearing. Everything I have to teach you is based on your ability to hear it, so I have to be sure you can hear what I say."

He pulled his mouth to the side, slanting his mustache. "So I could do this wrong, too? Hear things wrong?"

"No." She laughed. "You could have poor hearing, I suppose, but there would be nothing you could do about it."

He interpreted her answer as yes, he could fail here, too. He shook his head, then caught her hand when she reached to touch him again with the tuning fork. He said, "Let's do somethin' else. Let's talk. That's what you said we'd be doin' a lot of." From nowhere, he said, "Milton says you be gentry. Are you a" — he hesitated — "a baroness or somethin'?"

"No." What in the world? "I have no title." Then, yes, she thought. Conversation to distract him. Absently, she corrected herself as she set the fork humming again. "Oh, I'm still technically, I suppose, Lady Edwina Bollash, daughter of the sixth Marquess of Sissingley." He withdrew slightly, but let her put the fork on his bone. "Say, will you, when it stops humming."

After a few seconds, he nodded.

She quickly put the fork to her own ear. Nothing. "Good," she said, then struck it again, holding it this time to her ear first, continuing, "When my father died, someone else inherited the marquisate. I don't use the courtesy title.

There's no point." At her ear, the hum of the tuning fork faded.

She quickly moved the instrument toward Mr. Tremore. "Do you hear any —" She went to take his chin as she did with her lady students, but as her fingers grazed his jaw the feeling of stubble — more than a dozen hours beyond a shave — startled her somehow. She withdrew her hand, lowering it, burying it in her skirt as she stopped the tuning fork against her bosom. For a moment, the fork hummed against her chest.

She sat there a little bit taken aback. She'd done this a thousand times. It was quite ordinary.

"What?" he asked.

"Sorry." She shook her head, laughing nervously, and struck the fork again. "Let's have another go at that. Tell me if you hear anything when I touch it behind your ear."

They were both silent as she performed the second part of the test, this time without touching his chin. It went smoothly.

"Good," she reported again.

"You was rich?" he asked.

She lifted her eyes to him. "Pardon?"

"When your father was alive, you was rich?"

"My father was. But I'm not poor now."

"I can see that. But I can see your house ain't what it was. Was it ever fancy and right?"

She pondered the question. Right. Was this house ever right? "I suppose. Though the really fine one is — well, you'll see it. It's where the

Duke of Arles holds his annual ball now: in the house where I was born, my family's old estate."

"The duke inherited your house?" The look on Mr. Tremore's face said he could hardly believe that fact.

She could hardly believe it herself some days. Still, twelve years later, she'd wake up some mornings and be surprised all over again that Xavier had everything, all she'd ever known growing up, while she had ended up here, a place she had only visited in her youth, a house in which she had only ever spent the night when her father had made trips to London, because he had papers to present.

She picked up a smaller tuning fork, struck it. "You'll tell me please again when you no longer hear the sound."

When she reached toward him, he caught her hand, taking the fork from her. "What happened to your old house?"

He was delaying after a long day of strange procedures and drills, all of which he'd trudged through but disliked. She answered anyway, mostly to be done with it, to be past the awkward questions. "Exactly as you said: When my father died the next male in line inherited his title, that person being my father's cousin. He wasn't a duke yet. That came three days later, when my grandfather, the fourth Duke of Arles, died, too. My cousin Xavier inherited it all. He became the Duke of Arles as well as Marquess of Sissingley and a host of lesser honors." She shrugged.

"Quite normal. Lines pass through their first-born sons." Indeed. Daughters of marquesses married to acquire land and money, only she hadn't.

Here was as far as she ever went aloud. Her history embarrassed her. She murmured, "Please give that to me." She held out her hand for the tuning fork.

Mr. Tremore watched her a moment, then struck the tines on his palm as she'd done. He held it to his ear, listened, then handed it back, tines first. When she grasped it, her fingers vibrated.

Within the hour, they finished up the last of the initial record-keeping and testing and began in earnest on articulation. Which left Mr. Tremore really at sea. They'd hardly started when he wanted to quit.

"I ain't used to bein' wrong at anything so much as you say I be here."

She could have countered that she wasn't used to a lot of what was happening either. A man in her house. Tuning forks handed back to her, humming. A student who leaned back on the rear legs of his chair and twitched a big, bristly mustache at her every time she said something he didn't want to hear.

She told him anyway, "It's to be expected that you'll say everything wrong at first. We're *looking* for what you say wrong. You just have to keep at it." She explained, "To learn a new sound, we'll steep your ears in it. You listen and listen, then

try it. I observe the movement of your lips and jaw, infer the position of your tongue and palate, the openness of your throat passage. By watching, I can often tell you what you're doing wrong, then help you get your organs of speech into the right position to produce the desired sound."

He smiled slightly at the term *organs of speech*. It was a game to him. He was bored.

She felt lost, a woman swimming in knowledge she didn't know how to get into him. She continued, "Occasionally I won't be able to tell by simply looking why your pronunciation is off. But there are other means of determining the problem. For throat sounds, for instance, there's the laryngoscope." She opened the table drawer and produced a small mirror fixed obliquely to a handle.

He glanced at it, and his smile became unsure, a half-smile of misgiving.

"You see, I hold this inside your mouth at the back and reflect a ray of light down your throat. This way, I can see in the mirror just how your throat is opening and closing."

He laughed uncomfortably, but kept listening.

"I can also objectively tell the positions of your tongue by exploring your mouth with my fingers —"

"Wait." He held up his hand, chortling now. "You gonna be puttin' your fingers in me mouth?"

"Perhaps. Most likely, just my little finger

against your gum so I can feel the position of your tongue."

His eyebrows drew up at that. He leaned back in his chair, folding his arms across his chest, smiling, shaking his head. "Well, this be gettin' good."

"*Is*," she said. "This *is* getting good."

"Bloody right, it is."

She squinted. *Is.* He used it correctly. But he had the wrong idea. "We'll see if you still feel that way after the palatagraphic."

"That'd be what?"

"*What is that?*" she advised.

"All right, what is that?"

"A thin artificial palate that goes into your mouth with some chalk dust on it. You say a sound, then I infer the position of your tongue on your palate from the contact marks."

"So you're gonna be in my mouth a lot tonight? Do I got that right?"

Impatiently, she told him, "Mr. Tremore, I'm not used to your bawdy suggestions with regard to what is my job and a serious business —"

"Bawdy?"

"Vulgar. Indecent."

"I know what *bawdy* means," he said. "I just be surprised you find me enjoyin' your finger in me mouth vulgar. You be the one puttin' it there." He shook his head, laughing at her. "You know, loovey, what men and women get up to ain't indecent. It's about the most decent thing on the English island. Even the good Queen went at it.

121

The whole world knows she was keen for Albert, and she got nine children, so that many times at least."

Edwina was unable to say anything for a moment. Nothing seemed more inappropriate than his implicating the Queen in one of his ribald digressions. "Sir," she said, "I don't know where to begin in telling you that what m-men" — she actually stammered — "men and women g-get up to —"

"Easy, loov. You be a virgin, I know that." He said it without batting an eyelash, as if this presumption of his, all the more annoying for being accurate, were supposed to console her.

Edwina opened her mouth, shut it, didn't know what to say for a good half a minute. Finally, she told him, "Gentlemen, sir, don't speak of such things."

He looked at her, tilting his head. With his arms crossed, his vest pulled across the back of his shoulders. Then he raised one arm off the vest and stroked his mustache, once, twice, with the back of his knuckle. "That be a fact?"

"Yes," she insisted.

"I bet gentlemen know the word *virgin*."

"Well, yes" — she struggled a moment — "I'm sure they do. But they don't say it."

He leaned toward her a little. "Then how to do they learn it? Someone says it."

Edwina pressed her lips together, a little annoyed, a little turned-around. "Well, they probably say it among other gentlemen —"

122

"This mornin' you told me you didn't know what gentlemen talked about when they be alone."

"I don't." She couldn't find her bearings in the stupid conversation. "So this must be one of the topics," she said quickly, "since they certainly don't speak of it around ladies. May we get back to the lesson now?"

"Suit yourself." He shrugged. "Looks like we got somethin' for me to say at least in a few weeks, when the ladies leave after dinner. I'll just open the conversation up with virgins."

She stared at him. A second later — one heart-stopping second later — she realized he was having her on, teasing her. His mouth drew up in that lopsided way it had, a full, toothsome smile that dimpled only one cheek.

Edwina didn't know whether to be offended or not. She could hardly credit it. Normally, she hated to be tormented. Yet she didn't feel hurt now. It made her feel . . . warm . . . foolish but not unpleasant. He'd somehow managed the miracle of turning her upside down, just for fun, without making her feel bad about it.

He grinned wider, then took her deeper into confusion. "You ain't never known a man, I know that. Not even kissed many."

What an outrageous — "One," she said, "you," then wished she hadn't. It called attention to the fact that no one else had ever wanted to, not even for the silliest, most lighthearted of reasons.

But that wasn't how he took it.

Mr. Tremor's expression changed. It became genuinely taken aback. He dropped his teasing mien and looked straight at her. Very seriously, he said with amazement in his voice, "Well, beggar me. That be just plain sweet, Miss Bollash. I feel right proud you let me."

She was too surprised to give his words the horselaugh they deserved. She sat there for several stupefied seconds before she found the refuge she knew best: speech. "Now, you see, Mr. Tremore," she said, "it would be better if you didn't say *beggar me* anymore."

He tilted his head, frowning slightly. "Wha'd'you want me to say?"

"Try: 'I'm astonished.' "

He laughed, though at the end, still smiling, he raised one brow — a look that certainly could have passed for ironic amusement — and said, "All right: I'm astonished."

He repeated the words exactly as she'd said them, so naturally and perfectly she was without response for a second. "Yes." She blinked and looked down. "Yes, that's right."

Then he really took her breath away. He murmured, "*You* astonish me."

Edwina looked up, frowning, squinting like a woman trying to understand the mechanism of a trick, a sleight of hand. Well-dressed, sitting there with his white-sleeved arm folded across his dark-vested chest, Mick Tremore looked so much the part: the English lord. With his sounding the part, too, well — he stopped her in

her tracks. As if all this talk about catching rats and Cornwall were the false part, the real part being what sat before her: a confident, well-dressed fellow whom she'd managed to astonish.

Oh, this was awful. It was painful. She couldn't keep doing it. And it was only the beginning. She had to find a way to make him stay who he was, for herself to see him properly and stop catching glimpses of this other man, this ghostly . . . what? viscount? who could inhabit his skin.

Her mouth went dry. Her skin grew hot. For several seconds Edwina looked at an English lord with graceful hands, one finger of which he used to stroke an unusually thick mustache in what was coming to be a characteristic gesture. Sometimes he did it with the back of his knuckle, sometimes with the inside of his finger as now. In either event, it always made him look pensive. Pensive and faintly wicked. She remembered how surprising it felt, soft and coarse, both, when it touched her mouth.

Oh, dear. Edwina lowered her eyes and put her hand to her throat, her palm circling her own neck, her collar, where her fingers found tiny steel beads on tulle over silk. An old dress. A dress made as stylish as possible again. A dress bought when the idea of courting was still a ridiculous possibility. When she'd had money and consequently had the interest of suitors.

What had she been saying? She couldn't remember. It was no use. There was no getting back to what they'd been talking about before all

this, no getting back to whatever it was she'd been trying to accomplish. She sat there staring at a tuning fork on the table. Inside, she felt like that, as if someone had lightly struck her and now she resonated from the contact, vibrating with something she didn't understand, that wasn't visible, yet that worked on her from the inside out while she fiddled with the beads on her collar.

Beyond the windows of the room, it had grown quite dark. The night, opaque at the glass, reflected the room back on itself. Only a distant street lamp indicated anything existed outside her laboratory. It was late. She didn't usually work so long. A bad idea. Time to call an end to it. They'd do better tomorrow.

"Well," she said. "That's enough, I think." She stood shakily. Her knees felt weak. "I think we should go to bed now."

As the words left her mouth, and Edwina heard them, she thought, No, I didn't say that. Not aloud. Mr. Tremore lowered his eyes. Or she thought he did; his eyes fell into the shadow of his deep, jutting brow. "I think we should go to bed, too," he said.

She blinked, frowned, swallowed. She wanted to snap at him, chastise him — for what? For saying exactly what she had just said. Only he didn't mean it as she had. He was being —

What?

She'd assume he wasn't. Pretend he wasn't. Excuse yourself, Winnie. Go to bed.

126

Only, for the life of her, she couldn't. Her arms, her legs wouldn't move. Instead, heat rose up into her face as if the door to a furnace had opened. Her cheeks, neck, shoulders grew hot from an embarrassment she couldn't contain. She'd said something risqué. Accidentally.

Mr. Tremore said nothing. He remained quiet. She was now, presumably, supposed to be grateful for his silence.

Fine. She attempted to speak. "W-well, yes, we may, um, could —" She swallowed wrong, choked. Her eyes teared instantly. Edwina found herself caught in mortified coughs and stammers, then was further obliged to feel, grudgingly, out-and-out indebted as Mr. Tremore took over, making excuses for her.

"A slip of the tongue, loov. It can embarrass the best of us. It's all right. I know what you meant."

Their eyes met, held. How odd. His angular brow or perhaps her own discomfort in meeting his eyes for very long had kept the color of his eyes a secret till this moment. She'd known they were fair, but they were more than fair. They were green. Not a hazel, but a true, fair beryllium green, steel-gray green around a black pupil, the iris ringed in a thin line of dark, vivid mossy green. Stunning eyes. Another detail she would just as soon not be aware of.

She was developing a schoolgirl infatuation for a ratcatcher.

Well, she simply wouldn't allow it. Though her

body demonstrated that some things could not be controlled: The bright embarrassment in her face spread down her arms, her body. Everywhere. She must have looked apoplectic, because the object of her discomposure reached across the table and patted her hand, then gently squeezed the backs of her fingers — his were strong and warm, sure of themselves.

He said, "Go on to bed now, loovey. I won't even walk up with you. You be doin' all right, Winnie. A good girl. Just a little shook up. It'll be okay in the mornin'. When you come down, I'll be sittin' at breakfast nice as you please — no dancin' with Molly Reed this time."

Molly Reed? Was this Mrs. Reed's first name? If so, Edwina had never heard it till this moment.

She felt momentarily disoriented. As if he were unearthing startling objects, dropping them before her, out of familiar terrain, terrain that was her own.

Oh, enough, she thought. She was about to take what was offered, a clean exit.

But Milton interrupted. He came to the door. "Is everything all right, m'lady?"

"Yes." She frowned around at him, a plea for rescue.

As if nothing were amiss, he went on. "I took Mrs. Reed home. Her son's horse threw a shoe. I've locked up. Is there anything else you need?"

She shook her head. If there was, she couldn't define it well enough to ask for it.

"Oh," Milton added, "and the dresses from

128

the seamstress arrived early this evening. I put the box on the table in your sitting room."

She nodded. What dresses? Oh, yes.

As if in echo, across from her a voice asked, "What dresses?"

"What?" She looked down.

Mr. Tremore's smile was gone, replaced by a strange, quizzical look. "New dresses?"

"No, old ones." She shook her head; it was of no consequence. "Brought up to date."

"Where?"

"Pardon me?"

"Where did you have 'em fixed?" It was apparently of consequence to him.

She frowned, wet her lips. "The seamstress's, Milly-something, off Queen's Gate." She remembered he knew at least the shop assistant there and couldn't resist asking, "How well do you know the ladies of that shop? Are they friends of yours?" *Until yesterday,* she wanted to add.

He didn't say yea or nay, though, only sitting back in his chair to stare at her, his attention so unwavering it could only be called rude.

After a moment, he shook his head, smiling slightly, shook his head some more, then looked down. He seemed almost embarrassed. Well, there was a change. *He* looked discomposed. One strange outcome for certain: He tried to speak, then couldn't. The man who loved talk was completely without words.

Chapter 8

Mick spent the better part of the next week gawking at Winnie Bollash's skirts, half-hoping his stares would burn a hole through them. God knew, for all that was going through his head — while he ogled the way the fabric of her skirts moved when she crossed her legs or when she stood or sat or stretched her long self out — hell, if a man's hot thoughts and stares counted for anything, her skirts should've bloody well been on fire by now.

They sat side by side today in her laboratory. He was going through a drill of vowels — she'd given him a pencil to point down the page, so he could follow along, sound at a time, with what she'd written out. He was supposed to mark the sounds he thought he was ready to record for the stupid gramophone.

Lessons. They'd been going at all kinds of tricks Winnie Bollash knew to make a man talk different, ten and twelve hours a day for a week. They'd had things in his mouth. Her taking notes. Him saying sounds that weren't even words. Or sitting alone much of the time repeating exercises for so long, that were so boring,

even Magic got up and left.

They worked at a table together now, her to his right, to his left a tall window that looked out onto the front street of her fine London neighborhood. For eight days, he'd woke up in the same bed, each day surprised to find himself there, each day amazed anew to get up and walk around a house where, from any window a man looked, he could see tall houses made of brick, clean glass blinking at their windows, flower boxes, trees neatly shaped, hedges, iron gates. He didn't feel like he belonged here, that he deserved this life — who did? he wondered — but he was happy that, for a change, the injustice of life was working for him, not against him.

He tapped the pencil on the page, looking at the sounds he was supposed to be saying to himself. He should've mentioned they were written out in a way that didn't make much sense to him. He was bored. He'd spent the morning on *is*'s, *am*'s, and *are*'s, *was*'s, and *were*'s. Yesterday, *ing*'s and *th*'s. He couldn't keep them all straight. He was ready for some amusement to break up the dreariness.

Winnie looked at him, at his hand tapping the pencil. His heart gave a little leap. She was going to talk to him. He loved to talk to her. He liked the sound of her, the way her voice was soft and classy, smooth and fine. He liked the words she used and how she used them.

The words she used this time though, as she glanced over the tops of her eyeglasses, were:

"You should really shave your mustache, Mr. Tremore. It doesn't have the refined air we are trying to cultivate for you."

He rolled his eyes, but she didn't see. She went back to writing. Bloody hell. She had only told him a dozen times to take a razor to the fine growth of hair on his lip. "I like it," he muttered.

He watched her touch the tip of her pen to her tongue to make the ink flow better. Without looking at him, she said, "It's not stylish."

"It's thick. Not many men can grow a mustache like it."

"Not many men would want to."

"Oh, I don't know about that." He touched the hair that grew under his nose. "It's funny, though, you think you got the right to get rid of it, like you can reach over and tweak my lip. Kind of brassy of you, when you think about it."

She looked up from her writing, her pen stopped over the page. "Brassy?"

"Full of yourself. Cocky, you know?"

She squinched up her face like she could, then laughed not unkindly, which made him feel a little bad. "I'm not the least bit" — she paused — "brassy, as you put it."

He was being testy, he knew, but he just felt . . . itchy or something lately. "Well, no," he conceded. "You're a nice woman. Gentle-like. You mean well. But you sure think you run everything."

"Ha." She put the pen down and looked at him. "I don't think anything of a sort. If I run

anything, it's my own legs. I'm usually running as fast as I can, figuratively at least. I'm scared most of the time." She made another face, sheepish, like she wished she hadn't admitted it. He liked her face, its funny features that could move so many ways, bend. She had a thousand expressions.

But one predominant state of mind. He said, "Scared 'cause the world ain't working to your plan. Scared someone's gonna find out and blame you for it."

"That's not true. And it's *isn't*."

"What?"

"Pardon?"

"Oh." She was fixing him again. *Isn't.* Right. He said, "Scared we all isn't falling into your line."

"Aren't."

Mick stopped talking, finding a back tooth to push his tongue against, twisting his mouth. Twisting his mustache at her. Stupid. All these different words for the same thing.

He pitched the pencil onto the sheets of paper in front of him. It tapped end over end once, making a light mark, then clattered still. He sighed. "All I can say, loov, is it must be hell running the whole blooming place. Especially when so much of it depends on things that are about as dependable as, oh, just one damn roll of the craps after another."

Whatever he was trying to tell her, Edwina didn't understand it. Though she knew, when he

made a faint grin and lifted his eyebrows at her, he was trying to jolly her out of any offense.

He picked up his pencil again, flipping it over in his hand, playing with it, then beat on the edge of the table. *Tap tap tap tap.* . . . He kept the rhythm going lightly as he said, " 'Course the chanciness is damn exciting, you gotta admit." He threw her an unaccountable smile. "Like now. Either of us could do *any*thing in the next second."

It was involuntary; she drew back. More of the capricious philosophies of Mr. Mick Tremore. She was always dodging them.

She might or might not, she thought, have him speaking and acting like a viscount by the end of next month, yet she had come to believe quite firmly that Mr. Tremore could grab hold of the lapels of a regius professor of philosophy on the street, expound in his face on one amusing topic after another, then let the fellow go, dizzy with his own sense of unoriginality when it came to words and theories on life.

"Speak for yourself," she said. "I couldn't do anything" — she paused, then used his word for it — "chancy."

"Yes, you could."

"Well, I could, but I won't."

He laughed. "Well, you might surprise yourself one day."

His sureness of himself irked her. Like the mustache that he twitched slightly. He knew she didn't like it; he used it to tease her.

Fine. What a pointless conversation. She picked up her pen, going back to the task of writing out his progress for the morning. Out the corner of her eye, though, she could see him.

He'd leaned back on the rear legs of his chair, lifting the front ones off the floor. He rocked there beside her as he bent his head sideways, tilting it, looking under the table. He'd been doing this all week, making her nervous with it. As if there were a mouse or worse, something under there that she should be aware of. It was never anything though. Or nothing he wanted to mention; she'd asked already more than once.

She phrased the question differently today. "What *are* you doing?"

Illogically, he came back with, "I bet you have the longest, prettiest legs."

"Limbs," she corrected. "A gentleman refers to that part of a lady as her limbs, her lower limbs, though it is rather poor form to speak of them at all. You shouldn't."

He laughed. "Limbs? Like a bloody tree?" His pencil continued to tap lightly, an annoying tattoo of ticks. "No, you got legs under there. Long ones. And I'd give just about anything to see 'em."

Goodness. She was without words again, nothing readily available to say to yet another of his impertinent comments.

And he knew it was impertinent. He was tormenting her. That much knowledge she had

gained of him. He liked to torture her for amusement, like a child pulling legs off a bug. Though something about him today felt at more extreme loose ends, more bored than usual, capable of "chancy" mischief.

He tipped back further on the rear legs of his chair, giving the waving front leg a quick double tap of the pencil, *ta-tick,* on his way to dropping his arm down, out of sight. His position was quite precarious, she was thinking —

She felt the tickle up her ankle before she understood what it was. His pencil. He ran the tip of it, quick as you please, up her anklebone along the leather of her shoe. It flipped the hem of her dress up.

She brushed it down. "Stop that."

He bounced the pencil once off the leg of the table, *tick ta-tick,* then puffed his top lip out, squelching air between lip and teeth to make a strange little rude sound; it bristled his mustache. Oh, that mustache.

Then she caught the word: *anything?*

To see her legs? Her legs were nothing. Two sticks that bent so she could walk on them. He wanted to see these?

For anything?

She wouldn't let him see them, of course. But she wasn't past provoking him in return: pointing out that, while some people wanted to see what they shouldn't, others were forced to look at what they'd certainly like to be rid of. "Well, there is a solution here then, Mr. Tre-

more. You can see my legs, when you shave your mustache."

She meant it as a kind of joke. A taunt to get back at him.

Joke or not, though, his pencil not only stopped, it dropped. There was a tiny clatter on the floor, a faint sound of rolling, then silence — as, along with the pencil, Mr. Tremore's entire body came to a motionless standstill. He was caught in that awful, boyishly crude pose, leaning back on the legs of his chair, a recalcitrant look on his face.

He opened his mouth as if to say something, then just wet his lips.

Edwina wasn't sure where the knowledge came from, but she understood with sudden, sure insight: He was keen to see a pair of legs that no one else cared a fig about. Long, rangy legs, their proportions to her body about as graceful as those of the legs on a colt.

As to her joke — oh, my. His expression said he was considering it as a genuine offer, an idea that made her more uncomfortable than she would have thought possible. His stillness, the look on his face . . . The combination made her run her hand over the tops of her knees, hold her dress against her shins.

He wet his lips again as if trying to lubricate speech. "Pardon?" he said finally. He spoke it perfectly, exactly as she'd asked him to. Only now it unsettled her.

Not enough though to relinquish the advan-

tage she seemed to have gained over him. "You heard me," she said. A little thrill shot through her as she pushed her way into the dare that — fascinatingly, genuinely — rattled him. She had at last set him on his ear as he did her so often. Ha ha ha, she thought. She wanted to clap her hands in delight.

She spoke now in earnest what seemed suddenly a wonderful exchange: "If you shave off your mustache, I'll hike my skirt and you can watch — how far? To my knees?" The hair on the back of her neck stood up.

"Above your knees," he said immediately. His amazed face scowled in a way that said they weren't even talking unless they got well past her knees in the debate.

"How far?"

"All the way up."

She frowned, then cautioned, "Just my legs though."

"Right. To the tops of your thighs."

"But I'm keeping my knickers —"

"Then I'm only takin' off half the mustache."

His mustache! "You'll take it off?"

He looked at her, thought about it. "You'll lift your skirts and let me see your legs?" He added, "Without your knickers."

"No, no." Instantly, she shook her head. "Certainly not. I won't take my knickers off."

He knew when he'd gone past the limit. "All right," he agreed quickly. "With your knickers on, but all the way up to the tops of your thighs."

They were silent a moment. How had they come to such a quick, insane place? Were they seriously negotiating for what was both trivial to discuss — hair on a lip, looking at legs, silly if she thought about it — yet in some ineffable way so significant they neither one should have been bargaining with what he or she had to lose?

Modesty and mustache.

Yet, Winnie thought smugly, when she dropped her skirts down again, her loss would be over and his lip would be bare. "Yes," she said.

"How long?"

"How long what?"

"How long can I look?"

She pinched her mouth. Oh, now he wanted all afternoon to stare at her. Well, he wasn't getting it. "A minute."

"Then no." He shook his head. "Longer than a minute."

"How long?"

"Fifteen minutes."

Blood rushed, making her arms, her hands, her cheeks hot. "I can't stand there for fifteen minutes, you dolt! That's absurd! Just standing there with my skirts up? My knickers hanging out?"

It was meant to be a ridiculous image. His face changed though. His expression relaxed into it. Oh, she hated to see that. She'd lost ground somewhere. He was winning again. His mouth drew up on one side, indenting his cheek with that single, deep dimple. A slow, sly smile spread

into his features. "Yes, fifteen minutes. And I get to touch your legs —"

"Now wait one instant, Mr. Tremore —"

He stopped her by coming forward onto the legs of his chair with a clunk as he pointed his finger at her. "You, Miss Bollash, want me to shave off my — well, my masculinity. The least I get for that is to know what those legs feel like."

She balked. No, this was not at all what she'd had in mind. Her idea was getting quite out of hand.

He wiggled his mouth at her then, making the mustache come alive on his lip. Oh, she hated that thing. Why? Why did she dislike it so much?

"All right," she said before he could ask for anything else. "But only ten minutes. And, if you have to, you can touch my legs." She restricted, "At the end," then cautioned sharply, "but just my legs. If you touch anything else —"

He grinned widely, crookedly. "Agreed. Just your legs." He laughed, showing a lot of good teeth. "And ten minutes is all right, but now. I want to see 'em right now." With the flat of his hand, he patted the tabletop. "Hop up here, loov. Let's see what's under those skirts."

Chapter 9

The way Edwina and Mr. Tremore worked it, since neither one trusted the other very well, was that he could see her legs now for five minutes, but not touch them. (Oh, so absurd! she thought, as she stood up shakily — and somehow euphorically — from her chair. She could hardly believe they were discussing the plan, let alone acting on it!) Then they would go upstairs together, where at his washbasin and mirror she'd watch him shave his mustache. Oh, yes! After which, he'd get to see her legs for the last five minutes. And touch them at the very end.

"Once," she said.

"Once." He repeated the word, but was so merry about the whole business, she didn't think he heard her. He stood briskly.

To her surprise, his hands landed on her waist, and then the ground came right out from under her. Simultaneously, as he lifted her up and over him, she said, "And I'm not getting on any table —"

She stood on one, looking down at him.

A strange perspective. Below her, she watched him drag his chair back a few feet. "I can't see ev-

erything proper unless it's at eye level," he said. He turned, grinning, and plopped himself into the chair, folding his arms over his chest.

And so he was: eye level with her skirts, about four feet away. She glanced over the edge of her lesson table. The floor seemed a chasm, the table a cliff. This wasn't right. It wasn't what she'd imagined. What *had* she imagined?

His lip lathered up, a straight razor neatly cutting through shaving soap foam. That was as far as her fancies had taken her.

The face of reality was a man with a sloping grin, his thick black mustache slanted at a triumphant angle, his spine scooted down in his chair, his legs wide, knees bent, his arms crossed over his well-cut vest.

"So?" he asked. When she gave him a frustrated look, he said, "Your skirts. Lift 'em up. Or are you already backin' out?" His arm rose off his chest so his finger could stroke the hair on his lip. He prodded, "The sooner you do it, loov, the sooner we go upstairs and get to what you fancy so damn much."

She nodded. Yes, of course. She put her hands in her skirts, grabbed fabric. Five minutes wasn't so long. The clock on the mantel behind him said twenty till eleven. At a quarter till, she'd be done, or half done at least.

Yet getting her skirt up was so much more difficult than she would have thought. He watched intently — he wasn't going to miss a second, his eyes not even attempting to look at her face. She

wasn't accustomed to a man's eyes openly fixing themselves on, well, *there* at the hem of her dress. It gave her a funny feeling, a frisson . . . not up her spine exactly, but a light downward ripple into her belly.

"You need some help, Winnie?"

She threw him a frown. She was going to say, *Miss Bollash*, but then she only wet her lips. She didn't bother. All her instruction in the matter so far hadn't done any good.

Just do it, she told herself. "No, no help."

Still she couldn't get her hands going. It was his fault. He was trying to —

Oh, bosh. It occurred to her. His triumphant smile. The challenging way he'd taken over. Mr. Tremore didn't believe her. He was having a good time because he thought he was calling a bluff.

The idea that he thought she couldn't do it made her feel positively audacious.

Without looking down, she made her hands work. Her fingers balled up fabric into her fists, bunching.

She watched him, still slouched in his chair, as a tension overtook him, his humor replaced with surprise — and an anticipation that was hard to miss. The way Edwina stared expectantly sometimes at the curtain as the big, bold first notes of the overture to a favorite opera sounded. She felt like that — kettle drums, cellos, heavy strings swelling, rising to sing in her veins. Yes. Do it. Shock him. An odd thrill

hummed her blood and tickled her chest.

She looked down at herself. There was an inch of shoe showing. Well! That wasn't so hard! She watched as her hands gathered up more, feeling the scrunch of silk and horsehair and linen.

An inch more of shoe leather appeared. The room grew still, not a sound except the slide and rustle of fabric. More and more of it accumulated, till it was too much to hold in her fists. She had to catch it against her forearms and thighs, gathering, catching, gathering. Till she was looking at all the laces to the tops of her shoes and an inch of shins.

Skin. She had to stem a nervous giggle. It was so silly, yet exhilarating somehow now that she was at it.

When her skirts were at her knees, a faint draft brushed against her legs. It moved up under her skirts. A giddy sensation. She wouldn't look at Mr. Tremore, though she knew he was there. She heard him shift in his chair, clear his throat.

She saw the knee lace of her own knickers at the same time as she heard a soft, kind of whistling word. "Ch-e-e-e-sus." Mr. Tremore. Excitement shot through her. Her stomach rolled over. Anxiety and pleasure. The combination brought such a pinching delight.

It was so strong, the feeling. Stronger than anything she could remember. From standing on a table and lifting her skirts till her legs showed from the knees down.

Yes, more. She wet her lips again, gathering

fabric as quickly as she could, not stopping, as if she were digging through it. Up, up, up, and there she was: all her legs in view. The last little bit, where she brought her skirts in a ball against her hips, gave her the most peculiar little sensation, a kind of electrical charge at her belly. A warm, melting tingle that felt actually, physically, present inside her — right there, under the bunch of skirts, as if a response to them somehow.

Good. Done. And quite successfully, she thought, elation lifting her, taking her up. Yes, yes, yes. Now all she had to do was stand here for a few minutes and —

"No, no," he said.

She jerked her head, frowned down over the table at him.

Mr. Tremore stared at her legs, with a kind of . . . involved expression, completely engaged by the sight, yet . . . uncomfortable. And dissatisfied.

"You, ah —" He moved his head back a degree, but not his eyes. They didn't leave her legs. "Your stockings," he said. "You have to take them off."

"I do not." She straightened, dropping her skirt. "We never talked about stockings."

He scowled at the dropped skirts, then lifted his scowl to her face. "We said *legs*. I was looking at stockings."

"You were looking at legs. You had a good, clear view of exactly what we discussed."

"We discussed legs, not stockings."

She glared. So was he telling her that he wouldn't shave his mustache now, unless he got to add more to his side of the bargain? Why, the conniving —

"It has to be legs," he said. "Really your legs."

She pressed her lips together. She'd gone this far. It hadn't been bad. And the stupid man was looking for a way out. Well, she wouldn't give it to him. "Turn around," she said.

"I don't have to turn around."

"You do. We didn't say anything about watching me take anything off. Turn around. I'll tell you when I'm ready."

He protested briefly, but then stood enough to swing a leg back and around. He straddled the chair, his back to her. Winnie bent over hurriedly, reaching up under her petticoats, pushing the edge of her knickers out of the way enough to get at the new garters the shopkeeper had sent. She quickly slid them down her legs, one then the other, pushing her stockings along with them to her ankles.

She stood, then pulled her skirts back against herself to stare at what she'd wrought: her silk stocking waded in a clumping ring about the ankles of her high-laced shoes. It looked stupid, foolish. Good, she thought at first. Then no. A kind of vanity took hold. There was no point, she told herself, in looking any more foolish than she already would.

She squatted, sitting back onto the table with a

bounce, lifting her foot immodestly to work at the ties of one shoe, then the other. There. Bare feet. She wiggled her toes. That looked . . . better. She stared at her foot. Better? It looked *something*.

"Are you ready yet? What's taking so long? I could take them off myself in less than a minute."

"Just wait. I almost have it." She got her feet under her, but as she raised up, unbending, she realized she could see his reflection in the window glass — his mustache a vivid bar at his mouth — which meant presumably he was looking at her reflection. They stared at each other in the glass.

Anger prickled the hairs up her arms. But its result was her digging in. No. She would not call it off, not slow it down, not give him one single excuse. She straightened completely, pulling her dignity up around her. "All right." She looked at the mantel clock behind him. "It's five minutes till eleven. You have till eleven o'clock." She'd be generous.

Because she fully intended to be merciless in the end.

His eyes lingered on the clock as he came around to face her. The game began again. He sat back, facing her, crossing his legs as if casually, one knee over the other — he did that in a way that couldn't be taught, in a rare way. Delicate, a refined air, particular and graceful, without being the least effeminate. Masculine, in

147

fact. She didn't know where he'd learned to do such a thing, but it added to the illusion of a gentleman.

Though no gentleman would do what he did after his crossed his legs. He laced his fingers together behind his head, elbows out, leaned back, stretched, and stared at her skirts again: waiting.

She made herself do it faster this time. Get them up; get it done. But she did the wrong thing, as it turned out. Instead of watching herself, her legs, she watched him. And what she saw not only fascinated, it all but undid her.

The sight of her bare legs affected him in a way he couldn't disguise. He tried to be nonchalant about it — the raised arms behind his head, his legs resting out. But after only a few moments, he'd grown tense enough that the posture no longer served him. He lowered his arms, leaning forward, elbows onto the tops of his thighs, staring as if his life depended on memorizing every inch of her bareness his eyes could cover.

She had power over him. Power that made her mouth dry. It made that feeling low in her belly roil around like something alive.

It warmed her to have his eyes on her like this. It made her face, her skin hot. As if the sun beat on her legs, as if its rays could insinuate themselves up into her. His gaze felt so tangible it seemed to touch her, brush her calves, push against the knickers at her thighs. It made gooseflesh run down the backs of her knees then up her shins, the sensation traveling further up and

up into the center of her between her legs. The same, strange place again.

She shifted on her feet, feeling the table under her naked soles. They stuck slightly to the wood, the contact cool, humid from her feet having just come from her shoes.

The feeling was more discomposing than she could have dreamed. His eyes ran up and down her legs, making her aware of how long they were, tree-like, yet somehow his appreciation was candid: burning. There was no other word. She shifted on her bare feet, unable to make herself be still. She could feel her heart thudding. How long had it been pounding like this? Was it healthy for it to pump at such a rate for so long a time as it seemed? Her breathing felt short; she couldn't get quite enough air. Or no, more as if she needed a greater amount than usual. Her palms grew hot and sticky where they clutched the wads of silk, making her dress damp.

The clock ticked. She and Mr. Tremore said nothing. His intense regard only broke once. He became briefly distracted by her shoes, stockings, and garters sitting beside her, fascinated by her pile of clothes for a moment.

She raised her eyes to the clock, trying not to think. Only a minute to go, with him having his eyes on her bare legs, the silence in the room becoming heavy. Her bare legs, she thought. Even she had never looked at them so much. No one had. No one else had ever been so interested.

Just before the clock began to strike, he broke

149

the stillness to ask, "Winnie, do you know how beautiful your legs are?"

She looked down, agitated, fidgety, wondering if he and she were talking about the same pair of legs.

Then he murmured, "I can't wait to touch them."

And her stomach rose up into her chest, turned upside down, then melted, sinking, into her pelvis.

Nothing she could do about it: He somehow had more control over her than she did. Their eyes met. She stared down from the height of the table at him, into light, greenish eyes beneath black eyebrows, coloring so unusual . . . including a mustache, glossy with health. With her gaze fixed to his, she felt that low place in her body roll again, the place between her legs, and as if in unison with her stomach, the goose-bump feeling lower slowly somersaulted over.

"I want to touch them with my mouth," he said softly, tentative. He knew he was on shaky ground, nothing they'd discussed. He wanted to woo a change into their contract.

No words. Winnie raised her eyes to stare across the room at her wall of books. Then didn't see them. Her vision blurred. She couldn't see for the heat at her eyes.

He continued. "I want to kiss the backs of your legs, behind your knees and up."

She shook her head. It was the closest she could come to contradicting him. *Once.* They'd

said he could touch her legs once. He could put his hand on one leg. Then he had to take it away.

A lot of kissing up the backs of her legs wasn't — Dear God, her head grew light, so light she thought she might faint. It was too much. She felt overwhelmed, unwell. . . .

The clock began to chime — a sobering, saving toll of grace.

Done!

Joy came into her chest with a burst of relief. It came out her mouth with gusto. "Your turn!" she announced.

She dropped hems and petticoats with a loud rustle of silk and linen and lace. Heavens, the sweet charity of being covered again. Who would have thought that to have one's legs bare, from only the knees down really — after all, she had on her knickers — could be such an ordeal?

"Not till the last chime," he said from his chair. Like some almighty emperor from the throne. "Bring 'em up again, Winnie."

"No."

They hassled back and forth as the last chimes struck. In the end, she had to pull her skirts up, let him look for ten more seconds, before she could get him moving toward the staircase.

Chapter 10

Edwina watched over Mr. Tremore's shoulder in the mirror, his reflection above the washbasin. She watched him touch his mustache. It was brief, just the tips of his fingers lightly combing it downward, almost with affection. She felt a small twinge of guilt. Ever so small. Then he rattled the shaving brush in the cup again and slopped lather onto his lip. He picked up the straight razor, taking hold of his face to make the skin taut. He rolled his lip under his teeth, then — *scritch* — he took the first swipe.

Oh! Edwina wanted to pat her hands together. Skin under the mustache! White, tender skin. She was gleeful to see it. She could barely be still for her feet's urge to dance.

He took another stroke of mustache off, glancing over at her, a deep frown. He returned his attention to the basin to sling the razor once, slopping foam into the bowl, then wiped the edge of the razor on a towel, raised his head, and scraped again. To get at the edge, he had to twist his mouth and hold his cheek, then had to make another contortion to get under his nose and over the curve of his teeth. Stroke, *scritch*, stroke.

It didn't take more than half a dozen good passes, before the thick, bothersome mustache was in the basin mixed with a lot of shaving-soap lather.

Edwina looked down. Seeing it there, she felt as if she'd vanquished a dragon. Or a caterpillar at the very least; something that had been eating holes through her.

Mr. Tremore laid the razor down, then bent over the basin as he poured water from the pitcher. He splashed his face, rinsing over the bowl. Then rose up partway and stopped. He looked at his own face in the mirror.

He startled, blinked. They both did. He slowly rose, staring at his image in the glass.

Goodness, he looked different. Sharper. Cleaner. Smoother, of course. But unpredictably somehow . . . more severe in his handsomeness. Mick Tremore, clean-shaven, looked like an idealized drawing for a shaving-lotion advertisement.

With the mustache gone, his eyes became his predominant feature, and they, of course, were stunning. Light, mossy green eyes set beneath a jutting brow in a plane perpendicular to a long, straight nose. The bones of his face came forth, a near-patrician facial architecture of strong, masculine angles and planes. Oh, she'd been so right to insist, Edwina thought. So right to get rid of that animal tuft.

Mr. Tremore stared into the mirror, his unusual eyes focused on the lower half of his face.

He put his hand over the wet, fresh-shaved skin, dragging his palm down his mouth, frowning. He pressed his lips, moving them, stretched his upper lip.

Whatever it felt like, he didn't dally with the sensation. He turned around just like that — they hadn't been in his bedroom a full minute, hadn't passed a dozen seconds beyond removing his mustache, when he pointed to the wood chair by the washbasin and said, "Get on that where I can get a good look. Then raise 'em up, Win."

Act II. Panic. She took a step back. "You're bossy."

"I'm not bossy. We're negotiating. I know what I want. Get on the chair."

"How did you get that right suddenly, all the *I'm*'s and *We're*'s. You're saying them correctly almost every time now."

"I've been listening to you. Stop stalling. We can be done in five minutes. Get on the chair."

"No." What she meant was she wasn't standing on anything.

How he took the reluctance in her tone though was, she wanted to back out of her second half of their agreement.

His face took on a look of genuine anger, a look, she realized, she'd never seen on him. It made her back up another step and talk faster than normal. "I'm not standing on the chair. The table downstairs —" She swallowed. "I didn't like it. It was too —" Awkward somehow. In some extreme sense.

154

Standing on the table downstairs, she thought, had made the strangeness at the end, the eerie feeling that had made her hot and light-headed. "I'm not doing that again," she reiterated. "You have to look where you are."

He twisted his mouth, an instant's displeasure, then pulled the chair he'd indicated around, straddling it backward. He dropped himself into the seat, bracing his arms on the back. "Fine," he said.

It was her word. He said it exactly as she often did. The man was a parrot today, soaking up more than she wanted at the moment. She backed a step further, staring into his newly revealed, somehow sharper features. He didn't look as kind without his mustache. She almost missed it for a moment. He didn't look himself.

"Take up your skirt," he said.

She let out a huff. "Don't make it any cruder than it is."

"I can make it any way I want: It's my turn."

He touched his lip again, and his brow drew into a deep, preoccupied crease. One elbow braced on the chair back, he absently fiddled with the newly shaved skin.

Edwina hadn't been aware she was retreating further until her bare heel stepped rudely into the baseboard. By then the weight and balance of her substantial body was already in motion. She collided, her shoulders hitting the wall.

"You gonna start, or do you need some help?"

She brushed at her skirts, getting herself set-

tled on her feet, wishing somehow for more time, a delay, which wasn't of course going to happen. Get on with it, she told herself. "No, I don't need any help." She grabbed her skirts, two handfuls, looking down at them.

"Good," he said. "Because I want to get to the last minute as quick as I can."

The last minute? Oh. Her stomach dropped. The touching part. She wouldn't think about it. She lifted her eyes — she would look at his clean lip and do what she'd done before.

It was harder this time. She had the memory of the odd, tingling embarrassment that in the last instant had just about leveled her. Added to this now was knowing that the odd sensation his eyes made on her would become somehow the concrete feel of his hand. How was she supposed to manage *that?* Just stand here? Let him walk up and put his — Oh dear heaven, she thought.

She stared at his lip and kept telling herself it was worth it: as she gathered up her skirts. She began again, taking the fabric up more and more into her fists. The air was warmer than downstairs. She felt a draft on her legs that was almost balmy as her hands claimed scrunching silk and underlinens. When her fists couldn't hold any more, she pressed the scroopy stiffness of her skirts back against her knickers, hiking, pushing skirts up under her forearms. Skirts rising, rising . . . bare feet then shins. When she saw her knickers, where they began at her knees —

She suddenly remembered what he'd said he

wanted, the part about kissing the backs of her legs. No. She looked at him. "You can't — you have to —" She couldn't say it. "You can't use your —"

"Mouth," he finished for her. He laughed, a release. Of sorts. It wasn't a particularly nice laugh — dry, ironic. There was a subtlety to him she hadn't given him credit for till now. He understood nuance. And perhaps even some sort of double entendre she couldn't grasp: "All right, loov. I won't put my mouth under your skirts where you don't want it. It ain't my intention to make you unhappy."

Ain't. The word let her breathe. Thank God he still said it occasionally. Still her Mick. Funny, joking Mick. Who wasn't joking now. He bit the inside of his mouth, a movement that sucked his lower lip in at the edge. His eyes were hooded, half-closed from watching the show that was lower to the ground than before. Looking, looking, not a moment's reprieve . . .

Winnie got the whole wad of her skirts pulled up into her arms and against her hips. She didn't know how long she'd stood there, fretting and rubbing her thumbs at the silk, standing with her skirts up in front of a man who gave the sight his full concentration. She only jerked to greater consciousness when he rose, swinging one leg back and off the chair, standing up to his full, rather imposing height. He seemed huge when he came toward her.

"What are you doing?" she blurted.

"I'm going to touch your legs. We agreed —"

"No, we didn't." The wishful lie choked out.

"Yes, we did."

"Once," she recanted plaintively. "We said you could touch one leg once."

He didn't answer but bent down on one knee in front of her. She looked down on his head, his glossy hair. He'd put himself at her legs, within inches. "Turn around," he said.

"No."

He glanced up. "Winnie, my mustache is in the washbasin. If you think I put it there for some child's game, you're wrong. I guess we said once, but it's gonna be a long 'once.' I'm touchin' you all the way up your leg. If you say I can't use my mouth, I won't. But turn around. I'm touchin' your legs at the back."

"*Leg,*" she said.

"All right, *leg.* But I'm sliding my hand up the whole, damn, gorgeous length, from your sweet heel there" — he pointed — "up the back of your calf, the inside of your knee, all the way up the back of your thigh" — his finger drew an imaginary upward path in the air that gave her goose bumps, then, when his hand got to hip level, his hands took real hold of her hips, turned her around by them, pointing in the process, still without touching — "to the curve right here under your bum. Thank you."

She was facing the wall.

She leaned her head against it, with the "curve under her bum" tingling. God help her, he

hadn't done anything yet, and she was in a state. Goose bumps kept running up her legs in waves. Her belly felt as if she'd swallowed something animate that squirmed to get out.

While uncertainty made every single sensation acute. She waited, a woman up in the air, kept aloft on emotions she hated — dread and suspense.

Yet there was another feeling here niggling, as she stood against the wall waiting for Mick Tremore to do something he shouldn't. Why did she allow him the leeway to turn her, to even consider touching her? She couldn't answer the question. She didn't *like* what was happening, she promised herself. She wanted it to be over. The tension it brought was abominable.

Yet as she stood there, waiting, tortured, unhappy, anxious, she was somehow also . . . thrilled beyond words.

Nothing she had known of life till this moment had ever been this exciting.

Mick, on the other hand, was fairly clear about what was happening. He had hold of a guilty virgin he was pushing a little harder than he should. He tried to calm her. He tried to feel bad about it. Winnie here was getting fairly wrung out, and he was the culprit, challenging a hesitant, fretful woman . . . who, buggeration, come to think of it, couldn't be all that timid, since she'd found the courage to have his mustache.

Anger again. It kept shooting through him in bursts, bright and startling like fireworks in the

night sky on St. Agnes's birthday. He told himself it was just that Winnie didn't know exactly
what she was doing here, how hard she was being
on him. She didn't have a lot of experience in
matters between men and women.

He murmured, "Just be still," thinking that
would help her get through it — he couldn't
make himself feel bad enough to let her off.

He put his hand to her ankle, and, with the
contact, his shoulders jerked. "H-h-h-h —" he
said, unable to hold it back: her aspirated H.
Here was how to get him to make the sound.
From pleasure. Pleasure honed on the sight of
her bare legs so that it cut into him like the edge
of a knife. Her skin was so bloody smooth . . . ten
times smoother than his. Her ankle was narrow,
the calf a long swell —

She jerked, pulled away, taking her leg with her
as she turned around. "There," she said. "You
did it. Your ten minutes are over." She let go of
her skirts.

He caught them and stood up, carrying them
to her waist.

He pushed the wad of dress at her, putting
pressure against her stomach. "I hate a cheater,
Winnie. Let's do that again. I know you're
scared, but you can get through this. Here. Take
your skirts."

She refused them. "You're done," she whispered, a little hiss.

"No, I'm not. You've been trying to short me
on this idea from the first second you thought of

160

it. Now, you notice, please, I came upstairs and took my mustache off in under a minute. I didn't dodge or argue or give you a moment of trouble. Now hold up your skirts and bear the last minute of the bargain *you* invented."

He held the bundle of skirts against her belly, leaning into them, letting her feel his existence on the other side of all the silky stuff of her clothes. He was scaring her, he knew. Winnie didn't like not to be in charge. Well, stuff her, he thought.

Except that was the point, of course. He couldn't. And the idea of "stuffing her" was pretty much running wild through his head. Ho-o-o-o, he wanted to have at her. He wanted to lay her so bad his eyes were hot at the backs from being so close to the burning thoughts in his head. He was trying to be rational, trying not to act as crazy as he felt — galled, goaded, teased, and naked. A feeling he'd known the instant he raised his head and stared into the mirror at his own bare lip. Stuff her, he thought again.

But since he couldn't, he descended down her body, inches away without touching, to do what she'd said he could.

Winnie watched him go, then lost sight of him. She could only stand rigid and stare at his shoulders over the bunch of silk she clutched. She felt his head brush against the wad of her skirts, then nestle into them a little. She could feel the warmth of his closeness at her legs, a sensation so extremely pleasurable it was horrible. She was

161

breathing with small vocalized gasps at the end of each breath, embarrassing mews she'd never made before. What was wrong with her? Her mouth was parchment from her trying to find air.

Mick meanwhile turned his head, and his cheek brushed where the hem of a petticoat hung down. The linen was still warm, fragrant from her body. Clean, sweet, starchy. A womanly smell that stirred up a lust the likes of which he hadn't felt since he was a boy just discovering the female sex. In half a second, he lifted in his trousers, all the way out to a full, stiff erection. Oh, bloody hell, he thought. What was he going to do with this? From here, touching her, and not having her, should be one great, big, old Buckingham Palace of torment. Halls and gardens and monuments to it.

No sooner had he grazed her calf, though, than she jerked and twisted away again.

She let out a panicked breath. "Enough. That's it. We're done."

Rage. It stood up with him, pure and clean. He couldn't remember the last time he'd known such a potent, simple emotion. "You cheat," he said. He stepped against her dress before it could fall all the way. He bent his face toward hers, almost touching her nose with his, eye to eye. He dropped his hands with force on the wall at either side of her shoulders — he watched her jump as his palms hit, the daylights all but leaping out of her.

She pulled back, hit her head on the wall. Old Winnie was going to brain herself before she accepted that right here was where her game had got her to and she wasn't going backward: She was going forward.

Forward into what? Mick stood there, blinking, panting, furious, flummoxed. He winced over how hard her head had clunked on the plaster — then the crack to her fool head knocked some sense into *him*.

He wasn't getting to touch her leg. She couldn't do it.

Mick wanted to howl at the injustice. He'd grazed her leg, thought about touching her. Hell, where he'd got to was worse than not touching her at all. He rolled his lips together into his teeth, feeling his upper lip stretch, cold, numb, and bare as a baby's.

They argued with their strength for a minute. Winnie was a sizeable girl. When she shoved him, he knew it. A big girl. The way her hands grabbed his shoulders, though, and pushed — hard, businesslike, not joking — it took more wind from his sails.

He started looking for options.

While Winnie was all but choking from how narrow hers were. Mick was all around her. She shoved, but his weight didn't budge. It didn't even lift.

In fact, she felt him shift. He stepped his feet apart, making himself as heavy and immovable as a boulder, then whispered into her ear, "So

what is the penalty for breakin' faith?"

Her heart leaped into her windpipe. "I didn't —"

"Oh, yes, loovey. Let's see. I think the knickers. They have to go."

"*Ac-k-k!*" That was all that would come out Winnie's mouth at first. Then, "N-no, absolutely not, you —"

"Now, now. You cheated. Or you've tried and tried to. You have to pay."

"No," she said. Her voice sounded pathetic, even to herself. What he was doing genuinely frightened her. It was too much. He asked too much.

He took pity. "All right, Win. You can buy your knickers back."

She let her anxious eyes find his. His face was so close, and oh, God, she'd somehow gotten her hands flat against his chest. It was wide, the muscles curved, warm, as hard as the wall behind her. And hair! God help her, at the edge of her thumb she could feel the light cushioning of hair that ran between contours of muscle. His body made her dizzy, near-delirious: as if one of the statues she'd admired had grown warm under her hands, then started to breathe.

"H-how?" she asked.

"Cooperate for a minute." He put his nose near her cheek, brushed it against her. She could hear the sound of air, his smelling her. He brushed his mouth along the same place, his clean, freshly shaved mouth. It set off a series of

shivers, little quakes through her.

She took her cheek away, bending her neck, and he put his lips onto the arch of it, lightly brushing his dry mouth up to where her jaw met neck at the back of her ear. They both grew still.

Winnie because she was afraid to move. He, she realized, to take the time to consider how and what to ask of her: The toad, the miserable, mean toad was making it all up as he went along.

He slowly told her, "I'll kiss you . . . I mean, really kiss you this time, Win . . . and you let me. You open your mouth —"

"Open my mouth!"

"Sh-h-h. I knew that was gonna get you goin'. Stop. Just listen. Don't fight me. You let me show you. You open your mouth and let me in. Let me kiss you like I want to." His face drew back, shadowed, but it smiled faintly. She watched the slightly crooked bend of lips that seemed almost familiar. His slanting lips without their mustache were full and neatly made, plump, perfectly chiseled like those of a wicked cherub, lips as no man should own. "That's it. Then I let you go, and we're done."

Oh, she wanted to be done. Finished, over with. Her chest hurt from a kind of thudding exhaustion, as if she'd been running for hours. She let his words console her, *then we're done.* Nor did she miss that he was letting her out of the most onerous part of her bargain, the leg-touching part that simply felt too wrong. She surveyed herself. Her blood pulsed at the insides of her el-

bows; her arms felt weak. Her whole body was like that, beating, beating, hot, squirming with energy while wanting to lie down, wanting to rest, to languish from an insane ennui.

God, oh, God, just to get it over with, she nodded her head, a quick jerk.

"Close your eyes and relax."

Oh, *that* would be easy. In the end though, she only nodded again as if she were going to be able to do it. She closed her eyes and tried to contain her wriggling restlessness.

His palm spread at the back of her shoulders, then his fingers combed up her nape into the back of her hair. Ooh, so pleasant . . . she wouldn't have thought . . . His hands spreading on her felt much nicer than she could have imagined.

He was gentle. As one hand cupped her skull, his other flattened against the small of her back and brought her against him. It was a gentleness, however, that didn't stop an insane pitch of panic when he brushed his lips across hers, then whispered, "Open."

She did slightly, and he pressed his mouth over hers — she could feel the strength in him, his holding it back, a constraint that was palpable. It brought a sharp, ambiguous zing: fright for the size of his strength, a brawn she sensed that could break her in half; paired with a mind-numbing, knee-bending urge to be wrapped in it, surrounded by it, invaded with it. His mouth coaxed hers open further. Then, turning his

head, he pushed his tongue deeply inside, between her teeth, against her palate, the insides of
her cheeks, pushing against her own tongue — a
full, openmouthed takeover of what Winnie had
never questioned was her space alone.

For a moment, her back stiffened, and she
jerked in his arms. His tongue in her mouth was
revolting . . . well, not revolting exactly. She
eased a little. Shocking. It was simply shocking
then, after a moment . . . interesting. It was
warm, very warm to feel his tongue move in her
mouth . . . and, well, it was an extraordinarily intimate thing to feel his strength *there,* his tongue
against hers. She could taste him — with sudden
vividness she remembered the orange he'd eaten
at breakfast an hour ago.

The man with the tangy kiss drew her from the
wall, sliding his hand down over her buttocks,
and pulled her, full length, up against him. The
kiss was instantly more potent. She didn't know
a kiss could be like this: teeth, lips, tongue . . . oh,
heaven, his tongue was bold. It went deep. It
stirred up an awareness, warm, liquid. It made
her tense, yet it felt . . . surprisingly right.

Then "right" and "interesting" slowly insinu-
ated themselves into "fascinating." She grew
aware of how solid he was, aware of his weight
and substance, of how deeply and languorously
he kissed her, how he put his whole body into it.
He leaned them both back into the wall again,
pressing her there, as if he wanted to be closer,
though heaven knew he was as close as another

human being could be. Hips, chest, arms around her, moving, pressing, sliding. She found herself pushing back as he kissed her, though not with struggle. A resistance that added something. A cooperation on her own that made her bones quiver.

With her rumpled skirts still caught between them, she could feel the brush of his wool trousers against her bare shins. She felt his hands dig into her buttocks, push her. They encouraged her to meet the force of him. He wanted the kiss to have a slow, deliberate rhythm — and her shivers became a kind of vertigo that raced her heart and spun her head.

His hands pulled her buttocks into him, pressing the wad of dress between them as, bending his knees, he flexed his hips forward and pushed. He did it again. Then again. While he groaned inside their kiss, satisfaction, as his tongue did a slow, rhythmic penetration of her mouth.

The horrible part was, though she had a vague idea what he imitated, she couldn't stop wanting the next full press of his hips, the next plunge in her mouth. She wanted him to kiss her just as he did, to touch her, and she wanted it with a vehemence that made her ashamed while it stole the strength from her legs; they wanted to fold.

She heard him draw a ragged breath as he lifted his mouth away, turned his head the other direction, then kissed her again. The sound of his rattled breathing matched her own. Then, as

if her spinning inability to get air weren't enough, she felt his hand play delicately at edge of her raised skirts: looking for what he'd asked for, the feel of her leg.

Her leg? She thought the kiss was instead of her leg. No. No, no. Then another, distant voice in her head said with grave curiosity, Yes.

Her emotions pitched. Fear, pleasure, panic, anticipation. Yet this time she let him without a moment's reproof.

His hand went up under her dress. Through the fine-weave linen of her knickers, she felt his palm lay itself, spread-fingered, onto the back of her thigh. With the touch, an acute, stomach-knotting jolt of pleasure shot through her so strongly it made her shiver and jump in spasm. Then the smooth warmth of his palm tentatively stroked her thigh up under the curve of her buttocks.

Oh, dear. So wrong. A man she hadn't known two weeks was rubbing his sublime hand under her near-naked backside. So wrong it made her stomach flip. So right she couldn't swallow.

He slid his hand lower, rubbing down her thigh, the back, the side, the front, the inside . . . ooh, the inside of her thigh. Bliss. Oh, to be touched by Mick Tremore. Pure sensory rapture. It set every hair of her body on end. Ecstatic. Dreadful in its power, its climb, its pure, blinding brightness.

This strong pleasure spread, expanded, threatening to usurp every logical thought. It ruled

from that low place in her abdomen, as if she were possessed there by a demon. Something was taking her over, turning her over into the hands of a commanding instinct she hadn't known she possessed. A vaguely terrifying "something," for it was a stranger. A fierce, frightening feeling that left the rest of her powerless. She shifted, made an instant of struggle.

"Sh-h-h," he said and stroked her where she liked, in the curve beneath her buttocks. The place that seemed safer. Only it wasn't that safe.

The strange new awareness in her tugged, pulling her toward what seemed a dark pit, a place where she dare not go further, dare not let herself fall. She feared her own unknown self. She was afraid of following him where he wanted, of not coming out again. Or not coming out the same: changed forever.

Her senses singing, full-voiced, Winnie stood shaking — seemingly complacently in Mick's arms — as she quietly grew frantic: poised on an overpowering brink of too much, too new, too strong, too different from any other experience she knew, her emotions carrying her to the edge of pure, guilty terror.

While Mick fought a singing urge of his own: He wanted to move his hand an inch toward the center of her body and touch what was so close and so on his mind. He *wanted* to lose control, take her with him. They were in a bedroom, ten feet from a bed.

He fought the urge valiantly. It was leagues be-

yond their agreement. He liked kissing her. He kissed her and kissed her there against the wall, pressing her and tonguing her first one way, then, turning his head, another, like he could put all his male self into the single act of penetrating her female mouth. He rubbed his body as close as he could to hers. He smoothed his hand along the contours of long, comely thigh. Soft along the inside, female. While the singing thought kept whispering, What you want is right there. An inch away. Have it. Touch her.

In the end, he wanted to so badly he simply couldn't *not* do it. He ran his hand all the way up to where her thigh gave into the delicate indentation, where her leg joined her torso. He drew his fingers along the bend to the ridge of tendon, then simply shifted his hand. He took firm, cupping possession of her between her legs, holding of her, feeling her. It was worth it: She was wet. Her knickers were soaked. Her body was ready, no denying how ready, his —

Winnie's head jerked. She let out a sharp yelp. It took him aback a little when, from here, she became a sudden tangle of arms and flailing legs and fists coming at him. With all her considerable strength, she was suddenly a whirling, thrashing animal, drawing its last ounce of spit to save itself.

Mick got a good, strong barefoot kick to his shin and a fist to the side of his face that about took off his jaw before he could catch her arms, draw them down, and step back. He half-

expected her to come at him again. She was that crazy. He guarded himself, hands and forearms up, breathing like a freight train.

But instead of more fight, Winnie turned to the wall, putting both her hands on herself where he'd touched her. Her head bent. Her shoulders hunched. And she burst out in sobs.

Mick couldn't've been more surprised if she'd pulled out a gun and shot him.

But, well, of course, he thought. He should've known. Winnie was the guiltiest, scaredest woman. He reached, touched her shoulder. "Sh-h-h," he said. "It's all right. I'm sorry. I shouldn't've done that."

So, so sorry. She cried like a child. A child who knew for sure she was getting no supper, getting a beating, sent to the orphanage, put up for adoption. He felt awful.

He put both his hands on her shoulders, rubbed up and down her arms. "It's all right. It's right normal, Win. It's what men and women do. But I shouldn't've. I —" He tried to turn her around and just hold her. She wouldn't let him though, so he only hugged her from the back, wrapping himself around her as he stroked his hand down one arm.

As he petted her, his own hand ended up near his face. He caught the smell of her there. He closed his eyes and resisted one second. But it was irresistible. He put his nose into his palm and breathed in the smell of Winnie's female sex, then discovered a place where his two fingers

met at the palm that was still wet from touching her. God bless, he held her there, soothing her, while behind her he opened his mouth on his own hand and touched his tongue between his fingers, tasting her. He shuddered.

How buggered-up was this? he asked himself. He wanted to bend his mouth into the curve of her neck. He wanted to rub her buttocks with an erection so hard and taut there was a delicate possibility for disaster. He had no business with Winnie in his arms here, no business consoling her, telling her that everything was going to be all right and that he was sorry — while he stood behind her, wanting to run his hand under her beautiful round bum, between her legs, get rid of the knickers, rip them if he had to, so he could put his hand directly onto her flesh, put his fingers into her, slide —

Mick, my boy, you ain't buggered-up. You are out of your bloody lunatic mind. Winnie would come at you like the Furies if she even knew what you were thinking. If she didn't kill herself first.

So, standing there with every one of his senses full of Winnie Bollash, Mick determined that all he wanted of her was bad for her. And, one of the hardest steps he ever took, he let go of her, stepped back, getting himself clear of her long, sweet body. Backing one footstep then two away, he left her alone at the wall.

Watching her there made him feel so small. If only it made his cock small, too, but it didn't. That part of him nosed rod-straight against his

trousers, still trying to do his thinking for him — Winnie had forgot to let go of her skirts. Her bare legs were bent together, one pressed against the wall, as she clutched her dress to her hips and cried and cried and cried. She was inconsolable.

He tried anyway though. He said, "Winnie, it's no secret now I want you. Let me be the one. Come lie down with me on the bed over there." He shook his head. He wanted to say all manner of things he was fairly certain a gentleman didn't say. How he wanted to put himself inside her. How he wanted to eat the freckles off her long legs. How he wanted to kiss her mouth till their tongues were sore and their lips were raw and make love to her till neither one of them could stand up straight. And then, after that, exhausted, he'd crawl down her body and kiss her between her legs like he'd done her mouth, long and deep, then fall asleep with his face there.

Wisely, he didn't mention these things. To him, they were beautiful. Poetry. To Winnie, he was right sure, they were crude. He wouldn't've been surprised if, on telling her all he might want from her, she bent right over and got sick.

Especially given that her next sobbing words were, "Y-you said you wouldn't t-touch me anywhere else."

There wasn't really any defense for what he'd done. Well, hardly any. He told her, "You liked it, Winnie."

"I did not."

More meekly, he chided, "All right, but you al-

most did. You would've, if you'd've let yourself. And God bless, Win . . ." He shook his head, a man who had bewildered himself, then spoke softly. "I bloody loved it. I bloody effing loved it." He looked at her with utter seriousness, trying to say what he felt. "I want to do it again. I can't tell you how much. I won't. I won't come near you again, if that's what you want. But Lord, Win." He shook his head. "You're amazing. You are the best handful of woman I've ever held in my arms, and I've held a few, loovey. But nothing like you. Nothing."

It didn't cheer her up. She cried like she was dying.

Mick put his hand to his lip, finding only damned, half-numb, smooth-shaven skin. Buggeration. He held his hand there, his thumb at his jaw, his fingers over his lips and mouth like he could cover it up, like he could hide what he'd done.

"What am I supposed to do, Win?" he asked.

She said nothing, but just sobbed there, her shoulders shaking.

He pushed his hand back through his hair, feeling it between his fingers, wanting to pull it out. "Should I leave?"

She didn't answer him.

"I mean, really leave. Take Magic and Freddie and go. I can forget about the hundred pounds. I'll earn it another way." He couldn't, of course, but that was a different matter.

She said nothing, though she took a long,

sloppy sniff of air.

He tried to tease her out of all her tears. "You want that I marry you?" He laughed at how stupid that was. Like she'd marry a ratcatcher.

She stopped her crying for a minute, long enough for another big, wet hiccup of misery. Then she looked at him, sort of out from under her pretty red hair what was coming down, and whispered, strong, mean, angry, "Don't laugh at me anymore. Stop it. Stop all your teasing! I'm not a joke!"

Right. If she'd've had the strength, she'd've slapped him. Right.

Married. Winnie should've been married. She was a fine woman. Nurturing, kind. She surely as hell shouldn't have been clinging to a wall because some Cornish miner's son had stuck his hand where it didn't belong.

Right, he thought again. A marrying joke. Pretty insulting to offer to make her miserable like she was for the rest of her life. But, see, he hadn't meant the insult toward her. He was making fun of *himself.*

Oh, he was good enough for her. It wasn't that. He just wasn't good enough in her mind, and not in the minds of the rest of the world either. He knew it, accepted it, and wasn't even bitter about it. It was just the way things were. But Winnie thought the joke was on *her.* She always thought it was her, no matter what happened. She carried the world on her shoulders, responsible for every little thing that happened in it. Or even for what

didn't happen sometimes like it should.

In her mind, Winnie ruled the world. And a fine old burden it was, considering she ruled a fickle place that ran on havoc.

And sweet Win here wanted a man, *needed* a man, but she didn't know how to get one. Or how to get one she wanted, since she wouldn't let herself have the one she accidentally got.

Mick forced a long, breathy sigh down his nose. The whole business made him just plain tired. His solution was easy. His solutions were always easy. As far as he was concerned, it was one of those situations where to shag her silly, he was fairly sure, would be a big favor to her. He half-wished he had the nerve to do it: just lay her down and get her past it. It'd be good for her. At least in one way. Of course, it might kill her in another.

Good thing it wasn't his job to worry over it.

"Okay," he said. "I'll go take Magic for a walk. Whatever you want me to do, put it in a note. Leave it by the basin. I'll come back. I'll read it. I'll do it." He couldn't resist a sarcastic snort. "Just don't use too many big words, all right, Win? So I don't have any trouble understanding what you want from me."

Mick couldn't find Magic at first. He went down the hall, calling him, then he had to hunt through Maj's favorite rooms. When he finally did find the stupid dog, he wanted to shoot him. He was in Winnie's laboratory, having a grand ol' time, chewing the elastic out of a fancy silk garter.

177

Chapter 11

The note Mick found was short:

Mr. Tremore,
Please let's not think about or discuss this morning further. We must go on as if it never happened. I'll meet you in the laboratory for our regularly scheduled lesson at three this afternoon. We have a great deal to do and too little time to do it.
Edwina Bollash

That afternoon, Edwina told Mr. Tremore, "The lady steps up into the carriage first. Offer me your hand." He did, though it took a moment for her to lay her fingers into his. With premeditated care, she grasped his extended hand. It was dry, warm, and unhesitant.

She paused with her foot on the step to her carriage. The vehicle didn't budge. It couldn't. No horse was attached. She had brought Mr. Tremore out to the carriage house in order to practice in her unhitched coach.

"Once I'm up," she told him, "you'll follow me in. You sit opposite me with your back to the

horses, or where the horses would be. You never sit beside a lady in a carriage, other than your own wife or daughter; you always sit opposite, always facing the direction from whence you are coming."

"Backward," he clarified. "I face backward."

"Correct."

He was paying attention, which was good. He could see apparently the immediate value in what they were doing.

She'd brought him out to the carriage house, knowing he'd learn more surely by doing than talking. She wanted him to begin moving through the night of the ball in his mind, knowing where to put himself, how to dance his way, so to speak, through the rules of politeness and protocol.

Also, if she were honest, she'd brought him out here because she couldn't face watching his mouth in the usual way of their lessons. She couldn't bring herself to stare at it for the rest of the afternoon, fussing over how he put his tongue against his teeth when all she could remember was how, earlier, he'd put it against hers.

She held on to his palm for balance as the vehicle rocked on its springs toward her slightly. She went up the steps. Mr. Tremore's fingers were strong in their grip of hers, helpful, steady. Nonetheless, she was eager to get her hand away. She let go the second she grasped the door frame.

Then, just as she ducked under the doorway, she was suddenly halted. She made a horrible leap, literally and figuratively — for she jumped

as if he'd yanked hold of the entire back of her dress, meaning to ravish her there on the steps of her coach. Behind her, she heard him say, "Sorry." Her skirts released.

He'd simply tramped on them.

She laughed nervously. "It happens occasionally." She tried to regain herself by backing out from under the carriage doorway and turning to stand up again. Edwina balanced on the top step, gripping the door frame on either side, both hands, in order to hold herself on the precarious little tread. She smiled down at him, or tried to. "And 'sorry' is perfectly fine." She did achieve a kind of smile, she thought. "Some gentlemen have more trouble than others with ladies' trains and sweepers." She paused, took a breath, then recuperated enough to say sincerely, "Let's try again, shall we? I don't doubt that you shall get it perfectly next try."

He did. On the second attempt, Edwina made it uneventfully into the carriage and onto her seat, then watched the athletic Mr. Tremore hoist himself through the doorway with an energy and lightness that defied explanation, especially for such a large man. She was going to correct him, make him get in more sedately, but then thought better of it. The ladies she knew would probably enjoy watching him do that, swing in like some sort of primitive.

He sat opposite her as instructed, then leaned to reach for the door.

"No," she said. "Don't get it. A footman will

close it on the night of the ball. Let him. You must become accustomed to people doing things for you. There will be servants everywhere."

He looked uncomfortable with the information, but sat back, leaving the door swung out on its hinges.

There they sat in the open-doored carriage in an open carriage house — they'd left the carriage house doors open as well to let in the daylight. A horse nickered down at the far end in its stall, the sound punctuating the tension of their first "lesson" since this morning. Winnie drew in a breath and took in the smell of hay and horses and well-oiled tack, while a rosy kind of light spun dust motes through the carriage doorway in a beam that ended in Mr. Tremore's lap.

She swung her head away, looking quickly out the window of her marooned carriage. Through the opening, she stared down a hay-lined corridor of horse stalls, most of them empty now. Without looking at him, she began again. "At the ball," she said, "when you enter the house or any room in it, you let the ladies of your party go in ahead —"

"There'll be ladies with us?"

"Possibly. The Misters Lamont, I imagine, will take you to the ball. They may bring wives or the ladies on whom they pay call."

"And you?"

"What about me?"

"Won't you be with us?"

"No," she said, turning to look at him with sur-

prise. "I'm just your teacher."

"I want you there."

"Well, I can't go."

"Why not?"

She paused, frowned. She didn't know how to explain; she didn't *want* to. "My cousin doesn't wish me there." She quickly added, "Nor do I wish to be in his house. As I was saying," she began again, "you open the door for any woman with whom you are walking, allowing her to pass through the doorway, then —"

"Why don't you want to go? It sounds like your sort of fun. All these rules, and you're good at them."

She made an impatient face. "I don't like my cousin, and he doesn't —"

"What's he like?"

"Who? Xavier?"

"Is that his name?"

"Yes. And he's very old, very charming, and very well-connected. You'll probably like him. Most people do."

"Not if he doesn't like you."

She opened her mouth, then closed it again without speaking. She wasn't sure whether to applaud or laugh at his loyalty. "All right, then you'll kowtow because you'll be afraid of him. Those who don't like him, fear him. He is powerful."

"You don't."

"Pardon?"

"You're not afraid of him."

She did laugh then, short and abrupt. "Yes, I am. That's why I don't go. May we continue please?" Without waiting for an answer, she said, "Above all, at the ball, please see to it that you do not allow yourself to be alone with a woman under thirty. Never. Not for a minute. It would be disastrous. A lady under thirty may be with a gentleman only in the company of a chaperone. Otherwise —"

"How old are you?" He leaned back, put one arm along the top of the seat, making himself perfectly comfortable. He could do that. Wherever Mick Tremore went — she envied the ability — he could make himself at ease.

She scowled a moment. "Nor does a gentleman ask a lady her age."

"Then how's he supposed to know if she needs a chaperone?"

She turned her scowl into a quick, fierce scrutiny, but his expression seemed to honestly question the logic. She muttered, "I'll be thirty. Thirty on the twenty-ninth."

"Of April?" This month.

"Yes." Her birthday was in three weeks.

He leaned back into the seat, smiling. "Then you need a chaperone."

"I most certainly do. But I can't afford one and my family doesn't care. I promise you, though, that the families of those ladies attending the duke's ball will ruin you if you take one of them aside —"

He laughed. "What? Will they cut my vast for-

tune out from under me?"

"No." He'd best understand. "They would find what mattered to you, then they'd take your ferrets, take your dogs, have you beaten, then thrown into jail. It would take you years to get out, if you ever could."

He sobered.

She tilted her head, looked at him directly. "Mr. Tremore," she said, "the people we are going to fool are the most powerful people in England." She let that sink in. "That's what I'm trying to tell you. Fooling them is one thing. But if you compromise one of their daughters, put her in a position to have to marry you, only to discover that you are entirely inappropriate for marriage, well, they will have your hide."

And mine, too, she might have added.

She let the picture she'd painted for him fade into silence. She didn't want to unnerve him, only be sure he was warned fairly.

The peculiar thing was, she wasn't afraid they would fail. She was afraid, in her worst moments recently, that he would succeed too well.

She looked at his clean-shaven face, his tall, well-favored looks. As if in complicity with her fears, he leaned just then, and light cut across the side of his face and shoulders, delineating how perfectly handsome he was. A tremor ran through her.

Heaven above, to pass him off, she had to teach him to be halfway consistent with his manners and speech — and, if she could, this man

184

was going to stop hearts. On the night of the ball, he would walk into that room and doctors were going to have to be called, because women were going to faint dead away, have seizures, heart attacks. He was the sort of man who sent female hearts pounding, sent windpipes into asthmatic fibrillations, who addled brains till nothing but nonsense came out.

God help the female upper class. Because if he polished up half as well as she was beginning to think he could, every woman in the ballroom, when he walked in, was going to become a raving idiot. Mindless giggles and fluttering fans would travel along with him like an epidemic of smallpox — no woman would go without a slight case; some, if allowed, would develop a fatal instance.

This singularly handsome man nodded now, then murmured, "I wish you were coming with me."

Oh, yes, that's what he needed. A gawky, six-foot-tall woman, whom Xavier had turned out into the streets, walking behind him like a lovesick calf.

A lovesick calf. Oh, dear. Edwina looked down. The shadows on her side of the carriage thankfully hid her, for she'd made herself blush. Poor fool, she was fascinated by the man who Mick Tremore was becoming. Or no. Idiot that she was, she was fascinated by the man who *resisted* becoming exactly as she tried to make him. Fascinated by him, appalled at herself. A confu-

sion that was becoming typical of her attitude toward him. Excited, boggled, frightened — unable to stop herself from wanting to stare at him, yet unable to look at him for more than a few seconds.

She could be one of them if she weren't careful, she realized. One of the brainless, fluttering nincompoops she was perpetually trying to educate to be better, stronger, more self-sufficient — sanguine yet open-eyed about what society truly had in mind for a woman.

Her gaze rested on her own folded hands in her lap. What had she been saying? She couldn't remember. She lifted her face, looked toward him, then spoke to the place where the coach ceiling came within inches of his head.

She began again. "When the carriage arrives, you alight first with the gentlemen, seeing to the ladies of your party, if you are the last man out." Yes, yes, out. She needed to get out of the carriage. Bringing him into it hadn't been the good idea she'd thought. "The footman holds the door. You step down, turn, offer your hand."

He said nothing.

"Do you have this then?" She glanced at him.

He leaned forward, his arms onto his thighs — and the beam through the doorway suddenly lit up the entire side of him. It made the sleeve of his shirt stark white, the silk of his vest sheen softly, and gave a round sleekness to the craggy breadth of his shoulders.

He nodded solemnly. Then let out a soft laugh.

"No. I don't have it." He shook his head almost fondly. "But you'll repeat it when I do it wrong. You love to tell me rules."

Possibly, she did. At the end, though, there was a surprisingly gentle moment that broke any rules Edwina knew.

He stood below her on the ground, offering his hand up to her exactly right, convincingly a gentleman. She gave him her hand, her fingers bending over the side of his as he pressed his thumb to her knuckles. Perfect, perfect. He did so much so well so quickly sometimes. Then he said from nowhere, "You all right then?"

When she'd stepped down, level with him, he squeezed her hand and held it. They stood, hand in hand, for a few seconds longer than was necessary.

What could he possibly mean? she thought. Here she was standing next to him, tidy, full of good information, in control of herself — doing her work with grave dignity. But, odder still, for one instant she wanted to answer his question by throwing her forehead onto his chest and wailing, *No, no! I'm not all right at all!*

She said, of course, "Yes. I'm fine."

He smiled, making a quick, little nod. "Good." He smiled wider, though his sideways, slanting good humor was almost a wince when he added, "Glad to hear it, loov." He nodded again. "No worse for wear?"

Ah. "No worse for wear," she repeated.

If she harbored any resentment for his part in their rough morning, she forgave him completely in that instant. She looked at his smooth lip and smiled.

"Good," he said again. "Good." And he meant it. Relief settled tangibly on him. "So shall we go in and do your vowels again then?"

She smiled perfunctorily, while thinking, Oh, no! She couldn't decide how to avoid spending this afternoon and all subsequent afternoons, evenings, and mornings for the next four weeks watching his mouth form sounds. She nodded, full of deceit. "Yes. Shall we?"

Chapter 12

As Edwina and Mr. Tremore crunched along the gravel drive that led back to the house, she asked herself, So what in the world were you thinking, when you suggested your game in the first place? That it would be innocent? That you could throw him out if it wasn't?

You misled yourself, Winnie. You set yourself up for a month of discomfort.

Indeed. The best that could be made of the situation, she thought, was to pretend that she hadn't made a horrible, indecent fool of herself and that he hadn't behaved like a bull in a mating paddock. This morning didn't exist. She wished he hadn't referred to it, even obliquely.

She wanted the idiosyncratic structure of his speech. She wanted to take it apart and rebuild it — something that could well yield a paper to read before the Royal Philological Society. It was a once-in-a-lifetime project that, on top of everything else, was free, since she was being paid to do it. He needed the money he could earn if he carried the bet off, and he might gain in the process a way to speak himself into a better station in life. They both had losses if they stopped and

advantages if they did not. Yes, here they were, treading along toward the house and an arrangement they neither could afford to back out of, not without great cost.

Moreover, either one of them would have been hard-pressed to explain what had gone wrong with a bet in which the Lamonts now had a great deal invested.

At the house, they discovered a pocket watch had arrived — Mr. Tremore held it up, delighting in it. It chimed in pairs, *ding-ding, ding-ding.* Inside the boxes that had arrived with it — that he and she opened instantly like curious children there in the hallway — were two pairs of day boots, some men's formal evening slippers, a pair of dark kid gloves, a pair of white formal ones, and two top hats, one for evening made of black silk and one for day, a dark brown thing made of beaver felt that was luscious to touch. Edwina hadn't seen anything like it up close in a dozen years.

Surprised by the man's day hat (for what purpose did the Lamonts think he needed it?), she raised it from its box, then stood there holding it balanced on her fingertips inside the crown. She turned it, imagining it on the head of a man who knew how to wear it. The crown was high, rigid, and perfect, with a black band, while the felt of the crown and brim were softer than the underbelly of a cat. It was lined in silk.

As she held the hat up, examining it, Mr. Tremore abandoned the watch. "Well, I'll be

190

buggered," he said, coming over. Then he corrected himself, laughing. "What an astonishing hat." It came out half-right — he found the *an* properly, but missed the H. *An astonishing 'at.*

He plucked it off her fingers and set it onto his head.

The astonishing hat fit him perfectly, of course; it had been made for him. But the way he set it on his head was the truly astonishing part: at an ever-so-slight angle, instinctively debonaire. Well, Edwina thought. She had wanted to see the hat on a man who knew how to wear it, and here he was.

She stepped out of the way, so he could see himself in the hallway mirror. His expression in reflection liked what he saw, then she watched a ripple of displeasure pass over his face as his eyes dropped to his upper lip. He truly did look different wearing a top hat — and no mustache.

"I'm sorry," she murmured.

He glanced at her. "About the mustache? Don't be. You didn't shave it off."

"I made you do it. I made us both feel awful."

He turned toward her, taking the hat off with a flourish of his wrist. The man loved style and show, and, honest to goodness, he actually had a little. He had a way about him. "You do this with everything, don't you, Winnie?"

"Do what?"

He shook his head. "All this thinking," he said. "It's like a superstition with you."

"Superstition?"

"Like throwing salt over your shoulder."

"Now, see here —"

"Winnie," he said, "let me tell you about my mum. Grand lady. Great mother. But a superstitious loon when it came to God. When I made her mad, she'd say" — he did a full Cornish accent quite well —" 'Yee be a bad boy, Mick, but yee'll git what yee deserve. God'll see to it.' Then I'd fall and skin my knee and she'd say, real smug-like, 'See?' like God had shoved me down, not my own clumsiness or hurry. In the end, she died spitting up stuff from her lungs."

He looked down a moment, frowned. Then continued, "Hard and ugly for her, you know. I told her she didn't deserve it, but she cried and cried, full of teary regret. Oh, the confessions we got. She was sure she had done something wrong or hadn't done something right. But, you see, none of us believed bad of her. It was impossible. She was the gentlest woman. Couldn't hit us. The only weapon she had, when we were bad, was to promise us damnation. While us children just rolled our eyes at her, 'cause, see, not a one of us believed we were mortal: We felt so safe in her care."

He grew quiet for a few seconds, then said, "Don't die like that, Winnie. Or live like that either. Like you can know every little thing before it happens or can explain a mess away by retelling it to yourself a hundred times."

She frowned at him. "Sometimes, Mr. Tremore, it's *good* to question oneself —"

He leaned toward her. "Winnie, what I did, I was lookin' for a way to do. You just gave me the chance. Maybe not even that much. It's over. Let it go. You worry too much over everything."

"I care about details and my own behavior. I like to look at what I can, then rethink —"

He interrupted, shaking his head sadly. "No, the nits and picks will give you the miseries, if you let them. They'll weigh you down like stones, make you sad and dotty. They did my mum. You didn't do anything so awful, so can we go on now? You're a good girl, Winnie Bollash. Kind and decent. Right generous with yourself. You ain't a snoot like I said when I first got here. I take it back." He grinned then added, teasing, "Or mostly you ain't."

"Aren't."

"Right." Mrs. Reed came into the hallway just then, humming and dusting knickknacks on a shelf a dozen feet from them. They both listened to her till she disappeared again. Mick lowered his voice, in deference to the intrusion, but he brought the conversation right back. "Serious now," he asked, "do you believe some word you say or don't say can shave the hair off my lip? You didn't do it — I did. And when I want to, I'll grow it back again." He laughed softly, then winked at her. "Which is better than you can say, Miss Bollash. 'Cause I'll always know you have the prettiest legs in all of England. Any time I want to see them, all I do is close my eyes."

Oh, the cheek of him. Winnie smiled when she

shouldn't have, then couldn't let him get away with being so self-satisfied. She said, "No, Mr. Tremore, imagination is a fine thing, but we both know there is nothing like reality. I can see your mustache is gone right here —" She touched his face above his lip before she thought not to. Taking her hand back quickly, she said, "I know reality. You have only what you are able to remember and daydream."

His eyebrows raised. He touched his own lip where her fingers had been the second before. He looked surprised, then not. He laughed, this time letting out that deep, low rumble he could make in his chest. It came forth through his easy, sideways smile. "Why, Miss Bollash," he said, "are you flirting with me?"

No. But heat began immediately to seep into her cheeks. She couldn't stop it. She couched her face, hiding it and the beginnings of a smile. "No, of course not."

"You are," he insisted.

"No." She shook her head vehemently, but the smile kept coming.

His finger touched under her chin, and he lifted her face to make her look at him. "You are," he said quietly, with utter seriousness. "Watch out, Miss Bollash. I like to flirt, but I like better where it gets me — and you don't."

She tried to absorb his admonishment as she stared into his eyes, shadowed there in the hallway. Smoky green eyes that made her heart thud; they took her breath away. He was right, of

course. *You watch out, Miss Bollash.*

Yet she couldn't make herself stop smiling slightly. He found her attractive. She truly might be attractive. She'd been turning that idea over and over in her mind since this morning. It wasn't just words any longer. She had felt how attractive he found her. And, oh, she discovered, what a greed she had for that notion. Attractive. In her way. To the right man.

Mr. Tremore broke in on this sweet thought by saying, "Don't dally with me, Winnie. I'll lead you down the path. Sooner or later, I'll have you." Then he used a word she'd used once half an hour ago: Carefully, thoughtfully at each syllable, he said, "In-ap-pro-pri-ate." After a pause, he took the word for his own by saying, "As inap*pro*priate as that'd be."

In that moment she understood: Mick Tremore was smarter, more attractive, and more aware of himself than she had ever supposed. And these marks in his character made him powerful. She was to be wary of that power; he understood it. She *was* wary. But she was something else, too. Her chin balanced on his fingers, she felt nothing ambiguous in one particular fact: Her blood came alive, as with nothing and no one else, when he stood near her.

That evening a tradition, born of cowardice, began. After dinner, Edwina still couldn't look a man in the mouth who was promising to lead her "down the path." Hunting for a way to sidestep

their usual focus on his organs of speech, she came up with what possibly would become her best idea for re-tailoring his words, even his thoughts.

"I'd like to go into the library tonight, where I'll read to you aloud." She suggested brightly, "We'll douse you in the sounds of proper English, while we educate you in the classics."

In the library, she drew down a book, and began to read to him — he on the sofa, she in a chair at the other side of an unlit fireplace.

She expected to read to him for only an hour or so. But as she began the stories — with Dryden's translation of Ovid's *Metamorphoses* — Mr. Tremore grew silent, rapt. He listened to the rhythm of English in heroic couplets, chosen so he'd hear the music of the language in a different way than prose exercises. Eventually, he scooted himself down onto the floor and lay nearer on the hearth rug, one arm over his head, the other fiddling with the brim of the hat on his chest — he'd worn it through dinner; he loved it.

While she read, he and she didn't argue. They didn't challenge each other. He stopped her occasionally for words he didn't know. That was the limit to his objection. He wouldn't let her speak a word, if he couldn't guess the sense behind it, not without her telling him the meaning — there were some they both had to look up. Winnie read for three hours through two different authors — he asked enough questions that she took down Bullfinch's *Mythology* — until at

last she grew hoarse.

At the end, he must have drifted off to sleep. She wasn't certain when. The hat had covered his eyes for the last half hour. Something now though in the rhythm of his breathing, the movement of his chest, made her stop reading. He said nothing, when up till this point, if she stopped, he lifted the hat and encouraged her to continue.

He lay there now on the hearth rug, completely relaxed, his dog stretched out beside him, both sleeping peacefully. Edwina sighed and smiled at the sight of the two of them, motionless, quiet. A rare state for either.

She closed the book in her lap, resting her hand on it. Then the pressure, the odd pressure as she stared at him, made her draw in a breath. Hesitantly, then intentionally, she pressed on the book, over where he had touched her today. There. Winnie had never imagined he might want to do that. It had been shocking: humiliating for him to know that animal part of her, to know her —

She couldn't proceed further in her thinking . . . but, oh, the feeling his hand had left on her. It was a constant battle not to remember the strong curve of his fingers, the feel of his hand when he curved it to —

Enough. She really had to *not* think about it. Yet more and more there seemed a bevy of things she was not supposed to think about — and by virtue of trying to remember not to, she hardly thought of anything else.

Shaking her head at herself, Winnie stood and walked to the bookshelf, where, as she replaced her book, the hair on her arms suddenly pricked with the full irony of what she'd been reading. The spine that she pushed into place read *Bulfinch's Mythology: The Age of Fable*, the last tale that she had pronounced aloud beginning:

Pygmalion was a sculptor who made with wonderful skill from ivory a perfect semblance of a maiden that seemed to be alive. . . .

Winnie glanced at the man asleep on her hearth. She was vain of how clever she was at teaching phonetics, how smartly she could break down the vowels and diphthongs of upper-class English, manufacture its inflections, feed its vocabulary, instruct on the human considerations that were its manners. That was partly what had gotten them here, her vanity. She was good at it.

An art so perfect, he fell in love with his counterfeit creation. . . .

Yet, today, she had stepped beyond her art, and she knew it. She pushed Mr. Tremore to embody her own conception of what a man should be — or rather what a gentleman should be, she corrected herself. She was limning out her own personal conception of what a gentleman should look like and say and how he should behave, while Mr. Tremore was grabbing up the notion, running like a racehorse with it, embodying her ideal more perfectly by the day.

And smoke roiled up . . . and Pygmalion made sacrifices on the altars of Venus. . . .

Part II

Winnie

The festival of Venus was at hand. . . . Victims
were offered, the altars smoked. . . . When
Pygmalion had performed his part of the
solemnities, he stood before the altar and
timidly said, "Ye gods, who can do all things,
give me, I pray you, for my wife" — he dared
not say "my ivory virgin," but said instead —
"one like my ivory virgin."

"Pygmalion," *The Age of Fable*
THOMAS BULLFINCH, LONDON, 1855

When Winnie was seventeen years old, her father died. This was eleven years after her mother had left them, only to die on some foreign continent — her mother had traveled so much after her departure that no one had been able to keep up with her. The letter announcing her death had been forwarded a number of times, leaving Winnie and her father with only the information that Lady Sissingley had died of pneumonia in Africa, India, or, possibly, China.

Winnie had been raised by a series of governesses and a father who — though he loved her, she was sure — was preoccupied with his own work. He was a linguistics scholar of some stature. Before he died, he'd written more than a hundred monographs on language-related topics and two textbooks. He was the foremost British theoretician on RP, received pronunciation — that is, the sounds that originated in upper-class mouths, how these sounds were formed, how they were perceived in the ear, and what subtle changes were happening to them as they were being transmitted via the public schools to the English middle class.

When Lionel Bollash — Regius Professor Bollash, Marquess of Sissingley by courtesy of being the fourth Duke of Arles's only son — died, everyone expected that his daughter would be taken into the household of his second cousin, Milford Xavier Bollash, who, up to that point, had been merely the grandnephew of the fourth duke, second in line, part of the family, but with no title other than the courtesy of "Lord" before his name.

To everyone's astonishment, however, when Xavier succeeded to the marquisate — inheriting not only Edwina's father's title, but every one of her family's possessions, the money, goods, and entailed estates that composed the full honor of being heir apparent to the duchy — he did not welcome her into his household. Winnie had barely absorbed the implications, however, when another calamity befell the family.

The hale and hearty fourth Duke of Arles, Winnie's grandfather and someone she might have counted on to lean on Xavier to sponsor her at least through a Season, to be of nominal support, while out on a walk at the ripe old age of one-hundred-three, was struck by lightning and smote dead on the spot. He followed his son to the grave by a delay of only three days. Xavier acquired the duchy of Arles in the same week he succeeded to the already vast and lucrative holdings of the Sissingley marquisate, ascending to the full roll call of honors: the fifth Duke of

Arles, Marquess of Sissingley, Count of Grenne-wick, Viscount Berwick — oh, there were more; she couldn't even remember them all.

At which point, Xavier told the seventeen-year-old Winnie quite plainly that, not only was she not residing under his roof, but: "There is no point in sponsoring you for a Season in London either, my dear. You are unmarriageable. You have no property to speak of. Heaven knows you aren't pretty. And, as if these facts weren't enough, you ruin what little femininity you have by mimicking your dotty father's obsession with how people talk."

He told her this by way of excusing himself for using her dowry to buy an elaborate custom crested brougham with eight matching bays and uniform livery for his footmen and coachman.

The day he packed her into this coach to send her off, one-way, he added, "You may as well be a man."

If only she had been, she would have been in line ahead of him.

But she was a girl, a funny-looking girl who, grieving for a father and grandfather, was ill-prepared. She — nor her father nor grandfather, she was sure — had considered for a moment that a cousin would not see to her at least modestly. She hadn't fully believed it, even as he was saying he wouldn't, till she was riding away in the coach with Milton, her butler, on her way to his sister's house. Her butler's sister's house, for goodness sakes.

Of course, by Arles's standards, he *had* seen to her: A year and a half later, when the Home Office caught wind of her situation (as it turned out, what Xavier had done wasn't quite legal) and said he must make restitution of her dowry — property he had sold, money he had already spent — he resigned claim to the only thing he didn't know what to do with: her father's library on human speech and the building it was housed in, the marquess's town house in Knightsbridge.

What was Arles like? Mr. Tremore had asked. Besides greedy? Old, but spry. When he had inherited the world, Xavier was already in his late seventies. All her life, he had stood at the self-assured center of her family. The witty one, the clever one, the one who entertained them all, the one who had the parties and the friends and connections. He loved power and influence; he cultivated them. He wanted to be adored and, generally, was.

Edwina had actually admired him. She had circled the little planet of her father — a father who floated in the solitary ethers of academia — in awe of her brighter, more gregarious second cousin, once removed. An obscure little moon to Xavier's sun.

She used what she'd acquired of her father's things and her father's knowledge to make ends meet in a way her father never could have imagined. Lionel Bollash had had no head for business; he hadn't needed one, having enjoyed, as his father before him and every other previous

Marquess of Sissingley, one of the most lucrative entailments in the empire. Edwina had come through, though; she was even proud of herself. She was happiest when she was working. She loved what she did.

Nonetheless, she retained a degree of rancor for Xavier and an odd sense of shame.

One of her first students, who knew of events, said, "Oh, it was perhaps for the best. These things happen." It was meant as consolation. Yet Edwina could not surmount a sense of horror to hear the words.

For the best? As if, given the choice, she should have wished all this to befall her? Sought it on purpose? Since it was so good?

No, she personally thought she could have done without it.

Oddly enough, the parents of the same student, when the duke had first dispossessed Edwina, had been outraged. People in general at the time were outraged. Then they weren't. Life went on. It took a year or more, but eventually everyone returned to making their morning calls on Xavier's wife, to seeking his support, to asking him to donate to the missionary fund, to invest in their projects. And they never stopped decking themselves out and going to his annual ball.

A ball that Edwina herself had never attended —she'd been too young, then too strained a relation. Nor could she call at Xavier's house. He wouldn't have allowed it; she wouldn't have

wanted to. Which made her feel more or less marooned, a little red boat in a dry basin at low tide. She could send other little boats out upon the sea of English high society. She could teach them to sail, to skim along the water with style and grace. While her own sails only luffed in the wind.

The next morning, Mick lathered up his chin and cheeks, but left his upper lip dry. In one night, he already had a dark shadow of stubble on his lip. He twisted his mouth, holding his cheek taut with his fingers, and shaved as usual: both cheeks, his chin, his jaw, his lower face, save the place under his nose.

He rinsed, stood up, then, as he toweled himself dry, stared into the mirror. The dark hair across his lip looked like dirt on his mouth. He'd looked better clean-shaven. In a few days, he'd look fine again, he supposed. His old self. But his new self stood there, cogitating, unhappy with an itchy lip that looked as if he'd been drinking stout and forgot to wipe his mouth.

So which self should I be? he asked.

Then the question unnerved him.

Which self? There weren't two of him.

Get rid of the thing, he told himself. Don't make it complicated. Winnie liked him better without it. Anything that reminded her that his sex was the opposite, the mate, to hers alarmed her. Fine, he could go delicate with her. He could become the most gentlemanly gentleman

she'd ever known. All her ladylike rules were a lot of bung, but he was beginning to understand why gents went through the ordeal.

He stared into the mirror, turning his head. A barber had come in last week and taken a razor to the hair at the back of his neck. There was a clean line where his hair met his collar, nothing scraggily on his neck. Neat. His shirt collar was high on his throat, snug. It half choked him sometimes to wear it. Milton had been showing him how to tie a necktie, but he'd made a tangle of it today. It draped, wrinkled from effort, on either side of his neck down his vest.

Outside he was looking more and more like — what was it they wanted him to be? A viscount? But inside he still felt like Mick from Cornwall who lived underneath a shoemaker's shop in London next door to the Waste Market.

Winnie liked the result, and that made half of him — the lower half of him — want to go on. He'd done crazier things to get up close to a woman he liked. The other half of him, though, hesitated.

More and more, he spoke differently. He acted different, too. But the strange thing was, sometimes he thought different lately. Differently. Hell, he worried over whether to say *different* or *differently*, when how the hell much could it matter? And why did he care?

He thought things like, Wouldn't it be nice to have a respectable woman like Winnie Bollash? When what he wanted of Winnie, of course, was

for her to be unrespectable with him. No, no, he corrected, not Winnie Bollash. He didn't want her; he couldn't have her. But . . . oh, a seamstress's assistant maybe. A woman *like* Winnie Bollash. Good-hearted, smart, hardworking. And faithful. Of the half dozen highborn women he'd been with, every one of them had been married. But Winnie . . . a woman *like* Winnie would be loyal. Hell, there she was yesterday, steadfastly trampling along beside him after he'd scared half the wits from her just hours before. And grit. She had grit.

He picked up the razor again, then spoke to the fellow on the other side of the mirror, taking exaggerated care with pronunciation. "I rahther think you should take the mustache off, old man. Jolly good idea."

Stupid toff. Except he liked that his room was dry. In the cellar under the shoemaker's, half the time when it rained, water seeped through the walls. He liked not being exhausted at the end of the day. Eating well and regularly had its advantages. And new words — especially finding new words, more particular words, and being *understood* when he said them — were bloody marvelous.

It felt surprisingly good not to be misunderstood most of the time — to have a thought, a feeling, and say it, then have others grasp what he was trying to get across. Expressing himself easily relieved a tension in him he hadn't known was there. And it was useful, being able to tell

people what he wanted. Milton understood what he said lately, and Molly Reed laughed at his jokes. Useful and enjoyable. And it would most surely be a help, when he next had to explain to some fancy housekeeper that he wasn't begging at her kitchen door, but offering to rid her of a chronic problem in London.

Useful. Mick looked down at the sharp razor itself, pearl-handled. It was the smoothest-feeling blade he'd ever held. He liked the feel of it on his skin. It cut clean.

He looked at the hand that had hold of it. There wasn't a mark on it, not a scratch or bite, because the hand didn't dive into the rat holes of life. If he wasn't careful, he'd have himself do-nothing gentleman's hands. Yes, hands that had time to think — but look what he thought. How to trade his good ol' flavor-savor mustache for a look at a pair of legs he wasn't supposed to touch. On a woman he couldn't have.

The really stupid part, though, was he picked up the shaving brush, clacked it around in the soap cup again, then lathered his lip up. He razored the damn beginnings of mustache off, shaving his lip again for Winnie. Because he was hoping for another damn, pointless look.

Ironically, down the hall, Winnie was also standing before a mirror. She had, however, a slightly different prospect. Ten feet from the mirror, she looked at the full-length reflection of her body, stark naked.

She could never remember taking off her clothes by the light of day before, simply to look at herself. She had never thought not to, she had simply never done it. This morning, though, with her nightgown off, before she drew a stitch over her head, she turned to the mirror to survey herself.

Her body. She was immediately struck by how long her legs were. She'd never thought of them. But yes, they were long, and their muscles were good, well-proportioned. Her legs were firm. They were pretty. It was the first time she could honestly like any part of herself. They'd always been covered up. She'd never looked. Now that she had — well, marvelous: The only part of her that was pretty was one that no one would see, not even the faintest shape.

And the rest of her — oh. Her breasts were two little funnels on her chest. Her waist was small, but her hips and buttocks offset any advantage that brought. They were too full, making her into a pear.

Her eyes settled at the top of her legs, at the apex between. The hair there was dense, tight-curling, and dark cherry blond, only slightly deeper in hue than the hair on her head. Winnie touched it. It was wiry. Like —

Like a mustache.

She tried to envision what Mick Tremore looked like here. She couldn't. The small bits she'd seen on stone cherubs, the baby penises (there, she'd thought the word!), had always

seemed so vulnerable. Cherub male parts in the flesh, she always thought, would look like little snails without shells — an idea that most certainly didn't suit Mr. Tremore. Adult stone men had fig leaves where their widges should be. She was sure that was wrong. Which left only imagination.

And a word. She formed it silently with her mouth. *Widge.* Her lips looked as if they were blowing a kiss. What did one look like? And hair. Did a widge wear a mustache?

She found herself feeling uneasy, silly, peculiar — giggling as she donned her clothes for the day. Just as she was getting her hair up, there was a knock at her door.

She jumped guiltily, then thought, Oh, goodness, Mr. Tremore was so forward. There he was outside in her sitting room, knocking on her bedroom door.

When she opened it, though, it was Milton. "May I come in, m'lady?" He looked grave.

"Yes. Certainly. Is something wrong?"

He frowned. He stammered. "I — Well, yes —" He finally said, "I've been with your family" — he cleared his throat — "for a very long time, and I have never intruded, my lady." She waited for him to go on. It took him a moment. "I was there on the night you were born."

"Yes, Milton. What's the point? What is bothering you?"

"Well." He drew his small frame up and stiffened his mouth. "Well," he repeated, "Mrs. Reed

211

and I were discussing it, and we think —" He blurted the rest. "We think it would be better if Mr. Tremore moved downstairs with me."

Edwina sank down into the chair by her bed. She stared at him. "Why?"

He frowned. "My lady, you are living upstairs with a man — well, who is — We didn't think — No one thought — But, well, now — And he clearly finds you —"

"You think it's immodest of me to have him staying above stairs, his room on the same floor as mine?"

"Yes, m'lady."

Goodness, such a judgment from Milton, who tended to be generous with her. Winnie nodded, expressing her understanding.

"There are eight empty rooms below stairs," he proceeded to tell her. "Mr. Tremore could have any of them. I can make one up, tell him, help him move —"

"No." She shook her head quickly. "I'll tell him."

Milton was right, of course. She couldn't have a . . . a gentleman sleeping under her roof, just him and herself alone upstairs. Why hadn't she thought of it in this light before?

She repeated, "I'll tell him. I'll explain." She glanced at Milton, the most loyal family she had. "I appreciate it," she said. "Thank you for saying."

He nodded. "Your best interests," he murmured. "I've watched you grow up into a fine

young woman, Lady Bollash." The form of address for the eldest daughter of a marquess; he had never made the transition, always addressing her with the same respect. He continued, "I am proud to work for you. I don't wish to see you" — he hesitated again — "unhappy when he goes. I'd stay by you, it's not that —"

Ah. It wasn't for form's sake that he wanted to move Mr. Tremore, not for the sake of gossip or appearances. He feared she'd succumb to ruin itself.

"It's —" He continued, "Well, I do think, if Mr. Tremore were to sleep downstairs in the room next to mine, it would be better."

"Yes, it would be." She nodded again, then repeated herself. "I'll tell him."

Winnie was going to make short work of the obligation. She would go downstairs, find Mr. Tremore, and tell him straight off. She'd explain that he'd become — what? A man. He'd become a man to her and to the others around them.

How awful. She couldn't say that. What had he been before?

God knew. She only knew that now he fit a different pattern. It didn't matter if a ratcatcher was given her finest room. But it mattered if Mick slept within tiptoe of her bed, especially given that she stood before it recently, looking at her own naked body while wondering about his.

It mattered. And she'd say.

Then she hedged. At the foot of the stairs, she veered toward her laboratory. There, she sat and stared blankly at her notes, trying to think how to phrase it.

Chapter 14

Winnie intended to mention to Mick all that day that it would be better, all things considered, if he moved himself and his things downstairs. She intended to, but didn't do it. She didn't know why she hesitated. It was her house. She could make the decision. Yet there never seemed an appropriate moment.

Moreover, Mick was moodier than usual, unsettled. It was a new or at least a less often seen side to him. All day long, he seemed lost in thought. She set him up to do his drills and exercises on his own, using a mirror and a gramophone. When she checked on him half an hour later, though, he only sat, staring into space, running his finger over his bare lip — surprisingly, it had been shaved again. The muscle at the side of his jaw, the one that squared it so perfectly, flexed morning till night. In the end, she simply flunked the task of speaking to him about moving downstairs. She'd do it tomorrow, she promised herself.

Then tomorrow came, and she couldn't find him.

Mick occasionally left for short periods of

time. "To attend to my business," he always said quite formally. Edwina was never sure exactly what he did. He had animals to which he attended, she knew. He had friends, she suspected, he taunted with his new wealth and manners.

She heard him return about noon. She was down the hall from her lab in the library, reading, when she became aware of him knocking around in the mudroom at the back of the house in a way Milton never did — Mick usually had mud *on* him. She could hear his kicking off wellies, as if he'd come up through the back garden.

A few minutes later, she recognized his footfalls in the hallway, coming toward her, though his tread was a bit heavier and more jangly than usual.

Then he appeared into the doorway and announced, "It's the carriage house."

"What's the carriage house?"

"The rats. That's where they are. They have a nest. Let's go get 'em."

She laughed. "You want me to catch rats with you?"

"It's fun," he said. He grinned, the most relaxed she'd seen him in a day or two. Fun. He was the Mick Tremore again who thought everything, life itself, was fun.

She sat back in her chair, smiling despite herself. It wasn't such a bad way to see things, she decided. She wished her existence were fun or at least that she thought it was as often as he did.

"It's work," she contradicted. And he was dressed for work. He was wearing heavy boots and old clothes.

He came over, lifted her, or tried to, by the arm. "True, but exciting work. Come on. You don't have to help or watch, but you should see what I'm talking about. It's your carriage house."

She let herself be stood up by the arm, then raised one eyebrow at him. "Do you kill them?"

"The rats? Of course."

She frowned. "Is it bloody?"

"Not for me, though I'm sure the rats think otherwise — the dogs and ferrets get messy." He made a mock-exasperated face. "Winnie, they're rats. They're dirty, ugly rats, who each have fifty or sixty babies a year, and those babies start dropping babies by two months. You figure it out. That's a lot of little things scooting around, eating your horses' oats, burrowing into your walls, getting up into your carriage —"

"Ewww," she shuddered, then wrinkled her nose. "Still, they're animals."

He laughed with that rumble that always caught her up into it somehow and made her want to smile back. "You're right, loov." She'd told him a number of times that it wasn't *loov* but *love,* and in either case that it was an unseemly form of address, yet still he insisted on using it. He said, pulling her forward, "We should go buy them cheese, leave it for them each night, maybe put a little bow on it. Oh, come on." He used her

217

arm to turn her and put her ahead of him, then he pushed at her back.

When, over her shoulder, she threw him a worried look, he only wiggled his eyebrows in that funny way he could when he was thrilled with himself. "Shiver me timbers, mate," he said gleefully. He did his old accent, only thicker: Cornwall, the land of pirates, with a Cockney twist. "We'll pint th' carrich 'ouse wiv ther blewd."

It was a relief to see him in fine spirits again.

She went out with him to the carriage house, thinking, Yes, here was the opportunity. While he was doing something that made him feel good, she'd tell him he was moving downstairs. Why was she making it such a tribulation? It wasn't. He'd shrug; he wouldn't even care.

At the end of her drive in front of the carriage house, she saw a donkey cart. He'd borrowed it from a friend to transport his dogs and ferrets. In the back of the cart, Mick's entire retinue barked and kicked up a commotion the moment he and she came into view.

From the wood cart, he unloaded half a dozen box-carriers, two ferrets to a box. Five small dogs clambered down, but not until Mick whistled for them. Magic jumped at his heels. The little dog was alert in a new way, more excited. Into the carriage house Winnie went, following this animal act — Mick with carriers under both arms, more dangling off his hands, dogs nipping at his heels, a bevy of small beasts to whom, it

seemed, he sang. Whether to control them somehow — for they seemed to follow with it — or as an expression of his own absorbed contentment, he hummed a low tune, the Pied Piper.

Inside the carriage house, he squatted, setting boxfuls of ferrets onto the floor. The dogs continued to make a ruckus. But when he moved his hand through the air at them and said, "Hey," every one of them quieted and sat — six motley little terrier faces looking up at him expectantly. "You wait," he told them.

She watched him move — he stooped, stood, bent to slide a ferret box across the floor, motioned to a dog, each of which listened with rapt attention — as he explained to her.

"Ratting's a sport where I come from. A useful sport that neighbors do together. Growing up, I ratted barns, poultry houses, and mines with sometimes as many as a dozen men. . . ."

He said more, but she heard only bits. She watched, mesmerized. Methodically, he sat dogs at intervals, then slid ferret boxes, turned them, looked, turned one a few more degrees. Periodically, he assessed the space, the placement, as if he had an analytical plan. All the while, he jangled — tools swung from his hips as he moved, off a wide leather belt he'd strapped on: collars with bells, a coil of string, secateurs, a long, slender wood club, a short metal cosh.

Over the edge of the belt against his hip was folded a pair of old leather gloves. He wore heavy boots. They clunked as he walked. His trousers

were tucked into them, while into the trousers was tucked a tight-fitting knit shirt, faded red, open at the neck. Old work clothes, similar to those the day she'd first seen him, though these had considerable more dignity, all fascinated properly, no one chasing him: Mick in control.

He was graceful and precise. He knew what he was doing.

He finished some sort of explanation. ". . . but only if you station the dogs in good tactical positions," he said. "Then you're ready to send the ferrets into the likely places. They raid the nest. What escapes them has to face the dogs. And me — I try to get any who get by the first two lines of attack."

It was a battlefield to him, a war to be waged with his animal army. Winnie shuddered again. She must have made a sound, for he stopped and looked around. "You're gonna go before I start. But I just wanted you to know, I guess, it's gonna be better when I'm done." As if she'd argued with him he said, "It's none worse than foxhunting. In fact, the terriers cut their teeth on foxes. Magic here'll go to ground for fox *or* rat, follow the darn thing right under the earth, then stay there barking till you dig him and the animal out."

She grimaced. "Heavens, if I even saw a rat —" She looked at him. "What's it like?"

"See them?" He laughed at her timid curiosity. "They're going to be jumping out of the woodwork, leaping everywhere." He shook his head. "It'll be about as crazy as you can imagine for a

few minutes, all of us chasing each other, with rats making us wild. It isn't pretty, Win, but it sure is exciting. You'd be safe up in the loft, if you wanted to watch."

"Safe?"

"Brown rats don't like heights."

"Um, no, thank you."

"It's a shame," he teased her. "You're missing about the most exciting thing you'll ever see in your life."

She doubted that. She suspected she was looking at the most exciting thing in her life. A man with coshes and belled collars hanging off him, in hobnailed boots that clacked like thunder on her floor, who wanted to make her carriage house "better."

"What?" he said. "Why are you staring at me like that?" He smiled, then, as if she'd accused him of something, said, "All right, I brought you out here because I wanted you to see how good I am at it. If you stayed, you'd be impressed." His face drew up further into his recklessly confident, left-tilting grin.

"I am impressed." She smiled back, if a little uneasily. Rats. Ugh. "I'm sure you're enormously competent." She shook her head. "You're good at a lot of things."

He tilted his head with interest. "You're always fixing me."

"You're good at a lot of things," she repeated.

"Do you think so?" He liked the idea.

"Yes."

She looked around. With a little shiver she could imagine his battle plan come to life. Yet it was too earthy and frightening to let her mind go very far with it. Though it would be triumphant, she didn't doubt. "So you have —" She didn't know what to call them then found, "customers and places you go?"

"Ace," he said, having fun with her.

"How do you remember where you've been and haven't been and who needs it done and how much you charge?"

He glanced over his shoulder as if she were crazy. "I don't remember it. I write it down."

"Where?" she asked. She envisioned scraps of paper or the back of his hand.

She received another glance that mocked her doltish lack of imagination. "In a book, Win."

"A ledger?"

He rolled his eyes. "You could call it that. I'm a businessman. I have a hundred regular customers, and every year I have to sell myself to a hundred new ones. I write down their addresses, where I've been, what they've said. I add up what I make — last year, I earned sixty-four pounds. That's not too bad for a bloke" — he corrected — "for a fellow like me. Damn good, in fact."

It was indeed. She was stunned. And he kept records?

He went on. "Joe there is Magic's son. The fellow with the cart has a bitch Maj is fond of. I traded first pick of the litter next time for second, in exchange for the use of his cart today."

222

"That was nice of you."

"No, it wasn't. That's what I'm trying to tell you. It's my business. I have to keep the fellow happy and making a living, or I don't get to use his cart; he couldn't afford to keep it. . . ."

He kept going, keen to talk about his work. He was proud of it. And Winnie surprised herself with how fascinating she found the ins and outs of ratcatching.

Mick took out a ferret, snapped on a belled collar, ". . . because this is the one going under the boards, and I want to know where she is." He held the little animal up. Her dark coat was glossy, mink-colored. "Pretty, isn't she?"

As he dropped it back into its box for the moment, Winnie thought, no, not the ferret, the *man* was beautiful, long-armed, long-legged, physical, robustly reeking of health. Even in rat clothes.

A ratcatcher. He *was* one. Imagine. And he'd kissed her: once gently, once with so much passion it had made her cry.

Oh, dear, dear, she reprimanded herself. Don't find him exciting. Or, no, why not hire a chimney sweep to clean the chimney, then kiss him, too? She could call the glazier to fix the front window and perhaps have a hug. And the plumber was a nice man — *smirk, smirk, smirk.* Oh, Edwina, she thought, get hold of yourself.

Rats, she thought. Goodness. Time to leave. He was set up, ready to begin. She turned. "Well —" she said.

Mick watched her and knew she was about to

go. For no better reason than he wanted to hold her there, he said, "Watch this."

He raised his arm over Magic, snapped his fingers. And ol' Magic did his old magic. Just for fun, just because Mick wanted him to, he started to jump.

Now Magic wasn't a good-looking dog. He had a white body, a whiskery-looking snout from the white fur flecking into brown, a short, shaggy coat, and a wizened little face. A scruffy little dog, barely a foot high at the withers. But Maj had the heart of a giant. If he did something, he put his whole, fearless self into it.

He jumped more than five feet into the air. Straight up. Then, his neat little feet no sooner touching the ground, he went up, straight up again. It delighted Mick to see the energy the dog put into it. Over and over. He wouldn't stop till Mick told him to. If Mick should die someday between when he told the dog to jump and the stop signal, Maj would jump himself to death.

Mick smiled at Win, at her face beaming with wonder. "It's like he has springs in his back legs," he said. "Have you ever seen anything like it? He's jumping five times his height. If I could do that, I could leap this carriage house."

She shook her head, glued now to the sight. He felt exhilarated, seeing her there, her expression amused, absorbed. Oh, he wanted to charm her. He wanted to woo her, make her stay. He just wasn't sure how to do it. Not by setting rats loose on her.

For Maj's sake, he gave a nod of his head, and the dog settled to earth, bright-eyed, happy, ready to go again the second he might be asked. Mick fed him a piece of apple from his pocket, something the dog loved, his payment — though had there been no payment that would have been all right, too; often there wasn't.

Mick knew Win wasn't listening as he told her about the dog; he was barely listening to himself. He wanted to say, *Don't go. Just stay. Stay and keep looking at me like that.* He rattled on instead, "Only once did a rat ever mess with this fierce little fellow, and the bite only made Magic madder. . . ."

He glanced at Winnie. She was enjoying the dog's antics, but she was dancing on her feet a little. The ratting made her nervous. She didn't like the atmosphere. She didn't want to watch rats killed.

Why had he brought her out here? He could have predicted her reaction.

He knew the answer, of course. Her face was the answer. Because he was so damn good at this that it was obvious even in the way he laid out his attack — and he was so damn awkward at every- thing else she was teaching him. He wanted to be . . . skillful, elegant at something in front of her. Ha. Elegant at being a ratcatcher. Now, there was a way to impress the ladies.

Thing was, it often did impress them. More than once, a lady had watched from over her up- stairs banister as he got rid of the brown rats

below. Brown rats on the ground floor, the milder black rats in the upper stories; it never varied. It was the order of the rat world. A few cats could take care of the black rats upstairs, but Mick was the man for the meaner ones who dominated the more accessible turf. More than once, a lady had watched him do the deed, shrieking in disgust but riveted. Then he'd clean himself up in her scullery or mudroom, and been invited for a cup of tea or a glass of claret, where one thing led to another.

"I have to go," Winnie said.

He looked up at her. "I know. I'll wash and change, then meet you for the afternoon lesson. I'll be on time."

"That would be good." She took a step, then rotated back. "Oh, and I have to tell you something. Milton," she said, as if the man should be forgiven for something, tolerated. Then she shook her head. "No, not Milton. Me —"

Mick waited. The blood in his body knew before he did. It reacted to her expression or reluctance or something. It started to pump hard, rush. He was going to be told something bad.

She said, "Um, I'd, uh — like you to move your things downstairs to the room next to Milton's. He'll help you do it."

More for her to deny it, he asked, "You want me to move into the servants' quarters?"

She shook her head no, but she confirmed it. "You'll be with Milton," like it was a big privi-

lege, "the room down one from his."

"Right."

Defensively, she added what he already knew. "I like Milton. He's more than a servant. He lives downstairs because he prefers to and because it's proper."

"And because he's your butler."

She frowned, opened her mouth, then said nothing, like she was angry at him for saying it out loud.

While the reality of it raced around inside him. He knew why he was being moved. Mick the rake, banished. Maybe she could remember not to kiss the help, if the East End hooligan-help lived a few feet further away from her. Bloody hell, she was welcome to try.

He didn't dare say anything for a moment. And he didn't want her to see his disappointment, so he turned his back, waving away her tongue-tied, irritated confusion. "No need to explain," he said. He stooped down and stroked his dog. "I'm as good as there, Miss Bollash. I'll do it as soon as we finish here. You better go now. I'm gonna start."

He stood, dusted his hands on his trousers, pulled his gloves off his belt.

Just then, a ferret down the way made an angry little sound at her coworker in the carrier. There was a hiss and a little *bonk* of soft bodies.

And, like that, Winnie was on him. Her weight hit him. She grabbed his shoulders and half-climbed his back to his neck. She all but knocked

him down, before he got a leg-hold of her with her clutching him by his chin and a handful of ear.

"Ferrets," he muttered as best he could with her arm under his jaw.

Her body relaxed a little, though she didn't relinquish her higher position. She had her legs wrapped around him like a vise, skirts and all.

"Just ferrets," he assured her.

He torqued at the waist and slowly pulled her down him, trying to lower a sizeable woman from an awkward position without dropping her. Oh, it was right odd and delicious, the feel of easing her down. He jerked when her parted legs slid for a second over the top of his thigh. She leaped, too, from the contact of their bodies, though she was more taken aback. Him, he was getting used to the jumps and jolts of their pleasure. It was a fierce thing. No help for it; it slammed them around.

He peeled her off him, his blood hopping. He could feel the place where her breasts had pressed into his back, the place where she'd straddled his thigh. Christ, he thought. He shifted her around in front of him, lowering her by her spectacular bum, down onto her feet.

And there she was, her face an inch away from his for a second, her body all but up against him. She paused, looking up. If he blew on her, her eyelashes would've fluttered from his breath. For one blistering moment, he was sure she was waiting — waiting for him to do what he nor-

mally might. If he wanted to kiss a woman who got this close, he didn't usually hesitate.

This time, though, he murmured down into her face, "It'd be my fault again, wouldn't it?"

"What would?" She wet her lips, staying right there, waiting.

Hell, he thought. He didn't do half bad, when he had some distance. But when she was this close, it just made him angry she wouldn't admit it. He asked bluntly, "Do you want me to kiss you?"

"No!" she said instantly. Though the shock in her face, he would've guessed, was more for having her mind read than from the idea.

He turned her loose, pushing her away. "Fine. If you ever do, just remember I like a little participation. A little share in the responsibility, Miss Bollash. If you want me to kiss you, it'd be right damn nice if you'd say so. Otherwise" — he reverted intentionally — "you ain't havin' a kiss from me."

She glared and pressed her lips so hard together, they turned white. Her face was full of havoc — frustration, vexation, bewilderment — for what had just happened.

Then the mean witch of a woman said, "Instead of *right* — *right nice* or *right fine* — you should say *quite* or *rather* or even *ratherish*."

He gave a snort. He wanted to hoot. "I'm not saying *ratherish*."

Then he wanted to laugh outright. Here they were, him and Winnie, going at it again. Jesus,

the woman was thick. Didn't she feel it? Hell, he wanted to shove her against the wall between bridle straps, pull up her skirts — Or no, maybe in the carriage, flat out on the seat or — Jesus, he couldn't think how to do it or, rather, he could think of a hundred ways he wanted to. He wanted to have her, just have her — maybe the floor would do, if the dogs and ferrets didn't mind.

He made himself ask instead, "What do you want me to say? What was the rest?"

She corrected him again. "*Pardon*. Remember you're supposed to say *pardon* when you want someone to repeat themselves."

He raised his brow with theatrical impatience and said, "Pardon, Miss Bollash? What the bloody foke do you want me to say instead of *right damn fine?*"

She stared fixedly. "*Quite fine*. Or *rather fine*."

"*Rather*," he repeated. Rahther. Mick could hear himself saying it right. He looked at Winnie. She waited for the whole phrase. Stupid woman. She was happier fixing him than admiring him. It was her way of connecting, her way of shagging him blind. "Rahther fine, Miss Bollash."

He wondered if maybe he still said it wrong though, because she blinked at him, stared. But then she said, "Well. Yes. That's quite good." She laughed. "Right damn fine, in fact." She had a bloody wonderful laugh when she let it out, which wasn't often. Then she murmured, without explanation, "I'm sorry."

Another apology, though he wasn't sure for what. But without a word more of explanation, she turned and bolted.

He watched her run from the carriage house, up her back garden, all the way to her back door and inside her house without stopping.

Bloody wonderful, Mick. You're a prize.

He pushed his hand back through his hair, then held a handful of it, closing his eyes. He breathed, only breathed, for a minute, letting his mind, his blood calm. God bless, the woman made him crazy.

He took it out on the rats.

He rid the place of them in short order — ferrets chasing and diving, dogs jumping, rats screeching and running everywhere. Ten minutes of pandemonium, which suited his mood perfectly.

At the end of it, he sat on the floor in the midst of mayhem. He took an accounting: several dozen dead rats, with a ferret and a dog bit, the dog pretty badly. Right, he thought. Right.

"She could have a point, you know," he told the little dog softly as he cleaned out its wound. "It's awful, isn't it? Look what they did to you."

Another reason to have brought Winnie out here struck him. Yes, he'd wanted to show her how good he was at something, but — maybe more so — he'd come out here to prove in his own mind he was still himself.

Only to succeed in proving he wasn't: The dog didn't agree with him. He hopped right up the

moment Mick let him, ready to do it all again. Stupid dog. Something always got ripped up by rat teeth, and though not often, more than he liked, that something on occasion was Mick Tremore. He had a place on his hand where a rat got it, a place on his shin. Ratting might be good sport, but as a line of work it was right disgusting.

Rather disgusting.

He let out a breath, a laugh, down his nose. It was *extremely* disgusting, which had never bothered him before. It was dangerous, but he'd never thought he had a choice. And there was the problem. Choices. New ones could be there for him, if he just looked.

Mick sacked rats with a hook, not touching them, then rallied his whole brood of animals and washed them out back. In cold water at the pump. He washed his dogs and ferrets to protect them from the diseases and vermin rats carried, the same as he'd wash himself.

As he poured cold water on Magic, though, he couldn't help be glad he had a hot tub to look forward to.

Then he heard himself thinking. Bloody hell, was he even liking baths these days? He was. He hated to pull the plug on the tub. He usually lay back and soaked himself wrinkled.

Being here in this house was having a more drastic effect on him than he had expected. He'd begun to like things he couldn't afford. Tubs. Gallons of hot water pumped in at a spigot.

Steamy rooms just for bathing.

He'd begun to want a woman he couldn't have.

It was funny how he trusted Winnie. He'd gotten used to her fixing him. He trusted her to look at him, then say, to listen and correct what might give him away in a few weeks. And lately, he'd begun to make notes in his head, things he liked that he was learning and intended to keep, things he would abandon the moment they were finished. He was getting more from her than a way to win a bet. He was getting new ideas. And Winnie was like a kind mirror. He could look into her and adjust himself to suit himself.

When she wasn't being stiff-necked, she was the friend he most wanted to talk to, who he couldn't wait to see each day. She came into his mind with the first ray of consciousness at day-break. He nodded off, smiling over her with his last, heavy-eyed blink before sleep. Sweet Win. Funny Win. Clever Win. Frightened, brave, careful, meticulous Winnie, trying to avoid the bite of the world by pretending it didn't have teeth.

No, he wasn't his old self. He wasn't sure what he was, except different. And to know it, to see himself a different way, was like looking for the first time at his bare lip again. It rattled him. It ran him off his rails. He felt turned around by the vague, untried choices that lay before him. He wasn't certain what he was beyond a ratcatcher who chummed with Rezzo and the others. He

233

couldn't say for sure where he was going, and it was right unusual — no, *rather* unusual — to feel so directionless. Which made him remember suddenly a swarm of words from his and Winnie's nightly reading, reading he liked so much, on one hand, while, on the other, it made him curse his good memory: disconcerting, confounding, addling, perplexing.

What was a ratcatcher going to do with these words?

After he was finished, he went to calm Freddie, his ferret who no longer worked but rather stayed in her cage at the rear of the carriage house. She had to have been "disconcerted" herself by what had gone on. Freddie was thirteen years old, when ferrets only lived ten or twelve years. She was feeble and near-blind. When he'd thought she was dying, he'd carried her in his pocket and made up excuses to people to have her with him. In her day, though, she'd been the bravest, craftiest ferret, the best of her kind. She'd fed him and his kin rabbits in Cornwall. She'd given him work when he'd brought her to London: She'd given him self-respect.

These days, she was getting around pretty well again. She was less thin. Her new surroundings agreed with her. So Mick stroked her and cooed and told her of all the rats that had gone under today as he fed her the liver of the healthiest kill. It cheered her, he could tell. While petting her, seeing her look good, certainly cheered him.

Chapter 15

Mr. Tremore wasn't very genteel about the move. He came in that afternoon, cleaned himself up, then threw his things into his bed's counterpane, yanked it all up by the corners into a knapsack, and hauled it and himself downstairs. He wouldn't take the room next to Milton's. He took the one farthest from the butler's, which happened also to be the smallest, but "more private, more my own." It was a room that would have belonged to the scullery, had there been one, a miserly piece of space with only one high window that looked out onto the sidewalk in front — onto the glow of a street lamp by night; by day, the feet of London passersby.

Fine, Winnie thought. At least they would get along better now. And so they did, in their way. She'd silenced him. It was an eerie silence though, much happening beneath it, invisible, undiscussed. Fine, she thought again. Just as well.

It took another few days for her finally, fully to return to her side of the table, to sit across from Mick and work with him — something, as she began again, she realized, she enjoyed too much to give up.

Mick wasn't educated very well, though not as badly as she'd first thought. The country school he'd been to in Cornwall had done a decent job on basic reading. Heavens, though, had he made the most of a fundamental education. His mind loved wordplay. It made teaching him language a pleasure. He was a classic case of the student, though less knowledgeable, keeping the teacher on her toes. He was always one step ahead of her, always leaping in directions she had never considered.

In particular, he took to the vocabulary exercises she gave him. Of course, he ended up acquiring favorite words, then couldn't be pried away from them. *Diabolical* was a standard he only moved from when he discovered others. Along with his avidity came, also, a mystery. From nowhere, he started using words she hadn't taught or read to him. He brought them like gifts, coming up with them on his own.

"Junoesque," he said one day.

She looked up and across the table. He was staring at her in that thoughtful way he had, contemplative.

He continued. "Callipygian."

She blinked. He couldn't possibly know the word's meaning.

But he did: "Having well-shaped buttocks."

"It has pear-shaped connotations. A large bum."

He smiled. "I know. Large and well-shaped. I wish I knew a word for a large, well-shaped bum

that goes into legs yards long and with more curves than an orchestra of violins."

She didn't know where to look for a moment. Boldly, she tried to hold his eyes. Well, she thought. An orchestra of violins. The Venus Callipygus. His references were certainly changing, if not the direction of his mind.

She lost the battle of eye contact when her gaze dropped a degree, to his lip where a mustache had been. It remained clean-shaven, but felt now somehow like a joke. He could shave the mustache, but a big, bristling masculinity remained in him.

There was a kind of virile swagger to everything Mick Tremore said and did, indomitable, in all his teasing and talk, his daily rituals, in his smallest duty or whim. It permeated even his silence. He had a masculine sense of himself that couldn't be tamed or turned into something else. He hadn't lost the animality in his mustache; he was only becoming more polite about it.

The odd thing was — a new perspective on herself that set her teeth on edge — she was fascinated by the very thing she abhorred, that she wished she could tone down: the unchecked, all but unvarnished, potent male energy of him. She half-relished the odd, anxious chagrin it brought. He seemed lately more complicated than anyone had realized, while — never mind the polish he was acquiring — she was more entranced by his raw edge than she liked to admit. And by the directness that went with it. And his good heart.

The mystery of how he learned the words was solved a night later.

Winnie awoke at two in the morning with a start and discovered herself to be crying — a frenzy of soft little sobs. After a few seconds, she was able to get hold of it, though her heart raced as she wiped her face. She lay there, puzzled. She'd been dreaming; she couldn't remember of what. She tried to grasp the content, yet was only able to recapture a sense of fury and deprivation — a wanting, a howling for something someone wouldn't let her have.

Sleep, she told herself irritably as she slid from bed. Something was keeping her from it lately. She hadn't slept decently in a fortnight, though tonight was the worst. Happy at least to be free of the mental debris of her dream, she went downstairs for a glass of milk.

Coming back upstairs from the kitchen, she saw light at the end of the ground-floor hallway. It came from her library. She didn't think about what she was doing any more than would a moth. She padded silently, then pushed open the door.

And there he was. Mick, sitting in an over-stuffed chair beside a reading lamp. He jumped when he saw her: caught. He had a book in his lap.

She walked in. They stared at each other. More dense silence, full of matter neither wanted to discuss.

Finally, he shrugged, smiled, and offered an explanation. "I like reading. I thought I should

238

read as much as I could, since I doubt I'll get another chance at so many books." He held out one hand, a gesture of bewilderment. "Twelve days," he said.

That many days till the ball. Yes, where had the time gone? The days, the hours lately seemed to go by in blinks.

He added, "I'll catch up on my sleep after I'm gone."

He'd said it: what Winnie had been avoiding thinking about. In twelve days they would no longer have any excuse to spend day in and day out in each other's company, no matter how strangely they were getting along.

She asked, "Do you have any trouble with your reading?"

"Yes. All the time." He laughed. He was still dressed from the day, though his cravat was loosened and his vest was open. The halo of the reading lamp put a slight golden glow to his white shirt. "I'm getting better though. It's mostly vocabulary."

"How do you manage?" It seemed impossible he could be teaching himself the words he'd been saying.

From the table beside him, from under the bright lamp, he lifted a collection of papers, half a dozen sheets, offering them.

On them were written words in a tight scrawl — *callipygian, Junoesque,* simpler words, too, *identity, banished,* more, pages of them — and marks. Beside each word, he wrote down the title

of the book where he found it, sometimes abbreviating it, a page number, then how many lines from the top or bottom with an arrow pointing up or down, indicating the exact location in the book where the word occurred.

"I look them up at the end of the night, then I go back to the pages and read the words again when they mean something to me. I go over them the next night. If I forget any, I look them up again." By way of apology, an excuse for such excessiveness, he shrugged again, helpless, and said, "I like words."

That, she knew. She smiled faintly. "Diabolical," she murmured.

"Felonious."

"Nefarious."

He blinked, smiling with wonder. He didn't know that one, but he liked it. He added, "Blackhearted."

She laughed. "All right. It's not that you don't know words, but you use them strangely."

"I like to play with them." From the beginning, he'd liked grand-sounding words that he could say majestically.

Or amusing words. Widge, she thought. "I know," she acknowledged. "But for the night of the ball you have to play with them less obviously. And you can't use certain ones."

His brow creased. A contemplation came over his face, a meditative look that would have suited a Cambridge don. His features, when still and serious, simply gave the impression of insight,

judgment, sharp mental activity. It wasn't true necessarily, she told herself. His mind could be as blank as a stone at the moment, but the structure of his face — the way the ridge of his brow tended to knit, the clarity and focus of his eyes, the high forehead — lent itself to the notion that he was intelligent, possibly profound.

She stared at his handsome face. The word *astute* leaped to mind, and it was from more than just the look of him. Canny, street-smart, cunning. She held his eyes and knew he was a sharp customer.

And that he was sizing her up.

She broke her gaze away, turning her head. "We'll give you some expressions." She cleared her throat. "Things to say, to remember for that night." She looked down at the sheets of paper he'd handed her, paging through them for something to do. "Actually, as we continue to fix your grammar and pronunciation, the way you like to use words may not stand out so baldly."

When she glanced up, he was still watching her, a disturbingly secure look on his face, a look that wanted to bore into her. He didn't think he used words badly. Differently, he might have said. Cleverly. And he wouldn't have been wrong.

It was she who judged too harshly, who jumped to wrong conclusions about him. She hadn't taken his measure correctly, not from the first moment. With condescension, she'd occasionally told herself that Mick was smart, clever.

No. Mick was brilliant. She'd never had a student learn so much as fast as he did. His abilities were outright eerie at times. He was smarter than she was.

She handed back his papers, then snugged her dressing gown up tight around her throat, crossing her arms over herself.

As he stared at her — his keen eyes a green found in the sea, the color of grass-bottomed inlets — she actually felt her face warm. For no better reason than his looking at her. She could feel her skin heating. She turned away from him, putting her palm to her face. A casual way to hide from him. Her hand felt cool on her cheek. Blushing. She couldn't believe she was blushing. Again. For nothing. He'd done nothing to warrant it.

He just sat there in the light of the reading lamp, Mick lit up, the rest of the world dark, watching, silent, though out the side of her vision she saw him tilt his head. The way his dog Magic did when a human being baffled him by one behavior or another.

Well, good. She baffled herself. She might as well baffle him, too.

Chapter 16

After almost five weeks of instruction, Mr. Tremore had all but mastered the structure of proper English and was well on his way to re-shaping his diction to an impressive degree. One lesson, though, Winnie delayed as long as possible. She might have avoided it completely, but since he was going to a ball, he had to learn to dance something beyond a jig around the kitchen.

She always taught her girls in the upstairs music room, a little room originally for the purpose of small gatherings of instruments and dinner guests that had occasionally, when her mother was alive and in the house, turned into extemporaneous dancing. Now it was a bare room, except for a big, black grand piano with a lot of broken strings and hardened pads. The bulky piano stood scooted back in a corner, un-used and slowly falling apart. Other than this, the hardwood floor was wide-open and spacious, if a little dusty. All in all, though hardly the size of a ballroom, there was still plenty of area across which to move.

Dancing lessons were not usually a chore to

Winnie. She loved to dance, and teaching foreign ladies or the gauche daughters of lawyers how to do it was her best opportunity to indulge herself in the entertainment. It was normally a favorite lesson. She brought in her gramophone, setting it on the closed piano lid, then cranked it up and ran full-volume the recordings she'd made of a trio playing Strauss.

With Mr. Tremore, she started the music, then went to position him. "Here now. You stand not exactly in front," she said, "but a little bit off, so our legs can go —" In between. She couldn't say it.

Then she didn't need to; he already knew. He took her hand into his and put himself automatically at the proper angle. She grasped the upper portion of his arm, the one he put round her waist. He knew to do that, too. She stood there for a moment in the marvel of it. The embrace of a dance — her own arm resting up his to the edge of his stone-hard shoulder, his palm flat to the small of her back.

She had to reverse her usual instructions. She told him, "You step forward, taking me with you to the count of three. . . ."

She had to step backward, the opposite direction she usually went, onto the opposite foot. He tightened his grip, moved her, and suddenly everything seemed upside down. *She* slipped, missed the step. She thought something rolled underfoot. Like a stone loose on the floor, though she couldn't imagine where that would

come from. So perhaps it was simply that she was her usual off-kilter self with him.

Before she could put anything right, something more went wrong. On the piano beside them, the gramophone found a scratch, and the needle stuck. "Oh, bosh," she said.

She took herself out of his arms to hunt through her stack of cylinders for a better recording. Oddly, a sound intruded into the silence of the room, and she looked up.

As Mr. Tremore waited, he made a faint jingle. A light, metallic *clink*. She stared at him a moment. He stood with one hand in the pocket of his trousers, the other tapping his leg.

Tap-clink-tap. How annoying.

He dressed the part of gentleman; no more ratting clothes, now that her carriage house was "better" than before. Today, green tweedy trousers, neat, worsted wool, lightweight in anticipation of summer, creased with a turnup. His vest, a light, muted brownish gray, fit snugly, it, too, cut for a warmer season. Low, it showed two studs, his cravat, which he had finally learned to tie, parted, folded, and tucked to expose the starched front of his shirt.

No, he appeared perfectly the gentleman. He had pulled together every last thread and seam of the look of an upper-class Englishman. He understood the style of one. But — *clink, clink, clink* — she frowned down the length of him again. What made that irritating sound?

Though in concept, Mr. Tremore was coming

along nicely, in the flesh, she found more and more he galled her these days. His perfections disturbed her. His silence exasperated. She especially took exception to the way he faced her now and then with regard to some of her improvements that he didn't seem to value as improvements: with an insolent self-assurance, as if he knew something she didn't. Worse, she resented her own horrible fascination with him at moments — the fact that, without his saying a word or lifting a finger, he could taunt and attract and make the hair on her arms lift.

Today the tension in him was palpable. It needed to tap.

Her temper was short. "Stop it," she said.

He looked right at her and continued, *jing jing jing.* In fact, if she weren't mistaken, he did it a little harder.

It didn't matter, she told herself. She went back to her cylinders, lifting one then another to read the scrawl on her own recordings — all the while thinking that the jingle was something in his pocket. What was in there? What did men usually keep in their pockets?

She remembered all the "usual" things Mr. Tremore possessed. Long, slinky animals that became fierce and dived into dark places. Coshes and bells. Bells? Would he keep bells in his pockets? She wanted suddenly to go through his trousers — go over to him and turn his pockets inside out, to be sure he didn't have anything, she told herself, that would give them both away

246

later. And she'd like to reach into his vest where a chain indicated she'd find, held by a vest pocket firmly against his abdomen, the chiming watch he so liked —

That was the sound. His watch chain clinking against the stone button of his vest as he moved his arm a fraction, whapping his hand on the side of his thigh. The sound and movement momentarily arrested her, captivated by his tapping his leg in idle impatience.

She shook her head free of it, then found another Strauss she liked that was slow enough for a beginner. She put it on, went back to stand before her student, then was unsettled again when he took hold of her as if he knew what he were doing.

He didn't exactly. It took them four attempts till they were finally moving. Or moving of sorts. He knew how to lead, yet still he and she weren't graceful. He didn't know the rhythm. He was used to dancing differently. He kept wanting her to put her arm all the way onto his shoulder so her hand would be at the back of his neck — till she finally told him, as inoffensively as possible, that his way of dancing was indecent. It put the couple too close.

He snorted and glanced her over, as if she invented the criterion. But he kept at the lesson, waltzing her way. While, every time the music and the room grew quiet, as if to punctuate their dance's ceasing, she could hear the faint chime of him clink to a stop.

When she went over to crank the gramophone for perhaps the sixth or seventh time, he followed her, poking through the cylinders himself. She doubted he could read her handwriting or, if he could, that he would be familiar enough to make sense of the names of composers or musical compositions. But he pulled one out after a moment and said, "This."

She looked at what he handed her. No, he didn't know the piece; he only liked the name. The "Thunder and Lightning Polka." Typical.

"It's not a waltz." She went to set it back into the box.

He caught her wrist. "I know that. But I know how to dance it better than a waltz, and you, I'd bet, don't. It might get us over your trying to steer me."

She looked at him, raising one eyebrow. "I don't steer you —"

"You do. Like a pushcart."

"I don't steer you like a pushcart!" Did she? She was both offended and taken aback.

"It's a damn wrestling match we're doing here, Winnie. Your wanting to lead is why we're having so much trouble."

"No, it's not. It's your inexperience —"

"My experience with a woman who's afraid to let me control her, who wants to mop the floor with me." Then with barely a breath between, he said, "All right, a waltz, but take off your shoes."

"Pardon?" She drew back. "I won't."

"Take off your shoes. You'll slide better. I can

248

move you easier. It'll help."

It also made her shorter. Her head came to just under his nose when she stepped forward in her stockinged feet to take his hand again. He pushed his advantage of her having less traction, her barely being able to keep her balance at places as he turned her on the smooth floor. It made her more fidgety still that she'd let him talk her into taking off her shoes. It didn't seem smart all at once.

Though he was right, it was good for their dancing.

No, it was wonderful for it. It put her somehow in a different state of mind. Eventually she followed, letting him find the movement he needed. Then, once he had the basic feel of the waltz, it was a fight to keep him from doing it double-time, spinning her — partly from delight (he was pleased to learn that some waltzes had a fast, spinning finish), though partly, she suspected, from his liking that he could make her body move with his, make her physically follow his will.

He was better at the spins than the slower movements. There, he needed practice. Practice with the slight bend in the knees, the left and right swooping turns of an English waltz. It was practice that seduced them both. He liked to dance. She loved to. He became increasingly good at waltzing, taking her round and round the room, moving her with a growing confidence she could feel in him, a masculine confidence that

danced her backward into a state of breathless appreciation of it. She waltzed in the large, dark shadow of her own awareness of him, a shadow so large she quaked to think of the dread attraction that cast it.

Dancing put him at his zenith. He didn't speak very much. He moved well. He looked marvelous — an uncommonly good imitation of English peerage on the wing. How dare he, she thought, irrationally. How dare he turn her like this: on her ear with his astounding adaptions, so vastly outstripping anything anyone expected of him, so far exceeding merely looking the part. How could she expect to stay stable through such a waltzing, vertiginous reality wherein what she heard and saw breathing before her contradicted what she knew to be true.

A ratcatcher! she told herself. A ratcatcher from the worst streets in London, formerly from the poorest district in Cornwall, with nothing to travel on but a rural education and a cocky, crooked smile.

As she cranked the gramophone for the dozenth time at least, he asked beside her, "Do you want to stop?"

"No," she said too quickly.

"Neither do I. Your face is pink though." He gave her a wry look. Two people having fun in a strained kind of way. With his having a seeming admiration for a face pinked from exertion and a strange stimulation.

It made Winnie laugh, despite herself.

Which made Mick laugh too, against his better judgment.

The tension between them broke slightly, though only for the moment. They had been like this for days, so he didn't expect it to go.

Oh, they were getting along like cats and dogs. Him chasing, wanting to grab her by the neck, her spitting and hissing every chance she got. If they didn't sleep together soon, they were going to kill each other. Except he couldn't explain that to her. She wouldn't hear it, even if she understood somewhere inside the truth of it.

Still, to enjoy her smile, even for a moment, was lovely — with its contradiction of shyness and slightly crooked teeth, of faint freckles and eyeglasses and downcast humor. Despite all their pushing and shoving at each other, despite the less than conventionally pretty elements of her person, the total of Winnie Bollash pleased him like no other woman in the longest while. When her mouth drew up into a wide smile, it made her eyes come alive.

Then her spectacles caught the light from the window, reflecting. The lenses blinked at him, obscuring what was behind them. On impulse, he reached and unhooked her eyeglasses, lifting them off.

With her, of course, grabbing and protesting. He won by the length of his arm; he held them overhead. Then, setting them down on the piano, he took hold of her and danced her away from them.

"I can't see." Worse and worse, Winnie thought. Barefoot and blind.

"What's this called?" He let go of her hand — it was like being left out on a limb, twirled in a blur. He touched the lace yoke of her dress at her collarbone before his hand came back to hers to guide her.

"What?"

"The word. Give me the word for it." He stared at her collarbone. With her spectacles off, her whole world was muted, narrow. Her myopic eyes could bring nothing into focus but him.

"Um, ah — Lace."

He raised a rueful eyebrow, the way he did when she didn't give him enough credit.

Only that wasn't the problem. It was a matter of trying to think when he put his finger on her collarbone as he waltzed her backward and stared down at her, nothing but a fuzzy room turning behind him.

"No," he said. "The stuff underneath, here" — again he let go, leaving her hand in the air, to point — "that you can hardly see."

She looked down, then missed a step. He put his finger in a hole between lace rosettes.

For a few seconds, she couldn't have told him her own name. Then she let out a light breath. "*Ah-h-h.*" A sound that was mostly air. "Tulle," she said. "The lace is crocheted onto silk tulle."

"Silk tulle," he repeated. Perfectly. "Silk tulle the color of flesh." Every sound correct. Then he grinned faintly and added, "Blimey." She

blinked. She wanted to hit him. He was having her on, playing with his old accent. While she tried to keep her equilibrium on a dusty floor in her bare feet, blind, with only his arm for balance, and his teasing humor.

"And your dress —" He arched back, his eyes drawing an X on the front of her, tracing where her dress crossed between her breasts. "What's it called when a dress does that? I like it."

"It's, um, ah" — she looked down, trying to think what he meant — "a surplice bodice." She scowled up. "You don't need this much information about ladies' clothes."

He was going to say more, but the gramophone groaned into its slowdown, preparing to stop. "Excuse me," she said.

On the piano, she found her spectacles. She put them on, shaking, angry. It took her two tries to hook the left earpiece back into her hair and over her ear. She tried to calm herself by hunting through her cylinders. Not a word registered. She couldn't read a name on one of them. While behind her, he said, "We dance at the Bull and Tun." Conversationally, he added, "You know, you've never danced till you've danced with someone you like who's kissing your mouth as you go." He added, "Let me know if you want to try it."

She turned to look at him, ready to knock him down. With narrow eyes, she watched him tap the side of his leg again, standing there in the center of the room as if having a casual dialogue

on the various styles of dancing.

Dancing with your mouth on someone's. No, she did not want to try it, thank you. She put the same cylinder on again. They could dance to the same thing over and over.

He waited as she got the music going. Then he took her hand and put his palm at her back as if nothing unusual had been said.

Good enough. She'd ignore it, too. She'd ignore the choler she felt; yes, she didn't doubt her face was red. She told him, "Let's practice the pivots."

They were fast, so he was good at them.

He was fast, she thought. In every sense.

She didn't like the idea of him dancing with his mouth on some woman. Or some woman's mouth on him. It wasn't proper. It wasn't decent. And she certainly didn't want him to do that to her.

Though she wondered for a second what it would feel like. *Let him know?*

She remembered in the carriage house that he'd said she had to tell him if she wanted him to kiss her, that he wasn't going to unless she did. Tell him? She couldn't. Even if she'd wanted him to, which she didn't, she could never have been so bold. For a lady to say something so forward was beyond the pale of decorum.

Besides, wasn't he the one who'd threatened in a hallway to take her "where flirting led"? So why was he making such a to-do over a kiss? Dryly, she told him as they danced, "All this commo-

tion from a man who, at one point, wanted to lead me 'down the path.' "

"Ah" — he laughed, taking her through a smooth turn — "so that's what you're hoping for. Not just kisses."

"I didn't say that —"

"No. You said *I* wanted it. But that's the way your mind works, isn't it, *Miss* Bollash?"

She hated when he said her name like that. She said, "Don't be vulgar —"

"Why? That's what you like so much about me. If I were a real gentleman, you couldn't blame me as easily. Hooligan Mick. Low-class Mick. Who has the poor taste to make you feel what you don't want to think about."

"Damn you!" She stomped her foot, which ended their dance. They came to halt. *Damn.* She never cursed. She was horrified to hear it come out of her mouth.

They stood there at the far edge of the floor, the tinny music across it continuing on without them.

He laughed, surprised by her cursing and thoroughly pleased with himself. "Nice," he said, with chuckling, wicked approval. "Congratulations, Win—"

She slapped him. Without thinking. Not once, but twice. She whacked the air with all her might and caught his cheek, a sharp smack. It was no accident. She meant to get it. Then, just because the contact felt so *damn* satisfying, she did it again. She would have hit him a third time, but

he stopped her. He grabbed her arm.

He stood above her, for a second as angry as she was, both of them engrossed in one another in this unholy way.

He slowly lowered her arm, then let go, though the air was charged. They neither would let the other break his or her eyes away. Until Winnie happened to see out the corner of hers a red splotch on his cheek. The place where she'd struck him began to glow, more intense by the moment. She watched her own angry handprint, the spread of fingers, the impression of palm, appear vividly on the side of his face.

"Oh," she said as she watched it get redder and redder. "Oh," with dismay. What had she done? She had never hit anyone in her life. Why Mick? Why him? "Oh, Lord, does it hurt?"

She frowned and winced and put her hand to his cheek. The handprint was hot. She caressed it, running her fingertips over the frightful mark she'd made on him. She put her other hand up and caressed his face, both palms.

He jerked as she embraced his jaw, but then let her touch him freely. Once her hands were there, they wouldn't stop.

His cheeks were smooth with the faint grit of a shave that was half a day old. His jawbone was hard, angular; his eyes, the regard in their greenish depth, as fervid as the imprint she'd put on his skin. Her fingers fluttered over this face, her palms smoothing and cupping the topography of it, the planes and hollows. Regretfully,

she retraced the livid red blotch up a cheek that had high, perfect bones. She drew the pads of her fingers down the cartilage of a narrow, straight nose, then along a mouth that —

He captured one hand and pressed it to his mouth, breathing into her palm, his hand clasping the back of hers. Then, licking a warmth into the center of her palm, he kissed the inside of her hand. As he had her mouth so many days before.

Winnie was speechless. She wouldn't have thought it were possible — he kissed her hand with a wet, open-mouthed kiss, with the push of his tongue, as he groaned and closed his eyes.

Goose bumps . . . chills . . . the hair at the back of her neck, up her arms lifted. Her belly rolled. The room did a slow rotation around them, while Winnie stood still.

Paralyzed. She wanted to take her hand away, but it wouldn't respond to her own volition, as if it didn't belong to her. When he raised his head, she made a fist, and he kissed her knuckles. She closed her eyes. Lord help her.

She used her other hand to reach and take her arm away from him. "I'm —" She could barely speak. "I'm not — not going" — her murmur broke again before she could finish — "down your path."

"Too late," he whispered. "You're already on it." He added in a tone that sounded more resigned than happy about it, "Too late for both of us."

The voice of the gramophone grew slow and

low again, then rasped to a stop with her standing there, staring up at him.

Then, clutching her tingling hand to her chest, she walked across the floor in her bare, stockinged feet. At the piano, she cranked the gramophone, round and round and round briskly. She wound it too tightly. The music started again at a high pitch, a crazy tempo.

She walked back to Mick, into position, then had to stand there in front of him, both of them waiting for the machine's music to gain some semblance of sanity.

The odd thing was, once it did, she couldn't. She was reluctant to put her arm on him, to reach up and touch him at all. The music played. Nothing happened. Until he slipped his hand under her arm, as if to begin dancing.

But his hand instead ran lightly down her back, the hollow of her spine, and he said, "Let's have your skirts up again, Win."

She couldn't have heard right. She let out a quick, nervous laugh when he actually took hold of a handful.

When she stopped him, he shook his head in reprimand. He said, "Be good, Win. Do what I say."

She let go, a reflex.

Good. She'd been good all her life. A good girl who felt muscles tense in the pit of her stomach when he invited her to be good his way.

He whispered, "So what did they tell you when you were bad, Winnie?"

"What?" She looked up at him, blinking. Her heart began to thud at the base of her throat.

As if he knew, with the edge of his thumb he touched her there, then traced her neck up the tendon to behind her ear.

She shivered and murmured, "Give me your hand. Put your hand at my back where it belongs. We're supposed to be dancing."

"Tell me about 'supposed to be,'" he whispered. "When you didn't do what you were supposed to, what did they tell you?" His face came closer. "What happened when you did what *you* wanted? What do I need to say to let you do what you'd like?" He changed tack. He said, "What I'd like is to kiss you. I would. But I'd like you to want it. Do you?"

"N-n—" She got that far, then stopped. She didn't know. She was reeling again, caught in the strange energy of him. She wet her lips. No, she didn't want it.

The music played behind them, its own little world, getting away from them. While he waited. Then touched her collarbone again, tracing it with his fingertip. She let him. The touch of his finger, so light, up then down her neck, was unearthly. Sublime.

She bit her lip, closed her eyes.

Then heard him say, "Fine," very softly, as he'd said once before. "When you can say what you want, you can have it."

Just like that, he stopped.

She opened her eyes to see him walk across the

room himself to the gramophone. It was groaning again. He cranked it, then two seconds later was pushing her backward into pivots around the floor, the jangle of a recorded violin moving them.

Let him know? she thought.

Kissing him, she remembered, "really kissing him," as he called it, had been . . . exciting. Such a surprisingly powerful and tender connection to him. Unforgettable. As she spun backward round the room — as he let go of the counting, gathering himself into the rhythm alone without it, incorporating it into himself — she remembered how vital it felt when his mouth opened hers and he breathed into it.

She was supposed to ask for this?

She couldn't. She murmured, "You want too much."

He danced and answered with his usual candor. "You criticize me and cry, Win. You curse me and slap me and move me downstairs." He shook his head at her. "Is it too much to want that you take a look at what you're doing?"

She was saved from having to think about what he meant. Just then, as they moved across the dusty floor, the ball of her foot stepped squarely on a small and sharp object.

"Ah — Wait — I've tramped on something." She halted them, hopping on one foot as she grabbed the other one under her skirt.

The music kept going, though it wasn't as pronounced to Winnie as the sound of their breath-

ing, both slightly breathless from waltzing and talking, both.

She was clutching his arm, holding her foot, trying to figure out what she'd done, while he supported her balance. He was close. His arm remained around her back. Her hand gripped his wide shoulder.

Yes, she thought, she wanted him to kiss her. Yes.

But she didn't want to say. How unfair. She frowned, then scowled. How miserably unfair. She stood there sluicing her eyes sideways at him, flat-footed in one stockinged foot. She opened her mouth, closed it, skewed it to the side, then looked up, scrutinizing him.

Chapter 17

Holding Winnie, with her standing on one foot by the piano at the side of the music-room floor, Mick watched her screwed-up face — her brow furrowed downward, her mouth twisted up. She was trying to say something —

By God, she was going to say it! he thought. He just knew she was. She clutched his back. He let her hang onto him. God bless, they were all over each other today.

He could almost see her mind review the problem — how to get kissed without admitting she wanted it — from a thousand angles, trying to process each one.

She opened her mouth.

He leaned forward so as to hear every syllable or to grab a shred of one, at least, if she couldn't get it all out.

Then Winnie said, "My foot hurts," and folded. Her long frame simply collapsed downward into her dress like a deflating balloon onto the floor.

Mick stood above her, stymied, not sure if this were a good sign or not. After a moment, he sat down beside her, tried to reach under her dress

for her foot, then got his hand slapped for it.

Glumly, he protested, "I was going to look at your foot, see if I could find anything. Is it a splinter?"

"No, I tramped on something larger than that."

"This?" he asked, rotating to lean out onto one arm and pluck a small black screw off the floor. He showed her.

She nodded. "It has to be from the piano. I slipped on it earlier, I think. I should have stopped. Look, it cut through my stocking." It made a pinprick of blood at the round swell of the ball, as if she'd tramped full force, all her weight.

He dropped the screw into her hand, then took her foot. Like everything else, they fought over it, but he won by massaging his thumb up her arch.

"Oh," she said. Then "Oh," again. "Oh, crumbs. What you're doing feels wonderful."

She leaned back as, reluctantly, there on the floor, she let him take her foot into his lap. She stared at the screw in her hand. "I think it's from the music stand. It fell off last week."

He rubbed her foot down the bottom strongly to the heel, then rotated her ankle.

"Oh," she said again. "That feels impossibly good."

He said, "So, when you were bad, what did they tell you? What did they do?"

Her eyes blinked up from where they were policing his possession of her foot, taken by sur-

prise to find the game on again. "Who?"

"Your parents."

"My parents didn't say anything."

"Truly? Not a word?" He was puzzled. "Someone then. Someone else."

She frowned and looked away.

"A governess," he suggested.

She whipped her eyes around to him, as if he'd read her mind.

"So what did she say? What did she do?"

"I had a lot of governesses." She frowned then said quickly, "Miss Nibitsky."

"Ah, Miss Nibitsky," he repeated, sliding his hand up her leg a little, kneading the back of her lower calf. "So what did Miss Nibitsky say when you were horrid?"

"She'd say, 'You little brat, if you don't do what I say, I'll break all your toys.'" Then she laughed shyly and looked down. "I've never told anyone that. How peculiar to say it to a grown man."

"No, no." He shook his head, surprised, interested. "Would she break them?"

She answered with a shrug. "I just stopped playing with anything I liked in her presence. One year, she canceled my birthday. She said I simply couldn't turn six. I'd have to wait till the following year."

"What a wretched woman." He didn't like any of this. He withdrew a little. He rubbed the bottoms of her toes and asked, "Didn't you tell someone?"

"Who? If I said anything to my father, he waved me away vaguely. If I told my mother, she got angry; she didn't believe me."

Mick frowned and tried to get hold of his original notion. "Then what?" he asked. "What if you still wouldn't listen?" There must have been gentler reproofs, he told himself. He wanted to use them, to see if he could counter all that held Winnie back with reasons to go forward expressed as rigidly. He rubbed up her ankle, playing at the hem of her dress. "What if you were just a little bit bad?"

She said nothing. He stopped, tilted his head. He had to look for her face. When he found it, the look on it — it was bloody terrible. "There was no 'little bit bad'?" he asked. Then he guessed more than he liked: "She hurt you," he said, "really hurt you."

Winnie defended her upbringing quickly, yet it shocked him. She said, "She only used a cane once. She said that, if I were a boy, I'd be in boarding school by now, where in a blink, when children were as bad as I was, they sent them to the headmaster who made them stand on a pulpit and —" Her voice broke. She stopped.

Mick let go of her foot and smoothed her dress down. He leaned back onto his arm, putting his hand up to his mouth, a finger across his bare lip.

"What's wrong?" she asked, as if she'd offended him.

In a way, she had. It was his turn to feel sick. He, who could cosh a rat bloody senseless, was

265

revolted by Winnie's childhood. It was a good thing her story took place a long time ago, because, if he ever saw this Nibitsky woman, he would want to do her violence.

"Did your parents know?" he asked.

"I think so."

All Mick knew about boarding schools was that they turned out snobs. He hadn't known about their discipline habits, and certainly had had no idea about evil governesses, though he understood what caning was from stories of orphanages and poorhouses.

"It wasn't really so —" She tried to shrug it off.

He was too distressed on her behalf to let her. He said, "No, Win. English gentlemen and gentlewomen don't deserve the word *gentle,* to put such fear into their own children. Or to pay someone else to do it. The upper class is" — he looked for something to say that was sufficiently disgusting, then found it in his growing stockpile of words — "barbaric."

"I was a frightened child before she ever —"

"I'm sure. All the worse."

She looked at him as it seemed to dawn on her. "It *is* horrid, isn't it, what she did?" She frowned at him. "Have I made you loathe me then?"

"No!" He laughed, then slid her around and pulled her up against him. "Sh-h-h," he said. "Oh, Winnie."

He felt homesick all at once, a sweet, sharp longing for rocky moors and jagged coastline, where a boy was never more than twenty miles

from the sea no matter where he stood. And always on solid ground with his family.

"Let me tell you about Cornwall," he said. He scooted her till she sat in the cove of his legs, nestled her into his arms, and kissed the top of her head.

He did: He told her of playing in Celtic ruins, ducking through half-tumbled-down archways, unmindful of the hands that built them. His castles. He told her of running along the sea with several of his brothers, then sisters, too, as more children came along, until he was running in a pack of fourteen wild siblings, some of them barely nine months apart.

"That's a lot of children," Winnie said.

"Mum was Catholic. She didn't believe in preventing a child the Lord wanted her to have. She even took in one He didn't put on her. My brother Brad isn't even hers. His mother died, then his father beat him, so he came and lived with us, the wild Tremore brood. He fit right in."

"If your mother couldn't manage you all, did your father do it?" Winnie wanted to know.

"God, no. My father left after the fourth or fifth one, I think."

She puzzled over the information. "Then how did the sixth one and the rest come about?"

He got a good chuckle out of that. "God did it," he said. "That's what my mother would say. The rest were all immaculate conception. She was a crazy one, my mum. Or else she thought we were." He laughed again, fondly. "She did her

best. She tried to put the fear of God in all of us, and always succeeded for a while with the littlest ones. But they'd come to me, crying, scared, you know, and I'd explain. 'No, God won't punish you. He loves you. And your mum does, too, only she's angry with you and can't give you the good swipe you deserve.'

"Being the oldest, I thought it my duty to put them on to her, wise them up, you know? No use scaring little children with a lot of talk about damnation. Then I'd say, 'But see, I can take a swipe at you, so do as you're told. Your mum's too kindhearted to hit you. That's why she invents all these things.' " He laughed. "It worked. We all helped her."

"You especially," Winnie said.

He ran his mouth down an inch of her crown, feeling her hair against his lips. "Yes, me especially. I pretty much ruled the roost as the oldest. It was my job to use that the right way, to help the rest with it."

She thought for a minute, then said, relaxed now, her body fitting sweetly against his chest, between his legs, "That explains why you act as if you're king sometimes then." She was teasing him.

"I am king," he said. "King of the life of Mick Tremore. And you, my pretty thing, are queen. Queen of yourself."

"Why did you leave if you liked Cornwall so much?"

"To feed us. After my mother died, we about

starved to death." He laughed. "I'll be honest, Win. I think some of my brothers and sisters were the result of my mother's enterprise." It was funny to him, sad, too; his mother struggling to feed her brood, but doing it in a way that only made her more children. "Anyway, with just myself and three brothers working in the mines, trying to feed fourteen, it wasn't enough. So I put my younger brothers and sisters with aunts and uncles then came to the city. I brought Freddie, a great ferret. You met her."

"Yes, you said she's your best."

"Was. I lied a little. She's old now." He paused, thinking. "Because of her, though, I sent home money my very first week, enough to buy food and a bit of clothes, something the younger ones sorely needed. We wouldn't have made it another winter. Freddie saved us. That's why I have to take good care of her, right to the end."

"Fourteen," Win repeated. "That's a big family."

"It is, but I managed and the older ones help now. Five brothers, eight sisters. My youngest sister is eleven. I support the ones who can't support themselves yet, with a bit left over for me after I give extra to the three aunts and an uncle who care for them. It works out. Don't know what I'd do without family."

"Or them without you," she pointed out.

He laughed. "I guess." Then he corrected himself. "I imagine." He refined it. "I rather imagine." He made a snort, a vocalized breath

that heard — but wasn't certain it liked — how upperclass he sounded. "Anyway," he continued, "it wouldn't even have occurred to me to keep the money all to myself." He made indirect reference to her cousin. "I mean, how could I enjoy it, knowing I had so much when they had so little?"

If she understood his expressed loyalty, she didn't acknowledge it.

They sat on the floor there in the dancing room, saying nothing for several minutes, just sitting together. He liked it. He brushed his lips across the top of her hair again. It was silky. Like the rest of her. It smelled lemony.

When he started wanting to eat it, to lick her neck, to pull her backward and down, roll on top of her . . . bloody hell, at that point, he slid away and stood up. "He doesn't *sound* pleasant, this cousin of yours." He was contradicting what she'd told him earlier, that he would like Xavier.

On the floor, she spun around on her skirts, pulling her knees against her chest. She arched her long, pretty neck to look up at him directly and said, "He tells good jokes," then laughed, shaking her head.

She bent it again, down till all he could see was the interesting way she held her hair up. With two sticks. It fascinated him. He couldn't understand how her hair didn't fall down. It looked heavy enough. It was abundant, shining; a light, coppery red. Lots and lots of colorful hair. Pretty.

She continued, "Someone said recently that he's changed. Not so funny, more solemn. But he wasn't when I last knew him. The day he inherited every last bit of family land, he was jubilant, the most miserably happy eighty-some-year-old man I've ever seen. Shortly after, by the way, he married a woman who was about my age now, a woman whom he'd adored for a dozen years. Can you imagine? That would make Vivian, let's see, about forty now. And I wish I could say she was a conniving, spoiled shrew who was only after his money, but the woman I met a dozen years ago was quite sweet. Shy. Obedient. People tell me she still is. The daughter of a rich Italian family, oh, with some title or other. Something high-and-mighty, since Xavier wouldn't have anything less. Very beautiful. She's with him still. She'll be there beside him the day he dies."

Mick sympathized. "That must annoy the hell out of you."

She laughed again, squeezing her knees. "Sometimes it does. It's as if one person, always one person, is dealt all the aces."

"It only looks like aces from here, Win. You don't know. You can't see — you can't play his hand, only yours."

She nodded. She was lost a moment, then looked at him. "Mick," she said. It was the first time she had ever used his given name, and it made his chest expand to hear it. It made him warm. "You are the most generous man I have ever met."

He liked that even better. He smiled widely. Then told her, "I'm not generous. It's just —" He shrugged. "Why blame people when they can't help their nature?"

She contemplated that a moment. Then she suddenly reached her arms out and lay straight back, all the way onto the floor.

"The ceiling is peeling," she said, then let out a long, delighted bubble of laughter, the sound of genuine humor.

Looking down at her, Mick thought: He'd stood too quickly. If he were down there now, he'd have stretched out beside her.

Before he could think of a way down to her, though, she reached up, holding her hands toward him, asking to be pulled to her feet.

He drew her up — and she made a little shriek. "Oh," she said, "my stomach lifts when you move me sometimes." Quickly, "So can you waltz, do you think?"

"No," he said gravely. "Or not like someone who's been doing it all his life. I need more practice." Dishonest again. Though not quite in the same formal manner as her way, he waltzed all the time at the Bull and Tun. He'd pretended not to know, just to spend the afternoon dancing with her.

And he wanted to "move" her some more. He held out his hand.

She put hers into it, and he took her into his arms in the proper manner, in the way she allowed. He began counting. "One, two, three.

272

One, two, three." No music. Or just the music of the two them together, his whispering in her ear as he spun her around.

She felt so loose in his arms, warm and smiling. Oh, he liked her like this: waltzing in the byways of one of life's finer moments, in one of its little contentments.

They danced through supper, till their feet hurt. Sometimes they used her gramophone, but often, when it *grog*ged slowly to silence, he took over. He made up waltzes, humming to her, loving the feel of her in his arms, her laughing and dancing with him.

At the end, he made a ballocks of it, of course. Somehow their mouths got close. When he drew closer, her eyes widened. They filled with wonder — she was perpetually amazed by his interest. And confused by it: Her eyes filled with that funny fear of hers, too. She braced herself, ready for him to push her into it, but not ready to invite him in. Her posture shot a jab of frustration through him, with enough pinch to it to make him wince. Damn her anyway.

"Winnie," he said. "I want to kiss you. I want to do a lot of things, and I've been about as forthright as a man gets about it. But it can't be all me every time. Me pushing, me seducing, me making you do what we both know you want to do anyway. I can't keep chasing you and chasing you, even if you like it, without your giving back, letting me know you want *me*. Own up to it."

Her expression wouldn't. Her mouth grew

into that tight pucker she could make. She didn't offer a word.

"Do you or not?"

"Do I what?"

He'd start at the most basic. "Want me to kiss you," he said.

She frowned down. She wanted him to.

"Say it," he said. "Say, 'Kiss me.' "

She opened her mouth, then closed it, shaking her head as if he'd asked her to fly up to the ceiling.

He continued, torturing them both. "Say, 'Touch me, Mick.' Oh, God, Win, I'd like to hear you say it. Say, 'Hold me, undress me, touch me, come inside me —' "

He had to look away. His mouth went dry saying the words. To the piano, he muttered a string of epithets under his breath, cursing himself, but her, too.

It rallied her sizeable frustration and rage. Starchy again, she said, "Most gentlemen don't swear as you do in front of a lady."

"Most gentlemen don't go through what I go through with you."

"You go through nothing —"

"I go through your tying my privates in knots, with you wanting to lather them up, me dodging, so as to keep you from shaving them off in a pique, trying to make me tame enough to get near." What a speech. He was half-sorry he said it.

Then sorrier it hadn't been worse, when she

said with sarcastic wonder, "Oh! Oh, yes!" With emphasis, "That was splendid! You are quite getting the hang of being a gentleman. Why don't you just stick your hand between my legs?"

That did it. He leaned toward her. "Well, you'd never have gotten any part of man stuck there otherwise. You're terrified of sexual relations. Hell, you're foking terrified of life. Whatever brought you to this place, *Miss* Bollash," he said, "it killed off every speck of spontaneity and adventure in you, if you ever had any to begin with."

She blinked, and the fight in her rose up. She came back with, "Spontaneity and adventure? What big words, Mr. Tremore, for *randy*. For being a rat who wants to climb up into the flounce and froufrou of every silk petticoat."

He saw red. He wanted blood. "Not yours," he said. "I'd rather be gnawed to death, thank you, than have to deal with what's under your petticoat. Every bloody moment'd be anxious. I'd be ready to shoot myself, trying to tow a line you'd snap in my face every ten seconds."

He'd gotten her, a direct hit. He wasn't proud of it the second it happened. Her face fell. He'd confirmed to sweet Winnie, who thought no man wanted her, that he didn't either.

He took a breath, then said quickly, "That's a lie. Winnie Bollash, I want you so badly, you're making me say things I don't mean." Then that was wrong, too. "No, you aren't making me do anything. I'm wagging my own tongue. Winnie,

275

I'm sensitive about the fancy ladies I've slept with. Oh, they all wanted me. For the day. I'm a good time, but nothing more. I'm tired of it." He took a breath, looked around, then stepped back and shoved his hands in his pockets. "You're right, I'm wrong. I wouldn't enjoy being a good time to you either in pretty short order. It would make me feel terrible." He shook his head, then looked at her.

She was wide-eyed.

"I'm going back downstairs now," he said. "Bloody hell," he muttered, exasperated. "If you need me, pull the bell cord. It'll ring below stairs, and I'll hear it. Me and your butler. Other than that, I'm staying away from you. That should suit everyone. Even me," he added.

Chapter 18

Edwina, Mick, Jeremy, and Emile Lamont awaited tea in her father's upstairs study. On the rare occasions when gentlemen called, she always felt it more gracious to speak to them in the room where her father had conferred with his colleagues. A room of large, heavy chairs and dark wood, of bookcases full of philology and linguistics as well as a bit of poetry and fiction that, she presumed, appealed to men. *Moby-Dick. The Strange Case of Dr. Jekyll and Mr. Hyde.* Richard Burton's *Arabian Nights.* The most delicate accouterment of the room was a cut-crystal brandy decanter that sat in a polished niche with two matching snifters set upside down.

Jeremy and Emile Lamont had arrived at a propitious time. She and Mick had been arguing over a bill that had come in the morning's post. It was from the tailor, for every piece of clothing Mick owned at present, and the bill was addressed to Miss Edwina Bollash.

Mick, of course, had rolled his eyes. "I think we should take as much back as the tailor will allow. Those two fellows —" He referred to the Lamonts, and, though he left the thought unfin-

ished, there was no doubt about his feelings for them. "We could end up having to pay for all this. They're up to something, Win."

She only shook her head. "You can't take anything back," she told him. "It's all custom-made. Besides, the bill is a mistake, a simple mistake."

And, of course, it was. These things happened.

Though Winnie realized how much Mick's suspicions were coloring her own thinking by the magnitude of her relief when Jeremy Lamont said, "Dear, dear!" He turned the envelope over, frowning down at her address on it. "They confused the address to which they shipped the parcels with the address where they were to send the bill." He looked at her with what seemed genuine regret. "I am so sorry. What an embarrassing confusion. Here."

He reached into his ever-deep pocket and took out the ever-full notecase. It was, as before, packed with bills.

He counted out several, then looked up at Winnie. "And how much do we owe *you*, Miss Bollash, to date?"

She glanced at Mick. Emile sat off to the side, Mick stood by the window, his hostility so dense in the air, it all but left a haze.

He had greeted them at the door a few minutes before like an ogre guarding its lair, then had been actually offended by their astoundment.

They kept looking at him now, then passing

looks between each other. There was no doubt that Jeremy in particular was thrilled by Mick's sound and appearance.

Winnie's own accounts were prepared. It was a matter of retrieving them from her sitting room, which she did. She hurried. Leaving the three of them alone in the study together felt chancy somehow.

When she returned, all three men were exactly as she'd left them, as if in her absence they had not moved or spoken, but only glared at each other. Oh, dear, oh, dear. She presented the list of her fees and expenses. She'd computed them carefully, hour by hour, and was prepared to go over them. She'd been generous, if anything.

Jeremy glanced at them, then, without question, counted out more crisp notes of British pounds sterling. He set a stack of them on the mantel, saying, "I've put in twenty pounds extra to cover anything that might come up till we're back. Emile and I are going to the coast for a few days, but we'll return the day before the ball. We'll bring the invitation then."

He looked at Mick over his shoulder, then, putting a monocle to his eye, he studied the man in the center of the room, up then down, walking around him. To which Mick responded by folding his arms over his chest and looking faintly truculent.

"I must say," Jeremy told her, "*Emile's* money is extremely well spent." He chuckled and glanced at his brother, a goad referring to the

279

fact that the loser was to reimburse the winner of their bet.

Emile remained in the far chair, though he studied Mick with no less interest, only less kindness. He said, "He hasn't done it yet, you know. Though I admit," he said grudgingly, "Miss Bollash has wrought a miracle. If I didn't know those clothes and that face, I'd say it was a different man."

It. "He," she corrected. "He's in the clothes you picked for him. They're excellent —"

"No, no," Jeremy insisted, "he greeted me at the door. His manner is completely different, and what I've heard him say sounds marvelous. You're brilliant, Miss Bollash."

Her pride puffed a little. Yes, she was doing first-rate work, it was true.

Mick snorted. "Right," he said. "You all have done a bloody fine job."

Ah. Winnie said quickly, "No, *we* all." To the Misters Lamont, she declared, "Mr. Tremore is the most able student I have ever taught. He is at the heart of the change."

Any rapprochement among the men her words might have won, however, was immediately lost when Jeremy said, as if he spoke to a trained monkey, "Say something. Talk."

Mick made a sideways pull of his mouth, then held out his hand. "Lemmy see them notes there, Cap'n. Pass 'em over, eh?" He put Cornwall into his voice as thickly as he could.

Alarmed, Jeremy turned to Winnie. "He

sounded better when I first came in."

"He's annoyed with you." She scowled.

Mick said, "I can speak for myself. Let me see the notes, mate." He pointed to the money Jeremy had stacked over the fireplace.

Jeremy raised an eyebrow in affront.

Mick looked at him levelly, unmoved.

A kind of tension grew.

Happily, Milton dissipated some of it by walking in just then with the tea tray.

As tea and biscuits were served, Jeremy sat. He balanced his hands in front of him on the ferrule of his cane. To Mick, he said, "I'm leaving the money here. Feel free to examine it, Mr. Tremore. Oh —" He threw a concerned glance at Winnie. "Which reminds me. We have to find a better name. I was thinking Michael Frederick Edgerton, the Viscount Tremore. It's not a real title, but has the advantage that if anyone calls him 'Tremore,' he'll respond. Meanwhile, if we are called upon to do so, we can claim the title for a remote viscountcy in Cornwall. Hardly anyone pays attention to that provincial tip of England." He turned to Mick and repeated, as if trying it out, "Michael?"

Mick snorted. "It won't be hard to answer to. It's my name. Michael Tremore."

"Well." He looked at his brother, as if to say, *More* surprise, *more* delight. Their evident pleasure seemed to grow by the second. "He does talk well, doesn't he? Isn't it amazing the change it makes?" To Mick, he said, "Perfect then. Mi-

chael it is." To Winnie, "You must call him 'Michael' from now on so as to be sure he's accustomed to it."

Michael, Winnie thought. Michael. Something inside squirmed, uncomfortable. He was Mick to her. It was hard to think of him differently.

"Say something," Emile said from his chair again. "Make him speak more. I want to hear it."

Mick turned toward him. For a moment, Winnie was frightened as to what he might say. God knew he could still be profane. She said quickly, "Read something, if you please." She pulled down a book and pushed Mick toward the desk.

He sat, disgruntled, but he opened the book. He began to read aloud a passage they'd read the night before. Everything, and then some, that a person might want to know about whales. He wasn't perfect with it — most of the sounds were right, but he struggled over a word here and there before he recognized it.

Still, he was amazingly convincing.

Listening to him, again Winnie felt that ghostly sensation. Another man, Emile had said. It was true. Mick's family in Cornwall, the friends he spoke of in London, the way he could mimic his old accent — his real life, she reminded herself — seemed sometimes just another one of his extravagant stories, another of his jokes. Here was the real man. Michael Whomever-They-Wanted-to-Call-Him, soon to

be the Viscount Whatever, world traveler, humanitarian, bon vivant, and wealthy member of English nobility.

And would-be suitor to Lady Edwina Henrietta Bollash, only child to the Marquess of Sissingley. Ah, now there was a lovely fantasy. Soon she'd be gathering pumpkins and mice, hoping for a fairy godmother to come along and turn them into a coach and eight.

Yes, someone, please turn my ratcatcher into a prince for me.

The someones who all but had stared at Mick — or rather, Michael — as he closed the book with a snap of its cover, a grip in one hand that would have allowed him to throw the volume across the room.

She quickly took it as Jeremy began, "That was" — he stood, as if for an ovation — "that was simply, well" — he could barely find words — "marvelous . . . unbelievable." Looking at his brother: "Can you credit it, Emile? Did you hear? Better and better — oh, I like it!"

Emile stood. Mick did, too. Nothing. There was nothing for anyone to disagree about, yet Winnie felt it expedient to get the Lamonts out the door as quickly as possible. She took Jeremy's arm. Emile followed. "You wait here," she told Mick, who wore consternation all over his face.

At the doorway, though, he stopped them by calling, "Will the invitation work to take her to the ball, too?"

She turned, sending him a sharp frown. "I don't need an invitation."

All three men paused to look at her. It was her tone.

She explained, "I'm invited every year. I send my regrets. Xavier only invites me for form's sake."

"Surprise him," Mick said. "Go." When she only scowled at the suggestion, he argued with her name alone, "Winnie —"

"*Winnie?*" Emile repeated, lifting an amused eyebrow.

"Shut up," Mick told him.

The room grew icy-quiet for a moment. Then Emile smirked and began, "Oh, no. This is too good to —" He stopped.

Mick glowered at him, a look of open, hateful animosity from a man a head taller and five stones heavier at least.

He presented enough threat that Emile raised his hands, a surrender. "Goodness," he said. He longed to say something more; his face twitched with it for a moment. Then he seemed to think better of it. "Well," he risked saying. "What an amazing afternoon."

Winnie hastily ushered the Lamonts out, thanking Jeremy profusely for the payments, seeing that he and his brother had their hats, canes, and gloves in their hands, then closed the door on them, as happy to see them go as she had been to see them arrive.

When she returned to her father's study, Mick

was still there: holding one of the banknotes up to the light.

He said, "It's good."

More relief — a sense of out-and-out deliverance. Which said a great deal about her own doubts.

He destroyed her peace of mind, though, by adding, "Extremely good. Better than what Rezzo and I ever came up with. It's on the right paper."

"Oh, stop it," she said, walking briskly over to him. She snatched the note away, then took the whole pile from the mantel into her possession.

He looked at her, offended. "Look at it, Winnie. It's all new. Not an old bill among the pack." He added, emphasizing the last diphthong, "Fresh-sh-sh."

She looked at the money in her hand. They were new bills, but no, she would not be impressed by the fact. She frowned at him. "The Bank of England does occasionally print new ones, you know."

"Then hand the whole stack over to two blokes who throw it around like" — he corrected — "as if it were water?"

"They're rich. Besides, we aren't. What could they possibly want from us?"

"What they're getting, I'd have to say."

That made her stop and think, then ask, "What are they getting?"

He lifted one shoulder. "I don't know. Your skill. Me, all decked out like a lord. It has to do with that ball." He paused, then said, "Winnie, I

want you to go with me." More quietly, "Don't send me alone. You know the people I'll be mingling with." He rephrased again. "With *whom* I'll be mingling. Things could happen I don't understand, and you'll know what they mean."

After a moment, she said pathetically, "I can't." Then, "If you're afraid, we'll tell them it's off. We'll stop."

He shook his head. "I don't think we can. I know this game. Jeremy is the good one, Emile, the bad. If we try to back out, there will be pressure. Jeremy will shake his head and apologize, while trying to hold his brother back, but he won't succeed. Emile will make threats and — well, I'm not sure how far he'll go. They have a lot invested in their game. They've gone to a great deal of trouble."

"If they become unpleasant, you could —" She didn't finish. What did she envision? Mick, the hero? Rushing in to protect her from anyone who became harsh with her?

"Thank you," he said, as if she'd made perfect sense. He smiled. "And yes, I bloody well could. But I don't want to stop them yet. I want to ruin them. I don't like being set up. I want to see what they're up to and shove it down their throats." He grinned lopsidedly. "Come with me. Do it with me."

"I can't." She tried a practical reason. "I don't have a dress."

"Let's find you one. What do you have in your wardrobe?"

A dress. In all her life, Winnie had never purchased an evening gown. She didn't even own one to alter. She'd been too young to have one when she'd been of a monied family. Now, of course, she couldn't afford one that would be appropriate. She ignored Mick's suggestion.

Besides, he was seeing shadows. There was nothing wrong going on here, aside from a little prank on her cousin who would never know. It was a bet, she told herself. A stupid, competitive wager between two rich brothers, nothing more. Mick was judging others by the fact that he'd run too many "games" himself. A classic case of the kettle calling every pot black.

He wouldn't let it rest, though. More ideas, more questions. "You must have connections. Can you ask someone about them?"

She looked at him, frowning at his concern. For no other reason than to please him, she nodded. "All right. I stay in touch with several of my former students. I'll ask them. I'll see what they know of the Misters Emile and Jeremy Lamont."

That very evening, she sent Milton with several inquiries. By morning, she had two responses. No, her contacts in the realm of high society knew nothing one way or another of a Lamont family, not good nor bad. By default, the Lamonts were in the clear.

Then after elevenses tea, she received a third correspondence. It was from the Duchess of

Wychwood, a delightful young woman, recently wed, and a student of Edwina's just the summer past.

Particularly happy to hear from the girl, Edwina quickly tore open what unfolded out into a lovely, long letter — or lovely until the last few sentences, which made her frown and reread them:

> *As to your new clients, I'm afraid I have no recollection of any Emile or Jeremy or Sir Leopold Lamont, nor does my mother. Mother mentions, though, that she heard of gentlemen twins in Brighton last season — she doesn't know their name — who ran some dubious investments out of the pocket of a cousin of the Marquis de Lataille. I sincerely hope your Misters Lamont are not the same men.*

Oh, crumbs, Edwina thought. All right, she reasoned, it didn't matter so much that no one knew the Lamonts; her lofty friends wouldn't necessarily know every member of every minor family of consequence. But this other —

No, no, she told herself, she would not believe the worst. There were many sets of twin brothers in England. Why, the two who'd caused trouble in Brighton could be any of them.

Besides, she reassured herself, there was no profit in taking a bogus nobleman to the Duke of Arle's ball for an evening.

Another voice whispered though: Profit or not, if the bet isn't legitimate, you have no reason to continue teaching Mick. You must stop; your association with him is over, here and now: sooner than expected.

She would lose their final week.

As she folded the letter, with its last dreadful sentences, back into its envelope, a part of her knew perfectly well that Lady Wychwood had just told her the Lamonts might well be as Mick suspected: some sort of confidence men involving him and herself in a fraudulent scheme of unknowable depth.

But there was the problem: the knowing part of Edwina didn't care what the truth was or what the risks were. She wanted the last days with Mick Tremore. They were hers. She'd counted on having them, and she would, come what may.

Chapter 19

"If I have to say that one more blasted time, I'm going to puke." Thoroughly exasperated, Mick twisted his mouth and looked at Winnie across a table on which — it was too splendid an image to forget — she'd once stood with her long legs showing.

"Well." She blinked and cranked her head at him. "That was perfect," she said. "Especially if you could think of something a little more genteel to threaten than puking." She laughed. She let go, a small, light peal of genuine delight. "Oh," she said, "you did the H just as it should be and every vowel perfect. *Hahff to, blahs-sted,*" she repeated. "You didn't even curse too badly, and the grammar was perfect. That was wonderful. And quite natural."

"Truly?" He laughed too. Though mostly at her. Her nose wrinkled when she laughed. It wiggled at the tip.

He'd said he'd stay away from her, but he couldn't. And she wouldn't let him anyway. No matter where he went in her house, she chased him down, then insisted they "get on with it." And so he put up with her "it," whatever "it" was

she was doing to him. Any contact seemed better than none. He put up with her moods and seemingly unassailable, stiff-necked propriety, and watched and waited and hoped.

"What a lovely nose you have," he said. He reached, thinking to touch it.

She pulled back. Her laughter stopped. Her eyes, a look in them, grew wary, almost hurt. He realized that she thought he was playing with her in an unkind way.

"I mean it," he said. "I love your nose."

Love. He'd said it. Though only for her nose. It was only her nose he loved.

Her eyes grew larger, wider behind her eyeglasses. She looked afraid, yet full of hope. She was dying to believe him about something she couldn't see in herself.

"I don't like my nose," she said.

"You're so hard on yourself. I think your nose is the best nose I've ever met."

She gave a little snort. "You see? The best nose. Honestly. You aren't supposed to notice a woman's nose."

"Why not?"

"It's supposed to blend in, be part of the overall beauty of her well-proportioned face."

"Yours is part of your overall beauty."

She made a face at him, complete with tongue stuck out.

Which made him laugh outright. It took him a moment to recover.

While she watched him with her wide blue

saucer-eyes, perfectly solemn, attentive. As he calmed, she asked, "Do you really think I'm hard on myself?"

"Yes."

"How?"

"You don't let yourself see how good you are. To begin with, how striking your looks are." *Striking*. It was a new word. He hadn't even planned on saying it. It simply came out.

She didn't seem to notice. She merely shrugged. "No one before you has seen me as striking."

"I doubt that. I'd bet dozens of men have eyed you."

"None that said anything."

"And if they did, you'd probably criticize their taste in women. That's what you do to me."

"I do?"

"If I say you're pretty, you tell me I'm wrong."

She looked puzzled for a moment. "Well, the people who were supposed to love me best never thought I was very presentable." She cast her eyes down. "My mother thought I was 'a fright of a child.' My father didn't see me at all. If you'd asked him what color my eyes were, he wouldn't have known."

"There must have been other people."

She shrugged. "Milton."

"There you go —"

"Look, Mr. Tremore —"

"Mick," he told her. She said it occasionally, though she tried not to.

"No, Michael, we've decided. Remember: Michael."

He nodded. "Right. Michael."

"Michael," she said, then realized she'd lost the volley of given names. She broke off, as if she couldn't remember what she'd been about to say. She exhaled a long, loud breath. "Don't be foolish, Mr. Tremore. My nose is huge."

He laughed. "Yes, it's a good-sized smeller, loov. If it weren't so pretty, I might have sympathy for you."

"Pretty?" She let out an insulted breath.

"Yes." This time, when he reached, she let him run his finger down the ridge of her nose before she jerked back. "So thin and delicate," he told her, "with long nostrils, and the nicest, slightest curve to it. It's upper-class, you know. You have a very classy nose, missus. Calls attention right away to your breeding. Wish I had one like that."

She twisted her mouth as if to say that, if he weren't out-and-out insincere, he was certainly misguided. "I have a funny face."

"Funny?" He stared. "I suppose. Your face *is* amusing. Like a pretty puppy's. You have a witty face, a lively mug of a face, Win. As if God made everyone else's then came back to you and gave you a few extra touches, to make you stand out; you're more interesting to look at than most women, Win."

"I'm not pretty," she complained woefully.

He frowned. "All right, perhaps you're not. But your face is much more riveting than a pretty

one. Pretty faces are a guinea a dozen. So predictable. I'm tired of pretty faces already. Your face, though, I'd never tire of."

That put a *clunk* in the conversation. Why had he said it? He shouldn't have. Of course he wouldn't tire of her face. He wasn't going to see it after three days more, was he?

Three days till a ball, when, it had only recently occurred to him, he wasn't even sure what a ball was. A lot of dancing, he thought. Saturday, though, he'd find out.

He changed the subject. "Let's go somewhere. Let's put me to the test. Let's take that pretty face of yours out of the house." He wiggled his eyebrows wickedly and leaned forward. "Let's go back to the tearoom," he said.

She let out one of her gasping laughs. "No! They'd know you."

"No, they wouldn't." He sat up straight, touching his mouth. "I have no mustache. I have a new haircut, all new clothes. I talk completely differently. How could they possibly know me?" He raised one eyebrow. "I'm not at all the same," then winked. "But I'll know them, and it would be great entertainment to see some of the fools who chased me wait on me all afternoon."

He grabbed her hand and stood. He tried to lead her up and away from the table. "Come on," he said. He remembered brightly, "Oh, and I can wear that top hat, the one we like." The idea was sounding better by the moment. Then he thought of something else and turned too quickly

— she ran right into him. He smiled down the few inches into her face and said, "No big hat. No big hat for you, all right?" His wagged his finger. "A little hat, if you have one. Or no hat. I want to see your funny face."

She squinched it at him, but her eyes behind her lenses were smiling. He laughed again, so amused by her. Oh, her sweet face . . . her dear face with all its infinite movements and twists.

She said, "No, sir. I'll wear any hat I choose, thank you. Now get out of my way. I want to dress for the occasion."

Winnie chose a little straw hat she hadn't worn in years, one with a small, forward brim. It was out of date, yet not too bad. Milly had put a new flower on it at the side and new ribbons. It was cheerful; yellow straw, little yellow roses, with dark green grosgrain.

Indeed, not too bad. Like Winnie herself. Not too bad from this angle or that, especially in a not-too-bad little hat. Yes, she had a strong, healthy, if quirky, sort of femininity, she thought. No nonsense. And then, of course, there were her legs, which were beautiful, she was coming to think. No matter what she believed, though, the amazing part was, when she looked in Mick's face, there was no mistaking his sincerity: *He* thought her pretty, and she could have looked at that information on his face all day long.

She looked forward to staring at it across a tea table at Abernathy's. Her heart was light, though

her nerves were frayed. She wasn't certain he was ready for public inspection. She wasn't certain she was, for that matter. She had never gone to tea with a man, other than her own father.

For all her own nerviness, Mick seemed perfectly calm, happy, in fact. Charming. He asked Mr. Abernathy for a table for two, please. "Yes, sir," the man said, and Mick laughed out loud.

Winnie loved watching him act the gentleman, yet it terrified her to see him do it, too. Like watching someone on a high wire, someone she had put there, who carried somehow her fondest hopes, high, high up in the air overhead. She wanted to stand under him with a giant net. No, she wanted to get up there with him, hold onto his shirt, tie strings around each of his ankles. Don't fall. Don't let anything bad happen.

As they walked behind Mr. Abernathy into his main tearoom, entering its refined air of soft chatter and long-fronded palms, questions popped into her mind. Did he know not to remove his hat? Not to raise his voice? Had she told him every single rule regarding a gentleman's behavior in public? Probably not. Could he extemporize his way through the moments that depended on what she'd forgotten to tell him?

"Will this do?" asked Mr. Abernathy. He was seating patrons himself today.

The teahouse wasn't crowded, though it was relatively full. He sat Winnie and Mick at a small table near the door. Good for a quick exit, she thought, then sat nervously, laughing at herself.

They ordered tea and cake. The first five minutes went well, and she relaxed a little. Mick was beyond gentlemanly. He was attentive. He touched her hand at one point, and she blushed.

In the heat that flushed through her, her mind warmed to a little fantasy. Suppose they went to tea together next Wednesday, too, after the ball was over? Suppose they went to tea next Wednesday, or perhaps the opera?

Oh, yes, she answered herself. Imagine that — because that is the only way you'll see it, in imagination. Mick at the opera. Pah. He wouldn't like it. It wasn't his sort of entertainment. No, they had no future, not even one of Wednesday-afternoon teas. He didn't fit into her life — passing him off for an afternoon or an evening wasn't the same as passing him off for a lifetime. And she was hardly suited to catching rats — she'd proven that, when she'd all but climbed him like a pole then run away from fright.

She watched Mick raise his teacup to his mouth, ever so beautifully, especially when she remembered the last time she'd seen him do it in this tearoom. But then his cup stayed in front of his mouth without his drinking. His eyes grew still and intent as he stared fixedly over the cup across the room.

"Oh, no," he murmured. Then, "Don't look. But brace yourself. We have a visitor."

The baroness from the seamstress's shop six weeks ago, the one who had bought Winnie her garters, came straight over to their table.

Ignoring Winnie, she said to Mick, "Lady Randolf Lawnhurst, the Baroness of Whitting." She added coquettishly, "Blanche," then extended her arm toward him, her hand dropped at the wrist. "And we know each other, I do believe." Her face was smiling, though puzzled, one eyebrow was arched high in question. With relief, he realized, she couldn't remember the circumstances under which she knew him.

Mick started to rise, being a gentlemen at the moment, when he would rather have told her to go jump in the Thames.

She stopped him. "No, no, don't get up. I don't mean to intrude." She already had, of course. "It's just that I'm sure we've met, yet I can't remember where." She was asking him to explain her own confused memory.

Settling back into his chair, Mick smiled and shook his head. In his best, most posh syllables told her, "I'm sorry. I don't believe I've had the pleasure." He tried to look dismayed, disarmed.

"Oh, but I'm sure —"

"No," he insisted, smiling, "I don't think so."

She tilted her head, frowned, then smiled, then frowned, like neon flickering in a glass tube, off and on, off and on, all the while studying him. She shook her head, then her smile widened as she announced cheerfully, "You're wrong. I know you, I'm certain."

Ah, well. Since she was certain. "You do look familiar," he allowed.

Winnie made a sound, a surprised, censuring

little click of her tongue. She was alarmed, no doubt, at hearing him go in this direction.

While the baroness openly flirted with him, flapping her eyelashes, rolling her shoulders under her boa. "Are you from here?" she asked.

"No," he said quickly.

"Where are you from?"

He blurted what was as far away as he could think of. "Paris."

Under the table, Winnie kicked him.

He laughed at the heady sensation of two women taking after him at once.

"Paris?" The baroness was delighted. "I love Paris! Where in Paris?"

He knew of only one landmark in that city, so he said it pleasantly. "The Eiffel Tower."

Behind the baroness, out of her line of vision, Winnie put her hand over her mouth, her eyes widening, part horror, part mirthful disbelief she held back.

"The Eiffel Tower," the baroness said, perplexed. "You live in the Eiffel Tower?"

He could hear in her tone this was wrong. "No, no," he amended, "I was suggesting we might have met there."

She thought the information over, as if trying to make his hypothesis plausible. "When did you last visit the Eiffel Tower?"

"Oh, I go there all the time," he said. When he saw on the baroness's face that this wasn't right either, he thought to add, "I know it's foolish. Even trite, since, well, the most common of per-

sons knows of the place. But I can't help myself. It's simply so —" He had no idea what he was talking about.

She finished for him. "Yes, so amazing. And the fountains —"

"Oh, yes, especially the fountains. And —" And what? What to contribute to the conversation? He held out his hand. "And the tower itself."

"Oh, yes. A marvel. Those French."

"Indeed." He smiled and said, "Well, it was lovely meeting you again."

She blinked, seemingly at a dead end. Thank God. "Yes," she said. "Very nice to see you." She turned to go. He thought he was free of her trouble, but she turned all the way, full circle, and came back after only moving away a foot. "Your name," she said and smiled. "I don't remember your name. Please remind me." She eyed him with an interest that was a shade warmer than was polite and so reminiscent of their last encounter he wanted to shake her.

Remind her indeed. He dare not. If he repeated the name *Tremore*, she might remember its context. He looked down at his teaspoon, turning it over. He read the names off the back and flipped them over. "Bartonreed," he said. "Michael Edgerton, the Viscount of Bartonreed."

"Bartonreed," she repeated blankly. She couldn't seem to think of anything further to ask. "Well, then, Lord Bartonreed." She wanted

more information, but had run out of latitude to acquire it. "A pleasure," she said.

Once she'd left, Winnie leaned forward and whispered, "You gave her the wrong name!"

"I couldn't give her *Tremore*. She knows it."

"She knows it!" she repeated, though her tone was more emphatic. It questioned him.

He didn't want to explain. Besides, they were past the problem.

Winnie, of course, didn't like to miss a chance to worry. "Oh, crumbs, oh, crumbs," she said. She put her long fingers to her mouth, pressing them, then spoke over the tips. "Now you have to remember 'Bartonreed' — where did you come up with that? — and answer to it. Will you be able to?"

"I'm sure. But we can go ahead and use —"

"No, we can't. She's the wife of the Master of the Hounds for the Queen. She'll be at the ball."

"Oh, bloody hell," he said and sat back. He did laugh this time, and richly. Bloody hell.

Winnie, though, was losing her sense of humor. "Stop it," she said. "You're going to mess this up."

"No, I won't."

She leaned toward him, her face furrowing, squinching up and down both, as it could. Intently, she asked him, "Do you know what it would be like to fail in front of the *bon ton*?"

"The *bon ton*?"

"Yes. Every. Single. Family in England that matters?"

He raised his brow. "Every single person at the ball matters to you?"

"Well, no." She made a befuddled frown, then shook her head. "Oh, I don't know. Some do; most don't. They all mattered to my parents."

"Ah," he said. He laughed gently at her. "Loovey, how sweet. I'll do my best. I'd love for your parents to be proud of me — and proud of you, too — even though they're dead."

She let out a laugh at this, a *squawk*, half of distress for being teased, half of release, then nodded, biting her lips together. She admitted, "I'm so nervous."

"I can see that." She nearly always was, bless her.

He hoped her nervousness this time didn't make her put her fingers into things beyond good judgment. He hoped she'd leave him be so he could do what he needed to his way. But she either would, or she wouldn't. He would deal with her as she came.

For now, he signaled the waiter, asking for milk instead of cream for his tea. As the waiter left, however, Mick watched trouble circle back around to them.

Smiling, a look of triumph on her face, the baroness left her own party once more to bear down on Mick and Winnie's table.

He leaned forward and whispered, "Finish your tea, loov. She's found something more to say to us."

The baroness walked up to their table again,

wagging a thoughtful finger at Mick, and said, "Niece." That was the word she used, though he was fairly certain she meant a place, when she continued, "In Nice at the Hotel Negresco. You were on the floor." She frowned, as if it were painful to draw so hard on a memory that resisted. She bridged her flawed recollection with an invention of her own. "Yes," she said with certainty now, "you were the one who found my cat. Positively heroic, you were." She frowned, then smiled, doing that flicker of uncertainty again. Then, as if perfectly logical, she let loose a torrent of what he thought to be French.

He nodded politely till she finished, then took a chance saying, "Excuse me, but my fiancée doesn't speak French. May I present Miss Edwina Bollash. We're to be married in June." That should shut the woman up and make her leave him alone.

But, no, she was fascinated. "Miss Bollash? Lady Bollash?" she corrected. "Lionel Bollash's daughter?" The baroness was surprised, but riveted.

Next to Winnie, however, the woman looked calm.

Win had been startled apoplectic by his announcement. "Michael," she began, then laughed, then couldn't get whatever else she was going to say out for a few seconds. "You're, um — ah, not supposed to say that. That is, *tell* people yet." To the baroness, apologetically, she said, "It's not official. We haven't an-

303

nounced it. We aren't really."

Mick reached across and patted her hand. "Winnie, my dove, don't start again. You promised. Don't say you're making me wait longer, because I can't. I can't wait to make you my own."

Win's jaw dropped. No halfway about it, her mouth looked unhinged for a second. Then she giggled, blushed, and looked away. The perfect picture of a sweet, shy bride.

Oh, to have it be true, he thought. Wouldn't that be something?

The baroness turned and studied Winnie now with rapt curiosity. She glanced at Mick, then once more attempted to speak to him in French.

He held up his hand, shaking his head, a man being firm. "In English, Lady Whitting. Please."

Lady Whitting, ha! He was enjoying himself! Nonetheless, he thought they should cut their tea short. His luck was holding, but he had no idea what the baroness might latch onto next.

To Winnie, he said, "Are you finished, darling?" He took out the chiming watch that he loved to look at for any reason, and that he was probably going to have to return. Too bad. He popped its cover. *Ding-ding, ding-ding.* . . . It continued to chime till the hour exactly. Four o'clock. "Goodness," he said. "I had no idea it was so late. We have to meet Lord Rezzo at five. We'd best be going." He stood. To Winnie: "Dear one, you gather your things, while I take care of the bill."

She grabbed his forearm. "You can't pay," she hissed, though suppressed laughter was now making her all but delirious. She tried to speak under her breath, but her voice carried anyway. "You have no money," she said.

"Of course, I do, dear heart. I have a fresh twenty." He turned toward her fully, wiggling his eyebrows, a gesture only she saw. "A very, very fresh-sh-sh" — he let the sound run — "twenty. Let's go see how it spends."

"Michael!" she said with giddy panic.

But he freed himself from her and backed with a slight bow from the table. Behind the baroness — who followed him, looking disappointed and bewildered — he watched Winnie put her hands over her face, aggrieved, laughing, hiding. He called to her. "Winnie, gather your things. We're leaving."

Indeed, they'd best be gone. He wondered if the baroness were truly going to the ball on Saturday. Or if any of the other upper-class women he knew, several of them more intimately, would be there. Bloody hell, what a shock to realize he might actually know people at the gathering. An ugly shock. He laughed. A challenging shock.

Outside, down the street, with Winnie's hand safely in his, he caught sight of an omnibus. A number six. Perfect. "Come on," he said. He started to run, pulling Winnie along.

She followed, still laughing, a gamine making her escape. He could hear her, delighted by their

strange encounter, drunk on it. "Where are we going?" she called.

"We're trying to catch that bus." He pointed and tugged, encouraging her to move faster.

"My carriage —"

"One problem at a time, loovey. Come on, be quick."

She wasn't as quick as he was. She held her hat and clopped down the pavement behind him, skirts kicking up around her wonderful legs.

They weren't going to make it. The omnibus stopped. One man got off, two women got on. Mick called to the driver, but he and Winnie were still too far for anyone at the bus to hear him. Mick slowed. Still a block away, the horses of the omnibus lurched forward.

"There'll be another," he said.

Then a woman across the street, closer to the vehicle, called to the driver. The omnibus slowed and Mick said, "Come on. Run."

Winnie did. She remembered the breathless chase he'd led the first day she'd set eyes on him. Now she ran with him, and it thrilled her. No other word to describe it. *Thrill*. Feeling his dry, warm hand around hers, his pulling her through traffic, then his arm about her back, her waist, lifting her, propelling her up a curb, taking her with him, then boosting her up the steps of the bus when she hesitated — oh, it was so bold and simply too much fun. She started laughing hard somewhere along the way, uncontrollably; she couldn't stop.

In this condition, Mick wound him and her both all the way up the steps to the roof of the bus, the bench seat. From the top, she stood on her knees and waved to Georges, the coachman she shared with two neighbors. He saw her, then a second later, her own carriage pulled away from the curb to follow. She turned around and slid down into the seat, and Mick's arm — he'd braced it on the bench back — slid down, too. He gripped her around the shoulders. He squeezed her to him as both he and she laughed without reserve.

As they clopped past Hyde Park, then along the side and around Buckingham Palace, the two of them laughed like fools, recapping the baroness's confusion and surprise till they were slouched against the seat and each other, gripping the arm pieces to hold themselves up, till Winnie was wheezing from it. She couldn't catch her breath from the wild run topped off by laughing too much.

When he became concerned with her breathing, she waved her hand. "It's all right. Asthma. It'll go away as soon as I settle down." She tried to get hold of herself, drawing in deep breaths, then letting them out slowly, with giggles.

As she wheezed her way into sanity again, Mick frowned, smiled, shook his head, then touched her cheek. "Oh, you are a mess, my sweet duck. Such a sweet mess."

He turned in the seat, his shoulder against the

bench, his chest close enough to her arm that she could feel his humidity and warmth. He wanted to kiss her. She was becoming aware of the signs, how he moved close, how he watched her face, her mouth. Then she remembered that he wanted her to say it, to tell him. He waited.

Oh, dear, if she were honest, she'd admit she loved all this kissing business. She could do it forever, give up eating, sleeping, just kiss his mouth, maybe lie down beside him, press her body against him. Just the kissing. She remembered it sometimes so vividly from that time in his room that memory brought a near-perfect echo of sensation, a lovely ripple of the same, if muted, pleasure.

Sometimes, too, she remembered the other thing he'd done. The way his hand had sought her lower, the way he'd so fiercely seemed to want to touch her there. When she thought of it now, it wasn't so awful. Only intimate. Very, very intimate.

Yes, she wanted him to kiss her, quick and strong; hard, as he had that time when his mustache was just freshly off. She wanted to say it. *Kiss me.* She wet her lips, opened her mouth — and her mind went blank. She sat there like a nit, nothing coming out but horrid, faint asthmatic wheezing. Which made her close her eyes in despair as a wave of the old feeling returned: a sense of being the least appealing woman on earth.

Why did she have to ask? Pretty women didn't,

she was sure. If she were only pretty enough, only a more powerfully attractive female, she'd have kisses bestowed . . . kisses everywhere . . . that would arrive on their own.

Since they wouldn't, though, she tried valiantly to get past her misgivings about her own worth so as to ask for what she wanted. The concept was simple enough. Yet she tried all the way down Birdcage Walk and onto Whitehall to no effect, save a lot of wheezing.

As they approached Trafalgar, Mick laughed beside her, then his lips brushed her cheek. "You're hopeless, Winnie," he said. "But it's a stupid game. Arrogance made me invent it, and I'm suffering now for it. We both are. I'm kissing you anyway. Just let me."

Then he lifted her chin, brought her face to his, and breathed into her mouth as if he could supply her oxygen.

God above. He may as well have. He certainly did something to the flow of her blood. It began to pound. Oh, yes.

He kissed her in front of all of London, on the rooftop of a horse-drawn omnibus as they trotted by Lord Nelson looking down on them from his granite column.

In front of the world, clever, handsome, humorous Mick kissed her, while her heart thudded and her belly squirmed and something low inside melted. Then better still, Mick moved her around, pulling her legs over him, and scooted her up into his lap.

Goodness. Oh, goodness. He pulled her against him as he kissed her strongly. She let him; she helped. She put her arms about his lovely, sturdy neck, reached tentatively into his hair, and kissed him back. She devoured him.

His soft hair. His hot, tender-wet mouth, reaching, wanting hers. He scooted himself down a bit, till her weight rested against his chest, until she lay against a hard, broad wall of muscle. Then something new and strange. Where she sat she could feel through her skirts the vague outline of him under her. He grew hard, becoming a noticeable, rounded ridge.

The sensation wasn't repellent, though she had believed somewhere it would be. Someone had left her with that impression, but, whoever they were, they were wrong. It was . . . mesmerizing. She could sense the length of him against her buttocks as well as a kind of heaviness, a substantive presence. He was changing right there under her, growing longer and thicker, information she acquired through the unlikely source of her bum, while he kissed her mouth. Heavens, what a sensation. She didn't know what to make of it. Too much to assimilate, too different from what, all her life, she'd thought a man would be: both more sleek — elegant — and more formidable.

It was the formidable part, of course, that gave her pause. She backed away from his face, looking into it, both of them knowing what she was feeling. The size of him felt threatening

when paired with what she knew of simple biology, with where he was supposed to put something that large. She couldn't imagine it.

She was saved from having to, then, when the conductor interrupted. " 'Ay, lovebirds." She and Mick both looked around to see the man's head up over the top of the steps. "How far, mate?" he asked. A Cockney. *'Ow far, mite?*

"Aldwych."

"Four P for two." *Far pee.*

Mick leaned to dig four pence from his pocket as Winnie slid herself back onto the seat, a more ladylike location. Goodness, what had come over her? she thought. In front of anyone who wanted to look up on top of a bus. Could people know? Could they tell what had been under her backside? She thought she should be embarrassed. She *was* embarrassed, she told herself.

Still, she hummed tunelessly to herself as they headed east.

When she asked Mick at one point where they were going, he said, "My part of town."

At first, this quieted her. She worried he meant Whitechapel. She'd been there once with her father; they'd gone to listen to voices. The sounds in that district, of purest, richest Cockney, were wonderful, but the atmosphere of Whitechapel was frightening. At the heart of the East End, it was a hard place of ragtag children, poverty, and narrow, sunless streets. It had been a seedy part of town; then, three years after her visit with her father, Jack the Ripper had made it notorious.

As they lurched through traffic, though, she felt Mick's arm bump her shoulder blades — it was stretched out along the bench back behind her. After that, it didn't matter where he was taking them; she wanted to go. She felt oddly confident of him: If he thought he could guide them without danger, then she would believe that he could.

It was a pretty, midweek late afternoon. London was still bustling as shops prepared to close for the day, people out on the streets, in transit; coming or going. The light breeze on the top of the bus was beautiful; the view was excellent. They left behind the spire of St. Martin-in-the-Fields, then passed Covent Garden, like a tourist's ride. Then at Aldwych, they got off.

"We have to walk from here."

They shooed pink-footed pigeons out of the way as they cut through a small churchyard. The smell of flowers wafted from somewhere, as if from a whole market of them, then this changed abruptly into the pungent smells of a brewery. Then music. Distant, but jolly.

They followed the music into back streets, and Winnie became turned around. They were burrowing their way into what was not a bad area so much as working-class: close flats, children playing in front of an eel-and-pie shop, a heavy cart-horse slipping on wet cobbles where a sewer drained, stomping and jangling its trappings.

And all the while, Mick held her hand, leading her along. His part of town. His warm, em-

bracing hand around hers. He could have led her to hell, and it would have been fine; pleasant, in fact.

Then she thought, How prescient. For he stopped, held out his arm, gesturing toward an overhead, swinging sign halfway down the block. The Bull and Tun. The music was coming from there. It was loud — a tinny piano played with a violin that sounded as though a gypsy worked it, along with some sort of percussion, perhaps a sack of tins. What the trio lacked in nuance they made up for in volume, as they played a lively, if slightly off-key rendition, of a cancan from *Orpheus in Hades*. Hell, indeed.

"Dancing," Mick said and smiled as if he offered a gift. "I can't guarantee what kind, but some of the people inside will dance before the night's over. Let's be two of them, Win."

Chapter 20

The Bull and Tun was little more than a large room with a bar and foot rail at one end. Its furnishings were simple — wood tables and chairs, the walls covered with ale signs, certificates of inspection, a dart board, all proudly displayed along with a large photograph of the Queen and a smaller one of the Prince of Wales. The public house's wood floors hadn't seen wax in a very long time. The brass at its rails was dented but shining. Nonetheless, the place had an air of goodwill that was attractive. As Mick and Winnie came in, a dozen people greeted them. Several greeted him by name. He was a regular.

At the back, the musical trio caroused through the Offenbach rearranged to suit working-class tastes. A man with a bald spot on his head played the piano so hard his hands bounced off the keys. A swarthy man with baggy eyes sawed a bow back and forth on a violin. A rather talented young man rattled sticks across glasses and cans and anything else he could hit. If people got within reach, he'd play their buttons.

Patrons sat at long tables together, elbow to elbow, though there were still places available.

On a small section of open floor, a dozen men and women did a fairly robust polka to the French music. Mick's dance. He wanted to join them. "We have to dance soon. It will be too crowded later."

First, though, he introduced her to a small, wiry fellow named Rezzo, then several other men whose names she hadn't heard before, and two women, Nancy and Marie. Marie liked him, Winnie knew immediately, though Mick didn't seem to be even faintly acquainted with the fact.

He was well-liked. And well-known — his friends wanted his jokes and philosophies, telling him, "No, no, do the voices, do the accents." They liked him to talk in dialects. It was odd, but during his introductions, she'd heard him attempt to sprinkle his speech with some of his old accent, to blend in, she supposed, but then he stopped. His friends teased him a little about the way his voice sounded these days; her, too, as if he and she had both been somewhere that flavored them differently, like pies in the larder set too close to the basil.

Accent or not, his friends wanted his reactions and ideas; they engaged him in conversation. If anyone knew what he did for a living, it wasn't a subject of interest. Here, Mick was the fellow who — someone let the fact out — danced well with all the ladies and spouted colorful stories with a clearsighted outlook that everyone loved to hear.

She looked at him among them. He wasn't like

them. His clothes were too smart, his speech and manner too polished. She looked at his hair, so dark and shining. It was well-cut. His eyes, oh, his beautiful eyes. Their steely green was so much finer than any other eyes here. Perhaps he never had been one of them, she thought, then laughed. Perhaps she was prejudiced. She thought him handsomer than any of the others. Cleverer. Taller, of course . . . kinder, friendlier, funnier. . . . The list went on.

After ten minutes of chatting with friends, with two men buying both him and Winnie drinks — Mick ale and Winnie lemonade — Mick wanted to dance. "In an hour, we won't be able to."

For him, it was simply a matter of dancing, of course. He was familiar with the way of the place, good on his feet, good at quick steps. Winnie was less able. It took a few attempts at each new rhythm to be graceful with it — though Mick exclaimed over and over how quickly she caught on and how good she was once she did. Still, she had good, if self-conscious, fun. He was always a pleasure to dance with.

Then a fast waltz played, and he leaped right into it.

With surprise and recognition, Winnie accused, "You knew how to waltz!"

He shrugged, smiled, and spun her to the music, left then right. "Not all the same steps and not the dignified way you do it, but yes." He laughed, then teased, "Still, you had so much fun

telling me how, I was happy to cooperate."

"And what else could you do before I ever tried to teach it to you?" She teased him back. "Could you talk like a lord all along?"

He grinned crookedly and said nothing, as if it were possible.

She remembered all the difficulty they'd had getting him to this point. Still, there were moments when she could almost believe their struggle had never happened. The sounds coming from his mouth tonight were so clearly upper-class — even if his knowledge about Paris was sketchy. Oh, she laughed to think of that foolish woman at the teahouse, flirting with him when there was no point.

He was hers.

She began to think this: hers. As they danced among his friends, and the floor grew more crowded. He was the only Cornishman, but not the only one from remote places. There were gypsy and Irish and Jew. She could hear in the voices that they danced among the grandchildren of the potato famine, the children of European pograms, all come to England for haven. And though Winnie knew that just a few blocks further east, it wasn't very safe at all, here felt haven to her, too. Here was light and laughter and ale and song.

And music. With Mick dancing her around to it. A rare opportunity. She warmed to the unusual music and the quick tempos. She danced, having her own little ball in a pub on the west

edge of the East End in London. She danced with Mick till they were bumping up against backs and shoulders, till they didn't have a square foot to move, till, when they wanted a drink to wet their throats, it took half an hour of wedging and working their way to get the fifteen feet to the bar. The room grew hot from the bodies alone. And still, people kept coming in. On a Wednesday night.

They brought tables from the back, filling the dance floor with them. The dancing was over, Winnie thought. Until the woman introduced as Nancy grabbed her arm and said, "Those of us who don't want to stop dancing, get up on the stage." She pointed.

The "stage" was three long wood tables put end to end. Several men, Mick one of them, helped maneuver the wood furniture into position. He saved Winnie and himself seats at the "stage." They pulled up chairs.

When the music started again, Nancy, her friend Marie, and two other women climbed up onto the three contiguous tabletops and began to move to the music. Though this dancing was different.

The girl, Nancy, swung her skirts, then kicked them up in back. She put her fists on her hips, still holding handfuls of skirt, and moved in a way that was provocative and sly, but rhythmic and beautiful to watch. The others showed their petticoats, too, laughing, dancing.

Winnie watched the four girls dance till they

were all perspiring, then watched with utter astoundment — horrified, but fascinated — as each and every one of them, one by one, shrugged out of their blouses. Not that they didn't have a great deal on underneath; there was much corsetry and underlinens, all very lacy and pretty. They exposed nothing indecent, or not exactly. But removing their blouses left their arms bare.

She looked to see what Mick made of this. He wasn't even paying attention. His head was bent in cheerful conversation with the fellow next to him; Mick was uninterested, as if he'd seen it all before.

Winnie hadn't. She couldn't decide what to make of it.

"Would you like something to eat?" Mick called over the music. Before she could say, he was up and answering his own question. "I'll bring you something."

As he left, Nancy's friend, Marie, climbed down, using his chair. On her way past, she smiled at Winnie and said, "All the single women are allowed to dance up here. Come join us."

Winnie drew back.

The girl added, "If you want to."

"I don't," Winnie said quickly. She pressed her lips together and shook her head.

Oddly enough, though, she didn't disapprove exactly. Or yes, she did, a little, but she also admired the dancers. She admired the girls' bold-

319

ness, their joie de vivre, their openhearted laughter and friendly manner.

"We're not whores," Marie called down to her, reaching over Winnie's head to accept a drink Nancy brought.

"Oh, no, I wasn't thinking that." Though, of course, the idea had been in the back of Winnie's mind.

"I work in a garment factory," Nancy said, "and Marie sells apples and flowers. We're good girls." She laughed. "But we love the fellows. And love to dance."

Yes. Winnie loved to dance, too. She tapped her feet to the music.

Other than toe-tapping, though, she had the presence of mind to sit, ladylike, and watch as Nancy, having swilled a half pint of ale in a single draft, stepped back up, from the floor to a chair to the tabletop again.

The piano went from a double-quick polka to a music-hall rendition of another of Offenbach's cancans, while underneath the table Winnie danced her toes in little steps.

On the tabletops, the girls broke into high kicks. Amazing. And bawdy. And slightly awe-inspiring. They bounced their knees into the air and circled their legs — their pretty, stockinged legs half-covered in lacy knickers. It made Winnie's heart pound to see it.

The oldest girl up there, she would guess, probably Nancy, was still at least five years younger than herself. They were all pretty girls,

one dark, another petite, another slightly plump; Nancy herself was fair, slender, and shapely.

From nowhere, Winnie remembered her mother. In the six years she had known the woman, Helen Bollash had paid as little attention as she could to her daughter, and when her attention came, it was inevitably harsh. Winnie had understood intuitively before she could talk that her mother didn't like children. The Marchioness of Sissingly had been young when she'd had her only child, eighteen; twenty-four when she'd left; then dead at twenty-six.

Winnie had never heard the word applied to her mother, but she didn't doubt that some said it: Her mother had been *wild*. Or as Mick would call it: spontaneous with a strong sense of adventure.

She wished she had a dash of her mother in her now, for, she felt sure, Helen Bollash would have thrown her head back at the suggestion of dancing in her camisole and shaking her skirt, of showing her legs. She'd have laughed sweetly, even squealed with delight, then leaped upon the tabletop. Her mother would have danced. And her father, even if he'd been sitting at the table, wouldn't have noticed — he wasn't indulgent so much as blind. Lionel Bollash was aware of his wife only insofar as she had a beautiful voice that spoke with clear, upper-class syllables. Lady Sissingly could even curse like a lord, but when she did, it came out with such soft, round sounds, with such dignity that people doubted

they'd heard correctly. She couldn't have said *that*.

Spontaneity and adventure.

Winnie watched. As she had watched her mother. She watched other people have an unconventionally good time, afraid to have it herself.

Finally, Nancy, with a stroke of insight, said, "Come on, love," and held out her hands, reaching down toward Winnie. "Come on. You don't have to take your blouse off. Just get up with us and dance. It's fun."

"I can't."

From behind, Mick spoke as he sat down into his chair, pulling it forward. "She can," he said. "She will. I can see her knees moving." He laughed.

She twisted, frowning around at him. "You're always watching my skirts."

He grinned, unapologetic. "I damn well am. I can't stop myself. Here," he said. He'd brought her fish and chips and a lemon shandy — lemonade and beer. More money; he shouldn't be spending it.

She sipped the shandy, her second of the night. Mick took a long draft of ale as he tipped back on the rear legs of his chair, then casually laid his arm across the back of Winnie's, wrapping his fingers around her chair back's far spindle, a possessiveness that somehow made her spine prickle with pleasure.

They watched for a while like that, eating their

fish and chips, a social couple; something she had never known and was keenly aware of. She couldn't sit back in her chair all the way for being nervous she'd lean into his arm, yet she loved knowing his arm was there.

Meanwhile, the girls entertained them, dancing for all they were worth. They were good. The music thumped in Winnie's chest. Now and then, Mick rubbed his thumb against her shoulder, a little brush in musical time.

"Come on," Nancy said when she came down for the third time. "I can see you moving to it. You don't have to do anything you don't want to, but come dance with us, dearie."

Winnie was susceptible enough to the girl's coaching that she leaned forward in her chair, wanting to get up, shy, uncertain. Then Nancy grabbed her at the elbows, Mick planted his palms squarely under her bum, and Winnie was levitated up onto the tabletop.

She straightened herself, turned, and looked down. Heavens, a tabletop again! The room below her was crowded, hardly an inch between people to move. Full of faces . . . strangers . . . who suddenly applauded a lady who would play their game. *A lie-dy who 'ill ply,* a man's voice called out.

And the music pounded; the crowd stomped. Winnie stood there a moment, dumbfounded, while the other dancing feet around her made the table hop under the soles of her shoes, making the rhythm of the music shake up her

legs. She could feel it.

Slowly — to please everyone, then she'd get down, she told herself — she allowed herself to be moved by all that was going on around her. When she took her first step, the men and women below her hooted good-naturedly.

"Come on, duckie! Let's see whot you're myde uv!"

Yes, her mother would have reveled in the attention, the same attention that embarrassed Winnie. She blushed. She looked for Mick.

He was just below, leaning back in his chair, precariously balanced and perfectly confident. His face smiled up at her, ready to accept anything she wanted. He'd get her down, if she asked for help. *Take me away.* He'd clap his hands in time to her movement, if she let loose and danced.

She shifted on her feet, making small, half-hearted movements, listening to an Irishman at an old English piano play a French bouffe song that had been turned into a fine East End rhythm. Her feet moved a little more earnestly. Then she raised her skirt enough to watch her own toes.

She danced — not like the others, not without restraint — but as she danced by herself sometimes at home, with demure little steps. But the music wasn't really for that, so she matched it a little better. Her steps grew daring. She made a little kick, then a small twirl, then a crossed-over step that became a kind of deep curtsy, from

which to recover she had to swoop herself up; she ended with a spin.

When she found Mick's face again, he was laughing, enjoying himself: enjoying her. He liked it. And his laughter, her own movement, her own feelings as she did it, these made her feel light — not the large, sometimes cumbersome woman she was, but light on her toes; light in her mind.

She must have been interesting to watch, because after a few minutes, Nancy and Marie and the other two stepped back and the whole room began to clap. Winnie was flustered when she realized they clapped to the music for her, encouraging her to turn and move and leap. Well. All right. She did it.

She danced. She danced down the tables then back. She kicked a beer over on purpose. The splash was perfect. It went with a jangle of the piano that made the little crowd roar with approval. She danced till her dress was sticking to her, till her hair was coming down in strings. She even kicked her foot high once and showed her legs — that was a truly popular step. The men — it seemed all the men in the room — made such a fuss. More than the commotion they made for Nancy or Marie or the others.

When she looked for Mick, he winked at her, wiggled his eyebrows, then dropped his gaze again and watched her legs the way he could. She would swear that the glow on his face was from pride and possessiveness and anticipation. His.

She felt like his, and it was a good feeling. And he, oh, he who was the finest man in the room; he was so hers. The tallest, handsomest, friendliest . . . warmest, earthiest. . . .

Anticipation. Her stomach rolled over again in that way it had weeks ago now, when she'd stood on a table in a room alone with him. Then more so, when he'd pressed her to a wall. She grabbed her skirts as the music went into a cancan again, raising them to shake them to the tempo and see how high she could kick. The whole tavern roared. The other men, no doubt, thought the whole thing saucy, a devilish good time, but when she saw Mick's face, it was something else. To everyone else, it was rollicking. But to him — she could feel it — he was watching a change happen, watching her do what she could sense in her blood: ease up.

Anticipation, she thought again. His gaze followed up her body once more till their eyes held . . . and, oh, the heat in his stare. His eyes, his lovely smoky eyes — green yet not, gray yet more — they wouldn't let hers go. Their intensity promised something.

What? Oh, what? she thought. She gave him a questioning look, saying wordlessly, *Why do you stare at me like that?* Her heart felt gay all at once.

Nancy grabbed her. "Your hair is falling down." She tried to repin a piece that lay on Winnie's shoulder, then leaned to her and said, "Take off your jacket and blouse, dearie. No one cares here, and it's cooler. You have plenty on to

cover yourself. Take it off or at least unfasten the collar."

Practical advice perhaps, but no, thank you.

Except, well, the collar. Yes. She let Nancy fiddle with it. Yes, it would feel good to release the high neck. Winnie tried to hold her feet still long enough for the girl to ease the hooks of the boned collar up her throat.

The fabric fell free, and Nancy quickly untied the little jabot and undid a few top buttons for good measure. Air found the moisture on Winnie's skin, cooling her. It felt wonderful.

"Come on, dearie," Nancy chided as she pulled at Winnie's coat, a little mutton-sleeved bolero that was showing dark, damp splotches. "Gawd love us," Nancy said, "but you have on more clothes than a nun on a winter's night. Here." She peeled the coat from Winnie's arms, turning her around as she did it, three hundred sixty degrees.

When Winnie faced the room again, she was oh-so-much cooler. And freer.

Nancy pinched two fingers' worth of blouse, pulling it from where it stuck to Winnie's chest. "If you get rid of this, your arms won't be so hot."

If she got rid of her blouse, she'd feel naked — despite, it was true, a camisole over a corset over a chemise corset liner over a ruffled bust-improver. She wore too much.

On her own, Winnie unbuttoned the sleeves of her blouse and rolled them back. Oh, to have air

on her arms! She danced more and harder, till she had to stop from asthma. She took a break, stepping down.

Her blouse was wringing wet. She could see through it to her skin and her corset liner where its ruffles came up over her corset to show in the low V of her camisole. A fine lot of good her blouse did her.

"Are you stopping?" Mick asked. "Do you want a drink?"

"No, and yes, please!" The wheezing eased a little. All she had to do was rest, then she could go back up again. Oh, she never wanted to stop.

When he turned and pushed into the crowd, she put her own fingers to the buttons up the front. She popped them through the button-holes, one, two, three, four. . . . She tapped her feet and hummed as she did it. Winnie took off her blouse and lay it over Mick's chair.

Yes, much better. And her arms weren't completely bare. The wide neck of her chemise, after all, ended in the little cap sleeves. She stretched her neck, her long neck, and put her hand to her bare throat. She felt exceptionally good, if a little tipsy. She was slightly drunk, she realized.

Not so drunk though that, as she stood there alone, she didn't know it when a man came up and flirted with her. He actually flirted with her! And she flirted back. Not because she liked him — she couldn't have remembered a single detail about him, if asked. He said his name, and she promptly forgot it. No, she flirted with him to see

if she could and because, with Mick gone, she wanted to practice for when he came back.

And because she was full of herself.

She wanted to crow. Goodness, she was having a good time as her mother used to. And so far it hadn't killed her. How grand! Oh, how grand it was simply to do what she felt like doing! How grand to be alive tonight!

Chapter 21

"Coo, ain't you fancy tonight," said Charlie behind the bar.

Mick smiled as he ordered another ale and shandy, trying some of his old patter with Charlie. It didn't work any better with him than it did with anyone else.

Oh, his mates were nice to him. He liked them; they liked him still. He laughed and talked to them, just as always. But when he tried to talk like them, it sounded wrong. Not for them, but for him. He didn't like his own voice when the same words came out that, a month ago, would have passed by his ear unnoticed.

A part of him must want to be a gentleman of some sort, he decided. He liked the new way he sounded; he even liked his new manners to some extent. He enjoyed bringing a sense of refinement to his life.

He might become a kind of gentleman after all. He'd spoken to Milton, asking him what other occupations the butler thought Mick might be able to do, and the butler had encouraged him with a few interesting ideas. He could work in a shop, maybe own one someday. He

could go into service; at the right house with the right pay, this had the advantage of fine living arrangements. There were other things he could do, none that caught his fancy, but Mick was fairly certain he could find something to do with his new self that suited him.

It was a little daydream these days that he'd do something that suited Winnie as well. They'll go off, find a little cottage, and live together forever as man and wife. Why not? He was honest and hardworking and smart. She could do worse, and she fancied him, he was sure of it. Of course, the two of them together, really together, wasn't a practical idea, but it certainly made a good daydream.

Standing at the bar now, waiting for his drinks, Mick turned to watch the room again, to watch its endless mixture of people and find Winnie among them — at which point he found himself staring at Why-not: Winnie, with her damn blouse off, talking to a toff out slumming.

Mick had seen the man come in. It happened occasionally. An upper-class fellow wandered over from Covent Garden after an opera or such, looking for a little . . . mud. The bloke was chatting Winnie up, probably thinking her a tavern wench. Ha, he was in for a surprise.

Mick, though, got a surprise, too. Winnie answered the fellow in a friendly manner, instead of with her usual tartness, and, of course, the moment she opened her mouth and her sweet, soft voice came out — the smooth-as-cream upper-

class tune in it — well, anyone could see the fellow's response from across the room. The man liked his surprise.

Mick didn't like his: Suddenly Winnie and the toff over by the dancing stage were having a fine old talk, two peas in a pod. She was laughing with the man, smiling at him, wagging her finger at something he said.

Charlie put the drinks down, a *thunk-thunk,* as Mick turned and left them behind.

He cut straight through the crowd, shoving people, using his size to get through. Damn it, he didn't like the way the man nodded and leaned toward her.

As Mick came up to them, the arsehole asked her, "So, having a little 'outing,' are we?" *We?* He and Winnie were no *we,* and Mick was about to tell him so.

He could have saved himself the worry. The second Win saw him, her face lit. She turned toward him, ignoring the other man. "Where are the drinks?" she asked.

He didn't have them. She laughed. Never mind. She grabbed Rezzo's beer from him, took a swill, then wiped her lips demurely with her fingertips. All was forgiven. Mick was confused. What had just happened?

Then more amazing: Winnie leaned forward onto her toes and planted a quick, damp kiss on his cheek. As she clambered back up onto his chair, then the table, he was left holding his face where her wet, cool mouth had touched him.

Stunned. Oh, Win. . . .

She began her dancing again. He laughed. A madwoman. Mad to dance. She couldn't get enough. She was too eager to be about her own entertainment than to be bothered with a toff out on the town. Mick let it go. She danced. He watched. So did the toff, he noticed. So did a lot of the men. Who wouldn't? Whenever she'd stop long enough to get a drink of water, the fancy fellow, though, tried to make conversation.

Mick listened to him ramble, paying less attention to what he said than how he said it. He put *bloody* into the middle of everything: hoo-bloody-rah, abso-bloody-lutely. When he asked Winnie to step out front with him "where it isn't so noisy," Mick interceded. He put his hand over the fellow's reaching arm and said, "Not bloody likely."

The man looked at him. Mick realized he assumed they were the same, two toffs wanting the same bit of wild skirt, a lady out for a good time. Hell, the man couldn't have been more wrong about everything, though it made Mick frown at Winnie. Something was different about her, something nice, something he liked. Though somehow it worried him, too.

Then she became reassuringly the same. With all the starchiness she was capable of, Winnie said to the man, as if he were insane to have imagined differently, "I'm not going anywhere with you." She looked perfectly startled to have to inform him of the fact.

Thank you, loovey, Mick thought.

The fellow accepted her decision, though he handed her a quinine, which Mick might have complained about if he hadn't forgotten his own drinks at the bar and Winnie hadn't looked so thirsty. While she drank it, in under a minute, the toff mentioned he was in London for a horse auction, obviously trying to impress her.

Mick folded his arms. Hell. In the minute, off-hand, in passing, they talked about breeding horses — for Ascot as opposed to good carriage horses — what it took to breed good hunting dogs, and where to buy a Van Dyke, whatever that was.

Winnie could talk to the fellow about these things. She knew all about them; she had lived in his world. Lived there still to a degree. He said to himself, She's the daughter of a marquess, for godssake, Mick. You're thinking you'll just up and marry a marquess's daughter? Then what? Haul her off to the country in a donkey cart? If you can find a donkey cheap enough?

What was so god-bless special about her anyway? Yes, she was quite the classy lady. Sweet, kind to people; kind to him. She was about as intelligent a woman as he'd ever known, and he liked that about her. He liked that she was sensitive and careful, even if she was so careful sometimes she made herself crazy. And pretty, Lord, she was pretty to him — in a unique way that no other woman could duplicate.

A smooth-skinned, strong-featured face. Very

English. Beautiful coloring. An elegant height. Substantial. With pretty little breasts. A fine, grand bottom. And, of course, the damnedest legs a man might ever know. Lord, he'd like to see those legs, bare again, just one more time before he died.

He loved Winnie's body. It was odd, but Mick could no long remember if he'd always liked this shape in a woman, then Winnie came along and filled the bill. Or if he liked this shape because it was the shape of Winnie Bollash.

When he came down to it, he just didn't know. It was a mystery to him why he liked her so well, why he wanted her. A mystery usually summed up with the phrase: *I'm in love with the woman.*

And there it was, for better or worse. His worry. He was in love with Winnie — with Lady Edwina Bollash — a lady he couldn't carry off and have forever. It was going to break his heart to leave her. But he was going to have to, and that was a fact. He was going to have to leave her to the likes of the toff.

By midnight, the crowd had thinned enough that in a cramped, crowded way, couples, now most of them to one degree or another drunk, clung to each other in what might have been called dancing. That section of the floor swayed again to the music, slowing along with the girls who moved more languorously on the tabletops — only three survived: Nancy, a girl named Lolly, and Win, his sweet Win. Mick didn't know

if Winnie were aware of it or not, but her own movements had become willowy, softly undulant. Sultry. He was riveted.

The lordly fellow hung on, too. He wouldn't leave, and he wouldn't stop staring. It hadn't bothered Mick that any man in the room looked at her, not up to this point. He was damn proud to know her, to watch her make herself happy in a way that didn't hurt anyone — in a way, in fact, that made a lot of other people damn blissful. The men in the room were pretty much mesmerized by tall Win moving her long body.

Now, though, even though the upper-class fellow was being perfectly polite about his interest, Mick wanted to throttle him. For no good reason at all. Or no, for the simple reason that he had the good taste to watch the prettiest woman in the room dance better than anyone else. Winnie certainly had a way of moving to music. She'd said it was Strauss in her blood, but tonight it was gypsy. Sweet gypsy Win.

He realized after a while that he and the other fellow were standing shoulder to shoulder, watching her, though his own shoulder was a good six inches higher.

The other man noticed, too. "Can't help but observe," he said, "we both have good taste." Then he asked, "Is she yours then, mate?" He didn't own the word *mate*; it wasn't his. He was being chummy, trying to adopt the vernacular of the place — possibly because he'd noticed Mick had command of it.

"Yes," Mick said. It was simpler than explaining.

Then stupid Winnie, fresh from huffing and puffing her way off the table, stepped down and chimed in, "I'm not his. I'm not anyone's." She looked right at Mick when she said it, as if he should contradict, but how could he? She wasn't.

The fellow arched a self-important, condescending eyebrow at Mick and shifted his gaze to her, smiling. "May I buy you a drink then?"

"No," she said cheerfully. "I'm drinking with him."

"I could buy you something much fancier. I'm a baron's son." The awkward announcement, if it were true, was meant to convey he had money, connections, a way of wooing beyond the Bull and Tun.

Mick told him, just as cheerfully as Winnie, "You could be the son of a whore, and no one would care."

The other man jerked, blinked at him. Mick half-hoped he would rise to the insult. He would have been happy to level the arsehole. He hadn't hit anyone in years, and tonight felt like a splendid night for it. He was angry over something — over something larger than a stupid nob making eyes at Winnie. Still, whatever it was, he'd be only too happy to take it out on a mouthy fellow with more gall than a monkey pulling his own tail.

Now, it was Mick's experience that other men

didn't lightly test out the truth behind his mean look. He didn't even have to make it all that hateful. It was one of the joys of being a tall, powerfully built man that his confrontations rarely escalated into physical matches of brawn. He was usually the declared winner by virtue of the other fellow taking a good look at him. So he let this other fellow study him.

Then Winnie pushed him. "Stop. Don't cause trouble." Oh, fine, now *he* was causing trouble. She looked down at his hands, both fisted together, and frowned. "Whatever happened to the drinks you were bringing us?"

Ah, the ale and shandy he'd left on the bar half an hour ago. They'd be gone by now. He tried to sidestep his way around her question. He didn't want to leave her, not now. But she was hot and thirsty, and there was no getting around her saying so.

"Go on," she told him and pushed him in the chest again. She used her full, flat palm, which he caught and held against him a moment, rubbing it up his shirtfront an inch, holding it to him. *Yes, touch me, Win.*

It felt so good, her hand on him. Better still, the way her eyes met his made him feel like a bloody king. The male grit and gripe of him relieved in one direction and expanded in another. He wanted her. He wanted her right now. If there hadn't been a law against it, he'd have thrown her on the table and had her. That is, if there hadn't been a law and a lot of people and if

Winnie herself weren't, almost certainly, opposed to the idea.

Unaware of the way his mind worked, she absently wet her lips and curved them up for him, her expression glowing — full of promise he doubted she understood, that she didn't mean.

"All right," he said. A drink for Winnie.

He went, watching her and the fancy, irksome fellow over heads and between shoulders as he shoved his way to the bar. Winnie didn't even look at the man, though, horse's arse that he was, he remained at her side, trying to get her to. At the bar, Mick played the same sort of game, torturing himself by looking for them through the crowd as he waited for the drinks. He tapped his fingers, hurried Charlie up, grabbed the mugs, then pushed his way straight back across the room.

Just as he came up, Winnie managed to rid herself of the upper-class nuisance. Yes, a nuisance, Mick thought. That's all the man was to her. Lord Baron's Son moved off, wisely shifting his interest to Nancy, telling her something that made her spill her beer laughing. Anticlimactic. One of Mick's newer words. It was perfectly accurate.

He was left with no place to put all the crazy feelings that raced around inside him.

He handed Win a half pint of straight ale. "Here," he said. "Drink up. You look as if you could use it."

She waved her hand in front of her face, an ex-

aggerated fanning gesture, and smiled. "Hot," she said.

Wisps of hair clung to her neck. Sweat ran down her throat in two neat rivulets, one of them sliding between her breasts as he watched, making him curve the tip of his tongue to the back of his teeth. Yes, Winnie was roasting, he thought. He watched her chug the ale a little quicker than she should. As she drained it, he caught her eye over the rim of the mug. He tipped his head sideways, a nod toward the door at the back. Night air.

She nodded quickly. "Oh, yes, that sounds good."

He set his own drink down, untouched, and took her hand. It felt thin and fragile, soft. He rubbed his fingers over the knuckles as he led her through the room to the back. There, he pushed the door open, then leaned, holding it to let her go first. She brushed his chest as she walked past, out into the night, out onto the stoop, then down the one step to the ground; she walked into the dark.

He followed. It was surprisingly cool outside, quieter, though the music still rattled behind them. He came closer to her as his eyes adjusted, then saw the glimmer of her bare arms as she wrapped them around herself in front. He watched her silhouette from the back. Her pale neck in the moonlight that came between buildings into the alley. Without all her clothes up around it, her neck was long and slender, supple.

Her shoulders were rounded. He knew from the shadows and her posture that the muscles of her back were lean and strong; she would have a beautiful back.

He reached, rubbed his palms over her shoulders and down her bare arms, to her elbows. She shivered, making a lovely, light sigh, then surprised him by stepping back against him. Ooh, more promises, Win. With her nestled there in his arms, he took his right hand and lifted a strand of hair that had fallen to her left shoulder. He brushed it back up then gently continued, pushing her head over to make an open place, opening up the vulnerable curve of her neck.

He bent his head into the exposed crook and kissed her there as he pulled her strongly into him, wrapping his arms around her. He more or less ate her neck — lips, teeth, tongue — all the way up to the edge of her jaw where it met the back of her ear, then all the way down again to where her collarbone met her shoulder. It was a delicious stretch of skin.

She shuddered and gave him access while molding her back against his chest.

His, he wanted to say. *Me. Only me.* But he didn't have the right.

Just a compelling inclination. A relentless drive down one narrow train of thought that carried him, again and again and again, to the same conclusion. He needed to have her. He needed to put himself inside Winnie, into the sweet, dark privacy of her, and stroke himself there till he

came — h-h-o, God help him.

Putting words to his strongest wish made his head swim. It made the world tilt under his feet. He told himself, Time to think with something other than what was coming to attention in his trousers. Get yourself on the straight and narrow here, Mick. Winnie wouldn't like all this.

But he kept kissing her neck, because Winnie wasn't the same tonight, and any fool could see it.

God help him.

He wanted a woman who could talk about horse auctions and Van-whatever-they-weres, who could teach a man to talk till his friends hardly knew him. Yes, God help him, he thought.

Because all he could think about was how to get this woman back further into the dark.

Chapter 22

The back door of the Bull and Tun gave onto a little alley lit only by the tavern sign's gaslight on the street, an illumination so faint Winnie hadn't noticed it till her eyes had gotten used to the dark. She stood at the edge of the alley, in front of a small, one-step stoop. There was a similar stoop down thirty feet, its door giving into another part of the public house, the dim filtered glow from it indicating it was a kitchen. Behind her, she didn't know what Mick was doing or why he'd stepped back. She turned, rubbing her arms, trying to find him in the shadows. He'd stooped. She couldn't see his movement. Then she realized he was anchoring the door open with a rock, letting some of the heat out for everyone else. The pub had become a furnace inside. How considerate of him, she thought. She waited, her neck feeling bare for his having left it, her arms and back cool from his absence, but she knew he wouldn't leave her here alone for long.

He'd brought her outside to kiss her, and she didn't even have to ask.

The music was softer here in the alley, though the rhythm was just as toe-tapping. Winnie felt a

surge of happiness as a breeze blew her chemise flat to her; it clung to her corset where it was wet from the perspiration of her body. She turned to stare back into the tavern a moment, through the doorway, grateful to be out of the humid heat of bodies.

Another wave of good cheer came over her. She felt lucky all at once, though she couldn't have said why. She felt fortunate somehow, blessed by life. The breeze whipped up again, cool, blissful on her skin. She could look up and down the alley; it was open, a little pass-through delivery road at the back of the Bull and Tun. A smell wafted on the wind. Winnie located it vaguely in the dark — ten feet away was a huge bin of bottles and pub accouterments, not the kitchen bin but the bar bin. Its smell was as yeasty as a brewery, earthy in a way that wasn't bad yet was strong enough to encourage her to move away.

She had to laugh at herself. Lucky. Lucky to be standing in an alley, damp, not quite wearing enough clothes for the night, while smelling old beer bottles and tap tubing.

Oh, yes, and this: Lucky to be caught around the waist by a long, muscular arm. She let out a delighted, long laugh as Mick took hold of her again.

"Come here," he said.

He pulled her into the dark that he'd made by opening the door. It cut off the light from the tavern sign at the street, while the light from the

kitchen wasn't enough to make it into the corner between stoop and wall. Oh, yes, so considerate. He'd made them a private, invisible niche.

This was where he first kissed her in earnest, really kissed her. He took her by the hips and guided her, backing her up against the bricks, putting her where he wanted, into this wedge of lightless space. Then he brought his body, his mouth up against her. No sight, Mick blocking off all the light. There was only the feel of him and the heat from dancing hard and the rich, organic taste of his mouth, malt blended with hops.

Oh, glorious, she thought, as his tongue touched hers. He pressed her mouth open, and she didn't even have to tell him she wanted him to. But she did, oh, she did. He kissed her openmouthed again, as he had that time in his bedroom. Exactly right, without asking. Oh, yes! It was perfect. A big, lush kiss with the full of his mouth, his hands down her back, his body pressed to her. How strange, how right. She didn't know what she was supposed to do from here, but she would let him figure it out, let him lead the way. She wanted more. More, Mick.

While Mick thought, What naïveté. He could feel her willingness to go beyond a kiss — just as he could sense her ignorance of what "beyond" meant.

He tried to tell her. "Winnie." He pulled back from kissing her neck. "Do you know I want your

skirts up again? I want your skirts up and these"
— he pulled at the ribbons and lace at her shoulders — "all these" — she wore all manner of covers and corsets and liners and lace — "down. I want your clothes around your waist."

His honesty took her aback, though she laughed at it. "You can't have that," she said.

"I think I can. That's what I'm saying. The time to change your mind is now."

She laughed again, so confident of herself in her innocence. "Fine, then," she said. "Let me go. I'll go in." When he said nothing, she said, "You agree not to then?"

"I agree not to make you do anything you don't want to."

This reassured her. Though he kept her pinned there in the dark corner between door and wall. He knew what business he was about.

Oh, he wanted to lick her body, gently bite the insides of her thighs — taste them, eat his way up. He had no idea what he was going to do exactly. He only knew that the flashing images in his mind were full of sexuality; he was steaming with it. He suspected he would shag her here, that when they went back inside, it would be without her virginity. She didn't take him seriously though.

So much for warning her. He kissed her again. Again, she opened to it; she warmed to his deep kiss, a woman of growing experience.

He should be warning himself, he thought. God bless, the large, bold physicality of tall

Winnie. So undeniable in sheer physical presence. If she had any idea how appealing she was, it would give her far too much the upper hand. He'd never tell her, he promised himself. She'd never guess. He'd never let her know the degree of attraction he felt.

As if he could keep it a secret. Delicately, as he kissed her, he rubbed his thumbs along the bone of her shoulder, till he managed to slide lace and ribbons and gauzy stuff down. Flesh. He shivered. He bent his head to kiss her bare shoulder. Then she jumped and caught her breath as he peeled the neckline a fraction lower and exposed a firm little breast.

"O-o-oh," she said in her soft upper-class voice. "Oh-h-h." As if exclaiming at a tea party. He loved the sweet, proper sound of her.

He loved making nonsense of it. Her breast jutted over the top of her rigid corset. It was tiny in his large hand, soft against the calluses at the inside of his knuckles. Kneading it made her go into a panting kind of flurry, not one of prohibiting him so much as trying to take all the newness of it in. He squeezed and tugged the nipple between his thumb and palm. So sweet. So small, and soft as down. God, how lovely she was.

She put her hand to his, trying quietly to inhibit it as she murmured complaint. "Too small," she said. Her breast embarrassed her.

"Just right. A mouthful." He bent his head and swallowed it up.

She leaped, started with a kind of mild, willing

panic. He could feel her heart. It beat so hard he could count the thuds through his lips when he took her breast all the way into his open mouth, pressing his lips to her chest. All the while, she whispered a kind of litany into the dark, "Oh, God. Oh god, oh god, ohgod, ohgod, ohgod. . . ."

From here, he tried to raise her skirts, but she wouldn't let him. She still had enough presence of mind to say, "No," quite clearly. It echoed softly in the dark.

All right. He pulled her floundering hands to his shoulders, laying them at the back of his neck to show her what to do with them. He bent his head again, suckling and nipping at the one breast, then, pushing the gauzy fabric and ribbons off the opposite shoulder, he exposed the other to the night air and his mouth. He wet first one, then the other with kissing. Her breasts, two perfect little bon-bon–sized bites he tormented with his tongue.

"Lord," she said, then repeated that, too, as if her mind when aroused were prone to sticking like a needle in the groove of her gramophone. "Lord. Lord, lord, lordlord, lordlord. . . ."

She became unintelligible, guttural, just sounds in her throat as he teased the soft little tip with his teeth.

She arched, knocking her head on the wall.

"Easy there," he whispered.

"Oh, stop, Mick. I can't — I don't —"

He used his knee to open her legs — and she

helped, a tentative little piece of cooperation. He leaned into her and, even with all their clothes between them, his body found the right place. Through their clothes, it dropped into the small cove of her sex, as if it had found home. He let out a long, deep groan, growl-like in his attempt to keep himself from calling out. God in heaven, he'd found paradise.

He wanted the impossible. More. "Straddle your legs." He breathed out soft laughter at his own nerve at what he was willing to say to Win. But he wanted it. "Do it," he said. "As if there were a horse under you. Make your legs wide, loovey, and bring one up. Here."

She let him find the back of her thigh through her dress, then lift her leg up and around his waist. He wrapped her long, luscious leg around and behind him, then pressed her heel into his buttocks. "Like that," he said. "Ooh, yes, like that." His head swam in carnal pleasure. He reeled from it.

If he could have gotten her skirts up, fine gentleman that he was, he would have had intercourse right then. He'd have plunged in, burying himself in her. Instead, he-didn't-know-how-many layers of fabric, skirts, petticoats, trousers prevented it. He was left with pressing his erection along her, rocking, stroking the full length of his penis in the slight depression of her female sex, through clothes and all.

He stroked himself, up then back, driving himself along her, till he throbbed, hot and swollen,

almost painful. He let out a groan, and it could have passed for anguish.

In a way, it was. "Aa-a-h!"

So harsh, their passion. So strong. If he could ever get her to release herself into it, they would climb mountains of it, sink into oceans of it, cleave the earth, if they weren't careful. The attraction between them was huge.

He tried to raise her skirts again.

"Someone will see," she protested.

Not unless someone walked outside, he thought, who could see in the dark.

He made note though: her objection was no longer her own, but belonged to "someone" else.

He might have simply proceeded from there to have her. In his arms, she trembled and shook. He sensed her will shift.

He owned it.

But the word *alley* sobered him. A miserable, rational voice said, Listen, Gentleman Mick, the reality is: you don't take a virgin for her first time, a kind, gentle lady who's been sheltered most of her life from the facts of men and women, in an alley behind a tavern. Whether you love her or not, you don't do it. If you love her, especially you don't.

Right. Yet another voice demanded, Now. Have her now. Just a little coaching, a little wooing, and she's yours.

Reality. He hated it. Someone truly could see, if they came out with a lantern. No, he should walk her back inside. He should be satisfied for

now — Winnie had surrendered. Out of respect for that, he should take her home and make love to her properly, where there was privacy and dignity and sweetness.

Yet something prevented him from letting go of the moment. Somehow, now, right now, it wasn't enough. His body — no, his spirit felt arched, taut and bent to the point of breaking. A voice howled, Not enough!

Before he could move from this place, he wanted to possess her in some way. He felt hungry for it, famished, emaciated, needy. Like a beggar in the street; give me. Like a thief; I want.

He began to make promises to himself. And to her. "Let me touch you," he said, gathering her skirts again slowly, trying not to frighten her into shoving them down. He put his foot on the edge of the stoop to better support her raised leg. "I want to touch you, then we'll go."

Winnie mumbled something. She made no sense. Her leg grew slack, relaxed over his. She was trying to pull the shoulder of her camisole up, but only succeeded in pulling the ribbon out of its casing. She wasn't able to pull herself together. And despite all good intentions, Mick didn't want to help her.

Not enough. It was heaven to hear the sound of her fluster. Winnie, undone, breathing like a woman aroused, talking like a woman in a stupor. Touch her. The thing he hadn't been allowed to do before. Do it now. Touch her between her legs. And not just through her

351

knickers. Touch her, really touch her.

What insanity. What an outrageous thing to want of her in an alley. As a token. Yet he'd never known her as she was, without her lists and organization and proper demeanor. How to keep her like this? How to never let her back into the safe place of her propriety?

Take her now. Yes, that would do it. You have her where you want her. Take her now. What if whatever had changed her here tonight is gone tomorrow? Or, worse, is gone by the time you get her into the carriage? What if it disappears between here and home? Take her.

No. No. Though, as a kind of compromise — a reward for his heroic self-denial — he kissed her again while, through her skirts, he grazed the front of her body. Through fabric, he touched across the private female place with the tips of his fingers. She jumped, but she didn't pull her leg away from him. He kissed her deeper, and she dug her heel into his buttocks, moaning softly.

He slid his hand along her raised leg, going along it up under her skirts. Along a silk-stockinged calf that went forever, up underneath the humid warmth of her to a knee inside the wide leg of her knickers. Though it was as wide as a small skirt, her knickers snugged toward her hips. He smoothed his hand across her knickers at her abdomen, then around. He explored where they met her corset with the flat of his hand, front and back, trying to understand the construction of her underdrawers, while he

fought a head-spinning delirium of lust. Her knickers buttoned down the back, he realized. Down the back all the way under the crotch to midway in front.

Well. What innovation. With the tips of his fingers, he found the strategic buttons and began flipping them through the buttonholes, opening her knickers down the low curve of her backside and under.

Then he slid his hand inside, touching the bare curve of buttocks, the cleft where the two moons of her rounded together — and the earth beneath his feet shifted under him. He gripped her as his hand found her bare bottom, the flesh soft, dewy, and smooth, like the petals of flowers. Oh, the pleasure of touching her. He thought he would die of it.

While Winnie felt herself alive with it. Her pleasure was nervous: excited, astounded; unknowing, apprehensive. Before, Mick had touched her through her knickers. Now his hand was inside them. Lord, what did that mean? This wasn't wild. It was impossible, unimaginable. And pleasure, oh, the pleasure of it.

He reached behind her and tugged her knickers out from under her corset. He found the rest of the buttons at the back. With one hand, he undid them completely, then folded them forward onto her own leg. Then, with no leave or hesitation, he slid his hand over her knickers, under her body, between her legs. His palm took possession of her naked pudendum.

She jumped then grew utterly still. Shame. That was what the word meant. *Pudendus*, the Latin for *worthy of shame*. And she felt it. Shameful, how her body sang at his touch. She wanted to close her legs for the disgrace of it, take her leg down; yet his elbow clamped her leg to his waist, holding it there, and she was glad.

"Let me," he whispered so softly it was without voice, just his air forming the words at her ear. More hushed sounds, he told her, "It will be all right." So quiet, she could hear the faint contact of his perfectly articulated T's.

She nodded, though her body kept spasming in strange reaction. Yes. If he wanted to, she trusted him. She let him have his hand under her skirts, her underthings down, her legs open to him; free rein.

Indeed, who else might she give this to but Mick? Who else could she follow into the world and all its experiences? Who else but the man she watched with unceasing interest? Whom she delighted in? The man who made her laugh and feel good, who responded sometimes more honestly than she did to her own hurt and joys?

Who else but the man she loved?

She let him slide his hand over her, inward, cupping, then out. In truth, she would have let Mick lay her down onto the cobbles of the alley, put his weight on her and do whatever a man did to a woman. All resistance left — she felt it go as if her veins opened — as he cupped his hand to her. If he had chosen to murder her in this mo-

ment, she would not have put up a fight.

She leaped slightly when his fingers burrowed slightly, then nearly climbed up over his back as they found her. So new, the sensation. And powerful. All her senses, her mind drew into focus on the spot where he pressed her flesh apart. His fingers touched inner layers. Slick. She was slick. Why? She was messy. That couldn't be right —

"Aa-ah," she said, her muscles jumping and jerking. His thumb found a sweet, secret place that, when he touched it, made her see stars. Little, ecstatic exclamation points of sensation.

She knew nothing of her body here. To find it all so sensitive amazed her. To discover he knew all about her body, more than she did, astounded even more. Thank God he did though. He stroked her exactly right; he knew better than she how to stir up pleasure, more than pleasure, a hypnotic, physical joy so compelling it absorbed every corner of her mind. She tried to analyze it, understand, but couldn't make her attention do anything for longer than a second. Her mind wanted to feel, simply feel, nothing else.

"Let go, Win," he murmured. "Stop thinking."

His head bent, his silky hair touching her chest as he lightly bit the tip of her breast. Then he slid his finger deeply into her, all the way inside her.

"H-hah, h-hah —" She jerked as her diaphragm sent spasms of air through her lungs. "H-ho, H-hooh —"

He drew his finger out, pulling more wetness

along her flesh. Her knee buckled. He had to support her. He touched what she wasn't sure she'd even known about, didn't think about, a part of her own body she had never looked at or touched. Absurd. His finger hit upon where his thumb had been before. More star-bright bits sparked in her mind. By comparison, they darkened everything else. Sensation became only this. The dark fog of his knowing fingers, sliding, warm . . . making sparks of perfect pleasure along her nerve endings, bliss so pure and glistening it was blinding. It obliterated the rest of her senses, incapacitated all other awareness. A steady heat built, one made up of these sparks . . . snapping, becoming more and sharper . . . a rising rapture taking her up and up to God knew where. She knew a tension . . . something coiling in her belly, tighter, stronger. Then it suddenly released in an instant of crystal-clear, physical euphoria at the center of her, a spilling of this so intense she let out a cry.

She tried to hold back her own voice, but sounds, soft animal noises erupted from her mouth, noises as she could never remember speaking. Low groans, strained mewlings that, had she allowed it, would have come out nearer to screams. Her body jerked from the effort of holding it back. The pleasure was so acute. . . .

Once, as a child, she'd been stung by bees. Half a dozen minute, quick, angry stings that hit her nerves, shooting their little pinpoints of pain everywhere. Her pleasure was like that, though it

spread more evenly, more liquid somehow, as if pinpoint droplets of stinging ecstasy dropped into her, a thousand tiny droplets of it hitting her then expanding across the surface of her senses until sensation ringed and rippled to silence.

She calmed slowly, smoothing out into a glassy peacefulness. She shivered once, then curved into Mick's chest. He kissed the crown of her head as he straightened her skirts, fixed her camisole at her shoulders; putting her right. She stood there inside his arms for a full minute at least, perhaps more, letting him rearrange her — aware that she had never in all her adult life known such a thorough trust.

Another person, a man — Mick, dear Mick — had done this to her. She'd given over all her defenses, and it had been just fine. Better than fine. Better than anything she could have thought of on her own.

"I'm taking you home," he murmured. "I'm taking you home and making love to you all night, Winnie." He lifted her face to him by her chin and kissed her mouth again, intimately but so gently this time. Mouth and tongue. Then softer still, he said, "Let's go rid you of your infernal virginity. I hate it. I want it gone."

Yes. She was absolutely in favor of the notion. She wanted to do away with it, too. She wanted to hand it to him like a gift. Here.

Chapter 23

Winnie followed Mick into the tavern, his warm fingers wrapped around her own as he pulled her lolling self along a bit faster than she might have chosen. She felt dreamy, unable to focus. She kept thinking, Mmmm, make love to her all night. Yes. Mick, with his strong body and knowing hands. Make love. Whatever that meant, she wanted it in all its glory.

In contrast, the man who dragged her along by the hand was a man on a mission, focused enough for both of them. Without breaking pace, he picked up her blouse and jacket and hat, his own coat. They were almost to the door when the baron's son, who'd given them a bit of trouble earlier, decided to go for broke.

"Well, well, well," he said. Winnie hadn't been aware he was near, till her grabbed her round the hips. She was pulled in two directions for a second, till Mick realized she was hung up somehow.

He turned, saw. Then even Winnie pulled back as far as his grip on her hand would allow. His face was frightening for a moment — she'd never seen such instant and open rage come over a man.

"Get your hand off her," he said.

The other man was drunk, she realized. He said, "Why don't we ask the lady? Perhaps she'd like someone who'd entertain her in the West End of town."

Winnie would never have believed what happened next if she hadn't seen it. Mick raised one eyebrow, lifted his head a degree, then his lip, a lordly sneer if ever she'd seen one. "You?" he said with a derisive snort. His posture changed. He was acting, but what an actor he was. He could have been on the stage. His stance became at once hostile and arrogant: the full male challenge of superiority.

The other man was briefly hesitant. He hadn't expected such an aggressive and immediate confrontation after Mick's last concessions to peace. Unfortunately for him, he recovered himself. He leered at Winnie — he honestly leered, which in a strange way flattered her. She hadn't realized she was sufficiently interesting to generate a leer. Then he floored her further: "I say the lady stays. I want to see her dance again with those long, beautiful legs."

Goodness, other men thought they were pretty!

To Winnie, the young blood said, "You are without doubt, miss, the most attractive" — he laughed — "and tallest woman I have seen all evening."

Winnie wanted to hug him, give him a big kiss for saying something so nice. Though of course

such behavior would never do.

Mick, as it turned out though, wanted to kill him for saying the same words. He clenched and bared his teeth, then spoke through them. "You aren't seeing anything, except possibly my fist in your face. Get out of the way."

"A baron takes precedence over —"

Mick interrupted with a snort, a truly convincing display of contempt, and talked over him to say, "What makes you think you're the only blood to slum on a Wednesday evening? What makes you think you are and I'm not, you silly pisspot?" He took a step toward the man, pulling Winnie around and behind him. "And I do believe a viscount goes in to dinner before a man who's not a baron but only a baron's son. You go in dead last. And with this lady you don't even start."

Well. He'd learned his lessons on protocol. How nice. Though she could think of better circumstances for him to use them.

The fellow made the mistake of believing, however — now of all times — that Mick was truly a gentleman: that he had some restraint.

He moved a step toward Winnie, and Mick hit him: in the face, the stomach, then kneed him in the groin. The precious gentleman out to see the "low sights of London" saw the lowest — the floor — so fast, Winnie didn't have time to screech till he was down on it, and there was no point in saying anything.

The sound that came out of her was a high-pitched chirp.

"Come on," Mick said to her. He took her hand again. To his friends behind them, he said, "Can you get the bloke some water, help him up when he gets his breath back?"

Winnie left feeling dizzy. Two men had fought over her, a baron's son had been leveled for want of her. She'd been the toast of a tavern. She'd kissed the man she loved in an alley till her nerves were jumping like a warehouse of fireworks touched by a match.

What a perfectly wonderful night!

In the carriage, Mick kissed her fiercely. He kissed her and kissed her and kissed her, but a strange thing happened. Instead of his doing all the horrible things he'd promised, as he kissed her he grew *less* ardent.

Till he suddenly stopped and moved away. For the last five minutes of the ride home, he stared out the window, not saying a word.

She'd done something, Winnie thought. She'd made him angry. She'd upset him. She'd behaved badly. Something.

Then no. It came to her: She had done absolutely nothing she could think of and, given that to be true, she needn't feel guilty about anything. She'd had a marvelous time and given him every — and she did mean every — consideration. He was being sullen all on his own.

Jealous. When the word came to her, it made her jubilant. Mick, so clever at everything he did, so smart and handsome, so convincingly anything he wanted to be. *He* was jealous of the

baron's son — a real, if insipid, example of what he played at with more style and force than all the barons in the Doomsday Book. Well. She could deal with a little jealousy. How utterly delightful, she thought. She felt like Delilah — dangerously powerful: desired. She laughed to herself. It was the crowning cherry on top to a night of her ego's eating pure cream till it bloated.

Still, Delilah wasn't all that good for Samson. That wasn't the feeling she wanted most to know in any consistent way. What she wanted to feel again was the warm sense of herself when Mick looked at her and saw the real Winnie. She wanted him to *love* the real Winnie, the one with her ups and downs. The Winnie trying to become brave enough to reveal herself to him as completely as a person could.

She wanted an emotional corollary to what she'd done physically with Mick in the alley. She wanted the afternoon on the dance-room floor, only more and without fear. Trust. She wanted to trust him with all of herself, her body, her spirit, her emotions, her mind, right down to the most delicate, sensitive places of her human existence. She wanted to turn it over into his hands and see what he did with it. And she wanted something similar from him. She wanted to know him and touch him and have him believe in her generosity toward him.

She began to talk to him, trying to draw him out. There was no reason to be jealous. She

thought it was as simple as that. She wanted closeness.

While Mick withdrew. He felt a distance coming between them with the speed of a whistling wind.

He stung from his encounter with the idiot-lord, an idiot who nonetheless was authentically what he himself only pretended to be. For all his bravado, Mick felt like a forgery. Like the money he and Rezzo had made downstairs in the Bull and Tun's cellar. Almost as good, yet no matter who accepted the tender it was still something to hide, to fight doing again, to worry over: not real.

He'd felt tonight like a king to be among his friends, like a king when he kissed Winnie. But the stupid toff had set the truth on him like a pack of dogs: In the real world, he was king of the beggars — a fake lord, a good fake, but a real rat-catcher: He would never be good enough for Winnie Bollash.

He and Winnie. Whatever they were to each other, to extend it into the realm of mating was sham. Their relationship in this regard was as fake as Lord Tremore himself: It had no future.

Unmindful of the fact, she chatted softly at him as they entered her house. The hallway was dim. There was only the sconce lit at the end to provide enough light to enter safely. He stopped her from putting on the brighter lamp on the side table. He was too depressed to want her to see him clearly.

Milton, happily, had gone to sleep already. At

least they weren't required to make explanations for the careless way she laid her blouse, jacket, and hat on the side table. She hadn't bothered to put them on again, presumably too warm from her thrilling night.

Oh, he knew she was thrilled, and he was happy for her. He just wasn't too thrilled with himself or the role he played. Where was his real self? Where did this game end and where did he begin? He felt confused. And tired. And unhappy.

As Win walked to the stairs, she rambled and digressed, laughing, whispering intimate things to him. He loved her openness; he hated it. The social gap between them made it feel awful, like looking at a kindred spirit across that river Styx.

Of course, he could invite her downstairs to his room for a little lovemaking. They could have a fine old time, so long as they didn't make too much noise and wake her butler. Or he could go upstairs to her room, upstairs with a fancy woman who wanted an earthy good time, as he'd done half a dozen times.

He muttered curses under his breath as he paused at the newel post. He didn't want either of these things, yet he could find no equal footing. Perhaps there was none. He resolved to say good night quickly. Alas, nothing seemed more appropriate than they part here, that she go up her polished staircase, while he took the service stairs down.

But at the base of her polished staircase, she

touched his arm, drawing him literally closer as she laughed her way into another of her stories. He tried not to be interested, but ended up being taken in. He couldn't help it. He found Winnie, her life, endlessly entertaining.

"I was very young," she was saying. "It was Easter, and the parish church asked the children to bring tins of food for the poor. Only I misunderstood somehow. 'Bring tins,' I heard. I was fascinated by tins myself. I played with them, put holes in their shiny metal for candle holders, beat on them for music. I was allowed to have them from the cook. Anyway, I interpreted the priest's directive to mean that I was to bring empty food tins. My mother insisted I was wrong, but I was adamant.

"Then destroyed: for when I got to the church with my empty tins, everyone of course had brought full ones, which, the second I saw them, made ever so much more sense. I felt utterly bereft. I cried and cried with a sense of hopelessness for myself. How could I have made such a stupid mistake? I was humiliated. My mother was mortified. She made her usual to-do. 'I told you. But it is so like you, Winnie, not to listen to a word I say. I don't know what's to become of you. You look like a mantis and think like a mule.' Oh, what a scene she could make, what drama. I was a pigheaded child, difficult, selfish, the bane of her existence. And, that day, I agreed with her. I still do at times."

She sighed, laughing at her own story. "Though

not tonight," she said. She leaned back against the rails of the balustrade, the banister slanting upward over her head. She looked inviting. Her chemise was damp, its lace lying wilted against the curve of her breast. "Tonight," she said, the gypsy come-hither aura shining shyly again in her eyes: looking to be fanned to life. "Tonight I was no mantis."

"No," he said sincerely, wishing he didn't feel the truth of his words as sharply as he did. "Tonight you were the most desirable woman I have ever looked upon, ever watched move or draw breath."

Her breasts, there in the dim light of the hallway, swelled as she softly inhaled his compliment.

It was crushing to watch her. She was so full of life. Her mind was shining, bright. The beauty of it, of her here in the hallway, pierced him, the pain as exquisite as catching his fingertip in the spring of a trap: a pinch so hard it brought tears to the backs of his eyes. It ravished him; it shimmered and blurred his vision. Winnie, the beautiful, could be his.

Till the end of the week.

Then she couldn't.

Next week, he'd become a ratcatcher again. Or a valet perhaps, though now the two felt almost the same in light of the fact that neither were good enough for Edwina Bollash. Sunday morning, when the impossible magic of Emile and Jeremy Lamont evaporated, as in the fairy tale,

Michael's fine horses and clothing would return to Mick's rats and rags once more. He and this remarkable woman would no longer struggle with the make-believe of him. When he walked out her door — whoever, whatever he was — the only thing certain would be that neither his "what" nor "who" would be the equal of Edwina, Princess of the Empty Tins.

She was waiting for him to respond. She expected him to kiss her.

Mick smiled, hesitated. God knew, nothing would be so sweet as to make love to Winnie the gypsy girl tonight. Nothing better, that is, than making love to her while knowing it was no magic or pretense or heedless moment: that he could make love to her as his own, his other half, his mate.

He could pretend a lot of things. He could fake much. Yet he couldn't fake this: He couldn't pretend tonight was forever. Such a lie would have made his chest so tight no air could enter.

So he laid his palm against her face, as if he could touch for a second what was inside her bright, waiting expression. He smoothed his thumb down her soft cheek and met her glistening eyes — they were fixed on him in a way he would not easily forget. He leaned, pressed his dry lips to her forehead, drew the smell of her hair into his nose, his lungs, held it there, then pushed himself back and spun on his heels.

He turned and fled down the hall, across the dining room and into the half-kitchen, then

down the stairs and into the servants' quarters where — Milton was right — he belonged.

He ran like Freddie. Too many dark, ugly things down there, Mick. And the teeth are sharp; I know. Can't knowingly jump down into a rat's nest anymore. You just got to understand.

And he did. Oh, he did. Too well.

Mick was undressing for bed, the placket of his shirt open, his trouser braces dangling, standing there in his bare feet, his back to the door, when he heard her. He turned, expecting the sound was his imagination.

But no, there Winnie was, framed in his doorway. She'd rallied the courage to follow him downstairs — now of all times suddenly uncowed by the fact that Milton was asleep only three walls away.

"Well," Mick said, then couldn't think how to follow the pointless remark. It seemed rude to ask simply, *What do you want?*

How funny: Her eyes fixed at his chest. She loved his chest, and he loved that she did. She eyed what she could see of him inside his open shirt. It was a strain for her to bring her eyes up to his face, even though, clearly, she had something to say.

Bloody hell, he thought. She was finally going to say it. Something brave and romantic. Too late, he told himself. They were past where it would do them some good. Still, he listened attentively. He waited, half-hoping, half-fearing he

might finally hear "Kiss me" or "I love you." *I love you* would have been nice.

Instead, her sweet-soft, classy voice said, like silk, in her tea-party singsong, "I figured out what I want. I want you to be as naked as a statue: I want to see you in the rude with your widge hanging out."

Chapter 24

Mick burst out laughing. He tried to contain it, then couldn't. What release. "My widge?" he said finally. And that started him all over again. "Oh, God," he said, trying to get hold of himself. He put his hand in his hair and leaned his shoulder on the bedpost. He didn't know where to look. His widge? She wanted to see his widge?

Winnie smiled at his discomposure. She liked it. It made her bold. She told him, "You promised. You told me when I could say what I wanted, I could have it."

And so he had. "Winnie —"

He didn't know what to tell her. He touched his lip, in his distress forgetting for the hundredth time his mustache was missing. He shaved it off every morning, then forgot he had, at least once a day. He brought his hand down and tried telling this unusual woman the truth. "Winnie, I'm in love with you," he said.

It was not what she was expecting. She glanced down quickly. She couldn't look at him for longer than a second at a time, but her face filled with wonder. She was happy one moment, then sad the next. She finally squinched her face and

held his eyes long enough to ask mildly, "So that means you can't make love to me?"

He shook his head. "It means —" He couldn't explain it neatly. "It means I want more than I can have. And having a little, a taste, might hurt worse than having nothing at all." He shook his head again, frowned. "I wasn't prepared to feel as I do about you, Win."

With a new curiosity and a kind of timid, but growing confidence, she stepped into the room. "Mick," she said, "don't worry about the future so much that you make our present less than what it should be. We could die tomorrow." She spouted his own philosophy. "Anything could happen." She came to a stop right in front of him and whispered, "Make love to me now. Please."

He shook his head, then muttered, "No escape." It was true. He laughed helplessly at where he'd gotten himself. Up to his eyeballs here in trouble, and only able to dig himself in deeper. Muttering, still laughing, he looked at her and repeated, "In the rude? Honest to God, Win. With my widge hanging out? Where did you hear such a thing?"

"You said it."

He did? He sat down on the end of the bed, bewildered.

In the end, though, he knew what to do. He lifted his arms and peeled his shirt over his head. He wore no underclothes; he hated them and no one knew the difference. Until now. Winnie looked rather amazed by the fact.

He tossed the shirt, then patted the mattress beside him. "Right here, loovey. Put it here. The wicked widge of Michael Tremore would love to make your acquaintance."

Winnie only stood there.

After a moment, he complained with humor, "You tell me to make love to you. I tell you how to start, what I want you to do, then you won't do it. You are not the obedient girl you once were."

"I know." She smiled and murmured, "I want to see. Show me."

"Aah. The widge," he said. He felt himself lift — from simply the sound of her voice, the cool-soft, feminine plush of her saying in her tony English, *Show me*. Yes, he was going to have something to show her. "Close the door."

Winnie turned and leaned against the door, watching as Mick's dexterous fingers undid the buttons of his trousers. His long-fingered hands moved with a slow grace that was almost courtly as he opened them for her. She wet her lips and watched with concupiscent curiosity. Then started at what dropped into view. He continued, shoving his trousers down his legs, not the least bit inhibited. Already barefoot and bare-chested, once he stepped out of the wool worsted, he stood naked in front of her.

A statue, yes. Warm and breathing.

She watched the rise of his chest as she walked forward. She already knew he was broad and muscular through the chest and shoulders, but

she hadn't realized how narrow he was through the hips. Sturdy, but slender. His thighs were long and cut with muscle. But between his thighs —

She walked close, riveted. She said, "*That* wouldn't fit under any fig leaf. In fact" — she looked up into his face with a sudden frown — "that won't fit anywhere I know of."

"Oh, yes, it will." He laughed at her. "And perhaps I might mention" — he mocked himself — "it ain't a widge, loov. Not now." When she knit her brow, he explained, "It's a widge when it's quiet. Or when it's nosing around just a bit. At some point, though, Win, it becomes a cock: mine especially."

Whatever he called it, it was as stiff as the boom on a ship. It stood straight up, slightly mobile in an upward-angled way. As she inspected him, he took her hand, then leaped and gasped as if surprised when he placed it on him. Covering the back of her hand with his, he put pressure, sliding her palm slowly up and down him, pushing forward with his hips. He groaned from it, a single deep rasp of breath.

Then took her by the shoulders and turned her around toward the bed. "You can look more later. I'm sick with waiting, Winnie. I'm having."

Indeed, they were both past ready. The backs of her legs hit the bed, and he pushed her. She fell, a delicious plunge through the air that lifted her stomach and ended on bouncing bedsprings. He lifted her skirt and pushed her legs apart at

the same time, then got his knee between, on the bed, as he put his hand on her, rubbing between her legs, through her knickers. He rubbed for a moment, hard, a few times, then said, "Let's have done with these. Lift up, loov."

He stripped her knickers off, just like that, then lay over her, bringing his naked weight on top of her. Oh, his body. Free of his trousers, his penis fell heavily, nestling naturally into the sensitive crevice of her. They both leaped, tensed at the contact, caught their breaths in unison. She tried to relax again, though relaxing wasn't exactly what she wanted. She closed her eyes, then found her mouth kissed. Mick's mouth touched hers and she opened it to him, then his tongue penetrated this intimate place. Tentatively, she let her tongue push into his. He groaned, twisted his head, and went at her mouth harder, his body curving to her in rhythm.

It was the last she knew of sanity.

She knew the sliding of his body, a desire for the contact of skin that became a sliding everywhere and particularly a rhythmic grind of hips. His hands went into her clothes, owning the inside of them and her naked flesh . . . then the inside of her. He reached between them and did what he'd already done once tonight. He touched her inside.

"Aah!" she called out.

He made a low sound, something near a growl of satisfaction.

Their communion became the way it always

was with them: rough — not for what either one did, but from sensation itself. She wanted whatever he would do with an intensity she could never foresee. Then, with each contact, the feeling was so powerful, it seemed to knock her senses flat. She jumped and gasped through his stroking her, his rubbing his face against her cheek, his chest against her breasts . . . his hips . . . his finger moving in her. She loved it, yet her own ears might have doubted she loved anything. Sounds came out, not unlike those from an animal crying out, beaten, torn apart.

They touched each other with relative gentleness, yet they each reacted as if from violence: bombarded with pleasure.

Mick flinched and let out a long, dragging rasp of air, when all he did was open her with his fingers, then draw the head of his penis down her — she shivered with enough power to shake the bed — to where he could guide it with his hand. He was shaking himself and muttering epithets as he planted himself into position, then with a thrust of his hips — one, single, swift, elegant deflowering — he buried himself deeply into her and they both buckled up into each other as if reacting to being scorched.

"Gaw-aw-awd bah-less-s-s," he breathed out. "Be still oh be still," he warned.

Winnie couldn't have been anything else. Her body had contracted around his, arms, legs, torso, the very inside of her. It felt like what it was: her flesh torn. A strong pinch, then a burning. She lay

375

there, aware of the fullness of him. An alien, thick pressure, a weight that was surprising, yet satisfying, indescribably satisfying.

He began to unfold himself, move again. The burning lessened through friction. He withdrew then thrust again with the sure force of passion, a thrust then pull, each time flinching, his breath rasping with his deep bass groan. While each stroke made her dizzier, consciousness itself in question at the peak of full penetration. He pushed his hips, as if he couldn't get himself deep enough, yet each time the heat of him went so deeply into her body that it moved something inside, something unearthly and wonderful.

Winnie let instinct take control. She returned Mick's strength. She savored his power and her own. She loved his movement and the vigor of him that translated into a hardness not just inside her body but everywhere along him, in his muscle and sinew and bone, while she clutched this rock-solidness in his flexed shoulders, dug her fingers into them.

A fever took hold as if it flowed in her veins, as if she had grabbed hold of an electric wire charged with pleasure. Volts and volts of it. It coursed through her, leaving her helplessly connected to it while it traveled up her nerves. It gripped her — him, too, for he called out as he convulsed — and drove them into each other. Till it grounded, like lightning, down her spine into the low center of her, between her legs, shocks of bliss. . . .

In the throbbing aftermath, she felt the ghost of Mick's masculinity inside her, as if it were thunder, rolls and rolls of it in the distance, continuous. It resounded through her veins, booming, as she lay exhausted, leveled by it. As if she were singed from the bolts of their contact. Struck. Love-struck. She understood the analogy all at once in more particular detail. Yet was bewildered to understand that it came from something so simple and seen daily: the skin and muscle and heat of Mick's male body.

Winnie had had no idea. . . .

Mick pursued sexuality the same way he pursued everything else. For the rich, full joy of it and for all he was worth. He had a penchant for whispering wicked things in Winnie's ear. Oh, the horrible-delicious things he promised to do. Attacks, atrocities, on her modesty. And he liked her up against walls and straddling him on chairs and in his arms, rolling around in bed, not to mention once rolling around in the grass of the back garden in the middle of the night. Oh, the fine old time they had.

Lovers.

They were naked for most of the next three days. Milton became so put out with them, he went to his sister's. Mrs. Reed mysteriously didn't come at all. Mick and Winnie had the house to themselves. And they put their privacy to good use.

"Look," Winnie said one afternoon. She was

exasperated. "Look at these pathetic things." She glowered down at her breasts. "So small they don't round even a little. They point."

There on the bed, Mick looked as if from politeness, since she'd asked him to. His eyes, when they rested on her naked body, darkened; they became the green of a still sea reflecting black clouds overhead, the sky closed off, a black green, deep in hue. These eyes didn't miss a spot on her. If she showed naked flesh, they found it and stared.

They looked directly at her breasts now. Then Mick smiled. "Here, you complain you aren't petite, Win, when you have two somethings that are petite and don't even appreciate them."

"Petite breasts! Who wants petite breasts!"

"I do." His hands took them, one in each, curving his fingers around them as he rubbed his thumbs over the nipples, back and forth slowly. Back — "They are the sweetest little things I ever laid eyes on" — then slowly forth again — "or mouth on." He bent his head.

He opened his lips over her breast, widening his mouth enough to take the whole of it. Inside, he tongued the nipple and the area around it, while her entire breast sat enveloped in the warm, slick softness of his mouth. Then he slid his lips back up the little mound out to tip, riding the breast as he closed his mouth, sucking as he went, then nipped the tip with his teeth. She shivered. Both nipples puckered tightly.

"M-m-m," he said. He did the same trick to

the other one, leaving both her breasts wet and cool to the air when he was finished, their nipples little hard pebbles of sexual awareness. "M-m-m," he said again. "Warm little dumplings, sweet as cream."

And so it went. A man of many talents.

He could make his erect penis nod yes and no, on its own. He could move it left and right. Neither trick impressed her so much, though, as the fond relationship he had with his body that made him willing to entertain her with it.

"Imagine," she said. She took him into the grip of her fist, making Mick huff as he tried to maintain composure. "And only a moment ago you were half this size. How do you do it? How does it work?"

"H-h-ha-a-ah," he said at first. Then, "H-h-hyou do it." He grabbed her hand and pressed it to him, as if the pressure would relieve some of the delicacy of feeling. "You know how you're always worrying that you've done something you didn't mean to do?" he asked, then made a wicked laugh deep in his chest. "Well, this time, you have." He repeated, "You do it."

"I don't do anything." She teased him. She wanted him to say more.

He leaned his face into her neck and touched his tongue lightly to the spot where her jaw and ear and neck all met, then whispered, "You do. You make me hard." He bit the lobe of her ear. "Hard and long and thick as a post. You've been doing that to me for six weeks."

She laughed and lay back, happy. "I am strong," she said. It amazed and pleased her to think so. "Potent."

She was glad when he understood what she meant. "You are indeed. Heady stuff, Win. You are two-hundred proof, loovey." He whispered, "Do it some more."

They played like children. Adult children playing games all through the house. The time went by so quickly.

Winnie had to watch herself. By Saturday morning, she was daydreaming dangerously: of picking up and moving somewhere, of passing Mick off forever as . . . oh, a country gentleman. He could hunt rabbits with ferrets as some rural squires did. He and she could find a little cottage, live off whatever lessons she could give to the local girls. He'd mill about, just like a true gentleman; no gainful employ.

They were in the half-kitchen behind the dining room, when Winnie mentioned her fantasy to him, just to see what he'd say.

He didn't react as she'd have liked. "Ah," he said. "Like all the other fancy ladies. You want to buy a man to play with?" He guffawed over it, thought it hilarious, then added, "I never could understand that about gents, why they'd *want* not to do anything, no skill, no trade, no service to God or England."

Winnie wanted to discuss it seriously, though. She wagged a sausage at him. They were cooking

380

themselves breakfast.

"I don't understand what the joke is," she said. "Don't laugh. I'm serious."

He grew grave. Without a speck of his humor, he asked, "What? I'm supposed to do nothing? Have nothing of my own? And you teach who" — he corrected — "whom? Country girls? Country girls don't care how they talk. I know country girls. Milkmaids. Farmers' wives. Daughters of shopkeepers. No. You need a city and society mamas. I need my business or something like it, nothing you would approve of, but it meets my bills — and will afford me a wife one day when I decide to have one. You think it's beneath you."

He was gaining steam. It was apparently something he'd thought a lot about. "I'm telling you," he said, "useful work well done is something to be proud of. Thing is, you're a bit of a snob, loov. Not horrible. But the saddest part is you're a snob about you — you're too individual to conform to bland standards. You make yourself crazy trying to, then you don't even like yourself. You won't even let yourself go to the ball and have fun. You should. You should go the duke's house, dance holes into your slippers, and foke the bloody bastards who don't like it. Foke them all."

What a speech.

Winnie tried to absorb it. It made her heart race.

To lessen its impact, she tried to dismantle it.

She told him, "I don't know what that word means, though I'd wager you're saying it wrong."

"Which word?" He frowned.

"Foke."

"Ay!" he said quickly, turning on her with the fork he was using to cook sausage in the pan. He waved the implement. "That's not nice, Win. Don't say it."

"You say it all the time."

"Do I?"

She laughed, a belly laugh at finding him in this rare ignorance of himself. "Oh, yes. And I think, when you say *effing,* it's short for *foking.* What *does* it mean?"

He grinned sideways, then wiggled his eyebrows. Raising one in humor, he said, "I could show you." He pulled her into him and pressed his hips once. "This." He moved them again, and she liked it. She always liked it; it was such a wonder, his touch. "It means —" He looked for a phrase, a good example. "It means, Have it. Take life by the balls, Win. Take her, have her, mean old thing that she is. Foke her silly. Lap her up. Love her, why not?"

She giggled. "Women don't have balls."

He laughed, nuzzling her. He said into her hair, "Life does. Life has it all. And I love it, Win." Softer, she thought she heard, "I love you," but she couldn't have.

He wouldn't have said that. *In love,* yes. But not *I love you.* Mick was honest. He wasn't a man to court a woman with lies.

Then he said quite clearly, "So how would it be, after breakfast, before those stupid Lamonts arrive" — they'd sent a note that said they were bringing evening clothes, the invitation, and themselves at noon — "I take you upstairs one last time before we go and foke you silly? What do you think about that?"

She bit her lip, then answered honestly. "It sounds very bad, terribly wicked." She whispered, "Do it."

Oh, she did revel in the secrecy of lovers. In Mick's dirty words and sweet words. In their private conversations that, murmured elsewhere, would have been horrid, beyond the pale. Yet between them in the kitchen or the music room or in the pitch dark of night, they were just right — because they spoke with different meanings to the words, meanings and sly degrees of meanings that they invented together, in a language that was just for the two of them.

A snob, though, Winnie wondered. Was she? A snob couldn't have Mick Tremore, that much she knew. So could she let go of her opinions of ratcatchers and poor Catholic Cornishmen? Surely she could.

Or was she fooling herself? It was more than snobbery to want comfort or even luxury. She looked around at a house that already had quite a bit less of both than the one she was born in. Sometimes she missed the old elegance of her upbringing. Sometimes. Could she leave even

this? Her bathroom and electricity and the luxury of buying any book she took a fancy to? Even she wasn't sure.

If he asked her to go with him, would she?

Meanwhile, Mick wasn't certain that the accusation didn't work equally well for him. No matter what he told her, he had a vague sense of not being good enough for her. All her family, education, culture, money, her house and skills — the whole of her he found bloody frightening, truth be told. How did he dare to want such a smart lady, a teacher, the daughter of a marquess, granddaughter of a duke — what a laugh.

He always knew he was ambitious, but this was going some, even for him. The son of a copper miner, whose family thought he was a bloody adventuring hero for going to London and making a ratcatcher of himself so as to send home more money than anyone there had seen in years. Ha. Honest to God. Winnie Bollash. Michael Tremore, you may as well try courting the Queen.

Winnie had been to university. She owned a fancy coach and two horses of her own, plus a carriage house to keep them in. She owned a house of three stories with a lower level for the servants. She had a cook and butler, for godssake, and a third of a coachman, whom she shared with two neighbors. Mick, he'd made the most of two dozen ferrets, most of which he'd bred himself, and five dogs, all of which he'd picked up off the street. He housed every last thing he owned in the

cellar where he slept, renting it off a shoemaker for nothing, in exchange for keeping his shop free of rats.

His absurd fantasy was for her to flee her high-class upbringing. She'd become the ratcatcher's wife — though he never mentioned his day-dream to her. And not because she wouldn't — though, of course, she wouldn't — but because she deserved more.

The fellow at the bar haunted Mick. The toff who raised horses was more her sort. Or some-one like him, but nicer. There were nice blokes, real gentlemen, who could give her a respectable place, show her off in society — Winnie could use that.

She could use a hundred years of admiration; she'd had too little in her life.

The Lamonts were late. "Happily," Mick said. Winnie knew they couldn't be late enough, so far as he was concerned.

When a box arrived just after lunch, she thought it had to do with them, but no, it had to do with Mick. When he realized it had arrived downstairs, he rushed to get it, as if relieved.

Relieved, elated, and almost fearful, he brought it upstairs to Winnie in her bedroom and presented it. It was a gift.

"Happy birthday," he said.

Oh, dear. She herself had forgotten. No one remembered her birthday. It was an un-event.

"Thirty," he said. "You are now as old as I am.

We're the same age."

He took the lid from the box, then, from the top of its tissue paper, handed her a pair of long white evening gloves. "Milly said you had to have these."

She took them, bewildered. They were kid; soft, lightweight, with twenty or more tiny buttons on each.

Then he pulled back the tissue paper and, inside, was a sunset. Winnie caught her breath.

"Tulle," he said, pleased with himself. He lifted it out, as if he could lift out light itself.

It was a dress of embroidered, glass-beaded, salmon pink tulle over darker taffeta — the beads almost as if they were dropped onto the net while liquid, on every other filament, the whole fabric glittering with tiny droplets of smooth glass. Between double shoulder straps, one to be worn just off the shoulder, the other down the arm, the little sleeves were sheer, nothing but tulle and glass beads.

She slipped her hand under one delicate sleeve. The tulle disappeared, while the beads shimmered, as if their sparkle had condensed on her skin.

"Oh, Mick. What have you done?" she asked. He had to have robbed a bank. Or stolen the dress. Or God, no: He must have paid for it with counterfeit money.

She would have to take it back. Though, for the time being, she would just look at it, hold it up to herself. The astounding thing — breath-

taking, in fact — was that it seemed it might fit.

"Try it on," he said.

She looked at it, holding it against her in the mirror. No, she shouldn't try it on. She would look . . . pretentious in a beautiful dress. As if she were trying to be prettier than she was. She shook her head.

"Try it on," he insisted. "I want to see you in it."

She turned her head, gazed at him, wanting to, yet feeling hesitant. She pressed her lips together between her teeth and stared at him. In this one regard, Mick saw her so differently from how she saw herself. And, oh, how she wished he were right.

"Come on, my loovey with the wide blue saucer-eyes. Don't look so distraught. Put it on."

It was exactly long enough in the hem, exactly right. The waist was perfect, narrow, and banded in velvet, the neckline square, flat to the breast, and low. The skirt flared in front then billowed in back, a froth of rich, bronzed rose organdy embroidered with silk floss and more glass-beaded tulle. It was an enchanted dress, a spell conjured up out of nothing. She wondered again how he'd done it, then lost herself in the feel of the gloves. They fit like a second skin up her arms, with tiny, graceful little wrinkles when she bent her wrist. She'd never had anything like them. The buttons, though, were a trial to fasten. Mick had to do her right hand, his fingers working with delicate attention up the inside of her wrist. An

amazing feeling. And an effect, in the end, that was stunning.

Winnie looked at herself in the mirror and felt . . . grown-up somehow. A grown-up woman in a grown-up dress.

Mick, meanwhile, walked around her, smiling and smiling and smiling as he took turns touching her and the dress, both. "It's really beautiful," he said. "I've outdone myself. I'll never pick anything more beautiful than this." He added, "Except you." He found her eyes with his and told her, "Now you have no excuse not to go with me."

She still wasn't sure she wanted to. Frowning, she told him, "You've robbed a bank."

"I did nothing illegal or immoral to get it."

She looked at her reflection, half-wanting to believe him, though to do so seemed like believing in sorcery.

She tried not to like the evening gown. "People will stare at me in it."

"They damn well should. I will, I can tell you that."

She furrowed her brow with concern and self-consciousness.

"Winnie, they looked at you when you took your blouse off and shook your skirts. This at least will be a little more demure."

He was wrong. That wasn't the problem. A ball would be very different. Especially a ball where her cousin and all his friends were there watching. Xavier, with his gregarious elegance

and easy self-confidence, his upper-class hauteur and haughty manners: he would take one look at her in this dress and break out laughing.

Yet, to her own eyes, she could not deny that the dress suited her or that it was lovely beyond imagining. The color made her freckles look . . . healthy. It made her hair seem a prettier color, a kind of strawberry gold.

She brushed its skirts. The beads weren't heavy. The fabric was light, as light as air. It whispered, running through her fingers, liquid and shimmery. She had never seen anything more beautiful. Never. And her mother had owned quite a few fancy ball gowns.

"How?" she asked, turning on Mick. How could he possibly have managed such a trick?

He waved his hands in the air, abracadabra. "Magic," he said.

It took her a second, then she frowned and looked around suddenly. "Where's your dog?"

It was a stupid question. His dog could hardly have brought this sort of dress. She realized, though, she hadn't seen the dog, not for several days.

"Where's your dog?" she repeated, this time with a sense of horror.

He frowned. "Win, I have something to tell you. I sold my dogs and ferrets at the beginning of the week, all my cages, my carrier boxes, all my equipment as well as my customer list. I won't be needing them.

"You see," he continued, "I think I'm taking a

job as a valet after we're done. Milton says his brother in Newcastle can get me a position." He let that sink in.

Her stomach went cold. He'd named a real place. He was going, and he had a destination. Newcastle.

"Milton says I have a style to me that would appeal to young gentlemen who can't match their stockings. I agree. I'd be good at taking care of a gentleman." He laughed. "Though after looking at that dress, I'd probably make a better lady's maid, but no one would hire me for that.

"Still, being a valet would be good for me, secure. Good for me and mine. And because I can write and do sums, they're talking about my balancing the gentleman's accounts and keeping track of his appointments, too. It would be at a good salary. It makes sense. Anyway, I won't be needing dogs and such to do it, and my animals weren't getting the exercise and attention they need anyway. Better for them to sell them. Better for me. Even Magic —"

"No," she said, appalled.

"He was worth the most, Win."

"He was your pet."

"He was my friend, he surely was. But you see, the place in Newcastle, they won't let me bring my dog." He stopped a second, looked at his feet. "Milton's brother said the gentleman in Newcastle has his own kennels. His dogs are pedigreed, and he wouldn't want them mixed up with mine." He smiled at her a moment, that cocky,

raffish grin he had, full of male bravado. "I mentioned to Magic how I could, you know, have him done, but he said he'd rather I wouldn't. He's wild for Rezzo's bitch. He just loves her. They've been having puppies once a year for a while now, and, truth is, their puppies go like fresh jellied eels first thing in the morning. There's a list of people waiting for them. It'd be selfish to take him."

She tried to accept the dog's absence as matter-of-factly as Mick did. She looked at the dress. It was lovely. But it made her cry. She put her hand to her mouth.

"What?" he said. "What? Don't." He took her shoulders. "No," he reprimanded. "I want you to have the dress. I'm nothing but happy to give it. Won't it do?"

"Oh, yes." She cried, trying to smile, a mess. She sniffed. "Oh, yes. It's quite marvelous, Mick. Quite marvelous." But him. Oh, him. He overwhelmed her. While the dress, the way she looked in it, frightened her.

Oblivious to her distress, since she wouldn't discuss it, he smiled, happy, then — silly man — he wiggled his eyebrows over his crooked grin. He said, "I'll be taking Freddie. If she's up to it. I'll sneak her into my rooms, if I have to." He added, "Just come with me tonight."

Winnie squinched her face at the dress, then at him in the mirror and the way it had all come about. She wasn't sure she should like an evening that he'd had to give up his dog to buy.

He knew her so well, though. He said, "Win, don't struggle with it. I can't have everything. But that's not bad: A poor man learns what he values better than a rich man. I loved that dog, but I love you more; and I want a life with hot baths, books, and enough money for the last of my brothers and sisters to get a good start. I'd have sold everything anyway, even if you had a dress. But since you didn't and since I'm going to a place where I'll have more spending money, well, why shouldn't you have this present?"

He smiled. "Besides, the magic isn't gone from my life." He touched her face with the backs of his fingers, brushing her cheek lightly. "Quite the opposite. I want us to have tonight. One, magic, singular night. Do you have shoes?" he asked.

"No."

He laughed. "Dance in your stocking feet then."

She snorted, a kind of laugh finally. Mick was consoling *her* for his having sold his dog to buy her a dress. How typical of the man. How purely, endearingly typical. Oh, how she loved him.

Mick's heart was noble. Inside, he was better than a gentleman; he always had been. A kind of stunning reality hit her: Life would not be the same — it would be less — without him.

The Lamonts were very late, if they were coming at all. In the interim, Winnie told Mick about the letter from her former student, the new duchess, then told him her theory:

392

"If they bring an invitation, they have to be legitimate. The duke doesn't invite any but those of the oldest, most reputable families to his annual event — the long-known, the bluest blood."

Yes. That was the test. She doubted that Jeremy and Emile would show themselves at her door if they couldn't procure an invitation, which would be fine. Or if they arrived and tried to travel on hers, she wouldn't allow it. In either case, neither she nor Mick would go. That would be the end of it.

And if the Lamonts did bring their own invitation?

In that instance, she told herself, she and Mick needn't worry. All his idle curiosity was pointless. No matter what the young duchess said or what Mick thought, if Xavier put invitations to his ball into the hands of the Lamonts, then the twin gentlemen with Brighton in their voices had the hardest to acquire, most eagerly sought reference that society deigned to give.

Chapter 25

As it happened, Emile and Jeremy Lamont did *not* have an invitation to the Duke of Arles's gala. Yet. But as they walked up the front walk of his London town house, they were fairly confident that, within the hour, they would be walking down it again, carrying one.

As they tapped up the wide steps of the duke's portico, they were still talking about their Cornish ratcatcher-cum-aristocrat.

"Quite the *gentilhomme*," said Emile with undisguised gloat. He was so happy with the way Tremore had cleaned up, he had to keep himself from rubbing his hands together. He could feel money coming toward them, buckets of it, dropping into his waiting arms. "I was hoping she could make him halfway presentable, but, by Jove, she's made him bloody royalty." He laughed. "He's perfect. Absolutely perfect." Jeremy joined him in chuckling yet another round over their good management.

At the door, they were greeted by the duke's butler. They'd made an appointment. The butler brought them into an entry hall, a room that was a hall in the sense of *town hall* or *public hall* — a

vast, open space where people might gather. This hall, though, was by no means so paltry as those found in public buildings. It was a simple, splendid arrangement of high, coffered ceilings inlaid with gold, marble floors, and rich Persian carpets. Its furnishings were spare in number and extravagant of design: Over the central medallion of the huge Oriental rug was a gilt Louis Quinze table that held fresh flowers arranged in a crystal ship. The arrangement stood eight feet high and was at least that wide. The only other furniture in the room was a series of matching gilt and velvet benches around its perimeter, broken only by the precise geometric placement of four small, Italian tile fountains. Water burbled in these, the sound a little, liquid symphony that played peacefully in the hush of a very formal house.

The effect of the duke's house in London wasn't pretentious so much as a genuine expression of staggeringly ridiculous wealth. And this house wasn't even the grandest one he owned, merely the most convenient to the amenities of London.

Emile and Jeremy walked along behind the butler, their steps cushioned across thick carpet. He escorted them to the front library, where they waited for the duke among his books and family portraits.

"Here it is," Emile told his brother, the moment the butler left them. He indicated one of more than a dozen dark, oil-on-canvas paintings

that broke up the bookcases of the room. "A portrait of the duke's son. He died years ago."

Jeremy stepped back to look at the painting. Then said, "My God." He was suitably impressed. "Tremore looks just like him! The resemblance is uncanny!"

Indeed, it was. Due to careful choosing, some similar clothes — and, more, to the miracle that Edwina Bollash had worked. Six weeks ago, no one would have believed it possible that Tremore was the son of the man in that portrait. The Cornishman had simply been too grimy and coarse. And, similarities or not, Emile knew his mark: The duke would have rejected such a fellow out of hand. Arles was a pompous old bastard. He would have sooner believed he was related to a monkey than consider himself related to an ill-spoken ratcatcher. They wouldn't have been able to get the fellow into the house.

Now, of course, Tremore was suitable to dance across the floor of the duke's ballroom at Uelle Castle. He could have a chat with the duchess — hang it, Emile thought, he could have a nice chat with the Queen herself, if she showed up tonight.

Further contemplation of his triumph, however, was cut short when the butler opened the door and an old, frail man hobbled in with the use of a cane.

Once of a stately stature, the Duke of Arles was now stooped. He moved slowly — with an hauteur, though, that was uncompromised by the indignities of age. Though he was old and infirm,

people joked that he had a mind upstairs in his attic slowly becoming senile, while the one that everyone dealt with was as sharp as a bee's quill. Emile had already told his brother: do not underestimate the old man.

Arles came into the room with the august decrepitude of ageless power. "I don't have time for this," he said.

He knew already what "this" was about. In order to gain the interview, Emile had sent him a note. It had said simply: *Your grandson is alive, and we know where he is.*

Jeremy was the one they had decided should begin. He said, ever so pleasantly, "We have found a man whom we believe is your grandson —"

Arles cut him off. "You haven't." His expression didn't change. "Is that all you have to say?"

He'd only come in as far as the chair closest the door, a man who didn't intend to enter further. He grasped the chair's back now for balance, as with his other hand, he leaned heavily onto his cane.

Emile came forward, as planned, the brute again. He asked bluntly, "Is the reward still being offered?"

"Emile," Jeremy said. He smiled his sincere smile — the best part about Jer's deception was that he believed it himself so well that he was utterly convincing. To the duke, "My brother can be so crass. I'm sorry —"

"Shut up, Jeremy. I'm not a rich man, and nei-

397

ther are you." Of Arles, he asked a crucial question. "There was once a reward of a hundred thousand pounds for the return of your grandson to you. Is it still available?"

The old man laughed with a dryness that ended in a slight cough. Then he said, "I haven't offered a reward for my grandson in twenty years. He's dead, you know."

"Is he?" Jeremy said. He furrowed his brow with his usual artless sympathy, and asked, "Do you hold no hope at all then?"

Arles's bony fist contracted around his cane as he pounded the end once with a sharp rap. Then he leaned on it toward them. "I can save you both a great deal of trouble. In the thirty years of my grandson's being missing" — he looked from one to the other — "I've had every swindler this side of the Atlantic try to sell me someone who looked vaguely as they imagined he might." He reached the cane, took a step away from the chair. "I don't know who you think you are, but you aren't going to get anything from me." He waved the cane once, surprisingly able to stand without it, then took a swipe through the air with it. "Except possibly the end of this. Now get out."

It was not precisely the reaction they had been hoping for.

Emile scrambled. "How old was your son in this portrait?" he asked and turned to look up. He needed time to think, time to sniff out a weakness in the old sturdy duke.

Only silence ticked by. Then behind him, he heard, "Thirty."

He turned around slowly, gauging, allowing a faint smile. "That is almost exactly the age of the man we wish to bring to you." He indicated the painting behind him. "And he doesn't look vaguely like anything: He is the spitting image of his father."

Arles's sharp, rheumy eyes narrowed. For a moment, he seemed interested, then his arm raised with a swiftness that surprised. He pointed to the door. "Get out!" he said. "Do you think you are the only ones to try to play on an old man's emotions? Do you imagine I am some sort of fool? Get out! Get out this instant!"

Emile glanced at his brother, who was already taking small sideways steps toward the door. The devil take him. His stupid brother was never any help, always the coward. Emile gnashed his teeth and said with just as much force as the high-handed old duke, "Listen to me, old man. You may have seen a lot of schemes, but this isn't one of them. I was here two months ago with a chap from your club. I saw the portrait. I heard the story. Then, last week, I met the son of the man in it. My brother and I have come to tell you. We'd like the reward, if you agree we're right. We're not rich as you are. But we aren't trying to swindle anyone. We're offering you a chance to see for yourself."

Arles was livid, but he didn't issue his command again. He listened.

Emile continued. "Michael," he said. "They even called him Michael. He is well over six feet, with your eyes and hair the color of jet —"

"Stop it!" The old man came at him. He raised his cane, swinging it this time. "Stop it!" Surprisingly, he was able to get it over his head. He thrashed the air.

It missed Emile, only because he stepped back. It clacked on a chair, splintering a piece from its carved wood.

"Get out!" he repeated. He limped forward, coming at Emile again. "Get out, you thief! You sleazy, venomous snake of a human being. How dare you start this again —"

"And his smile," Emile said, ducking another swift slice of the cane. He played his ace, the one that had taken the most patience as he'd studied men, looking for the right candidate. "It's like the one in the portrait. It's off-center. His smile lifts up on one side more than the other."

The old man hobbled to the side and pulled the bell cord, while through his teeth, he said, "Get. Out. Of my. House." He yanked the cord again, then again, then bellowed with great volume and strength, "Get out! Get out!"

That was it. Emile had played every card that he had and had lost, he thought.

Then something else, something inside the old man made him raise his eyes.

Emile turned. Jeremy looked, too. They all lifted their gazes to the large painting overhead, to its dark colors and moody look that seemed to

speak across their silence.

No, Emile thought, the similarities were perhaps not so great as he was making out, though they were profound enough that their ruse was tight. What luck, he thought.

Then, no, of course it wasn't luck. He knew all the facts. Twenty-nine years ago, just before the duke's grandson's third birthday, while everyone was asleep in the house one night, someone crept in and stole the small child from his nursery. The boy disappeared, no explanation; a child kidnaped, never to be seen again — though his family searched and called out every favor that was owed them. They put pressure directly and indirectly on friend and foe alike; everyone felt their furious, hysterical conviction that they could buy or negotiate or dictate their way out of their bereavement. The duke offered a spectacular reward. Yet, still, nothing.

Which, by Emile's standards, meant the child was already long dead. Though the idea of the lost baby, even thirty years later, provided a damn lively game.

When he turned around again, the old man was still holding on to the bellpull. He seemed, for a few seconds, almost to dangle from it. Then he lowered his haughty eyes, drawing himself up again.

Quickly, Emile said, "You can assess the truth of what we're telling you without risk."

The old man raised one contemptuous eyebrow.

"Give us invitations to the ball tonight at Uelle Castle. We'll bring the fellow. We'll dance him right out into the center of your ballroom. You can look him over. If you agree with us that he's your grandson, we get the hundred thousand pounds. If not, he dances out the door, and nothing more is made of the matter." Emile held his hands out and smiled. What could be more simple?

"Pah," the duke said in a burst of air. "If he's not, I'll have you all arrested for fraud and —"

Not if Emile had any say in the matter. He and his brother had train tickets to Southhampton and a dinner in Brussels tomorrow.

The old duke scowled, truculent, but he'd stopped arguing.

Jeremy was helpful. At last. Soothingly, he asked, "What do you have to lose?"

The old man sent for his secretary who brought them invitations. The duke himself, by then, was long gone. There was a hiatus between when the secretary left them, before the butler came to escort them out.

In the interim, Jeremy dallied, staring up at a portrait of a man long dead. A tall man with a deep brow and strikingly black hair.

He murmured, "You know, brother, the likeness is so amazing, it makes me wonder if we might truly have found the old fellow's grandson."

Emile, too, paused for a moment to look up

402

and contemplate, in awe, the possible convolutions of their own chicanery.

Then he sniffed and said, "Yes, but he's not. Jeremy, we've bought him clothes in the same color scheme as those, in the same general style, only undated. We've cut his hair nearly the same, and, happily, Miss Bollash talked him out of his mustache. Then, too, don't forget: He *has* a family. He's from Cornwall, for godssake."

"I picked very well," he said, taking credit where credit was due. "And remember what he was like when we first saw him," he reminded. "A slimy Cornishman who lived among Cockneys and chased ferrets." He tapped his brother on the shoulder. "Let's go, Jeremy. I want to find a servant or someone in this house who knew the child. I want to gather a bit of personal information. We have to *make* this work. We can't expect it to, or it won't."

When his brother only stared up at the portrait, as if transfixed, Emile cuffed him along the ear.

Jeremy jerked around, scowling and holding the side of his head. "Don't do that."

"All right, but don't become sentimental or romantic. *We* are making the stupid ratcatcher into a duke's grandson. *We* are doing it, along with Bollash's help. Don't start believing your own hoax, idiot."

Chapter 26

The Lamonts arrived with the coveted invitation — a mere five hours late. They brought evening clothes for Mick, along with the tailor himself for some last-minute adjustments. Mick stood in his former room upstairs before the large, full-length mirror, his arms out, while a black tailcoat with satin facings was adjusted at the cuff.

On the bed lay a voluminous cape of black worsted with a deep velvet collar and a lining of midnight purple silk. He wore black trousers held in place by wide, white, elasticized braces. In a moment, though, he would cover them up with a white waistcoat that was cut deep to show the pleats of a white shirt. A white silk tie lay draped about his neck; he didn't know how to tie it. By a chair sat evening boots, a silk top hat, and white gloves, all ready to go.

Mick looked at himself, coming together in the mirror, as the tailor finished then packed up his needle and thread. Yes, he thought, quite the posh getup. Meanwhile, the Lamonts kept staring at him and exchanging looks.

"My God," Jeremy said finally, "he looks so like —" After a pause, he finished, "A gentleman."

He saw the tailor downstairs and out, while his brother, sitting on the windowsill, began feeding Mick a history they'd invented, "if anyone asked." A history with the oddest details. Trains. He was supposed to love trains. What did he know about trains? Aside from the fact that the fellow who wanted him to work in Newcastle had sent him a ticket for a ride on one — it had arrived in the afternoon's post.

"And purple. You love the color purple."

Mick dropped the waistcoat down his upraised arms onto his shoulders, then he turned the edge of it out to show the lining. Purple. He said, "You allowed me to select the lining, remember? I do like purple, so we have no problem there. But trains. I know nothing of trains." He shrugged, offering, "Except that in America the red car at the end is called a caboose."

Jeremy returned to the room just then, overhearing. As if the fact were an event, he asked his brother, "He knows the word *caboose?*"

"Indeed." His brother laughed.

Jeremy frowned at Mick, then his eyes widened. He said, "The lining of his vest is purple!"

Emile laughed again. "He likes the color. It's his favorite."

"You're bloody kidding," Jeremy said with genuine wonder.

Mick couldn't grasp their mood. He said, "Well, not my favorite, I don't think —" Though he had picked a lot of purple. He'd selected the lining for the cape as well, if he remembered cor-

rectly. He frowned, looking at it on the bed.

"How do you know about cabooses?" Jeremy asked. He sounded almost irritated.

Mick shook his head. "I read it somewhere, I think. Is it significant?"

"No." Emile queried, "Do you like the word?"

"Caboose?"

"Yes."

Mick puzzled over their fascination with the topic. "I suppose," he told them. "It has an interesting sound. *Caboos-s-se*," he repeated.

They looked flummoxed for a few seconds, as if he'd told them a joke they were having difficulty sorting out. In the mirror, Mick watched them look at each other. Emile shrugged and shook his head; Jeremy nodded — a strange little pantomime between twin brothers who were already a fairly remarkable sight.

Jeremy moved on with: "We should come up with an explanation why no one knows of the viscountcy we've invented."

"It's a Cornish viscountcy. No birth records," Mick suggested. He wrestled the bow tie, not paying much attention to anything but trying to tie it. He was making a regular mess of it. After a few moments of silence that became noteworthy for its lengthiness, he found them again in reflection, one at the window, one directly behind him.

Both had turned toward him again, both frowning deeply, identically.

Mick turned his head to face them over his shoulder. "What?"

"The birth records in Cornwall."

Since they didn't seem to understand what he was getting at, he explained, "Births aren't recorded out in the country. There could easily be a peer in Cornwall whom no one knows about, a peer whom no one is aware of until he comes to London. Perhaps he's come to sit in Parliament and reestablish the title."

Jeremy glanced at his brother, more agitated. Then he said to Mick, "Michael." As if the name itself had a bearing. "How old are you?"

"Thirty. Why?"

"Ah." This somehow relieved him. "Two years too young," he said.

"Too young for what?"

He didn't explain, but only laughed, then said, "You are incredible. The way you talk, the way you look. *What* you talk about. Goodness, even we, who know better, believed for a minute you were —" He paused, then said, "A gentleman." He said to his brother across the room, "This bloke is brilliant! And he looks so like —" Another halt, then, "A peer. He's perfect. What a find you are, Tremore!"

"Happy to please," Mick told him, though he was more mystified than anything else.

What *were* they up to with purple and trains and Michaeling him suddenly?

The Lamonts had brought their own evening clothes. They had brought not only an invitation for Mick, but invitations for themselves as well — then had been surprised to learn Winnie in-

407

tended to use hers. They seemed happy enough to allow her to come with them. Perhaps they realized that she was, for Mick, an unnegotiable part of the evening.

Perfect. No, Mick didn't feel perfect. He felt annoyed with himself. He knew the Lamonts were setting the game further, deeper into what they intended to accomplish, yet for the life of him he couldn't get a foothold into what it might be. Purple. Michael. Cabooses. What idiotic game was this?

Then, on top of everything else, he went out to give Freddie a quick bite to eat, and there she was: lying on the bottom of her cage, looking tired and hungry. She hadn't eaten what he'd given her this morning. When he took her out, she was weak. She couldn't hold her head up well.

"Ah, Freddie," he said, stroking her fur. "Ah, Freddie," he crooned over and over. "Don't pick tonight, duck. Not tonight."

All three men waited at the front door for Winnie, while they took turns fussing with Mick's bow tie. Both Jeremy and Emile wore one. Emile's was pre-tied and hooked into place. Jeremy could tie his, but he couldn't reverse the process and make it work at Mick's neck.

"I can do it."

They all turned, looking up. And there was Winnie, standing at the top of the stairs, and, oh, what a sight.

She'd run out and bought shoes, little satin slippers that were pretty on her feet. She carried her mother's purse, with its jeweled metal frame and gold tassels that looked like acorns, made of wrapped metal threads. The only other accouterment she wore were opals, also her mother's. Mick had never seen opals until Win had taken them out this afternoon. They gleamed now at her throat, showing off her long, graceful neck. She shone like them, pale, iridescent.

As Mick's eyes rose to her face, he found another small alteration that he liked particularly well: While out buying her shoes, she'd found a jeweler who was able to mount the rimless lenses of her spectacles into a pince-nez on a satin string, a stylish solution to her nearsightedness that, as she raised the elegant article to look at him, caught pleasing light. An edge glinted warmly, playing hide-and-seek with the blue of her eyes.

Even Jeremy and Emile caught their breaths. Princess Edwina, with her hair piled up on her head. Oh, she looked the part tonight. Tall, willowy, elegant. A vision of opals and salmon-rose light and long white gloves.

Mick beamed at her. "You are gorgeous," he said. He went to the foot of the stairs and offered her his hand.

She came down only so far as the last step, though, then, looping her evening bag over her wrist, began tying his tie. Her fingers were shaking. He looked at her. She was excited. She

was terrified. How very much like Winnie.

She did what no one else could — tying his tie in a few seconds — while looking as if any loud noise might make her race back up the stairs and decide not to go.

He touched her arm. "You'll do fine."

She made a face, unconsoled.

He shook his head, trying to smile reassuringly. At his timid, long-legged fairy. His tall, tetchy imp-face who had no breasts to speak of, full hips, and perfect legs. And whose idiosyncratic, capricious pieces came together somehow in a way that was so amazingly attractive his chest ached at seeing her.

Outside, they all ascended into Winnie's carriage, which then rolled out into the street at about six in the evening. They would miss dinner. They were going to be quite late, with Uelle Castle still an hour southwest of London.

In the carriage, the three men sat opposite Winnie for the first five minutes, then Mick thought, The hell with etiquette, and shifted over to sit beside her. He took her hand. She smiled briefly, letting him, then stared out the window, tense but quiet. Poor thing, he thought. Yet once they arrived, they would surely enjoy themselves: better they had this night than nothing.

Their emotions seemed to joggle along in tandem as they rode, she perhaps a little sadder, while Mick felt resigned; the two of them together in an understood bittersweet harmony.

410

One way or another, an exciting night lay ahead. Then nothing. They wouldn't speak of it; there was no more to be said. When Mick tried to imagine his walking out her front door tomorrow morning, on his way elsewhere, he couldn't envision it. Literally, he couldn't. Nothing. As if he would step off her threshold into a void.

Eventually, from simple, baffled irritability over the fact that Emile Lamont watched him with a small, self-satisfied smile on his face, Mick said, "Why are you so happy? You're about to lose a very large bet."

The man's smile didn't change, faint but smug as he said, "Merely seeing if you can pull this off — the pure dangerous mischief of it — intoxicates me. It's worth it, even it I lose, to watch you do it." He laughed. "And of course Jeremy is going to squirm with worry all night. That's always fun."

His brother huffed, then interrupted, cutting off further exchange between Emile and Mick. Wisely perhaps. He involved Winnie in conversation, something about the Royal Enclosure at Ascot.

Mick was becoming accustomed to discussions of topics he had no knowledge of, discussions that Winnie's bearing, her accent, something about her, generated when anyone came near who could engage in what he thought of as toff conversation. It didn't bother him. He settled back, listening, the rhythm of her voice reminding him of good music played well on a

fine instrument. He let the sound of it lull him into daydreams as he watched the sun set into the horizon. Whenever the carriage turned a little southward, these last, gold rays would cut across Win's face, and he'd watch her mouth.

Watch what you can see of my tongue, she'd told him as she'd shown him her teeth, making an *Eee*. Oh, yes. Whenever he listened to the tune of her voice, he wanted to lean toward her, up onto his own arms for balance, and bend down into her mouth. *Watch what you can see of my tongue.* He wanted what he could feel of it. He wanted to touch into her well-spoken *E*, into teeth with a space between, to twist his head and press himself into her clever mouth. He wanted to make her his own again for the night. Ah, tonight, he thought.

Possession. He'd tried not to want Winnie, but he did.

He wanted her so much it made him shudder to think of it. With delight. With dread. Wanting Winnie, so far above him, was as practical as wanting to walk on water. Even as he enjoyed her — the miracle of floating, the sparkles and ripples beneath his feet — he knew that to sink was inevitable. What he feared, in fact, was that he had succeeded too well, that he'd gotten out too deep with Princess Winnie of the Empty Tins and now all that was left was to drown.

There was no bridging the gap between them.

When he thought of her with her linguistics and her house and her students, it was hard to

412

imagine a life more removed from his in White-chapel or even his new possibilities in New-castle.

Hard to imagine a life more removed, that is, until the place where she was born came suddenly up over the horizon.

The road curved, a zigzag that turned the carriage south along with the river. Winnie pointed. Mick leaned to look out her window: and there it was. Uelle. *Yule.* Like the pagan festival. A celebration of stone and fire, of Thor. Of power. And eternity.

Against the darkening sky, the seat of the marquisate of Sissingley rose up and onto a south bank of a bend in the river Thames. A spreading rise of yellowish stone, it extended itself out and up, the setting sun's colors sheeting up steep walls and limning a crenellated skyline of towers and sentry walks, casting the whole in an aura of a golden, pinkish orange light.

Mick blinked for a few seconds, squinting as if he might bring it into more realistic focus. *This* was the home where Winnie had lived? This was what she had lost?

The structures that made up Uelle were as numerous as those of the town where he was born. They took up more space. A massive gatehouse before a high barbican. A huge, central octagonal keep. A high-spired chapel built in the shape of a cross. Square towers set into walls with arching gates, nestled against round towers that extended upward into turrets. Behind all

this, a separate, long, flag-flying hall, with high, imposing bay windows down its entire length.

It was a congeries of civilization, like an old medieval village, yet orderly, the buildings — there were corridors of them — arranged in courtyards around gardens, squared, their corners rising in massive, castellated towers. Uelle was larger than Buckingham. It was older, more a fortress, yet grand, beautiful. And more dramatic for sitting on the far side of the river, alone in the midst of darkening English countryside, meadow and hedgerow.

Princess Edwina. How astonishingly accurate. A princess, deposed, her fall from grace the scope of a chasm: come to reclaim her place, Mick hoped. If only for the night. And he would help.

He'd help, that is, if whatever Emile and Jeremy were planning didn't bind him, hand and foot.

He happened to catch glimpses of their perfectly replicated faces as they leaned forward to stare out the carriage window. Neither man had ever been here before. The fact was written all over their gaping awe; they were as impressed as Mick by the small town of a castle toward which they all headed. So how the bloody hell had they gotten invitations? It was the question of the hour.

He hoped it wouldn't be the question of the evening. It was past time to find out.

Chapter 27

Uelle. Winnie was surprised to know it still moved her to see the old place. It was a large, squared, battlement affair overlooking the river, though to call it so was truthful without conveying the effect.

Tonight, the torches were lit. As the carriage clattered across the river, the air drifted with the smell of rosin burning at regular intervals in small iron baskets along the bridge. They didn't show up well at sunset, but she delighted to glimpse their fire; they would light up the night. She could see more cressets atop the rampart that rose up from the banks of the river, cups of flame that guttered in the wind, extending in both directions, up and down along the whole length of the castle. An architect, a century ago, had turned the rampart into the wall along a wide promenade that, all along the riverside of the castle, looked down into the Thames. The river below was already coming alive with reflections of flickering light.

After the bridge, the carriage plunged into a tunnel lit by torches, then it climbed out again at the first gate, upward into the lower ward. As

they went under the gate, she called to Mick, "See the slits overhead?" He angled his gaze to look out and up, and she explained, "They're for pouring boiling oil down onto the castle's enemies." She shivered and laughed.

They passed under the iron and wood grate, a portcullis, that could be raised thirty feet into the air. Its full drop took less than thirty seconds, its iron spikes coming down with the force of two tons — guaranteeing for centuries that no one entered Uelle without invitation.

Up they climbed through a corridor of guardhouses and outbuildings, their crenels and merlons having once hidden legions of archers. It made her skin prickle. Oh, Uelle, she thought, such a lovely, shivery place — and so suitable for the duke's ball. A place built for the sake of intimidation. An elegant, embattled fortress, the home of knights from centuries past who had brought back treasures that had remained.

They pulled into a courtyard, and footmen rushed forward from the shadows to help Winnie descend into an Arabian-tiled coach entrance. Mick came down behind her as more servants scurried toward them from a dark illuminated by tall windows that bent long, bright, paned rectangles of light over bushes and ground. The sound of people and music rang from inside.

Winnie gripped the hand loop of her evening bag, clutching her own squeaky-gloved fingers. The Lamonts walked past, while she remained transfixed.

Mick hung back with her, silent, taking everything in. She wondered what he'd been expecting. Not what stood before them, it was safe to say. Unless he'd ratted Buckingham Palace, he had no reference point, nothing in his experience against which to measure this.

He wasn't silent, she feared, so much as dumbfounded.

She herself felt a stab of faintheartedness, and she *knew* the rooms they were about to enter. Though she didn't know them as they were — not lit, full of people, an orchestra playing, not as an adult admitted to partake. It was so unnerving. Poor Mick, she thought.

She heard her carriage roll away to take its place in the line of carriages that would wait all night, then before her two doormen pulled back heavy double doors.

Light and music and chatter poured out, amplified, dignified, clinking with crystal, humming with sociability. Inside would be people whom Winnie hadn't seen, save her own students, in a dozen years. Why had she chosen to return? Why now?

To see a joke as she'd imagined six weeks ago? The joke of sending — no, bringing, as it turned out — a ratcatcher to dance in her cousin's ballroom? It had seemed like such a good idea then. Now, if it were a joke, it was no longer funny.

Then, worse, when she glanced over her shoulder for reassurance, she got none: for the man she looked at wasn't a ratcatcher.

417

Instead, she saw a tall gentleman standing beside her, straight-postured, his top hat at an insanely right — rakish — angle, his shoulders wide as the wind off the river billowed his long dark cloak. Mick. He was shadow and light standing there in the nightfall, the back of him only a glow across his shoulders from the torches, the front of him stark, his shirt and vest a snowy contrast to the black of his evening suit.

And his face. Dear Lord, his face. The brim of his hat cast his eyes into perfect obscurity, while the light from the reception room made the rest — the angles of his cheekbones, his straight nose, the wide, masculine set of his jaw — simply and stunningly handsome. At her side was a mysterious gentleman in a cloak blown by the wind, a cloak that cast shadows across him, its lining flapping eerie bursts of vivid, sheening purple.

For a moment, she didn't know who he was, why he stood there, or why she was beside him. To be here felt unreal.

Then he asked, "Shall we?" And a smile she knew, yet didn't, crooked up sideways, devastating.

She was so taken aback, she asked, "Mick?"

The hat turned, looked right at her, responding to the name. In a whisper, she asked a question in her own mind. "Are you sure you wish to go through with it?"

Without hesitation, he said, "Damn right." She felt a strong arm loop about her waist. He whispered, "I wouldn't miss it."

His hand came up, and his head came closer. He was about to remove his hat to kiss her. But she quickly braced herself, holding him back. She felt a tension in his arm, in his chest where she pushed.

And knew: God help them both, he wasn't intimidated. He was excited.

Full of himself, she thought. His confidence panicked her. "Remember the rules —" she murmured.

"Oh, Winnie," he answered softly. "Don't you know by now? There are no rules." Then he pulled back and laughed — at her, she feared.

She was going to lecture him, bring him down to earth. But as their bodies separated, she felt something — a small, soft weight between them that rested in the lining of his cloak.

"Do you have your gloves?" she asked.

"On," he told her.

"What's that then?" She reached for the weight.

He drew back. "Freddie," he said.

"What!" Her heart lurched quite nearly out her throat. Then, with sudden relief, she put her gloved hand against her chest, onto her shoulder cape. She shook her head. He was tormenting her. "Goodness," she said, "I almost thought you were serious. Don't be so unkind. You terrify me."

He said nothing, only staring at her for a moment. Then quite seriously, he murmured, "I don't want to terrify you."

"Then don't tease me."

Nothing again. Until he said quietly, "All right."

"Are you two lovebirds coming?" Emile Lamont called from ahead. With his brother, he stood just inside the doorway.

Mick offered his arm. Winnie linked hers through it, and she marched forward.

They left their wraps with the servant in the cloakroom with only minor incident. Mick hesitated to turn his handsome new cloak over to the attendant till she encouraged him. "It's fine," she whispered. "He'll keep everything sorted and watch over it. You can leave your things. Everyone does."

That was the last of any awkwardness on his part. Shed of their wraps, he took her gloved hand and threaded it through the crook of his arm. All awkwardness became hers: She felt like a cliff-diver as they walked out to be announced. Once, she'd gone with her father to watch a man who dived from cliffs at Dover into a deep shoreline pool of the English Channel. She couldn't understand why the man kept doing it or how he did it at all without dying.

That was how she felt, as if called upon to participate in a free fall that might kill her, when she heard: "Lady Edwina Henrietta Bollash and Lord Michael Frederick Edgerton, the Viscount Bartonreed."

She and Mick walked out onto a huge landing that overlooked a monumental staircase leading

down into the ballroom. Winnie drew herself up, having to remind herself to breathe.

Mick, it seemed, had to remind himself to proceed slowly. As they began down the stairs, he murmured under his breath, "Oh, look at the size of this room! Oh, my God. I can't wait to dance you out onto that floor — look at the size of that floor!"

And the number of people. Dear Lord.

And every single one of them seemed to stop and stare up.

As they made their way down, Winnie stole sideways glances at him, looking for a kindred spirit: and not finding one. He held his head up, a faint smile on his face, perfectly calm, as if he walked down a hundred twenty-seven wide marble stairs — she had counted when she rolled jacks and balls down them as a child — every day of his life. Dashing. That was the word for him. Dashing, handsome, perfectly pressed, perfectly tailored, and poised.

The poise was his own. The rest was a complicated overlayer of clothes, speech, and manners, applied to a ratcatcher whom she kept trying to see, yet couldn't. Where was Mick?

Instead, she watched the ghost who had materialized now and then in the course of Mick's instruction. Only now, the ghost had taken over his skin. When she was younger, she would have had difficulty speaking to such a man as walked beside her. Words would have stuck in her throat.

Where was Mick? She couldn't find him.

Could anyone else?

She lifted her pince-nez when she thought she recognized the Baroness of Whitting from the teahouse. Indeed, it was — the woman saw them, too, and began toward them from the far end of the room. The baroness's presence was expected. Less expected, Winnie saw two couples she was fairly certain had been in the same teahouse six weeks before on the day Mick had made his less than graceful entrance into it. Oh, dear, oh, dear. She spotted also several of her former students. One of them, the lovely young duchess, turned the moment she saw Winnie, lifting her skirts in a careful, ladylike hurry, waving as she approached — which she was not supposed to do.

Nonetheless, Winnie felt nothing but relief to see the greeting. She smiled back, trying to appear cheerful.

She wanted to enjoy herself, she really did. But how? She couldn't with so many people watching. And Mick — he was worse than the dress he had brought her. He attracted attention. People stopped to stare at him. New blood. New gossip. A new bachelor for the mamas to look over, for the papas to chat up. And for the young ladies to sigh over. By the hush, it was obvious the entire room was studying him for one reason or another. Him and the tall, freckled woman who came down the stairs on his arm.

The orchestra in its balcony overhead came to the end of one waltz, then without hesitation

swirled into the notes of a new one — the opening strains in praise of another river, a beautiful blue one that flowed through Austria.

Then, on the last stair, just before she and Mick touched down into the room itself, a little gathering at the side opened up to reveal at the end of a corridor of stiff, staring people —

An empty chair. A woman came around it toward them. Vivian, if Winnie remembered correctly, Xavier's much-younger wife.

There was a carpet that ran from the stairway to the empty chair, like a pathway to homage. Only the man to whom one usually paid it at this point was nowhere in sight. Mick and Winnie followed the carpet toward the duchess, making the required approach. She met them halfway, as if to make up for, to hide, the insulting, empty chair — an indication of what the duke thought of her arrival, Winnie feared.

She brooded over what to say, how not to whimper out something meek and self-effacing to Xavier's wife. How to respond after so many years, with apparently still so much resentment between Winnie and a cousin who absented himself from his own gathering. Mick, however, solved the problem.

He bent in a low, graceful bow before the duchess and said, "Your grace. Good evening. Thank you for inviting us." He was happy to be here and said so.

Winnie followed suit with a deep curtsey, wondering with bewilderment what could be sim-

pler. Sincere appreciation, directly expressed.

The duchess seemed relieved herself. She nodded.

Then before anyone could agonize further, Mick pulled Winnie by the hand, taking her by the waist, and drew her into a turn. He spun them both out into the room.

He smiled as he did it, as if to say, Xavier could be rude, but they needn't be. They could enjoy themselves. Well, he could anyway. Winnie looked up into his face, into his confidence and perfection and . . . frowned; she quaked. How had he done that? So unruffled. Without a moment's distress.

He reminded her of . . . someone. Of someone who made her feel timid and disheartened without lifting a finger.

He undid her tonight. He turned her around, inside out.

"What's wrong, loovey?"

She glanced up at the endearment, biting her lip. For a moment, he was her sweet Mick. "You overwhelm me," she said.

He clicked his tongue. "No, no, loov. Don't let it happen. I'm just playing. Play with me." As if to illustrate, he said in an ever-so-dramatically upper-class voice, "Aah, Miss Bollash, you do dance divinely." Then he winked at her and added, "Of course, you do have the best equipment for dancing of anyone in the room."

Her legs. The thought made her smile. Then frown, then blink, then smile and frown, both,

shyly and perpetually dazed by the seeming earnestness of his admiration.

He pulled her closer, too close for etiquette, but the best distance for pivots. He took them into this step. Round and round they went till she was faintly dizzy from it, held against his starchy shirtfront, her nose filling with the warm, lemony talc scent of his fresh-shaved cheek.

He eased and led them into a fluid waltz rhythm. She kept up, moving with him smoothly, with growing satisfaction. Yes, they did move remarkably well together. Let people watch if they hadn't anything better to do. She tipped her head back, enjoying the twirl of their waltzing under a ceiling of paintings coffered deeply into other paintings, a ceiling of cherubs and gods, wreaths and battles, ornaments, clouds, all sixty feet or more overhead.

"Look up," she said. And he did. They spun in the light of old-fashioned chandeliers aflame with real, flickering candles, illumination augmented discreetly with gas jets.

"What a place," he said as they passed a woman who waved her fan at them. The Baroness of Whitting, becoming rather bold in trying to gain their attention. Or Winnie thought it was she. She wasn't certain, she couldn't see perfectly without raising her lenses, which she pointedly refused to do. They danced past a man who, she believed, was one of the Lamonts, movement and lack of eyesight making him, too, impossible to determine precisely. They left

them all behind as Mick said again, "What a place, Winnie."

Yes. She loved Uelle. Uelle itself was something. She had just breathed her first easy breath inside its walls again, just gathered her first nice moment, when Mick said, "Suppose the Lamonts brought me here to pose as someone."

She frowned, saying quickly, "They didn't."

He only laughed at her. She stared up into his crooked, handsome smile.

"Suppose," he continued, "I'm to impersonate someone. Who?"

"Oh, Mick, don't. Don't weave stories or start trouble."

"I'm not starting any. I'm going to end it." He wiggled his eyebrows in his wicked way, then told her, "I'm going to catch rats."

"No! Oh, no," she groaned. "You mustn't! Mick, I'm so nervous. Don't complicate things."

It was like pleading to a wall, though. His mind was elsewhere. He couldn't stop speculating. He said, "So this person I'm to impersonate likes purple and trains. No," he corrected, "cabooses. Purple and cabooses. Someone whose name is perhaps Michael. Do you know anyone who fits that description?"

She shook her head, lamenting his obsession with the Lamonts. "Oh, Mick, do you seriously believe Jeremy and Emile have set up something so elaborate? Then would try to carry it off here, of all places?"

He took her aback. "Without doubt, Win," he

answered. Then repeated, "Purple and ca-booses."

She frowned at him. "It sounds like a child."

"Yes!" he said. "A child, yes!" He thought a moment. "A child, grown up into me." He pondered the idea to a left turn then a right. "And money," he added. "There's money in it somewhere, for me being this child." He frowned, perplexed. "Can you think of anything from there?"

"No." She shook her head and danced with a man who moved as naturally as if he'd waltzed all his adult life.

He kept them dancing, turning, swooping to the music as they avoided everyone who might want their attention.

Then *Winnie* missed a step. "Wait," she said. Oh, no. She frowned. She half-hated to tell Mick, but something did occur to her. She said, "The year I was born, there was a tragedy. I only heard about it. But one of my cousins" — she thought it out particularly — "my second cousin once removed was kidnapped: Xavier's grandson." She looked up into Mick's face, pressing her lips together. She truly didn't like the rest of what she had to say. She sighed, disappointed to lend credence to his theory that the Lamonts were swindlers. "There was a very large reward," she said. "Oh —"

He broke away.

"Wait. Where are you going?"

He headed toward a doorway through which a servant had just come into the room, a servant

carrying a tray of champagne. Winnie followed. He stopped the fellow long enough to take two glasses, handing one to her.

"Wait," she called again. Then repeated the question he hadn't answered, "Where are you going?"

He pointed to another servant, whose champagne tray was empty. "Wherever he goes," Mick answered. "I'm going down into the kitchen, wherever I can find a servant who might have been here thirty years ago. I want to know more about this grandson."

"Oh, Mick —"

He was gone. He disappeared between the arches into the series of anterooms that ran along one side of the ballroom.

Winnie stood there, holding a cold glass of champagne, feeling uneasy. She took a sip, then another, then a long swill. It was good. She took another drink. Then she blinked, for it seemed she saw Mick again, only walking between the same arches in the other direction. She lifted her pince-nez to confirm the oddity. It was indeed Mick, going the wrong way. He was carrying something. Food.

She called, "No. You want the door at the other end."

He started, as if surprised to see her still standing there, watching him through her spectacle lenses. Then he smiled, shrugging off his momentary fluster, and answered, "I decided to get my cloak first. I think I left something in it."

His cloak? She tilted her head, puzzled. He was taking food to his cloak?

Mick was taking food to Freddie. He stood out on the river walk in the dark, his cloak over his arm, that hand holding a plate, while his other dipped into the place in the lining he'd made for the animal. He pulled her out. She felt listless, but warm and breathing, happy to see him. And well she should be: He offered her slices of cooked liver he'd found in an antechamber that was serving it. He'd found, in fact, a virtual ferret feast: liver, some of the fattest, biggest goose liver he'd ever seen, some sort of fish roe with cream, and chopped, hard-boiled egg; plus he'd brought the champagne. Surprisingly, the ailing ferret ate the liver. She loved it, then liked the fish roe even better. She lapped up the thick cream, nibbled some hard-boiled egg, but wouldn't touch the bubbly wine.

"There you go, duck," he told her, pleased to see her eat. "You fight the good fight. Keep your strength up."

Once she'd finished, he settled her back into his cloak, smoothing it over his arm, feeling her weight in its lining. Then he walked around the corner, out of the dark, and smiled at the servant who held the door for him. "Fine night," he said.

The fellow looked startled, then smiled. "Yes, m'lord." The man seemed quite cheerful to have been addressed.

At the cloak counter, Mick handed the gar-

ment back to the fellow who would hang it. "No," he said sadly. "I didn't leave my notecase in it. Nor it is outside where I thought I'd dropped it. Sorry to trouble you. Hang it carefully, please."

Half an hour later, Winnie was standing with Mick, a member of Parliament, and the MP's wife, when the baroness finally caught up with them. She waved at Winnie, still several heads away, just as the MP asked Mick, "Bartonreed, how long have you been in London?"

"Six weeks." Mick didn't even hesitate.

After more than an hour, Winnie knew him to be frighteningly good, frighteningly bold in his charade. She kept watching people, waiting for someone to call him out over the hoax. No one did. No one even seemed to suspect. In fact, people liked him. As the evening had progressed, more and more he was sought out.

"Six weeks? Yet we haven't seen or heard of your being here," said the MP's wife. She smiled and batted her fan against her chest, *thwap, thwap, thwap.* "Where have you been hiding yourself?"

Mick lowered his eyes as if hesitant to say, then smiled and explained, "Lady Bollash has, um, taken most of my time."

Winnie looked at him. Oh, no, she thought. He wasn't going to begin with his courting-her nonsense again, was he?

Then worse, the Baroness of Whitting wiggled

her way through the last cluster of people, calling, "Michael!" She thought to add, "And
Winnie!"

The MP and his wife turned, making a place
for the woman among them.

"Oh, Michael," continued the baroness. "And
Win. How lovely to see you again." She leaned
and bussed both their checks like old friends.
With a look of smugness, she announced to the
others, "Winnie and Michael are engaged. Isn't
that delightful?"

"No, no —" Winnie protested.

"Unofficially," the baroness corrected, then
winked, pleased with herself.

"Your lordship," the MP's wife asked, "where
are you from?"

The baroness chimed in, "Paris."

The other woman frowned at her. "That's odd.
He doesn't sound as if he's from Paris."

"Actually I'm not," Mick said. "I'm from
Cornwall. I'm sorry" — he reached for her name
then, surprisingly, found it — "Blanche. I was
having you on a bit."

The baroness loved the use of her given name
with its implied coziness.

The other woman didn't. She questioned
Mick, "Well, you don't sound as if you're from
Cornwall either."

"Ah." He looked around for a reason, then
found, "That's because I was educated elsewhere."

Winnie was entranced. He simply kept going,

431

spinning bits of the truth into long, believable threads, while no one seemed to think anything of his ludicrous answers.

"Where?" the MP asked affably.

Mick frowned at him. "Where what?"

"Where were you educated?"

He was only nonplused a moment, then smiled in Winnie's direction. "Why, um, the same place Winnie was," he said, taking her hand.

"Girton?" his wife asked. "Girton is a girls' school."

"No, not Girton," Winnie said, giggling nervously. "Cambridge. I was at Girton when Michael was at Clare. That's how we met, at Heffer's, the bookstore. I dumped over a stack of books, and he helped me pick them up."

Mick stared at her, then beamed.

A few minutes later, as they danced, she told him, "It was rather fun, that last bit. I saved you."

"You did."

But who would save her? She danced with a man who was bold beyond her bravest dream, who moved as easily in this crowd as the one at the Bull and Tun. Confident, elegant — It suddenly occurred to her whom he reminded her of, and the notion made her stumble and stop: Xavier. Only younger and handsomer. And kinder.

Though this fact disturbed her, Winnie managed to relax a little. The evening became pleasurable in its way. She caught up with two friends who had tried to stay in touch, but whom she had avoided because she'd been too ashamed of her

circumstances. How ridiculous. It was pure fun to hear about their lives and realize she still liked them very much.

Mick disappeared again. Sometimes she spotted him among people. Sometimes he was nowhere to be found. Mostly, she enjoyed suddenly coming upon him in a crowd. She played a game, Find the Ratcatcher, as she tried to catch glimpses of the man he used to be.

He seemed to control it. He could smile out at her, call her *loovey,* then disappear behind Lord Bartonreed — a man who nonchalantly named himself after the sterling on his tea table, then carried the masquerade off as seamlessly as if he were truly the lordly fellow he pretended.

She realized it wasn't the ghost of the English lord she feared. It was the real gentleman, the sterling article she didn't feel up to.

As she watched Mick, she thought, her problem was not as she'd supposed, that she couldn't run off with a ratcatcher. Oddly enough, that didn't sound so difficult anymore. No, her problem was that she was afraid of Lord Bartonreed. The man whom everyone looked at, who could have any woman he chose, who, if he lived among these people, would be deluged with finer possibilities than an elocution and deportment teacher.

Empty tins. Empty again. Insufficient. When everyone else's seemed full.

Winnie stood talking to her former student,

the young duchess, while waiting for Mick in the antechamber near the servants' door. He'd gone downstairs again. A footman had arranged for him to talk to a cook who'd been in the duke's household for years. As Winnie spoke with her friend, Jeremy Lamont caught her attention. He came toward her, looking harried, then motioned her aside with urgency. She excused herself to speak with him.

Jeremy shook his head, unhappy, then told her, "Arles wants you in his study." He pointed to a room at the other end of the long anteroom, the distress on his face compounding. He gave her a pained look. "We hadn't planned on an interview, but he wants Tremore, too. He wants to talk to him, to talk to all of us. Where is he?"

"Who? Mick?" She pretended to look around, then shrugged. That was when she saw him. She couldn't believe it.

Winnie lifted her pince-nez and frowned through the lenses. Yes, Mick entered the room at the far end, coming from the reception room again. He'd gotten to it somehow through another service stairway. The man was certainly familiar with below-stairs avenues.

Then as she stood there with Jeremy squirming, full of anxiety, a horrible feeling of her own suddenly descended into the pit of her stomach. Mick's cloak. He kept leaving and was clearly doing something more than talking to servants. She remembered once before, when his ferret

had not been doing well, he'd taken the creature into his pocket.

And tonight, when she'd felt something small and soft in his cloak, he'd even admitted it. Freddie.

No, she thought. Oh, no. Not tonight, Mick. No one could overlook a ferret. Not with several people in the room who had even been in Abernathy and Freigh's when Freddie had last made herself publicly known. No, oh, no, she groaned inwardly.

To Jeremy, she said, "There he is. You go on. I'll get him."

Winnie avoided Mick instead, racing toward the cloakroom. A ferret. Only ratcatchers had ferrets. Gentlemen had . . . horses and setters or perhaps a pet parrot. But ferrets . . . Oh, they would be discovered. She would be humiliated in front of — if not *by* — a cousin who enjoyed humiliating her.

She told the man who watched over and fetched people's wraps, "I've left my face rouge in my fiancé's cloak. It's the long black one with the dark purple lining."

He wouldn't let her take it, but only come into the back to go through its tucks and pockets. Happily, someone else came along, needing the man's attention. Winnie wedged herself between a pile of hats and a rack of hanging wraps. There she ran her hand down Mick's cloak and — oh, with a plummet felt the soft little weight.

"O-o-oh, no," she groaned.

She reached into the pocket in the lining, squinching her eyes tight, clenching her teeth. She had to get it out, get rid of it, but, *ewww*, what was it like to touch? She felt around, digging down into the cloak lining, then suddenly she had it. Through her glove, it was smooth-coated, warm and wiggly — like a snake in a slippery-slick mink coat.

Ugh. She let go with a choked little breath, her hand coming out empty. She had to steel herself to try again. Calm down, she told herself. Get the thing into — what? Her purse. Would it fit into her purse? Yes. Put it in your purse, she told herself, then carry it out to Georges at the carriage. He could take it back to London, give it to Milton, who could put it in its cage, then come right back. If Georges left now, he'd return just in time to take them home.

That would do it. Perfect. She reached in again. The little thing was frightened. So was she. She rubbed the back of her gloved knuckle along it, feeling the resistance of bone, possibly a little skull. She got her fingers under its belly and lifted, aware of its little bones, the way it braced its claws, fearing her, trusting her.

With her back to the room for shelter, Winnie pulled the little animal out into view — oh, ugh, she thought again and shivered. She looked it in its little animal face, and it made a little sound, a kind of hiss at the back of its throat. Its parted mouth, the view of its tiny teeth, made Winnie

shudder again. Then the ferret took a good look at her and began to run its legs, wiggling its body. It didn't like her holding it any more than she liked having it in her hand.

She lost her grip of it. Freddie dropped into her skirts, a light plop, then slid down the silk, making Winnie squeal and step back from fright. The thing looked stunned for a second. She thought she'd killed it. Oh, God. A new dread. Mick would be furious. But the second Winnie reached for the ferret again, it skittered — straight into the coats and wraps, burrowing into them.

She dug through for a few moments.

Someone — the man who checked and watched over the coats — tapped her shoulder. "Miss, may I help you find the gentleman's cloak?"

She looked up and around. "No, I have it." Indeed, she still held Mick's evening cloak. Which left her with no excuse to keep digging.

"What are you looking for then?"

She didn't dare say. "Nothing." Out the corner of her eye she saw a little brown tail-thing skitter out the door and into the main reception room. "Oh, dear God."

She threw the cloak at him and ran after the ferret. The reception hall, though, was crowded. The last she saw of Mick's ferret was its tail as it disappeared between the trouser legs of a lordly secretary from the College of Arms.

A moment later, Mick appeared at the far end

437

of the entry room. He spotted her, but it took a minute or more for him to make his way to her. A full minute to suffer over what she had done.

Oh, what to say, what to tell him? Her apprehension grew, spiraling into gigantic proportions.

As Mick came toward her, suavely excusing himself past people, smiling as he went, she wanted to shake him. She wanted to scream, *Stop!* Stop it! Stop being as I remember Xavier, only more so. Stop being so . . . frighteningly competent and polished, so damnably fearless.

Lord, he reminded her of Xavier's hauteur when he moved, of the cocksure way that Xavier had carried himself years ago. Mick was taller and more limber, but he had something like Xavier's bumptiousness to him, a manner that everyone had put up with in Xavier because, like Mick, he had somehow managed also to be charming — and because her cousin had been the most likely heir to a duchy. No, part of her *wanted* the ratcatcher revealed. This man, this Lord Bartonreed, made the hair on her neck stand on end.

As he came nearer, she shrank back, determined to say nothing about the ferret, like a miscreant under death-sentence, waiting for the axe. He'd find out. But until then, distraught at what she'd done, she would hide there inside her own quiet.

Yet Mick was wrong to have brought the animal, wasn't he? For a moment more, she felt

confused: ashamed and fearful, but angry, too. The old terror didn't quite take hold. Worse than empty tins, she reprimanded herself. You look like a mantis and think like a mule.

Yet no. She hadn't meant for this to happen. Her original intent had been to safeguard them, not expose them further. She had meant to take good care of the ferret. And besides, a voice said, you needed to be a mule to survive your upbringing. Outwardly shy and retiring, a proper young lady; inwardly as strong as a donkey.

As Mick smiled and touched her shoulder, Winnie frowned, putting the tips of her gloved fingers to her mouth. Then she brought them down and told him, "I lost your ferret."

"You what?"

"Freddie. I thought I was sending her home, but she got away from me."

"What the hell —" He didn't like it.

"Don't be angry."

"She's ill."

"She certainly ran fast enough."

He scowled. "Where did you lose her?"

"Right here somewhere."

"Why did you do it?" he asked. He bent toward her, putting himself nose to nose with her.

She whispered, vehement, "Because at least two of the couples from the teahouse six weeks ago are right here —"

"It would have been fine —"

"It would have been odd beyond measure: A gentleman does not bring a ferret to a ball."

"You don't know that." He made a harsh, put-out face. "There could be a ferret in every cloak here: You didn't look. You expect everyone to play by the same rules you do."

And *still* she didn't crumble. It amazed her. "I'm sorry," she said. "You're right. I shouldn't have done it. I should have spoken my fears to you. But I didn't. Now help me find her."

They tried; they looked. They wandered through the crowd, communicating with each other through heads to ask by facial expression, *Have you seen her yet?*

The answer was always no. Then Winnie lost sight of Mick entirely. She could find neither. Not Mick. Nor Freddie.

Someone grabbed her elbow. Emile. He hissed. "He *wants* us now. We're late. Get going."

Oh, grand. Xavier. This was all she needed. Now of all times to have to face him. But there was no help for it. She would go and placate him till Emile or Jeremy were able to bring Mick along.

When Winnie walked into the study, Jeremy was already there. Emile came in a few minutes later. He'd spoken to Mick who was coming. Shortly, he hoped. On their way here, they'd been separated when an animal of some sort had attacked the Russian caviar and crème fraiche, then beat a path through the foie gras. Mick had gone berserk trying to catch the thing.

The ferret. Since it was just the three of them,

she told them about the animal, two souls with whom to lament. They all groaned.

"And Xavier will make us wait at least half an hour," she told them. "He likes to keep people dangling."

So they sat, while her stomach churned.

She felt ill. Oh, and she thought she'd been embarrassed — shamed — before. Wait till everyone heard *this*. Winnie Bollash was thrown out of the Duke of Arles's ball for having brought a ratcatcher and a ferret to it. No one would ever bring their daughters to her again, no matter how good she was at phonetics.

They only waited a few minutes, however, before the duke's study door creaked open, and a stooped old man came through it, walking slowly with the use of a cane, a woman hovering behind him.

Xavier. He was thinner and more feeble than Winnie remembered. She lifted her pince-nez and had a good look.

He was himself, yet he wasn't. She could barely credit how he'd changed. Withered and bent, he had to have help — his wife attended him — all the way to the desk, where he sat like a bag of bones dropped into the chair.

"You let go too soon," he snapped at her, his voice raw. She stepped behind him, less the trophy than Winnie had imagined, more a nursemaid. Attentive, fussing, she reached for his arm, trying to take his cane. Imperiously, he snatched it out of her reach. Then from his chair, as from a

throne, he settled the cane across the desk and stared about the room, glowering at everyone.

Oddly, he didn't seem powerful so much as crotchety. Though, no doubt, he had power. Just not the kind Winnie had always accorded him: He had no power over her.

His wizened body didn't keep him from quick words. The second his eyes settled on her, anger straightened him like a rod down his spine.

"You stubborn, obnoxious girl," he said. "Like all the rest, you come to play on an old man's pain. Well" — he looked around, speaking to them all — "where is he, this Michael?" He said the name with distaste.

"He's coming," Emile told him.

"I've seen him," the old man said directly. "I looked him over when he came down the ballroom stairway, then I left. That was enough. He's an imposter." He added, "Whom I shall unmask with a few pointed questions, then have you all thrown in jail."

Jail. Winnie's heart sank. They were all going to jail.

Just then, footfalls outside the room made everyone's head turn. Just beyond the door, footsteps approached. They were Mick's; Winnie knew their confident rhythm. They tapped, separating out of the crowd in the anteroom, came closer, then paused, and the knob turned.

Mick stepped in, handsome, dashing, looking as if he could carry off anything. Ah, there was what she wanted. There was what she stood to

442

lose that was greater still. How to have him? How to get out of all this somehow and run away with him somewhere?

He stared from one to the other, puzzled by the gathering. Then his eyes stopped on the old man behind the desk, and a look of surprise crossed his face.

After which a single word came out Mick's mouth, with his looking more surprised still, as if it came out on its own and he couldn't hold it back.

"Poppy," he said. The way someone might ask, *Poppy, what are* you *doing here?*

Chapter 28

Xavier Bollash's chin tightened till it dimpled. He brought his lip up, mashing it against his teeth, while his glaucous, watery eyes grew fierce.

While he stared at Mick, he spoke under his breath with chilling quiet. "Get out." Then louder and firmer, "Get out." He lifted himself precariously to his feet, and, from here, he flew into rage. "Get out, get out, get out!" He pounded the desk. "Get out, all of you! He's not my grandson! This is a hoax. I won't have it!"

His pursed lips began to tremble until the movement was so violent he had to put his hand up over his mouth.

Winnie watched Mick take a step toward him, his brow furrowed in concern.

He seemed about to say something, when the old man swung his cane through the air. It cleared everything off the desk. Pens, a book, a pair of glasses moved with such force that they hit the bookcase to the side before they clattered to the floor.

Thumping his cane down, he hobble-pounded around the desk. "You! And her!" He swung his

cane to point at Winnie. "Don't think I don't know what she does. This time she goes too far with her passing off her damned creations on me." To Mick, "I saw how you danced with her. The conniving witch is trying to regain her lost property through a man she's invented. Well, I'm not having it." To the room at large, "You're all pretenders, all of you, scoundrels. This is too much! All of you, get out!"

His wife cautiously approached him, trying to help him without being hit by the cane, while the old man was so unpredictable, no one else dared move. With shuffling steps that couldn't match his rancor, he made his way toward the door — "getting out" himself, since no one else seemed inclined to.

He seemed infuriated by his own slow progress, muttering as he went, "So what? So he looks like my son. My grandson wouldn't dress like that. He wouldn't wear a vest with such a loud lining." He looked from one person to the next, as if he didn't know to whom he was addressing the remark. He frowned at Mick, stared a moment, then looked away. "Though he might wear purple," he grumbled. "He loved purple." At the door, he glanced at them all again, issuing another fierce scowl, then asserted finally, as if it were proof positive: "But he wouldn't dance all night with Winnie Bollash, not when there was a roomful of prettier women. *My* grandson would have taste." He stabbed at the floor again with the walking stick as his wife opened the door.

He would no doubt have loved a clean, brisk exit. But physical feebleness dictated he scoot a step, Vivian Bollash taking his elbow, then scoot another step. She guided him as he stabbed at the floor for traction. Stab, *step,* stab, *scoot.* Shaking with age, infirmity, and a strong desire to deny what he obviously feared to believe, he made his feeble way out, his wife at his elbow.

After such an astounding departure, utter silence reigned in the room for at least ten seconds. No one had expected anything like this.

Then Emile Lamont looked at Mick and said, "That was cute. Where did you dig that up?"

"What?" Mick looked distracted: as if trying to grasp the meaning of a seemingly huge, unforeseen possibility.

Could he really be Xavier's grandson? Winnie wondered.

She stepped toward him, laying her hand on his arm as she tried to explain his use of the nickname away. "He must have learned the name downstairs when he went to talk to the cook's assistant." She changed the subject. To the Lamonts, she said, "You have attempted to trick my cousin, but it didn't work —"

"Oh, it worked," Emile said. He turned more fully toward her, folding his arms and leaning a hip on the desk. "He's shaken. But he'll come around and fairly soon." To Mick, "He believes you're his —"

"No," Mick said, stepping toward him. "No. You're finished now. So am I. I was coming up

446

here to tell Arles the whole story. The bet, how you made me seem like the grandson he still longs for, and how" — he paused — "how it just isn't true."

Emile snorted. "Right. That's why you called him that name when you came in. Because you were going to tell him the truth." He snorted again. "*Poppy*. Nice touch, Tremore —"

Mick leaped at him, grabbing him by the front of his coat, walking — slamming — the man backward with the momentum of his anger. He rammed Emile's back into the bookcases against the wall.

"Mick —" Winnie called.

He didn't listen, but lifted the struggling, furious Lamont slightly onto his toes. Into his face, Mick said, "What I 'dug up,' arsehole, is you are conning this old man for a hundred thousand pounds and using me to do it. Well, you're finished; it didn't work." He glanced over his shoulder at Jeremy, who, now pale, had stepped toward the door. "You won the bet," he told him. "Everyone here thinks I'm a viscount. Your brother owes you money —"

Emile hissed vehemently, "There was no bet, you stupid —"

"Shut up." Mick shoved him harder, til the man let out an *ooof* of breath.

"Mick, don't be —"

"I'm not hurting him, Win. Not yet anyway." To Emile, he said, "My obligation to you was to fulfil my part in a bet. I did. You owe me a hun-

447

dred pounds, because I pulled it off. And then you're leaving. You are *not* using me to milk money and heartache out of an old man, no matter how much he might deserve it. And you are not staying here to cause trouble."

He let the man go and stepped back so suddenly that Emile stumbled down the length of one bookshelf. His face, when he turned, though was livid. Leaning toward Mick, he whispered, furious, "The reason you don't want us to have the hundred thousand is you see it coming out of your pocket now: You intend to con him out of the entire duchy, you ungrateful, greedy son-of-a —"

Mick grabbed him by the back of the coat, moving him toward the doorway, escorting the two brothers out.

Winnie followed, frowning. So *did* Mick hear the nickname downstairs? Was he attempting to assume a duchy? By virtue of six weeks' instruction on how to be an English Lord? *Her* instruction? She wished for a moment that she didn't know him to be so . . . quick-witted, so adept at improvising and taking advantage of whatever came his way.

As Jeremy and Emile were handed their things from the cloak attendant, Jeremy stammered, "W-we'll call the police on you, Tremore. We won't let you get away with this."

"I've done nothing wrong." He pushed them toward the main front doors, then stepped out behind them into the night with Winnie fol-

lowing. "Have a good walk to London," he told them.

"You won't get away with this. I'll see that you —"

"You won't see that I'm anything. Tomorrow morning I'm turning over your counterfeit bills to the authorities. If you have any sense, you'll be as far from England as possible by then. Don't ever come back."

Jeremy let out a high, foolish laugh that came out in a giddy burst. He stood under the portico, silhouetted against the river torches, his hat in his hand, his cloak clutched to his chest. "You — you —" He struggled for words for a moment. "You *rat*catcher." Rather prosaically, he added, "Who do you think you are?"

There in the odd light from the riverwalk, Mick blinked, frowned, then shook his head. He looked down. "I don't know," he said, "I don't know."

In the entry alcove as they came back in, Winnie leaned toward Mick and asked, "Did the cook's assistant tell you the name?"

Mick bent his head to her, touching her back, her spine. "No," he said, "but I don't think that means anything." His voice grew more hushed as they whispered together. "She told me about the kidnapped grandson and the reward from years ago. I was going into Arles's study to tell him, to set the record straight from one end to the other. But when I saw him —" He broke off. "I can't

449

explain it. He so reminded me of my own grand-father. That's what I used to call him. *Poppy*. The name isn't that unusual, is it?"

Winnie took his arm. Such a warm, muscular arm beneath his evening coat. Then he lifted it to put it around her shoulder, and they leaned into each other. They stood there almost as if consoling one another.

"I don't know how unusual it is," she told him. "I don't know what to think."

He brushed the crown of her head with his lips.

No, she didn't know what to think, except that she loved him, whoever he was.

When they returned to the ballroom, the most amazing thing happened. As they entered, a small commotion was already in progress. Winnie raised her pince-nez. And — egad! — she watched a small tail-thing scoot from the sidelines out among the dancers in the center of the ballroom floor.

Pandemonium. The dancing stopped. The orchestra faltered. Men called out as women screeched, lifting their skirts and trying to flee out of its way as it darted between feet and around dresses.

Winnie — Winnie herself — took off after it, leaving Mick behind. She ran straight out into the middle of the huge dance floor and held up her arms. "Don't anyone move," she said. "You'll frighten her. It's Mick's ferret. She's gotten loose."

She glanced at Mick and saw him, his head

tilted at her, smiling the sweetest smile.

Everyone grew still, exactly as she'd asked. The little thing skittered around feet, visible one moment, lost the next. A man near Mick — the very man who was part of the couple who'd been at Abernathy and Freigh's when the ferret had last gotten lose six weeks ago — said, "Oh, I hope you can get her. My pet monkey ran out of the house last month, and we never found him. I've been distraught ever since."

People bent down — though a few, mostly women, climbed onto chairs.

Someone called, "Here it is!" Then, "There it goes!"

For the most part, the gathering tried to help the new young lord in their midst locate his unusual pet.

The ferret didn't matter. Because there was something about Mick that wasn't a fake anything. And Winnie herself felt more real somehow, running around, looking for the little animal that meant so much to him.

Alas, though, Freddie eluded everyone again. Mick called her and called her, but she was either too frightened or too weak to come.

He was philosophical about it. He shrugged as they began dancing again. "It's all right," he said. "The night is won. We did it. Let's enjoy our success."

Surprisingly, it wasn't hard to do. Winnie found herself smiling and smiling at Mick. She worried for him a little, because he didn't always

smile back. He was quieter than usual. But the music and the swirling rhythms of dancing seemed eventually to penetrate his mood. Indeed, the night was won. Mick made a brilliant English lord. And she celebrated a success of her own: With a freedom much as she had at the Bull and Tun, she cane back to Uelle — to the ease she had known within its walls only rarely since childhood.

Somewhere near midnight, Mick said, "I want to ask you something."

They were dancing in the thick of the crowd, in a sea of shoulders that swirled in unison. Her face felt flushed from exertion. She was happy. "Ask away," she said innocently.

"Winnie," he began, "when I ask you this, I want you to understand, it's just Mick asking. As nice as this evening is, I'm not a viscount or marquess or heir to a duchy, nor do I want to be."

She only smiled. She knew who he was. Her Mick.

He halted a moment, a man facing his misgivings. Their gazes caught, eye to eye, and her smile seemed to give life again to his. After a moment, he let out a snort of humor, shrugged, then laughed outright. He said suddenly, "I love dancing with you like this." He leaned toward her, dancing much too closely, and murmured, "I love you, Win."

Goodness. Her chest filled with warmth, a rush of pure, physical joy to hear the words aloud. He loved her.

"I love you, too," she said, the silly exchange of lovers.

"I know."

She laughed. "You would, of course."

He stared fixedly at her, still smiling as he turned them in waltzing rhythm. "So I was thinking that I'm good enough for you, Winnie Bollash, good enough to ask at least. My question is, Will you marry me?"

She stared. Marry him? She'd dreamed of his asking, of her doing it. She'd played with the idea. But he was joking surely. Still, she smiled so widely at the notion, it made her cheeks hurt. Oh, this man. This bold ratcatcher she had taken in six weeks ago knew no limits, no boundaries. "You know," she said, "you remind me of someone."

"Who?" He made a put-out face. "And that is not an answer, you witch."

She laughed. A witch. Oh, yes. "You remind me of Xavier."

"No-o-o-o." He rolled his eyes. "What an awful thing to tell me." He laughed. "Here I offer to make an honest woman of you, and you say I remind you of your atrocious cousin." More seriously, though, he added, "Winnie, don't kid yourself. That's what I was saying: You're in the arms of Coornish Mick" — he used his old accent — "the soon-to-be-valet who'll have a nice income with a retirement sum one day. And the immediate use of his own cottage on a picturesque estate in a town that could possibly use a

resident scholar who writes her papers in New-castle, then has to take the train to present them in London." He took a deep breath after all that, then said, "Winnie, find a way. Make it true. Marry me."

She frowned. He wanted it to be real. Marry him. What would she do with her tutoring? What would Milton do? How would she sort herself out in a community where she was the wife of a gentleman's gentleman?

The practicalities of it boggled her mind. Yet, try as she might, the idea so pleased her, she embarrassed herself. She looked down at their feet. And, goodness, their feet. How well they moved together! In and out, in and out, between each other's legs. She shook her head, grinning foolishly. Oh, dear. What was she doing? Everything around them, people and ballroom, blurred as she looked up again to meet Mick's gaze.

She nodded. "All right."

He missed a step. "All right?" He stopped entirely, his face full of wonder. A couple ran into them before dancers knew to detour around. "All right?" he repeated.

"Yes."

He didn't know what to say. He looked about them a moment, then grabbed the first person to dance within reach. He told a surprised, elderly woman with a tiara, "We're engaged." As if she'd disputed it, he added, "No, truly. We truly, in fact, are engaged. We're to be married."

He grabbed hold of Winnie then, taking one

hand tightly in his, his other palm pressed her back, and pulled her up against him, flat against him, as he danced them in pivots, round and round, double-time. Then he kissed her on the mouth, still dancing. *Dancing with your mouth on someone you like.* It was harder than she'd thought, bumpier, but nice.

He laughed at her gracelessness with it, then danced them some more. If she'd thought people would disapprove, she'd been wrong again. A little space cleared for them, and people began to applaud.

"Tell me again," Mick said. Over and over, "Tell me again, tell me again. . . ."

"Yes." And again, "Yes, yes, yes." She was delighted with his elation, his candor. More practically, she couldn't help asking, "Can't we stay in London? Do you really want to go to Newcastle? Do you really want to be a valet? I don't know what I want exactly or how to manage it all. Could you give up something so I could be in London a little —"

"Shush." He put his finger over her lips as they danced. Then, making his ridiculously fine half-smile up one side of his face, he said, "We'll bargain. Figure out what you want most, and it's yours. You're the queen of propositions, Win."

Chapter 29

The next day, Winnie and Mick were awakened by the arrival of an urgent message from Vivian Bollash.

HE WANTS TO SEE YOU. HE ISN'T WELL.
PLEASE COME SOON.

Lady Arles greeted them herself at the front door of their London home. "I have something I want to show you first."

Winnie and Mick followed her through a vast entry room with thick carpet and trickling fountains. It took Mick somehow aback. He halted when he first saw it.

He murmured to Winnie, "I think I ratted this place once. I know this house."

He seemed disoriented when they entered the front library. Then out and out stunned, as was Winnie herself: In the center of the far library wall was a portrait. "Oh, my Lord," she whispered, grabbing Mick's arm as if she could hold him back from looking.

The painting, five feet high and placed prominently in view, was of a man in his thirties, a man

who wore clothes from decades ago, yet who, other than that, looked so like Mick, it was hair-raising. The man in the oil portrait had Mick's long bones, his deep brow, his black hair.

And a faint, lordly version of his perfectly crooked smile.

"His eyes are blue," Mick said as if in contradiction to something.

"Xavier's are green," she murmured. "You look like this man. Exactly like him. Mick —" She left the thought unfinished.

He put his hand up over his mouth, thinking, then he turned around, scanning the books on the shelves, then the room. His eyes slid along a heavy desk the size of a grand piano to the lamp on it that dripped with crystal. A tray beside the lamp held glasses of cut crystal. He frowned at this, then looked at Vivian.

"Was there ever a decanter on that tray?"

She looked at the desk, frowned, then shook her head. "I don't know. Oh, wait. How odd." She turned again and reached toward the portrait, its frame. "Here," she said. "I've never seen a decanter in this room as long as I have been here, but Xavier won't fix the picture frame. He says his son did this."

She ran her hand over a gash in the side of the wood, then explained, "He told me his son broke a decanter on it, when he threw it against the wall. He had quite a temper apparently." She looked at Mick. "Do you suppose it's the same decanter you remember?"

457

Mick shook his head. "I don't know. I'm not even sure it's significant." He shrugged. "Winnie has one, too. They're not so uncommon."

They walked upstairs then into the darkened room of Xavier Bollash. They could hear him before they entered. He was cursing someone, complaining that people were always trying to trick him, take his money, that no one ever told him the truth. That no one ever loved him enough.

It was his doctor, who was packing up, leaving, disgusted with him.

"What's wrong?" Winnie asked from the doorway. Xavier was in bed. He didn't look strong enough to be sitting up, though he was.

He turned toward them. "I've had a heart attack is what's wrong."

"Oh, no," she said. Then, "I did this by bringing ferrets to your ball and by —"

He cut her off, saying, "I'm ninety-six years old, you arrogant girl. Who do you think you are? God? I'm dying because I'm old, and nothing works anymore." Then he motioned them close, to stand by his bed.

There, Winnie looked down and saw a surprise.

"My God!" Mick said.

It was Freddie. The ferret lay on the old man's chest, snoozing.

"It's yours, isn't it?" Xavier's crackly voice asked. "Do you know it only eats foie gras, crème fraiche, and Russian caviar? An expensive little

458

beast." He laughed, rasping and coughing again as the complacent animal allowed him to pet it despite his joggling it on his chest. "What's its name?" he asked.

"Freddie."

His eyes brightened, a genuinely lively burst, and he smiled without reservation, delighted, surprised. "Freddie," he repeated, settling back again, stroking the shiny brown fur. "I should have known."

He lifted his gaze to Mick's as the small, pointed tip of his tongue came out, trying to wet lips that looked as dry as paper. His eyes grew round and glassy. "My grandson loved animals," he said. "Of course, what child doesn't? But he was marvelous with them. At two and a half, he would call; they would come to him. They weren't afraid." He closed his eyes, remembering, a beatific look of bliss coming over his face. "Oh, he was a magic child." Then he opened his eyes and scowled at Winnie. He pointed a long, boney finger at her, shakily. "Instead we were stuck with her. A girl. And an ugly one at that."

Mick didn't like the remark, but he sat down on the edge of the bed anyway. Very quietly, he began to explain, "Sir," he said, "we've come because you asked. But you have to know: I'm not your grandson. I had a mother. I have a family. I come from Cornwall."

The intransigent old man, though, would only smile and shake his head. "No," he insisted,

"you're my grandson. You're Michael. Though I called my grandson Freddie. They wouldn't name him after me, so to confound them, I called him by his middle name, my father's name." He smiled with vindictive pleasure.

Mick glanced at Winnie, glad he hadn't been raised by the fellow. Glad he had nothing to do with him. Sorry that she had.

The old man crooked his finger, inviting them both closer. When Mick leaned forward, the old man said, "You are Michael Frederick Bollash, the sixth Duke of Arles by nightfall, I would guess."

"Now, now," Mick said quickly. "Let's have none of that." He frowned. "I'm telling you: I had a real, loving mother. She always said that she nursed me too long, and I was a difficult birth."

No help at all, Winnie asked, "Mick? Don't you think it's a rather large coincidence that your name is Michael and you named your ferret Freddie?"

"Yes." He grew annoyed with both of them. "I do. A coincidence. Let's not call it more than what it is." When he looked at her, though, she believed it. She thought he was the duke's grandson. "I'm not," he told her. "I'm not."

He didn't want to be. Despite the fact that Winnie might deserve a fancier husband, he didn't want the absurd wealth he saw around him. He felt a real and sure attachment to his own family in Cornwall. Moreover, he certainly

didn't want to be related to the self-centered old man lying here in bed.

Meanwhile, the self-centered old man, his eyes still closed, his mouth faintly smiling, spoke into the room as if for all posterity. He said, "My grandson's wet nurse was Cornish. I don't remember her name, but she wouldn't wean him, so we dismissed her. She was too lax, too indulgent. She went back to Cornwall." He shifted grammatical person. "And your birth *was* difficult. My daughter-in-law almost died."

The old man believed it, too.

He added, "The wet nurse was Catholic, deeply religious. We worried she would turn him into a Papist."

Mick, the Papist, remained unconvinced. There were many parallels, but many gaps. "I remember nothing, not any of this."

"Two and a half," Winnie told him. "The child was only two and a half when he disappeared, Mick."

The duke said, "She took him. We let her go months before he was kidnapped. It never occurred to me *she* might have been the one, but now it makes sense. She'd lost a child just before she came to us. She knew the house, our schedules, where to find him. He would have gone with her happily. After all these years, I remember now her saying she thought we were a terrible family, that he should have a better one." He chuckled. "Can you imagine? A Cornish wet nurse thought she was better than the heir to a

461

duchy and all his blood, lineage, and kin." As he nodded off, he muttered, "What an idiot." He settled to sleep.

Vivian asked if they could stay for dinner. She looked harried and alone. Winnie wanted to, so Mick agreed. They stayed, taking turns sitting with the cantankerous patient upstairs. Xavier awoke several times, but seldom for very long. Mostly, he slept with short bursts of demanding one thing or another in fits.

It was Winnie's turn when he awoke, saw her, and motioned her over. Once she was beside him, he patted the bed.

She sat down nervously on the counterpane.

Just then, Vivian brought in his dinner. The moment she entered, he was distracted.

Winnie had already noticed that he never took his eyes off his young wife when she was about. He watched her with ceaseless interest, while she was polite to him. Sweet. Obedient. If he asked for water, she put her sewing down and fetched it for him. When he asked for tea, she went down-stairs to brew it herself.

After she'd gone again, Xavier looked at Winnie. Then he whispered in his hoarse voice, "She doesn't love me. She never loved me." His teeth found the edge of his lip. His round, milky eyes filled with tears that didn't flow. Rather the tears sat in small pools in the bags of his lower lids. He wiped them away with his hand, then tried to bring all his emotion into a bitter laugh that only ended in coughing. His hand found the

ferret. Odd, the way the two of them had found each other. Freddie seemed to like his attention.

Petting the animal, Xavier told Winnie, "I've lived for a dozen years right beside what I've always wanted most, what I thought everything else would bring." Then he shocked her by saying, "But, no. She's still in love with the man I stole her from." He added bitterly, "Though I gave her everything. I gave her a hundred, a *thousand* times what he could have." He curled his lip. "Would she even pretend though —" Even he realized the thought was unworthy. He let it go.

How strange that she had imagined he didn't suffer. How foolish to think, because he was rich and powerful and mean as the blazes that he somehow had life by the tail.

His eyes held Winnie's. She patted his hand. He nodded once — in a kind of thank-you, though she wasn't certain for what. For a moment, his watery eyes clung to hers, hungry for something. She would have given it, if she'd known what it was.

Then she watched as Milford Xavier Bollash slipped out from behind his eyes. They glazed, staring sadly at her, seeing nothing; seeing eternity.

She reached and closed them for him.

It was only when Mick came upstairs that they noticed that Freddie had slipped away, too. The old man and the ferret had wandered off together.

Even for a man of ninety-six, for whom everyone expected that death wasn't too far away, it was a shock. Mick and Winnie stayed to help Vivian through the worst of the first twenty-four hours. Mick took care of the practicalities, organizing the servants, the particulars of the room, calling the doctor, while Winnie fixed Vivian tea with brandy in the kitchen.

As the duchess's husband had imagined, she was not struck down by his going. She was quiet. Quietly set free, Winnie suspected.

She must have been preoccupied though, because she didn't remember to give them an envelope till it was well past midnight and they were leaving.

"I almost forgot. Oh, dear. Here. He said to give you this when he died. I just didn't expect — well, you know. I didn't expect it to be today."

She handed the envelope to Mick, a letter from a dead man.

He opened it as the three of them stood in the severely formal entry room, fountains trickling. Then he had to sit on one of the stiff velvet benches.

"Dear God," he said, then handed the letter to Winnie.

I, Milford Xavier Bollash, fifth Duke of Arles, do hereby acknowledge that the man who presented himself at Uelle Castle this evening, the nineteenth of

464

May eighteen hundred ninety-eight, as Michael Frederick Edgerton is my grandson, son of my own blood, Phillip Samuel Bollash. I do hereby recognize him as my heir and proclaim him due all hereditary honors and properties associated with the duchy of Arles, including the title, and all subsidiary titles, the Marquess of Sissingley, Viscount Berwick, Viscount of Meadborrow, Baron of Berchester.

The letter was dated yesterday evening, signed by the duke with his ducal seal, and witnessed by four men, including the lord secretary of the College of Arms and the Home Secretary himself.

That night Mick dreamed of legs, though it was an odd dream. He dreamed of fine, sturdy legs. Men's legs, women's legs. Beloved legs. Legs lost to him. New legs, strange legs. And all the legs in a dream that was overrun with them were so tall he only came to their knees.

Epilogue

Winnie married Mick anyway, even though he was a duke.

They traveled to Cornwall for the wedding, where they were united as man and wife in a small ceremony followed by a fine, jovial dinner at Mick's aunt's house. Mick's family was in great attendance: two uncles, three aunts, two cousins, and twelve of his brothers and sisters — one brother being unable to come because he wouldn't leave his wife; she was pregnant with their third child and too close to term. The celebration afterward was a gay affair filled with Cornish voices, much dancing, and warm laughter.

Unavoidably, Winnie noticed that Mick didn't look a thing like his brothers and sisters. He was a head taller than the tallest of them. They were all brown-eyed with pinker complexions. No one seemed to notice though; they all adored him. He was fond of each, from the youngest early adolescent rapscallion to the eldest after Mick himself, a shy sister.

Not a one of them thought a thing of the fact that Winnie's few guests — Milton, several of her

former students, and a few of her old friends with whom she had reconnected after the ball — kept addressing herself and her new husband as "your grace."

In general, London society was greatly put out that the new duke should be so private and remote in taking a bride. But it was a precedent. The new duke showed no desire to occupy the center of society in the way the old duke had. Very quickly, people learned the new lord prized above all else family, his wife especially, and the company of dogs, especially terriers — in the first weeks of his marriage, he acquired several from the stock of the famous Reverend Russell.

In London, Mick signed the official marriage documents with his new name, which ironically did not change his wife's name at all — other than to make her the Duchess of Arles. As a matter of course, the new duke granted the dowager duchess the use of the house in London where she had lived with her husband, "for as long as she should want to live there." No kinswoman of his, Mick determined, would struggle to have a good roof over her head. Much to the mystification of London, he granted a family in Cornwall — one by the name of Tremore — the use of the duchy's four lesser estates.

Thus Winnie Bollash, the only daughter of the Marquess of Sissingley, had a remarkable thing happen: Not only did she marry the man she adored who became the Duke of Arles, but through a circuitous route of second cousins,

once removed, she regained her family home, Uelle Castle, which was where she and her husband chose to live.

Mick was out on the river promenade, waiting for her the day she came home from London, having gone to discuss and deliver a copy of her paper on Cockney speech to a playwright who was researching the concept for a play based on the myth of Pygmalion.

"Mick!" she called as her carriage rolled across the bridge. "Mick! Come see!" She had her driver pull right up onto the river walk. "Look what I've brought!" When Mick came close enough, she said the line that she had been rehearsing: "Everyone can always use a little magic."

Then she leaned out the window of the carriage, not even bothering to open the door, and handed him a warm, wiggly puppy.

"Oh, a mongrel terrier!" he said. "My favorite."

"No, a little Magic."

Then she opened the carriage door and let another dog bound out, a dog that leaped up on seeing Mick; it high-jumped five feet into the air.

"Magic!" Mick said. The dog was as pleased to see him as he was to see the animal.

Winnie stepped down from the carriage herself, saying, "He's only visiting. Rezzo won't sell him. But he gave us the puppy as a wedding present." She took the puppy from Mick, letting him deal with Magic, who was beside himself with joy;

jumping, jumping. She brought the puppy against her nose, rubbing his tummy. "Ooh, he smells so good." She grinned over his little, round belly, her eyes smiling at Mick as the puppy stretched his head backward to look at him upside down. She assured him again, "He's Magic's son."

Mick nodded, too content to answer.

"How are the ledgers coming?" she asked. She knew, he was overwhelmed by them some days.

He looked up from the dogs. They had already relieved his preoccupation with all he had to learn — all he and she *both* had to learn — about running an estate. He spent hours over its books, trying to make sense of them. "Getting better," he assured her. "The whole thing is rather like breeding ferrets. Once you know who's who and what strengths are where, you start to know which assets to match up with what liabilities. We'll make a lean little animal of this estate yet."

She watched him playing with the dogs, so seemingly at ease in his bespoke clothes — he liked them and had a wardrobe of them — and new responsibilities. Still, though, she wondered if he missed the more rag-tag lifestyle of making his own business pay by the seat of its pants. From nowhere, she found herself asking, "Are you happy, Mick? Really happy?"

He looked up, surprised. "Aren't you?"

"Me?" She laughed. "I've landed in heaven. I just worry."

"About what, Win? I love you. I want to be with you."

She shook her head. "No, not that. The life here —"

He winked at her. "Loovey, the life here is grand. I've ended up with my Cornish mother's love, my grandfather's money, and you in a castle on the river. What could be better?"

"Well, there's one thing that could be better," she said. She was sheepish, but grinned in spite of herself. She announced, "I've missed my second menses, Mick."

His eyebrows went up. "Oh." He smiled, abandoning the dogs. "Oh, loovey, that's marvelous."

"Really?"

"Abso-bloody-lutely."

She cackled at that — and with delight as he scooped her up against his chest.

"M-m-m," he said, pressing his face into her hair. "I want a lot of children. I come from a very large family, so large it's two families, in fact. M-m-m," nuzzling her more, "that's wonderful, Win. Really wonderful."

How could a person be more content? she wondered. How could anything be better than this?

Then he showed her: Very softly as he nuzzled her, his mouth near her ear, he began to sing. "I'm so happy with you, la, la . . ." A plant-song. Only this time she let him sing it to her.

That night, in the huge bedroom neither one of them were quite used to, in a high new bed, on a new feather mattress, Winnie said to him in the dark, "Grow your mustache back."

Mick lay beside her, his long body still. She thought he didn't hear her at first. He looked unconscious in the moonlight as it came through the high windows. It was a balmy night. The sheer, flowing draperies that lined the heavier damask ones blew out into the room. They and the moonlight made Mick's face into a play of shifting shadows. Winnie stared, doubting herself for a moment, as she watched his lips curve in a barely discernable smile.

His head turned toward her, and he opened one eye. He gave her a one-eyed, inquiring look, then he let his head rock back. He closed his eyes again, while she thought she saw a smug smile spread.

With his eyes still closed, he said, "What'll you give me, if I grow my mustache back?"

"Pardon?"

"I have an idea."

"What?"

"You go over to the wall, Win, and lift your nightgown up. All the way up over your bum. Then turn around and put your head like you did that time against the wall. I get to kiss my way up your legs. You can't stop me, no matter what I do, for ten minutes. If you can do that, I'll grow the mustache back. Just for you."

"No," she said, laughing, a little bit nervous. "We're married now. We're not doing — um, that. We don't do *that* anymore."

His head turned toward her again, one sleepy eye slitting enough to look at her. "Winnie, I think in this area you better let me decide what

we do and don't do. For a while yet." In the purple-gray of the room, she watched his head roll back again, his expression relax.

What she could see of his smile was faint, fond — and wistful in a way that could only be called wicked.

From the shadows, he said, "You be the student. I'll be the teacher now."

When she said nothing, he rolled his head toward her again and gave her another slitted look, this time with both eyes. "What are you waiting for, loovey? Come on. To the wall with you."

She didn't move.

He nudged her, then he came up onto one elbow, over her, and said, "Do you want the mustache back or not?"

"Um —" It seemed like a trick question. "Um, yes."

"All right, then. You can have it, but up with you now." He gave her rump a push. He was serious. "To the wall, Win. And I'm putting you on notice." He bent his lips down her ear. The heat and humidity of his breath tickled as he whispered, "I'm kissing the backs of your legs all the way up to your bum, and anyplace else I want. For ten minutes."

Winnie lay there on the pillows, speechless. For a full two seconds. Then she laughed and said, "Fifteen." She changed her mind. "No, twenty!"

Ah, what a good bargainer she'd become.

The Proposition

Published in 2000 by arrangement with Avon Books, an imprint of HarperCollins Publishers, Inc.

G.K. Hall Large Print Core Series.

The text of this Large Print edition is unabridged.
Other aspects of the book may vary from the original edition.

Set in 16 pt. Plantin by Minnie B. Raven.

Printed in the United States on permanent paper.

Library of Congress Cataloging-in-Publication Data

Ivory, Judith.
    The proposition / Judith Ivory.
      p. cm.
    ISBN 0-7838-9057-5 (lg. print : hc : alk. paper)
    1. Women linguists — Fiction. 2. London (England) — Fiction.
 3. Large type books. I. Title.
 PS3559.V5 P76 2000
    813´.54—dc21   00-036981

The Proposition

Judith Ivory

Large
Print
Fiction
Ivory

G.K. Hall & Co. • Thorndike, Maine

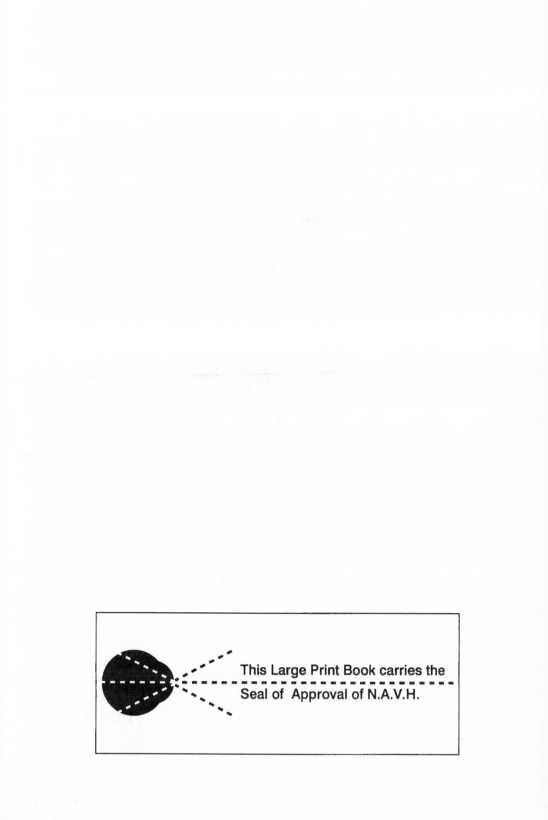

This Large Print Book carries the
Seal of Approval of N.A.V.H.

W9-BTK-019

1997, missed the shift to digital wireless technology by just a year or two. In that sliver of time, Nokia, a hitherto unknown company, perched on the edge of the Arctic circle, became the world's new number one. A decade earlier Nokia had been making snow tires and rubber boots; suddenly it was one of Europe's fastest growing high-tech companies. For Motorola, regaining its top spot will be a Herculean task.

○ Want to build a world-beating Internet portal site? Sorry, too late. If you're a traditional entertainment or media company like Disney, Bertelsmann or Viacom and you want to grab a few million online eyeballs, you've probably already missed the boat. AOL and Microsoft, both media newcomers, built commanding positions in the online world while most of the old line media companies were otherwise occupied.

○ You might be surprised to learn that the fastest growing sector of the commercial aircraft market, regional jets, is dominated by two comparative newcomers: Canada's Bombardier and Brazil's Embraer. Airbus and Boeing have been virtually foreclosed from this booming market. And should they commit themselves to recovering the ground they've lost, they can expect a brutal fight with their new rivals.

Yes, incumbency still matters. This is a lesson that more than a few dot-com start-ups learned to their sorrow. But it is also true that incumbency matters less than ever before. Schumpeter's gale of "creative destruction" has become a hurricane. New winds are battering down the fortifications that once protected the status quo. Economic integration has blown open protected markets. Deregulation has destroyed comfortable monopolies. *Easily bored customers have become ever more promiscuous in their loyalties.* Online search tools have created a class of almost perfectly informed customers.

Compaq, Novell, Westinghouse, Kodak, Kmart, Philips—these and a hundred other incumbents have found themselves struggling to stay relevant in this new topsy-turvy world. Just as the Age of Reason undermined the authority of organized religion in matters secular, this age of revolution is undermining the authority of the world's industrial incumbents in matters commercial.

Consider some evidence. If you're an American over the age of 40, you may remember Main Street—that humble row of shops operated by neighborly souls who knew your kids by name and catered to your every need. All that is gone now, replaced decades ago by look-alike shopping malls with Sears at one end, JCPenney at the other, and a row of specialty shops such as B. Dalton and KB Toys in between. Then, when you weren't looking, those suburban malls started down the long road toward retail irrelevance. Category killers like Toys "R" Us, The Home Depot and Staples slowly crushed many of the specialty retailers that once made the malls work, and Wal-Mart displaced Sears as America's biggest retailer. But what's the chance that the retailing revolution stops with Wal-Mart and Toys "R" Us? None. Consumers aren't going to spend the rest of their lives wandering the soulless canyons of Wal-Mart to save a couple of bucks on a hammer. Woolworth's never escaped Main Street. Sears got stuck in the mall. And all those "big box" retailers afloat in a sea of asphalt may one day find themselves on the wrong side of yet another retailing revolution.

Or consider one of America's most venerable brands—Coca-Cola. A Morgan Stanley survey of 25,000 consumers in 2001 found that the Coke brand was weaker among young people than at any time in recent memory.[1] The culprits? A slew of hip, new beverage brands from Red Bull to Starbucks to SoBe. With their increasingly eclectic and hair-trigger tastes, young consumers are less and less likely to be satisfied with the same-old same-old. In the age of revolution, great companies are as vulnerable as they are venerable.

If you have any doubts about the waning power of incumbency, consider for a moment all the goods and services you buy from companies that are no more than a generation old—airline tickets from Southwest Airlines, furniture from IKEA, mutual funds from Charles Schwab, computers from Dell, collectibles via eBay, video games from Nintendo, coffee from Starbucks, books from Amazon.com and so on. Never has the world been a more hospitable place for unorthodox newcomers.

Of course, industry newcomers are just as vulnerable as the firms they displace. During the 1990s, Gap Inc. was one of retailing's hottest stories. The company had transformed itself from a pile-them-high purveyor of Levi's and T-shirts into a trendy retailer of Gap-branded fashion basics. Yet as the century turned, The Gap's clothing and its store format were no longer fresh and hip. A slew of competitors— some new, some old—had copied many of The Gap's retailing ideas, and the company seemed incapable of refreshing its image and strategy. In recent years, CNN, the pioneer of 24-hour television news, has seen a significant number of its viewers jump to Fox News Channel, MSNBC, CNBC and other newbie news channels. Incumbency may be worth less than ever, but the wet cement of orthodoxy and dogma sets fast in even the most revolutionary of newcomers. In an age of revolution, the trip from insurgent to incumbent is often a short one.

Just as the collapse of communism gave us a new world order, the decline of incumbency is giving us a new industrial order. In the new industrial order, the battle lines don't run between regions and countries. It's no longer Japan versus the United States versus the European Union versus the developing world. Today it's the insurgents versus the incumbents, the revolutionaries versus the landed gentry.

Royal Dutch/Shell is one of the world's premier oil companies, with a history as old as the industry. Yet one day Shell awoke to find that a supermarket, Tesco, had become the largest retailer of "petrol" in Britain, one of Shell's home markets. How do you handle that? You've spent hundreds of millions of pounds over several decades trying to convince consumers that your brand of petrol is better than the next guy's, and suddenly it's being sold as a loss leader along with milk and eggs.

Starbucks has become America's premier coffee brand with the most loyal clientele of any retailer in the United States—the average Starbucks customer visits a store 18 times a month! (You'll have to find your own legal drug to sell—caffeine's already taken.) So picture all the brand managers sitting at Nestlé headquarters in Vevey, Switzerland, running Nescafé, the best-selling coffee in the world. Do you think they ever wondered how they could entice bus drivers and schoolteachers to line up five deep to pay three bucks for a latte? No? What were they worrying about? What color cans to put on supermarket shelves? How to beat Procter & Gamble? The result? In mid 2000, Starbucks had a stock market value of $9 billion—11 percent of Nestlé's market value, yet Starbucks' revenues were a scant 4 percent of Nestlé's. All too often, industry incumbents mistake historical rivals for the enemy—a potentially catastrophic mistake in the age of revolution.

Industry revolutionaries will exploit any protective urge, any hesitancy on the part of the oligarchy. Any attempt to hunker down, to fall back and regroup, or to disengage will be seized as an opportunity to claim more ground. **First the revolutionaries will take your markets and your customers.** Southwest Airlines might have started in Texas, but it's not just serving the Southwest anymore. It now serves virtually every major city in the United States. **Next they'll take your best employees.** Think about it: if you're a bright young executive eager to make your mark, who would you rather work for—Hewlett-Packard or Dell, United Airlines or NetJets (the pioneer in fractional jet ownership)? Sooner or later, bold thinking and growth attract the best talent. Finally, they'll take your assets. How unexpected that eBay acquired the third largest auction house in the United States, Butterfield & Butterfield. How surprising that Vodafone, still in its teens, bought Mannesmann, one of Germany's oldest and proudest companies. How weird that AOL's leadership team would end up in control of a postmerger AOL Time Warner. The barbarians are banging on the gate—and if you're not careful, they'll be eating off your best china. This is the old guard versus the vanguard. The power of incumbency versus the power of imagination.

While the battle is always between new thinking and old, it is not always between newbies and veterans, much less between the "new economy" and the "old." As it turns out, many industry revolutionaries are large, well-established companies—they are newcomers insofar as the incumbents are concerned, but they aren't new companies. Bombardier had a long history as a snowmobile manufacturer before it acquired Canadair, a near-bankrupt manufacturer of executive jets. It was this acquisition that established the platform for Bombardier's expansion into regional jets. Likewise, Hughes Electronics had a history as a manufacturer of military and commercial satellites before it challenged the monopoly of America's cable television companies with its DirecTV service. These companies were newcomers to aerospace and television, respectively, but they weren't start-ups. Though the odds don't always favor it, new thinking can be found in old companies. When "gray-haired revolutionaries" combine their substantial resources with a revolutionary spirit, they are often able to surprise the incumbents *and* squash the start-ups. The future belongs to the unorthodox and the agile—be they start-ups or giants.

LIMITED ONLY BY IMAGINATION

Every age brings its own blend of promise and peril, and the age of revolution has plenty of both. But there is reason to be more hopeful than fearful, for the age of revolution is presenting us with an opportunity never before available to humankind: For the first time in history we can work backward from our imagination rather than forward from our past. For all of history, human beings have longed to explore other worlds, to reverse the ravages of aging, to transcend distance, to shape their environment, to conquer their destructive moods, to share any bit of knowledge that might exist on the planet. With the International Space Station, genetic engineering, videoconferencing, virtual reality, mood-altering drugs and global search engines, we've begun to turn each of these timeless dreams into reality. *Indeed, the gap between*

***what can be imagined and what can be accomplished has
never been smaller.***

We have not so much reached the end of history (as Francis
Fukuyama claimed) as we have developed the capacity to interrupt
history—to escape the linear extrapolation of what was. Our heritage is
no longer our destiny.

Today we are limited not by our tools, but by our imagination. Those
who can imagine a new reality have always been outnumbered by
those who cannot. For every Leonardo da Vinci, Jonas Salk or Charles
Babbage, there are tens of thousands whose imagination cannot escape
the greased grooves of history. For though there is nothing that cannot
be imagined, there are few who seem able to wriggle free from the
strictures of a linear world. Like a long-captive elephant that stands in
place out of habit, even when untethered, most minds have not
grasped the possibilities inherent in our escape from the treadmill of
progress. Yet individuals and organizations that are incapable of escaping the gravitational pull of the past will be foreclosed from the future.

To fully realize the promise of our new age, each of us must become
a dreamer, as well as a doer. In the age of progress, dreams were often
little more than fantasies. Today, as never before, they are doorways to
new realities. Our collective selves—our organizations—must also learn
to dream. In many organizations there has been a massive failure of
collective imagination. How else can one account for the fact that so
many organizations have been caught flat-footed by the future?

THRIVING IN THE AGE OF REVOLUTION

Somewhere out there is a bullet with your company's name on it.
That bullet may be a company that's eager to exploit a disruptive technology, it may be an impending shift in customer preferences, a demo-
graphic change, a lifestyle trend or a regulatory upheaval that will
render your strategy obsolete. You can't dodge these bullets—you're
going to have to shoot first. You're going to have to out-innovate the
innovators.

When Bill Gates says, "Microsoft is always two years away from failure," he's not defending himself yet again from the charge of being a
monopolist. Gates understands the competitive reality of the new age.
He knows that it's not only product life cycles that are shrinking; strategy life cycles are getting shorter, too. An almost stupefying pace of
change ensures that any business concept, no matter how brilliant, will,
over time, lose its economic efficiency. The difference between being a
leader and a laggard is no longer measured in decades, but in years,

and sometimes months. Today, a company must be capable of reinventing its strategy, not just once a decade or once a generation in the midst of a crisis when it trades out one CEO for another, but continuously, year after year.

The fact that few companies are capable of making right-angle turns is evidenced by the increasing number of CEOs who lose their jobs every year. Apparently, investors and boards have concluded that the only way to revector a large company is to jettison its CEO and bring in a new leader. While this is sometimes effective, it doesn't address the deeper problem—the inability of companies and leaders to renew themselves in the absence of a crisis. Indeed, too many companies are like Third World governments—banana republics where the only way to effect a change in policy is to depose the despot. Changing the CEO is an expensive and wrenching process—and too often happens only *after* a company has missed an important turn on the road to the future. **WHAT WE NEED ARE COMPANIES THAT ARE CAPABLE OF SELF-RENEWAL, ORGANIZATIONS THAT ARE CAPABLE OF CONTINUALLY REINVENTING THEMSELVES AND THE INDUSTRIES IN WHICH THEY COMPETE.** We need fewer stories about heroic and belated turnarounds, and more stories about perpetual revolutionaries.

Microsoft is unlikely to oust its chairman anytime soon. Instead, the company is dealing with the threat of unconventional competitors and new business models by launching a blizzard of new services and products—including Passport, Hailstorm, the X-box and a host of others. Microsoft's ".Net" strategy—the label for a cluster bomb of innovation initiatives—is aimed at nothing less than remaking the company. Bill Gates and his team at Microsoft understand that in the age of revolution, there is no defense, there's only offense. Those who live by the sword will be shot by those who don't.

Gates isn't the only corporate leader who understands the dynamics of the new industrial order. In a Gallup survey I authored,[2] approximately 500 CEOs were asked, "Who took best advantage of change in your industry over the past ten years—newcomers, traditional competitors or your own company?" The number one answer was newcomers. They were then asked whether those newcomers had won by "executing better" or "changing the rules of the game." Fully 62 percent of the CEOs said the newcomers had won by changing the rules. Despite this, how many times have you heard a CEO or divisional vice president say, "Our real problem is execution"? Or worse, tell people that "strategy is the easy part, implementation is the hard part." What rubbish! These worthless aphorisms are favored by executives afraid to admit that their strategies are seriously out of date, executives who'd prefer their people stop asking awkward questions and get back to work. Strategy is easy only if you're content to have a strategy that is a derivative of someone else's strategy. Strategy is anything but easy if your goal is to be the author of industry transformation—again and again. It is, however, immensely rewarding. What could be more gratifying than putting one's fingerprints all over the future?

One CEO put it to me this way: "I used to spend most of my time worrying about the *how*—how we did things, how we operated, how efficient we were. Now I spend much of my time worrying about the *what*—what opportunities to pursue, what partnerships to form, what technologies to back, what experiments to start." The point is simple. By the time an organization has wrung the last 5 percent of efficiency out of the how, someone else will have invented a new what. Inventing new whats—that's the key to thriving in the age of revolution.

RADICAL INNOVATION

The signal accomplishment of the industrial age was the notion of incremental, continuous improvement. It remains the secular religion of most managers. Its first incarnation came in Frederick Winslow Taylor's scientific management. Its many descendants include the Japanese concept of *kaizen* and the oh-so-'90s notions of reengineering and enterprise resource planning. Taylor is the spiritual godfather of every manager or consultant who has ever sought to describe, measure and streamline a business process.

Organizational learning and knowledge management are first cousins to continuous improvement. They are more about getting better than getting different. The final accomplishment of the age of progress was to turn knowledge into a commodity. Today you can buy knowledge by the pound—from consultants hawking best practice, from the staff you've just hired from your competitor, and from all those companies that hope you'll outsource everything. Yet in the age of revolution it is not knowledge that produces new wealth, but insight—insight into opportunities for discontinuous innovation. Discovery is the journey; insight is the destination. You must become your own seer.

In a nonlinear world, only nonlinear ideas will create new wealth. Most companies have reached the point of diminishing returns in their incremental improvement programs. Continuous improvement is an industrial-age concept, and while it is better than no improvement at all, it is insufficient in the age of revolution.

Radical, nonlinear innovation is the only way to escape the ruthless hypercompetition that has been hammering down margins in industry after industry. Nonlinear innovation requires a company to escape the shackles of precedent and imagine entirely novel solutions to customer needs and dramatically more cost-effective ways of meeting those needs.

In tough economic times, there are always those who urge top management to get "back to basics." I agree with this sentiment. I have long argued that the foundation for radical innovation must be a company's core competencies (what it knows) and its strategic assets (what it owns)—you can't get any more basic than that. Unrelated acquisitions, new venture divisions and corporate incubators seldom if ever bring genuine renewal. They are tangential to the core and typically leverage little of what a company already knows and owns. Yet to argue that a company must leverage its core is not to argue for inch–by–inch incrementalism. Nor is leveraging the core simply a matter of finding obvious "adjacencies"—nearby channels and customers (à la "Baby Gap," "Cherry Diet Coke" and "Double Stuf Oreos"). Instead, leveraging the core is a matter of reinterpreting the very essence of a company in ways that allow it to create completely new market space. This is what UPS did when it built a billion–dollar–a–year logistics and supply chain management business. Who would have guessed that a package delivery company could win a contract to deliver Ford cars to dealers across the United States or mend Compaq and HP computers in a huge UPS–owned repair facility?

And what about the core business? Here the goal is pretty simple: to grow revenues, pump up prices and reduce costs. Other things being equal, this will yield real earnings growth. Having discovered, to their chagrin, that earnings actually matter, investors are once again in search of companies that can deliver sustained profitable growth. They are demanding that companies get back to basics. In recent years, CFOs regularly tested the outer limits of investor credulity and generally accepted accounting principles in hopes of somehow disguising faltering growth rates and shrinking margins. In the wake of Enron's collapse—engineered by a swashbuckling finance function that was, to use the British expression, "too clever by half"—investors have said "enough is enough" to the "extraordinary" charges, off–balance sheet financing and pro forma accounting that have so often been used to divert attention from a slowly atrophying or nonexistent business model.

But here's where back to basics runs straight into a brick wall. Growing the top line, raising prices and cutting costs are hard and getting harder. In fact, without radical innovation, they're near impossible. In the summer of 1999, Procter & Gamble announced 15,000 layoffs around the world and warned investors of a potential $1.9 billion charge against earnings. This despite the fact that in 1995 P&G set itself the ambitious goal of doubling its revenues to $70 billion by 2005. This would have required a 10-percent annual growth rate. In 1999 P&G was a long way off that pace.[3] For the last several years, McDonald's growth engine in the United States has been sputtering. In a heavily touted move, the company introduced a new cooking system that promised made-for-you hamburgers even quicker off the grill. Will this solve McDonald's growth problem? It might, but maybe McDonald's should ask itself if Americans are already eating as many hamburgers as they're ever going to. Maybe Americans have reached their cholesterol limit. In a recent survey across 20 industries, I found that only 11 percent of companies had been able to grow revenues twice as fast as their industry over a decade, and only 7 percent had been able to grow shareholder returns at twice the industry average.

In 1999, DoCoMo, a division of NTT, Japan's largest telecom company, gave the world its first large-scale packet-switched mobile phone network, iMode. With their always-on, data-enabled phones, DoCoMo's customers could get instant news updates, automatic downloads of cartoons and horoscopes, weather reports and much more. By the end of 2001, the service had attracted 30 million customers—probably the fastest growth for any new consumer service in history. The message is clear: If you're an established company in a "mature" industry, it's impossible to significantly grow the top line in the absence of radical innovation.

What about raising prices? In a world of ever more powerful customers, and relentless competition at home and abroad, few companies have the luxury of raising their prices. In the good old days, when inflation moved along at a double-digit clip, it was easy for companies to hide their price increases in the upward spiral of inflation. But with inflation now at less than 2 percent per annum in most of the world's developed economies, there is little scope for hidden price increases. The only way to raise prices is to find a truly novel way of differentiating your product or service. In Britain, you can buy lunch at Burger King for a pound or two less than you can at Pret A Manger (prêt-à-manger is French for "ready-to-eat"), a chain of trendy fast-food outlets where every sandwich is made fresh on the premises each morning. Pret's hundred-plus stores are testament to the fact that many customers are willing to pay a premium for gourmet fare like a Thai Chicken Miracle-Mayo sandwich. Despite its decentralized production system, Pret's cost structure is low enough to give it margins that match those of its most efficient fast-food competitors. Accountants and imagination-challenged executives often forget that productivity has two components—the efficiency with which you use your inputs (labor and capital) and the value that customers place on your outputs. Too many managers know everything about cost and next to nothing about perceived value. Pret willingly adds cost to its sandwiches—fresh, additive-free and sometimes exotic ingredients—because the quality and flavor of those sandwiches commands a price advantage (over a typical fast-food "value meal"). Pret's example suggests that it's possible to charge a price premium—but not unless you have a unique value proposition—and you're not going to get one of those without radical innovation.

Another response to razor-thin margins is to whack away at the cost structure. Yet with virtually every company on the planet thoroughly committed to cost cutting, what is required is not another incrementalist margin-improvement program, but a radical reinvention of the cost structure. Wal-Mart's superstores and its pioneering use of information technology have allowed it to reap unmatched economies of scale and scope. Southwest Airline's point-to-point route system, its 737-only fleet and its multitasking employees produce a level of capital efficiency unmatched by any traditional rival. IKEA's flat-packed furniture, manufactured at global scale and sold in warehouse-style stores, offers frugal customers "affordable solutions for better living." Indeed, IKEA claims that in its never-ending attempts to drive down costs, "the only thing it doesn't skimp on is ideas." Finally, Dell's lack of vertical integration and its direct, Internet-based distribution model allow it to make hundreds of millions each quarter while its competitors are losing a similar amount. Each of these companies brought radical innovation to the cost side of the equation, and each views every market downturn as an opportunity to acquire market share from less efficient competitors who have no choice but to retrench when demand goes slack.

So while the basics never change, "more of the same" is no longer enough if the goal is sustainable, profitable growth. If you're trying to grow revenues or slice costs with a straight line approach, you're going to find yourself facing an "innovation gap" with competitors who have managed to break conventions and achieve step-function changes. Soon the world will be divided into two kinds of organizations: those that can get no further than continuous improvement and those that have made the jump to radical innovation.

Now, let me be clear: there is nothing wrong with incrementalism. Gillette used to make razors with a single blade. Later, one of its diligent students of stubble asked, Wouldn't two blades be better than one? Thus was born the Trac II. Next came—guess what?—a razor with three blades—the Mach III. I love Gillette razors—use one every morning—but they are examples of incremental innovation. Incremental innovation is desirable, indispensable and, in a discontinuous world, insufficient—that is, if your goal is to create *new* wealth, year after year.

Tough economic times can make timidity seem like a virtue. A CEO or business leader struggling to "make the quarter" may view radical innovation as—well, too *radical*. The unstated assumption is that incrementalism is low-risk and radical innovation high-risk. Yet in a fast-changing world with few second chances, more of the same often represents the biggest risk of all, as the recent histories of Xerox, TWA, Kmart and dozens of other incumbents so clearly show.

Without doubt, innovation can be risky—think of Motorola's multibillion-dollar bet on satellite telephony, Iridium, which ultimately went bust. Innovation risk is determined by four things: first, the size of the irreversible and nonrecoverable financial commitment that must be made to get a project off the ground; second, the degree to which the new opportunity departs from the company's existing base of technical and market understanding; third, the amount of irreducible uncertainty surrounding critical project assumptions (particularly with respect to the nature of customer demand and technical feasibility); and fourth, the time frame required for ramp-up (the longer the time scale, the higher the risk). Against all these criteria, Iridium was a high-risk project. But there's no reason radical innovation has to be high-risk. As we will see, it is possible to de-risk bold new strategies through low-cost, low-risk experimentation. **Imagination and prudence are not mutually exclusive.**

I believe that many companies are *too* willing to make big, risky bets. Between 1996 and 2000, companies in the S&P 500 wrote off more than $226 billion in the form of extraordinary charges against earnings. During this time they recorded only $62 billion of extraordinary gains. A significant proportion of the write-offs came from acquisitions that failed to live up to their (typically overhyped) advance billing, from new business bets that never paid off and from venture investments gone bad. Let's be honest: In recent years investment bankers and VCs have talked big-company executives into doing the *stupidest* things. The challenge is not to avoid taking risks, but to get much, much smarter about how to de-risk grand aspirations.

I believe in revolutionary goals and evolutionary steps. When Julian Metcalfe and Sinclair Beecham, the founders of Pret A Manger, set out to create food that was fresh, preservative-free, healthy, tasty *and* affordable, they were embarking on a revolutionary journey. The first Pret store opened in 1986, the second in 1990. In the intervening four years, the founders lurched from challenge to crisis and back again as

capacity for radical innovation. Shareholder wealth may be the score-board, but the game is radical innovation.

TOWARD CAPABILITY

Any company that hopes to stay relevant and vital in turbulent times must be capable of creating strategies that are as revolutionary as the age we live in. This raises a question you may already be asking yourself: Where do new wealth-creating strategies come from? The strategy industry—all those unctuous consultants, self-proclaimed gurus and left-brain planners—doesn't have an answer. They all know a strategy when they see one—Look! Twenty-two "profit zones"!—but they don't know where new strategies come from. They don't have a theory of strategy creation, much less any insight into how to build a deeply embedded capacity for strategy innovation.

Perhaps strategies come from the annual planning process—that well-rehearsed ritual found in almost every organization. Consider the planning process in your own company. What adjectives would best describe it? Those in column A or column B? Unless your company is truly exceptional, you'll probably have to admit that the descriptors in column A are more apt than those in column B.

__A__	__B__
Procedural	Creative
Reductionist	Expansive
Extrapolative	Inventive
Elitist	Inclusive
Easy	Demanding

The notion that strategy is "easy" rests on the mistaken assumption that strategic planning has something to do with strategy making. Of course strategy appears easy when the planning process narrowly limits the scope of discovery, the breadth of involvement and the amount of intellectual effort expended, and when the goal is something far short of revolution. The assumption that strategy is easy says more about the inadequacies of our planning processes than the challenge of creating industry revolution.

Giving planners responsibility for creating strategy is like asking a bricklayer to create Michelangelo's *Pièta*. Any company that believes planning will yield revolutionary strategies will find itself caught in a prison of incrementalism as freethinking newcomers lead successful insurrections. If the goal is to create new strategies, you might as well dance naked round a campfire as go to one more semisacramental planning meeting.

No wonder that in many organizations, the whole notion of strategic planning has been devalued. How often has it produced any radical value–creating insights? No wonder corporate strategy has become little more than deal making. No wonder consulting companies are doing less and less "strategy" work and more and more "implementation" work.

Perhaps revolutionary strategies come from "visionaries" like Bill Gates (Microsoft), Anita Roddick (The Body Shop), Jeff Bezos (Amazon.com), Howard Schultz (Starbucks) and Michael Dell (Dell Computer). Many, if not most, industry revolutions have their genesis in the vision of a single individual who often ends up as CEO or chairman. Yet today's vision is often tomorrow's intellectual straitjacket. **All too often a company outruns the visionary's headlights, and then crashes and burns.** Just remember Apple Computer, where Steve Jobs, the poster boy for missed opportunities, resisted efforts to license the Macintosh operating system to other companies. Improbably, after having been booted from the company he helped to create, Jobs got a second chance when he took up the CEO reins again in 1997. Yet however miraculous Apple's more recent turnaround, the company will forever be a footnote in the history of the computer industry—in large part because of the myopia of the company's founders. Likewise, Dell Computer will be similarly doomed if its top management is unable to escape a PC–centric view of the computer industry. The mainframe was eclipsed by the minicomputer, which was in turn eclipsed by the personal computer. DEC became the second–largest computer company in the world when IBM was slow to respond to the threat of minicomputers, and Dell became the most dynamic company in the PC business when IBM, Compaq and others were slow to reinvent their business models. Yes, there will one day be a post–PC world, and if Dell is going to thrive in that world, it will need to reinvent itself just as thoroughly as it has reinvented the PC industry.

Visionaries don't stay visionaries forever. Few of them can put their hands on a second vision. Worse, their compatriots become dependent on the visionary's prescience, thus abdicating their own responsibility for envisioning new opportunities. More times than not, a fading visionary who is also CEO or chairman unwittingly strangles a company's capacity for radical innovation. That is why visionary companies seldom live beyond their first strategy.

Of course most companies are not led by visionaries; they're led by administrators. No offense, but your CEO is probably more ruling-class than revolutionary. So don't sit there staring at the corporate tower hoping to be blinded by a flash of entrepreneurial brilliance. Administrators possess an exaggerated confidence in great execution, believing this is all you need to succeed in a discontinuous world. They are accountants, not seers. Visionary CEO or sober-suited apparatchik, neither is likely to be an ever-flowing font of radical innovation.

Maybe some of you have sat through a business-school case study—a 90-minute striptease where some creaky professor undresses a management principle that has been enrobed in 20 pages of colorless prose. Suppose the case being discussed concerns a hugely successful company, and the professor is in the midst of an elaborate and elegant post hoc analysis . . .

> . . . So you see, they developed a killer application by exploiting a disruptive technology that allowed them to capture increasing returns from their unique core competencies, thereby creating a new ecosystem with a deep, untapped profit pool.

In the midst of such blather did you ever think to yourself, "Wait a minute, was this success the result of some terribly incisive strategic thinking, or was it pure dumb luck?" Luck or foresight? Where does strategy come from? That's a damn good question.

Consider the genesis of three revolutionary strategies:

> When her husband left their home in Littlehampton, England, to pursue a lifelong dream of riding horseback from Buenos Aires to New York, Anita Roddick was left to fend for herself and her daughters. To support her family, Anita opened a small cosmetics shop in nearby Brighton, filling cheap plastic bottles with goo. From this seed grew The Body Shop, a worldwide retailer of funky, politically correct cosmetics.

Just before his 58th birthday, Mike Harper, the acquisitive CEO of ConAgra Inc., suffered a heart attack. After an extended stay in intensive care, Mike left the hospital with a commitment to changing his dietary habits. The newly health-conscious CEO challenged his company to create a line of good-for-you products that would be equally great tasting. The result was Healthy Choice, a line of nutritious frozen dinners that quickly became the leader in its category. The Healthy Choice brand now spans more than 300 products—from breakfast cereals to snack foods to deli meats to ice creams—that had more than $15 billion in sales in 1999.[4]

What do Pez dispensers—those little plastic heads that dole out candy—have to do with one of the world's hottest Internet start-ups? Plenty. Just ask Pierre Omidyar. His fiancée was a committed Pez collector. How, Pierre wondered, could he help his girlfriend feed her Pez passion? The answer: an online, person-to-person trading community where Pezheads could buy and sell their weird collectibles. Pierre's idea blossomed into eBay, the Web's premier auction site, where more than 2 million members place a million bids a day. As eBay's founder, Pierre is credited with transforming everything from classified ads in small-town newspapers to the pompous practices of the world's elite auction salons.[5]

Luck or foresight? Where do radical new business concepts come from? The answer is this: **New business concepts are always, always the product of lucky foresight.** That's right—the essential insight doesn't come out of any dirigiste planning process; it comes from some cocktail of happenstance, desire, curiosity, ambition and need. But at the end of the day, there has to be a degree of foresight—a sense of where new riches lie. So radical innovation is always one part fortuity and one part clearheaded vision.

If the capacity of an organization to thrive in the age of revolution depends on its ability to reimagine the very essence of its purpose and destiny and to continually create for itself new dreams and new destinations, we are left in a quandary. How do you increase the probability that radical new wealth-creating strategies emerge in your organization? Can we turn serendipity into capability?

The quality movement provides a useful analogy. Thirty years ago, if you had asked someone, "Where does quality come from?" they would have replied, "From the artisan" or perhaps, "From the inspector at the end of the production line." Quality came from the guy with magical hands at Rolls-Royce, who spent weeks hammering a fender around a wooden form, or from the white-coated inspectors at the end of the Mercedes-Benz production line. Then Dr. Deming came along and said, "We must institutionalize quality—it has to be everyone's job. That guy down there on the shop floor, with ten years of formal education and grease under his fingernails, that guy is responsible for quality." With 30 years of hindsight, it's easy to forget how radical this idea was. In Detroit, auto execs said, "You gotta be kidding! Those guys down there are saboteurs."

It took many companies a decade or more to grasp the notion of quality as a capability, and American car makers have still not closed the quality gap with Toyota and Honda. But the challenge is no longer quality. Neither is it time–to–market, supply chain management or e-commerce. Today the challenge is to build a deep capability for business concept innovation—a capability that continually spawns new business concepts and dramatically reinvents old ones.

Like Deming, Juran and the early leaders of the quality movement, we're going to have to invent new practice. If you had wanted to benchmark best–of–breed quality in 1955, where would you have gone? The answer's not obvious. There was no Deming prize; no ISO 9000. Yet the quality pioneers were undeterred. They invented new practice, built on a new philosophical foundation. Like them, we must aspire to more than "best practice," for most of what currently passes for best practice innovation is grounded in the age of progress; it's simply not good enough for the age of revolution.

Creating a companywide capacity for radical innovation will be no less challenging than creating an organization infused with the ethos of quality—and this time it can't take ten years. And it won't—not if you're willing to kick off the lead boots of denial; not if you're willing to dump all that useless management theory you picked up back there in the age of progress; not if you're ready to climb over the walls of your cubicle and take responsibility for something more than your "job."

THE POSTINDUSTRIAL ENTERPRISE

Reflect for a moment on just how little management wisdom has changed over the past hundred years. At the beginning of the twentieth century, Frederick Winslow Taylor was the world's best–known management guru. His principles were simple: Decompose your processes into their constituent parts, excise or redesign activities that don't add value, then put your processes back together again. For one hundred years Taylor's "scientific management" was masquerading as reengineering, business process improvement, and ERP and CRM and a dozen other acronyms for faster, better, cheaper.

Nearly everything we know about organizing, managing and competing comes from an age in which diligence, efficiency, exactitude, quality and control were the complete secrets to success. The management disciplines we inherited from the industrial age are the unquestioning servants of optimization. These disciplines are the product of a world where industry boundaries were inviolable, where customers were supplicants and where business models were assumed to be nearly eternal. That world may be long dead, yet optimization still regularly trumps innovation.

And despite all the pro-innovation rhetoric that one encounters in annual reports and CEO speeches, most still hold the view that innovation is a rather dangerous diversion from the real work of wringing the last ounce of efficiency out of core business processes. Innovation is fine so long as it doesn't disrupt a company's finely honed operational model. A hundred years on from Frederick Taylor, innovation is still regarded as a specialized function (the purview of R&D or product development), rather than as a corporation-wide capability. In most companies, the forces of perpetuation still beat the forces of innovation to a pulp in any contest. As change becomes ever less predictable, companies will pay an ever-escalating price for their lopsided love of incrementalism.

In the years ahead, we must build companies that are as full of radical innovation as they are of diligent optimization. There can be no either/or here, there must be an *and*. In the end, the goal is not innovation for its own sake. Given a choice, most of us would prefer quiet continuity to perpetual revolution. But the choice is not ours. Discontinuous change is the defining characteristic of the postmodern world. Even so, radical innovation is simply a means to an end—and that end is "resilience"—both corporate and personal: the capacity to thrive no matter what the future throws at us.

Resilience is what has allowed America to prosper for more than 225 years with only a single major internal disruption—the Civil War. Over that long span, America has changed all out of recognition—culturally, materially and technologically. It has metamorphosed from an agrarian society to an industrial powerhouse—and morphed again to become a supercharged information economy. It has cleansed itself of slavery, defeated the barbarisms of Nazism and Communism—and set back the ticking hands of the Doomsday Clock. More recently, it has led the international community in defending civil society from the scourge of terrorism.

In contrast, hundreds of governments and scores of constitutions have come and gone in the past two centuries—houses of straw against the gale force winds of change. America's resilience, like that of all long-lasting constitutional democracies, is based on a series of seemingly irreconcilable opposites, tensions held in perpetual creative balance: Coherence and diversity. Community and activism. Strength and compassion. Bravery and prudence. The spiritual and the material.

Resilience is based on the ability to embrace the extremes—while not becoming an extremist. As Charles Simeon, a prominent eighteenth-century English pastor, put it: "Truth is not in one extreme and not in the middle, it is in both extremes." The thesis and antithesis of the modern corporation are optimization and innovation. Both of these extremes must be embraced and transcended.

MOST COMPANIES DON'T DO PARADOX VERY WELL. They are filled with accountants and engineers who have an instinctive aversion to dichotomies and contradictions. But the postindustrial company can't be all one thing or all another. Instead, it must be all of many things—all focus *and* all experimentation, all discipline *and* all passion, all evolution *and* all revolution, all optimization *and* all innovation—*all*. Discipline, alignment and control will always be virtues, but they can no longer be the only or even the dominant virtues. Any company that hopes to survive the next ten years, let alone the next hundred, will have to be a paragon of penny-pinching efficiency on one side and unbridled creativity on the other. The accountants and the engineers are going to have to learn to love the poets and the dreamers.

It's easy to forget that the large-scale industrial company is the product of human imagination. Go back 150 years and you find chaotic and fragmented craft-based industries. In mastering the virtues of scale, control and discipline companies such as Du Pont, General Motors, Siemens and Shell invented the modern corporation. In so doing, they created incredible efficiencies and brought a cornucopia of goods and services within the reach of Jane and John Mainstreet. Now the times call for another burst of organizational invention, for we can be sure that the companies that learn to flourish in the age of revolution will be as different from the paragons of the industrial age as those companies were from their craft-based predecessors.

The good news is that no company has yet managed to build the epitome of a postindustrial enterprise, though a few companies like GE, Nokia, UPS, Cemex and Charles Schwab have challenged themselves to do so. So you're not starting from behind. The bad news is that creating an organization that is fit for the age of revolution is a lot harder than digitizing your business model. While there are a clutch of industrial-age virtues that will survive the shift to a postindustrial world, there are great swaths of management and organizational orthodoxy that will not. Expunging these superannuated beliefs won't be easy; making innovation a systemic capability will be even harder. Yet the payoff is nothing less than the chance to soar on the winds of change.

Whether what you now hold in your hands is simply shelfware or a powerful tool for radical innovation depends on you. You've been told often that change must start at the top—that's rubbish. How often does the revolution start with the monarchy? Nelson Mandela, Václav Havel, Thomas Paine, Mahatma Gandhi, Martin Luther King: Did they possess political power? No, yet each disrupted history; and it was passion, not power, that allowed them to do so.

Most of us pour more of our life into the vessel of work than into family, faith or community. Yet more often than not the return on emotional equity derived from work is meager. The nomadic Israelites were commanded by God to rest one day out of seven—but He didn't decree that the other six had to be empty of meaning. By what law must competitiveness come at the expense of hope? If you're going to pour out your life into something, why can't it be into a chalice rather than down a drain? For every one of us, it is our sense of purpose, our sense of accomplishment, our sense of making a difference that is at stake—and that is more than enough.

Never has it been a more propitious time to be an activist:

○ Intranets and corporation-wide e-mail are creating something close to an information democracy. The information boundaries that used to delineate corporate authority are more permeable than ever.

○ More than ever, senior executives know they cannot command commitment, for the generation now entering the workforce is more authority-averse than any in history.

○ It is universally apparent that we are living in a world so complex and so uncertain that authoritarian, control-oriented companies are bound to fail.

○ Increasingly, intellectual capital is more valuable than physical capital, and it is employees who are becoming the true "capitalists."

○ Millions of employees are now shareholders as well—they are suppliers and owners.

Activists are changing the shape of companies around the world. At Sony, a midlevel engineer challenges top management to overcome its prejudice against the video-game business. "We don't make toys!" they protest. He badgers, plots and schemes. Against all odds he persuades Sony to develop the PlayStation—a phenomenally successful video-game console that in 1998 accounted for more than 40 percent of Sony's profits. He keeps pushing. Finally Sony sets up a Computer Entertainment division and commits itself to making the computer more than a soulless business machine.

A Web-besotted computer scientist and a gadget-loving market planner join forces at IBM in the early 1990s. Their quixotic goal is to turn IBM into an Internet-savvy powerhouse. They establish a bootleg lab and begin building Webware. They organize an underground lobbying effort that turns a disparate and far-flung group of Webheads into a forceful community of Internet advocates. Their grassroots efforts become the foundation for IBM's emergence as the e-business company.

So don't tell me it can't be done. Only ask yourself if you have the guts to lead the revolution.

Dream, create, explore, invent, pioneer, imagine: do these words describe what you do? If not, you are already irrelevant, and your organization is probably becoming so. If you act like a ward of your organization, you'll be one, and both you and your company will lose. So if you're still acting like a courtier or a consort, bending to the prejudices of top management, buffing up their outsized egos, fretting about what they want to hear, getting calluses on your knees—stop! You're going to rob yourself and your company of a future that's worth having. No excuses. No fear. If you're going to make a difference in your company, these have to be more than T-shirt slogans.

In the new industrial order, the battle is not democracy versus totalitarianism or globalism versus tribalism, it is innovation versus precedent. Ralph Waldo Emerson put it perfectly when he said, "There are always two parties—the party of the past and the party of the future, the establishment and the movement." Which side are *you* on?

Just as nineteenth-century America opened its doors to all those who believed in the possibility of a better life, the twenty-first century opens its doors to all those who believe in the possibility of new beginnings. In the age of revolution it will matter not whether you're the CEO or a newly hired administrative assistant, whether you work in the hallowed halls of headquarters or in some distant backwater, whether you get a senior-citizen discount or whether you're still struggling to pay off school loans. Never before has opportunity been more democratic.

Do you care enough about your organization, your colleagues and yourself to take responsibility for making your company revolution-ready? If you do, you have the chance to reverse the process of institutional entropy that robs so many organizations of their future. You can turn back the rising tide of estrangement that robs so many individuals of their sense of meaning and accomplishment. You can become the author of your own destiny. You can look the future in the eye and say:

I am no longer a captive to history.
Whatever I can imagine, I can accomplish.

I am no longer a vassal in a faceless bureaucracy.
I am an activist, not a drone.

I am no longer a foot soldier
in the march of progress.

I am a Revolutionary.

2
FACING UP TO STRATEGY DECAY

BEYOND THE BOOM

In the last, long economic boom, companies were often able to deliver respectable shareholder returns despite a dearth of any real business innovation. Six things made this possible: first, a doubling of the P/E ratio for shares listed on the New York Stock Exchange (fueled by a massive inflow of funds from retirement-conscious baby boomers); second, an unprecedented attack on corporate inefficiency, which buoyed earnings in many companies; third, a superheated market for acquisitions, which drove up corporate valuations; fourth, an army of newbie investors eager to bet big on fast-growing, loss-making companies; fifth, dozens of creative CFOs who, in their quest to report rapidly escalating earnings, were willing to push generally accepted accounting principles to the breaking point; and sixth, a huge boom in capital spending as companies poured billions of dollars into computer and networking equipment. The confluence of these forces produced the longest bull market in history. Between 1995 and 2000, the NASDAQ Composite Index rocketed from 755 to 4,696 and the Dow Jones Industrial Average climbed from less than 4,000 to nearly 11,500. There were many who claimed that the long stock market rally was proof that the business cycle had been suspended and that a new age of unprecedented productivity growth had dawned. They were wrong.

Trees don't grow to the sky. P/E ratios can't rise indefinitely. Efficiency programs eventually reach the point of diminishing returns. The scope for industry consolidation is finite. Naïve investors inevitably discover that earnings matter. Sleight-of-hand accounting can't forever disguise a decaying business model. And sooner or later, CEOs discover that IT spending doesn't always, or even often, lead to fatter margins. During the boom, a rising tide lifted all boats—some of which weren't entirely seaworthy. It was all too easy for top management to take credit for financial results that were attributable to the incredible and unsustainable dynamics of the stock market rally. In the end, the belief that a 20- to 30-percent annual stock market return is somehow "normal" was revealed to be a temporary, though potent, collective delusion. Over the long term, it is impossible for share prices to rise faster than corporate earnings. And during the next decade, earnings growth is going to be harder than ever to come by—thanks to more powerful and fickle customers, diminishing returns to efficiency programs, the relentless onslaught of disruptive technologies, the consultant-aided spread of "best practices" and the consequent erosion of firm-specific advantages, the corrosive impact of e-business on prices, more aggressive enforcement of antitrust law and the entry of new competitors from at home and abroad. In the post-bubble economy, every company is suddenly alone with its bootstraps. Given that, any company that hopes to outperform the mediocre average is going to have to make innovation an all-the-time, everywhere competence.

STRATEGY DECAY

Even in the midst of a stock market boom, it is not easy for companies to deliver top-quartile shareholder returns for more than a few years at a time—a fact that becomes immediately apparent if one studies the recent performance of the companies that make up the S&P 500. Because the S&P 500 is a listing of America's most valuable companies, the population of this index is constantly changing—companies that have fumbled the future fall out while fast-rising newcomers earn their way in. At the end of 2001, there were 284 companies that had managed to hold a spot in the index for every year since 1991. Of these companies, 15 failed to deliver top-quartile shareholder returns in even one year out of ten; 74 companies achieved top-quartile results in one year out of ten, 69 companies made it into the top quartile in two years out of ten, and 61 were standout performers in three years out of ten. There were only two companies—Centex and Computer Associates—that delivered top-quartile shareholder returns in as many as seven years out of ten, and no company did better than that. General Electric, one of America's most-admired companies, was one of 40 companies that achieved top-quartile results in four years out of ten. In total, there were only 25 companies, or less than 10 percent of the entire population, that managed to deliver top-quartile returns for five years or more out of the ten-year period. These are the odds your company faces if it hopes to outperform its peers. The odds are long because all strategies decay—they lose their economic potency over time—and because few companies know how to reinvigorate old strategies and invent new ones.

Just how much life is left in your company's strategy?
How confident are you that your company's strategy is up to the task of delivering superior returns over the next several years? No company will embrace the cause of radical innovation unless it believes that strategy decay is inevitable. Companies that fail to face up to the reality of strategy decay suffer an all-too-familiar fate: They get "resized" in accordance with their suddenly diminished fortunes. The commitment to making radical innovation a corporation-wide capability should come long *before* your company's strategy starts to sputter. So you and your colleagues may want to ask yourselves the following questions:

- How much more cost savings can our company wring out of its current business model? Are we working harder and harder for smaller and smaller efficiency gains?

- How much more revenue growth can our company squeeze out of its current business model? Is our company paying more and more for customer-acquisition and market-share gains?

- How much longer can our company keep propping up its share price through share buybacks, spin-offs and other forms of financial engineering? Is top management reaching the limits of its ability to push up the share price without actually creating new wealth?

○ How many more scale economies can our company gain from mergers and acquisitions? Are the costs of integration beginning to overwhelm the savings obtained from slashing shared overhead costs?

○ How different from each other are the strategies of the four or five largest competitors in our industry and how different from our own strategy? Is it getting harder and harder to differentiate our products and services from those of competitors?

○ How much competitive differentiation is our company's IT budget actually buying? Does it feel like our company is locked in an IT spending arms race with our competitors?

If you answered "not much" and "yes" more than a couple of times, your company's business model is already showing signs of strategy decay. The only way to confirm these suspicions is to dig deeper into the evidence.

UNSUSTAINABLE COST CUTTING— GETTING BLOOD FROM A STONE

Over the past decade the pressure on executives to produce an escalator of steadily rising earnings has been intense. This pressure spawned a myriad of initiatives aimed at cutting overhead, reducing labor and material costs and improving capital utilization. Outsourcing, six sigma programs, reengineering, e-procurement, restructuring, ERP and downsizing are all examples of efficiency-oriented programs. In many companies, this single-minded assault on inefficiency produced several years of double-digit earnings growth. Indeed, in many cases, earnings growth far outstripped revenue growth.

In the short run, profits can grow much faster than revenues. We often see this phenomenon in the early years of a major corporate turnaround. Corpulent companies go on a crash diet. Head count is slashed, assets are sold and costs cut. While revenue growth remains sluggish, margins quickly improve. But there's ultimately a limit to how much profit even the best-managed, most efficient company can squeeze out of any fixed amount of revenue. And as the most egregious inefficiencies get excised, it becomes harder and harder to reap big cost savings.

We have to be suspicious of any company that has been growing earnings substantially faster than it's been growing revenues, especially if it has been doing so for more than a couple of years. Let's take a few examples. Between 1995 and 2000, the ratio of net income growth over revenue growth was 67 for Cigna, 48 for Computer Associates, 43 for Colgate–Palmolive, 27 for ConAgra Foods, 18 for AMR (the parent of American Airlines), and 13 for Northrop–Grumman. Ask yourself, How long can a company grow earnings 13 times, 38 times or 67 times revenue? The answer is, Not for long. My research indicates that if a company's earnings growth exceeds its revenue growth by more than 5 to 1 for more than three years in a row, there's an 80–percent chance that it will face a major earnings shortfall sometime in the next three years. Put simply: There's a limit to liposuction.

While cost cutting has a way to run in Japan and continental Europe, many American and British companies have already reached the point of diminishing returns in their efficiency programs. In 2000, the average operating margin for the nonfinancial services companies in the S&P 500 was 16.2 percent. In 1996, the average operating margin for these same companies had also been 16.2 percent. Whatever the contribution of downsizing, ERP and other efficiency programs to lower costs, these initiatives haven't done much to fatten margins—at best, they've simply helped companies ward off the effects of steadily declining real prices.

This doesn't mean that companies should abandon their zeal for cost cutting. But it does suggest that unless a company has a way of reducing costs substantially faster and deeper than the industry norm, it will gain little in the way of an earnings or share price advantage.

UNSUSTAINABLE REVENUE GROWTH—
SPINNING YOUR WHEELS

Downsizing is a harrowing experience. A lot of former efficiency addicts are now eager to grow. But focusing on growth, rather than on the challenge of radical innovation, is as likely to destroy wealth as to create it. After some point, trying to squeeze more revenue growth out of a moribund business model is no easier than trying to squeeze out more costs. In the absence of radical innovation, a blind allegiance to growth can suck a company into zero–sum market–share battles or seduce it into paying exorbitant sums for customer acquisition. Worse, it can lead to an ill-conceived acquisition. When Daimler–Benz acquired Chrysler, it became a bigger company, but the hoped–for economies at DaimlerChrysler have yet to materialize. Interestingly, Porsche and BMW, both of which make many fewer cars than DaimlerChrysler, have much better margins.

The result of a growth obsession is often bigger revenues but not much traction in terms of additional profits—this seems to have been the case for many Internet start-ups. Let's flip our earlier ratio and look at revenue growth over earnings growth. If the ratio of revenue growth to earnings growth is more than 5 to 1 and has been so for a year or two or more, it suggests that a strategy meltdown is in progress or, in the case of a start-up, a solid business model has yet to be found. After all, a "revolutionary" strategy that doesn't produce earnings growth isn't revolutionary at all—it's just dumb.

Between 1995 and 2000, the ratio of revenue growth over earnings growth was 28 for Cinergy. For Nextel the ratio was 21, 15 for WW Grainger and 7 for Nike. Despite growing its top line by 2,633 percent, Waste Management saw its bottom line contract by 431 percent. While Staples' revenues grew by 248 percent over the five-year period, its earnings contracted by 19 percent. **Clearly, growth by itself is no substitute for radical innovation.** This is particularly true when growth is the product of a pyramid of acquisitions.

Companies that can grow revenue only by "giving away value" at close to zero profit are spinning their wheels—the engine's racing, but there's not much forward progress. Of course, there will be times when profits are scarce as a company "builds out" its strategy and amortizes its start-up costs (think Hughes and DirecTV). But in an existing business, a declining ratio of earnings growth over revenue growth is a sure sign of strategy decay—the strategy may not stink yet, but it's sure dead.

On the other hand, many companies have had a reasonably balanced ratio of revenue growth to earnings growth. Charles Schwab, FedEx, General Electric and Washington Mutual are just a few of the companies that delivered balanced profit and revenue growth in the years 1995 to 2000. While a balanced ratio is no guarantee of a sound strategy, a seriously unbalanced ratio usually indicates a decrepit strategy.

UNSUSTAINABLE GROWTH IN SHAREHOLDER RETURNS—
THE LIMITS OF FINANCIAL ENGINEERING

It is fashionable today to talk of "unlocking" shareholder wealth. The metaphor is telling. The assumption is that the wealth is already there—it's already been created—and with a little financial engineering, it can be set free.

To unlock shareholder wealth you get out of bad businesses—as Jack Welch did when he took over GE. You spin off companies that may command a significantly higher P/E than the parent company—witness the recent appetite for spin-offs and de-mergers at 3M (Imation), Hewlett-Packard (Agilent Technologies), AT&T (Lucent Technologies and AT&T

Wireless), PepsiCo (Tricon) and a host of other companies. You try to dump inflexible and expensive capital assets onto someone else via outsourcing. Of course there's a limit to how many bad businesses a company can divest and how many of its assets it can transfer to someone else's balance sheet. It's not surprising that after a couple of rounds of corporate restructuring, CEOs turn to share buybacks as the easiest way of plumping up share prices.

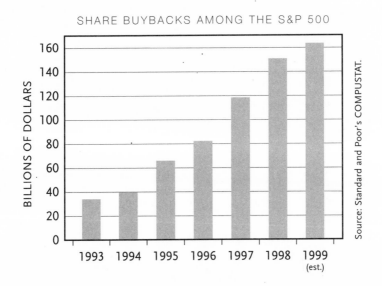

SHARE BUYBACKS AMONG THE S&P 500

Source: Standard and Poor's COMPUSTAT.

Share buybacks are one of the simplest and perhaps most simple-minded ways of unlocking shareholder wealth. Fresh out of ideas? No compelling investment opportunities? No problem! Take the cash being produced by today's businesses and return it to shareholders. We shouldn't be surprised that we've witnessed a record level of equity buybacks in recent years (see the graph "Share Buybacks Among the S&P 500"). After all, there's nothing on this earth with a shorter time horizon than a 60–year–old CEO sitting atop a mountain of stock options, racing his first coronary to the bank. And there's no way to get the share price up faster than buying back your own stock. Not surprising, then, that the number of share buybacks has grown apace with the number of share options held by senior executives in America's largest companies.

If downsizing is the quick fix for corporate obesity, buybacks are the instant cure for an anemic share price. In the five years through 1999, companies as diverse as Toys "R" Us, Cigna, PG&E, General Motors, US Airways, Times Mirror, Maytag and Bear Stearns bought back shares

BUYBACK CHAMPS: CUMULATIVE ANNUAL BUYBACKS AS
A PERCENTAGE OF MARKET CAPITALIZATION, 1994–1999

US Airways	66	Dow Chemical	31
Times Mirror	60	R. R. Donnelley & Sons	31
W. R. Grace & Co.	57	General Motors	30
Tandy	53	Union Carbide	30
Reebok International	44	Autodesk	30
Knight-Ridder	43	DuPont	26
Ryder System	40	AMR	26
PG&E	39	Phelps Dodge	25
ITT Industries	39	Sunoco	25
Liz Claiborne	36	Nordstrom	24
Cooper Industries	34	Deluxe	23
Adobe Systems	34	Hershey Foods	22
Hercules	33	Delta Air Lines	22
Maytag	32	Textron	22
IBM	31	Allstate	21

Source: Standard and Poor's COMPUSTAT; Strategos calculations.

worth more than 30 percent of their market capitalization (see the table
"Buyback Champs"). Buybacks are a way of rewarding shareholders
despite a lack of apparent growth prospects. Indeed, between 1995 and
2000 the average compound annual revenue growth rate of the top 50
buyback champs was a measly 4 percent. That rate for the S&P 500
was 13 percent, and the 50 fastest-growing companies averaged 50–
percent compound annual revenue growth. "Here," buyback CEOs
seem to be saying. "We don't know what to do with the cash. You
take the money and go see if you can find some better investment
opportunities." Of course this is exactly what a CEO bereft of new
strategy ideas should do! But it's no more sustainable than selling off
assets.

There are dozens and dozens of companies that have, over the past
few years, delivered healthy shareholder returns, but have at the same
time generated little or no growth in their overall market value. (A few
are listed in the table "Growth in Shareholder Returns Versus Growth
in Market Capitalization.") These companies haven't created much new
wealth.

When growth in shareholder returns significantly outpaces growth
in a firm's market value (i.e., when share price is going up faster than
the overall value of the firm), you can be sure there's a bit of financial
legerdemain going on somewhere. A company that is relying exten-

	Shareholder Returns 1994–1999 (annualized)	Growth in Market Cap 1994–1999 (annualized)	Difference
W. R. Grace & Co.	18.3	(31.2)	49.5
Dun & Bradstreet	12.9	(15.4)	28.3
Times Mirror	27.2	(2.3)	24.9
Fortune Brands	9.2	(7.4)	16.6
Philip Morris	8.5	(6.4)	14.9

Source: Standard and Poor's COMPUSTAT.

sively on sell–offs, spin–offs or buybacks to drive up its share price is admitting, however inadvertently, that its strategy is wheezing. Look down the list of the buyback champs and you won't see too many industry revolutionaries.

De–mergers, spin–offs, share buybacks and other techniques for unlocking shareholder wealth have built–in limits—at some point, there's no more wealth to "unlock." At some point you actually have to *create* new wealth. Stewards unlock wealth, radical innovators create wealth.

Of course, worse even than the share buybacks are the accounting gyrations that some companies go through in a vain attempt to prop up a feeble business model. Stuffing the channel at the end of the quarter, issuing pro forma earnings reports that ignore significant non-recurring charges, taking "extraordinary" write–offs in an attempt to boost future earnings growth by lowering the baseline, using off–balance sheet financing to deflect attention from a crushing debt load—a reliance on such devices is prima facie evidence of a significantly challenged business model. Having endured a painful lesson on the limits of aspirational accounting, post–Enron investors are demanding new accounting standards and even more transparency. In this climate, even the most imaginative CFO is going to find it hard to pretty up a butt–ugly business model by draping it in a gossamer veil of creative accounting.

The point is this: In too many companies, senior management has mistaken the scoreboard for the game. Quarterly earnings are the score; customer–pleasing, competitor–slamming innovation is the game. Wildly manipulating the numbers on the scoreboard is no substitute for learning how to play the game.

There is yet another option open to executives who are exhausting internal cost–cutting possibilities and have already pushed their accounting practices to the limit—the mega–merger. Hoping for a temporary respite from the law of diminishing returns, companies spent the last few years merging and acquiring at a record pace. The value of mergers and acquisitions announced globally in 2000 amounted to nearly $3.5 trillion (see the graph "Value of Announced Mergers and Acquisitions Worldwide"). In the United States alone, announced M&A activity totaled more than $1.7 trillion, roughly 14 percent of the value of all publicly listed companies in America. Nineteen out of the top 20 mergers in history, by size, were announced in the 18 months leading up to the end of the century. With virtually every company "in play," this superheated merger activity helped to buoy stock prices ever higher. But sadly, there is an in–built limit to industry consolidation. After all, if industry consolidation proceeded for another seven or eight years at 2000's breathless pace, there would be only one firm left in America. This seems an unlikely outcome! Indeed, in 2001, global M&A fell by half, amounting to just $1.7 trillion, and investment banks slashed more than 30,000 jobs.

Over the past few years it has been hard to pick up a financial magazine and not feel like someone who's just been transported to Jurassic Park. Everywhere you look there are dinosaurs mating: Exxon and Mobil, BP and Amoco, J.P. Morgan and Chase Manhattan, Norwest and

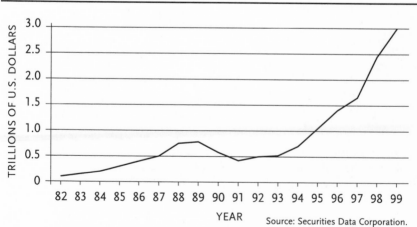

VALUE OF ANNOUNCED MERGERS AND
ACQUISITIONS WORLDWIDE

Source: Securities Data Corporation.

FACING UP TO THE REVOLUTION

More than 50 percent of the senior executives of America's largest companies derive a significant portion of their compensation from stock options. Indeed, a $100 million stock option payout is not unusual. A few executives have reaped close to half a billion dollars in a single year by exercising their accumulated share options. And these are not hot, young CEOs building new fortunes, but tenured administrators running legacy companies. While the theory was that option-owning managers would work even harder to create new wealth, the reality has been somewhat different.

With most of their assets tied up in stock options, it's difficult for top management to diversify their own shareholdings. Hence they cannot easily offset the risk of holding a large hoard of one company's equity. Thus it's not surprising that option-rich executives are likely to be even more conservative and short-sighted than the average investor who has the freedom to diversify across many companies. With so much of their net worth riding on a single stock, and retirement just a few years away, senior executives can be expected to prefer low-risk strategies for pumping up the share price. Buying back one's own shares is a safer bet than betting on novel business concepts.

Most option plans are not tied to the relative performance of a company against the S&P 500 or any other index. According to the *Wall Street Journal*, of the 209 big stock option grants made by large companies in 1998, only 36 had any type of performance trigger.[a] Thus an executive could underperform the average and still cash in, as his company's stock price was on the rise. Worse, options are frequently repriced if a stock falls below the strike price——an option not open to outside investors who may find themselves underwater thanks to management's malfeasance. Even the *Wall Street Journal*, hardly known for begrudging wealthy CEOs their due, had to conclude that "these days CEOs are assured of getting rich, however the company does."[b]

A few compensation committees do set specific stock price hurdles that must be reached before the options can be exercised. Level 3 Communications grants its top executives options that can be exercised only if the company's stock outperforms the S&P 500 stock index. General Mills requires executives to hold on to most of the shares they buy when they exercise their options.[c]

The law of unintended consequences is ever at work. Rather than getting CEOs focused on growing the long-term value of their companies, stock options have seduced many into short-term, one-shot, price-pumping schemes such as share buybacks, spin-offs and mega-mergers. In too many cases executives are not managing in the best long-term interests of their shareholders; they are managing in the best short-term interests of themselves.

[a] Joann S. Lublin, "Lowering the Bar," *Wall Street Journal*, 8 April 1999.
[b] Ibid.
[c] Tamar Hausman, "Predicting Pay," Wall Street Journal, 8 April 1999.

Wells Fargo, American Airlines and TWA, Daimler-Benz and Chrysler, International Paper and Champion, Bell Atlantic and GTE, SBC and Ameritech, Pharmacia and Upjohn. Hundreds of other copulating couples dot the landscape. While some of these mergers are propelled by truly strategic considerations—global market access or industry convergence—many are simply the last gasp of cost-cutting CEOs who hope that by slamming together two lumbering incumbents, they will be able to lop off another $1 billion or so of shared overhead and show another 10,000 employees the door. Yet shareholders lose more often than they gain from such mergers. A 1999 study found that of the 700 largest deals completed between 1996 and 1998, more than half had actually diminished shareholder value.[1] These mergers follow a familiar course. The share price takes a bounce on expectations of future efficiencies, top management in the acquired company gets a Midas-like payout and in the months that follow the deal, the usual postmerger turmoil and ever-escalating integration costs wipe out nearly all of the expected benefits.

A recent study in the pharmaceutical industry suggests that the most notable impact of a merger is the loss of market share by the participating companies. Furthermore, the study finds little evidence that bigger companies are any more productive at discovering new drugs.[2] A significant minority of mega-deals, such as AT&T's purchase of NCR, Novell's acquisition of WordPerfect, Dow Jones & Co.'s purchase of Telerate and Quaker Oats's acquisition of Snapple Beverage (which was eventually sold to PepsiCo), turn out to be monumental stinkers, with the acquired company sold after an enormous write-off. Putting two drunks together doesn't make a stable person.

If there is a secondary logic to the wave of mergers sweeping the planet, it is the simple arithmetic of oligopoly. If you reduce the competitive intensity in an industry by reducing the number of independent competitors, profits are likely to go up. It's hard not to conclude that this logic has driven a number of telecom deals such as that between SBC and Ameritech. The industrial oligarchy loves an oligopoly: just enough competition to avoid direct government control; not enough to threaten a profitable sinecure.

Defending their merger plans, CEOs are often quoted as saying, "You have to be number one in your market to make any money" or "Only the biggest will survive." This rationale is largely specious. Size doesn't inoculate a company from rule-busting innovation. **Bulk is no bulwark against the onslaught of revolutionary new competitors.** And it's hard to mate and run at the same time. The merger-obsessed thinking in some executive suites seems to go something like this: "If we're a really, really big dinosaur, maybe we can survive the Ice Age."

In fact, for the top 1,000 publicly listed companies in America, the correlation between company size (revenues) and profitability (operating margins), whether measured over three, five or ten years, is no more than .004—a result that isn't statistically significant.[3] Put simply, there is no reason to expect that being bigger will make a company more profitable. Company size and imagination of the sort that produces new wealth–creating strategies are not correlated. Sure, size brings advantages, but in the age of revolution those advantages are often offset by disadvantages—inflexibility, internal politicking and sloth.

A final rationale for many mega–mergers is "synergy," or its twenty-first-century counterpart, "convergence." These words should send investors racing for the door. Here's what AT&T's CEO said in 1991 when his company acquired NCR: "I am absolutely confident that together AT&T and NCR will achieve a level of growth and success that we could not achieve separately. Ours will be a future of promises fulfilled." Here's what AT&T's CEO said in 1995 when NCR was spun off to shareholders: "The complexity of trying to manage these different businesses began to overwhelm the advantages of integration. The world has changed. Markets have changed." No shit, Sherlock. That's the age of revolution for you—all that damn change. Well, then, be careful about loading up the balance sheet with billions of dollars of fixed assets on the basis of something as ethereal as "synergy" or "convergence."

Yeah, there are going to be a lot more mega–deals in the years ahead, particularly in Europe and Asia, where there are still too many national-scale banks, airlines, car companies and insurance companies. And yes, a well-thought-out program of disposals and acquisitions can sometimes play a critical role in revitalizing a company's core strategy. A series of bold deals, culminating in the acquisition of Seagram's Universal unit, helped transform a 150–year–old French water treatment company, Générales des Eaux, into Vivendi Universal, one of the world's top three media and entertainment giants. But once the ownership cards have been reshuffled, top management still has to produce sustainable, profitable growth. And that takes genuine innovation. The 1990s produced a crop of ravenous deal makers—from Sandy Weill at Citigroup to John Chambers at Cisco to Bernie Ebbers at WorldCom and Chris Gent at Vodafone, from Bernie Arnault at LVMH to Dennis Koslowski at Tyco and Jean–Marie Messier at Vivendi Universal, among many others. In a few cases, the deal making was based on sound business logic. In other cases, the orgy of buying was nothing more than a giant pyramid scheme: Use a spate of acquisitions to fuel top-line growth; talk investors into giving your company a nose–bleed share price based on its growth record; use your vaunted share price to make yet more acquisitions, etc., etc. In the long term, such a strategy is completely unsustainable; but in the short term it can turn a vision-challenged CEO into a demibillionaire. In the end, deal making is no substitute for strategy innovation. Investment bankers can make a company bigger, but they can't make it more innovative.

STRATEGY CONVERGENCE—
THE LIMITS TO BEST PRACTICE

In a recent survey, I asked more than 500 CEOs whether they believed the strategies of their major competitors had been getting more alike or more dissimilar. The number one answer: more alike. This is not good news. Do you remember Economics 101 and the idea of "perfect competition"—when everyone in an industry followed an identical strategy and had similar resources? You probably also remember the textbook result: Every company made just enough profit to survive and no more. It's the business equivalent of a subsistence economy. That's the inevitable result of convergent strategies.

In nearly every industry, strategies tend to cluster around some "central tendency" of industry orthodoxy. Strategies converge because successful recipes get slavishly imitated. All you computer industry executives who've been trying to imitate Dell's build–to–order business model, raise your hands! All you car company honchos who spent two decades trying to duplicate Toyota's lean manufacturing model, fess up! All you department store execs who've been using Wal–Mart as a case study in how to manage logistics, go ahead, admit it. Nothing wrong with imitation, of course, as long as you've achieved strategy differentiation in other areas of your business. *But all too often, a successful new business model becomes the business model for companies not creative enough to invent their own.*

Aiding and abetting strategy convergence is an ever–growing army of eager young consultants transferring "best practice" from leaders to laggards. When some big consulting company whispers in your ear, "We have a really deep understanding of your industry," what are they saying? Simply this: "We'll infect you with the same orthodoxies we've infected everyone else in your industry with." The challenge of maintaining any sort of competitive differentiation goes up proportionately with the number of consultants moving management wisdom around the world.

Outsourcing has been another powerful force for strategy convergence. As companies outsource more and more, the scope for competitive differentiation gets narrower and narrower. There's a reason Dell Computer hasn't outsourced its core IT processes and is no friend of cookie-cutter ERP solutions. Dell's business model is based on creating unique advantages out of IT—that's something that can't be easily done with off-the-shelf solutions.

Executives who spend much of their time attending the same trade shows, reading the same industry magazines and listening to the same e-biz pundits accelerate the pace of strategy convergence. In the end, strategies converge because everyone defines the industry in the same way, uses the same segmentation criteria, sells through the same channels, adopts the same service policies and so on. In fact, the typical definition of an "industry" is simply those companies that are all operating with the same business model.

In the airline industry the strategies of American, United and Delta are virtually indistinguishable—at least from the perspective of a customer. If tonight, while everyone was asleep, we randomly reassigned the top hundred executives from each of these airlines to their competitors, would you expect anything substantial to change in your flying experience? Despite a vibrant economy, the U.S. airline industry's return on sales was a meager 5 percent in 1999. With every downturn, the incumbents engage in a sort of intra-industry cannibalism, slashing prices in an attempt to steal each other's customers. Of course, cheapskate flyers will heartily applaud the spectacle of contestants chewing off each other's limbs, but investors may be less amused.

Or think about department stores. May Department Stores, Federated Department Stores, JCPenney, Sears and Dillard's have all underperformed the S&P 500 in the last decade. And no wonder—store layout, merchandise selection and service policies are boringly similar. Wal-Mart, Best Buy, Target and Kohl's are the standout performers. Each has a strategy that's distinctly different from traditional department stores.

In general, wealth-creating champions possess highly differentiated strategies. Sure they face competitors, but they have unique capabilities, unique assets, unique value propositions, and unique market positioning. You won't mistake a flight on Virgin Atlantic for one on United. You won't mistake a sandwich at Pret A Manger for a production-line burger. If a strategy ain't different, it's dead. At one time, Bernie Ebbers, the rebel who built WorldCom, claimed to be an enemy of strategy convergence. A stock analyst once asked Mr. Ebbers whether he was going to buy up cable television properties as AT&T's Michael Armstrong had done. Bernie's reply: "We're not going to do anything that he's doing."[4] How then, Bernie, do you explain your acquisition of MCI, a long–distance telephone company that competes head–to–head with AT&T? If ever there was an industry where strategies have converged, it's long–distance telephone service in the United States. Quick—name an important difference between the service offered by Sprint, AT&T and WorldCom MCI. You get my point. Bought for $30 billion in 1998, MCI was estimated to be worth around $3 billion in June 2001.[5] Not surprisingly, many observers now view MCI as an albatross round WorldCom's neck.

So how do you know if your strategy is converging with everyone else's? Well, if your company's revenue growth, return on investment, operating margins or P/E ratios are tightly clustered around the industry average, it's a good bet that strategies are converging. Have a look at the performance of the major U.S. airlines over a ten–year period (see the table "Key Financial Indicators for Selected U.S. Airlines, 1989–1999"). Who do you think has the most differentiated strategy here? Southwest's earnings grew nearly twice as fast as the industry average and its revenues even faster. It also has the healthiest operating margins by far. It should be no surprise that Southwest also has the most highly differentiated strategy. Southwest said, in effect, "If we're going to treat customers like cattle, we might as well develop a business model for cattle—no reserved seating, no meals, no fancy lounges and no in-flight entertainment." The airline industry is not unique. Strategy convergence tends to produce margin convergence—around a relatively low average.

Without radical innovation, a company will devote a mountain of resources to achieve a molehill of differentiation. The amount spent on advertising indistinguishable soft drinks, the millions of direct–mail so-

KEY FINANCIAL INDICATORS
FOR SELECTED U.S. AIRLINES, 1989–1999

	Average Operating Margin 1990–1999	Compound Annual Growth in Net Income 1989–1999	Compound Annual Growth in Revenue 1989–1999
AMR (American Airlines)	6.1	3.7	5.4
Northwest	4.9	16.2	4.6
Delta Air Lines	4.2	9.1	6.2
UAL (United Airlines)	3.4	14.3	6.3
Southwest	**11.6**	**20.8**	**16.7**

Source: Standard and Poor's COMPUSTAT.

FACING UP TO THE REVOLUTION

licitations trying to induce customers to switch from one credit card company to another, the millions of "free" miles given away by airlines to induce customers to remain "loyal" in the face of uniformly lackluster service, the marketing investment needed to get investors to pay attention to any one of the more than 3,500 mutual funds available in the United States, the resources expended in producing half a dozen look-alike television newsmagazines, the "incentives" car companies have to pay to move indistinguishable autos off dealer lots—these are just a few examples of the high-cost, low-impact futility of carbon copy strategies.

Is your company a victim of strategy convergence? If you have to answer yes to the following three questions, it probably is.

1. **Have we let others define customer expectations?** Sears, Roebuck let Wal-Mart and Target set customer expectations for value. Target went a step further and created a shopping environment substantially more inviting than Wal-Mart's warehouse format. Target's payoff: loyal shoppers from across the entire socioeconomic spectrum.

2. **Does competition within our industry feel like a zero-sum game where the only way to gain market share is through cutting prices and margins?** This has long been true within the American long-distance telephone business, where pricing gimmicks seem to be the only way to grab customers. In this case, tit-for-tat price battles serve only to ratchet down industry profitability.

3. **Are our performance metrics (revenue growth rate, operating margin, P/E ratio, asset turn, etc.) within a standard deviation of the industry average?** Performance metrics that conform to the industry average are usually evidence of a strategy that is no more than average.

Occasionally, strategy convergence verges on mass hysteria. This is, of course, what produced the dot-com bubble. While some observers, reflecting on the dot-com crash, have argued that the Internet spawned too much business innovation, the opposite was actually nearer the truth. Literally thousands of B2C and B2B companies were created between 1998 and 2000. Most of these companies had virtually identical business models—indeed, it was often possible to find 20 or 30 companies vying for the same narrow niche (e.g., creating an online market for buying and selling bulk chemicals). Moreover, each of these companies believed resolutely in first-mover advantages and therefore attempted to outspend competitors in building early market share. Services were given away for free, small fortunes were spent on advertising and computer capacity was built far ahead of demand. Of course, to get a first-mover advantage, you actually have to be a first mover, that is, you have to arrive at a truly unique point of view about a new opportunity *before* anyone else. This was the case for eBay, for Amazon, for ICQ (the instant messaging pioneer later bought by AOL) and for the handful of other Internet pioneers still standing. To reap a first-mover advantage, a company must be able to buy market share at a discount. This is possible only if potential competitors have not yet awoken to the new opportunity and are not, therefore, going to attempt to outspend you. When a clutch of companies all share the same broad view of a future opportunity, are building roughly similar business models, are equally well funded and intent on spending whatever it takes to build a preemptive market position, there is virtually no chance of buying market share at a discount. In such a case, there is no first-mover advantage—just a bloodbath. As the vast majority of dot-com entrepreneurs ultimately discovered, the fact that a business model is Net-based doesn't make it "revolutionary"; it is revolutionary only if it is different in some substantial, and profitable, way from other Net-based business models.

Gray-suited executives are just as susceptible to mass hysteria as T-shirt–wearing entrepreneurs—how else can one explain the $130 billion that European telecom companies dumped into third-generation wireless licenses in an orgy of competitive bidding? Outbidding similarly intentioned and deep-pocketed rivals for the right to spend further billions building out an infrastructure for a service facing uncertain demand is bold—but not necessarily smart. A folly of similar proportions occurred between 1997 and 2001 when, in a headlong rush, a few dozen United States–based start-ups buried $90 billion worth of fiber optic in the ground. A score or more of companies with identical visions and willing bankers managed to borrow nearly $400 billion and raise hundreds of billions more through equity offerings. At the end of this orgy of tunneling, less than 3 percent of the fiber was actually in use and dozens of bankruptcies had been announced, including PSINet, Winstar Communications, NorthPoint Communications and many more. A mania, defined as an excessively intense enthusiasm, is not the same thing as a competitively unique strategy. And when a mania is widely shared, there are going to be tears all around.

Right now, thousands of managers are spending boatloads of bucks to webify their business models—without any real understanding of whether those investments will create competitive differentiation. Efficiency–besotted execs can be forgiven for falling prey to the lurid come–on of IT consultants: Slash your inventories, cut your working capital, replace your call centers and get rid of all those paper–pushers. There is no doubt that e–business transformation yields unprecedented efficiency gains. Yet it's not easy to turn productivity into profits. And in the absence of competitive differentiation it's impossible.

If the Net's efficiency bonanza doesn't end up on the bottom line, where will it end up? In the pockets of customers. The thought that you can spend a couple of years and a mountain of cash turning your company into an e–business and end up with your margins just about where they started is none too comforting. But for many, probably most companies, this is exactly the fate that awaits them in the brave new world of e. Lest you think this is scare–mongering, consider, for a moment, the profit impact of the original e—electricity.

In their provocatively titled report, *Is the Internet Better than Electricity*,[6] Martin Brookes and Zaki Wahhaj, a pair of Goldman Sachs economists, studied the process of electrification at the beginning of the twentieth century. Their aim was to glean insights into the Internet's potential impact on productivity and profits. Electrification provides a useful analogy because, like the recent wave of IT spending, it produced dramatic efficiency gains and a redistribution of profits among various sectors of the economy. The fruits of electrification were divided among four groups: companies like General Electric and Westinghouse that made the equipment for electricity generation and transmission (think Accenture, Sun, IBM, Intel, et al.), companies that generated and distributed electricity (e–business consultants and application developers like Oracle and SAP), industrial companies which invested heavily to electrify their businesses (the bulk of the Fortune 500) and consumers.

During the more than 40 years covered in the Goldman Sachs study, the makers of electrical gear enjoyed the biggest profit boost, in part because of their lock on key patents (a particularly robust form of competitive advantage). Electricity generators did well for a while, then suffered dwindling margins and declining share values as competitors multiplied. But what was most remarkable was the impact of electrification on the profits of the industrial companies that rewired their factories and redesigned their processes to take advantage of the new technology. It is worth quoting Brookes and Wahhaj on this point:

> The industrials sector experienced profits growth below the growth of nominal GDP in each of the periods considered. Companies were becoming more efficient, using the technology of electricity to produce output more cheaply. But they were forced to pass these gains on to the consumer in lower prices instead of increasing profit margins. [p. 16]

Of course a few industrial companies grew their profits faster than GDP, but these were the exceptions. In the battle between producers and consumers over the spoils of increased productivity, the consumers won—at least in the case of electricity. Will the Internet be different? Certainly it will bring a productivity bonus to the U.S. economy. Robert Litan of the Brookings Institution and Alice Rivlin, a former Federal Reserve vice chairman, predict Internet-related savings ranging from $100 billion to $230 billion between 2001 and 2006. But that doesn't mean these savings will fatten corporate profits. Indeed, over the past decade, the share of U.S. capital spending going into IT zoomed from less than 20 percent to nearly 60 percent. Yet, as we saw earlier, average operating margins have barely budged over the last several years.

There are two reasons why the twenty-first-century version of e may be even harder on profits than its twentieth-century counterpart. First, to the extent that the Internet succeeds, over time, in reducing economic "friction," it will also zap profits. While Web-heads celebrate the dawn of "frictionless capitalism," they typically fail to note that companies often owe a majority of their profits to friction. Profit-producing friction comes in many guises:

- For banks, insurance companies, auto dealers and many other industries, customer ignorance has long been a source of friction and a reliable profit center. Before the Internet, consumers found it difficult and time consuming to compare prices and features across multiple suppliers. Now we are moving toward a world of perfectly informed customers and zero search costs. Many companies are going to get a surprising lesson in the difference between customer inertia and real customer loyalty.
- In the past, jewelers, bookstores, radio stations and all those category-killer retailers often enjoyed local monopolies. Minimum-scale economies limited the number of retailers that

could profitably serve any particular geographic area. But today, customers can shop the globe for the best deal. There are no more hostage customers.

○ Accountants, lawyers and financial advisors have long exploited knowledge asymmetries. They knew something you didn't know and charged you hefty fees to share their wisdom. But the cost of putting information on the Web is close to zero, so the margins from knowledge arbitrage are bound to fall.

○ Asymmetries in bargaining between buyers and suppliers are yet another source of friction. B2B exchanges threaten to even out these differences. A group of 40–plus retailers with nearly three–and–a–half times the buying power of Wal–Mart have come together to form the World Retail Exchange. On the flip side, Procter & Gamble, Coca–Cola, General Mills, Kellogg, Kraft Foods and other grocery suppliers have invested more than $250 million to build Transora, their own B2B mega–market. Whatever the out–come of these efforts, most suppliers will soon be facing a world in which there are no more weak customers. Every buyer will wield Wal–Mart's bargaining power.

○ Transaction costs, which represent information asymmetries between buyers and sellers, are another artifact of friction. In the years ahead, market makers of all sorts are going to find it harder and harder to make a living as the Net drives transaction costs ever downward.

Friction props up prices. As friction disappears, the challenge will be to invent new forms of competitive advantage faster than old ones disappear. For companies that have grown fat on friction, this will be no easy task. It doesn't take a heap of imagination to exploit the advantages of friction. But in our hyper–transparent world where the Net has left mediocrity no place to hide, competitive advantage will increasingly rest on an ability to create products, services and business models that are unique and utterly compelling. In the past, it mattered less that few companies were adept at radical innovation—they could coast on friction instead. So although e–business offers enormous scope for cost cutting, it may well be that the price–deflating impact of the Web, in the form of reduced friction, will overwhelm the efficiency–enhancing benefits of the Web for the vast majority of companies. This is not to argue that the Web will fail to offer companies the chance to invent new sources of friction—you can be sure Microsoft is working day and night to do just this. Microsoft's hope is that its Passport e–commerce registration system will be the turnstile through which every online shopper must pass, depositing his or her identity and a few coins along the way. Neither is the Internet going to erase all forms of off-line friction overnight. But in the medium term, the Net is going to exert a powerful deflationary impact on prices—of that there can be no doubt.

There is a second, subtler way in which the Internet may prove to be the enemy of profits: e-business transformation may contribute to strategy convergence. More and more, companies are using the same software platforms, be it SAP's R/3 ERP solution or Oracle's 9i database. More and more, companies are relying on the same handful of IT consultants—all of them organized along vertical industry lines—the better to share *your* best practice with your competitors. More and more, companies are outsourcing critical IT functions to a small club of specialists like EDS and IBM Global Services. And if the IT vendors have their way, erstwhile rivals will adopt common procurement policies and combine their purchasing power in B2B exchanges.

For too long, CIOs have seen their role as improving operating efficiency rather than creating competitive differentiation through radical innovation. As long as this is true, they will fall victim to e-biz vendors who bleat about the importance of IT as a source of competitive advantage, then urge their clients to outsource rather than operate, buy rather than build and embrace the best practices of competitors. If your company is going to spend better than half of its capital budget on IT, it better have a point of view about how it's going to use IT to create advantages unique to the industry!

Of course a Web-based strategy *can* create competitive advantage. AOL accomplished this with instant messaging. eBay did it with online auctions. In the pre-Web world, information technology powered innovative business models at Wal-Mart, Federal Express and a handful of other companies. But if you expect the Web to create wealth for *your* shareholders, your e-strategy better come wrapped inside a truly novel business model, one that offers customers unrivaled efficiencies or truly unique products and services. And these things aren't for sale by any e-consultant.

The collective delusion of the dot-com mob was that clicks, hits and visits could be readily translated into customers and revenues. The collective delusion of the Fortune 500 aristocracy is that productivity gains automatically translate into plumper profits. Any company that plans to make money from e will have to have a Web strategy that creates *unique* value for customers, confers *unique* advantages in delivering that value and is tough to copy. As different as Mustique is from the Jersey Shore—that's how different your company's Web strategy needs to be if it's going to create real competitive advantage. Of the many things the so-called new economy didn't change, here's one more: Sameness still sucks.

So no, Virginia, the Internet is not some profit bonanza—not even for big companies with seemingly well-entrenched positions. The Internet is simply one more force chipping away at profits and thereby increasing the importance of rule-busting, expectation-shattering innovation.

HONESTY FIRST

If you want to escape the cul-de-sac of diminishing returns, the first step is to admit that your current strategy, your dearly beloved business model, may be running out of steam. ***Strategy decay is not something that might happen; it's something that is happening.*** And it's probably happening faster than most folks in your company are willing to admit.

Working ever harder to improve the efficiency of a worn-out strategy is ultimately futile. Think of all those CEOs leading all those depressingly mediocre companies. How many of them are willing to stand in front of their shareholders or their employees and own up to the obvious—"Our business model is busted"?

Dakota tribal wisdom says that when you discover you're on a dead horse, the best strategy is to dismount. Of course, there are other strategies. You can change riders. You can get a committee to study the dead horse. You can benchmark how other companies ride dead horses. You can declare that it's cheaper to feed a dead horse. You can harness several dead horses together. But after you've tried all these things, you're still going to have to dismount.

The temptation to stay on a dead horse can be overwhelming. Take one example. In a recent six-month period, the percentage of teenagers who named Nike as a "cool" brand shrank from 52 percent to 40 percent.[7] By the time teenagers are sporting T-shirts that read, "Just Don't Do It," it's a bit late to start work on revitalizing your brand. The time to begin searching for new wealth-creating strategies is long before the horse stumbles. Today's stock market darlings would do well to reflect on the fate of Hewlett-Packard, Xerox, Compaq Computer, Novell and dozens of other highfliers that fell to earth when they couldn't escape the gravitational pull of moribund strategies.

Sun Microsystems' chief technology officer has estimated that 20 percent of his company's in-house technical knowledge becomes obsolete each year.[8] Sun sees itself as being on a never-ending hunt for new strategies. America's major television networks, dusty relics in an era of 500-channel satellite television, have been somewhat less than attentive to the risks of strategy decay. It's been nontraditional channels like MTV and Comedy Central that have pioneered edgy new shows (though it's hard to argue that *South Park* advances the art of television programming). Twenty years ago, television networks were a bit like *Time* magazine—broad and shallow, with something for everyone. Now television is like a 30-foot-long magazine rack filled with specialty rags: The Classic Movie Channel, The Golf Channel, Animal Planet, MTV and dozens more. Television has been parsed into hundreds of tiny markets. Just over the horizon looms full video Webcasting, which will turn television into a whatever-you-want, when-you-want-it medium. In the 1991–92 season, the four major networks had an audience share of 76 percent. By the 2000–2001 season that had tumbled to 51 percent.[9] Says Robert A. Iger, the former head of ABC and now president of Disney, "We used to think the possibility existed that the erosion was going to stop. We were silly. It's never going to stop. As you give customers greater and greater choices, they are going to make more choices."[10] **DENIAL IS TRAGIC. DELAY IS DEADLY.**

Why do so many companies once a decade have to suffer through a performance crisis and the management upheavals that typically ensue? The answer is that they can't bring themselves to abandon a seriously out-of-date business model. To create new wealth, a company must be willing to abandon its current strategy, at least in part, before it goes toes up.

In the age of revolution, the future is not an echo of the past. While every executive understands this intellectually, it is quite another thing to stand in front of the members of your organization and your investors and boldly confront the demon of decay. But investors and employees are smart enough to know that sooner or later every company has to do a strategy "uninstall."

Without an explicit recognition of the onset of decay, there is little incentive for a strategy reboot. It is imperative, therefore, that you and everyone else in your organization be alert to the signs that your company's business model is approaching its "sell by" date—unless, of course, you particularly relish the chance to manage a turnaround.

So start with the truth. Executives must be willing to be brutally honest about the rate at which their current strategy is decaying. Most senior executives grew up in a world where business models aged gracefully and where incumbency was often an overwhelming advantage. That world is gone. Get over it. Anyone who fails to recognize this fact puts his or her company's future success in grave jeopardy. Executives and employees in every company have a set of little lies they tell themselves to avoid having to deal with the reality of a faltering strategy. Like an alcoholic who claims to drink only socially, managers often claim a dead business model is only sleeping. Here are some of the most–used lies:

"It's only an execution issue."
"It's an alignment problem."
"We just have to get more focused."
"It's the regulators' fault."
"Our competitors are behaving irrationally."
"We're in a transition period."
"Everyone in our industry is losing money."
"Asia/Europe/Latin America went bad."
"We're investing for the long term."
"Investors don't understand our strategy."

Sometimes people in a company will walk around a dead strategy for years before admitting that it has expired and gone to strategy heaven.

So what are the little lies that get told in your company? Recently, I came across the corporate magazine for one of America's largest insurance companies. In this magazine the CEO was quoted as saying, "Insurance is very complex, I think people will always need agents." That's at least a medium–size lie. Quotesmith.com, along with a bunch of other new insurance infomediaries, can easily imagine a world without agents, as can anyone who has bought insurance this way. Oh yeah, we may still need claims agents for a while longer, but sales agents? Don't be too sure. Every business model is decaying as we speak.

If you want to lead the revolution you have to search for signs of diminishing returns in your efficiency programs, for evidence of unsustainable revenue growth or creeping convergence. Be honest: Has "corporate strategy" been more about financial restructuring and mega–deals than about business concept innovation? Are you counting on some e–business whitewash to cover the cracks of a crumbling business model? You have to have the courage to speak candidly about the fragility of success in a discontinuous world. Never forget that good companies gone bad are simply companies that for too long denied the reality of strategy decay.

The nub of the matter is this: What will it take to get your company to reinvent itself? Will it take a competitor's success—a benchmark so clear and unequivocal that you will be forced to move? That's what it took to prompt Merrill Lynch to embrace online trading. But if you wait until a competitor hands you a paint-by-numbers kit, you're going to end up producing something highly unoriginal. Will it take a direct and immediate crisis—a threat so close you can smell failure on its breath? If the threat is already breathing in your ear, you're unlikely to escape without a mauling. Or does it take only a sense of the enormous possibility that exists in the age of revolution to get you and your company totally jazzed about the opportunity for radical innovation? In 1986, Lorenzo Zambrano, the newly installed chairman of Cemex, a regional Mexican cement producer, saw the chance to turn the global cement industry on its ear. Over the next 15 years, Cemex became the fastest-growing *and* most profitable cement company in the world. It's no coincidence that Cemex was also widely regarded as one of the most innovative companies in the world.

In the age of revolution, every company must become an opportunity-seeking missile—where the guidance system homes in on what is possible, not on what has already been accomplished. A brutal honesty about strategy decay and a commitment to creating new wealth are the foundations for strategy innovation. But you can't be an industry revolutionary unless you've learned to see the unconventional. You won't have the courage to abandon, even partially, what is familiar unless you feel in your viscera the promise of the unconventional. And you can't create radical new business concepts, or reinvigorate old ones, unless you first understand what a business concept actually is. So that is where we will turn our attention next.

3
BUSINESS CONCEPT INNOVATION

CAN YOU THINK BEYOND NEW PRODUCTS?

Can you think beyond "more of the same"? Can you imagine products and services that have the power to profoundly change customers' expectations? Can you conceive of entirely new business models? What about unconventional strategies for breathing new life into old business models? Can you envision pulling apart an industry and putting it back together in a way that creates new value? In most organizations there are few individuals who can think holistically and radically about *business concept innovation.*

Say the word "innovation," and the average middle manager will conjure up an image of a product-line extension (Diet Coke with Lemon) or a big bucks R&D project (nanotechnology, fuel cells, pharmacogenomics and the like). The first type of innovation seldom produces a torrent of new wealth, nor is it likely to arrest the fading fortunes of a firm stuck with an out-of-date business model. The second type of innovation occasionally produces big returns (like the multibillion–dollar payoff on a blockbuster drug) but also requires an appetite for equally outsize risks. Product development and corporate R&D are well–recognized functions in most companies—yet radical, rule–busting innovation seldom comes from either of these traditional sources.

Product–focused innovation is often more incremental than radical—it seldom challenges the basic conception of the product or the service. Of course there are exceptions—real product breakthroughs occasionally change the future of an industry. The video tape recorder, the Apple Macintosh computer, the ATM card and AOL's instant messaging service are some standout examples. **INCREMENTAL INNOVATION IS BETTER THAN NO INNOVATION AT ALL, BUT IN AN INCREASINGLY NONLINEAR WORLD, ONLY NONLINEAR IDEAS ARE LIKELY TO CREATE NEW WEALTH.**

Radical innovation is innovation that has the power to change customer expectations, alter industry economics and redefine the basis for competitive advantage. The notion of competitive advantage is very important here. An idea may appear to be radical in the sense that it changes customer perceptions (for example, the ability to buy pet food online), but if the idea doesn't produce a defensible source of competitive advantage, it is radical only in the most superficial sense—a point many dot–com entrepreneurs failed to understand. By definition, a bona fide competitive advantage is both unique and difficult to duplicate. A central goal of radical innovation is the invention of new sources of competitive advantage. Few product–line extensions or product enhancements (for example, a TV with a built–in DVD player) meet the test of radical innovation. Correspondingly, they have limited power to generate new wealth.

Virtually every industry can be characterized by a set of improvement curves that define the pace of progress. One of the most famous is Moore's Law, which posits a doubling of the ratio of semiconductor performance to price every 18 months or so. An improvement curve measures progress in a key performance metric over time. Typical metrics include cost of customer acquisition, time to market, direct manufacturing cost per unit, number of defects per thousand products and reported customer satisfaction. When it is successful, radical innovation dramatically alters the shape of an important improvement curve. For example, when Kodak pioneered the single–use camera, it created a significant dislocation in the cost curve associated with the manufacture of 35mm cameras. Indeed, Kodak's cheap and cheerful cameras sell for less than the annual cost savings typically achieved by Canon or Nikon in the production of traditional 35mm cameras. The single–use camera also changed customers' perceptions and habits. How many parents would trust a ten-year-old with a Nikon camera? Yet few would think twice about giving a child a disposable camera to use at the beach or a friend's birthday party. This kind of innovation is far more profound and has far more impact than incremental product enhancements.

Another limitation of traditional product innovation is that it is often confined to the physical product or the actual service. Yet the product is only one of several components that comprise the overall business concept. Thinking in terms of business concepts rather than products significantly extends the potential scope for innovation. It may be possible, for example, to build a radically different business concept even when the product itself is a virtual commodity. This is what Dell Computer accomplished in the PC business. A personal computer made by Dell is virtually indistinguishable from one made by HP or Compaq. Dell is not a product innovator. Yet Dell has innovated extensively in the way it builds and distributes PCs. And the 2:1 margin advantage that Cemex enjoys over its traditional competitors in the cement business is not the result of product innovation. It derives instead from Cemex's ability to spawn and deploy a steady succession of process innovations.

A product-centered view of innovation leads to blind spots—neglected opportunities for new thinking that are likely to be exploited by less myopic competitors. Product innovation is to business-concept innovation as bicep curls are to strength training—important, but only a small part of a much bigger challenge. Our interest is in innovation that is not only *radical* but also *extensive* in that it views every component of the business concept as a potential candidate for rule-breaking innovation. A business concept that differs from industry conventions along several dimensions is typically the most difficult for convention-bound incumbents to emulate.

Every new idea can be judged in terms of these two criteria: To what degree does the idea depart from industry norms (how radical is it)? and to what extent does the idea stretch beyond the product to encompass other elements of the business concept (how extensive is it)? Using these criteria, it is easy to see why companies like IKEA, eBay, Southwest Airlines, MTV, ReplayTV, Dell Computer, NetJets, Starbucks, Kohl's, Pret A Manger and XM Radio, among many others, truly qualify as industry revolutionaries.

Ask yourself what percentage of your company's product development projects, improvement initiatives and capital investment programs are aimed at producing radical innovation? Any company that

		Incremental	Radical
Industry		• B2B and supply chain integration	• Inventing new industry structures
Business		• Re-engineering business processes	• Creating entirely new business concepts
Product or Process		• Refining products & processes	• Reconfiguring products & processes

How Broad? (vertical axis)

Incremental   **Radical**

How radical?

hopes to outperform its mediocre peers will need to have a significant percentage of its projects, programs and initiatives in the upper right-hand quadrant of the matrix above.

So what about science? What about the kind of innovation that wins Nobel prizes? Companies like Boeing, Merck and Intel depend on R&D to produce breakthrough products and to redefine the performance envelope of existing products. R&D can be outrageously expensive (in 2002 the cost to develop a new drug was around $800 million).

Struggling as it does to push back the frontiers of knowledge, R&D is beset by uncertainties. Multimillion-dollar R&D programs often grind to a halt when they encounter intractable scientific problems. And even in the best cases, payback periods can stretch out to a decade or more. As an example, it took JVC and Sony nearly two decades to master the science of video recording. Given this, it shouldn't be surprising that technological prowess is no guarantee of above-average returns. In a recent five-year period, each of 21 U.S. companies was awarded 1,000 patents or more. These companies are America's technology superstars. Yet as a group, their earnings per share grew only 70 percent as fast as the average for the entire S&P 500 over the same five-year time frame. No wonder many companies are reining in corporate R&D and tying research budgets ever more tightly to the near-term priorities of operating units.

Science seeks to discover what is not yet known. Business concept innovation has a more modest goal—to imagine what has not yet been done. While the financial rewards can be spectacular in both cases, business concept innovation is, on average, less risky than fundamental technology innovation (where risk is the probability of failure multiplied by the minimum required investment). New scientific knowledge typically comes at a steep price. By contrast, **the imagination required to invent new business concepts comes cheap.** And while business concept innovation is never risk-free, there are ways, as we will see, of reducing those risks through low-cost experimentation and short-loop market feedback cycles. Radical innovation does not need to entail radical risk taking, nor should it.

Many companies have a difficult time in assigning an exact dollar value to the returns they get from their R&D spending—yet year after year they devote 2, 5 or even 10 percent of revenues to it. I would argue that companies should be spending a like sum on experiments aimed at reinventing existing business concepts and inventing new ones. One company with which I am acquainted recently decided to set aside 10 percent of its billion-dollar-a-year capital budget for projects that met the test of being "radical." Over each of the next five years, an additional 10 percent of the capital budget will be devoted to projects that challenge conventional thinking. If divisional managers fail to come up with such projects, their capital budgets will be cut proportionately. In this case, the CFO is sending a clear message to operating executives: Above-average performance requires investment proposals that defy industry-average thinking and deliver better than industry-average rates of improvement.

In the end, it is imagination, not investment, that drives innovation. The goal of this chapter and the next is to help you improve your capacity for the kind of radical, extensive innovation that thrills customers and dismays competitors. In the chapters that follow, you will meet some of the individuals and companies that have become adept at business concept innovation. But first, let's get some practice in thinking radically about business concepts. Let's speculate about what could be. As a start, let's imagine a radically new business concept—a global cyber business school.

CYBER B-SCHOOL

Maybe you're midcareer and would like to go to business school but don't relish the prospect of uprooting your family and putting your career on hold for two years while you attend a top-flight B-school. Or maybe you simply can't afford the exorbitant fees charged by those ivy-clad institutions. Could the way you buy business education change as dramatically over the next ten years as the way you buy books (Amazon.com), trade shares (E*TRADE), or get your news (Yahoo!)? You bet. Let's try a little thought experiment, one that will illustrate the kind of wrenching innovation that will destroy old business models in the age of revolution.

Start with the salient characteristics of a typical top–ten B–school:

○ *Geographically defined:* Faculty and students live within 20 miles of campus.
○ *Tough to get in:* Admission requirements include an honor-student GPA and a ninetieth percentile score on the Graduate Management Admissions Test—for starters. On average, fewer than one out of five applicants gets accepted.
○ *Classroom-based:* The typical format is one professor, 80 students, and a badly photocopied case.
○ *Few "stars":* Twenty percent of the faculty have world–class reputations as "gurus," the rest don't. Stars earn as much as 90 percent of their income from outside teaching and consulting.
○ *Egalitarian pay structure:* The salary differential between the "stars" and newly hired assistant professors is typically no greater than three to one.
○ *Publish or perish:* To get promoted, young faculty must publish within a narrowly defined "discipline." Peers within that discipline review their research. Faculty are generally unwilling to participate in multidisciplinary research and teaching.
○ *Young customers:* For the core M.B.A. program, customers are college graduates, roughly 25 to 30 years of age, with three or four years of work experience.
○ *Student numbers:* Top business schools admit anywhere between a couple hundred and around 1,000 M.B.A. students per year.
○ *High tuition:* Fees can amount to as much as $20,000 per year and even more.
○ *Inflexible program of study:* The M.B.A. program comprises two years of intensive residential study with 20 classroom hours per week and classes offered at set times.
○ *Academic research:* For faculty, the unstated goal is to publish "the maximum number of pages in journals read by the minimum number of people." Most research never gets applied. Even the best faculty find it difficult to pry research money out of the dean.

The top ten business schools in America turn out fewer than 7,500 M.B.A. graduates a year. In a world of 6 billion people, what is the size of the unfilled demand for high-quality business education? The vast majority of would-be business students is relegated to a second-class education or none whatsoever. As market economies take root in Eastern Europe, Asia, Latin America, and the Indian subcontinent, the demand for management education will soar. Failure to meet this demand could slow the speed of economic development in some parts of the world. Is there room for a new business model in business education? Yeah, acres of room.

Imagine that Paul Allen, co-founder of Microsoft, or George Soros, the global financier, decides to establish a cyber management school—let's call it the Global Leadership Academy. The first step is to skim two or three star professors from each of the ten best business schools and ten or so of the most cerebral partners in the leading consulting companies—the ones who've written groundbreaking books. Faculty are attracted to GLA by the chance to make a global difference in the quality of management—something that's difficult to do when your distribution channel is limited to a few hundred 27-year-olds each year. Faculty members are given equity in the new venture and a guaranteed income of $1 million per year. The new venture can afford these salaries because it is built on a very different economic model from a physical B-school. Instead of putting one professor in front of 80 students, GLA puts one professor in front of 100,000 students—through live satellite broadcasts and Webcasts. GLA also builds a network of local tutors around the world, affiliated with second-tier universities. These tutors meet occasionally with students and can facilitate online discussions of cases and lectures. Students can share insights in custom-designed chat rooms.

GLA's admission requirements are unlike those of traditional B-schools. To enroll, an applicant must simply submit three letters of recommendation from individuals outside his or her family. The first letter must describe some sort of "against the odds" accomplishment—perhaps overcoming drug addiction or helping to raise younger siblings after the death of a parent. The second letter must describe the applicant in a leadership role, however humble, and the third must outline a contribution the applicant has made to the community.

GLA's costs are largely unrelated to the number of students it serves. Indeed, it wants as many "customers" as possible in order to better amortize its fixed investment in online courseware and faculty salaries.

Though the entrance requirements may appear to be "soft," there is a demanding exit exam. Those who pass it get a degree from GLA. Those who don't get a certificate outlining their specific educational accomplishments. GLA charges students a flat fee of $2,000 per year, irrespective of how quickly they progress through the program. Dedicated students can finish the program in three years.

In some traditional business schools, students are given a limited number of "points" with which they can bid for admission to the classes of the most popular teachers. There are no oversubscribed courses at GLA. Every student learns from the best. The elite faculty supervises the development of Internet-based curricula and delivers key lectures.

GLA abandons the traditional discipline-based M.B.A. program and opts for an issue-based curriculum instead. Courses include "Profiting from Strategic Alliances," "Unleashing Innovation," "Building Digital Strategies," "Accessing Global Capital Markets," "Inspiring a Gen-X Workforce" and other cross-discipline issues.

With a 50 percent gross margin, GLA is able to build a first-rate research team around each faculty member. Freed from the burden of repetitive teaching, and with a cadre of first-rate researchers, faculty members dramatically raise their research output.

While GLA doesn't have a hundred-year history as a noble university, the chance to study with the world's best business minds attracts a flood of students. The collective "brand" of the faculty soon outshines the brand of any offline university.

GLA's early success astonishes traditional business schools. Unlike first-generation distance learning programs pioneered by Duke University and other schools, GLA offers its students the very best faculty in the world, rather than those willing to live near some particular university. Business education begins to resemble investment banking and basketball, where the stars get paid star salaries. Traditional business schools that seek to emulate GLA find themselves caught in a thicket of intractable issues:

> How do we sign up faculty from "competing" business schools?
>
> How do we manage the tensions when one faculty member gets paid 10 or 20 times what another faculty member gets paid?
>
> How do we pay star rates, given a brick-and-mortar overhead structure?
>
> How do we blow up the functional chimneys that prevent us from building an issue-based curriculum?

How do we justify high tuition fees when students can get the best faculty in the world for 90 percent less?

After three years of dithering and debate, Harvard, Wharton, Michigan, Northwestern and the London Business School join forces and launch their own virtual B-school. But internal squabbling and the challenge of managing a five-way alliance hamper their efforts. Oxford, Cambridge and other universities still struggling to build old-economy business schools simply give up.

An all-star B-school in cyberspace. Will this new business model materialize? Without a doubt. **New business models are more than disruptive *technologies*, they are completely novel business concepts.** They are more than *replacements* for what already is. Instead, they open up entirely new possibilities.

BUSINESS CONCEPT INNOVATION

New business models sometimes render old business models obsolete. For example, it's easy to imagine Internet-based phone calls, based on packet switching, largely supplanting phone calls made on dedicated voice circuits. More often, new business models don't destroy old models, they just siphon off customer demand, slowly deflating the profit potential of the old business model. Sears still has a hardware department, and Craftsman is a great brand, but The Home Depot has captured a huge portion of the burgeoning demand in the do-it-yourself market. Digital photography is not going to kill the film business in one fell swoop, but it may maim it by capturing a significant part of the "imaging" demand.

The goal of business concept innovation is to introduce more strategic variety into an industry or competitive domain. When this happens, and when customers value that variety, the distribution of wealth-creating potential often shifts dramatically in favor of the innovator. It's not value that "migrates" within and across industries, but the locus of innovation. Companies in one part of an industry will sometimes sit idly by while their strategies converge, while elsewhere some radical upstart creates a new business model and a gusher of new wealth. For example, Wal-Mart's bargaining power has allowed it to suck a lot of wealth out of its suppliers, but it would be only half right to say that value has "migrated" toward Wal-Mart. What actually happened was that Wal-Mart succeeded in doing something that few of its suppliers or competitors had done: inventing an entirely new and oh-so–attractive business concept—the super efficient hypermarket with "everyday low prices."

Business concept innovation is *meta*–innovation, in that it changes the very basis for competition within an industry or domain. The *American Heritage College Dictionary* defines "meta–" as "beyond" or "more comprehensive." Because it is nonlinear, business concept innovation goes *beyond* incremental innovation. Because it takes the entire business concept as the starting point, it is more comprehensive than innovation that focuses solely on products or technology.

Let's take cosmetics as an example. **When was the last time you caught your breath as you walked past the cosmetics counter in some big department store?** When was the last time you stopped, looked around and thought, "This is *so* cool"? Never? Well, that's no surprise. The way cosmetics are merchandised and sold has hardly changed over the past couple of decades. If you parachuted into the cosmetics section of a major department store, could you immediately tell whether you were in Macy's, Saks Fifth Avenue, Bloomingdale's or one of their competitors? If the product names were disguised, could you immediately distinguish the Estée Lauder counter from the Lancôme counter? Probably not. No wonder the cosmetics industry has been in a funk.

Think for a minute about the cosmetics business concept. High–end beauty products are sold almost exclusively in upscale department stores and account for as much as 20 percent of store profits. Manufacturers jealously control the display of their products, with counters and staff dedicated to each brand. Salesclerks, who are often paid by the manufacturers, are on commission and trained to be pushy—to *sell* you something rather than just let you *buy* something. If you want a lipstick of a particular shade, you'll have to wander from counter to counter, trying to remember if that Chanel lip gloss over there is an eensy-weensy bit less pink than the Lancôme lipstick you're holding in your hand. Many times you have to ask a clerk to see a particular product—most are displayed under glass–topped counters. Merchandising often relies on a "gift–with–purchase," a freebie that shoppers increasingly take for granted.

Sephora, a French–born cosmetics chain, recently acquired by the luxury giant LVMH, is on a global growth tear. Why? Because it's been ripping up the cosmetics rule book. Walk into a Sephora store, and you'll be blown away. In front of you is a wall of video screens. The staff are robed in black, each wearing one black glove, the better to show off delicate perfume bottles. They work for a flat salary. The store layout is black and white and oh–so–sleek. You'll find beauty–related books, magazines and videos; poetry inscribed on gleaming columns; and more than 600 different brands. But the biggest wow factor comes from the way Sephora displays the merchandise. Virtually every perfume in the world is arranged alphabetically along a wall. There's a lipstick counter with more than 365 hues, arranged by color. Face and body products are organized by category, rather than by manufacturer. You'll find everything from the hip (Urban Decay) to the *très chic* (Lancôme). Premium and mass–market brands often end up side by side. There's a fragrance organ—a multitiered rack of essences—where staff can tell you just what's in your favorite perfume and direct you to other similar fragrances. All the products are on open display. Pick them up, test them—even the lipsticks. There are no gifts. This is a temple of beauty, with the consumer as goddess.

Don't take my word for it, listen to Marianne Wilson of *Chain Store Age*:

> By the combined force of its ambience, design and merchandise mix, Sephora blows away all other competitors in its category. And it does so without the gift–with–purchase clutter, hard sell and often haughty sales people that define much of department store beauty retailing. In fact, what I most liked about Sephora was the egalitarian way it treats both shoppers and merchandise.[1]

By the spring of 1999, Sephora had captured 20 percent of the French retail cosmetics market. Within 18 months of opening its first U.S. outlet in Manhattan, Sephora had opened an additional 49 stores across the United States, and had plans to open as many as 200 more. Myron E. Ullman III, architect of Sephora's international expansion, has his own view on what Sephora is all about:

> Retailing is about change. I can't think of a single retail concept that hasn't changed that is now doing very well. That's why we have a group in Paris who sit around and do nothing else but think of different ways to do things. Chief among their tasks is to keep [our] flagships so stunning that people are compelled to walk in. When our customers stroll down Fifth Avenue, we want them to say to themselves, "Should I go to the Museum of Modern Art or should I go to Sephora?"

Sephora has trashed the typical cosmetics business model:

	Traditional Model	Sephora Model
Sales staff on commission	Yes	No
Gift with purchase	Yes	No
One brand per counter	Yes	No
Manufacturer controls display	Yes	No
Easy to sample	No	Yes
Shop unmolested	No	Yes
Easy to compare products	No	Yes
Customer in control	No	Yes

Without a doubt, this is business concept innovation.

With Sephora, the cosmetics makers lose their control of the sales force, product display and merchandising—the very things they relied on for competitive differentiation at point of sale. Major ouch! Some cosmetics manufacturers, afraid of angering department stores, have refused to let Sephora handle certain product lines. You won't find Estée Lauder's MAC, Bobbi Brown and Aveda lines at Sephora. Nor will you find Chanel's makeup lines—not, at least, for now.

Business concept innovation starts from a premise that the only way to escape the squeeze of hyper-competition, even temporarily, is to build a business model so unlike what has come before that traditional competitors are left scrambling. **When it's most effective, business concept innovation leaves competitors in a gut-wrenching quandary:** If they abandon their tried-and-tested business model, they risk sacrificing their core business for a second-place finish in a game they didn't invent, with rules they don't understand; yet if they don't embrace the new model, they forgo the future. Damned if they do and damned if they don't—that's business concept innovation at its best.

Business concept innovation is not a way of positioning *against* competitors, but of going *around* them. It's based on *avoidance*, not *attack*. Here's the key thought: *what is not different is not strategic*. To the extent that strategy is the quest for above-average profits, it is *entirely* about variety—not just in one or two areas, but in all components of the business model. Business concept innovation often falls short of this lofty goal, but that's the objective.

Consequently, a capacity to first identify, then deconstruct and re-construct business models lies at the heart of a high-performance innovation system. If your company is not experimenting with radically different business models, it's already living on borrowed time.

UNPACKING THE BUSINESS MODEL

To be an industry revolutionary, you must develop an instinctive capacity to think about business models in their entirety. There are many ways of describing the components of a business model. I have created a framework that is complete, yet simple.

A business concept comprises four major components:

○ Core Strategy
○ Strategic Resources
○ Customer Interface
○ Value Network

Each of these components has several subcomponents, which will be described later in this section. For each element I have also suggested a few questions that should help you think more deeply and deftly about opportunities for business concept innovation. The fact is that most companies have *business concept blind spots* that prevent them from seeing opportunities for innovation in many parts of the business concept. In this chapter we'll remove those blind spots.

The four core components are linked together by three "bridge" components:

○ Core Strategy → *Configuration* of Activities → Resource Base
○ Core Strategy → Customer *Benefits* → Customer Interface
○ Resource Base → Company *Boundaries* → Value Network

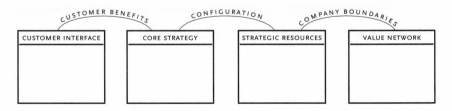

Underpinning the business model are four factors that determine its profit potential:

○ Efficiency
○ Uniqueness
○ Fit
○ Profit Boosters

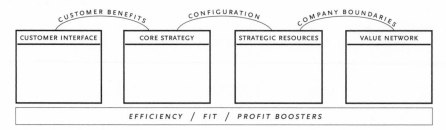

Core Strategy

The first component of the business concept is the *core strategy*. It is the essence of how the firm chooses to compete. Elements of the core strategy include the business mission, product/market scope and basis for differentiation.

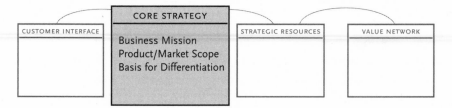

1. **The Business Mission:** This captures the overall *objective* of the strategy—what the business model is designed to accomplish or deliver. The business mission encompasses things such as the "value proposition," "strategic intent," "big, hairy, audacious goals," "purpose," and overall performance objectives. It implies a sense of direction and a set of criteria against which to measure progress. It is often unstated and often constrains a company's view of potential business concepts. A change in a company's business mission doesn't necessarily result in business concept innovation. But when a company brings a new or very different business mission into an industry dominated by companies with roughly similar business goals, the result may be business concept innovation. This was the

case when Virgin exported its lifestyle-oriented, entertainment-focused business mission to the airline business. Traditional air carriers had business missions focused on maximizing the operational efficiency of their airlines. Virgin's business mission was focused on fun, value-for-money and customer feel-good factors. Anyone who has flown on Virgin will have noticed the difference this makes.

Example: Although it has long styled itself as "The Document Company," Xerox's implicit business mission has focused on copiers and copying. This definition created a *business concept blind spot* that allowed Hewlett-Packard to build a commanding lead in the printer business. With most of their documents stored electronically, individuals use their printers, rather than copiers, to reproduce documents. You can argue that HP is also a "document company," but its business mission focused on printing rather than copying. After falling far behind, Xerox amended its business concept to include printing. 'Tis a pity for Xerox that this business concept innovation didn't occur a decade earlier.

Ask yourself: What is our business mission? What are we becoming as a company—can we describe a "from" and a "to"? What is our dream? What kind of difference do we want to make in the world? Is our business mission sufficiently broad to allow for business concept innovation? Is our business mission as *relevant* to customers as it might have been in years past? Most important, do we have a business mission that is sufficiently distinguished from the missions of other companies in our industry?

Thought: A business school that sees its business mission as granting degrees to residential students, rather than addressing the world's "management deficit," will have little incentive for business concept innovation.

2. Product/Market Scope: This captures the essence of *where* the firm competes—which customers, which geographies, and what product segments—and where, by implication, it doesn't compete. A company's definition of product/market scope can be a source of business concept innovation when it is quite different from that of traditional competitors.

Example: Amazon may have started as an online bookseller, but its goal is to become the Wal-Mart of the Internet—offering products as diverse as videos, personal electronics, lawn and garden supplies, tools, toys and much more. Leveraging its easy-to-use customer interface, Amazon seems intent on increasing its share of online purchases to the detriment of single-segment Web retailers.

Ask yourself: Could we offer customers something closer to a "total solution" to their needs by expanding our definition of product scope? Could we increase our "share of wallet" as well as our share of market by expanding our scope? Would a different definition of scope allow us to capture more of the life cycle profits associated with our product or service? **Are there types of customers that have been generally ignored by companies in our industry?**

Thought: What if banks expanded the scope of their debit card offerings to include children? Wouldn't it be great if your daughter had her own debit card and her allowance was automatically transferred to her bank account each month? She could spend the available funds with her debit card. No more worrying about lost allowances, and no more arguments about whether you remembered to pay her or not. 'Tis a pity that Visa or MasterCard haven't thought of this.

3. Basis for Differentiation: This captures the essence of *how* the firm competes and, in particular, how it competes *differently* from its competitors.

Example: You don't know Jonathan Ives, but you know his work. At 30 years of age, the quirky Londoner was appointed head of Apple Computer's industrial design division. It is Ives, after all, who was responsible for the iMac, the curvy, translucent machine that has redefined what a computer should look like. For years, the PC was the ugliest thing in your house. It looked like a disemboweled robot with cords and cables spilling everywhere. And it came in only one color—deadly, boring beige. Why? Because most of the companies making PCs had an industrial products heritage—they were filled with engineers not artists. The iMac sold 400,000 units in the first month after its introduction, and introduced an entirely new dimension of differentiation—aesthetics—into the computer industry. And in early 2002, Apple did it again with the new iMac—a radically new computer design with a footprint smaller than a dinner plate and a new ergonomic "floating" flat panel display.

Ask yourself: How have competitors tried to differentiate themselves in our industry? Are there other dimensions of differentiation we could explore? In what aspects of the product or service has there been the *least* differentiation? How could we increase the differentiation in some of these dimensions? Have we searched diligently for differentiation opportunities in *every* dimension of the business model?

Thought: You can take $250 out of a cash machine with a piece of plastic. But if you want to check in to a $250-per-night hotel room, be prepared to give your life history at check-in. This is absurd. You take money out of the ATM, but you take nothing from the hotel but the soap. By the time you arrive, you've already guaranteed your room with a credit card, and they have your name on file, so why do you have to go through the whole check-in rigmarole? Why not use your credit card as a room key? Will it happen? Yep. Holiday Inn is planning a new hotel near the Atlanta airport where consumers will be able to use their credit cards as room keys.[2] Hey guys, ATMs have been around for years—what took you so long?

CUSTOMER INTERFACE	CORE STRATEGY	STRATEGIC RESOURCES	VALUE NETWORK
	Business Mission Product/Market Scope Basis for Differentiation	Core Competencies Strategic Assets Core Processes	

Strategic Resources

Every competitive advantage worthy of the name rests on unique firm-specific resources. Dramatically changing the resource base for competition can be a source of business concept innovation. Strategic resources include core competencies, strategic assets and core processes.

1. Core Competencies: This is what the firm *knows*. It encompasses skills and unique capabilities.

Example: Disney, a company with roots in animated films and theme parks, has become a force to be reckoned with on Broadway. Theatrical productions are lavish entertainment, and who knows lavish better than Disney? By transporting its core competencies in stage design (what is a theme park, but a giant stage?) and storytelling to Broadway, Disney's blockbuster *Lion King* was the winner of six Tony Awards and one of the highest-grossing musicals of all time. *Lion King* quickly became more than a Broadway production and a movie, launching a blockbuster franchise that spawned TV spin-offs, books, toys and theme-park attractions. When, on occasion, Disney has diversified into areas where there is less of a core competence connection, as with its purchase of the ABC television network, success has been much harder to come by.

Ask yourself: What are our core competencies? What do we know that is (a) unique, (b) valuable to customers, and (c) transferable to new opportunities? What are the deep benefits that our core competencies allow us to deliver to customers? How could we deploy those benefits in new ways or in new settings? What difference could our core competencies make if we introduced them into industries where competitors possess very different skills? Are there skills we don't currently possess that could undermine the role our traditional competencies play in some overall customer solution? What new competencies should we be adding to our business concept?

Thought: The skills eBay applies to the problem of creating an online, consumer-to-consumer marketplace are very different from the competencies a newspaper relies on in running its classified ads section. A newspaper would face a daunting challenge if it wanted to run real-time, coast-to-coast auctions. When business concept innovation changes the competence base of an industry, it puts traditional players at a profound disadvantage, which is, of course, the goal of business concept innovation.

2. Strategic Assets: Strategic assets are what the firm owns. They are things, rather than know-how. Strategic assets can include brands, patents, infrastructure, proprietary standards, customer data and anything else that is both rare and valuable. Using one's strategic assets in a novel way can lead to business concept innovation.

Example: I think it's unlikely that Barnes & Noble will ever match Amazon.com's success as an online retailer. But Barnes & Noble has one strategic asset that Amazon.com can't match—its prime retail locations. Barnes & Noble has used this asset to deliver new forms of value to customers. First it sprinkled comfy sofas and overstuffed chairs amid the acres of books. Next it built coffee bars in its bookstores. Then it started scheduling poetry readings and music recitals. All this has transformed Barnes & Noble into a leisure destination—something more akin to a community center or the old town square than a bookstore.

Ask yourself: What are our strategic assets? Could we exploit them in new ways to bring new value to consumers? Could our strategic assets be valuable in other industry settings? Can we build new business models that exploit our existing strategic assets—that is, can we imagine alternate uses for our strategic assets?

Thought: How likely is it that a company making earth–moving equipment would become a fashion icon? Despite the long odds, this is exactly what Caterpillar, the macho manufacturer of heavy machinery, has managed to do. Caterpillar started selling "Cat" branded work boots in 1995 and sold 3 million pairs that first year; by 2000 they had sold 26 million pairs. Cat branded shoes, apparel, toys and accessories will be sold in over 600 stores by 2003. Caterpillar's worldwide sales of licensed merchandise totaled nearly $1 billion in 2000. Making it one of the most powerful licensed brands in the world—up there with Coca–Cola and Harley–Davidson. *The raw mechanical power of the Caterpillar brand, that yellow-and-black image of heavy machinery once known only to construction workers, is now attracting hip young urbanites.* What strategic assets has your company overlooked?

3. Core Processes: This is what people in the firm actually do. Core processes are methodologies and routines used in transforming inputs into outputs. Core processes are activities, rather than "assets" or "skills." They are used in translating competencies, assets, and other inputs into value for customers. A fundamental reinvention of a core process can be the basis for business concept innovation.

Examples: Dell's build-to-order system is one of its core processes and a powerful example of business concept innovation. Drug discovery is a core process for every pharmaceutical company. It is also a process that has been radically reinvented in recent years through bioinformatics, which makes it possible to rapidly screen thousands and thousands of compounds. Toyota's lean manufacturing was a process innovation that turned the car industry on its ear.

Ask yourself: What are our most critical processes—that is, what processes create the most value for customers and are most competitively unique? What is the rate at which we are improving these processes? Is that rate of improvement accelerating or decelerating? Can we imagine a radically different process that would deliver the same benefit? Are there opportunities for step function improvements in the efficiency or effectiveness of our processes? Could we borrow nonlinear process ideas from other industries? Conversely, could we use our process expertise to transform some other industry?

Thought: Have you ever had a house built? How long did it take? A year? Two years? A few years ago the San Diego–based Building Industry Association sponsored a seemingly ridiculous contest. Two teams were pitted against each other—each would try to build a house in less than four hours, using traditional materials. The teams planned every second of the building process with military precision. They struggled to invent new technologies, such as cement that would dry in a matter of minutes. They broke the work down into subtasks that could be carried out in parallel. While one group was laying the foundation, another would frame the walls, and another would build the roof. The frame would get bolted to the foundation in large sections, and the roof would be lifted onto the framing with the help of a crane. Each team brought hundreds of construction workers to the site, and every tradesman was given an intricately choreographed role to play. Improbably, one team managed to build its three–bedroom bungalow, complete with landscaping, in less than *three* hours. Of course the contest had a logic—**ONLY BY PUSHING THE PEDAL TO THE METAL, BY REACHING FOR THE SEEMINGLY IMPOSSIBLE, IS IT POSSIBLE TO ESCAPE THE LIMITS OF CURRENT PROCESSES AND DISCOVER NEW POSSIBILITIES.** But don't you dare call *this* process reengineering—it's far more radical. So what kind of process innovation would allow you to transform *your* industry?

Configuration

Intermediating between a company's *core strategy* and its *strategic resources* is a bridge component I'll call *configuration*. Configuration refers to the unique way in which competencies, assets and processes are *combined* and *interrelated* in support of a particular strategy. It refers to the *linkages* between competencies, assets and processes and how those linkages are managed. The notion of configuration recognizes that great strategies (and great business models) rest on a unique blending of competencies, assets and processes.

> **Example**: Prior to its ill–fated acquisition by Daimler–Benz, Chrysler had gained a substantial amount of advantage from the way it uses "platform teams" to orchestrate the functional disciplines involved in producing and marketing a vehicle. Most car companies are organized by function–design, engineering, manufacturing, marketing and sales. Employees sit in functional "silos" and are often more loyal to their function than to any particular car program. The result is a lot of friction, suboptimal trade–offs and development delays. Chrysler used a new building to unite functional specialists around vehicle platforms, employing a team structure it first used in the development of the built–to–thrill Viper sports car. Each platform team has representatives from every function.

They sit together in a stadium–sized room, where each employee has a line of sight to every other employee. In the new configuration, it's clear that an employee's first loyalty is to the success of the program he or she is working on, not to some distant functional head. Chrysler's American competitors possess roughly similar technical knowledge, strategic assets, and processes, but Chrysler was the first American car company to configure all of these into boundary–breaking platform teams. This is one reason Chrysler came to be regarded in the 1990s as one of the most innovative car companies in the world.

Ask yourself: How do we manage the interfaces between different assets, knowledge and processes? Have we configured our assets, skills and processes in unique ways? Has anyone in our industry or domain configured their strategic resources in an unconventional way? Do they gain any advantage from this configuration? Can we imagine very different configurations from what we have at present?

Thought: If your bank is like most, it sends you one statement for your credit card, another for your mortgage, another for your checking account, another for your savings or investment account, and still another for your car loan or any other borrowing you may have. The blizzard of statements you receive each month reflects the internal configuration of most banks—each product area is a separate profit center. It also reflects banks' eagerness to borrow money from you at one rate (what they pay you on a certificate of deposit, for example) and lend it back to you at a higher rate (the interest you pay on your credit card debt, for example). Virgin Money, the innovative financial services arm of Sir Richard Branson's far–flung empire, offers customers a radically different approach based on a completely different configuration of banking resources. The Virgin One account works like this. Imagine you have a $200,000 balance on your mortgage, with an 8 percent interest rate. Imagine further that your monthly paycheck amounts to $8,000. When your paycheck is electronically deposited into your Virgin One account, your mortgage balance is immediately reduced by $8,000. Then, as you write checks during the month from the same account, your mortgage balance creeps back up. In this way, you're earning the equivalent of 8 percent on the money from your paycheck that sits in your One account. Compare that with what most banks give you on your checking account. Now let's say you splurge on a Tahitian holiday and end up with $10,000 of credit card debt. Instead of paying this down over a period of months and being subject to the typically exorbitant interest rates charged by credit card companies, you pay the credit card bill out of your One account. Your debt goes up by $10,000, but you're being charged interest at only 8 percent. And when, a few months later, you pay in that $20,000 inheritance from grandma, it reduces your debt by a similar amount, and there-fore earns an effective 8 percent interest rate—far better than what you could get on a deposit account. The radical premise behind the Virgin One account is this: you are one person with a single overall level of indebtedness. Your bank shouldn't treat you like you're suffering from a case of multiple personalities, nor should it gain financially from the fact that it is configured in a way that makes it impossible to consolidate your borrowing and savings into a single account.

CUSTOMER INTERFACE	CONFIGURATION		
	CORE STRATEGY	STRATEGIC RESOURCES	VALUE NETWORK
Fulfillment & Support Information & Insight Relationship Dynamics Pricing Structure	Business Mission Product/Market Scope Basis for Differentiation	Core Competencies Strategic Assets Core Processes	

Customer Interface

The third component of the business concept, *customer interface*, has four elements: fulfillment and support, information and insight, rela-tionship dynamics and pricing structure. The Internet has caused a radical shift in how producers reach consumers.

1. Fulfillment and Support: This refers to the way the firm "goes to market," how it actually "reaches" customers—which channels it uses, what kind of customer support it offers and what level of service it provides.

  Examples: Commercial radio, a $17 billion industry that has seen little technological change since FM 40 years ago, is ripe for revolution. If you commute to work by car in the United States, you have probably endured hours of bland, commercial–ridden radio. Most urban markets offer a scant handful of programming formats: Top 40, country music, classical music, hard rock, news radio and maybe a sports station or two. And if rush hour traffic wasn't frustrating enough, drive–time radio typically subjects the harried commuter to 20 minutes of advertising per hour. And if your journey spans a few hundred miles, you'll find that your favorite station soon fades to static. Thankfully, XM Radio and Sirius Satellite Radio are reinventing the way news and entertainment get delivered to your car. Both companies offer a "satellite radio" service that pumps out up to 100 channels of CD–quality radio to a small satellite receiver that can be mounted in a car or at home. The service, which covers the United States, costs listeners $10 per month. Within a few months of its launch, XM Radio had become the fastest–selling new audio product in 20 years. Satellite radio's new best friends are car companies, and factory–installed satellite radio will soon be available from GM, Honda, DaimlerChrysler, Ford and BMW. Sony and other consumer electronics firms are offering after–market radios that can be plugged into the car or carried indoors. A compact Walkman version is on the way. No longer will radio listeners be hostage to the bland and banal advertising–supported stations that typically populate the radio dial. Will folks pay $10 a month for something they used to get for free? **Well, water is free, and broadcast TV is free, and yet Perrier and DirecTV have managed to take billions of dollars out of consumers' pockets.** XM Radio might just be the next blockbuster based, as it is, on a radically different fulfillment model.

With iPhoto, Apple is transforming the way the humble snapshot gets stored, printed and shared. A key spoke within the iMac's digital hub, iPhoto helps shutterbugs import, organize, edit and store digital images with a graceful GUI that makes removing red–eye, cropping images and producing soundtrack supported slideshows intuitively simple—all without the need of third–party software. Among iPhoto's menus is a "share panel" that provides the option of one–click ordering of prints in various formats, from contact sheets to greeting cards. Images can be easily shared by posting them to an Apple–provided personal home page. If that weren't enough, iPhoto offers photographers the option of having their pictures professionally published, quickly and effortlessly, in a custom-made book of photographs and captions printed on acid-free glossy paper and bound in an elegant linen cover. As competitors focus on bulking up RAM and ROM, Apple has realized that digitally savvy customers also value memories of a more personal nature.

Ask yourself: How do we reach customers? What does a customer have to "go through" to buy our products and services? To what extent have we built our fulfillment and support system for our benefit rather than our customers' benefit? Could we make the process of fulfillment and support substantially easier or more enjoyable for customers? What would it look like if we designed our support and fulfillment processes from the customer backward? Could we dramatically reduce search costs? Could we provide customers with truly honest data for comparison shopping? Have we removed every element of customer aggravation in the support and fulfillment process?

Thought: Today Americans give to charity a smaller percentage of their income than ever before. We are so wrapped up in our lives, so constantly busy, that we have hardly a moment to think about doing good for anyone but ourselves. Could business concept innovation change this? Is there another way of linking donors to worthwhile causes—another "fulfillment" mechanism? Of course. One thing that blunts the impulse to give is the bureaucracy that intervenes between the giver and the beneficiary. You give to United Way or some religious organization that pools your money with other gifts and directs those funds to projects around the world. You have only a vague sense of where your money goes and no direct feedback on the difference it makes. Most of us wouldn't consider putting our financial investments in a "blind trust," but this is essentially what happens when we give to charity. What if you had the chance to pick the exact projects to which you'd like to contribute? What if you got a monthly report on the good that was being done? What if you were able to pick projects that were sized to the amount you could afford—projects where you could feel your contribution made a critical difference, whether it was $100, $1,000 or $100,000? What if you could easily build a portfolio of specific charity projects that reflected your own personal interests—be it abolishing hunger, ending child labor, reducing deforestation or saving souls? Instead of United Way, it would be Your Way.

So let's establish a website called givemore.org. A small team of people will vet charity projects submitted from around the world. They will be assisted by local review teams. One project might be to build an orphanage in Rwanda, another to help a struggling church in Byelorussia and another to help teens at risk. Each project will be posted to the Web. While today you can get a long list of charities on the Web, you can't easily make donations to specific projects. At givemore.org, project listings will include the amount of funding needed, the expected benefits and the supervising organization. The review team will rate each project on some cost/benefit criteria. You will know what portion of your contribution is going to be absorbed by overhead and administrative fees. Projects will be posted by government agencies, churches, long–standing charities and responsible individuals. Potential donors will go online and select a project from a menu of worthy causes organized by need and geography. They will get regular e–mail updates on the progress of their projects. Every year givemore.org will arrange a trip for large donors so they can review the impact of their giving on–site. With givers no longer divorced from the heartwarming gratitude of recipients, giving just might soar. Is this all a fantasy? Yeah, but it'll happen. **Do you have a fantasy about how your company can reinvent its connection to customers?**

2. **Information and Insight:** This refers to all the knowledge that is collected from and utilized on behalf of customers—the information content of the customer interface. It also refers to the ability of a company to extract insights from this information—insights that can help it do cool new things for customers. It also covers the information that is made available to customers pre- and postpurchase.

   Example: Dell Computer uses information to link itself tightly to its customers and to build barriers to entry for less Web–savvy competitors. Dell's largest customers, big companies that buy millions of dollars of hardware every year, access Dell products via custom–tailored "Premier Pages." These Web pages are configured to reflect the IT and procurement policies of each corporate customer. An employee who wants to buy a computer from Dell will have access to a special page that generates dynamic price quotes based on prenegotiated volume discounts. The Premier Pages also let employees know what product configurations have been approved by their company's IT executives. Corporate procurement managers can view each outstanding order submitted by their company's employees, give their approval and submit the order to Dell. By tightly coupling its online selling process with the procurement policies of its big customers, Dell has given itself a powerful "easy to do business with" advantage. Dell exploits information in other ways, as well. Each time it builds a PC, it gives the machine a unique five-digit alphanumeric code. A customer can go to Dell's support site, enter that code and get the original configurations of that machine as it was shipped, the days left on its warranty, where it was shipped and all the driver files and utilities. No monopoly lock-in here. Rather, Dell uses the twine of information to bind itself ever more tightly to its customers.

Ask yourself: What do we actually know about customers? Are we using every opportunity to deepen our knowledge of our customers' needs and desires? Are we capturing all the data we could? How do we use this knowledge to serve them in new ways? Have we given our customers the information they need to make empowered and intelligent purchasing decisions? What additional information would customers like to have?

Thought: A senior executive of a large supermarket chain once told me of some research that suggested a top-quartile customer in an average store would spend 50 times more in a year than a bottom-quartile customer. The top-quartile customer lived locally, shopped a couple times a week, had a family and was reasonably well off. The bottom-quartile customer was just passing through or didn't have a family, and wasn't so well heeled. I started thinking about this data. What if it were true? Every supermarket has an express lane for customers with "10 items or less." But who uses that lane? Bottom-quartile customers. Top-quartile customers are waiting in line with an overstuffed cart—they've come to buy more than beer and cigarettes. Why, I began to wonder, wasn't there a line for customers who spend $5,000 or more in a year? Why didn't these shoppers have someone to help them load their groceries into their BMWs and Volvos? While many supermarkets give loyalty cards to their customers, few seem to have used the information gathered to provide truly differentiated service to their best customers.

3. **Relationship Dynamics:** This element of the business model refers to the nature of the *interaction* between the producer and the customer. Is the interaction face to face or indirect? Is it continuous or sporadic? How easy is it for the customer to interact with the producer? What feelings do these interactions invoke on the part of the customer? Is there any sense of "loyalty" created by the pattern of interactions? The notion of relationship dynamics acknowledges the fact that there are emotional, as well as transactional, elements in the interaction of producers and consumers, and that these can be the basis for a highly differentiated business concept.

Example: There's probably no company in the world that works harder to build genuine relationships with its customers than Harley–Davidson. The Harley Owners Group boasts 450,000 members. Every year Harley–Davidson sponsors a rally where the tattoo contest is one of the most keenly anticipated events. As the company says, **"It's one thing for people to buy your products. It's another for them to tattoo your name on their bodies."** BMW makes awesome motorcycles, but when was the last time you saw a bicep that read "Bayerische Motoren Werke"?

Ask yourself: How do we make our customers *feel*? What is the range of emotions that a customer experiences in his or her interactions with us? Have we invested in our customers? Could we reinvent the customer experience in ways that would strengthen the sense of affiliation the customer has with us? Where can we exceed customer expectations and raise the hurdle for competitors? What are the dozen greatest customer experiences in the world? Is there anything about those experiences we could replicate in our relationship with customers?

Thought: Perhaps nowhere is the alignment between customer expectations and the actual service experience more out of whack than in health care. A senior health–care executive recently described the current state of the U.S. health–care experience as follows: "Prison inmates and hospital patients have a lot in common. Both are subjected to excessive questioning, stripped of their usual clothing and possessions, placed in a subservient, dependent relationship and allowed visitors only during certain hours." Adventist Health System, one of the largest church–affiliated hospital groups in America, is seeking to change this sorry state of affairs. It has examined each stage of the patient experience and has identified opportunities to revolutionize service delivery. A couple of examples: Instead of answering the same questions over and over again, patients will be given a Web-based "portable health record" that travels with them from clinical experience to clinical experience. Another innovation is the elimination of visiting hours. Family members will have visiting privileges 24 hours a day, even in the emergency room. While creating some inconvenience for the staff, this idea has greatly reduced litigation expense in the hospitals where it has been instituted. When a health event goes wrong, the family is less likely to point fingers at anonymous health–care providers if they were there and know the doctors and staff did all they could do for the patient.

4. **Pricing Structure:** You have several choices in what you charge for. You can charge customers for a product or for service. You can charge customers directly or indirectly through a third party. You can bundle components or price them separately. You can charge a flat rate or charge for time or distance. You can have set prices or market–based prices. Each of these choices offers the chance for business concept innovation, depending on the traditions of your industry.

   Examples: While traditional insurance companies are just that—traditional—devoting themselves to the age–old practice of selling fixed–rate auto insurance policies by the year, Britain's Norwich Union has overturned this industry orthodoxy by offering its customers insurance by the mile. Rather than pay to protect a car that is sitting in the garage while you work from home, carpool or travel by train or plane, you just pay for insurance when you're actually on the road. Using a global-positioning system, pay–as–you–drive customers are charged an insurance premium that is based on how often, when and where their cars are used. A novel pricing structure, to be sure.

In pre–Web times, when you purchased a CD, you were compelled to buy whatever tunes the producer chose to include. Consumers rebelled against this model in amazing numbers with the launch of Napster in 1998. Napster's users, as many as 20 million at its peak, weren't looking primarily for "free" music—they just wanted to make their own choices of which songs to include on their CDs. Since the days of Napster, a whole industry supporting user–selected downloadable music has emerged, including producers of portable MP3 players, CD–R drives and software for organizing and sharing playlists. Napster's legal successors, PressPlay and MusicNet, although backed by big record labels, have not yet achieved the Napster magic with their limited selection, crippled song versions and digital time bombs which disable your downloads should you stop subscribing to the service. Sooner or later, someone will invent a music download service that captures the hearts and wallets of Napster's former fans. At its heart will be a new pricing algorithm—one that allows customers to buy individual tracks and record them on any device of their choosing.

Increasingly, General Electric, Rolls–Royce and Pratt & Whitney—the world's leading makers of jet engines—don't sell a product. They sell "power by the hour." When airlines buy one of Boeing's ultra–long–range 777s, scheduled for launch in 2003, they'll get a pair of GE 90 engines that come with a fixed–price maintenance agreement pegged at so many dollars per flight hour. After all, airlines don't really want to own jet engines; they want guaranteed up time. Many Internet service providers used to charge by the hour for connect time. No more. Most now have a single monthly charge no matter how long you're online.

Ask yourself: What are you actually charging for? What is the dominant pricing paradigm in your industry? Can you break it? Do you really know what customers think they're paying for? Can you more closely align what you charge for with what customers actually value? Does the existing pricing structure implicitly penalize some customers and subsidize others? Can you change this?

Thought: What you charge for and what your customers think they're paying for are often quite distinct. Your pricing structure and a customer's value structure are not the same things. When I buy a magazine I pay for information or entertainment. When I buy a razor I pay for a cleanly shaven face. A company that understands a customer's value structure—the value that is placed on each of the benefits received—is in a great position to be a pricing innovator. If I visit the *New York Times* or the *San Jose Mercury News* online, I get the reporters or columnists that write for those particular papers. But why can't I go to a site that lists the top–100 columnists and news reporters, along with the titles of their latest stories or editorials? That way, I'd pay for and get to read the writers I most enjoy.

Customer Benefits

Intermediating between the *core strategy* and the *customer interface* is another bridge component—the particular bundle of *benefits* that is actually being offered to the customer. Benefits refer to a customer-derived definition of the basic needs and wants that are being satisfied. Benefits are what link the core strategy to the needs of the customer. An important component of any business concept is the decision as to which benefits are or aren't going to be included in the offering.

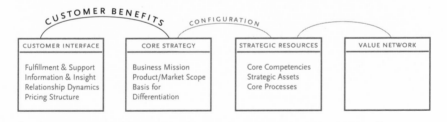

CUSTOMER INTERFACE	CORE STRATEGY	STRATEGIC RESOURCES	VALUE NETWORK
Fulfillment & Support Information & Insight Relationship Dynamics Pricing Structure	Business Mission Product/Market Scope Basis for Differentiation	Core Competencies Strategic Assets Core Processes	

Example: It used to be that when you bought a car, you bought sheet metal and rubber. Now, if you buy a luxury sedan, you get a car bursting with ancillary benefits: 24/7 roadside service, expense reimbursement when your trip is interrupted by car trouble, a loaner when your car is in for major service and a free car wash with every service. GM's OnStar system provides a 24–hour concierge who can secure a restaurant reservation or direct you to the nearest zoo. If your airbags deploy, OnStar automatically contacts emergency services and gives them your location. Having trouble locating your car in an airport parking lot? Call OnStar from your cell phone, and they'll flash your car's lights and sound its horn. They'll even unlock the doors remotely if you've been a particularly silly prat and locked your keys inside. OnStar may fall short of industry revolution, but it's certainly raising the ante for luxury car makers and it's just the beginning of what car makers hope will ultimately be a cornucopia of services that will generate a continuing stream of revenues long after the vehicle has been purchased.

Ask yourself: What benefits are we actually delivering to customers? Are there ancillary benefits that the customer might value? What's the core need we're trying to address? Have we defined that need broadly enough? Conversely, are we delivering benefits that customers don't really care about? Can we change the benefit bundle in ways that will surprise customers and frustrate competitors? What's the context in which the product or service is used? Does that context suggest the possibility of enlarging the benefit bundle?

Thought: Imagine you want to build a patio behind your house and you go online to check out a DIY superstore. You provide some information on the size of patio you want to build, the style of your house and your budget. A virtual architect then presents a couple of dozen plans from which you can choose. The program automatically resizes each plan to fit your available space. Once you've made your selection, a virtual contractor generates a list of all the tools and materials you're going to need and a construction blueprint. You can remove from the list any item that you already have. In a few hours a truck delivers everything you're going to need on one pallet. You print out a detailed construction guide from the website. When you make your purchase you get a telephone number to call for help if you should run into any problems. Now that's a

CUSTOMER INTERFACE	CORE STRATEGY	STRATEGIC RESOURCES	VALUE NETWORK
Fulfillment & Support	Business Mission	Core Competencies	Suppliers
Information & Insight	Product/Market Scope	Strategic Assets	Partners
Relationship Dynamics	Basis for	Core Processes	Coalitions
Pricing Structure	Differentiation		

uniquely tailored bundle of benefits, and it could be the basis for some real business concept innovation for The Home Depot, Orchard Supply or some other big home-improvement retailer.

Value Network

The fourth component of a business model is the *value network* that surrounds the firm, and which complements and amplifies the firm's own resources. Today many of the resources that are critical to a firm's success lie outside its direct control. Elements of the value network include suppliers, partners and coalitions. The design and management of the value network can be important sources of business concept innovation.

1. **Suppliers:** Suppliers typically reside "up the value chain" from the producer. Privileged access to or a deep relationship with suppliers can be a central element of a novel business model.

   Example: Pret A Manger, the UK-based fast-food chain specializing in freshly made gourmet sandwiches, uses a network of mostly small suppliers to provide it with a broad range of additive-free ingredients. Since ingredients are delivered fresh to each Pret store every day, there are no long supply lines of frozen French fries or sesame-coated buns. This allows Pret to change their menu frequently—adding a new menu item every two weeks or so. It also minimizes inventory costs. Pret's imaginative suppliers are always on the lookout for new and interesting ingredients. One supplier located a source of crayfish, flown in daily from China. In early 2002, the most popular sandwich on Pret's UK menu was a crayfish and rocket lettuce sandwich. Burger King may have a hyperefficient supply chain, but when was the last time a supplier brought forward an idea that turned into a BK menu favorite? Beating the hell out of suppliers over price may be fashionable, but this isn't likely to be a recipe for business concept innovation.

   Ask yourself: How effectively are we using suppliers as a source of innovation? Do we regard them as integral to our business model? Do we gain competitive advantage from the way we manage the linkage with our suppliers (lightning speed, dramatically reduced inventory costs, etc.)? How closely are our business goals aligned with those of our suppliers?

Thought: Now more than ever, it is possible for companies to off-load noncore activities onto suppliers. Technology has steadily reduced the costs of communication and coordination. Industry standards, such as GSM in the cell phone business, have simplified the interface between different components of a system. Enormous economies of scale in the manufacture of high-volume "core products" such as semiconductors have made it necessary for downstream assemblers to rely on just a few suppliers. Add to this ever shorter product life cycles and a premium on flexibility, and it is easy to see why companies are becoming less vertical. Yet every company must guard against "outsourcing" things that might become critical sources of competitive differentiation. Once you've outsourced something to some big IT company, you can write it off as a source of competitive advantage.

2. **Partners:** Partners typically supply critical "complements" to a final product or "solution." Their relationship with producers is more horizontal and less vertical than that of suppliers. ***An imaginative use of partners can be the key to industry revolution.***

Example: The success of Microsoft's Windows platform is in large part due to the support Microsoft has lavished on its software development partners. Making it easy for independent software vendors (ISVs) to write for Windows increases the number of applications running on Windows and further strengthens its market position. Microsoft's support includes offering development tools to ISVs that make it easier to write software for the Windows O/S, helping young companies get access to capital and offering them co-marketing opportunities, hosting dozens of developer events around the world and running a dedicated website that provides developers with extensive online support. In 1999, the Microsoft Developer Network included over 10,000 ISVs.

Ask yourself: Can we look at the world as a global reservoir of competencies? What opportunities might be available to us if we could "borrow" the assets and competencies of other companies and marry them with our own? How could we use partners to "punch more than our weight"? How can we use partners to achieve greater flexibility, focus more tightly on our own core competencies, build a first–mover advantage or offer a more complete "solution" to customers?

Thought: A lot of "suppliers" would like to become "partners"— that is, they want to be more than order takers competing on price. Here's what this implies. First, you have to take responsibility for something more than a minor component in the overall solution. You need to take responsibility for an entire system or product. Second, you may have to be willing to share some of the commercial risk. To win an exclusive contract from Boeing to supply jet engines for a super–long-range derivative of the 777, GE had to behave like a partner. It agreed to put up as much as half of the $1 billion needed to launch the 777 derivative, thus reducing Boeing's development risk. Third, you have to work hard to make sure that your contribution is truly differentiated in a way that makes a difference to end consumers. This means you can't rely on your immediate downstream customer for your understanding of end–consumer needs. You must build your own point of view about what those end customers really want. If you're Dell or HP, the Taiwanese company that makes your computer monitors is a supplier. Intel is a partner. Every supplier would like to become "Intel Inside." But this won't happen unless you stop thinking of yourself as a supplier.

3. Coalitions: Business concept innovation often requires a company to join together with other, like–minded competitors in a coalition. This is particularly likely to be the case where investment or technology hurdles are high or where there is a high risk of ending up on the losing side of a winner–take–all standards battle. Coalition members are more than partners, they share directly in the risk and rewards of industry structure innovation.

Example: Airbus Industrie, a consortium of France's Aerospatiale Matra, Germany's DaimlerChrysler Aerospace Airbus, British Aerospace, and Spain's CASA, is one of the world's most successful coalitions. In 2001 Airbus rang up 274 orders for new aircraft compared to Boeing's 272. This was the second time in three years that Airbus booked more orders than Boeing. With Lockheed gone, and McDonnell Douglas now part of Boeing, Airbus is all that stands between the world's airlines and a Boeing monopoly.

Ask yourself: Can we look beyond our own resources and markets and imagine new resource combinations that could create new markets and services? Can we co-opt other firms into a "common cause"? Can we use their resources to alter the competitive dynamics of an industry? Can we use a coalition to bring a highly risky project into the realm of feasibility? **Can we use a coalition to attack the entrenched position of an industry incumbent?**

Thought: Business-to-business "hubs" and "exchanges" have yet to live up to their promise, but they represent a potentially intriguing new type of coalition. In April 2000, 11 of the world's largest retailers, including Target, Safeway, Marks & Spencer and Tesco, announced the formation of the Worldwide Retail Exchange, a global buying consortium. Within two years of its founding, the WWRE had grown to 59 members. Sears, Carrefour, Metro AG, J Sainsbury plc and Kroger joined forces to form a competing B2B market, GlobalNetXchange. In both cases, member companies hope the exchange will help them counter the enormous buying power of Wal-Mart, which emerged at the end of 2001 as America's largest company, with $217 billion in revenues. Wal-Mart has its own proprietary exchange, Retail Link, and any supplier that wishes to do business with Wal-Mart must do so over this private exchange. Whatever the ultimate fate of these new coalitions, it is a good bet that they will ultimately change the distribution of bargaining power within the grocery industry. Through the 1990s, companies merged in hopes of capturing global procurement economies. Hubs and exchanges may eventually

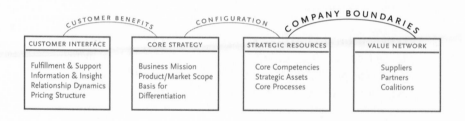

CUSTOMER BENEFITS	CONFIGURATION	COMPANY BOUNDARIES	
CUSTOMER INTERFACE	CORE STRATEGY	STRATEGIC RESOURCES	VALUE NETWORK
Fulfillment & Support Information & Insight Relationship Dynamics Pricing Structure	Business Mission Product/Market Scope Basis for Differentiation	Core Competencies Strategic Assets Core Processes	Suppliers Partners Coalitions

constitute a kind of "virtual" merger that allows companies to pool bargaining power while avoiding the panoply of complex integration issues that bedevil full–fledged mergers.

Company Boundaries

Intermediating between a company's *strategic resources* and its *value network* are the firm's *boundaries*. This bridge component refers to *the decisions that have been made about what the firm does and what it contracts out to the value network*. Again, an important aspect of any business model is the choice of what the firm will do for itself and what it will outsource to suppliers, partners, or coalition members. Changing these boundaries is often an important contributor to business concept innovation.

Example: The PC industry's spectacular growth was driven by innovative boundary decisions by IBM, Microsoft and Intel. Twenty years ago the computer industry was dominated by vertically integrated companies such as IBM, Data General and Digital Equipment Corp. These companies made their own silicon chips, created their own proprietary operating systems, manufactured their own computers and often wrote application software. The PC, with its open standards, changed all that. Microsoft did the operating system. Intel did the chips. Hundreds of suppliers from California to Taiwan to Ireland made specialized components such as SCSI cards, sound chips, monitors and disk drives. Thousands of independent software vendors wrote applications, and assemblers, such as Dell, shipped the finished products to customers and handled technical support. Horizontal specialization allowed component manufacturers to reap enormous economies of scale as they were no longer limited to selling through their own channels, under a single brand. It gave the assemblers complete freedom to incorporate the very latest technology and the most cost–competitive components in the finished product. Indeed, it is difficult to believe that a vertically integrated company could have sustained the pace of innovation witnessed over the past couple of decades in the PC business.

Ask yourself: Have you looked critically at where you draw the boundary between what you do and what you don't do as a company? Is there a chance to change industry rules by "deverticalizing" your industry, as Microsoft did in the computer business? How explicitly do you think about the opportunity to change the boundaries, vertically and horizontally, that distinguish the activities of various industry participants?

Thought: In the age of progress, companies were organized like hierarchies, where internal transactions were governed by some central authority and every business unit was 100 percent owned by the parent company. While this structure allowed, in theory, for a lot of internal coordination, as, for example, when General Motors sources engines for several model lines from a single factory, the sheer size of these hierarchies, and top management's distance from the market, often made them slow and unresponsive. In our increasingly turbulent times, resilience has become a critical virtue. The pursuit of flexibility and resilience has had a profound impact on corporate boundaries. In recent years, companies have been eager to shed fixed assets by outsourcing their manufacturing to companies such as Flextronics and Solectron, and turning their data centers over to EDS, IBM Global Services or other IT service providers. Companies have increased their workforce flexibility by hiring thousands of contract workers who can be let go when demand retracts.

Even pharmaceutical companies are beginning to question the benefits of vertical integration. Many of the big drug companies have been shedding functions amid the growth of new horizontally oriented pharmaceutical companies. Traditional drug companies are finding that clinical trials are becoming increasingly expensive, with clinical approval times nearly doubling in the last few years. In response, they are handing this function over to a growing number of CROs (contract research organizations). Covad, one of the largest of the CROs, uses its proprietary IT systems to manage patient data and rapidly screen the results of biochemical assays, all with the goal of quickly deciding which trials are worth pursuing and which should be abandoned. As drug companies struggle to cope with steadily escalating R&D costs owing to breakthroughs in genomics and proteomics, they have started to selectively outsource drug discovery to the new biotech companies and to companies that specialize in the various phases of the drug discovery process. Drug marketing is the latest of the major drug company functions to be outsourced.

FINDING THE REVOLUTION

A growing number of marketing service companies are focused on crafting new product launch strategies, drafting marketing plans and designing customer pull-through programs.

Undoubtedly, deverticalization and outsourcing decisions are occasionally no more than quick expedients for CEOs under the gun to shave expenses. In these cases, the quest for resilience may jeopardize important core competencies. Yet the fact remains that vertical integration, which was in the past a response to high transactions costs (which could be lowered by bringing key functions inside the corporate boundary), is becoming less critical in a world where real-time information allows for transparency and trust between business partners. Nevertheless, something that is outsourced usually ceases to provide a competitive advantage, unless a company has a unique and proprietary relationship with its partners. While being "virtual" may bring flexibility, the capacity to earn above-average profits still depends on having a defensible competitive advantage.

Wealth Potential

To be an industry revolutionary you need a point of view about how you're going to use each component of the business concept as a lever for rule-breaking innovation. You also need a compelling story about how this innovation will generate new wealth.

There are four factors to consider in determining the *wealth potential* of any business concept:

○ the extent to which the business concept is an *efficient* way of delivering customer benefits;
○ the extent to which the business concept is *unique*;
○ the degree of *fit* among the elements of the business concept; and
○ the extent to which the business concept exploits *profit boosters* that have the potential to generate above-average returns.

Let's take each of these in turn.

Efficient

To create wealth, a business model must be efficient in the sense that the value customers place on the benefits delivered exceeds the cost of producing those benefits. Many new business concepts founder on this very point—there's just no margin! Many Web–based retailers started with the idea that they could survive by selling goods below cost. The hope was that advertising revenues would compensate for negative retail margins. That dog didn't hunt. The largest of the large online retailers, ValueAmerica, went bankrupt in August 2000, and another, Buy.com, subsequently announced a new policy of "selective price increases."

Examples: Southwest Airlines has a business model that delivers air travel to budget–minded fliers more efficiently than any of its major competitors. With its point–to–point route structure, all–737 fleet and flexible work practices, Southwest has the lowest seat–per–mile cost of any major airline. Despite Southwest's low fares, it has one of the healthiest margins in the airline business.

However, having an efficient business model does not mean having the lowest costs. Midwest Express Airlines doesn't match Southwest's fares, and Southwest would never claim to deliver the "best care in the air," as Midwest does. Filet mignon with lobster, a roll with butter, spinach, mandarin salad and chocolate banana–split cake—when was the last time you ate like this in coach? That's a typical meal on Midwest Express. The company spends an average of $10 per passenger on meals, compared with Southwest's 20¢. (You can get peanuts really cheap when you buy in bulk.) Midwest offers its coach passengers two–by–two seating, with five more inches of knee room and four more inches of hip room than usual coach seats. Midwest earns healthy profits because it tightly controls costs in other areas—

it flies an older fleet of mostly DC–9s, and it operates out of a low-cost hub, Milwaukee. The same coach fare that would buy a distinctly mediocre service experience on American or United buys a near–first-class experience on Midwest. No wonder the airline has been rated by *Travel & Leisure* magazine as the best domestic airline, and no wonder its stock has outperformed the Dow Jones Industrial Average. While Southwest offers less service for a much lower price than traditional airlines, Midwest offers more service for about the same price. Both companies have highly efficient business models.

Ask yourself: Have we tested our assumptions about the value customers will actually derive from our products or services? Do we understand in detail the costs we will incur in providing that value?

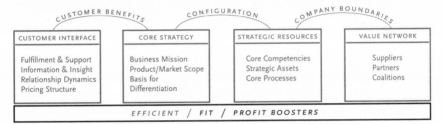

CUSTOMER INTERFACE	CORE STRATEGY	STRATEGIC RESOURCES	VALUE NETWORK
Fulfillment & Support Information & Insight Relationship Dynamics Pricing Structure	Business Mission Product/Market Scope Basis for Differentiation	Core Competencies Strategic Assets Core Processes	Suppliers Partners Coalitions

EFFICIENT / FIT / PROFIT BOOSTERS

Fit

Consanguinity is a ten-dollar word that means "fit." A business concept generates profits when all its elements are mutually reinforcing. A business concept has to be internally consistent—all its parts must work together for the same end goal. Almost by definition, a company with mediocre performance is a company where elements of its business model work at cross-purposes.

Example: Four Seasons Hotels and Resorts, Inc., based in Toronto, runs the largest chain of luxury hotels in the world and defines "pampered" in nearly 20 countries. The company's success comes from the fact that every aspect of its business model— property location, staff selection and training, architecture, quality of decor, service levels and catering—is focused on making you feel like a head of state. Few companies achieve the kind of consistency so much in evidence at Four Seasons. For example, on a recent first-class flight from San Francisco to London, on an airline that shall remain nameless, there was an elegant caviar service at the beginning of the flight, and a breakfast at the other end that featured a plastic tub of Wheaties with a pull–off paper lid. Talk about a jarring inconsistency! This is how cereal is sold at McDonald's, and not quite what is expected for a $10,000 roundtrip airfare.

Ask yourself: Do all of the elements of the business model positively reinforce each other? Are there some elements of the business model that are at odds with other elements? What's the degree of internal consistency in our business model? Is there anything that looks anomalous to customers?

Profit Boosters

Of course what you actually want to know is not whether your business model is going to be profitable, but whether it's going to be *really* profitable. **THERE ARE A DOZEN PROFIT BOOSTERS THAT CAN PUSH PROFITS INTO ORBIT.** The trick is to figure out a way of bolting one or two of these profit boosters onto your business concept.

These profit boosters can be grouped under four categories:

- ○ Increasing Returns
- ○ Competitor Lock–Out
- ○ Strategic Economies
- ○ Strategic Flexibility

You need to get acquainted with each of these profit boosters. They are what distinguish so–so profits from returns that make investors swoon.

The first two, *increasing returns* and *competitor lock-out*, are synonyms for monopoly. Business concept innovation is, after all, the search for temporary monopolies. While revolutionary business concepts tend to undermine entrenched monopolies, a business concept with strong monopolistic tendencies can often withstand a prolonged assault from would–be rivals before crumbling. In general, the stronger the monopoly, the greater the innovation necessary to unseat the incumbent. In this sense, business concept innovation is the quest for strategies that are, insofar as possible, impervious to further bouts of business concept innovation. Got that? To be clear, I am not using the word "monopoly" in a legal sense—I am merely referring to strategies that tend to be self-reinforcing. You don't have to engage in predatory tactics or set out to be a robber baron to create a business concept that ends up yielding monopolylike profits.

Economists start with an assumption of perfect, atomistic competition. They look at any firm earning above-average profits as an anomaly. Industry revolutionaries start with an assumption that the entire goal of strategy is to create *imperfect* competition. To them, strategy is all about building quasi monopolies. To an economist, above-average profit represents "market failure." To a strategist, it represents a killer business concept. The problem for economists is that there are a lot of anomalies these days. Microsoft's Windows operating system, Delta's control of gates in Atlanta and Salt Lake City, Intel's PC architecture and the patents behind the DVD are all examples of quasi monopolies. Recently, economists such as W. Brian Arthur and Paul Romer have discovered what savvy innovators have known all along: some business models, by their very nature, have built-in monopolies.

Increasing Returns

Founded more than 800 years ago, Oxford and Cambridge universities are two of the oldest examples of "increasing returns." Their continued dominance in British higher education is attested to by the fact that they are often known simply as "Oxbridge," a class of two that eclipses all other British universities. Imagine you're a brilliant young physicist who one day hopes to win a Nobel Prize. Where do you want to go to do your post-doctoral research? That's simple—to a university that already has a clutch of Nobel Prize winners. You also want access to the best Ph.D. students, who are, of course, attracted to the best faculty. The best attract the best— this virtuous circle has allowed Oxford and Cambridge to dominate British academia for the better part of a millennium. It wasn't Microsoft and W. Brian Arthur that invented increasing returns.

The term *increasing returns* simply refers to a competitive situation where the rich tend to get richer, and the poor, poorer. It denotes a flywheel effect that tends to perpetuate early success. Those who are ahead will get farther ahead, and those who are behind will fall farther behind. Perpetual motion is almost as rare in business as it is in physics, and every business model ultimately encounters some sort of friction, but a business concept characterized by increasing returns can produce fat profits for an immodestly long time. The notion of increasing returns is subtly different from the notion of scale. In an industry such as chemicals, which is characterized by significant economies of scale, you have to be big to win. In industries with increasing returns, if you win early, you're likely to *get* big. Economies of scale are largely static; increasing returns are dynamic.

To benefit from increasing returns, a business model must harness one of three underlying forces: network effects, positive feedback effects, or learning effects.

1. Network Effects: Some business models benefit from a strange kind of value multiplier known as the "network effect." In some cases, the value of a network increases as the *square* of the growth of the number of "nodes," or members in the network. If you model the growth of a business concept that exploits the network effect, you get a diagram that looks like the power curve for nuclear fission or the infection curve for a virulent virus.

Examples: eBay is a classic example of network economies. You wouldn't go to an auction site that had only a dozen items for sale. But as the number of participants (nodes) increases, the chance you'll find what you want, or find a buyer for what you don't want, goes up geometrically. If you have something to buy or sell online, why *wouldn't* you go to eBay? With 42 million registered users and over 79 million items for sale in 8,000 categories, eBay has exploited the dynamics of the network effect to the hilt. Where the value of the network is a function of the *number of members in the network*, there will be increasing returns for those who start earliest, work hardest and build the biggest network. As their network gets bigger and bigger, it gets harder and harder for latecomers to build equivalent networks, and there is less and less incentive for customers to switch networks.

Network effects also account for the triumph of Visa, Master-Card and American Express as truly global credit cards. The more merchants who accept these cards, the more likely you are to carry them. The more likely you are to carry them, the more merchants are apt to accept them. Another virtuous circle.

Ask yourself: Do we have a business concept that taps into the network effect? Can we find opportunities to create network economies where none currently exist? If not, can we somehow hitch our business concept to the network multiplier?

2. Positive Feedback Effects: *Positive feedback effects* and *increasing returns* are sometimes used interchangeably to denote a situation where success breeds success. But I'd like to use *positive feedback effects* in a more limited way—to refer specifically to the way one uses market feedback to turn an initial lead into an unbridgeable chasm for competitors. A firm with a large base of users, and a way of rapidly extracting feedback from those users, may be able to improve its products and services faster than its competitors. As a result, its products become better yet, and it captures even more customers. Another virtuous circle ensues.

Example: AOL has systematically exploited insights derived from its customer base to provide the easiest online service, and has steadily pulled ahead of other branded Internet portals. The better the content and online experience, the more users AOL attracts. The more users AOL attracts, the more advertising revenue it gets. The more advertising dollars it gets, the more it can afford to invest in upgrading and expanding its services, thus attracting more users. This positive feedback effect also works with advertisers. The more users, the higher the ad rates AOL can charge. The higher the ad rates, the more AOL can spend on differentiating its site and offering. The more it spends on making its site and content even better, the more users it attracts. Positive feedback effects are the hub in the virtuous circle of customer learning and improvement.

Ask yourself: Where's the flywheel that will perpetuate our early success? Where are we creating a virtuous circle of increasing returns? Where could we create positive feedback effects within our business model? Can we set up a very short learning cycle that will allow us to improve our products and services faster than anyone else? Should we be heavily discounting our products or services, or giving them away for free as a means to generate positive feedback effects that would allow us to outpace competitors?

3. Learning Effects: More and more industries are knowledge-intensive. A company that gets an early start in accumulating knowledge, and then continues to learn faster than its rivals, can build an almost insurmountable lead. Knowledge accumulation is often highly correlated with experience. (Remember

Boston Consulting Group's experience curve?) **The notion is simple: the application of knowledge begets new knowledge.** This is particularly true in cases where the critical knowledge is both complex and tacit—complex in the sense that it represents the fusion of several different types of knowledge, and tacit in that it is not easily codified.

Example: In an industry—be it manufacturing semiconductors or strategy consulting—characterized by strong learning effects, it is difficult for latecomers to intercept the knowledge-building progress of the leaders unless they change the knowledge base of the industry. Learning effects gave Sharp and Toshiba dominant positions in the manufacture of flat screen displays. In the early years, flat screen manufacturing yields were disastrously low. But perseverance paid off. For a long while, Sharp and Toshiba enjoyed virtual monopolies in the single most valuable component of a laptop computer. Hundreds of millions went to the bottom line. Of course, over time all knowledge tends to get commoditized—it gets acquired from suppliers, equipment manufacturers, ex-employees or through reverse engineering. As this has happened, new competitors have entered the flat screen display business.

Ask yourself: What parts of our business model might be subject to learning curve effects? Where does accumulated volume count, and how much does it count as a percentage of total costs? Are we taking full advantage of every opportunity to learn? Are we building that learning into our products and services on a real-time basis?

COMPETITOR LOCK-OUT

When you find a window of opportunity, the goal is to crawl through it and lock it behind you. You want *all* the loot, and you don't want to have to fight for it. Ghastly business, fighting. Always a chance that some of *your* blood may get spilled. **That's why really slick business models lock competitors out through preemption, choke points and customer lock-in.**

1. Preemption: Where there is great potential for increasing returns, merely being first may be enough to put competitors out of contention. It's terrific when the first punch is a knockout blow. In industries that are R&D–intensive or that have high fixed costs, there's often no second place—you're either first or you're nowhere.

Examples: Imagine that Early Bird, Inc., has just sunk $200 million into developing a new software product. In its first year of operation it finds 5 million customers for its WormFinder software, which sells for $250 a pop. That's $1.25 billion in revenue. With a variable cost of $50 per copy (to cover manufacturing, distribution, advertising, and admin), Early Bird's direct costs amount to $250 million. That leaves $1 billion—a 500 percent return on its R&D investment. If it's smart, Early Bird will sink a couple of hundred million dollars back into R&D to bolster its lead. Slow As Snails, Inc., enters the market 10 months late with a competing product and manages to sell only 1 million copies. At $250 a pop, Snails' gross is $250 million. With variable costs of $50 per copy, Snails' gross profit is $200 million. That barely covers its own development costs. Going forward, there's no way it will be able to match Early Bird's escalating R&D investment. Now Early Bird has the chance to play vulture. It drops its price to $150 and the market expands to 11 million customers, of which Early Bird has 8.5 million. Its revenues inch ahead to $1.275 billion, but it is still making a very healthy gross profit of $850 million. Meanwhile, Slow As Snails matches Early Bird's price and rakes in only $225 million on 1.5 million customers. After deducting direct costs of $75 million, Slow As Snails can afford only $150 million for ongoing R&D. It may take another couple of rounds for the fight to be over, but Slow As Snails is going down. A business concept with this kind of fixed–cost leverage offers the fleet of foot the chance to create an almost unassailable position.

First–mover advantages are never absolute, but they are often pivotal in industries with a rapid pace of technological development and relatively short product life cycles. If you get in late, you're going to be fighting the U.S. Marines with slingshots and bottle rockets. Preemption requires a great product, a capacity to learn fast, and a willingness to double up your bets. Being first means nothing if you're trying to sell something nobody wants or if it takes you forever to respond to customer input. Apple may have been first with handheld computers, but the Newton was so woefully underdeveloped that it left the door wide open for the PalmPilot.

Johnson & Johnson pulled a Newton with its groundbreaking coronary "stent," a tiny metal frame that props open cholesterol–clogged arteries. Three years after the product's launch in 1994, it was closing in on $1 billion in revenues, and had a 90 percent market share and gross margins judged to be as high as 80 percent. But J&J left the stent window wide open. The company's overambitious pricing ($1,595), sluggish pace of product refinement, and offhand treatment of cardiologists opened the door for followers like Guidant Corp. and Boston Scientific Corp. Forty–five days after it launched its competing product, Guidant claimed a market share of 70 percent. J&J ultimately abandoned the market. Preemption without follow–through ain't worth squat.

Ask yourself: Do you risk becoming a perpetual follower? Are there any first–mover advantages implicit in your business concept? Where do you plan to preempt, and how do you plan to follow up on that? How are you going to turn being first once into being first again and again?

2. **Choke Points:** The famed military strategist Karl von Clausewitz called it the "command of heights." My colleague Peter Skarzynski calls it "choke point control," but the idea is the same. Whether it's 1452 and you're Sultan Mehmet II building a fortress to control the Bosphorus or it's the new millennium and you're trying to gain control of the cable television infrastructure that will allow broadband Webcasting, the logic is the same. Whoever owns the choke point collects the toll. If you're unwilling to pay up, you're locked out.

Examples: In 1984, AT&T gave up direct access to its customers by agreeing to spin off the Baby Bells as part of its divestiture agreement. With this decision, AT&T not only gave up the physical line into the home but also the right to bill those customers, as long–distance billing was included in the local bill and the Baby Bells became sole owners of the local customer data. Now, as the dust settles from the great telecom shakeout, it is glaringly apparent that what still really matters is the physical connection to the customer. As digital subscriber line (DSL) providers like Covad, NorthPoint, Teligent, Winstar and countless other newcomers file for bankruptcy, the Baby Bells have emerged from the shakeout as the winners in the local market. The Telecommunications Act of 1996 was supposed to open the local market. But the Baby Bells had no incentive to give up their chokepoint—control over all connections to the local network—and they didn't. While staying within the letter of the law, which required that new entrants be allowed to connect to the local phone switches, the Baby Bells found amazingly creative ways to slow this process down—to the point where many newcomers either gave up or went bankrupt. With the local line still the bottleneck and the last-mile rollout of DSL slowed to a snail's pace, most of the so-called Next Generation backbone carriers, companies such as Williams and Level 3 that had been busy laying high bandwidth fiber between major cities, also found themselves in deep pooky. (If you need a picture here, imagine a super highway with no exit ramps.) And it wasn't just the DSL entrepreneurs and the fiber optic barons who paid the price for the Baby Bells' stranglehold on local access. As the broadband rollout faltered, so too did the prospects of companies making telecom hardware, providing Web-hosting services or hoping to provide interactive television and a host of other bandwidth-hungry services. The telecom shakeout serves as a multibillion-dollar lesson in choke point control. But the fact is that the stronger a company's choke point, the greater the incentive for competitors to blast a path around it. The Baby Bells' stranglehold on local access, and their leisurely approach to rolling out their own DSL services, provided a big opening for cable television companies eager to sell high-bandwidth cable modems to residential customers. Many tele-com experts believe that the Baby Bells overplayed their hand and will ultimately lose a big chunk of the broadband future to the cable television companies, which also own a last-mile connection to the home.

Microsoft's Windows may be history's most effective choke point. It is virtually impossible to build a PC, write a software application or create a document without, in some way, sending a check to Microsoft. All of us who've passed through the Microsoft toll gate should be thankful for one thing: Internet Protocol (the standard that governs how packets of data are sent across the Internet) and HTML (the standard that governs how information is displayed on the Internet) are not only open, they're in the public domain. That must drive Bill Gates nuts, yet he should be grateful, for if anyone owned IP and HTML, Bill would probably be the second–richest person on the planet.

Choke points come in many shapes and sizes: a technical standard, control of some costly infrastructure, preferential access to a government buyer, a patent or a prime location. Other choke point examples include the "anchor" store in a mall, Gatorade's prime position on the sidelines of every NFL football game, De Beers' historic control over the distribution of diamonds and a critical patent. **A truly strategic business concept lets you command the heights.**

Ask yourself: Is there some standard, some protocol, an interface or a bit of infrastructure that you could uniquely own? Are you creating any assets that will be critical to the success of other companies—so critical that you can effectively charge a "toll"? Are there some scarce assets or skills that you'd like to deny your competitors? Can you lock up these assets or skills in some way?

3. **Customer Lock-in:** Competitor lock-*out* often means customer lock-*in*. But even when you can't lock out *all* your competitors, you can lock in *some* of your customers—through long–term supply contracts, proprietary product designs that keep them coming back for upgrades and add–ons or control over a local monopoly. There are many ways you can tie up your customers, but you have to be careful. A customer that *feels* locked in is a particularly angry beast. You gotta use velvet ropes.

Examples: U.S. airlines have earned graduate degrees in customer lock-in. First there's the matter of gates. Competition–phobic air carriers moved swiftly after deregulation to consolidate their control over so–called fortress hubs. During the 1980s, the Justice Department approved every airline merger that was presented to it. The result? A fellow traveler can tell where you live simply by looking at the frequent–flyer luggage tag that adorns your carry–on—yeah, that gold–colored emblem of your slavery. You got a US Airways tag? You probably live in Pittsburgh or Charlotte. Continental? Houston or Newark.

America West? Phoenix. TWA (poor sod)? St. Louis. Northwest? Detroit or Minneapolis, maybe Memphis.

Fortress hubs have been wildly successful, as lock-in strategies go, provoking some in the U.S. Congress to label airlines "unregulated monopolies." Few fliers are dumb enough to believe that the new spate of proposed semi-mergers and co-marketing agreements (American and US Airways, United and Delta, Northwest and Continental) is really about "seamless travel." They're about better lock-in.

Frequent-flyer cards are an even more intricate set of mana-cles. Fail to fly enough with your airworthy monopolist, and you'll get stuffed into steerage on *every* flight. You'll never tally up enough miles for that second honeymoon either. You're not Platinum? Not 1K? Then don't even bother to ask an airline employee for a favor unless you're fully prostrate or more than halfway through a myocardial infarction.

Customer lock-in is just a fancy way of saying "switching costs." Once you've bought Microsoft Word and learned to navigate its Byzantine "features," you'll be well and truly on the hook. To Microsoft you're more than a customer, you're an annuity. Unless someone comes along with a truly radical new software business concept, you're going to be buying upgrades from Microsoft for a looooong time. Indeed, in a recent year, around half of Microsoft's software revenues came from upgrades. Talk about customer lock-in! You could escape the clutches of Philip Morris and a two-pack-a-day nicotine habit easier than you could wriggle free of Redmond Bill.

Only Intel has anything close to Microsoft's lock on customers. A few years ago Intel's co-founder and chairman, Gordon Moore, was asked whether he had been worried that his company's x86 chip architecture would be supplanted by new technologies such as RISC (reduced instruction set computing). His answer was telling: "No ... we had this tremendous advantage: all of the software that people had bought that ran on our instruction set."[5] Intel may be paranoid about many things, but a new chip architecture that would knock it out of the PCs is probably not one of them. Customer lock-in? Handcuffs, straitjacket and leg irons. Indeed, after years of trying, AMD has only recently taken a significant chunk of the microprocessor market in low-end PCs. And customers are glad for the alternative.

GE's jet engine deal with Boeing is a rather more palatable form of customer lock-in. GE's financial support for Boeing's development of the long-range 777 came with a price—Boeing would agree to sell the new 777 with GE engines *exclusively*. Lock-in is okay when the customer asks to be tied up.

All in all, be careful of customer lock-in. Lock-in is great while it lasts, but the moment those cuffs are off, your customers may well go for your throat.

Ask yourself: Could this business concept reduce our customers' ability or desire to buy from other suppliers? Is there anything in this business concept that would induce customers to limit their freedom of choice? How could we bind our fate with the fate of our customers even more tightly?

Strategic Economies

Unlike operational efficiencies, strategic economies don't derive from operational excellence, but from the business concept itself. Strategic economies come in three varieties: scale, focus and scope.

1. Scale: Scale can drive efficiencies in many ways: better plant utilization, greater purchasing power, the muscle to enforce industrywide price discipline and more besides. Industry revolutionaries often consolidate fragmented industries. Any company that gets caught behind the consolidation curve and misses the chance to build scale advantages will be left at a notable disadvantage.

Examples: Wal-Mart consolidated Main Street retailing and reaped unimagined scale economies in logistics and purchasing. While scale economies tend to perpetuate the success of big incumbents, revolutionaries look for industries that are still fragmented or for scale advantages that haven't yet been tapped. Imagine starting a business one day and 16 months later having your 29 percent stake valued at $315 million. Another sickening Internet story? Not quite—it's a story about Brad Jacobs and heavy equipment rentals. Jacobs got his start in the garbage hauling business. Having watched that business consolidate, he thought there might be a chance to bring scale economies to the highly fragmented rental market for air compressors, cranes, forklifts, generators and the like. United Rentals has consolidated more than 200 companies. After merging with a big competitor, United Rentals surpassed Hertz to become the largest equipment renter in the country, with over 600 locations.[4]

Ask yourself: Does our business model offer us the chance to build scale advantages? Where does size pay off in this business concept? Will the scale advantages outweigh any loss in flexibility?

2. Focus: A company with a high degree of focus and specialization may reap economies compared with competitors with a more diffused business mission and a less coherent mix of services or products. Focus is not about efficiency in a cost sense; it's about efficiency in a don't–get–distracted, get–all–the–wood–behind–one–arrow sense.

Examples: Focus is how little Granite Construction, Inc., of Watsonville, California, competes successfully with industry giants such as Morrison Knudsen and Bechtel. Granite Construction doesn't build chemical plants, and it doesn't do urban rail projects. It will, however, pave just about anything, be it an airport runway, a driveway or a section of interstate highway. Sales amounted to $1.2 billion in 1998, double what they were five years before. The company has a portfolio of more than 30 gravel pits that supply paving materials. It also makes its own ready–mix concrete and asphalt.

Focus is what lets BMW take on the might of Ford and GM in the luxury car business and win. Large companies often impose competing and ambiguous demands on their various divisions. Certainly this seems to be the fate that befell Cadillac—how can one explain products like the Cimarron and the only slightly less insipid Catera? What BMW loses in scale, it makes up for in single–minded zeal. Is there anything else on this planet so tightly put together as a 325i? BMW is a pure, sweet note; Lincoln and Cadillac have often sounded like ill–disciplined orchestras still tuning up. If BMW is ultimately swept up in merger fever, its new owners would do well to leave the Bavarian car–meisters alone.

Ask yourself: Does our business concept have a laserlike focus? If not, do we run the risk of trying to "boil the ocean"? What advantages would we gain by being more narrowly focused? What economies of scope would we lose if we were more focused?

3. Scope: The idea here is almost the inverse of focus. A company that can leverage resources and management talents across a broad array of opportunities may have an efficiency advantage over firms that cannot. Scope economies come from sharing things across business units and countries: brands, facilities, best practice, scarce talent, IT infrastructure and so on.

Example: Maybe you drink Moet & Chandon champagne, or perhaps your tastes run to Dom Perignon and Krug. Perhaps you carry a Louis Vuitton handbag or briefcase or wear a Tag Heuer watch. Your fragrance may have come from Christian Dior or Givenchy. And maybe that soft cotton shirt you're wearing came from Thomas Pink of Jermyn Street. Buy any of these brands and you're enriching the substantial coffers of LVMH, the world's premier luxury brands company. The company's chairman, Bernard Arnault, a.k.a. The Pope of Fashion, built LVMH into an $11.6 billion high–fashion juggernaut to capitalize on the substantial economies of scope that exist in manufacturing and marketing luxury goods. Scope economies come in a variety of flavors: channel power and ac-cess to distribution channels, economies in buying ad space and running high–tech distribution centers and the chance to move experienced management teams into acquired businesses to help revitalize elite but stuffy brands. While Prada and Gucci have recently made significant acquisitions of their own, they lag far behind LVMH in the race to build a *de luxe* powerhouse. No one in the rarefied world of platinum–plated brands doubts that Bernard Arnault is an industry revolutionary.

Ask yourself: Where are the potential economies of scope within our business concept? Can we find any "dual use" assets— things we can exploit in more than one business? What skills could we leverage across businesses, countries, or activities?

Strategic Flexibility

In a fast–changing world, with unpredictable demand cycles, strate-gic flexibility can generate higher profits by helping a company stay perfectly tuned to the market and avoid getting trapped in dead-end business models. Strategic flexibility comes from portfolio breadth, operating agility and a low breakeven point.

1. Portfolio Breadth: Focus is great, but if the world moves against you, you may lack other options. Linking the fortunes of your company to the fortunes of a single market can be a high-risk gamble. A company with a broad offering may be more resilient in the face of rapidly shifting customer priorities than a more narrowly focused competitor. **A portfolio can consist of countries, products, businesses, competencies or customer types.** The essential point is that it helps to hedge a company's exposure to the vagaries of one particular market niche.

Examples: Given the vagaries of drug development and approval, most pharmaceutical companies feel it necessary to support the development of a broad portfolio of drugs. A broad portfolio increases the chances that a company can sustain high levels of R&D year in and year out, rather than have its R&D budget whipsawed by the changing fortunes of one or two products. It also raises the odds of coming up with an out-and-out blockbuster.

Ask yourself: What are the advantages of a wide portfolio of products or businesses? How can we hedge our bets in this business concept? Does this business concept force us to put all our eggs in a rather small basket? Is the reduction of earnings variability, for example, a positive strategic benefit?

2. Operating Agility: A company that is able to quickly refocus its efforts is better placed to respond to changes in demand and can thereby even out profit swings.

Example: Given the fact that Dell Computer owns few fixed assets, it is able to quickly reconfigure its selling approach and product line to suit changing market conditions. As one senior Dell executive put it, "We don't have to change bricks and mortar to change our strategy." Contrast that with Sears's 800-odd stores or GM's aging plants. Some business models are inherently easier to reconfigure than others—these are the ones that will endure in the age of revolution. Web-based businesses may offer the ultimate in flexibility. You can change a product description overnight, test a dozen different ad ideas and have the data back in 24 hours, and experiment with different price points—it's as if Web business concepts were made out of Play–Doh instead of steel and cement.

Ask yourself: How quickly does the demand function in our business change? Is there an advantage to investing in flexibility (i.e., in processes and facilities that would allow us to respond rapidly to shifts in demand)? Could we earn consistently higher profits if we were able to respond more quickly to changes in demand, or to changes in input needs (e.g., were able to quickly incorporate the latest components in our designs)?

3. Lower Breakeven: A business concept that carries a high breakpoint is inherently less flexible than one with a lower breakeven point. Capital intensity, a big debt load, high fixed costs—these things tend to reduce the financial flexibility of a business model. In doing so, they also reduce strategic flexibility, in that they make it more difficult to pay off *one* thing so that you can go on and do *another* thing.

Example: For several decades Japanese car companies have been working to reduce the breakeven point of a car model. If you can break even on 50,000 units, instead of 250,000, you can trade that for a broader product range aimed at narrower consumer segments. More recently, the advantages of strategic flexibility have induced many companies to "de–capitalize" their business models.

Ask yourself: Does our business concept give us a lower breakeven point than traditional business models? How could we tweak the business model to lower our breakeven point even further? What would be the benefits of a lower breakeven point? Could we use a lower breakeven to buy ourselves more flexibility or deliver more variety to customers?

Of course, none of these profit boosters can turn an awful product into a smash hit. On the other hand, a great business concept can sometimes compensate for a mediocre product—indeed, for years this is just what drove Apple aficionados nuts about Microsoft's success. For more than a decade, Microsoft's operating system was much less user-friendly than the Mac's, but Microsoft's profit boosters yielded an unprecedented financial windfall.

BECOMING A BUSINESS CONCEPT INNOVATOR

There are two reasons you must develop an instinctive ability to picture innovation in terms of novel business concepts, and competition as rivalry between business models. (Remember, the building blocks of a business concept and a business model are the same—a business model is simply a business concept that has been put into practice.) The first is so you can construct a well-developed business case around *your* billion-dollar insight. **Half-baked ideas don't get funding.** The second is so you can escape the hold the existing business model has on your imagination and your loyalties.

A successful business model creates its own intellectual hegemony. Success turns *a* business model into *the* business model. In *Dealers of Lightning*,[5] a cautionary tale for any preternaturally prosperous company, Michael Hiltzik pins down the reason Xerox failed so miserably to capitalize on the innovations that poured out of its Palo Alto Research Center. In the copier business Xerox got paid by the page; each page got counted by a clicker. In the electronic office of the future, there was no clicker—there was no annuity. How would one get paid? The hegemony of the pennies-per-page business model was so absolute that it blinded Xerox to an Aladdin's cave of other possibilities.

Many of the choices that define your company's business model were made years ago. Those choices were shaped by the logic of another age. In the fading glow of success, they may seem like inevitabilities. But they're not. It is your job to turn those inevitabilities back into choices. You do this by subjecting each element of the existing business model to fresh scrutiny: What are the alternatives? Does this choice still have merit? How would a company free of our prejudices tackle this? In decomposing the existing business model you create degrees of freedom where tradition reigns.

There are 25-year-old engineers in Silicon Valley who dream in Technicolor business concepts. But if you've been stuck for a decade in some functional chimney or you inherited a strategy from the village elders or you were taught to venerate "industry best practice," then thinking in terms of business models won't be a natural act for you.

So begin to practice. Pick the worst service experience you've had in the last year, and think about the business model that failed to meet your expectations. How would you change it—element by element? Find an industry where everyone seems to be stuck in the same cul-de-sac, and invent an exit strategy for one of the companies. Pick a company you care about—one you think deserves to be more successful than it is—and try to imagine a breakout business concept, your own equivalent of the cyber B-school. The great advantage of a business concept is that it is infinitely malleable. It is, at the outset, only an intellectual construct. So pretend you're a kid again—with a very big Lego set, one that allows you to remake the very foundations of commerce. This isn't some meaningless exercise. This is mental training for industry revolutionaries.

4

BE YOUR
OWN SEER

DO YOU HAVE THE PENETRATING AND UN-
clouded eyes of a revolutionary? Do you just know what's coming next? Is it real and inevitable and three-dimensional for you? Can you see, really see, a kick-ass opportunity for business-concept inno-vation? Is it so seductive that you can't even imagine turning your back on it?

Are you the voice of opportunity in your com-pany? Are you the champion of the unconven-tional? Do you know how to break through the hard, parched soil of ignorance and dogma to find a gusher of an opportunity? Are you a source of strategic diversity? In the age of revolution you have to be able to imagine revolutionary alterna-tives to the status quo. If you can't, you'll be rele-gated to the swollen ranks of keyboard-pounding automatons.

There are too many individuals who can-not yet escape the dead hand of precedent. Too many who are not fully vested in the future. Too many who cannot distinguish between their heritage and their destiny. Is this you? Wanna do something about it?

Look around you. Look at the individuals and companies that have been champions of business–concept innovation. Do this, and you will see that rule–busting, wealth–creating innovation doesn't come out of corporate planning. It doesn't usually come from some corporate "incubator" division. It doesn't come out of product development. And it doesn't often come from blue–sky R&D. More and more, innovation comes, not from the triumph of big science (important as it is in removing physical constraints to innovation), but from the triumph of contrarianism (which leaps over the mental constraints). It is the idiot savant, who asks a fresh question and then answers it using parts that already exist, who is so often the author of the new. That's because industry revolution is conceptual innovation. It comes from the mind and soul of a malcontent, a dreamer, a smart–ass, and not from some bespectacled boffin or besuited planner.

FORGET THE FUTURE

From Nostradamus to Alvin Toffler, individuals and organizations have long been obsessed with trying to see the future. The goal is to somehow get advance warning of "what will be." Yet in my experience, industry revolutionaries spend little time gazing deeply into the future. While there are some aspects of the future that are highly probable—the cost of bandwidth will go down, our ability to manipulate genes will go up—most of what will constitute the future simply can't be known.

In 1984 the *Economist* magazine conducted a little study.[1] They asked 16 individuals to make predictions about 1994. Four Oxford economics students, four finance ministers, four corporate CEOs and four London dustmen ("garbage collectors" to Americans) were asked to predict the pound/dollar exchange rate ten years hence, the rate of inflation among OECD countries, the price of oil, and other macroeconomic unknowables. Not surprisingly, when 1994 rolled around, the forecasts turned out to be wrong. For example, the consensus forecast for OECD inflation was 8 percent. In actuality, it was barely 4 percent. Think about the difference that makes if you are trying to pick a discount rate to apply to a long–term capital investment. Interestingly, it was the finance ministers who made the least accurate forecasts. The best were made by the CEOs—who tied for first place with the dustmen. Yet even they produced forecasts so wrong as to be worthless.

Recently I heard the chairman of one of America's leading high–tech companies poke fun at a *Popular Science* article of some decades back that had predicted that the world's first computer, then just invented, would one day weigh one ton instead of 20. The corporate boss then made his own prediction: Within the next 20 years it would be possible to store the visual and aural data of an entire lifetime—the entire multimedia experience of a person's life—on a device no bigger than the proverbial credit card. I couldn't help but wonder whether someone writing 20 years from now would find this prediction equally amusing. When it comes to predicting the future, humility is a virtue.

Forecasting attempts to predict what will happen. This is largely futile. As Samuel Goldwyn once said, "Only a fool would make predictions—especially about the future." Recognizing this, companies have sought ways of coping with the future's inherent unpredictability. One response is to rehearse a range of futures via *scenarios*. Scenario planning speculates on what might happen. The goal is to develop a number of alternate scenarios as a way of sensitizing oneself to the possibility that the future may be quite unlike the present. By focusing in on a few big uncertainties—what might happen to the price of oil, how the Green movement might develop, what could happen to global security—scenario planning lets a company rehearse a range of possible futures.

Scenario planning has many strengths, but it is not, by nature, proactive. Its implicit focus is on how the future may undermine the existing business model. In that sense it tends to be defensive—what might that big bad future do to us?—rather than offensive—how can we write our will on the future? There is little in scenario planning that suggests a firm can proactively shape its environment, that it can take advantage of changing circumstances right now. At least in practice, it is more often threat-focused than opportunity-focused. It is more about stewardship than entrepreneurship. Companies must do more than rehearse potential futures. After all, **the goal is not to speculate on what might happen, but to imagine what you can make happen.**

Another response to the future's inherent unpredictability is to become more "agile." Strategic flexibility is certainly a virtue in uncertain times. The ability to quickly reconfigure products, channels and skills is essential to maintaining one's relevance in a world that is shaken, not stirred. But agility is no substitute for a vision of a radically different business model. Agility is great, but if a company is no more than agile, it will be a perpetual follower—and in the age of revolution even fast followers find few spoils. **Companies fail to create the future not because they fail to predict it but be-**

cause they fail to imagine it. It is curiosity and creativity they lack, not perspicuity. So it is vitally important that you understand the distinction between "the future" and "the unimagined," between knowing what's next and imagining what's possible.

To even talk about "the" future is a misnomer. There is no one future waiting to happen. While certain aspects of the future are highly probable (the earth will still be spinning tomorrow), there is little about the future that is inevitable. IKEA didn't have to be. eBay didn't have to be. Southwest Airlines didn't have to be. The future is the creation of millions of independent economic actors. Was Cubism inevitable in art? Was deconstruction inevitable in literature?

SEE DIFFERENT, BE DIFFERENT

You can't be a revolutionary without a revolutionary point of view. And you can't buy your point of view from some boring consulting company. Nor can you borrow it from some rent-a-guru. You have to become your own seer, your own guru and your own futurist.

Seeing over the horizon, finding the unconventional, imagining the unimagined—innovation comes from a new way of seeing and a new way of being. Learn to see different, learn to be different, and you will discover the different. Not only that: You will believe it—deeply. And maybe, just maybe, you will build it. How to see. How to be. Two more critical steps in your training as an industry revolutionary.

Listen to Amazon's Jeff Bezos, talking to *Wired* magazine:

> People have been telling me that everything that could be invented has been invented. This is insane.
> Look at Napster—this guy in his dorm room, one person with no funding, a little bit of software, and he launches this thing and nine months later the music industry is petrified. Think what this implies about the power of an idea to change the world.

Well, maybe the idea behind Napster, downloadable tunes, hasn't yet changed the world, but it's certainly forcing some big changes in the music industry. If truly novel ideas are rare, which they are, it isn't because they are inherently scarce, but because few people are capable of first recognizing and then challenging the dogma that surrounds them.

A company that has not cultivated a capacity to imagine radical new business concepts, or is unable to dramatically reconceive existing business concepts, will be unable to escape decaying strategies. You know that tired old saw, "You have to be willing to cannibalize your own business"? Well, how likely is it that a company will cannibalize an existing business unless it has some incredibly compelling alternatives in view? I don't think the problem is that companies are unwilling to cannibalize themselves. I think the problem is that they don't have enough good reasons to cannibalize themselves. When was the last time you hung on to a good option when you had a much better option in view? It's simple. You have to have some very attractive birds in the bush to loosen your grip on the bird in your fist. But it's not always easy to spot the birds in the bush. That's why you must learn to see different and be different.

Many times, what's required is not a vision of an entirely new business, but a fresh view on how to reinvent an existing business. Too many companies are too quick to give up on what they perceive as a mature or unattractive business. When Cemex, the Mexican cement producer, felt itself threatened by the specter of foreign competitors entering its home market, it sold off its noncement interests and proceeded to reinvent its core business so thoroughly and profoundly that the company ended up with gross margins nearly double the average of its global rivals. So yes, you need to be on the lookout for good reasons to cannibalize yesterday's success, but new thinking can also help you reinvent yesterday's success. After all, however attractive, a bird in the bush is still in the bush.

Alan Kay, who fathered the personal computer while at Xerox's Palo Alto Research Center, is a font of zippy aphorisms. One of my favorites: "Perspective is worth 80 IQ points." Alan knows that **A FRESH WAY OF SEEING IS OFTEN MORE VALUABLE THAN SHEER BRAIN-POWER.** Impressionism. Cubism. Surrealism. Postmodernism. Each revolution in art was based on a reconception of reality. It wasn't the canvas, the pigments or the brushes that changed, but how the artist perceived the world. In the same sense, it's not the tools that distinguish industry revolutionaries from humdrum incumbents—not the information technology they harness, not the processes they use, not their facilities. Instead, it is their ability to escape the stranglehold of the familiar.

The essence of strategy is variety. But there is no variety in strategy without variety in how individuals view the world. Do you see differently? Do you have a point of view that is, in at least some respects, at odds with industry norms? The point is simple: You're going to have to learn how to unlock your own imagination before you can unlock your company's imagination. You must become the merchant of new per-spective within your organization.

So what are ways we can school ourselves in the art of seeing past the familiar to the truly novel? The rest of this chapter describes a variety of disciplines that will help you imagine what could be. They fall into two broad categories: Be a novelty addict, and be a heretic.

BE A NOVELTY ADDICT

A whole lot of what's changing simply can't be seen from where you're sitting. You have an obstructed view. You have to get off your butt and search for new experiences, go to new places, learn new things, reach out to new people. In the age of revolution, the most dangerous words are "need to know." How the hell do you know what you need to know? You must find a way of continually surprising yourself. Sure the future is unpredictable, but what you don't know but could is much more important than what you don't know and can't. You must become a novelty addict.

FIND THE DISCONTINUITIES

Would-be revolutionaries, intent on discovering uncontested competitive space, think about the future very differently from prognosticators and scenario planners. They know you can't see the future. Their goal is less to understand the future than to understand the revolutionary portent in what is *already changing*. More specifically, they are looking for things where the *rate of change* is changing—for inflection points that foreshadow significant discontinuities. Those who fail to notice these nascent discontinuities will be rudely awakened by those who were paying attention.

They are also looking for things that are changing at *different rates*. Sooner or later, the thing that is changing more quickly will impact the thing that is changing more slowly—in other words, rates of change between different phenomena ultimately converge. For years the cosmetics industry assumed that women were interested only in glamor, that their sense of self-worth was directly proportional to the sparkle in a man's eye. As Charlie Revson, the founder of Revlon, once put it, "We sell hope in a bottle." As women gained their economic independence, the image of women as "eye candy" lagged farther and farther behind the reality of their changing self-perception. This lag was exploited by The Body Shop, Lush, Aveda and other New Age cosmetic brands with their implicit message that glamor is fine, but sometimes you just want to pamper yourself a bit and take good care of your skin. *Change differentials* often point to revolutionary opportunities.

Here's a visual illustration. Imagine that you attach one end of a piece of elastic to a hardback book. You begin pulling the other end. Slowly the elastic stretches. The book doesn't move. But when you reach the limit of the elastic, the book starts moving with a jerk. The "slack" disappears when some revolutionary says, "Wait a minute. Why is this thing just sitting there when everything around it is moving?" The car selling paradigm in the United States is stuck in neutral. While "category killers" consolidate distribution in other industries, car retailing remains a patchwork of mostly local dealerships. While you can get 24/7 tech support for your home computer, you can get your car serviced only between 8 A.M. and 5 P.M., and only Monday through Friday. While you can comparison-shop a dozen different TV brands at Best Buy, no equivalent auto superstore carries the full range of leading brands. Yeah, there are a lot of legal restrictions that have delayed dealer consolidation, but sooner or later it's going to happen. Right now, auto retailing in the United States is a glaring anomaly.

Or think of how little auto styling has changed over the last decade. Can you tell an Altima from a Camry from an Accord at 100 meters? Parking lots are seas of conformity. Now visit a dance club in Tokyo filled with Dankai Jr. kids—the rebellious offspring of Japan's baby boomers. You'll find multihued hair, clothes that are aggressively ugly and fashion colors that are so loud they practically scream at you. In short, you won't find anything that reminds you of Japan's blue-suited, look-alike salarymen. So why hasn't this new style been reflected in auto design? That's exactly the question Yoshiki Honma, a boyish 33-year-old designer at Honda, asked himself. His answer? The Fuya-Jo, a slab-sided vehicle that is one part car and one part dance club. The car has seats that look like high-backed barstools, mammoth speakers in the doors, a gearshift that looks like a microphone, an instrument panel meant to resemble a deejay's mixing table and storage space designed for skateboards and snowboards.[2] For now the Fuya-Jo is just a concept car, but it reflects a recognition at Honda that youth culture has changed a lot faster than automotive design over the past decade. This change differential creates an opportunity for a company with the courage to abandon conformist styling norms.

It's not enough to know what's changing. You also have to be aware of things that are changing at different rates, for it is the juxtaposition of the two that points to opportunities for industry revolution. Discontinuities and change differentials—that is where you look for inspiration.

Try to find the pattern in these three revolutions in sports equipment:

○ A couple of decades back, Prince pioneered oversized tennis rackets, and it is still the number–one brand in the industry. The frying–pan–size rackets have a giant sweet spot that helps propel off–center shots across the net.
○ Calloway invented the Big Bertha line of golf clubs, and Eli Calloway has become the patron saint of hackers everywhere. With an enlarged hitting area and perimeter weighting, the clubs dramatically increased the odds that high–handicap golfers could get the ball airborne and flying straight.
○ Elan was the first ski manufacturer to introduce super–sidecut, or "parabolic," skis, an innovation that has given the ski equipment industry a much needed boost. With a broad tip and tail, and a narrow waist, the new skis help even the most nonathletic skiers lay down curvaceous tracks.

What discontinuities were these three innovations exploiting? Beyond materials technology, they were exploiting the fact that baby boomers are the first generation in history that refuse to grow old. They may not have the hand–eye coordination they used to have, but they still love the sound of a tennis ball hitting the sweet spot. They don't have quite the rotation they used to, but they still want to hit the living daylights out of a golf ball. Their knees are a bit dodgy, but they still want to make turns like Hermann Maier. Come to think of it, Viagra's been exploiting the same discontinuity: Seniors who refuse to grow old gracefully and want great sex right up to the end.

Here are some essential questions for every wannabe revolutionary:

○ Where and in what ways is change creating the potential for new rules and new space?
○ What is the potential for revolution inherent in the things that are changing right now or have already changed?
○ What are the discontinuities we could exploit?
○ What aspect of what's changing can we come to understand better than anyone else in our industry?
○ What's the deep dynamic that will make our new business concept oh–so–relevant right now?

If you don't have an answer to these questions, there is virtually no chance you or your company is going to be an industry revolutionary.

Nearly two decades ago, in his book *Megatrends*, John Naisbitt posited that information would become a critical source of competitive advantage and that the "information float" would disappear as a way to make money. He argued that customers would demand a combination of "high tech" and "high touch." Instead of forcing technology on consumers, companies would learn how to use technology to improve service. He described a world in which hierarchies would give way to networks, and companies would become more virtual. He also hypothesized a shift from reliance on institutional help to more self-reliance in everything from health care to pensions. He foresaw a world in which consumers would use their wallets to enforce their values. Data mining, call centers, 24/7 customer support, outsourcing, supply chain integration, "green" energy, companies against animal testing—all these things are logical outgrowths of the forces Naisbitt described in 1984. How effective was your company in harnessing these discontinuities to create new business models and new sources of competitive advantage? If your company got caught behind the curve, it wasn't because these trends were invisible; it's because they were ignored. If you're paying attention to discontinuities, there's little that will surprise you. It's pretty simple. **Individuals who get startled by the future weren't paying attention.** One person's inevitability is another person's rude awakening. The question is, are you paying attention?

If you're an American, I'd like to give you a little test. How often did you watch ABC's *Monday Night Football* last autumn? If you're a middle-aged man, chances are you saw several games. Now ask yourself, how often did you watch an entire episode of TNN's *Raw*, a production of the World Wrestling Federation, which is also broadcast on Monday nights? Chances are, you didn't see even a single show. And you probably didn't read *If Only They Knew*, the best-seller co-authored by Chyna, one of the WWF's so-called divas. And yet, in a recent television season, *Raw* outdrew *Monday Night Football* by 47 percent among males aged 12–24. Now I'm not suggesting you watch the sweating hulks and surgically enhanced women who populate the WWF. On the other hand, if you work for a company that wants to sell something to young American males, you may need to get a bit closer to this particular fringe.

Or let's say you're in the music business, or the fashion industry, or merely want to know where the tastes of Gen Y urbanites are heading. Better get yourself down to one of Rio's funk balls in order to experience the world's most exotic and electrifying urban dance scene. The music, with its highly explicit lyrics and pounding rhythms, is the cultural signature of young Brazil. Having grown out of Brazil's *favelas*, the hillside shantytowns that are home to millions of Brazil's poor, funk is now going mainstream, just as rap did in the United States. Reaching far beyond Brazil, "favela chic" is inspiring fashion designers and music producers around the world. So have you done anything in the last year that has given you the chance to immerse yourself in something new, something strange, something that is on the verge of *happening*?

A novelty addict is always on the hunt for what's new, what's different, what's unexpected and what's changing. Every discontinuity prompts a "where does this lead" question. Let's practice. We'll start with a particularly noisome discontinuity. A recent study suggested that the average middle manager gets 190 messages a day: 52 phone messages, 30 e-mail messages, 22 voice mails, 18 letters, 15 faxes and so on. I don't have to tell you, this is a discontinuity. In the old days, when someone sent you a letter, they didn't expect to receive a response for at least a week. When they sent a fax, they expected a next-day response. Now, when they send an e-mail, they expect a reply within an hour or so. But it gets worse. With instant messaging, people know when you're online, and when they send you a message, they expect you to interrupt what you're doing and answer them immediately. It used to be that secretaries kept the world at bay—until downsizing turned middle managers into receptionists and filing clerks. It may be that we've taken accessibility to the point where meaningful work will simply grind to a halt. How ironic that in a world populated by "knowledge workers," there is virtually no time left to think. You may be able to manage the present in tiny splinters of time, but you certainly can't innovate if your attention has been smashed into minute-sized shards. This is a discontinuity. Can you see an opportunity in this? Let's take it a step further.

In a recent cartoon, a dad and his young daughter are walking along a beach. The dad is dressed in suit and tie and has a briefcase in one hand. His daughter is wearing her bathing suit. As she vainly tugs at her father's sleeve, he says, "Not now, dear, Daddy's working." Where don't you work these days? We are tethered to our jobs to an extent that is almost feudal. But there are opportunities lurking inside the insidious discontinuity of 24/7 accessibility. What about an electronic gatekeeper that could scan phone calls, e-mails, voice mails and even faxes? Caller ID? Hah! I want automatic message screening. Every couple of hours a little menu would pop up on my computer screen telling me who was queuing for my attention. I could tell my digital gatekeeper who I was willing to communicate with in a given day or week and how important it was that I make contact with any given individual. I could also tell it when I was willing to be interrupted and when I was not. (Imagine never, ever having a telemarketer interrupt dinner again!) I could assign a different level of "interruptability" to different times of the day or week. People and issues that exceeded some urgency threshold would get to break through into my consciousness. People below the threshold wouldn't get through. I could also give a few people (family) an "attention override" privilege that would let them intrude anytime. Trust me, some revolutionary is going to help us regain control of our fragmented lives. There's a billion-dollar opportunity inside this discontinuity. You get the point? Keep asking yourself, What's changing? What's the opportunity this presents? Do this at least a dozen times a week. Get addicted to change.

Imagine the possibilities when an entire organization is alert to discontinuities. Recently, General Motors launched a number of initiatives aimed at getting everyone plugged into the future. In one, a diverse cross-section of individuals identified 19 broad change categories (e.g., global urban culture, entertainment in everything) that encompassed more than 100 discontinuities. Every discontinuity was illustrated by a visual image in order to help individuals connect with what's changing. The goal was to use this inventory as the backdrop for every serious strategy discussion. After years of playing catch-up, GM is learning that you have to pay close attention to the discontinuities if you're going to get anywhere close to the bleeding edge of change.

SEARCH OUT UNDERAPPRECIATED TRENDS

There is no proprietary data about the future. Whatever you can know about what's changing in the world, so can everyone else. So you've got to look where others are not looking. The good news is that *most people in an industry are blind in the same way— they're all paying attention to the same things, and* not *paying attention to the same things.* For example, if you work at Shell or Schlumberger, you know a lot about the three-dimensional representation of complex information. Complicated computer models portray seismographic data in a rich graphical format. This is how petroleum engineers "see" underground. Likewise, the folks at Pixar, the computer animation company, are experts at visualization. Now talk to a senior partner in a big accounting company. How much does this person know about complex graphical modeling? Not enough. If you want to understand the financial performance of a large global company, you have to comb through columns of black and white data, searching for variances and calculating financial ratios. Ugh! Why isn't this information presented in three dimensions, dynamically? Why can't you "fly" over the globe, and "drop into" your German subsidiary? See that red mountain over there? That's inventory, and it's growing. See that lake over there? That's one of those famous "profit pools," and it's shrinking by the hour. See all those people massed at the border? Those are your employees leaving for better opportunities. You get the idea. But you can't get the picture—yet, at least not from any of the traditional financial software vendors. Odds are it won't be an accounting company or a well-known software company that reinvents the display of accounting data. But there's little doubt that Excel will one day look as antiquated as green ledger paper.

Next time you go to an industry conference or pick up a trade magazine, ask yourself, What is *no one* talking about? Search for what's not there. There's a reason that outsiders typically reinvent industries. The outsiders come from a different context—one that allows them to see new possibilities. William Gibson puts it beautifully: "The future has already happened, it's just unequally distributed." The future may not have happened yet in your industry, or your company, or your country, but it has happened somewhere. Revolutionaries are experts at *knowledge arbitrage*—moving insights between the hip and the un-hip, the knowing and the unknowing, the leading edge and the trailing edge. So get a bigger keyhole!

FIND THE BIG STORY

Next, search for transcendent themes. One of the reasons many people fail to fully appreciate what's changing is because they're down at ground level, lost in a thicket of confusing, conflicting data. You have to make time to step back and ask yourself, **What's the big story that cuts across all these little facts?** For example, consider five seemingly unrelated trends:

○ In most developed countries, people are getting married later in life. No longer do people expect to find a mate while still at school.
○ More people are telecommuting or working from home. Home-based businesses are one of the fastest-growing parts of the economy.

- The number of single-parent families has been steadily increasing. Single parents are run ragged trying to balance work and family—personal time is a rare luxury.
- New social standards governing the behavior of people at work make it ever more difficult to form romantic relationships with co-workers.
- E-mail and the Internet absorb more and more of people's time. All the hours in front of the PC are hours of aloneness—unless virtual communities fill all your social needs.

Can you see an overarching theme here? It's individual isolation. We're living in a world where it is more and more difficult for people to find time to connect. So you should have been able to anticipate the success of online dating sites like Matchmaker.com and AmericanSingles.com. Right? Recognizing patterns in complex data is a bit of an art. Some of it is just raw, conceptual ability. But if you've ever won a game of Scrabble or solved a challenging puzzle, you'll do fine. Keep a list of things that strike you as new or different. Every once in a while, scan that list and search for broad themes. If you can get above the trees, you'll have a view that few others can match.

FOLLOW THE CHAIN OF CONSEQUENCES

The world is a system. Something changes here, and it will affect something over there. Yet most people stop with first-order effects—they don't have the discipline to think through the knock-on effects. Jim Taylor, coauthor of *The 500-Year Delta* and dedicated trend-watcher, predicted a 10,000 Dow Jones Industrial Average in 1992. Here's how he did it:

> I saw a number that estimated how much people were going to save as they got older. About 15 million people a year would become 50 years old, and they would throw a lot of liquidity into the market. So I made a prediction that the Dow would pass through 10,000. When you see a trend, it's a matter of asking, "What would this mean?"

Paul Saffo, director and Roy Amara Fellow at the Institute for the Future, makes the point this way:

> I think about it as "orders of impact." First order, second order, etc. When an earthquake happens you have a whole series of waves

that follow. The first order of the auto was the horseless carriage. The second order was the traffic jam. The third-order impact was the move toward the suburbs. This led in turn to the creation of huge metropolitan areas.

No executive or manager should be surprised by the recent spate of books on corporate values and "loyalty." This concern around how to build organizational cohesion is the second-order effect of a first-order change: the steadily declining ratio of supervisors to operators or managers to staff in corporations. To cope, companies need a solid value system because more and more they must rely on people's judgment. Whenever you see something changing, begin to work through the chain of consequences. Get in the practice of asking a series of "and then what" questions. As you learn to do this, the future will become less and less of a surprise to you.

DIG DEEPER

Sometimes creating proprietary foresight is just a matter of slogging through more data. You can't create economic value out of a superficial understanding of what's changing. For example, a short news item noting that some teenagers are spending more time online than in front of the TV is of almost no value. The real question is, Which kids are going online? Where are they going online? What, exactly, is it about the online experience that is more compelling to them than television? How much time do they spend online in a given day or week? What do they find cool or geeky online? And so on.

Faith Popcorn's BrainReserve interviews 4,500 consumers across 16 product categories every year. They also have a TalentBank of 6,000 experts globally who are subject area experts. No wonder Popcorn sometimes sees the tectonic plates moving before others do—she's digging deeper. You probably can't spread your interests this broadly, but you can pick a few things to understand far more deeply than you do. Genetics, Generation Y, deregulation, ubiquitous computing, the market for online software services, the global revolution in how pensions are funded—every year pick a couple of the big things that are changing and resolve to dig deep.

KNOW WHAT'S NOT CHANGING

The deep needs of human beings change almost not at all. Go back to Aristotle and the wants of man—little has changed. What changes is how we address our wants. Change gives us better tools. Opportunities come when we can imagine how to use our new tools to address our deepest desires. As Jim Taylor puts it, "The nature of human beings is the eye in the middle of the hurricane." We want to be loved, we want to be known, we want to communicate, we want to celebrate, we want to explore, we want to laugh, we want to know, we want to see new vistas, we want to leave some footprints in the sands of history. Any discontinuity that allows you to slake one of these thirsts more fully is an opportunity in the making.

If you think about human beings for a minute, you shouldn't be surprised that the Web was a chat room before it was a department store, or that Internet porn generates as much revenue as online book sales, and ahead of online airline tickets.[3] To be an industry revolutionary, **you must be as perfectly attuned to the timeless as to the ever-changing.** You must also let yourself be informed by the recurring themes of history. History has much to teach you about how discontinuities will play themselves out. For example, advances in genetics are slowly turning humans into creators. History suggests that the battle between the spiritual and the scientific over the proper use of genetic knowledge may be as heated as Galileo's clash with the Catholic Church over humankind's place in the cosmos and Darwin's run-in with creationists.

The speed of the Internet's takeoff surprised most people, but that it happened should have been no surprise—because the interstate highway system provided an almost perfect historical analogy. The automobile had existed for around 50 years before the interstate highway system began to connect communities across America. Within a decade of the interstate's introduction suburbs were springing up, city centers were withering, corporations were building office towers in what had been cornfields and commuters were commuting. It wasn't the car per se, but the ability to connect communities that changed the distribution of work and commerce. Likewise, computers had existed for about 50 years before the Internet took off. Before the Net, computers had been islands of computational power. Once connected, they began to transform society in ways even more dramatic than the interstate highway but also in ways that are entirely consistent with timeless aspects of human nature.

SEE IT, FEEL IT

You don't fall in love with a photograph or a resume, you fall in love with the experience of being with someone. In a similar way, you can't understand a discontinuity merely by reading about it, you can understand it only by living it. To be fully grounded in what is changing, you must move from the analytical to the experiential. Let me share a couple of examples. A few years back I was working with a large Nordic firm, perched on the edge of the Arctic Circle. This company was filled with brilliant engineers who designed technologically brilliant products that were boring to look at and sometimes difficult to use. I broke the bad news—if they wanted their products to be highly desirable and highly relevant, they were going to have to learn something about global lifestyles. Off the engineers trooped—to Venice Beach in California, to Greenwich Village in New York and down The Kings Road in London. They saw trendy style–setters wearing the latest fashion accessories. They came across people who had pierced every possible protuberance. They saw how designers in other fields were using colors and shapes in new ways. And they didn't see any of their competitors. How do you explain lifestyles with an overhead projector? Face–to–face with the edge, the engineers "got it." They went back and designed products in crazy hues with edgy designs and easy–to–use customer features.

People don't embrace an opportunity because they see it, they embrace it because they feel it. And to feel it, they have to experience it. If you want to teach someone in your organization about a discontinuity or give them a glimpse of a bold, new opportunity, you're going to have to design an experience. To create a demo, or a prototype, or even tell a compelling story, you have to do some mental prototyping. You need more than a fragment of an idea. You have to build a story around it: why this is important, what difference it will make, who will care, how people will use this, what it will look like, taste like and more. Radical alternatives are hard for people to imagine. You have to build a bridge between the world you're living in and the world everyone else is living in.

It's not always easy to make something new and ethereal, real and tangible. But think of this: Ask just about any kid to draw a picture of heaven, and you'll get back an imaginative illustration. If an eight–year–old can draw a picture of paradise, you have no excuse.

GET A ROUTINE

Swim in the new. Sounds easy, but the ocean is a big place. How do you avoid drowning in data? You need some kind of routine. I can't tell you what your routine should be, but I can say what works for some folks.

John Naisbitt's routine for finding the edge is simple: He reads newspapers from around the world for several hours each day, hunting for patterns in things that get reported but don't yet generate a lot of ink. Marc Andreessen, the inventor of the Internet browser, has a different routine:

Pay attention to things that are taking off, even if they're only taking off at a small scale. One of the things that surprised me about the Internet is the number of things that I was aware of when they were small–scale things, not commercial, that are now picking up users and attention. Even if I was skeptical at the time, in most cases these are now billion–dollar companies. So you want to pay attention to small–scale successes because they're probably going to become large–scale successes.

What are your routines? How often do you pick up a magazine you've never read before? How often do you go to an industry convention for an industry you know little about? How often do you hang out with people who are very different from you? Are you on the fringe or in the hinterlands? Can you name a half dozen nascent trends? Find the small things, play an imaginary game of "scale up," and then ask, If this thing became really big, what kind of a difference would it make? Who would be affected?

Each of us tends to discount what is new and small. As a discipline, **start exaggerating what is new and small.** You're not investing in these things, for goodness sake, you're simply opening your mind to new possibilities.

Faith Popcorn's BrainReserve is a lightning rod for cultural discontinuities. Says Popcorn:

We do something called "Brailleing the Culture"–monitoring the top 10 of everything. Anytime we see something that is weird, we key in on it. We look for things that are not part of the puzzle. How come *Touched by an Angel* was big on TV? How come the Dalai Lama is on posters? Don't dismiss the weird.

We ask people, "What's sitting on your night table?" We're looking for culture hogs. They have to see everything, go everywhere. They're always on to the next thing.

We look for cultural lingo. We review the soundtracks of sitcoms. We review the top 10 CDs, and what the artists are saying.

I love to watch what new 12–step programs are emerging— recent ones are for people addicted to chat rooms or online pornography.

Popcorn isn't looking for fads, for cultural ephemera, but for the tip of deep icebergs, for leaves carried along by powerful currents that would otherwise be almost imperceptible. The weird are the harbingers. If you dismiss the stuff that strikes you as weird, you have virtually no chance of finding the new. What's the hippest club in your city? Have you ever been there? What's the trippiest video game out there? Have you played it? Go ahead, do a little cool hunting.

Jim Taylor of Iomega takes yet another tack:

> I watch the evolution of art, especially folk art. It's a wonderful precursor of what's changing in society. Look at the cubists in the 1930s. First it was art, then the structure of building and finally the structure of most organizations. Right now we're seeing the "outsider" movement in art—it's creating a sense that everyone is an artist.
>
> I also pay attention to a set of deep underlying questions: What's the big idea in society and how will it play itself out? What's the latest technology that's about to be generalizable [about to go mass market]? What's the latest organ they can grow in a test tube?

Artists have few constraints. Like magnifying glasses, they collect and concentrate the diffused light of cultural change. Taylor knows this. He also knows that if you develop a set of questions to ask yourself as you encounter the unfamiliar, you will increase the odds of actually taking away some meaningful insights.

John Seely Brown, for years the head of Xerox's famed Palo Alto Research Center, favors travel as a routine for discovering the new. A while back, he took a 7,500-mile motorcycle trip across America, entirely on back roads. Hundreds of conversations with people across America put Seely Brown in touch with what's changing away from the coasts. Says Seely Brown, "Everywhere one goes there's a chance to learn something. You keep asking, 'What's causing this?' ... for example, a teenager doing something weird on the street. It's really active listening."

Insights come out of new conversations. All too often, strategy conversations in large companies have the same ten people talking to the same ten people for the fifth year in a row. They can finish each other's sentences. You're not going to learn anything new in this setting. Travel is still the fastest way to start a bunch of new conversations. It has the added benefit of turning the background into the foreground. When you travel to an exotic destination you're suddenly reminded of how much you take for granted and how there are alternatives to the familiar habits of your life. It was his experience with the casual warmth of Italian coffee bars that gave Howard Schultz the idea for Starbucks.

Familiarity is the enemy. It slowly turns everything into wallpaper. Travel makes you a stranger. It puts you at odds. It robs you of your prejudices. If you can't travel, find a good bookstore and pick up the *Globe & Mail* (Toronto), *The Daily Telegraph* (London), *The South China Morning Post* (Hong Kong), *The New Straits Times* (Singapore) or some other foreign newspaper, or find them online. If your understanding of what's changing in the world comes from network television news, the *Wall Street Journal*, and *Time* magazine, you're going to miss the future.

BE A HERETIC

It is not enough to be a novelty addict. You must be a heretic as well. Heretics, not prophets, create revolutions. You can immerse yourself in what's changing, but you'll only see the opportunities to leverage change in novel ways if you can escape the shackles of tradition. There is much that individuals cannot imagine simply because they are prisoners of their own dogma. In this sense, the challenge is not long-term thinking but unconventional thinking. **The real issue is not the present versus the future but the orthodox versus the heterodox.**

There is an enormous danger in viewing what's changing through the lens of what already is. People saw plastic, when it was first invented, as a substitute for existing materials—steel, wood and leather. (Remember Corfam shoes?) Eventually, plastic got the chance to be plastic. Can you imagine a hula hoop, compact disc or videotape made out of anything else? In the age of revolution the future is not just more of the past—it is profoundly different from the past. Whether or not you succeed in escaping the past is, in a way, quite irrelevant. The future's going to get invented, with you or without you. But if you want to build the new, you must first dismantle your existing belief system and burn for scrap anything that is not endlessly and universally true.

Ask yourself this question: What are the industry dogmas my company has knowingly chosen to violate? Can't think of any? Then don't expect to outperform industry averages. Industry revolutionaries create strategies that are subversive, not submissive. To do this, you must deconstruct the belief system that prevents individuals in your organization from imagining unorthodox strategies.

In most companies it is virtually impossible to redesign business models without first challenging the dominant mental models. Mental models spring out of and reinforce the current business model. A business model is a "thing." The mental model is a set of beliefs about the "thing." The mental model reflects the "central tendency" of beliefs around the key business concept design variables:

- ○ What is our business mission?
- ○ What is our product/market scope?
- ○ What is the basis for differentiation?
- ○ What core competencies are important?
- ○ What strategic assets do we need to own?
- ○ What core processes are critical?
- ○ How can we best configure our resources?
- ○ How do we go to market?
- ○ What kind of information do we need to serve customers?
- ○ What is the kind of relationship we want with customers?
- ○ How do we price our products and services?
- ○ What is the particular benefit bundle we deliver?
- ○ How do we integrate with suppliers and partners?
- ○ What profit boosters can we exploit?

The more successful a company has been, the more deeply etched are its mental models. In even moderately successful companies, most people take 90 percent of the existing mental model as a given. Design choices made years earlier are seldom revisited. It's difficult to imagine revolutionary strategies when you start with nine-tenths of your brain tied behind your back. Design choices of long ago are seldom challenged in the absence of a crisis. Even then, it often takes a new management team to pull out the old beliefs by their roots. You and your colleagues must learn how to systematically deconstruct the existing set of beliefs around "what business we're in," "how we make money," "who our customers are" and so on.

The first step in your training as a heretic is to admit that you are living inside a mental model—a construct that may not even be of your own making. Alan Kay tells a wonderful little story about how he came to recognize this deep truth:

> On the third day of a conference at a Buddhist center, I asked
> people why they put their palms together several times a day.
> The Buddhists believe that the world is an illusion, but we have

to go along with the illusion for efficiency reasons. When they put their hands together it is a semicolon, an acknowledgement that whatever they may think is going on right now is largely a fabrication of their own mind.

For much of life we simply go along with the illusion—yeah, this is the only way to sell a car, get a date or sell perfume. But every once in a while you need to put your palms together, pause, step outside yourself and examine what you believe and why. And in the age of revolution you have to do this more consistently and consciously than ever before.

You have to know that things are not as they seem—and you must know this at such a deep level that you can challenge the very foundations of what others regard as axiomatic. We are all caught inside theories, inside constructs. Most of us spend our lives elaborating someone else's theory—about how to run an airline or publish a magazine or sell insurance. New facts are either absorbed into the construct or rejected. Seldom do the constructs themselves get altered. The challenge is to break the construct—or at least bend it a bit. To do so, you must first acknowledge that you are inside the construct. Jim Taylor puts it like this: "The more you pay attention to information that supports your worldview, the less you learn. There tends to be a convergence in what any group of people believe is important, despite what might really be important out there."

The problem with the future is not that it is unknowable. The problem with the future is that it is different. If you are unable to think differently, the future will always arrive as a surprise. You know that old bumper sticker, "Question Authority"? Well the authority you most need to question is the authority of your own long-held beliefs. This isn't about pricking someone else's conventions. We are all reassured when the world conforms to our prejudices. But confirmation of what you already believe is a complete waste of time. **YOU MUST LOOK FOR DISCONFIRMING EVIDENCE, FOR THINGS THAT DON'T FIT, FOR THINGS THAT ARE AJAR.** This is hard, because it forces you to write off your depreciating intellectual capital—you must admit not only that you do "not know" many things but that you "wrongly know" many things.

SURFACE THE DOGMAS

So how do you cultivate contrarian tendencies and surface the dogmas in your company? One simple device is to ask yourself and your colleagues, What are ten things you would never hear a customer say about our company or our industry? For example, no customer is ever going to say, "The airline treats its customers with dignity and respect." Few customers would ever say, "It's easy to shop for a better rate on electricity." Fewer still would say, "Banking is fun," or "Hotels always have great food." Once you've identified what customers wouldn't say, ask yourself why they wouldn't say those things. What orthodoxies do they reveal? What opportunities do these orthodoxies create for some unorthodox newcomer? And finally, what would happen if we turned this orthodoxy on its head?

Another way in is to ask, What are the ten things that all the major competitors in this industry believe in common? Then ask, What would happen if each of these assumptions were inverted? What new opportunities would present themselves? How would customers benefit? Clearly, not all industry beliefs are stupid. There's a difference between dogma (the earth is flat) and physics (things fall downward rather than upward). It is seldom a good idea to defy physics. Nevertheless, much of what people in an industry will tell you is God-given is merely human-made. It is your job to turn certainties back into choices.

Time again for a little practice. Think for a moment about the orthodoxies in the American health-care industry. The sick are considered patients, not consumers. Health-care providers dispatch cases, they don't build relationships. The goal is to cure illnesses rather than promote wellness (you don't get reimbursed for wellness). Insurers are in the business of dodging risks rather than improving the health of a population. The entire industry has been organized from the payor backward rather than from the consumer forward. This has led to the greatest orthodoxy of all: Americans spend too much on health care. Says who? As compared to what? Do doctors perform unnecessary procedures? Yes. Do hospitals perform needless tests? Sure. Is there room for huge economies? Yup. So cut the waste. But before going any farther down the health-care rationing road, someone needs to challenge the assumption that American citizens believe they are devoting too much of their resources to health care.

How can anyone say what percentage of their income aging baby boomers might be willing to pay for health care? The question's never been put to them. Today it is employers who decide how much is too much when it comes to health care. It is employers—who are purchasing agents, not consumers—that contract with health-care providers and insurance companies. Imagine if we let purchasing agents choose our toilet paper, or our cars or the kind of food we eat. We'd all be using single-ply toilet tissue, driving puke-green Chevy Luminas and eating the kind of food you buy in bulk at warehouse clubs. We wouldn't put up with that. Why do we put up with employers telling us how much health care we can have? Managed care, which is more accurately described as managed reimbursement, isn't a revolution—it's just the health-care version of vigorous cost-cutting. There's nothing nonlinear about it. Whether we ever get a real revolution in health care will depend on whether anyone ever succeeds in taking a wrecking ball to the edifice of industry orthodoxy.

NEVER STOP ASKING WHY

Like children, heretics play an endless game of "why" and "what if." If you've been paying attention to what's changing, you can play a very intelligent game of "what if." For example, What if everything in the world were able to communicate with everything else? What would a vending machine want to talk about? "Hey, it's hot, and at this rate I'm going to be out of orange sodas in a couple of hours." What would a fuel pump say? "Oh, hi there, Jaguar XK8. I know you need premium fuel. That's what I'll pump." What would a refrigerator say? "My sensors tell me there's something rotten down in the crisper drawer."

Wayne Huizenga asked "why." Before AutoNation, no major car dealer had ever gone public. Says Huizenga:

Every one of the dealers told me that Ford and General Motors and all the manufacturers would never let a publicly held company own a new-car dealership. And I'd always ask, "Why?" I never got a good answer. So we put some gentle pressure on the manufacturers and made it happen.

Revolutionaries simply ask "why" more often than the rest of us.

CELEBRATE THE STUPID

We've all been taught that good answers are more important than good questions. What was true in first grade is infinitely more true when you're in front of the board or your boss. But new questions are at the heart of business concept innovation—and if you're going to ask "why," you've got to be prepared to look foolish once in a while. Listen once more to Marc Andreessen:

If your goal is to create something new and big, you're going to have to do something that everybody else will laugh at—so that becomes the test. If they're not laughing at it, and you don't get turned down a few times, it's probably not a great idea. In other words, if it's something that makes everybody nod their heads and say, "Yeah, that makes sense," there are probably already a dozen people doing it.

Only stupid questions create new wealth. Of course, there are stupid stupid questions, and there are smart stupid questions. I remember asking a senior executive in one of America's leading hotel chains, "Why is it that someone who checks in at two in the morning has to check out at the same time as the guy who checks in at two in the afternoon?" When I got a blank stare I barged ahead. "Why can't you just have everyone check out 20 hours after they checked in? If I arrive at three in the afternoon, I'll have to check out at eleven the next morning. But if I arrive at ten in the evening, I can keep the room until six P.M. on the day of departure." The hotelier looked at me with a face full of condescension. "Gary," he said, "you don't understand the hotel industry." "*That*," I replied, "is my comparative advantage." I suggested he go study Hertz. When you rent a car at Hertz, they don't ask you to bring it back at noon. You have it for 24 hours. And the hotel operator has an advantage Hertz doesn't have—the rooms never move. No one promises to leave the room in Chicago and ends up leaving it in Milwaukee instead!

Or take another hotel example. Have you ever noticed that hotel hangers are often designed to make them impossible to use at home? The implicit message to guests is this: We think you're a thief so we've designed our hangers to be unusable anywhere else. Hmmm, not a very welcoming thought, is it? Now, what if you take something from the minibar and forget to report it when checking out? You'll still get charged for it—that's why the hotel takes your credit card data. Can you already see the unconventional solution to the problem of disappearing hangers? Put a sign behind the closet door, "Hangers $5, help yourself." Presto, you've turned the closet into a profit center. How hard was that? And the person who checks the minibar—well, he or she can check the closet as well. The point is, guests sometimes need an extra hanger. Here's a way to meet their needs and make a buck or two at the same time. So why is it that no one in the hotel industry has thought of this? Maybe it's because you don't ask stupid questions—like, how could we make the closet profitable—when you're an industry expert. What makes this particular bit of conventional thinking even more absurd, is that one of those useless hangers may well be holding up a bathrobe with a little card tucked into the pocket that reads, "If you choose to take this robe home with you, a $75 charge will be added to your account." But trust me, every industry is filled with dozens of similarly silly absurdities—but you won't spot them unless you're willing to ask a few silly questions.

In many companies the premium placed on being "right" is so high that there is virtually no room for speculation and imagination. If you insist on being incontrovertibly right, you will never be new. It's that simple. The fear of being wrong is so strong in many organizations that any idea not backed by a Dumpster of data is automatically suspect. The training given M.B.A. students and managers reinforces this tendency. In course after course the message is driven home: The quality of your analysis counts for more than the quality of your imagination. John Naisbitt explains:

> Academics are afraid to go beyond their data. Alfred North Whitehead said that a proposition doesn't have to be right, it just has to be interesting. Academics don't understand how liberating it is not to have to be right. When you have to be right you become a prisoner.

So students get steroids for the left side of their brain, while the right side gets put on a starvation diet. How absurd. Analysis can help you avoid truly bad strategies, but it will never help you find truly great strategies.

GO TO EXTREMES

Pick a performance parameter that's important in your business—time, cost, efficiency, quality, speed, whatever. Push this to extremes and ask, Why not? Pushing boundary conditions to the limit is one of John Seely Brown's favorite tricks for blowing up orthodoxies.

> My heuristic is, "Take it to the limit and see what happens." Xerox wants to make copiers that make less noise. I told our people that this wasn't an interesting problem. If you ask us to make a machine that makes no noise, that gets interesting. They said, "That's impossible." I said, "Not if the copier has no moving parts." The question led to a radical shift in architectures in terms of how to think about copiers, printers and mechanical systems. You'll see some radical products from Xerox that came from exploring impossible questions.

Think of every strategy conversation as your own personal version of the X Games. Get radical.

Revolutionaries find a way to transcend trade-offs. They just hate it when someone says you can have A or you can have B, but you can't have both. Toyota's "and" was a car that was economical to buy *and* of high quality. Where Mercedes-Benz and Chevrolet gave consumers an either/or, Toyota offered an "and." Look around. Where have people accepted "ors" when they would have rather had "ands"? Take one example. There are many who believe we have an educational crisis in America. Our kids live in a culture literally saturated with entertainment. The number of alternatives to homework grows each year: *South Park* or algebra—that's a tough one. Unless teachers can find a way to make learning educational and fun, media moguls will be the real teachers in America. "Edutainment" was the original idea behind *Sesame Street*. No wonder it became one of the most popular kids' shows in history—it offered an "and" instead of an "or."

This is how John Naisbitt puts it:

> You just have to hang out with the paradoxes, hang out with the contradictions until you understand them. When there is a perceived contradiction, I like to look for something that helps to resolve the contradiction. A lot of people have an either/or mentality. We get the Internet and everyone says, "Well newspapers are going to go away." It's not either/or. There will be a change in the mix, that's all.

Bridle whenever you hear an "or." Search for novel solutions that make trade-offs unnecessary.

DISTINGUISH FORM FROM FUNCTION

Why did people think the Internet would kill newspapers? Because they saw newspapers as a form (ink smeared on dead trees) rather than as a function (sifting through all that happens in a day and selecting out what's really important). While the form of a newspaper may disappear, its function certainly won't. If a newspaper company sees itself in the business of running giant printing presses and distributing newsprint, it may one day be rendered irrelevant. If it sees itself as a current events editor, it will learn to live as happily online as off.

One way of distinguishing function from form is to substitute a verb for a noun. Richard Kovacevich, chief executive of Wells Fargo bank, provides an example: "Banking is essential, banks are not." Banks are things—bricks and mortar. Banking is a function. If I can divorce the function from the thing, I can think about how to deliver the function in radically different ways.

There are some IT executives and technologists who argue that computing is about to enter the "post–PC era." High–capacity networks, linked by powerful hub computers, will feed data to millions of information appliances. International Data Corporation has estimated that by 2005 more information appliances—including set-top boxes, screen phones and handheld computers—will be sold than PCs. Couple this with online application service providers that remove the need for you to load up any software other than a browser, and you have a major threat to the existing PC business model—a threat that Microsoft is taking very seriously. The company's .Net initiative is aimed at using its XP operating system as the base for a wide range of new Web services. The company is also experimenting with set-top boxes for interactive television, has launched a video game device, is working with Intel on a new software/hardware platform for mobile phones and more besides. Yes, the PC will probably survive for another decade or two, but there's little doubt that the form of computing will change dramatically over the next few years. Any company that can't distinguish between form and function will get caught inside an obsolete form factor.

START A NEW CONVERSATION

In most companies there is no distinction between a conversation about radical new possibilities and a conversation about how to eke out another percentage point of gross margin. The same standards of analytical rigor are applied to both—whether the subject is the return on a new piece of production machinery or the chance to create an entirely new market. Strategy conversations at GE Capital are labeled "dreaming sessions." Questions about internal rate of return and EVA are disallowed. No one mistakes them for budget meetings. A conversation about an opportunity for radical innovation is supposed to be fun, open–ended, and inquisitive. It ends with a set of hypotheses to be field–tested. An operational conversation is supposed to be business-like, bounded, and filled with certainties. It ends with an implementation plan. In fact, there are a number of ways in which an operational conversation can be distinguished from a strategic conversation.[4]

	Operational	Strategic
FOCUS		
	Present focus	Future focus
	Certainties	Possibilities
	"Real"	"Play"
NATURE OF KNOWLEDGE		
	Knowledge confirmation	Knowledge development
	Static language	Dynamic language
	Analytical	Experiential
	Authoritative	Hypothetical
CONVERSATIONAL RULES		
	Advocacy	Dialogue
	Reach for closure	Open new conversations
	Need for expertise	Need for generalists
	Get a decision	Test a hypothesis

The next time you toss out an idea for turning your industry inside out, and someone asks you for an NPV, take a minute to educate them on the difference between a strategy conversation and an operational conversation. Then tell 'em to cut you some slack! The disciplines I've described here are reliable ways to help you discover opportunities for business concept innovation. Yet there's no surefire, mechanical process for creating a bold new "aha." Instead, you must marry a thorough understanding of your company's existing business concept with the wide-eyed curiosity of a precocious five-year-old. Phrases such as "disciplined imagination," "routine creativity" and "informed intuition" capture the challenge. You already understand the part about being disciplined, well informed and following a routine, but what about imagination, creativity and intuition? These qualities have been bred out of you—first by school, then by work. **Yet you can, and must, regain your lost curiosity. You must learn to see again with eyes undimmed by precedent.** What is familiar and drab must become wondrous and new. The goal of this chapter has been to help you regain your innocence.

Profound insights come out of a cocktail of unexpected problems, novel experiences, random conversations and newly discovered facts. The goal is to mix this cocktail again and again. Indeed the goal is to be the mixer—to encompass within yourself and your team all the elements that combine to produce bursts of deeply creative insight. Not only is this an individual imperative, it is an organizational imperative. No single individual can encompass all that is changing in the world. Your cocktail shaker is just so big.

5
CORPORATE REBELS

YOU UNDERSTAND THE REVOLUTIONARY

imperative. You feel it in your bones. You're vibrating with excitement at the thought of doing something new, building something radical, and you can't shut up about it. But your industrial-era boss, with a black belt in corporate gamesmanship, is immune to your ramblings. Every time you start to pitch your idea you get "the look"—you know the one I mean—the look that says, "Who hired this idiot, anyway?"

So whaddya do? Beat your head against the walls of your cubicle? Throw yourself in front of the chairman's limo? Bide your time until the morons recognize your genius and promote you? Take early mental retirement? Enroll in a seminary? Steady on. There's another option—a path, too-seldom trod, that is rocky and steep but leads to opportunity. It is a path unfamiliar to corporate types, but well known to thousands of otherwise powerless individuals who've succeeded in knocking history out of its grooves.

A middle-aged woman who takes on the Marcos oligarchy in the Philippines. An African-American woman who refuses to sit in the back of the bus. A group of mothers who press lawmakers to stiffen drunk-driving penalties. A 12-year-old kid who founds an environmentalist group that ultimately attracts 25,000 members. A Czech poet who stands up to totalitarianism. These are the people who change the world. And you can't change your own company? Give me a break.

Of course no one is going to give you permission. You're not going to get a "mandate" from on high. But you've got to decide. Are you a courtier, kissing corporate butt? Or a rebel challenging your company to reinvent itself? Are you there to buff up top management's outsized ego, or are you there to help your company stay relevant in a revolutionary world? If it's the latter, you're going to have to learn to punch more than your weight and to cast a much bigger shadow across your organization than you do right now.

FROM SUBJECT TO CITIZEN

Let's start with the facts. Big, complicated social systems (such as the company where you work) don't get changed from the top—not unless they're already on the verge of collapse. To understand why, take a minute and imagine the traditional corporate pyramid, with senior management at the top and the minions—sorry, I mean the valued "associates"—at the bottom. Where in the pyramid are you going to find the least genetic diversity? Where are you going to find people who have most of their emotional equity invested in the past? Where will you find the folks who are most tempted to venerate history? The answer to all three questions is "at the top." Now ask yourself, Who holds the monopoly on setting strategy and mapping out corporate direction? The same small group. Is this stupid or what? No wonder there is so little business concept innovation in most companies. No wonder it's newcomers who create most of the new wealth.

The organizational pyramid is a hierarchy of experience. Senior executives got promoted for doing one thing very well. But sooner or later, the organization must learn how to do another thing. Today the competitive terrain is changing so fast as to make experience irrelevant or dangerous–you can't use an old map to find a new land. If you're a senior executive, ask yourself, After two or three decades of industry experience, am I more radical or more conservative? Am I more willing to challenge conventions or less willing? Am I more curious than I've ever been in my adult life, or less so? Am I a radical or a reactionary?

Am I learning as fast as the world is changing? Senior executives have the same chance to be radicals as everyone else—but it is hard, because they have more to unlearn. Look at a company that is underperforming, and invariably you will find a management team that is the unwitting prisoner of its own out–of–date beliefs. When it comes to business concept innovation, the bottleneck is at the top of the bottle.

Rousseau once said, "Law is a very good thing for men with property and a very bad thing for men without property." The worshipful observance of precedent is a very good thing for those who sit at the top of organizations, because precedent protects their prerogatives. It rewards the skills they've perfected and the knowledge they've acquired in running the old thing. But precedent and a narrow distribution of strategy–making power is a very bad thing for anyone who wants to create a new future.

For business concept innovation to flourish, the responsibility for strategy making must be broadly distributed. Top management must give up its monopoly on strategy creation. In this sense, you can't have innovation in business models without innovation in political models.

Every company is comprised of four distinct models (see the figure "Creating Space for Business Concept Innovation"). On the bottom is the "operating model." This encompasses what people actually do on a day–to–day basis—how they're organized, what activities they perform, how they interact with customers and what processes they run. Sitting atop the operating model is the "business model." This represents all the choices, conscious and unconscious, the company has made about the various components of its business concept. On top of the business model is the "mental model," which encompasses all the beliefs that in-

CREATING SPACE FOR BUSINESS CONCEPT INNOVATION

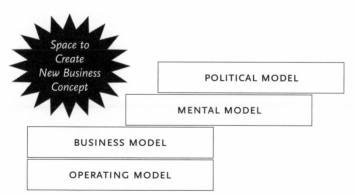

dividuals hold about what drives success in their industry. It is the pre-vailing set of dogmas or orthodoxies about what customers to serve, what those customers want, how to price, how to organize, which distribution channels to use and so on. Finally, on top of everything else is the "political model."

The political model refers to the way power is distributed throughout an organization and, in particular, the distribution of power to enforce mental models. So ask yourself, Who in your organization has the power to kill an idea and keep it dead? Who can make you feel like an imbecile just by saying, "We tried that five years ago and it didn't work"? Who can rule unconventional options "out of bounds"? Who has the last word on whether to try a new experiment? In most companies, political power is highly concentrated at the top of the organization, and precedent is a despot.

In a highly successful company the operating model, business model, mental model and political model are all perfectly aligned—each one sits squarely atop the one below. Human resource professionals call this "alignment." And **alignment is fine——if the world isn't changing. But perfect alignment destroys any chance of innovation, because it brooks no dissent and allows no alternatives.** Alignment is the enemy of business concept innovation.

In a discontinuous world, business models don't last forever. And when they begin to decay, the temptation is to pour human energy and capital into improving the efficiency of the operating model. But better execution won't fix a broken business concept. Ultimately, you need to invent new business concepts or dramatically reinvent those you already have. Yet there is no way of innovating around the business concept unless you can first move your company's mental model off dead center. You have to upend deeply cherished beliefs. You have to create some misalignment between the mental model and the business model. This is why you must learn to be a heretic. But there's a hitch. You won't succeed in changing your company's mental model unless you first push the political model off-kilter and temporarily redistribute the power to make strategy. Put simply, if the power to create strategy and enforce mental models is narrowly distributed, you may find it difficult to get heard. When's the last time your CEO invited *you* to address the Executive Committee? When's the last time your boss's boss told the board that the company was counting on *you* to come up with the next great business concept?

So how do you overthrow top management's monopoly on strategy making? Well, you're not going to stage a palace coup. You're not going to shoot a senior vice president. Instead, you must become an activist. You must build a powerful grassroots constituency for business concept innovation. You must help to build a hierarchy of imagination, where an individual's share of voice in strategy making and innovation is a function of imagination and passion, rather than position and political power.

The good news is this: rule-busting change can start anywhere. Ever hear someone say, "Change must start at the top"? What utter rubbish. How often does the revolution start with the monarchy? Have you ever seen Queen Elizabeth II out in front of Buckingham Palace, waving a placard that reads, "We want a republic"? Nelson Mandela, Václav Havel, Mohandas Gandhi, Susan B. Anthony, Martin Luther King—how often has profound change started at the top? Indeed, the fact that America has suffered but one civil war owes much to the principles of constitutional democracy enshrined in the Constitution. These principles create ample opportunity for change to emerge from below. It is not Congress that sets the social change agenda in America, it is activists.

Do the names Peter Benenson, Florence Kelly, Samuel Hopkins Adams, Irving Stowe, Sarah Brady and Linda Carol Brown mean anything to you? Perhaps not, but you may well have enjoyed the fruits of their activism. Benenson was the founder of Amnesty International. Kelly was a consumer and labor activist who established the National Consumer's League and fought for the passage of minimum wage, child labor and working hour laws. Adams was a muckraking journalist who was instrumental in getting the Pure Food and Drug Act passed in 1906. Stowe helped organize Greenpeace. Brady, whose husband James Brady was shot during the attempted assassination of Ronald Reagan, is one of the most effective gun-control activists in America. Her lobbying helped bring about the Brady Bill, which requires a five-day waiting period on all gun purchases. Brown was the gutsy, young African-American student who tried to enroll in an all-white school in Topeka, Kansas, in 1950, prompting the landmark Supreme Court case *Brown vs. Board of Education of Topeka*, which declared the racial segregation of schools to be unconstitutional. These individuals and thousands of less celebrated activists badgered, harangued, organized, plotted, schemed and ultimately prevailed. What they lacked in power they made up for in passion. They were citizen-activists.

The resilience of a democratic government rests not on one person, one vote, but on its capacity to give voice to the activists, provide a platform for the aggrieved, and harness the energies of those dissatisfied with the status quo. A democracy is a free market for causes—be it feminism, environmentalism, right–to–life, racial equality, or a hundred other movements. Those who lead these causes and shape society's agenda are truly citizens. The rest of us are subjects. It is unfortunate that the idea of democracy has become so enervated and the individual's sense of responsibility to the community so diminutive that they both can be summarized in the slogan, "One person, one vote." One person, one vote represents not the full ideal of democracy, but its most minimal precondition. If you exercise the rights of citizenship only once every four years, at the polling station, can you really claim to be a citizen? Likewise, if you willingly relinquish your responsibility to influence the destiny of the organization to which you devote the majority of your waking hours, can you really claim to be anything more than an employee?

Take a moment and reflect on the tragic price humankind so often pays when a society is unable to reshape itself through peaceful activism, when there is no escape valve for the disaffected and the disgruntled. Genocide, coups and bloody uprisings become the only way to alter policy. Is it any different inside companies? Many companies suffer for years under mediocre leadership before the generals, sorry, the shareholders demand a change of the guard. Instead of being tied to a stake and shot, discredited CEOs take early retirement for "personal" reasons.

American constitutional democracy has survived two and a quarter centuries of unprecedented social and technological change. Democracy in America and elsewhere in the world provides more than an escape valve for the disgruntled; it provides the means for altering the very foundations of the political institutions themselves—in the case of the United States, through the legislative process and, ultimately, Constitutional amendments. In the same way, if companies are going to thrive in the age of revolution, they are going to have to become less like autocracies and more like democracies. And if you want to be a corporate citizen, rather than a subject, you're going to have to learn to be an activist.

Activists are not anarchists. They are, instead, the "loyal opposition." Their loyalty is not to any particular person or office, but to the continued success of their organization and to all those who labor on its behalf. They are patriots intent on protecting the enterprise from mediocrity, narrow self-interest and veneration of the past. They seek to reform rather than to destroy. Their goal is to create a movement within their company and a revolution outside it. Here's how Webster's defines a movement: "a series of organized activities by people working concertedly toward some goal." By contrast, a revolution is the "overthrow of a government, form of government, or social system." A movement is what you create to raise consciousness and mobilize resources inside your company. A revolution is what you want to foist on your competitors.

Activists are "tempered radicals."[1] They are committed to their company, but they're also committed to a cause that is at odds with the pervading values or practices in their organization. They behave as responsible members of their organization, but they are also a source of alternative ideas and transformation. They challenge the status quo in two ways: first, by their refusal to "fit in" and, second, through their intentional acts to unbalance the status quo. They are idealists and nonconformists. But they're also street-smart pragmatists who know how to bend the political system to their own ends. They are cold-blooded hotheads.

You're probably asking yourself two questions: first, Why should I care? Why should I take a risk for a company that considers me expendable? Second, Is it really possible to change the direction of something as big and unwieldy as a company, particularly when one doesn't hold the levers of power?

For a decade now, senior management has been telling employees that they have no entitlements. There's no job for life, no sinecure, no guarantee. Take responsibility for your career. Stay current. Justify your job. But the flip side of no entitlements is no dependency. For years companies mistook dependency for loyalty. But you're no longer dependent, you have choices. Nevertheless, there are three good reasons to put your head above the parapet.

> **Reason #1:** You deserve something more than a paycheck and stock options. Do you remember that famous line often attributed to John Lennon: "Life is what happens while you're busy making other plans"? Yeah, maybe there's a hereafter, but that's no excuse to treat life as a dress rehearsal. Ask yourself, Have you done anything in the last three years that you will talk about for the rest of your life? Just what are you working for? Material well-being, granted, but is that it? Individuals become activists because they know that their

self-worth is determined by the causes they serve. You need a noble cause.

Reason #2: The organization isn't "them," it's "you." Stop whining about "them." That's just an excuse you use to justify inaction. Start thinking of your company as the vehicle for your dreams, as you writ large. That's not an ego trip, that's the truth. Every organization is no more or less than the collective will of its members. And you can shape that will.

Reason #3: You owe it to your friends and colleagues. Your company has a face—you see it every time you peer into the next cubicle or share a table in the cafeteria. Like you, these people deserve the chance to make a very cool difference in the world. They may lack your courage, but they yearn to create, and they're ready to dream. You're not doing this to pump up the value of the CEO's stock options; you're doing it to give ordinary people the chance to accomplish extraordinary things.

That's why you bother. But can it be done? Yes. You're about to meet several corporate activists who succeeded in changing the direction of some of the world's largest companies.

JOHN PATRICK AND DAVID GROSSMAN: IBM'S WAKE-UP CALL

Do you remember when IBM was a case study in complacency? Insulated from the real world by layer upon layer of dutiful managers and obsequious staff, IBM's executives were too busy fighting their endless turf battles to notice that the company's once unassailable leadership was crumbling around them. The company that took the top spot on *Fortune's* list of Most Admired Corporations for four years running in the mid-1980s was in dire need of saving by the early 1990s. Fujitsu, Digital Equipment Corp. and Compaq were hammering down hardware margins. EDS and Andersen Consulting were stealing the hearts of CIOs who had long been loyal to IBM. Intel and Microsoft were running away with PC profits. Customers were bemoaning the company's arrogance. By the end of 1994, Lou Gerstner's first full year as CEO, the company had racked up $15 billion in cumulative losses over the previous three years and its market cap had plummeted from a high of $105 billion to $32 billion. Armchair consultants were near unanimous in their views: IBM should be broken up.

Despite Gerstner's early assertion that IBM didn't need a strategy (the last thing he wanted was to start another corporationwide talkfest), IBM was rudderless in gale force winds. Yet over the next seven years, IBM transformed itself from a company that primarily sold boxes into a company that sold services and delivered end-to-end IT solutions. IBM Global Services grew into a $30 billion business with more than 135,000 employees. Fine, you may say, but IBM was still playing catch-up to Andersen, CSC, EDS, and a host of other IT service companies. Perhaps, but IBM's more recent transformation into the world's premier supplier of "e-business" solutions cannot be so easily gainsaid. By the end of 1998, IBM had completed 18,000 e-business consulting engagements, and about a quarter of its $82 billion in revenues was Net-related. In a few short years IBM had gone from being a metaphor for corporate sloth to being the first stop for any large company eager to become Net-enabled. Now how weird is that? **How did a company that had lagged behind every computer trend since the mainframe catch the Internet wave—a wave that even Bill Gates and Microsoft originally missed? Much of the credit goes to a small band of activists who built a bonfire under IBM's rather broad behind.** This is their story.

The first match was struck in the backwoods of IBM's empire, on a hilltop in Ithaca, New York, by a typically self-absorbed programmer. David Grossman was a midlevel IBMer stationed at Cornell University's Theory Center, a nondescript building hidden away in the southeast corner of the engineering quad. With access to a supercomputer connected to an early version of the Internet, Grossman was one of the first people in the world to download the Mosaic browser and experience the graphical world of the Web. Grossman's fecund imagination quickly conjured a wealth of interesting applications for the nascent technology. But it was an event in February 1994, as snow dusted the ground around the Theory Center, that hardened his determination to help get IBM out in front of what he knew would be at least "the next big thing," and might be "the ultimate big thing."

The Winter Olympics had just started in Lillehammer, Norway, and IBM was its official technology sponsor, responsible for providing all of the results data. Watching the games at home, Grossman saw the IBM logo on the bottom of his TV screen and sat through the feel-good ads touting IBM's contribution to the event. But when he sat in front of his

UNIX workstation and surfed the Web, he got a totally different picture. A rogue Olympics website, run by Sun Microsystems, was taking IBM's raw data feed and presenting it under the Sun banner. "If I didn't know any better," says Grossman, "I would have thought that the data was being provided by Sun. And IBM didn't have a clue as to what was happening on the open Internet. It bothered me."

The fact that IBM's muckety–mucks were clueless about the Web wasn't exactly news to Grossman. He remembers when he had landed at IBM a few years earlier, and everyone was still using mainframe terminals: *"I was shocked. I came from a progressive computing environment and was telling people at IBM that there was this thing called UNIX, there was an Internet. No one knew what I was talking about."*

This time, though, he felt embarrassed for IBM, and he was irked. After logging on to the corporate directory and looking up the name of the senior executive in charge of all IBM marketing, Abby Kohnstamm, Grossman sent her a message informing her that IBM's Olympic feed was being ripped off. A few days later, one of her minions working in Lillehammer called Grossman back. At the end of a frustrating conversation, Dave had the feeling that one of them was living on another planet. Ever persistent, Grossman tried to send the Olympic marketer some screen shots from Sun's website, but IBM's internal e–mail system couldn't cope with the Web software. That didn't stop IBM's diligent legal department from sending Sun a cease–and–desist letter, which succeeded in shutting down the site. Most frontline employees would have left it at that. But there was a bigger point that Grossman felt the rest of IBM was missing: Sun was about to eat their lunch. After everyone had come back from the Olympics, he drove down to IBM headquarters, four hours away, in Armonk, New York, to show Kohnstamm the Internet himself.

When he arrived, Grossman walked in unattended, a UNIX workstation in his arms. Wearing a programmer's uniform of khakis and an open–necked shirt, he wound his way up to the third floor—the sanctum sanctorum of the largest computer company in the world. Borrowing a T1 line from someone who had been working on a video project, Grossman strung the line down the hall to a storage closet where he plugged it into the back of his workstation. He was now ready for his demo—a tour of some early websites, including one for the Rolling Stones. As sober–suited IBM executives scurried through their rounds, Mick Jagger could be heard wafting out of the closet.

Two people in addition to Kohnstamm were present at that first demo. One was Irving Wladawsky-Berger, head of the supercomputer division where Grossman worked. The other was John Patrick, who sat on a strategy task force with Wladawsky-Berger. Patrick, a career IBMer and lifelong gadget freak, had been head of marketing for the hugely successful ThinkPad laptop computer and was working in corporate strategy, scouting for his next big project. Within minutes, Grossman had his full attention. "When I saw the Web for the first time," says Patrick, "all the bells and whistles went off. Its ability to include colorful, interesting graphics, and to link to audio and video content blew my mind."

Not everyone saw what Patrick saw in that primitive first browser. Says Patrick:

> Two people can see the same thing, but have a very different understanding of the implications. When Java first came along and you saw a little clown dancing on the Web page, some people said, "So what?" and others said, "Wow, this is going to change everything." Part of it is, I'm always intrigued by anything new. A lot of people did say, "What's the big deal about the Web?" but I could see that people would do their banking here and get access to all kinds of information. I had been using online systems like CompuServe for a long time. So for people who weren't already using online systems, it was harder for them to see.

Their passions fueled by the Web's limitless possibilities, Patrick and Grossman would become IBM's Internet tag team, with Patrick doing the business translation for Grossman and Grossman doing the technology translation for Patrick. Patrick would act as a sponsor and broker for resources. Grossman would develop intimate links with Netheads in IBM's far-flung development community. "The hardest part for people on the street like me," says Grossman, "was how to get senior-level attention within IBM." Patrick became his mentor and his go-between.

After seeing Grossman's demo, Patrick hired him, and they soon hooked up with another Internet activist within IBM, David Singer. Singer was a researcher in Alameda, California, who had written one of the first Gopher programs that fetched information off the Net. Grossman and Singer started building a primitive corporate intranet, and Patrick published a nine-page manifesto extolling the Web. Entitled

"Get Connected," the manifesto outlined six ways IBM could leverage the Web.

1. Replace paper communications with e-mail.
2. Give every employee an e-mail address.
3. Make top executives available to customers and investors online.
4. Build a home page to better communicate with customers.
5. Print a Web address on everything, and put all marketing online.
6. Use the home page for e-commerce.

The "Get Connected" paper, distributed informally by e-mail, found a ready audience among IBM's unheralded Internet aficionados. The next step was to set up an online news group of the sort that allowed IBM's underground hackers to trade technical tidbits. "Very few people higher up even knew this stuff existed," says Grossman. Within months, more than 300 enthusiasts had joined the virtual Get Connected team. Like dissidents using a purloined duplicator in the old Soviet Union, Patrick and Grossman used the Web to build a community of Web fans that would ultimately transform IBM.

As Patrick's group began to blossom, some argued that he should "go corporate" and turn the nascent Web initiative into an officially sanctioned project. Patrick's boss, Jim Canavino, disagreed. "You know," Canavino remarked to Patrick, "we could set up some sort of depart-ment and give you a title, but I think that would be a bad idea. Try to keep this grassroots thing going as long as possible." Patrick needed to infiltrate IBM rather than manage some splendidly isolated project team. It would be easy for others at IBM to ignore a dinky department, but they couldn't stand in the way of a groundswell. Still, Canavino wasn't above using his role as head of strategy to give the fledgling ini-tiative a push. To avoid the danger of IBM quickly going from having no Web site to dozens of uncoordinated ones, Canavino decreed that nobody could build a website without Patrick's approval. Though few in IBM had any inkling of what the Internet would become, Patrick had become IBM's semiofficial Internet czar. Pretty good for a staff guy.

Patrick's volunteer army was a widely dispersed group of Net ad-dicts, many of whom had been unaware that there were others who shared their passions. "What John ended up providing," says Grossman, "was the ability to articulate and summarize what everyone was doing and to open a lot of doors." In turn, "the kids in black" introduced Patrick to the culture of the Internet, with its egalitarian ideals and trial-by-fire approach to developing new technologies. When the Get

Connected conspirators gathered for their first physical meeting, re-members Grossman, **"the question on everybody's lips was how do we wake this company up?"**

Patrick gathered a small group of his Get Connected renegades, in-cluding Grossman, at his vacation house, set deep in the woods of west-ern Pennsylvania. There they cobbled together a mock–up of an IBM home page. The next step was to get through to Gerstner's personal technology advisor, who agreed to make Lou available for a demo of the prospective IBM corporate Web site. When Gerstner saw the mock–up, his first question was, "Where's the buy button?" Gerstner wasn't a quick study, he was an instant study. But Dave and Patrick knew that an intrigued CEO wasn't enough. There were thousands of others who still needed to get the Internet religion.

Their first chance for a mass conversion came at a senior manage-ment meeting of IBM's top 300 officers on May 11, 1994. Having schemed to get himself on the agenda, Patrick drove his point home hard. He started by showing IBM's top brass some other Web sites that were already up and running, including ones for Hewlett–Packard, Sun Microsystems, the Red Sage restaurant in Washington, D.C., and a page for Grossman's six–year–old son Andrew. The point was clear: on the Web, everyone could have a virtual presence. Patrick ended the demo by saying, "Oh, by the way, IBM is going to have a home page too, and this is what it will look like." He showed the startled executives a mock-up of www.ibm.com, complete with a 36.2–second video clip of Gerst-ner saying, "My name is Lou Gerstner. Welcome to IBM."

Still, many IBM old–timers remained skeptical. Recalls Patrick: "A lot of people were saying, 'How do you make money at this?' I said, 'I have no idea. All I know is that this is the most powerful, important form of communications both inside and outside the company that has ever existed.'"

Shortly after the May meeting, Patrick and a few colleagues showed up at one of the first Internet World trade conventions. The star of the show, with the biggest booth, was rival Digital Equipment. Like Gross-man before him, Patrick's competitive fires were stoked. The next day, when the convention's organizers auctioned off space for the next show, Patrick signed IBM up for the biggest display at a cost of tens of thousands of dollars. "It was money I did not have," admits Patrick, "but I knew I could find it somehow. If you don't occasionally exceed your formal authority, you are not pushing the envelope." Now that IBM's name was on the line, Patrick had a rallying point around which he could gather all of the company's various Internet–related projects.

Patrick was as concerned about the internal audience he wanted to reach as he was about the outside world. Here was his chance to seed his message across the entire company. He sent letters to the general managers of all the business units asking for anything they had that smelled like the Internet. They would only have to put in a little money, and he would coordinate everything. It turned out that IBM had a lot more Web technology brewing than even he had expected. But none of it was really ready to go to market. Still, by that December, Patrick was able to showcase IBM's Global Network as the world's largest Internet service provider and a Web browser that preceded both Netscape's Navigator and Microsoft's Explorer. IBM stole the show and became a fixture at every Internet World thereafter.

Constantly fighting IBM's penchant for parochialism, Patrick took every opportunity to drive home the point that the Web was a company-wide issue and not the preserve of a single division. At the next Internet World, in June 1995, he challenged his compatriots to leave their local biases at the door: "The night before the show, I got everybody together in an auditorium and said, 'We are here because we are the IBM Internet team for the next three days. You are not IBM Austin or IBM Germany.' That is part of the culture of the Internet: boundary–less, flat." The huge IBM booth generated a lot of curiosity among the show's other participants. When people asked Patrick to whom he reported, he said, "The Internet." When they asked him about his organization, he replied, "You're looking at it, and there are hundreds more."

Patrick was a relentless campaigner, spreading the good word about the Internet in countless speeches both inside and outside IBM. "Somebody would invite me to talk about the ThinkPad," he recalls, "and I would come talk about the Internet instead. I'd use the ThinkPad to bring up Web page presentations rather than PowerPoint slides." He also made himself very accessible to the media. People inside IBM would learn about what Patrick was doing by reading the newspaper. But even when talking to the media, Patrick's prime constituency was still the vast swath of unconverted IBMers. He just couldn't shut up about the Internet. Says Patrick: "If you believe it, you've got to be out there constantly talking about it, not sometimes, but all the time. If you know you're right, you just keep going."

While Patrick and his crew were throwing Internet hand grenades into every meeting they could wheedle their way into, Gerstner was fanning the flames from above. Gerstner's early belief in the importance of network computing dovetailed nicely with the logic of the Internet. Having bought into Patrick's pitch, Gerstner was ever ready to give IBM's Webheads a boost. He insisted that IBM put its annual and quarterly reports up on the Web well before most other companies were doing so. Gerstner also signed up to give a keynote address at Internet World, saying that the Internet was really for business. This was while Bill Gates and others were still dissing the Web as an insecure medium for consumer e–commerce.

Within IBM, Patrick became a trusted emissary between the company's buttoned–down corporate types and the T–shirted buccaneers who were plugged into Net culture and living on Internet time. Patrick had the ear of IBM's aristocracy, and his message was simple and unequivocal: "Miss this and you miss the future of computing." At the same time, Patrick convinced Grossman and his ilk that not everyone at head office was a Neanderthal. Says Grossman:

> I used to think that IBM at senior levels was clueless, that these guys had no idea how to run a company. But one of the many things that has impressed me is that the people who are running this company are really brilliant business people. Somehow we connected them to the street. Knowing how to shorten paths to those decision makers was key.

When IBM finally set up a small Internet group, with Patrick as chief technical officer, he insisted that the team stay separate from IBM's traditional software development organization. Patrick's logic: "I do believe there's a benefit in being separate, otherwise we'd have to start going to meetings. Pretty soon we'd be part of someone else's organization, and a budget cut would come along and we'd be gone."

Many of the folks in Patrick's fledgling organization weren't old enough to rent a car, and many were younger than his daughter.

Although IBM now had a formal Internet organization, Patrick and Grossman didn't disband their grassroots coalition. As the 1996 Summer Olympics approached, this group went through several watershed events. Patrick loaned Grossman out for 18 months to corporate marketing, which was in charge of the Olympics project. For the first time, the Olympics would have an official website, and IBM would build it. Grossman launched himself into building the Olympics website and was soon begging Patrick for extra bodies. "Patrick did the magic to get them hired," says Grossman, "and I morphed from doing the grunt technical work to being Tom Sawyer and getting other people to help whitewash the fence." Ultimately, more than 100 IBMers got involved.

To prepare for the Olympics, Grossman and his team had started developing websites for other sporting events such as the 1995 U.S. Open and Wimbledon. For the U.S. Open site, he gave a couple of college interns from MIT the task of writing a program to connect a scoring database to the website. "By the end of the summer," remembers Grossman, "we were sitting in a trailer, barely keeping together a website with a million people a day pounding away at it for scores. It was held together by Scotch tape, but we were learning about scalability." It was amazing, thought Grossman, that all of these people would come to a site merely for sports scores. IBM's second surprise came when it was caught off guard by the flood of global interest generated by a chess match between world chess champion Garry Kasparov and an IBM supercomputer named Deep Blue in early 1996. Corporate marketing had asked Grossman earlier to build the website for the match, but he was booked with too many other assignments, so the site was outsourced to an advertising agency that did little more than put up a cheesy chessboard. The day of the first match, the site was overloaded with traffic and crashed.

"Nobody had any idea this was going to be such a big deal," says Patrick. IBM went into panic mode. Grossman and a handful of IBM's best Web engineers jumped in to take over the site. They had about 36 hours to completely revamp the site before the next match. They got Wladawsky-Berger to pull a $500,000 supercomputer off the assembly line. The site didn't crash again, but the incident raised the anxiety level about the upcoming Olympics. If IBM was having difficulty running a website for a chess match, then what were the Olympics going to be like? The incident also succeeded in convincing a few more skeptics that the Internet was going to be beyond big.

IBM had to build an Olympics website that could withstand anything. Patrick went tin-cupping again, asking all the general managers to loan him their best people and their best equipment. He got not one supercomputer, but three. Grossman's team eventually grew to about 100 people. IBM was learning in the crucible of the world's most visible sporting event. By the time it was over, IBM had built the world's largest website (at the time), which withstood up to 17 million hits a day with few shutdowns. The content on the site was replicated in servers across four continents. IBM even learned how to do a little e-commerce when a demo site for online ticket sales attracted a flood of credit-card numbers and $5 million in orders.

For Patrick and Grossman, the Olympics was just one more high-profile way to show IBM the possibilities of the Internet. It was also an easy way to get funding for development. Admits Grossman:

I used the Olympics as a front basically. What I was doing, without telling anyone, was getting computing resources. I also thought the fastest way to get IBM to change was to work from the outside in. If IBM saw itself written about in the papers, then it would change faster than if we got mired in an internal process.

Grossman's on-the-fly development, in public no less, was the complete antithesis of IBM's traditional way of doing things, which was to push developers to perfect products before letting them out the door. It was the difference between improv comedy and a carefully rehearsed Broadway play. The old model didn't make much sense on the Web, where if something breaks, you can fix it universally without sending out millions of CD-ROMs with new software. You just fix the software on the server, and everyone who logs on automatically gets the new version. In the superheated development climate of the Web, there is a big premium on getting stuff out fast, learning quick, and improving the breed as you go along. Grossman and Patrick quickly concluded that creating Web-enabled software called for a new set of software development principles, which they summarized and shared with the burgeoning Web community within IBM:

Start simple, grow fast
Trial by fire
Just don't inhale (the stale air of orthodoxy)
Just enough is good enough
Skip the krill (go to the top of the food chain when trying to sell your idea)
Wherever you go, there you are (the Net has no bounds)
No blinders
Take risks, make mistakes quickly, fix them fast
Don't get pinned down (to any one way of thinking)

Much of the technology that Grossman and his crew first prototyped would later make its way into industrial-strength products. For instance, the Web server software developed for the Olympics evolved into a product called Websphere, and much of what his group learned formed the basis for a Web-hosting business that today supports tens of thousands of websites.

Following the Olympics, the Internet group turned its attention to proselytizing within IBM. Grossman, who had become the senior technical staff member on Patrick's team, set up an Internet lab to bring in executives from all over the company so they could experience the Web's possibilities. The group started a project called "Web Ahead" that worked to revolutionize internal IBM IT systems that had always had a low priority. For instance, the team took the old terminal–based corporate directory and wrote a Java application that gave it a great graphical interface and cool features. With a few clicks, employees could look up a colleague, see what computer skills he or she had, and then ask the directory to list every other employee at IBM with those same skills. These "Blue Pages" were an instant hit across IBM.

Patrick and Grossman never rested in their campaign to infiltrate the rest of IBM with their Internet thinking. The Internet group had only a few dozen people officially working for it, so Patrick was constantly pleading to borrow people (who were usually already part of his virtual team) from other departments. His most important ally was the team's ever–lengthening list of success stories. People could argue with position papers, but they couldn't argue with results. Repeatedly, Patrick put his whole organization on the line, and taking that risk and delivering results gave him credibility no fancy title or mega–budget could match. Patrick recounts how he co–opted line executives into sharing their resources:

> I have never been turned down on anything I have asked for,
> and I have asked for a lot. There was a lot of evangelizing and
> selling. I would go to a general manager and say, "I need you to
> pull some disk drives from the assembly line and I need your top
> engineer. What you will get out of it is unique. Your guy is going
> to come back to your group, and you are going to have a hell of a
> reference story to talk about. It will be great PR. We will make
> your stuff work on the Internet." I never did any name–dropping,
> but I didn't have to. Also, I was making a real commitment. I had
> 20 people working on these things.

Patrick was hard to refuse, partly because it was clear that he was fighting for the interests of all of IBM, rather than for the interests of his own little group. As he explains:

> I didn't have any allegiance to any one product group. Although
> I had a budget that came out of the software group, I didn't think
> of us as part of the software group. When somebody calls us and
> asks for help, we don't ask them for a budget code. We say, "Sure."

We have never been a threat to any other part of the company. From the beginning our goal was to help IBM become the Internet Business Machines company.

Patrick was quick to assure would–be donors that the relationships he was forging worked both ways. He would borrow people from various business units, but at any given time about a quarter of his own people would be out on loan to other units. Further, Web Ahead alumni were regularly posted to permanent positions across IBM. When that hap–pened, he would tell his remaining staff, "We did not lose Bill, we colo–nized the network hardware division. Now there is one of us living there." Patrick also helped start an internship program called "Extreme Blue" that paired some of the brightest engineering students with top IBM researchers. When IBM later hires these students, few come to work in Patrick's group, but all will be part of his virtual network.

Again and again, throughout their Internet campaign, **Patrick and Grossman broke long–standing IBM rules and overstepped the boundaries of their own authority.** But because their cause was so thoroughly righteous and their commitment to IBM's success so visibly selfless, they got away with things that had often sunk careers at IBM. Then and now, Patrick is unapologetic:

> If you think of yourself as being in a box, with boundaries, you're not going to have any breakthroughs. I expect this of my people on my team, if they come to me and say, we failed because we didn't have the authority to do something, I'll say that's crazy.

Inside IBM and out, Patrick and Grossman are today recognized for their pivotal contribution to IBM's e–business metamorphosis. John and Dave's excellent activist adventure is full of lessons:

○ They were relentless in getting their message across.
○ They ignored hierarchy and directly lobbied Gerstner and his deputies for support.
○ They borrowed resources from wherever they could find them.
○ They enrolled true believers from the distant reaches of the IBM empire in a virtual network.
○ From the Kasparov–Deep Blue chess match to the Summer Olympics to the Blue Pages, they put their butts and their reputations on the line to prove new technologies and build demos that would make the Internet's possibilities real to the uninitiated.

○ Web Ahead developers produced the seeds of dozens of commercially viable products and services, which legitimized not only their own Web projects but everyone else's as well.

These two unlikely heroes—a software nerd and a corporate staffer—along with a pro–change CEO, helped give IBM the chance to do something it hadn't done for a couple of decades: lead from the front.

KEN KUTARAGI: SONY'S DIGITAL BANDIT

Throughout its history, Sony has had a knack for coming up with gee-whiz products, from one of the world's first transistor radios to tiny TVs to the Walkman, CD player (with Philips), and 8mm camcorder. Its archrival, Matsushita, may be bigger, but Sony's relentless innovation has made it synonymous with what's new and cool. Yet by the mid-1990s, Sony was in a deep funk. Its profits had sunk from a high of $1.3 billion in 1992 to a loss of $3.3 billion in 1995. Its foray into Hollywood had proved expensive and embarrassing, generating a $3 billion write-off in 1995. More worrying, Sony had mostly missed three of the biggest opportunities in consumer electronics: personal computers, cell phones, and video games. Compaq, Dell, HP, Toshiba and a dozen other companies had trounced Sony in PCs. Motorola, Nokia and Ericsson had run away with most of the cell phone business, and Nintendo and Sega had staked out the video game market.

All these new markets were either based on or quickly moving to digital technology. Yet Sony's historical strengths lay with analog technologies—of the sort found in televisions, VCRs, and tape players. With the exception of a handful of engineers scattered throughout the company, few at Sony were in tune with the digital revolution that was rendering analog technology obsolete and fueling entirely new businesses. One of the few cognoscenti, buried deep in a corporate R&D lab, was Ken Kutaragi. Lacking any formal mandate, Kutaragi launched a bandit project that eventually led to the establishment of the Sony Computer Entertainment division in 1993 and the introduction of the PlayStation video game console the following year. Less than five years later, the PlayStation business had grown to comprise 12 percent of Sony's $57 billion in total revenues, and an incredible 40 percent of its $3 billion in operating profits.[2] But more than simply being an astounding financial success, the PlayStation provided the springboard for Sony's leap into the digital age.

From his earliest days, Kutaragi had been infused with an engineer's curiosity. At the age of 10 he built a guitar amp for a friend. By the time he was a teenager he was putting together go-carts from old scooters. Unlike most of his peers, he grew up in an entrepreneurial household, working after school in the printing company his father had started following his return from World War II. After graduating from engineering school in 1975, Kutaragi applied for a job at Sony. The oil crisis had put a damper on hiring, and Kutaragi was one of only 46 male university graduates Sony took on that year.

Kutaragi's first job was to work on a liquid crystal display for calculators. The potential of LCDs captured his imagination. He explains:

I thought it would be nice not just for calculators, but also for future televisions. I created a very small LCD TV set. Unfortunately at that time Sony was making CRT [cathode ray tube] TV sets, so this was not a mainstream area. I was the only one pushing for flat screen displays, and I was just an insignificant engineer.

His mini-TVs, which prefigured the Sony Watchman by about a decade, got stuck in the lab. Still a tinkerer, he was fascinated by the brand-new microprocessors that companies such as Hitachi, Intel, and NEC were just beginning to produce. He bought samples of the first 4-bit and 8-bit chips and reverse-engineered their simple instruction sets. He also explored the intricacies of CP/M, an early personal computer operating system. With this knowledge, Kutaragi created a computer system in the tiny laboratory he occupied. "It was a nice toy for me," he recalls.

Kutaragi's digital hobby came in handy in the early 1980s when Sony began replacing some of the electromechanical components in its tape decks and video recorders with digital microcontrollers. His frustrations in designing a chip to measure sound levels convinced Kutaragi that the development tools provided by the chip companies were inadequate. In response, he created his own hardware and software tools for developing chips aimed at audio and video applications. Ultimately, these tools became standard issue for all Sony engineers. By the mid-1980s, Kutaragi had become fully convinced that the digital revolution was inevitable. With dozens of companies being formed around the world to exploit the new technologies, Kutaragi started to get an entrepreneurial itch. "I was in corporate R&D, but I wanted to enter the business area," he says. In R&D he was heading up part of a project to develop the first-ever digital camera for the consumer market, the "Mavica." Instead of using film, it stored its images on a two-inch disk.

It was during this time that Kutaragi purchased one of Nintendo's first-generation, 8-bit video games for his eight-year-old daughter. "She begged me to play every day," says Kutaragi, though he readily admits he needed little encouragement. But two things about the Nintendo system disturbed him: its sound was awful, and the games were stored on magnetic cartridges. Ever the technical perfectionist, these shortcomings irritated Kutaragi. "Why," he asked himself, "did the game use such an unsophisticated magnetic storage system with such a sophisticated 8-bit processor?"

Convinced that he could make Nintendo's product better with the floppy storage system he had developed for the Mavica, Kutaragi tracked down the one salesman in Sony who had a relationship with Nintendo, and the two of them met with the game maker's head of technology. Kutaragi would have preferred to help Sony get into the video game business, but he couldn't find anyone internally who shared his enthusiasm for digital entertainment. Indeed, recalls Kutaragi, "When Nintendo introduced its first 8-bit system, no one in Sony mentioned it. They hated the product. It was a kind of snobbery. For people within Sony, the Nintendo product would have been very embarrassing to make because it was only a toy."

So began Kutaragi's collaboration with Nintendo and his bandit project. Ultimately, Nintendo decided not to use Kutaragi's floppy disk technology. Yet several of Nintendo's senior managers were intrigued by Kutaragi's unorthodox views and invited him to an offsite meeting in 1986 to further discuss the company's upcoming 16-bit system. Kutaragi suggested that Nintendo should let Sony make a special, digital, audio chip for its next game system. The new chip would greatly improve the machine's sound. Nintendo accepted.

Kutaragi's bold proposal left him with a problem. He was a researcher, not a businessman—he had no authority to strike a deal with Nintendo. To complicate matters, Sony had just embarked on an ill-fated foray into 8-bit computing with its line of MSX personal computers. Hoping to create an alternative to Microsoft's DOS operating system, a number of Japanese companies had converged around the MSX standard. The MSX project was something of a sacred cow within Sony as it was led by the son of Akio Morita, Sony's much-revered founder. Still, Kutaragi was unimpressed: "I hated the idea. We wanted to sell the MSX. But we saw the MSX as a subset of the PC. The MSX was no good at real-time graphics. Nintendo realized the importance of real-time entertainment. The architecture was totally different."

So Kutaragi kept his deal with Nintendo a secret. Only his boss, Masahiko Morizono, the head of R&D, was made aware of the budding relationship with Nintendo. Says Kutaragi, "I realized that if it was visible, it would be killed."

As the launch date for the new machine approached, Nintendo sprung a surprise on Kutaragi. The game maker wanted to release a joint statement touting Sony's new sound chip. Kutaragi's boss could no longer protect him. The project was out in the open. Kutaragi would have to come clean. Thus, he found himself in the unenviable position of standing in front of a group of furious senior executives trying to explain why Sony was helping a rival. Remembers Kutaragi: "They were upset. The executives hated to know that we were allied with Nintendo and were competing with an internal product [the MSX machine]. Many of them wanted to kill our project. But Ogha–san protected us."

Ogha–san was then president Norio Ogha, who later became Sony's CEO and chairman. Ogha was intrigued by the new market. In the end Nintendo was given permission to use Sony's chip, and the product's success brought Kutaragi some credibility—at least outside of Sony. When Nintendo started to think about developing a 32–bit system in 1989, the company wanted Kutaragi to contribute to its design. In addition to a better sound chip, Kutaragi still wanted to replace the magnetic–based storage device—this time with a CD–ROM drive.

Within Sony, Kutaragi was viewed with suspicion. If he was going to continue his collaboration with Nintendo, he would need to find someone who could help him make his case to top management. Trolling for sponsors, Kutaragi approached Shigeo Maruyama, one of Ogha's disciples within Sony Music Japan. Maruyama expressed interest in the project because a CD–based system would be able to play not only games but music as well. Using Maruyama as a conduit, Kutaragi asked Ogha to create a dedicated group around the Nintendo project that would sit outside Sony's major businesses. Kutaragi feared that without this separation, his project, and his dream, wouldn't survive. Ogha, who had years earlier resorted to the same tactic in creating the music division, agreed to put Kutaragi's fledgling business in a separate unit.

This was a very lonely time for Kutaragi. He felt isolated from the rest of the company. "I was the outsider," he says. "No one would use my team's technology for internal projects." Here he was, developing key components for Nintendo's next game machine, which was likely to generate hundreds of millions of dollars, and his colleagues were ignoring him. Kutaragi recalls: "We were in a separate facility. No one accepted our project. This was a very difficult time for me. I moved my project out of the headquarters building, and located in a different area of Tokyo."

Then in 1991, just when he thought things couldn't get worse, Nintendo backed out of the deal. This change of heart came after Kutaragi had already devoted two long years of his life to the project. Nintendo was frightened that a CD–ROM drive might weaken Nintendo's hold over the production of game software. Magnetic cartridges required longer lead times to produce and were much more expensive than CD–ROMs, but it was a technology that Nintendo controlled. Nintendo was concerned that a CD–based machine might weaken the company's position in the game software business, which was where the real profits lay.

With his project in tatters, Kutaragi was more lonely than ever: "People inside Sony hated us. I was aligned with Nintendo, so when they cancelled the project I was homeless. I was arguing that computer entertainment would be a very important area for the future of Sony, but no one agreed."

Undeterred, he once again approached Ogha through Maruyama. Kutaragi recalls: "I wanted to convince Mr. Ogha that we needed to make Sony a digital company, and the video game was the only project I could think of that would let us take a first step in this direction."

The MSX project, Japan's attempt to create its own PC operating system, had sputtered and died. Kutaragi saw game machines as Sony's best chance at becoming a digital company. But more than that, he wanted the company to make a commitment to computer entertainment. Sony sold millions of CD players, and by then there were digital components in most of its consumer electronics, but it still did not see itself as a digital company. The CD was seen as a replacement for vinyl records, rather than just one example of what would become an explosion of digital media. Kutaragi lobbied tirelessly to change this view. He explains:

> I convinced them that computer entertainment would be very important for the future of Sony. Sony's technology was analog-based. Analog would be finished by the end of the century in terms of being able to make a profit. The first age of Sony was analog, but it had to convert to a digital, information-based company in the future. No one realized that.

To underscore his commitment to the project, Kutaragi threatened to leave Sony if he wasn't allowed to proceed with his video game project. Not only that, he made an outrageous promise: If the company would fund his R&D efforts, he would create a platform for Sony's future growth. Ogha's go-ahead, when it came, reflected not only his reluctance to lose a creative engineer, but his annoyance that Nintendo had breached a contract with his own signature on it. Thus Nintendo's fears pushed the start button on Sony's PlayStation.

Kutaragi wanted to give the project a grand name, Sony Computer Entertainment, to match his grand vision for how chip technology would one day carry Sony far beyond games. At first, Ogha wasn't convinced. Recalls Kutaragi:

> I proposed the name to Mr. Ogha. I didn't want the project to be seen as games, I wanted a more sophisticated image. Mr. Ogha, said, "It's a very big name." Sony Music Entertainment, that's big business, but what is Sony Computer Entertainment? That is not a big business like Sony Music or Sony Pictures.

Despite the reservations, Kutaragi's project got the outsized name.

Already Kutaragi could envision an opportunity to vest bland business computers with fun, personality and emotion. Two years of development came and went before Kutaragi and a handful of engineers completed the PlayStation. The 1–million–transistor chip underneath its plastic shell was one of the first to combine a 32–bit processor, a graphics chip, and a decompression engine on the same piece of silicon, otherwise known as a *system-on-a-chip*. Launched in Japan at Christmas 1994, the PlayStation was the first 32–bit game machine on the market. It would be a full year and a half before Nintendo released its next-generation system, the Nintendo 64. In a market where being first with the fastest is everything, Sony had pulled off a coup.

Sony's sterling brand name and the machine's engineering superiority gave the PlayStation a rapid liftoff. As sales shot skyward, Sony Computer Entertainment was awarded divisional status within the company, but Kutaragi was not immediately appointed as its president. Instead, he was asked to head up the division's engineering efforts.

Where Nintendo had been notorious for taking a tough line with game designers, Sony coddled independent game developers and made it easy for them to design games for the PlayStation. The PlayStation quickly became the world's top-selling game machine. Kutaragi, the onetime outcast, became CEO of the division in March 1999, when his boss moved on to become Sony's deputy CFO. By the end of its 1999 fiscal year, Sony had sold 55 million PlayStations worldwide and 430 million copies of video game software. Over 3,000 different game titles were available. All told, Sony Computer Entertainment racked up $6.5 billion in revenues, with a mouth–watering 17 percent operating margin, compared with 5 percent for the company as a whole (see the table "Sony

Computer Entertainment Growth in Revenues and Operating Profits as Percentage of Corporate Profits").

	FY95	FY96	FY97	FY98	FY99
Sony Computer Entertainment Revenue	35	201	408	700	760
Sony Computer Entertainment Operating Income	n/a	(9)	57	117	137
Sony Corporate Operating Income	(167)	235	370	520	339

Kutaragi had proved himself. Former critics were now praising his courage and perseverance. He had made good on his promise. The returns on his bandit project had kept Sony afloat through the Asian financial crisis in 1997 and 1998, contributing nearly half of the company's profits. And Sony Computer Entertainment had become the company's second-largest business, surpassing Sony Music and Sony Pictures and second only to Sony Electronics. For a company that had staked billions on hardware-software synergy, Sony Computer Entertainment was proof that integration could pay off. Sony's software partners would sometimes spend as much as $40 million developing and marketing a single new game—that's the kind of budget more typically associated with Hollywood blockbusters. Video game software had come to generate more revenue than movie ticket sales. Nor was the PC safe from the onslaught. In 1998, software produced for dedicated game machines captured more than two-thirds of all the revenue derived from entertainment software. PC-based titles took the other third.

But Kutaragi's ambitions for Sony were far from sated. With sales of the PlayStation still climbing, Kutaragi began working on his next development masterpiece, informally known as the PlayStation II. Even though he was now CEO of Sony Computer Entertainment, he led the engineering team that set out to design the new machine. More than just a game machine, the PlayStation II would be built around a 128-bit processor called the "Emotion Engine," a chip Sony claimed to be three times faster than a Pentium chip of the same vintage. The new chip would be able to render images and movement more realistically than a Silicon Graphics workstation. Costing a cool $1 billion to develop, the chip would be powerful enough to recognize speech and render characters that could be controlled down to their facial expressions. The PlayStation II would play DVD movies, as well as all 3,000 CD–ROM games developed for the original PlayStation. Its graphics would be comparable to an animated movie, its sound quality superior to that of a music CD and its computing power more than that of a high–end PC. Plus, it would connect to the Internet because, as Kutaragi says, "Communications is the biggest entertainment of all for humans. Even the telephone is a form of entertainment." Kutaragi's hope was that the PlayStation II would become a "home server" that would link households to all kinds of broadband services. A senior executive at Sony described the PlayStation II as an entirely new *dohyou*, using the Japanese word for sumo ring.

But even this groundbreaking product was just one step toward an even bolder goal. Explains Kutaragi:

> My intent is to create a new type of entertainment. Music has a 1,000–year history, movies have a 100–year history, but the computer is new. The microprocessor is a 30–year–old product, and IBM and Intel want to use it as an enhanced calculator. They are focused on productivity in the office, not entertainment. Spielberg saw our demonstration and he said, "Wow." Lucas thinks the PlayStation II can deliver his dream to the home. They did not expect that this type of technology would be available in this decade.

What Kutaragi is describing is nothing less than some future melding of TV, film, computers, music, and the Internet. Whether Sony will actually make this happen remains to be seen. But there is no doubt that the PlayStation II is more than just a game machine, and a few of the world's digerati wondered whether Sony might have Intel or Microsoft in its sights.

Yeah, Kutaragi could have left Sony and started his own video game company, but then he wouldn't have been able to leverage Sony's considerable marketing muscle, manufacturing capability and money. Kutaragi muses:

> If I had started this business as a venture outside a big company, it would have worked, but the moving speed would not have been fast enough. Sony had great human resources, capital and

manufacturing capability, but it did not have a vision at that time. But my team had the vision. We wanted to use Sony's infrastructure to enhance the time to market. If we were a Silicon Valley company, we would have created another Silicon Graphics. But our ambition is bigger than to be another Silicon Graphics.

In spring 1999, Sony announced a restructuring that placed Sony Computer Entertainment at the core of the company, and Kutaragi joined Sony's corporate management team. Kutaragi's odyssey from ignored engineer to corporate mogul provides a real-life seminar in what it takes to make a great company greater still:

○ Start with a vision that is so bold and seductive that it is capable of sustaining you when others try to shut you down.
○ Don't start with grand projects; start with something you can achieve right now, with your own resources (such as that first sound chip for Nintendo).
○ Go underground if you have to, even if the price is isolation.
○ Don't ask permission until you have achieved an early success and are ready to scale up.
○ Be willing to put your job on the line for what you believe.
○ In a world where most people can't see beyond the next quarter, perseverance pays.

In his new role, Kutaragi is no less intent on changing the world than he was as a lonely engineer. From exile to divisional CEO, an activist indeed!

SHELL'S RENEWABLE RADICAL

When he joined Royal Dutch/Shell's planning group in 1993, peering into the future was Georges Dupont-Roc's job. But Dupont-Roc was more than a soulless planner playing scenario mind games. He was a dreamer and a doer. He could see a world of opportunities for Shell that lay beyond fossil fuels, a world so compelling and real that he was willing to abandon the safety of his anonymous staff job to become a highly visible champion of renewable energy. Before he was done, Dupont-Roc had convinced his century-old company to make renewable energy Shell's fifth core division, alongside exploration and production, chemicals, oil products and natural gas.

As head of planning for the energy group, Dupont-Roc's job was to "look at the world energy scene and understand long-term issues that might have an impact on various sources of supply." In doing so, he became intrigued with the challenge of meeting the energy needs of a world with a rapidly increasing population in a way that would be environmentally sound and capable of sustaining economic development. Eager to deepen his thinking, Dupont-Roc sought out the world's energy experts at both universities and other corporations. He visited experts at MIT, Berkeley, Boeing and Mercedes-Benz in his quest to develop a view on how the world energy system would evolve and what role renewable energy sources—such as sun, wind and wood— would play. In 1994, he put his findings into a seven-page report, immodestly titled "The Evolution of the World's Energy Systems."

The report looked out not 5 or 10 years, but more than 50! **Even for an oil company accustomed to making investments in exploration that don't pay off for 10 or 20 years, the scope of Dupont-Roc's report was audacious.** But it was also grounded in a wealth of hard data about the progress of energy over the previous 100 years and what this might mean for the future. During the past century, world GDP had grown an average of 3 percent a year, supported by a supply of available energy that had grown at a 2 percent annual rate. During that time, the annual worldwide consumption of energy had increased from the equivalent of 4 barrels of oil per person to 13. Given these historical trends, Dupont-Roc came up with two potential story lines for the next century. The first one, which he labeled "sustained growth," assumed that energy consumption would continue to grow at its historical rate, in which case people would be burning the equivalent of 25 barrels of oil per capita by 2060. The second alternative, dubbed "dematerialization," assumed that energy growth would become somewhat disconnected from GDP growth as information technology, biotechnology and lighter materials improved energy efficiency. In this case, people would be consuming the equivalent of only 15 barrels of oil a year by 2060.

In Dupont-Roc's view, the sustained growth scenario was the most probable. It assumed that energy efficiency would continue to increase at 1 percent a year, the same as it had for the past century. For the dematerialization scenario to occur, energy efficiency would have to increase at twice the historical rate, a phenomenon that had never occurred for more than a few years at a time. Even if dematerialization did take hold, it would begin in the fully developed nations and take several decades to spread to underdeveloped regions. However Dupont-Roc cut the data, he couldn't see any way to avoid an energy supply squeeze as the world's population grew and as the environmental perils of fossil fuels became ever more inescapable. Says Dupont-Roc: "I saw the potential for renewable energy sources to reduce their cost and take market share from traditional energy sources, going from a small niche to a serious competitor in the way that oil did at the beginning of the twentieth century."

To convince his skeptical colleagues, Dupont-Roc drew a powerful analogy. He pointed out that in the beginning, oil had been a niche product, used almost exclusively in lamps and stoves. In 1890, even after 20 years of 8 percent annual price declines because of improved refining and production techniques, the market share for oil was still only 2 percent compared with coal and wood. It wasn't until Winston Churchill switched the British Navy from coal to oil, in order to give ships more power and make their emissions less visible, that oil started to become the world's dominant source of energy. Dupont-Roc was simply reminding his colleagues of what they already knew: energy markets take a long time to develop. Every time energy consumption increased, the market diversified to meet those growing needs—from coal to oil and from oil to gas and nuclear. Wasn't it possible that renewable energy would come next—both from existing renewable sources like solar and wind and from other renewable sources yet to be exploited? Wasn't renewable energy one of history's freight trains? You could either jump on board before it gathered speed or get run over. Under the sustained growth scenario, Dupont-Roc figured that renewable energy would be fully competitive with oil, gas, and other traditional types of energy by 2020 (see graph "Energy Market Share, 1860–2060").

Dupont-Roc reminded his colleagues that, in the early stages, it was impossible to predict exactly which technologies would eventually triumph. In the early part of the century, for instance, the zeppelin looked like a surer bet than the airplane, and even electric cars looked more promising than those powered by combustion engines. An aluminum car powered by an electric battery broke the land speed record in 1899, clocking in at 105 kilometers per hour. On the last page of Dupont-Roc's report were excerpts from an article titled "What May Happen in the Next Hundred Years" from the *Ladies' Home Journal*, December 1900. One of the entries predicted, "There will be Air-Ships, but they will not successfully compete with surface land and water vessels for passenger traffic. They will be maintained as deadly war vessels by all military nations."

Obviously, there is no such thing today as British Blimpways. Dupont-Roc was saying that the future's big trends, such as how much energy 10 billion people will need, can be fairly guessed at, but the details, exactly which technologies will provide that energy, are more difficult to discern. For this reason, he advocated a technology–agnostic approach to renewable energy: experiment with everything from solar to wind to biomass (burning wood and other renewable resources) to geothermal. The goal would be to take options on a wide range of renewable energy sources.

Dupont-Roc wanted more than a nod to renewables from Shell's top brass. He was after more than a PR campaign to assuage the environmentalists. He wanted an ironclad corporate commitment. But first he would have to buttress the case for renewables. Dupont-Roc argued

ENERGY MARKET SHARE, 1860–2060

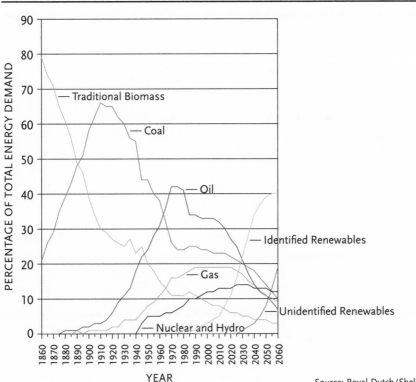

Source: Royal Dutch/Shell.

that the cost of making solar panels, growing trees and converting wind into electricity would drop at a rate similar to the decline in the cost of producing oil during the late 1800s. His report showed that during the 1970s and 1980s the cost of making solar panels declined 15 percent a year and that during the 1980s and early 1990s the cost of electricity from wind turbines had drifted downward at the rate of 10 percent per year. Wind energy was already competitive in some markets. Solar panel costs would continue to decline through advances in silicon manufacturing, thin–film technology and the scaling up of manufacturing. Through better cloning techniques and genetic manipulation, trees could be made to grow faster and burn hotter. In the meantime, production of hydrocarbon fuels would continue to rely on mature technology, and oil companies would be forced to go deeper offshore or look for smaller pockets of oil in older fields.

"I wasn't saying that oil was a dead business," recalls Dupont–Roc, "but that new energy segments would be able to improve their productivity faster and become competitive in the marketplace." Under his sustained growth model, the use of fossil fuels would continue to rise moderately until about 2020 or 2030, when renewables would come into their own and allow the total energy supply to keep growing at a time when energy from fossil fuels would be hitting a plateau.

Not everyone was immediately convinced by Dupont–Roc's thesis. In part, their skepticism was based on the disappointing results achieved in Shell's earlier experiments with renewable energy. In the 1970s, the company started a small solar energy project. But by the mid–1980s, after having spent about $100 million, it shut the business down. Photovoltaic energy was simply not cost–effective yet. In the 1980s, Shell also experimented with nuclear energy in a joint venture with Gulf, a dalliance that produced a $500 million write–off. By 1994, all that had survived of Shell's earlier experiments were a small photovoltaic research unit in Holland and a small forestry business with operations in Uruguay and Chile.

Undeterred, Dupont–Roc published his short strategy paper and began spreading the word about the new promise of renewables. He traveled from one Shell operating company to another, giving 80 speeches in 20 countries over the span of 18 months. Says Dupont–Roc, "Shell people were surprised that we were saying this sort of thing. **IT WASN'T PO-LITICALLY CORRECT TO TALK ABOUT A WORLD IN WHICH FOSSIL FUELS DIDN'T DOMINATE.**" Others suspected that it was all just a PR exercise. Yet every time he told his story, it got stronger:

People would contribute to my stories by giving more examples and providing clarification, which I would feed back into my model. It was a bit of a democratic debate. The biggest thing I learned was not to be arrogant. Shell people have a reputation for being arrogant, of trying to push a story instead of sharing it and trying to hear what other people have to say.

Finally, Dupont–Roc got his chance to give his presentation to Shell's executive management committee. He received a cautious endorsement. His case was helped by the steady trickle of positive feedback Shell's top management had been getting from country managers who were pleased to see Shell leading a dialogue about new energy sources. The fact that Greenpeace had succeeded in mobilizing public opinion in opposition to Shell's plans to sink an old oil platform in the North Sea also added urgency to the renewables cause. With Shell getting pummeled in European newspapers, top management was especially receptive to any ideas that would make their company more environmentally friendly.

The executive committee asked Dupont–Roc to prepare a business plan outlining how Shell might poke its toe into the water of renewable energy. They were perhaps looking for nothing more than a token, but this was just the opening that Dupont–Roc needed to make his concept of a renewable energy business a reality.

Tree huggers notwithstanding, Dupont–Roc knew that he had to make his proposal financially credible if it was ever to see the light of day. He was certain that renewables would become economical over the next couple decades, but couldn't say exactly when or how. During the mid–1980s Dupont–Roc had been leading a drilling project in the North Sea when the collapse in oil prices forced everyone to find innovative ways to reduce the project's costs (through three–dimensional seismic technologies, subsea satellites and unmanned platforms). He was sure a similar wave of innovation would one day push renewables into the energy mainstream. But if Shell waited for that inflection point, it would be too late. Shell would lack the experience to catch up to those who had started earlier.

In the fall of 1995, Dupont–Roc sidestepped all of Shell's numerous barons during a one–hour meeting with the chairman in which he asked for $25 million to test the commercial potential of some renewable energy business concepts over a three–year period. Dupont–Roc wanted to concentrate on the two areas where Shell already had some competence: solar energy and biomass (specifically, the growing of trees for power generation). In photovoltaics, he wanted to automate the way solar cells were made and increase energy plant production from the equivalent of 2 megawatts of power a year per plant to 20 megawatts a year. His goal for biomass was to demonstrate that Shell could grow trees sustainably, harvest them and produce wood fuel for no more than the cost of natural gas. "We had to convince the chairman that Shell could do something real and credible," says Dupont-Roc. By the end of the meeting, the chairman gave him his $25 million.

Dupont-Roc had the cash, but he still had to enlist the support of the local line executives who control people and facilities across Shell's global empire. Applauding his speeches was one thing, but actually dedicating resources to a nascent business project was another. With his little band of warriors, which included three other people at Shell Central in London, he embarked on a new campaign. "It was very exhausting. We had to convince the chief executives of the operating companies to help us," he says. Dupont-Roc chose his targets carefully. If the operating companies were too big, the project would get lost. If they were too small, it might prove too distracting. So he focused on about two dozen of Shell's medium-sized operating companies. Typical reactions would be, "We are sorry, we're trying to rationalize our oil operations," or "The local strategy cannot support renewables—although we support you." Finally, his team narrowed the candidates down to about a dozen medium-sized subsidiaries. These test beds had the advantage of representing different types of economies and climates. Some of the experiments failed, and some were unqualified successes. In Germany, for instance, Dupont-Roc had to temper the local enthusiasm. He reflects:

> You have to keep a balance between retaining some type of central steering and letting the local initiative develop. In Germany, they went a little overboard. They started looking at solar heating, wave power, and wind power, which was good, but it was trying to do too much. We said, "We don't want to go that far right now." You have to remain focused or you will fail.

By the time the executive committee reviewed Dupont-Roc's progress in December 1996, he was well ahead of plan. His group had planted 300 hectares (741 acres) of trees in Uruguay and had set up a 3-megawatt, photovoltaic demonstration plant in Holland. The committee was thrilled. Even though the three-year trial period was not yet up, it asked him to come back with a plan to substantially expand his renewable activities. This time he developed a broad 15–year business plan for an entirely new division, which would not only expand the scope of Shell's biomass and solar power activities but also create a platform for entering two new areas: wind and geothermal. In preparing the plan, Dupont–Roc consulted about 20 senior executives throughout Shell who helped him fine–tune the commercial aspects of the plan. They would grill him: "What are you selling me? How will you produce it? In what countries? Who will find the customers?" When he finally presented the plan to the executive committee in June 1997, it was concrete. Its target was to create a portfolio of businesses by 2010 with assets in at least 20 different countries, $100 million in profits, and a 15 percent annual earnings growth rate. The businesses would be run locally, but a central team in London would assist in replicating successful ventures across the corporation.

Shell now faced a choice: it could either house the subsidiary within an existing division or create an entirely new one. It decided to pursue the latter option so that the business would be more visible and have a chance to grow. In the fall of 1997, the company established Shell International Renewables with a commitment to invest $500 million in the venture over the following five years. While Dupont–Roc was gratified that all his speeches and lobbying had finally paid off, he was profoundly disappointed that he wasn't asked to head up the new unit. Unfortunately, Shell was still an aristocracy, and he wasn't a blue blood. The job went instead to a more senior executive who had recently been reorganized out of his job in the chemicals division. Nevertheless, Dupont–Roc was heartened by the fact that his vision, aligned as it was with the tides of history, had helped to create the first major new division in Shell in decades. After staying to help the ex–chemicals executive set up the new renewables business and jump–start a geothermal energy project, Dupont–Roc quietly resigned to work for the French energy company TOTALFINA.

Despite his departure, Dupont–Roc left an indelible mark on Shell. By 1999 the first batch of trees, which had been planted in Uruguay under his watch in 1996, was ready to be harvested, and a new 20–megawatt solar panel factory was up and running in Germany. In South Africa, Shell International Renewables was marketing home solar systems to 50,000 people who lived too far away to get electricity from the power grid—the largest commercial rural electrification project ever to be based on solar power. It was also installing 10,000 solar home systems in Bolivia. In Germany and Holland, it opened a handful of solar-powered service stations where people driving electric cars could charge up in an environment-friendly way. And it was combining solar home systems with biomass-fueled power plants in a "Sun Station" project that provided electricity for 80 homes, a mosque, a government building and 11 street lamps in a village in Indonesia.

Back when the renewables business was still a $25 million project trying to prove itself, Dupont-Roc received a postcard from a politician in the French Alps, where he had grown up. The postcard showed two children playing in front of an extraordinary mountain scene, with a quote from the French novelist Antoine de Saint-Exupéry: "We do not inherit the land from our forefathers, we borrow it from our children." Shell's chairman Mark Moody-Stuart would later repeat these words in a 1998 letter to shareholders.

Dupont-Roc's success is instructive:

○ Invest relentlessly in your own learning. The endless meetings with experts and academics gave Dupont-Roc the weapons and armor he would need to win his arguments inside Shell.
○ There's no substitute for impeccable data. While data alone is seldom enough to convince a company to do bold, new things, shoddy analysis will sink an activist's career before it even begins.
○ A great cause (e.g., a cleaner planet and sustainable development) is as important as a great business case.
○ If you're not willing to be an apostle, don't expect anyone else to be.
○ Use analogies and experiences from your company's own history to buttress your credibility. Dupont-Roc's analysis of how oil, natural gas, and nuclear power had come to complement earlier energy sources was a powerful argument for renewables.
○ Start small. Small successes are the platforms for big successes.

David Grossman, John Patrick, Ken Kutaragi and Georges Dupont-Roc. They worked within the system, fomenting discontent, mobilizing kindred spirits, leading outlaw projects and, ultimately, changing the destiny of some of the world's largest, most complicated companies. They were citizen-activists.

So where do you start? How are you going to organize a movement? Do you have what it takes? What can you actually learn from Ken and Dave and John and Georges? Read on.

6
GO AHEAD!
REVOLT!

EVERY DAY COMPANIES GET BLINDSIDED

by the future. Every day dozens of organizations find themselves suddenly on the defensive, struggling to adapt a decrepit business model to someone else's business concept innovation. Yet the future never arrives as a surprise to *everyone* in an organization. Someone, somewhere, was paying attention. For these heretics and novelty addicts, tomorrow's opportunities are every bit as real and inevitable as today's sunrise. But too often the seers feel isolated and impotent. They don't know where to begin in building a grassroots movement, even though the principles of activism aren't classified and there's no secret handshake. Over the decades, social campaigners of all types have constructed a highly practical theory of activism. How sad that the principles of activism are virtually unknown to citizens of the corporate realm.

Every senior executive claims to "embrace change," and every CEO solemnly warns that "change is the only constant." Isn't it rather odd, then, that the principles of activism haven't been drilled into the head of every employee? After all, most social systems get changed by activists not by the elite. Yet I've never come across a company–sponsored training program that teaches the rank and file how to be activists. Let's end this strange omission, shall we? There's plenty we can learn from Dave Grossman, John Patrick, Ken Kutaragi, and Georges Dupont–Roc, profiled in the previous chapter, about how to organize a movement.

HOW TO START AN INSURRECTION

STEP 1: BUILD A POINT OF VIEW

As an activist, you need a point of view (POV), which includes the following:

○ What is changing in the world?
○ What opportunities do these changes make possible?
○ What are the business concepts that would profitably exploit these changes?

If you understand the principles of business concept innovation, if you've learned how to be your own seer, then you're well on your way to developing your own POV.

It is rare to come across an individual who has a well–developed point of view about an opportunity for industry revolution. **Most folks stand for nothing more than more of the same.** This is much to your advantage. A sharply articulated POV is a sword that lets you slay the dragons of precedent. It's a rudder that lets you steer a steady course in a world filled with people blown about by fad and whim. And it's a beacon that attracts those who are looking for something worthy of their allegiance.

A POV must meet four tests: it must be credible, coherent, compelling and commercial. To be credible it must be based on unimpeachable data. A POV can be as bold and far–reaching as your aspirations, but it must have a foundation in fact. Georges Dupont–Roc demonstrated clearly and unequivocally that several renewable energy sources would become cost–efficient by the year 2020, if not before. He showed Shell's executive team that the cost per kilowatt–hour of renewable energy had been falling around 10 percent to 15 percent per year for several years. Project that forward, add in the cost of meeting stringent environmental standards for fossil fuels, and you can make a well-informed judgment about the point at which renewable energy sources will become a viable alternative to carbon fuels. It's also clear, given the technical hurdles involved, that any company that hopes to reap profits from renewable energy sources needs to start investing now.

John Patrick and David Grossman also had the tide of history on their side. Although the Internet was still a nascent phenomenon when they began agitating within IBM, there was plenty of hard data describing its rapid growth. There were also many analogies from history that suggested the inevitable triumph of any technology that would allow people to better connect and communicate. They may have been in front of the curve, but there was a curve. Rhetoric isn't enough. You need to wade hip-deep in data to make sure you really understand what's going on. You have to be ready to back up your bold assertions. And you must clearly separate what can be known from what is unknowable—don't claim to know things you can't.

A POV must be coherent. The pieces of your POV must fit together and be mutually reinforcing. Corporate executives and their well-trained attack dogs will sniff out the slightest bit of inconsistency in your story line. Logic lapses are not allowed. This doesn't mean you have to have perfect perspicuity, but there's no excuse for muddled thinking. I often see would-be activists demolished when, in their enthusiasm, they defy logic. I witnessed one young activist in a large software company pitching a new product to his CEO. "This will be on everybody's computer. Everyone will use it every day," he gushed. The CEO's eyebrows moved closer together. "Other than the browser, e-mail, and word processing, what applications get used by everyone, every day?" he inquired. The activist's balloon starting hissing air. "Well, none," he had to admit. "And what is it about your application," the CEO pressed further, "that will create some new standard of ubiquity?" The balloon was now a flaccid bit of rubber. The would-be activist never got a second chance. Passion is no substitute for a coherent point of view.

Facts and logic are not enough, though. If you're going to enroll others in your dream, you must speak to their hearts as well as their intellects. You must be ready to tell people why your particular cause will make a difference in the world. If you can present your POV as a story (what happens to the world if we *don't* harness renewable energy sources) or as a picture (like the Web page featuring Grossman's six-year-old son), it will be that much more emotionally compelling. Many assume that only numbers talk. That's stupid. Only economists think we're perfectly rational. Beauty, joy, hope, justice, freedom, community—these are the enduring ideals that attract human beings to a cause. What is the ideal that makes your POV truly worthwhile?

If you want your company to *do* something, your POV must be commercial as well as emotionally compelling. If you can't describe how your business concept will generate wealth, you won't get far as a corporate activist. This doesn't mean you have to have a pro forma P&L accurate to two decimal places. It does mean your POV must point to a bona fide commercial opportunity. Anticipate the basic commercial questions: What's the value proposition for a customer? How will this create competitive advantage? What are the cost dynamics? Where is the flywheel of increasing returns? Your business concept may not yet be fully fledged, but you must demonstrate you are attending to these questions. Somewhere in all the enthusiasm and purpose must be the beginnings of a story about wealth creation.

A POV that is credible, coherent, compelling and commercial may rise to the standard of an *ideology*, which the *Random House Webster's College Dictionary* defines as "a body of doctrine or thought forming a political or social program." Civil rights is an ideology. Democracy is an ideology. Christianity is an ideology. A vision of computers vested with the power and intelligence to display human emotion is an ideology. A belief in the power of renewable energy to sustain economic development without imperiling the planet is an ideology. **AS AN ACTIVIST, YOU MUST BUILD YOUR OWN IDEOLOGY.** Start your journey with a sense of destiny. Don't be afraid to dream big, like Kutaragi-san and Dupont-Roc. As one of my activist friends once put it, "If you're going to fish, use a big hook." Setbacks are inevitable. You will lose many battles in the process of winning the war. It is your ideology that will sustain you and from which you will draw courage. Know that you have a *righteous* cause—one that is in tune with what's changing, one that is inherently worthwhile, one that will help your company stay relevant in the age of revolution.

STEP 2: WRITE A MANIFESTO

These are the times that try men's souls. The summer soldier and
the sunshine patriot will, in this crisis, shrink from the service
of their country; but he that stands by it now, deserves the love
and thanks of man and woman.

George Washington ordered these words read to his soldiers at Valley Forge, on Christmas Eve, shortly before crossing the Delaware. They are the first lines of a polemic written by Thomas Paine, the American revolutionary and pamphleteer. Paine's most famous work, *Common Sense*, was the manifesto for the American Revolution. Over the course of two centuries his powerful words and timeless principles have been used again and again to resist the authoritarian designs of despots and dictators.

You, too, must become a pamphleteer. It's not enough to have an ideology; you have to be able to pass it on, to infect others with your ideas. Like Thomas Paine, you have to write a manifesto. It doesn't have to be long. A contagious manifesto will do the following:

○ Convincingly demonstrate the inevitability of the cause—here's why it is right, right now.
○ Speak to timeless human needs and aspirations—here's why you should care.
○ Draw clear implications for action—here's where to start.
○ Elicit support—here's how you can contribute.

There are hordes of people in every organization who bitch and moan about what their company *should* be doing. But how many ever take the trouble to write a passionate and well-reasoned call to arms? Ideas that are flaky appear even more so when committed to paper. Conversely, ideas that are inherently strong get even stronger through the discipline of writing.

Think of your manifesto as a virus. What can you do to make it even more infectious?

○ Search for "data bombs" that will explode upon reading— incontrovertible facts that challenge prejudices and create urgency.
○ Find simple phrases and powerful analogies that people can use as "handles" to pick up your ideas and pass them around. (Don't you love the description of the PlayStation II as an "emotion engine"? Those two words say loads about Sony's view of the future of computing. They make a very complicated idea instantly portable.)
○ Stay constructive. Don't criticize. Don't rehearse past failures. Don't look for culprits.
○ Provide broad recommendations, but don't argue for a single, do-or-die course of action. Remember, you're launching a campaign

that will need to go forward on several fronts. At this point you have to stay flexible on tactics.

○ Keep your manifesto short. You're not getting paid by the word. Patrick's "Get Connected" was a simple 6-point treatise on how the Web would transform business and large-scale computing. Dupont-Roc's manifesto, "The Evolution of the World's Energy Systems," was only 7 pages. A 40-page white paper isn't a manifesto—it's a consultant's report, and it will never get read.

○ Make it opportunity-focused. A manifesto is more likely to get passed around if it focuses on the upside rather than the downside. Where's the big win?

○ Sometimes you need a stick. There are some whose love affair with the status quo borders on obsession. Like a reluctant Pharaoh, unwilling to free the Israelites from bondage, the only way they're going to change their minds is if you convince them that things are bad and getting worse. Every company sits on a burning platform. If you don't know where yours is burning, go find out. Maybe it's an online competitor that's about to rip your margins to shreds. Maybe it's just the hard fact that your company is underperforming and you've run out of ideas for propping up the share price. Maybe it's that you're living on Internet helium and you have no idea how to produce sustainable profits. Do a fast-forward—make it abundantly clear when and how the existing strategy is going to run out of steam.

Expect to hear dozens of reasons for *not* doing something. When timid, backward-looking souls go scrambling for an escape hatch, bolt it shut.

Escape hatch: "It's not happening as fast as you say."
　　　Bolt: "Oh yes it is, and here's the data to prove it."

Escape hatch: "You can't make any money with that kind of a business model."
　　　Bolt: "Someone already is, and here's how they're doing it."

Escape hatch: "We don't have the skills to do this."
　　　Bolt: "But we could get them, and here's how."

Escape hatch: "We don't have the bandwidth to deal with this right now."
　　　Bolt: "We have no choice. Here's what we should stop doing."

Escape hatch: "Someone already tried this, and it didn't work."
Bolt: "They didn't try it *this* way."

Your manifesto must build a case for your *intellectual* authority. The depth of your analysis, the quality of your thinking and the clarity of your reasoning must shine forth from every page. It must also wrap you in a cloak of *moral* authority. Moral authority comes from a cause that is both economically sound and undeniably in the best interests of the organization and its members. Your manifesto must contain nothing that would suggest your primary motivation is selfish. You're not some product champion trying to get your little widget built, or some corporate hack trying to defend a budget. You can't afford to be sectarian or parochial if you want to change the world. Martin Luther King spoke for African-Americans, but he called on all Americans to embrace justice and equality. Unlike Malcolm X, he was inclusive rather than exclusive. He understood that America could never live up to its promise if it relegated some to a permanent state of despair. It is no crime to be self-interested, but if you are *only* self-interested, your manifesto will be quickly and rightfully dismissed.

Your manifesto *must* capture people's imagination. It must paint a vivid picture of *what could be.* It must inspire hope. Your manifesto must challenge people to look the future in the eye, however disconcerting it may appear. It must deal forthrightly with the little lies that people tell themselves to avoid the discomfort of change. It must make inaction tantamount to corporate treason. But most of it all, it must ignite a sense of possibility.

STEP 3: CREATE A COALITION

You can't change the direction of your company all by yourself. This is a lesson that even corporate chairmen eventually learn. As founder and chairman of Silicon Graphics, Inc., Jim Clark fought a long-running and often bitter battle with SGI's CEO, Ed McCracken. Clark was eager that SGI go "down market" and produce workstations at the upper end of the PC price range. McCracken was loath to sacrifice fat margins to serve "out-of-scope" customers. Unable to change McCracken's mind, Clark eventually quit.

Even chairmen have to seduce, cajole, and convince to get things done. Granted, it's easier when you control capital budgeting and compensation, but it still ain't a walk on the beach. Most CEOs are good at exhortation and arm twisting, but this is seldom enough to re-vector a large company. To do that, you have to build a broad coalition. **In**

building a coalition, you transform individual authority into collective authority. It is easy to dismiss corporate rebels when they are fragmented and isolated, and don't speak with a single voice. But when they present themselves as part of a recognizable coalition, speaking in a single voice, they cannot be ignored. This is the simple principle behind all collective action, be it a labor union organizing a strike or a trade association lobbying politicians. I have yet to see a company in which a few hundred or even a few dozen like-minded employees can't substantially impact corporate direction. The very fact that they *are* organized and *are* speaking from conviction is a powerful message to corporate leaders.

There is another reason to build a coalition. Most new opportunities don't fit neatly into any of the existing organizational "boxes." While there were scores of Netheads spread out across IBM, the Internet opportunity couldn't be shoehorned into any one division. Likewise, computer entertainment at Sony and renewable energy at Shell lacked natural organizational homes, at least to begin with. In creating a cross-company coalition, one is recognizing that the resources, brains and passion needed to bring a new opportunity to fruition are broadly distributed. You are creating a magnet for people who harbor the same revolutionary tendencies you do, wherever their current organizational home is. A movement is not a box on the organizational chart; it's an ink blot that has bled all over the formal org chart. It's a splat, not a department.

The first step in building a coalition is to recognize that you are not the only prescient, frustrated, yet ultimately loyal individual in your company. You're not the only one who "gets it." The second step is to begin to identify potential recruits. Start by asking these questions:

○ Who is already in your orbit? Surely you've already been talking to some folks about your revolutionary ideas.
○ Are there staff groups or task forces in the company that might be naturally inclined toward your point of view?
○ Are there any cross-company initiatives you could tap into?
○ Who across the organization might have a stake in the success of your campaign?
○ What are the news groups or e-mail distribution lists you might hijack?

Maybe you can't write like Thomas Paine, but then he didn't have the Web. Put your manifesto up on an internal website. Build an e-mail list of those you think might share your views. Create an online forum where people can share their perspectives and help elaborate your manifesto. Locate outside experts who can lend your cause credibility. Invite network members to brown–bag lunches and after–hours soirees where you can scheme and plot and remind each other that you're not all crazy. Create opportunities to work together on some ad hoc project. Coalitions get stronger when they focus on a common task. Be inventive. Look for involvement vehicles like the Internet trade shows John Patrick used to mobilize IBM's early Internet converts.

Stay underground, at least initially. Use the network to help strengthen your business case and identify opportunities for early action. As your recruits start talking to colleagues in their own spheres of influence, the virus will spread. Don't be impatient. If you map the infection curve of a virus, it is initially flat. But at some point the exponential arithmetic of the network effect takes over, and the infection rate soars. Don't be overquick to present top management with a go/no–go decision. It's easy to shoot one pheasant out of the sky; it's a bit harder to bring down an entire flock. Keep building your flock.

And remember, you have an advantage that top management often doesn't. Most of the folks who report to them are conscripts, but you're building an all–volunteer army. Conscripts fight to stay alive, volunteers fight to win. Your goal is to enroll and embolden the latent activists. If you build strength from below, top management will ultimately come to you. Georges Dupont–Roc got his chance because a chorus of support for renewable energy was echoing off the walls of Shell's worldwide organization.

STEP 4: PICK YOUR TARGETS AND PICK YOUR MOMENTS

Sooner or later, the movement has to become a mandate. The "Get Connected" coalition became "IBM, the e–business company." Dupont–Roc's informal network of renewables fans turned into a $500 million commitment. In most companies, these commitments aren't made by the Birkenstock-wearing, Volvo-driving, ponytail brigade. Activists create movements, they don't create mandates. That's why **activists always have a target——a someone or group of someones who can yank the real levers of power.** You need to know who in your organization can say "yes" and make it stick. It may be a divisional vice president, it may be the CEO, or maybe it's the entire executive committee.

At Sony, Kutaragi knew his project was doomed unless he got the CEO onboard early. Sony's aristocracy was actively hostile to the idea of video games. After trying several approaches, Kutaragi established a relationship with Maruyama, who helped him lobby the CEO. At IBM

Grossman managed to engineer an Internet demo for Lou Gerstner. Later, when Gerstner's likeness spoke from a Web page to a throng of IBM senior managers, the Internet die was cast. For Dupont-Roc, the pivotal moment came when he was asked to present to Shell's senior executive group.

All too often, corporate rebels are inclined to look at senior management as out-of-touch reactionaries, rather than potential allies. This is self-defeating. Their support is the object of the whole exercise. Few of them are stupid, and most are no more venal than you or I. Arrogant? Sometimes. Ignorant? Often. But that doesn't make them irredeemable. You must find a way to help them see what you see, to learn what you have learned and to feel the sense of urgency and inevitability you feel.

So you've identified your targets. The next step is to understand them. What are the pressures they face—from Wall Street, from customers and competitors? What issues top their agenda? What objectives have they set themselves and the company? Which of them is searching for help and ideas? Be ready to bend your objectives to fit their goals. Sony had been struggling to demonstrate that hardware/ software synergy was more than a concept. After Sony's initial debacle in Hollywood, Ogha was eager for another chance to justify Sony's foray into software and media. Kutaragi was ready to scratch Ogha's itch. Do you *really* know where the top guys itch? You gotta find out.

Often the top guy is easier to convince than the divisional barons one level down. Shareholder expectations hang over the head of the average CEO like Damocles' sword. With a corporate vantage point, the CEO is often less likely to be defensive and parochial than a divisional VP. In many companies, you find the "Gorbachev syndrome": there's a cautiously unorthodox leader at the top and a sea of discontent down below. Like Gorbachev, the CEO wants the organization to adapt and change. Likewise, ordinary citizens want a better life. It's all too obvious to them that the system doesn't work. The ones that are most difficult to convince are those in the middle—the city bosses, the *nomenklatura*, the vice presidents who feel most threatened by a new order of things. The recalcitrant middle can long resist the exhortations of an isolated and embattled CEO. But it's much more difficult for them to hold out when they are caught in the vise of a reform-minded CEO and a committed and revolutionary rabble. Savvy corporate leaders, such as Ogha and Gerstner, know this. They're more than willing to use the heat of the activists' passions to thaw the frozen middle in their own organizations.

Getting access to the top isn't always easy. "Invitations" often have to be engineered. Court the executive assistants, the adjutants and the bag carriers. Find out who the top guy respects and relies on. Find out who writes the speeches. Know what customers the senior execs care most about—they may provide a back channel of influence. In other words, plot all the various avenues of influence that lead to your desired targets. Invite these people to your offsites, hook 'em up to your e-mail list, do a demo for them. Use your network to work all the approach routes simultaneously.

Make a list of all the events and occasions when you might get a chance to directly influence your targets. What are the meetings, workshops or conferences that your targets regularly attend? See if you or one of your network members can get on the agenda. Keep your pitch short. Entice and intrigue, don't harangue. Think of the gatekeepers and high-profile events as "strategic infection points"—opportunities to educate, entertain and enroll. To activists, the whole world's a stage. Every event is an opportunity to advance their POV. Patrick and Dupont-Roc gave dozens of speeches. As with skilled politicians, it didn't matter what question they were asked; they gave the answer they wanted to give. They were endlessly opportunistic. Every impromptu meeting, every hallway conversation was a chance to win another convert.

Sooner or later, you'll want to go one on one with your targets. Pick your moment carefully. You're waiting for the stars to align—you want the groundswell to have reached a critical mass; you want to catch your targets at a point when they're rooting around for a new idea; and, in an ideal world, you'll time your big pitch to some external event that adds credibility and urgency to your case (such as the frenzy of environmental outrage produced by Shell's decision to sink an offshore platform). Get all this right, and top management won't think you're a rebel; they'll think you're a godsend.

Your big moment may not be planned. It may happen unexpectedly—in a company cafeteria, at a trade show. Always have your elevator speech ready. Know what you want to ask for—keep it small and simple. Make it easy to say yes.

STEP 5: CO-OPT AND NEUTRALIZE

Saul Alinsky was one of America's most accomplished twentieth-century radicals. His book on how to organize a movement, *Rules for Radicals*, is a classic.[1] In the mid-1960s he went to Rochester, New York, to lead a campaign on behalf of the city's black community. Mary Beth Rogers describes his approach:

Alinsky, in something of a self-parody of his own tactics, threatened to buy 100 tickets to one of Rochester's symphony concerts and feed the predominantly black members of the local organization a dinner of baked beans a few hours before they went to the concert. The resulting "stink-in" would be a surefire attention getter. . . . There was no law against it. It might be fun. And it would probably get action quickly because the social elite wouldn't want "those people" to invade their activities again.[2]

Such tactics may work in the public sphere, but confrontation and embarrassment are seldom effective in a corporate setting. You are trying to disarm and co-opt, rather than demean and confront. Temper your indignation with respect.

John Patrick was extremely successful in drafting IBM's big guns into his cause. Given the scope of his ambition—to make the IBM Corporation Internet-ready—he realized that Gerstner's support would be necessary but hardly sufficient. With virtually no resources of his own, Patrick had little choice but to co-opt IBM's feudal lords. This took more than concerted lobbying. Patrick constructed a set of win-win propositions for key divisional leaders: Lend me some talent, and I'll build a showcase for your products. Let me borrow a few key people, and I'll send them back with prototypes for cool, new Internet-ready products. Patrick knew that reciprocity wins more converts than rhetoric.

Patrick didn't belittle, and he didn't berate. He worked hard to avoid an "us versus them" mentality. He wasn't trying to suck people and resources out of other divisions. He wasn't trying to build his own corporate fiefdom. He wasn't out there competing with the rest of IBM for customers. Divisional presidents saw him as a catalyst for change rather than as a competitor for resources and promotion. He wasn't cannibalizing their business; he was helping those businesses get ready for the future. In everything he did, it was clear that Patrick had the interests of the entire IBM Corporation at heart. In the beginning, he even lacked a formal organization. For all these reasons, he presented a very small target to his opponents.

Win-win propositions. Reciprocity. A catalyst not a competitor. Big impact, small target. These are vital principles for *your* campaign. Of course, it doesn't always work like this. The top brass at Sony saw Kutaragi's project as an impertinent challenge to their own MSX initiative. Companies have a finite number of resources, so expect a tug-of-war from time to time. But whenever you can, avoid expending political capital in highly charged head–to–head battles. At Shell, Dupont–Roc drew little fire because he never argued that renewables would replace fossil fuels. Indeed, he didn't think they would become fully competitive until 2020, long after the retirement of the existing divisional leaders. So yeah, you can stand on your soapbox and rant at the VPs. But to change your company, you're going to have to learn to co–opt at least some of the aristocracy into your revolutionary cause.

STEP 6: FIND A TRANSLATOR

You've been at it a while, and despite your best efforts you're having trouble getting heard. You talk, but you're not sure they comprehend. Don't be surprised. The very things that make you a revolutionary make it difficult to build a base of common understanding with the disciples of orthodoxy. Imagine how a conservative dad might look upon a kid who comes home with green hair and an eyebrow ring. Well, that's the way top management is likely to view corporate rebels. **Different experiences. Different languages. Different values. Different planets. This is why corporate revolutionaries need translators.**

John Patrick was a translator for Dave Grossman—someone who could build bridges between the Internet cultists and IBM's corporate cardinals. Patrick was a translator between geekdom and officialdom. But he did more than explain the intricacies of HTML to guys still in love with Big Iron. He helped to translate between the apparent chaos of the Web and the discipline of large–scale corporate computing; between the culture of "just enough is good enough" and the ethos of "zero defects"; between a half–baked technology and a zillion–dollar opportunity; between the agenda of the true believers (we just want to do "cool stuff") and the priorities of top management (those demanding shareholders, again). Patrick was also a credibility bridge. When top management asked, "Who *is* this guy, Grossman, and these kids in black?" he had an answer. "These guys care about IBM, they're not bomb throwers."

Patrick was also a translator between present and future. He found tangible ways of folding the future back into the present, starting with the Web sites built for sporting events. Each successive project gave long–term IBMers a better sense of what the new business model might look like in practice.

So if you're stymied, go find a translator—someone who is plugged into the future, who is naturally curious and who may be shopping around for an interesting point of view to sponsor. Senior staff and newly appointed executives are often good prospects. Both are typically in search of an agenda to call their own.

People can argue with position papers, but they can't argue with success. All your organizing efforts are worth nothing if you can't demonstrate that your ideas actually *work*. Start small. Unless you harbor kamikaze instincts, search for demonstration projects that won't sink you or your cause if they should fail—and some of them will. You may have to put together a string of demonstration projects before top management starts throwing money your way. You don't run pell-mell down an unfamiliar path on a moonless night. Nor do companies blindly throw resources at untested business concepts. Commitment to a new business concept should never be presented as all or nothing—unless you're already way behind the change curve and some other company has taken all the risks. You have to help your company feel its way toward revolutionary opportunities, step by step.

Successful activists engineer a set of escalating experiments designed to test the new business concept and justify additional increments of investment. Without the original sound card he designed for Nintendo, Kutaragi would never have won the chance to do the PlayStation. Without Lillehammer, Deep Blue and a dozen other small wins, Patrick and Grossman would have never pushed IBM out in front of the Internet curve. Without a success in his first $25 million demonstration project, Dupont-Roc would have never shaken half a billion dollars out of top management's pockets. Activists are not daredevils. Revolutionary goals, but evolutionary steps—that's the way to think.

Be careful not to overpromise. Patrick's team called its alpha projects "experimental applications" to clearly distinguish them from IBM's thoroughly tested market-ready applications. There will be some who will wish you to fail. If your early experiments are too grand or you claim too much for them, and you then falter, you will provide enormous satisfaction to the skeptics. Search for small projects that offer the greatest potential impact for the smallest number of permissions, projects that will engender maximum visibility with minimum investment risk. You may have a grand strategy in the back of your mind, but you need to start with some little "stratlets." Keep asking yourself, What would constitute an early win? What could we do, right now, with the limited resources available within our network to build our credibility?

What could we do that would surprise the skeptics? What kind of success would others find compelling?

STEP 8: ISOLATE, INFILTRATE, INTEGRATE

Experiments that stay experiments are failures. The objective is to turn early experiments into radical, new wealth–creating business models with the power to change the direction of your company. For this to happen, you must eventually push your brood of baby projects out of the nest. In the early stages of your activist campaign, you may want to *isolate* your projects from the rest of the organization. Kutaragi moved himself and his team to a distant precinct in Tokyo, out of the line of fire of hostile executives. With a similar logic, IBM's PC business was originally housed in Boca Raton, Florida, far from meddlesome corporate staff and antagonistic vice presidents. To grow, new opportunities need to escape bureaucratic controls and orthodox thinking. They need their own place—a place where new ideas, new values and new teams can grow unmolested. This is the logic behind corporate "incubators," "internal venture divisions," and "skunk works." Sadly, most projects never escape the incubator, which is often little more than an orphanage for unloved ideas. Malnourished and secluded, few projects ever find foster parents.

Companies are often advised to "protect" new initiatives from the overweening control of the old guard, particularly when the new projects are built around a competing technology. But extended isolation will kill any project that requires a significant input of talent or capital or that is in any way complementary to existing businesses. For example, while IBM succeeded in "protecting" the PC business, that protection carried a stiff price. Physically cut off from the rest of IBM and from its broad base of capabilities, the PC development team had no choice but to turn to Microsoft and Intel for key software and hardware. The rest, as they say, is history. A similar fate befell many of the innovations spawned by Xerox's Palo Alto Research Center. Being 3,000 miles from headquarters guaranteed PARC a large measure of freedom, but it also made it difficult for Xerox to profit from PARC's endless stream of world–changing ideas. It's hard to drink through a straw that's 3,000 miles long.

Let's assume you are campaigning on behalf of something *big*. Sooner or later, a large–scale opportunity will require a large–scale resource commitment. This commitment is unlikely to be forthcoming if your project has been locked up too long in some business incubator.

You will need to convince a broad cross–section of key executives that your new business concept is essential to your company's future. Only then do you have a chance at winning the battle over resources. **To attract resources, you're going to have to make the leap from isolation to infiltration.** A powerfully argued position paper, regular speech making and high–profile demonstration projects helped Dupont–Roc to infect Shell with the renewable energy virus. He knew that if he couldn't get the rest of the organization to share his intellectual agenda, the renewables opportunity would never win the battle for resources within Shell. The resources that will make your dream a big commercial success have to come out of somebody's hide. Whoever's wearing that hide needs to be an ally. That will happen only if you've run a successful infiltration operation.

Sometimes you need more than resources. Sometimes the opportunity is not a *new* business, but a dramatic reconfiguration of the *existing* business. If you're a drug company, you can't put genomics in solitary confinement. If you're a retailer, you can't relegate e–commerce to some offline business incubator. Here you need more than infiltration, you need integration. Patrick wanted to change the very essence of IBM—rather than simply launch a new business. To this end he courted executives from IBM's operating divisions, searched for projects they would find relevant, trained and returned their people, and put his alpha–stage projects up for early adoption. It wasn't enough for Patrick to infiltrate IBM with his POV about the Internet; he needed to *integrate* the early experiments of the Get Connected cohort into IBM's major business groups. He didn't want the Internet to be a pimple on IBM's backside; he wanted it to be a virus in its bloodstream.

Sometimes an innovation makes it out of the incubator, but never gets integrated. GM's Saturn division is more than just an experiment. Saturn's sponsors were successful in infiltrating GM with their POV about the need for a "fresh–start" small car brand. Yet it is unclear just how many of the lessons learned in Saturn have been woven into the fabric of Chevrolet, Oldsmobile, Pontiac and GM's other brands. Indeed, in recent years it has appeared as if Saturn has become more like the rest of GM than the reverse. Integration requires more than a shared intellectual agenda. You are asking for more than capital and talent; you are asking the company to reinvent the core of who it is and how it competes. Your experiments must do more than attract resources away from incrementalist projects; they must take root throughout the organization and send out runners that will transform the landscape. It was John Patrick's hope that the Internet projects he transferred into IBM's operating divisions would ultimately seed a forest of local Web initiatives, and they have. This is the ultimate measure of success for a corporate activist.

Isolate. Infiltrate. Integrate. If you really want to change your company, you have to do it all.

ACTIVIST VALUES

Activists are the coolest people on the planet. They change big, complicated things with their bare hearts. They punch more than their weight. And when they fail, they fail nobly. To be an activist you need more than an agenda and a clever campaign. You need a set of values that will set you apart from the courtiers and the wannabes.

Honesty: Activists are truth tellers. They are authentic. They don't sacrifice their integrity for personal political gain. Their views cannot be bought and sold in the marketplace for perks and prestige. They speak the "unspeakables."

Compassion: Activists love the entire community. They are not interested in securing narrow sectarian advantage. Their goal is to create as big a legacy as possible for as many as possible.

Humility: Activists are terribly ambitious for their cause, but personally humble. They are arrogant enough to believe they actually can change the world, but they're not glory hogs. Their egos never get in the way of making something happen.

Pragmatism: Activists are more interested in action than in rhetoric. They're not searching for Utopia; they're trying to make stuff happen right here, right now. They prefer real progress to grand gestures.

Fearlessness: Activists are courageous. Their passion for the cause regularly overrides their sense of self-protection. They don't jump on land mines for the hell of it, but neither are they afraid to do battle with the defenders of the status quo.

Courage is, perhaps, the most important attribute of all. I have sat through hundreds of meetings where low-level employees soft-pedaled their convictions in an effort to protect the delicate sensitivities of top management. What came across as bold and uncompromising in a dry run presentation to their peers ended up as mushy and unconvincing when presented to top management. Afraid of bruising an ego or challenging a dogma, many would-be activists pull every punch and saw the sharp end off of every challenging point. In the end, every argument is so thoroughly padded with contingencies and qualifications that they might as well be firing cotton-ball bullets.

After Stalin's death, Khrushchev addressed the Supreme Soviet and denounced his predecessor's horrific crimes against the Soviet people. Many in the audience were stunned—the scale of Stalin's evil was mind-boggling. Finally, from the back of the hall, a voice rang out: "Comrade Khrushchev, you were there. You were with Stalin. Why didn't you stop him?" Momentarily flustered, Khrushchev's eyes raked the assembly. "Who said that?" he demanded. "Who said that?" he roared again. Those around the impertinent questioner sank lower in their seats. No voice was raised. No hand went up. After a terrible silence, Khrushchev said, "Now you know why." The questioner that day was no more willing to stand up to Khrushchev than Khrushchev had been willing to stand up to Stalin. The point was made. Luckily, there's no gulag in most companies. But activism still takes courage.

Listen, again, to Thomas Paine:

> Let them call me rebel and welcome, I feel no concern from it;
> but I should suffer the misery of devils, were I to make a whore
> of my soul.

If you find yourself saying a quiet "amen," then you're an activist.

The burden of radical innovation is not yours alone. To survive in the age of revolution, companies must become places where rule-busting innovation flourishes. In the next chapter we'll dig deep into several companies that have reinvented themselves and their industries again and again. From their experiences we can identify the key design criteria for building companies that are activist-friendly and revolution-ready.

7
GRAY-HAIRED REVOLUTIONARIES

ACTIVISTS SHOULDN'T NEED THE COURAGE OF Richard the Lion-Hearted, the patience of Job or the political instincts of Machiavelli to make a difference in their organizations. Sincere but bumbling activists often find themselves outgunned and outmaneuvered by those who've sworn allegiance to the status quo. In the age of revolution we need organizations that celebrate activism. Is this possible? Can the fires of revolutionary fervor be made to burn brightly throughout an organization, rather than only in small pockets of insurgency? As you'll see, the answer is a resounding "yes." Indeed, unless a company can institutionalize activism, it's unlikely to be able to meet the twin challenges of the age of revolution: reinventing itself and reinventing its industry.

REVOLUTION AND RENEWAL

Every organization, large or small, public or private, must be capable of innovating in two quite different ways. First, it must be capable of innovating with respect to its more orthodox peers. Consider, for a moment, the success of the University of Phoenix. With nearly 110,000 degree-seeking students taking classes on 110 campuses spread across 36 states, Puerto Rico and Canada, the University is the largest for-profit educational institution in America. While most universities see their "customers" as 18-year-olds, the University of Phoenix serves working adults of all ages who are eager to complete their university education. Founded in 1976, the University of Phoenix is truly an industry revolutionary. While the school doesn't have an Ivy League pedigree or endowment, its parent company, Apollo Group, has managed to build a business with a market value of more than $5 billion.

But it's not enough to innovate with respect to convention-bound competitors. A company must also be able to innovate with respect to its own past—this is often the more difficult challenge. The University of Phoenix has made a great start at reinventing its core business. The school currently has nearly 34,000 students enrolled in its pioneering online programs. Indeed, on its own, the University of Phoenix Online is bigger than all but a handful of traditional universities. With its own share listing, UoP Online was worth $350 million in early 2002. It's not a coincidence the overarching corporate values of the Apollo Group are innovation and inspiration.

Companies that are incapable of changing either themselves or their industry have no alternatives to retrenchment. They are the dead and

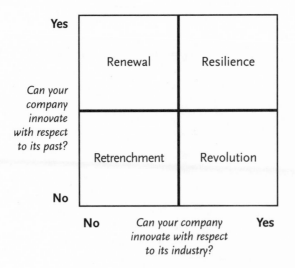

the dying, the no-hopers. They're acquisition fodder for more imaginative companies that will redeploy their skills and assets.

Companies that are incapable of leading an industry revolution are often slow-moving incumbents caught in perpetual catch-up mode. Think of Merrill Lynch and online trading, or Motorola and digital mobile phones, or Xerox and printers. All too often, incumbents reinvent their strategies only under duress—only when it becomes patently and painfully obvious that they've missed a critical opportunity. When they finally get around to the challenge of renewal, they do little more than ape the strategies of less orthodox competitors. However successful the ensuing makeover, top management deserves little credit, and even less recompense, for tagging along at the end of someone else's revolutionary parade.

On the other hand, the world is filled with one-strategy wonders—industry revolutionaries that were capable of changing an industry, but have yet to demonstrate that they are capable of changing themselves. Even the most brilliant strategy loses its economic effectiveness over time—this is the process of strategy decay. Any company that can't uncouple its long-term sense of identity from its initial strategy will end up as an industry footnote. Apple Computer, Body Shop, Kmart, Novell—these are just a few of the one-time industry revolutionaries who've never led a second revolution. Companies that have come to rely on a strong, entrepreneurial CEO find it particularly difficult to reinvent themselves. The simple fact is that most visionaries don't stay visionary forever. Renewal can't depend on a single individual having a second epiphany; rather the capacity for renewal must be baked deeply into the organization—into its attitudes, values, processes and systems.

Companies that are capable of both revolution and renewal are truly resilient—these are the companies that have the best chance of prospering in the tumultuous times that lie ahead. As we will see, there are revolutionaries like Charles Schwab (the pioneer of discount stock trading) that manage to reinvent themselves. And there are near hundred-year-old incumbents, like UPS and Cemex, that are able to reinvent both themselves and their industries. These are the "gray-haired revolutionaries," and they are the rarest breed of all. **Their gray hair comes not from years, but from the experience of having lived through several strategy "lifetimes."** They have done more than extend a legacy or enlarge a franchise. They have repeatedly turned themselves inside out and their industries upside down.

For every gray-haired revolutionary, there are dozens of incumbents still living off momentum and hundreds of start-ups that can't see beyond their IPOs. Even among the thin but vaunted ranks of gray-haired revolutionaries, there are no unqualified exemplars. There are no "excellent" companies. No company has totally cracked the code of the new innovation agenda. No company has yet fully internalized the new innovation regime with its focus on big, rule-busting ideas and radical entrepreneurship. But we can learn a lot from those that have made a start. In the pages that follow we'll learn from UPS, a company that has leveraged its unique competencies and assets to create a new multibillion-dollar business. We'll review the history of Charles Schwab, a serial innovator that has transformed itself into a quintessential e-business. Finally, we'll take an inside look at the unlikely success of Cemex, a company that has not only created new businesses and reinvented its core business, but has also committed itself to making innovation an everywhere, all-the-time capability.

UPS: GETTING OUTSIDE THE TRUCK

If you've ever had a cell phone break while under warranty, you know that all you had to do was call your wireless carrier and by the next day a new phone was on its way to you along with a prepaid postage label and a box to return the faulty phone. But did you know that if your carrier is Sprint PCS, the phone you sent back was never touched by a Sprint employee? Neither was the phone that was sent back to you. That new phone came straight from one of 500 warehouse and stocking locations throughout the country maintained by UPS, and the broken phone went to a cavernous UPS facility in Louisville, Kentucky, where its Service Parts Logistics business operates a repair operation. That's right, UPS brought you your new phone, and repaired your old one. And you thought all "Brown" did was deliver packages.

What is even more surprising is that this relatively new, and certainly creative, business is able to flourish in a highly disciplined, 95-year-old company like UPS with $30 billion in revenues and 370,000 employees. This is a company where, only a decade earlier, the decision to let employees decide how often to wash the company's ubiquitous brown trucks was hailed as a major break with the past. (Previously, a corporate policy had decreed that each truck was to be washed every day, whether dirty or not.) It's hard to imagine how such a buttoned-down place could give rise to a business that repairs returned cell phones, computers and medical equipment, and handles all the logistics to boot. Yet just two years after it had been formed, the

Service Parts Logistics was already ringing up hundreds of millions in sales. Moreover, this business is part of a larger UPS Logistics subsidiary that stores and delivers all Nike.com's shoes and helps Ford move its cars from factory to showroom. It took a mere five years for UPS Logistics to go from launch to an annual revenue run of $1 billion. "Within ten years," predicts former UPS Logistics CEO Dan DiMaggio (now president of UPS Supply Chain Solutions), "people will see us as a supply chain management company."

For most of its history, whether it was delivering parcels for department stores in the 1920s or for e-tailers in the 1990s, UPS maintained a maniacal focus on moving small packages efficiently from one place to another. In an engineering culture that prided itself on timeliness and accuracy, its drivers were measured to the second and trained in everything from how to hold their keys to what foot to put in their trucks first. In 1991, its highly focused corporate strategy statement was to "achieve worldwide leadership in package distribution." By 1999, that had changed to the much more expansive aspiration to "enable global commerce." UPS is aiming to do more than simply help its customers move their packages; it also wants to help facilitate the movement of the information and funds related to those goods. "We are always thinking about how to expand the definition of our markets," says recently retired senior vice president of corporate strategy Jack Duffy, of the company's new attitude. "We have all been trained to be constructively dissatisfied." It is that constructive dissatisfaction which helps UPS avoid being trapped by the constraints of its 95-year-old core business.

CEO Mike Eskew agrees with DiMaggio and Duffy's assessments of how the company is changing. "We've always been real good at analyzing the movement of goods as they go through our system," says Eskew, "and at trying to determine where to build buildings, and what kind of planes to buy, and where to position them. What we are doing more of now is helping our customers understand their information better, helping them streamline their processes, minimize their inventories and help them save some money. Really, what we are doing is to help streamline their supply chains."

This new outlook has been ten years in the making. UPS is a company that pays attention to small details and deviations. Duffy, a 30-year veteran, remembers working in New York City as a regional operations manager in the early 1990s: "Every day I would have to give a report to my executives about vehicles that broke down, the 100 packages that didn't get delivered, about the conveyor belt that broke down." It was this low fault-tolerance that alerted its executives to the early, subtle signs of strategy decay. UPS was still growing in the early 1990s, but the rate of growth, both in revenues and in the number of packages carried, was slowing. Margins were flattening. And the customer and employee satisfaction indexes that UPS measures religiously had peaked and were also flattening or declining slightly.

Rather than wait for a full-blown crisis, UPS decided to tackle the problems head-on, while the company was still healthy. It pursued a massive reengineering effort in which drivers were given more flexibility to determine their routes and generate sales leads. Suddenly it was okay to do things differently, as long as it did not affect the integrity of UPS's delivery network. The management ranks were trimmed 16 percent. Perhaps more important, the company's performance hiccup caused some to begin to question UPS's existing business definition.

This shake-up was all the more remarkable given that the company was still private at the time (its $5.5 billion IPO in 1999 would be one of the largest ever). For most of the century, the company was run as a partnership, which instilled a deep sense of responsibility in the senior executives. "We had a sense that we were given something, and we had to make it better," says Duffy. The senior management at the time decided to encourage some new conversations focused on a future that might extend beyond package delivery. They also came to the difficult conclusion that UPS would have to be willing to experiment with projects whose risk of failure was substantially greater than zero—not an easy decision for a conservative company, dominated by efficiency-minded engineers ever mindful of guaranteeing on-time deliveries.

Within this context, a group of about a dozen next-generation leaders in the company were chartered in 1995 to meet twice a month to explore possible new directions for the company. Named the Information Technology Strategy Committee (ITSC), the group included Duffy, soon-to-be CIO Ken Lacey and Eskew (who was then an industrial engineering VP). There were also representatives from international, UPS's package delivery airline, sales and engineering. "People got involved," recalls Duffy, "because here was a chance to reinvent the company—to create the future." The group's title reflected a belief that information technology would increasingly define the company's future. At the time, senior executives were also concerned that UPS was relying too much on outside vendors and consultants to keep abreast of changing technologies. The problem was, if UPS was hearing about some cutting-edge barcode technology from Gartner or a consultant, so were its competitors. The committee was a way for UPS to develop its own over-the-horizon radar.

UPS had already made a serious commitment to technology. It had introduced its electronic clipboard, the DIAD (delivery information acquisition device), in 1990 to replace the mounds of paperwork drivers previously had to fill out about each pick-up and drop-off. Information from each DIAD's barcode scanner poured into one of the largest private databases in the world and when the DIAD went wireless in 1993, UPS started leasing the largest private cellular network in the world. The company had a huge data center in New Jersey, and was building a redundant one in Atlanta, complete with server banks, mainframes and two sets each of power lines, fiber feeds, water mains, back-up generators, emergency battery rooms and hurricane-proof concrete walls. But the company had to figure out a way to make this information available to its customers while at the same time creating more efficiencies within its operations. But even as UPS's leaders were turbo-charging the core business with technology, they were also beginning to mull over the question of whether UPS had a future that extended beyond package delivery.

The goal of the ITSC was to create some time and space for reflection and exploration in what was otherwise a tightly controlled and tightly focused organization. The committee afforded its members the chance to learn about new trends, new technologies and new customer needs. Beyond that, it was a safe, nonhierarchical forum in which the implications of those needs, trends and technologies could be debated. The discussions ranged across a diverse set of subjects—from the implications of the then a-borning Internet, to bleeding-edge developments in robotics and mechanical engineering to ideas for how customers could benefit from the masses of information that coursed into UPS's vast data warehouses. Ultimately, the committee would bring in people from all over UPS (it touched at least a thousand other managers) in an attempt to mine the well of pent-up imagination that existed in the company. It also sought the views of outside experts and entrepreneurs. The members frequently went on field trips, and were taught early on how to use the Internet so that each of them could better understand its potential impact.

The ITSC was part seminar and part laboratory, part skunk works and part incubator—a place to think deeply and experiment quickly. Its members had the authority to decide whether or not to try experiments in each of their particular functions. "The group launched hundreds of projects and experiments directly, and probably inspired a lot more," says Duffy. The first thing it did was intercept e-commerce. Already in 1995, rogue Internet users within the company were putting up presentations, marketing materials, sales reports and other information on internal websites. Committee members interviewed these early users and came up with a set of best practices and guidelines for the company's internal use of the Web. They also recommended making package tracking information available to customers on the company's public website, which UPS did in 1995. The group authorized the development of software for large shippers that would link back into UPS databases, and the creation of software modules with standard interfaces that would plug into the enterprise software that its customers had already purchased from vendors such as SAP, PeopleSoft, Oracle or i2 Technologies. Customers such as eBay or Amazon.com would also use these interfaces as they sought to integrate UPS package tracking and returns management software into their own websites. UPS even created a corps of special e-commerce account managers whose job was to infiltrate customers' websites with these tools.

The committee also focused on improvements in material handling, which led to a five-year project to dramatically raise the level of automation at the company's main distribution hub in Louisville, Kentucky. The giant four-million-square-foot facility is filled with conveyor belts zig-zagging about, shoots, slides, digital cameras and barcode readers. Every night, UPS planes disgorge a mind-boggling multitude of packages into this labyrinth that then sorts them at a rate of 300,000 pieces an hour. What used to require legions of human package sorters is now done effortlessly by computer-driven machines. "A fundamental insight came out of the ITSC," says Duffy. "An understanding that we are a technology company with trucks versus a trucking company with technology." This significant insight was to prove the launching pad for a dramatic push into new market territory.

To get an early peek at emerging technologies, the committee created a corporate venture fund. The Strategic Enterprise Fund was started in 1997 and pretty much paid for itself through an early investment in an Atlanta-based B2B software start-up called Tradex which was sold to Ariba, netting UPS $200 million when it sold its Ariba shares near their peak in 2000. But unlike other corporate venture funds that were little more than an attempt to ride the dot-com boom, the UPS fund was set up from the get-go as a way to garner strategic insights. For instance, UPS was able to both profit and learn from Tradex, which helped UPS fine-tune its own software modules by being the first external company to adopt them.

"If you are going to have a venture fund, it should contribute back to the core entity," says John Wilson, who now runs the fund. "Before we make an investment," he explains, "both the fund and an operating unit within UPS have to agree there is a learning opportunity. It prevents an operating unit from making a bad investment and me from falling in love with a company." UPS always asked for board observation rights in the companies in which it invested, and that observer would always be pulled from the sponsoring operating unit. This helped to ensure that learning opportunities were fully exploited and that the Strategic Enterprise Fund didn't spend its money on completely tangential opportunities.

The venture fund served as a listening post, keeping UPS executives attuned to the ever-changing winds of technology and to innovations occurring outside the boundaries of their own experience base. It also helped them test their own conceptions of what business opportunities UPS might pursue in the future. The fund's purpose was threefold: to learn about new technologies that might be useful to UPS or its customers (and learn about them early); to be aware of rapidly emerging markets for which UPS might want to create new products or services; and to study novel business models to understand whether they posed any threat or could be adopted within UPS. So, for instance, the fund invested in a start-up called Savi Technologies to gain insight into the progress of radio frequency ID tags. While the cheapest tags (which currently cost about fifty cents each) are still too expensive to affix to every package, they could become a viable alternative to barcodes as their price drops. Similarly, the Strategic Enterprise Fund invested in Air2Web, a company that specializes in putting software applications on wireless devices. UPS also adopted Air2Web's technology and began to offer it as an additional way for customers to track packages, locate drop-off centers and figure out shipping costs.

The fund also helped UPS de-risk new opportunities in unproven markets and business models. One investment in particular prevented UPS from potentially wasting hundreds of millions or even billions of dollars. The start-up, Highpoint Systems, was developing specialized order entry software for grocery chains that needed to respond to the spate of home-delivery competitors such as WebVan and Peapod. In the fall of 2000, Highpoint's president helped UPS design a pilot delivery project with eight nonbranded trucks in a Northeastern city. The project tested the viability of delivering both groceries and dry cleaning. "We determined that the business economics would not be sustainable," says Wilson. Try as it might, UPS could not get the density of deliveries per hour up to a high enough level (six to eight was the goal) to make the business profitable. Everyone wanted deliveries at night, so the trucks and drivers stood unused during most of the day. Through its relationship with Highpoint, UPS confirmed that other such e-commerce grocery delivery businesses were running into the same problems. After a relatively inexpensive experiment costing a few million dollars (including the $1 million invested in Highpoint), UPS pulled the plug, an option that a company like WebVan did not have. In the end, it was a way for UPS to take an appropriately tentative stance on an opportunity riddled with uncertainty.

Though the strategy group was tasked to look beyond UPS's existing businesses, it didn't regard its mission as developing a diversification strategy. Rather, it was to find ways of leveraging the company's strategic assets and core capabilities to *create* new billion-dollar businesses under the broad umbrella of "enabling commerce." For instance, the committee pondered the fact that its drivers captured millions of signature every day on their DIADs, and wondered whether those signatures could constitute a proof of delivery, which would trigger an automatic payment between the recipient and sender. It was ideas like this that led to the launch of UPS Capital, which was established in 1998 as a separate subsidiary to create financial products related to the movement of goods. These included expedited C.O.D. payments, trade credit, credit insurance and electronic invoices. The strategy group also contributed to the formation of the service parts business in the same year.

Over the past five years, UPS's sense of what it is has changed dramatically. Who the company regards as its competitors has also changed. As the supply-chain outsourcing market develops, it will open up UPS to competition from more than just FedEx, Deutsche Post's DHL and the world's mail carriers. "We will end up competing with Accenture and IBM," says Duffy.

Going into logistics represents a major broadening of UPS's scope of operations. The small package delivery market is about a $100 billion industry, and UPS owns 30 percent of that. However, the global logistics and transportation industry is worth approximately $3 trillion— this includes about $1.5 trillion for physical transportation and another $1.5 trillion in other logistics-related services such as warehousing. That's a big opportunity—even for a $30 billion company. DiMaggio, who oversees the combined sales, product development and supply-chain consulting efforts for the logistics, freight forwarding and customs brokerage businesses, thinks the near-term addressable market within that much bigger opportunity is at least $150 billion—that's $150 billion worth of services that lie outside of UPS's traditional package transportation business. That's enough opportunity to keep UPS busy for quite some time—and to drive a whole lot of new growth. Indeed, while UPS's top-line growth was just 3 percent in 2001, the company's nonpackage segment, of which UPS Logistics is the biggest chunk, grew by an impressive 42 percent.

UPS will do anything it can to get a piece of that $150 billion market. Its UPS Logistics subsidiary manages warehouses, trucking fleets, ships, air cargo and all the information transfers required to get customers' inventories from factory to market. Sometimes it uses UPS trucks and planes, sometimes it contracts out to third parties—whatever makes the most sense for the customer. Of course, more than half the time it ends up using the UPS delivery network, driving even more volume through the UPS system and thus keeping it fully utilized.

As UPS broadened its vision to include the world of logistics, it was quick to realize that it didn't possess all the competencies that would be needed to succeed in the logistics space. Working diligently to acquire the new skills, the company has purchased a handful of smaller logistics players. Acquisitions were important in accessing new skills, but so were new hires. About three quarters of the employees who work at UPS Logistics come from outside the parent company and are conversant in the unique logistical challenges of industries such as health care, electronics and apparel.

By 2002, UPS had invested $800 million in its logistics business. But the $800 million didn't get spent all at once. Over and over again, DiMaggio has had to earn the right to up the stakes by meeting strict revenue growth and operating margin targets. UPS isn't going to take a flyer on some far-fetched dream. The logistics business has had to earn its right to explore new opportunity space, dollar-by-dollar.

"I'd be very disappointed if our growth rate in the logistics business was less than 25 percent," says DiMaggio, who sees his role as helping to decommoditize UPS's revenue streams. For instance, in a deal closed in early 2002, UPS won the right to revamp and manage the entire global supply chain of semiconductor equipment manufacturer Applied Materials. After months of carefully studying Applied's various logistics networks, DiMaggio's team suggested ways to rearrange the relationships between Applied and its customers and suppliers. "We're almost like consultants solving their business problems," says DiMaggio. He wants his customers to think of him as a trusted adviser, just like they would Accenture or IBM. Only UPS brings 88,000 trucks and 600 airplanes, as well as systems and software.

The story of how UPS created its service parts logistics business is indicative of how the company works its way into new opportunity areas. In 1998, the ITSC was looking at UPS's IT infrastructure and wondering if perhaps it could outsource some excess capacity in its warehouses, call centers or data centers. It explored these notions for six months, asking customers for their input. The data center management business proved untenable. There were also some challenging barriers to developing a third-party call center business. Michael Dell told a visiting UPS delegation that he would never outsource his call centers because that is one of the key ways his company learns about consumer desires and frustrations. But as the team kept mulling over ways in which it might use its assets to build businesses that would be nonthreatening to its current customers, it struck upon a quite different opportunity.

When UPS went to talk to computer makers like Dell and Hewlett-Packard, it noticed a common, albeit unvoiced, need. Hardware manufacturers all seemed to be having problems with managing their spare parts inventory. Duffy explains: "We came across an inefficiency that [original equipment manufacturers] had in terms of parts replacement—each OEM had their own system, even though most of the parts were standard. We realized that if we could consolidate all this, and then go to the IBMs, Compaqs and Dells, we could help them manage their parts inventory much more efficiently." Not knowing what repair challenge they might face next, computer technicians tend to keep a broad range of spare parts in the trunks of their cars. In an industry where the value of parts goes down every week, and many become obsolete within a matter of months, this "trunk inventory" was a huge waste.

For a company that makes a science out of getting things in and out of vehicles as quickly as possible, the very notion of "trunk inventory" was abhorrent to UPS. There had to be a better way. UPS could place the parts in a nationwide network of stock houses and manage them so that it could get a part to a technician within four hours of a call. UPS could also supplement these stock houses with same-day air delivery service via Sonic Air, a company UPS had acquired a few years earlier. After the service parts business was launched Sonic Air's revenue growth went from the low-single digits a year to 100 percent a year.

One key to renewal is the capacity to reinterpret your own history. In a way, the service parts logistics business was a reprise of an earlier UPS strategy. In the 1920s, department stores like Macy's, Saks and Gimbles each maintained their own fleet of trucks, just like IBM, Dell and HP maintained their own inventory of service parts in the 1990s. At the time, UPS founder Jim Casey convinced the otherwise fiercely competitive department stores to let UPS consolidate their deliveries. More than 70 years later, UPS would be consolidating and managing the global flow of spare parts for a group of otherwise bitter rivals in the computer industry.

Renewal is also about balancing what you are with what you could be. UPS has been able to do that by managing the tension between the need to experiment and grow while maintaining tight operational discipline within the core business. "We have [new] subsidiaries," explains Eskew. "They are nimble, entrepreneurial, innovative, quick. We tell them to try new things and fail small and fast. That is what our subsidiaries do. On the other hand our core company requires precision. You have to be deliberate and consistent across 200 countries because customers expect the same experience all across the world." The new and the old are tightly intertwined at UPS. New businesses such as UPS Logistics and UPS Capital are demand multipliers for the core business. Additionally, they leverage the enormous breadth of competencies UPS has assembled over the years. The new and the old play equally critical parts in the mosaic of enabling global commerce. A decade ago, few would have guessed that a company so disciplined in its quest to optimize what already is, could successfully create a capacity to explore what could be. Yet this is exactly what this gray-haired revolutionary has done.

LESSONS FROM A GRAY-HAIRED REVOLUTIONARY:

The essential foundation of UPS's capacity to leverage its assets and competencies are these:

○ An *out-sized aspiration* to grab a big chunk of the $1.5 trillion global logistics business—a sense of an enormous opportunity, there for the taking.
○ A *broad definition of business boundaries* (not package delivery but enabling global commerce), based on a deep understanding of the company's core competencies in transportation logistics, package tracking and handling and information systems.
○ A *learn-as-you-go* approach to new business development, which puts a premium on experimentation and rapid learning.
○ A willingness to bring in *new voices* to fuel the innovation effort. The ITSC tapped the imagination of hundreds of UPS employees as it explored the new growth options.

There are precious few companies that ever manage to create new multibillion-dollar businesses from within. Even more rare is an ability to reconfigure the profit engine in a company's core business. This is akin to changing jet engines in mid–flight. Yet this is exactly what Charles Schwab has accomplished—more than once.

CHARLES SCHWAB: BRICKS AND CLICKS

David Pottruck, president and co–CEO at Charles Schwab, puts it this way: "We're change junkies. We're addicted to change." Born a rule–breaker, Charles Schwab & Co. led its first revolution when it helped to create the discount brokerage industry by undercutting the steep fees of traditional brokers such as Merrill Lynch and PaineWebber. Its second revolution came with OneSource, a mutual fund supermarket that eventually let investors choose from more than a thousand different funds. Before OneSource it was difficult for investors to move assets between funds, and anyone with more than a few investments received a bewildering array of statements every month. By the late 1990s, Schwab's convenient one–stop shop for mutual funds had accumulated 10 percent of America's mutual fund assets in no–load funds and the company no longer relied so heavily on trading revenues. Between 1993 and 1998, the percentage of Schwab's revenues coming from commissions on stock trading had declined from 75 percent to 58 percent, attesting to the revolution in Schwab's business concept. Schwab's metamorphosis from discount broker to mutual fund powerhouse is only one of several strategy transformations Schwab has accomplished. Each metamorphosis has threatened to undermine historic sources of profitability, yet each has ultimately paid off by bringing customers fundamentally new benefits. Before OneSource, Schwab charged its clients a fee for the convenience of buying mutual funds in one place. Customers could avoid the fee by buying their no–load funds directly from the issuing investment companies. Irked that customers should have to pay more at Schwab than elsewhere, David Pottruck, then an executive vice president, was one of those who argued for doing away with the fee. Others at Schwab protested that this would cut the profitability of the company's mutual fund business in half. Ultimately the interests of the customer prevailed, and Schwab was able to recoup the lost fees by charging a small processing fee to the companies whose mutual funds Schwab was selling.

Schwab fought the cannibalization demon a second time when the company morphed itself into the nation's leading online broker. Deciding to make cheap Web trading available to all its customers was a gut–wrenching decision that slashed the company's commission for those trades by more than half. But by late 1999, Schwab boasted three million Internet customers with more than $260 billion in online assets (rival E*TRADE's assets were only one-tenth that size). With its Web offerings, Schwab recast itself as a new kind of full-service broker and entered the Age of Advice, coming full circle from its early days when it thought "advice" was a dirty word. "We are reinventing the full-service investing business and ourselves at the same time," says Pottruck. Schwab's conception of who it serves has also been a moving target. During its first decade, for instance, Schwab thought of itself as a no-frills broker that catered to sophisticated traders. Yet even within the discount brokerage industry, Schwab bucked conventional wisdom. Instead of sticking to a low-overhead, phone-based business, it started to build a network of branches. Chuck Schwab figured that people wanted to feel physically close to their money. This insight paid off handsomely when the company began to broaden its target audience. As investing became democratized—first through mutual funds, then via the Web—Schwab found that its branches were terrific for capturing neophyte investors because they gave Schwab bricks-and-mortar credibility. In 1999 customers opened more than one million new accounts at Schwab. Many of these investors had never had a broker before. In the process Schwab became one of the first "clicks-and-mortar" companies, with a business concept that optimized both its online and its offline presence.

Schwab's knack for reinvention and finding new business models has allowed it to thrive where others have foundered. It long ago zoomed past Quick & Reilly, its toughest competitor in the 1970s. From 1993 to 1998, Schwab's revenues grew at an average annual rate of 23 percent to $2.7 billion, and its earnings grew at an average annual rate of 24 percent to $350 million. During the same period, its stock price zoomed up 1,072 percent, as compared with 218 percent for Merrill Lynch and 164 percent for the S&P 500. In December 1998, Schwab's market capitalization surpassed that of Merrill Lynch for the first time ever. No one in the brokerage industry doubts that Schwab has been a revolutionary more than once.

IN LOVE WITH CUSTOMERS

SCHWAB HAS NEVER LET ITSELF BECOME TRAPPED IN ANY ONE PARTICULAR BUSINESS MODEL. Jeff Lyons, head of mutual fund marketing, says, "We have a hard time defining ourselves. We're uncomfortable with any of the labels." Rather, Schwab has always defined itself in terms of its cause, which is to serve investors by doing whatever it takes to help them secure and improve their financial lives. "When Chuck Schwab started the company," says John McGonigle, who runs the mutual funds group, "his goal was to make it a place where he would feel comfortable doing business as an investor. Chuck is the voice of the customer." One of the company's widely communicated and deeply held values is customer empathy, and Chuck Schwab is its foremost apostle. Says Bob Duste, CEO of Schwab Europe:

> I have never heard Chuck raving on about returns, profits or the share price. He is always talking about customers. He believes we need to do more to teach people how to invest—not for us, but for them. If we do right by the customer, he knows profitability will take care of itself. Chuck goes once a month to serve soup to old people at a Salvation Army kitchen. He says, "If they would have started early and planned, they could have avoided this, and it just breaks my heart. We have to have better products and reach more people."

Schwab's rank and file see their jobs not just as processing transactions, but as protecting some of the most precious things in a customer's life: the ability to send a kid to college, to support an elderly parent or to retire stress-free. "We think we're curing cancer," says chief strategist Dan Leemon.

Schwab has repeatedly found the courage to challenge industry dogmas by working from the customer backward. While other parts of the financial services industry seem to look on customer ignorance as a profit center, Schwab always assumes it is serving a very discerning customer—even when it is not. Comments McGonigle: "What distinguishes Schwab from most of the other financial services companies is that we presume that our customers are really smart and we're not going to pull anything over on them. We don't think we can fool them on fees or execution."

Schwab's unconventional strategies have often left competitors scrambling. It took Fidelity six years to fully embrace the idea of a mutual fund supermarket like OneSource because it was loath to carry competing products and surrender some of its management fees to other companies.

Schwab complements its customer worship with bold growth targets. Says Art Shaw, a senior VP:

Every year we feel we have to grow 20 percent. Every year we have to say that last year is over, and we're starting from zero. This creates an incredible desire to innovate. Only about 10 percent of large companies have grown both their revenues and earnings 20 percent per year for five years in a row.

Schwab sees itself as addressing a nearly limitless market. Of America's $15 trillion in savings, only 4 percent sits in discount brokerage accounts, and Schwab itself holds only about $600 billion. Its goal is to grab $1 trillion worth of assets before 2005 and nearly double its number of active customers to 10 million.

Besides its ardor for customers and ambitious growth goals, there are two other forces powering innovation at Schwab. The first is the opportunity that every employee has for wealth creation. Every employee at Schwab is a shareholder. Says CFO Steve Scheid, "One of the best financial disciplines is having your largest shareholder walking the halls thinking about serving customers." McGonigle, who previously worked at a giant bank, says, "At Schwab, the customer and the shareholder are preeminent. At my bank they were theoretical constructs."

The other spur for innovation is a meritocracy that welcomes new ideas. At Schwab the champions of innovation have been consistently promoted out of rank and out of order. Jeff Lyons, John McGonigle and Bob Duste were all activists who got early passes to an executive suite. "Everyone in top management had a big idea when they were more junior," says Susanne Lyons, Jeff's wife and another innovation activist at Schwab. She adds, "Each of us did something with our idea and got rewarded for it." Around Schwab, Susanne Lyons is known as the "Queen of Segmentation." When she first arrived at Schwab in 1992 from Fidelity, Schwab's approach to customers was pretty much one size fits all. Every customer had to call the same 1–800 numbers and got the same plain–vanilla service, whether they had $3,000 in their account or $300,000. But Lyons noticed that an elite group of customers known as the "Schwab 500," which included some of Chuck Schwab's friends and acquaintances, was getting special, personalized service from a small team of eight account representatives. She thought, "Why not replicate this on a much bigger scale? We could have these small teams serving affluent investors." Her enthusiasm ran headlong into a wall of resistance because most folks at Schwab thought the notion of a premium service conflicted with the company's core value of treating the small investor well and every investor alike. So she started collecting data on Schwab's more affluent customers and its most active traders. She discovered that although they represented only 20 percent of Schwab's customer base, they accounted for an astounding 80 percent of its trading revenues. Now she had the ammunition to argue for the expansion of the Schwab 500 and to help her colleagues rethink their definition of "fairness." Why shouldn't investors who brought more value to Schwab get more value in return? Wasn't that simply fair? This logic won most people over.

Starting with the customers already in the Schwab 500, Lyons launched the service in 1994. It was targeted at investors who traded more than 48 times a year (later reduced to 24 and then to 12) or people with more than $100,000 in assets. Schwab started using Caller ID technology to automatically route calls from high–asset individuals to the special teams. A live person was available 24 hours a day, thus providing a level of round–the–clock personal service unmatched by traditional brokerages. Each eight–person team was given responsibility for a specific set of accounts, so that a customer could be assured of always talking to someone who really did understand his or her particular situation. Each team comprised individuals representing a broad spectrum of investment expertise. By 1999, around 750,000 customers were enrolled in Schwab 500, which had been renamed "Signature Services."

LEAPING ONTO THE WEB

Susanne Lyons's story is not unique. **Most of Schwab's mega-innovations have been built on a series of mini-innovations, driven by individuals who've learned to live inside their customers' skins.** Dramatic business concept breakthroughs such as Signature Services and schwab.com are more often the product of a string of rule-bending experiments than some grand strategic leap— more like a tireless climber bounding up a spiral staircase than Superman leaping over tall buildings in a single bound. In the same way that Schwab 500 prepared the way for Signature Services, a long string of technology–oriented experiments helped Schwab beat many of its traditional competitors to the Web.

A few of Schwab's early experiments with technology, such as its StreetSmart dial–up trading software, were modest successes, but most were dismal failures. In 1982, for instance, Schwab came out with the PocketTerm, a bulky, portable contraption that could receive stock quotes over the airwaves. In 1985, it unveiled SchwabLine, a device that, when connected to a phone line, would spit out quotes on an extra–wide roll of adding machine tape. Schwab also developed a slew of stock–trading software programs that bombed. Nevertheless, the young innovation addicts at Schwab were encouraged to build these early flying machines.

Every so often, Schwab's penchant for experimentation would turn up a winner. TeleBroker was an idea that came from outside Schwab. In 1989, a small start–up came to Schwab and demoed a technology that would allow investors to check quotes and trade stocks using the keypad on a Touch–Tone telephone. Schwab's call centers were constantly busy, and here was an inexpensive way to increase the number of calls it could handle without hiring more people. Duste, who was head of software engineering at the time, took the idea to a senior VP in the retail service group. He ran straight into trouble. Recalls Duste: "The business people thought this was a terrible idea. They thought customers would reject it because customers want to speak with a real person, or wouldn't be able to use the keypad. They couldn't understand it, because they couldn't imagine how it would be used."

Instead of arguing with them, Duste had two of his developers build a demo and roll it out in a pilot test. Customers found its deep, automated voice soothing and telephone trading highly convenient. Within six months, TeleBroker was available to all of Schwab's customers. As one Schwab manager puts it, "Around here the pilot is the first week of the rollout."

By 1995, about a fifth of Schwab's trading volume was going through TeleBroker and StreetSmart. And with the promise of the Internet glistening on the horizon, Duste worked with a few passionate technologists to build another demo to show Pottruck and Chuck Schwab that they could do TeleBroker on the Web. When Schwab saw the demo, he was dumbfounded. "I fell off my chair," he later told *Fortune*. Duste and his colleagues didn't write an elaborate strategy paper on how the Web would transform investing. Instead they gave Schwab and Pottruck a first–person, hands–on experience of Web trading. Pottruck immediately set up a Web–trading unit called e.Schwab. It was up and running on the Web by mid–1996 and attracted 25,000 customers in its first two weeks.

But as the Web blossomed, cracks in the e.Schwab business model started to appear. Customers who used e.Schwab were given a 40 percent discount off the company's usual charges, but Schwab was still twice as expensive as E*TRADE. And there was another catch: Schwab's online clients were not allowed to call Schwab's phone representatives or visit its branches—they had to agree to do all their business over the Web. A traditional Schwab customer who wanted to trade online had to set up a new account. Pottruck wanted to do away with this dual structure, but there was a lot of concern among the senior officers that doing so would hammer profits. They thought that encouraging traditional customers to trade online would cannibalize transaction fees. Conversely, it was feared that the fees generated by new online customers wouldn't be sufficient to cover the cost of in-person service at Schwab branches or phone help from Schwab's call centers.

But once again, the desire to do right by the customer overcame the initial concern over cannibalization. As one senior executive put it:

> We asked ourselves whether Internet trading was the right thing to do for the customer—and the answer was "yes." It would mean better information, more timely information, quicker access to their account, and so on. Once this was clear, we knew we had to make the move sooner rather than later. We couldn't wait until we had an ironclad business case. It's our responsibility, not the customer's, to figure out how to make money in the new Internet business model.

In January 1998, Web trading was opened up to all Schwab customers and e.Schwab was rechristened schwab.com. By the end of the year, 61 percent of all Schwab's trades were being completed over the Web. Between the first quarter of 1998 and the first quarter of 1999, Schwab gained nearly one million new customers (almost all of them online), commissions increased 60 percent, online assets doubled and total assets were up 33 percent.

Could Schwab have beaten Merrill Lynch and other traditional brokers to the Web without a succession of earlier mini-innovations? Most at Schwab doubt it. Customer behavior and business concepts seldom get changed in one fell swoop. **Schwab's relentless pursuit of a better customer experience had once again paved the way for a radical rebirth of the company's strategy.**

OVERCOMING ORTHODOXY

Success typically turns beliefs into unquestioned orthodoxy. Yet unlike most companies, Schwab has again and again challenged its deep-seated beliefs. For example, since the company's founding, Schwab has had an aversion to giving advice and hawking proprietary products. As a result, the company has avoided the kind of conflict-of-interest dilemmas that have bedeviled other investment firms. Schwab's image of studied neutrality has long been highly valued by customers. But a wave of newbie customers, who are far less sophisticated than Schwab's original high–volume traders, has forced the company to revisit this particular bit of dogma.

Explains Pottruck:

> For a long time we thought advice was a self–serving path. That was the reality we saw in the rest of the investing industry. Advice always had a self–serving motive, whether it was to push proprietary products or to get paid for the trade. So we said, "We don't give advice." We no longer have that luxury. Today, in excess of 50 percent of our new customers have no investing experience. They don't want us to just give them a brochure.

Schwab was able to move beyond the advice/neutrality impasse only once it realized that this was a false dichotomy—that values and habits could be separated. Says Art Shaw:

> Giving advice has nothing to do with our values, but avoiding conflict of interest does. Advice had a lot of connotations from the world we left behind—we had an allergic reaction to advice. So we had to ask a new question: "How do you give advice without a conflict of interest?"

So in 1994, Schwab launched AdvisorSource, a network of some of its independent money managers to which it began to refer customers who felt they needed counsel. The company has also launched several index–linked funds under the Schwab brand name, a move that lets Schwab keep more mutual fund profit in–house, but keeps the firm out of the stock–picking game. And of course it provides investment research tools on the Web as a form of self-directed advice.

The double whammy of September 11 and the economic recession pummeled the earnings of every financial services company—and Schwab was no exception. Like many other brokerages, Schwab announced a loss for the fourth quarter of 2001—its first loss since the stock market crash of 1987. But with client accounts totaling more than $840 billion, Schwab is still the undisputed king of the discount brokers. And those who know Schwab's people and their penchant for unconventional thinking and customer–centric innovation have little doubt that the company will emerge from difficult times stronger than ever. After all, innovation can't protect a company from a macroeconomic meltdown, but it can soften the blow and raise the odds of a rapid rebound.

LESSONS FROM A GRAY-HAIRED REVOLUTIONARY:

Schwab's capacity for relentless innovation is a product of:

○ *Outrageously ambitious growth* objectives that are simply unattainable without business concept innovation.
○ A *heart-felt customer empathy* that ensures that employees are always working from the customer in, rather than from their existing processes and offerings out.
○ An *innovation meritocracy* where great ideas win out, no matter where they come from.
○ *Rapid experimentation and prototyping* that let innovators test and define new ideas at a speed that leaves traditional competitors breathless.
○ A *loose and evolving definition of the service offering*, which ensures that Schwab doesn't get boxed in by its own orthodoxies.

So maybe your company isn't in a business that is quite as exhilarating as stock trading. Given all the changes in financial services over the past decade (deregulation, the explosive growth of the mutual fund industry and the market rally of the late 1990s), there have been a lot of opportunities for nimble incumbents and ambitious upstarts to change the rules. Perhaps you're asking, how do you innovate in an industry that seems completely and utterly boring? Good question. Where would you begin if your core business was cement?

CEMEX: NOTHING IS SET IN CEMENT

If there was ever any question that adversity breeds creativity, one need only take a drive through the hardscrabble city of Monterrey, Mexico's industrial capital and the headquarters of Cemex, the country's most innovative multinational cement producer. The cement industry isn't the most obvious place to search for examples of revolution and renewal, but then again, neither is Mexico. But Cemex is no ordinary clinker. As the third–largest cement company in the world, Cemex enjoys operating margins that are nearly twice as high as those of its two global rivals—France's Lafarge and Switzerland's Holcim. In 2001, a tough year in general for the world economy, Cemex's sales managed to expand a healthy 23 percent to $6.9 billion, and its profits grew at about the same clip, to $1.3 billion. Success on this scale would have seemed wildly improbable a scant decade earlier, when Cemex's very independence was threatened by the decision to open the Mexican market to foreign competition. With a peso–denominated balance sheet, Cemex faced a significant cost of capital disadvantage vis–à–vis its international competitors. (The 1994 peso freefall did not help matters, either.) But hardship isn't exactly a novelty in Northern Mexico, and Cemex's disadvantages forced the ambitious company to innovate in ways few of its competitors could have anticipated or matched. Along the way, Cemex proved there's no such thing as a mature industry, only mature thinking.

Cemex is proof positive **that new attitudes and new values can change an old industry**—in the case of Cemex, attitudes like curiosity and experimentation, and values like ambition and persistence. To put it simply, the more conventional the industry, the greater the power of unconventional thinking. "We understand our real business is helping our customers complete their construction projects," CEO Lorenzo Zambrano told a Stanford University audience in January 2002. "At the end of the day, no one *wants* to buy cement; they *want* to build a house or a bridge or a road." In contrast, the conventional attitude in this industry is: We make the cement, the customer worries about what to do with it. At the root of the company's restless innovation is an inbred dissatisfaction with the status quo and an unquenchable thirst for growth. "There is this ever-present search for something that is better than what we are doing," says executive VP of Planning and Finance Hector Medina. "We have a passion for growth," adds Juan Romero, president of Cemex Mexico.

This passion has spawned dozens of growth initiatives across the company—from GPS-guided delivery trucks to cheaper fuels to new methods for building houses in the developing world. Cemex has demonstrated a capability to reinvent its core business while exploring white spaces where new businesses may emerge. It stokes the fires of innovation by combining and recombining networks of curious people with diverse backgrounds who together find unorthodox solutions to customer problems.

Founded by Lorenzo Zambrano's grandfather in 1906, Cemex remained a venerable, family-owned enterprise until 1976 when it first offered shares on the Mexican stock exchange (its ADRs began trading on the New York Stock Exchange much later, in 1999). Zambrano, an engineer and Stanford-trained MBA, took over as CEO in 1985. Eager to push the company beyond its tradition-bound roots as a regional cement producer, Zambrano started by broadening the company's management team, hiring executives from a range of other industries. One of Zambrano's key hires was Gelacio Iñiguez as chief information officer. Starting from scratch, Iñiguez committed himself to building a common IT infrastructure throughout the company so that executives and plant managers could learn from each other and build a foundation of common business knowledge. "I knew we had to remove any barriers that would inhibit human interaction," recalls Iñiguez. "We needed to share practices from north to south and east to west."

Understandably, plant managers were less eager to remove the barriers that had long protected their local prerogatives. In the late 1980s, even basic phone service was often patchy. It was common practice among plant managers to tell their secretaries to take messages for incoming corporate phone calls, knowing it would take three or four hours for the caller to get another connection. In the meantime, the plant manager would be able to develop a well-reasoned answer to the corporate inquiry. This practice highlighted the appalling lack of communication within the company. Not surprisingly, one of Iñiguez' first steps was to install satellite phones at every plant.

Iñiguez was up against more than antiquated technology. Some of the more tradition-minded executives at Cemex thought that spending money on IT was a frivolous waste of money. They were initially dismissive of Iñiguez' efforts: "We don't need this approach—cement sells itself." At the time, this was a common perception both inside Cemex and across the industry. Demand for cement went up and down with GNP growth—that was simply a fact of life, or so the thinking went.

Undeterred, and with Zambrano's backing, Iñiguez pushed on. The satellite system served as the backbone for Cemex's budding internal computer network. It allowed Iñiguez to begin to install a computer platform that linked all the company's plants, warehouses and office locations. The goal was not standardization for its own sake, but rather a common platform that would enable common performance measures and the development of a common base of business knowledge. Once every plant was online, and reporting daily and monthly performance statistics, it would be easy to pinpoint opportunities to transfer local innovation across the company. While this was not exactly a new idea, it was a new idea for the cement industry. Around the world, cement was a classic local-for-local business. Transportation diseconomies limited the catchment area of any individual plant. Even large cement companies treated their plants as autonomous and largely disconnected outposts. From the beginning, Cemex management believed that ideas could be transported

around the world, even if cement could not. They were eager to build a platform that would expedite the spread of new ideas across Cemex.

The IT system was an essential tool for spreading information and learning among Cemex's plants. Before, if a plant manager wanted to improve a production process, he would have to send a written request to the central office for approval. All the reporting and approval lines ran vertically, up to headquarters in Monterrey. There was little sharing of information horizontally across production facilities and commercial organizations. Capital budgeting and planning were centralized but not terribly well coordinated. Plant managers regarded head office bureaucrats as poorly informed and prone to interfere, and were to be avoided at all costs (hence the drawn–out games of phone tag). Local managers reaped few benefits from being part of a company with operations across the Mexican isthmus.

The new IT system started gathering core production and sales data from every plant, making it available to executives on their desktops. The data was presented in a way that even a technophobe could understand—a map of Mexico served as the graphical user interface. The map was dotted with a dozen icons representing each plant. Any executive could click on a dot to obtain a chart of relevant operating data from that business unit such as sales, average energy consumption, number of work stoppages or raw material inventories. Zambrano became one of the most avid users of this system. "Every day at noon, Mr. Z. religiously would log into the executive information system and check what had happened in the last 24 hours," reports Iñiguez. The dots were color–coded green, yellow and red, with a red dot indicating that a plant or sales center was behind its budget forecast. If Mr. Z saw a red pulsating dot, he would personally call the manager of that plant and ask some rather pointed questions.

Suddenly tethered to headquarters by a reliable satellite phone system and computer network, local managers quickly learned that they had better have good answers when Señor Zambrano called. In self-defense, they started using the system themselves. If they saw a sister facility was achieving better results in, say, energy utilization per ton of cement produced, they'd call that manager to find out what he was doing differently. In this way, standard measures and transparent performance metrics fostered greater sharing and cross–collaboration between managers who had only recently ruled over cement-producing islands.

While Zambrano was shaking up the culture internally, he was also expanding externally. He watched warily as the cement industry began to consolidate in the developed economies. He realized that sooner or later Mexico would be compelled to open its long–protected domestic markets. With this in mind, Zambrano moved to sell off Cemex's mining and petrochemical interests—businesses he believed would be a distraction in the coming battle to defend Cemex's core business from foreign invaders. "We saw that our global competitors were all focussed on cement and that they were making investments all over the world," recalls Medina. It was clear to Mr. Z and his top lieutenants that Cemex would have to become a global consolidator itself, or else risk becoming consolidated. "We had to do this to survive," says Medina. So with the proceeds from the divestments, Cemex began doing some acquiring of its own, plunking down $1 billion for competitors in Mexico that might otherwise be attractive acquisition targets for Lafarge, Holcim or some other multinational.

Ever mindful of the company's high cost of capital (which hovered in the high teens, versus the middle single digits for its European and American counterparts), Zambrano challenged the organization to innovate in ways that would more than compensate for this cost deficit. The result: hundreds of opportunities for improvements in the manufacture and distribution of cement—improvements that rapidly migrated from plant to plant. One barometer of the way in which these mini–innovations produced macro results: Between 1989 and 1995, the company cut its workforce in half to 7,500, yet increased its cement–producing capacity by more than 20 percent. Another barometer: For the entire period between 1990 and 2001, sales increased at a 16 percent annual rate, while headcount only increased 4 percent.

Bulking up at home also prepared Cemex for its own preemptive leap overseas. Having used the specter of foreign competition to turbocharge innovation at home, Cemex was ready to export its learning via foreign acquisitions. In 1992, Cemex made its first foray overseas with its purchase of two cement companies in Spain. Those were followed by a buying spree that took the company from Venezuela, to Colombia, Egypt, the Philippines and the United States. Having once acquired a foreign cement company, Cemex was able to raise its operating margins as much as 20 percent. And with each acquisition, the timetable for achieving these results got shorter. It took 18 months for Cemex to bring its Spanish acquisitions up to the company's demanding benchmarks, while Southdown, a Houston–based cement company acquired in 2000, came up to standard in only four months.

Everyone at Cemex realized that the faster the company integrated a new acquisition, the faster it would earn back its investment, which would help to lower its effective cost of capital. Cemex found other creative strategies for addressing its cost of capital challenge, including placing its international assets on the books of its Spanish subsidiary (whose accounts were denominated in dollars) and pursuing a sophisticated interest-rate hedging strategy. By the end of 2001, Cemex had worked its cost of capital down to a competitive 8 percent.

In many companies, there is an unspoken belief that new ideas start at the top, with corporate R&D or new product development—and proceed from the center out. But the goal at Cemex is not centralization but learning. Zambrano, Medina, Francisco Garza (head of North America) and other senior executives realize that a lot of innovation is local. Correspondingly, operating units need the freedom and encouragement to try new things. In their quest to ensure that innovations don't stay local, Cemex executives have created a wide variety of cross-pollinating mechanisms such as cross-cultural teams that oversee merger integration, in-person monthly meetings of country managers, and computer-based performance metrics. For its part, Cemex never set out to build a computer network, *per se*; rather, it set out to build a learning and innovation network. And even the parent can learn. When Cemex acquired its Spanish operations, it noticed that the plants there were using coal as fuel. Cemex had spent years trying to figure out how to use cheaper coal for fuel, but had repeatedly failed to achieve the necessary fuel efficiency. Within months of the Spanish acquisition, the coal fuel technology had been transferred back to Cemex's Mexican operations.

Cemex is able to integrate its acquisitions rapidly because it possesses common processes and a common scorecard by which to measure performance. This allows Cemex to quickly determine where a newly acquired company needs to improve, and, just as important, where it may be able to contribute new learning to the rest of Cemex. The Cemex Way, as it is known, is implanted in newly acquired companies via a postmerger integration (PMI) team, whose members are among the most talented managers and functional experts in the company. Having landed on-site, the PMI team actively looks for frustrated innovators and savvy operators who have been ignored or undervalued by the previous management team. Unleashing this pent-up energy and imagination is a key part of the integration process. Sure, GE Capital and other serial acquirers rely on similar integration teams, but like its earlier IT innovation, this was a first for the cement industry. **And being first in your industry is all that is required for innovation to pay off.**

Cemex's $3 billion acquisition of Southdown in 2000 provides a case in point. Southdown was the second-largest cement company in the

United States when acquired by Cemex, yet its operations were highly decentralized. The central dispatch system used in Florida, for example, was not used in California. Each plant had its own IT and accounting department. There was no common performance scorecard, and thus no common "language" for sharing ideas. Francisco Garza, president of North American operations and trading, explains how Cemex reined in this accounting mish-mash: "Some plants would include their environmental costs [in their monthly reports], and others wouldn't. In the past, each plant would buy its own fuel oils. No more. These are non-negotiable. On the other hand, we allow them to try new fuels—in some places we can use waste oils or tires. They don't have to ask permission [to try something new] if it brings in more profit." So, crucially, the scorecard is not a straitjacket. It's not conformance that Cemex is after, but the freedom to pursue opportunities for radical improvement and visibility for new ideas that deserve to be widely emulated.

It is this tension between ensuring respect for best practice and, at the same time, encouraging innovation, that is the essence of the Cemex Way. The trick is to get rid of gratuitous variety without killing off experimentation. "We tackle this," says Medina, "by declaring very firmly that the way we do things is not established. If you have a better way to do things, people will be interested in spreading that practice around."

At Cemex, innovation is a collective act, not just the product of a single, brilliant thinker. It occurs at the juncture between different attitudes, outlooks and life experiences. Thus it requires people with a combination of skills working together to solve problems, who feel jointly responsible for success. If collaboration and trust are absent, innovation becomes difficult. That is why the PMI team does not arrive like a conquering army, giving orders and demanding compliance. Instead, they talk to the existing managers and employees, delve deeply into existing practices, and together come up with a better approach. "There is a lot of innovation that we do locally, but we are obsessive about transferring that from one country to another," says Juan Pablo San Agustin, head of Cemex's new business incubator, CxNetworks. Sharing best practices is fine, but it won't keep you ahead very long unless new best practices are being created and shared all the time. For instance, the Mexican plants adopted the coal-burning methods of the Spanish subsidiary in the early 1990s. More recently, another Spanish plant figured out how to use an even cheaper fuel in its kilns: petroleum coke. Normally, when petroleum coke is burned it produces gases with high sulfur content that build up in the kiln and cause blockages in its pre–heating tower. But a kiln manager in Spain found a way around this problem by changing the chemical composition of the raw materials so that they bind with the sulfur upon heating. Now this method, which has the added benefit of being more environmentally friendly, is being spread to Cemex's subsidiaries across the globe.

Sometimes outsiders can see opportunities that time and familiarity have rendered invisible to insiders. It was this thought that prompted Garza, then head of the Venezuelan operations, to suggest that the company convene a PMI-like team from managers of acquired companies and challenge them to come up with ideas for radical improvements to the operations back in Mexico. Garza led a group of 45 managers from Spain, Colombia, Venezuela and elsewhere who came to crawl through the mother ship. "The chairman was skeptical at first," says San Agustin, then a young Spanish executive who worked for Garza on this team, "but in six months we found close to $100 million in annual operations savings." Among other contributions, the multinational team found a way to streamline logistics, allowing Cemex to close two cement plants. As a result of this exercise, talent from the various countries began to cycle more regularly through executive positions within Mexico. "We decided that if we were going to be a truly multinational company, we would need to be multinational even at home," says San Agustin. These intersecting career paths are yet another highway for innovation at Cemex.

This collaborative approach to solving business problems is ingrained in the Cemex culture. For example, in the early 1990s, a group of Cemex managers, including Iñiguez, were trying to figure out how the company could take orders for ready–mix cement and deliver them on the same day. Because contractors often change their orders at the last minute, Cemex veterans believed that the idea would only work if Cemex was prepared to punish customers who changed their orders by charging a change fee. Moreover, giving customers the right to order with less than 24 hours' notice would dramatically complicate production scheduling. Iñiguez remembers telling the skeptics, "This is crazy, you can't punish customers." If simple logic wasn't enough to win the day, maybe a real world example would sway the skeptics. So Iñiguez and his fellow zealots pulled together a microcosm of Cemex—plant managers, salesmen, credit managers—and packed them to Houston to visit the city's 911 call center. After visiting the 911 dispatch center, the visitors retreated to a hotel to discuss what they had witnessed. Using the power of analogy to expand their horizons, Iñiguez asked, "A month ago you said it was impossible to put cement in a truck without more than 24 hours' notice—so how is Houston able to assemble a team of paramedics inside a truck within ten minutes in order to save a life?" Iñiguez made his point.

As a result of this thinking, Cemex set up a GPS dispatch system which was christened the Dynamic Synchronization of Operations or DSO. Today, Cemex's fleet of 1,500 cement-mixing trucks in Mexico are equipped with GPS locators and data terminals which allow them to be routed to construction sites based on ever-changing demand. The dispatchers are now able to guarantee delivery of cement within a 20-minute window, instead of the three hours that was previously the norm. Not only do customers get a substantially more responsive service, Cemex's delivery costs for ready-mix cement have also dropped by 35 percent. (Ready-mix cement accounts for about a quarter of Cemex's revenues, with the rest coming from bagged cement powder sold to contractors and consumers who mix it themselves.) Initiatives like the DSO are the reason Cemex is now a global benchmark for the innovative use of information technology.

Thus, the Cemex Way is not only a method for integrating acquisitions, it is also a recipe for collaboration that is replicated again and again across the company. "We bring together a network of people involved with any issue, and let them talk about the problems that come from a lack of collaboration or coordination," says Iñiguez, explaining Cemex's approach to problem solving in general. Cemex has been able to create a culture of experimentation where probing minds are welcome. "We are very good at hiring people who have this attitude of curiosity," says Medina. "They have a researcher's attitude."

WHAT MAKES CEMEX ONE OF THE MOST HIGHLY REGARDED EMPLOYERS IN MEXICO IS NOT THE, AHEM, GLAMOR OF THE CEMENT INDUSTRY, BUT THE OPPORTUNITY THE COMPANY AFFORDS TO AMBITIOUS AND CONTRARIAN INDIVIDUALS. They may be making cement, but no one at Cemex believes they have to live by the limits that constrain their competitors. As Mr. Z put it in that Stanford speech: "The Cemex Way ... [is] aiming at nothing less than to reinvent our company and our industry." Ask yourself, how often have you come across a company where dramatic reinvention is the cornerstone of the firm's espoused values? The key to keeping the spirit of reinvention alive, says Medina, is "to make sure that people don't think they've arrived, that they don't believe that success can be taken for granted."

Within Cemex, one of the most critical mechanisms for sharing ideas and challenging conventional thinking is the monthly country managers' meeting. Each month, Señor Zambrano meets with all of his country managers, sometimes in Monterrey, but often in cities outside Mexico. Few multinationals bring their country managers together on such a frequent basis, but Cemex believes frequent face-to-face communication is critical to the cause of innovation. At the meetings, executives compare detailed performance data and share breakthrough ideas. New approaches quickly rise to the surface in this setting, and the close personal relationships among key executives grease the skids for the staff transfers that are often required to move ideas across oceans. The top 50 officers, who make up what is known as the Key Value Creators group, also communicate regularly among themselves. And they, in turn, each mentor five to seven younger managers who are considered to be rising stars.

At lower levels, new ideas are developed and distributed via expert groups, or e-groups, that form around various processes and functions. For example, there is an e-group focused on plant operations that includes the best kiln operators, plant managers and cement grinders, who get together to swap ideas about how to cut energy costs, move to alternative fuels or find better sources for raw materials. There are also e-groups for logistics, finance, sales and so on. They communicate via discussion boards on the corporate intranet, by telephone and by occasional face-to-face meetings. Again, out of this diversity of viewpoints and interplay of ideas springs innovation.

Cemex sometimes goes to extreme lengths to foster a customer-centric view of its markets among its managers. For instance, consider its attempt to better understand the housing and construction needs of the urban poor in the developing world. Housing is one of the most basic human needs, yet many of world's poor find it difficult to afford even rudimentary shelter. Despite their meager means and lack of credit, some do manage to scrape together enough to build modest dwellings for their families. Cemex wanted to understand how its poorest customers managed to do this, and what, if anything, the company could do to help the poor house themselves. To this end, a team of Cemex managers put itself in the shoes of the poorest of the poor—literally. The company sent a group of about a dozen junior executives from logistics, sales, operations, planning, and marketing to live and work in a poor neighborhood of Guadalajara for a year. "In this year, we learned many things we didn't know because we are very far from these people in our thinking and way of life," reports Romero, who visited the colony himself, as did several vice presidents who reported to him.

Out of this cultural immersion came two new financing projects aimed specifically at the poor. In studying how the residents of one poor Guadalajara neighborhood saved money, the Cemex team discovered that many families participated in a sort of lottery, organized by a trusted community member. Each week, several dozen families would contribute a preset amount to the lottery. And each week, one family would claim the entire pot—enough to build a modest addition to a house. The lottery would continue, week after week, until everyone's number was eventually called. Those who won early would continue to contribute until the last family had received its pay–out. In effect, the lottery was a community–run savings plan. Drawing on their hard–won insights, Cemex marketers approached some of the organizers of these lotteries, typically women, and suggested that Cemex might help them set up similar financing pools with the exclusive goal of funding home–building projects. They called the program Patrimonio Hoy, which means "have your savings today." The idea was warmly received and soon Cemex had a team of women, the Avon ladies of cement, going door–to–door, signing up families for the new scheme. As an incentive, Cemex volunteered to provide construction advice, blueprints and a small amount of financing projects for the members of the pools. After the third year of the project, 13,000 families were participating. And the default rate on the incremental loans provided by Cemex was practically zero.

Cemex extracted a second insight from this field study. Much of the money used by local families to purchase building materials came from relatives working in the U.S. Further research revealed that of the estimated $8.5 billion that Mexican workers send back to their families every year, about 20 percent is used for construction. But much of this money is wasted because migrant workers are often compelled to pay substantial commissions, sometimes as much as 12 percent, to transfer their money. Moreover, once the funds arrive in Mexico, family members often spend the money on a party or on some other less–than–vital need. Another complicating factor was the fact that the wife or mother receiving the money in Mexico might not know how to get the best deal on construction materials. To address these issues, Cemex started a pilot project in Los Angeles in 2001 called Construmex. Under the scheme, Mexican workers can go to a Cemex office in L.A. and get help picking out the plans and material for a particular project. After being paid, Cemex communicates with a local distributor in Mexico, who assembles the materials and delivers them to the expatriate's relatives. The reinvention of the community lottery and the development of the expatriate funds-transfer service are both typically Cemex—

unconventional yet eminently practical ideas that were eagerly sponsored and quickly prototyped. And in both cases, the outcome was more customers buying more cement.

In the past few years, Cemex has begun taking steps to expand the scope of its business from merely making and selling cement to providing distribution and logistics services across the whole spectrum of the construction industry. "We have been working to become a complete supplier of construction materials, not only cement and concrete," says Romero. One way Cemex has done this is through Construrama, a franchising program for distributors and construction supply stores. In Mexico, more than 75 percent of Cemex's sales come from bagged cement powder. These bags are typically sold through small construction supply stores where cement makes up about half of their business. Cemex selected 1,000 distributors, out of 4,000 in the country, and started wrapping valuable services around its cement. "Our goal was to create competitive differentiation for something that is a commodity," says one executive. It may sound strange to treat cement as anything other than a commodity, but then, **does anybody fault Perrier for treating water as something more than H$_2$O?**

Cemex invested \$10,000 in each store—enough to pay for a new Construrama storefront, Cemex signs, a computer and inventory-tracking software. Cemex also trained the distributors in marketing, financial planning, tax accounting and inventory control. "You are using your distributor as your hands," says Romero. Instead of just delivering cement to these distributors, Cemex now helps them design their stores, provides them with a barebones IT infrastructure, and helps them pool their purchasing power. In return it gets brand loyalty.

After being perfected in Mexico, Construrama is now being rolled out in other countries as well, but it's just one piece of a much larger puzzle. Cemex's goal is to become a mega-supplier of all construction materials to these distributors. Cemex doesn't intend on manufacturing a full range of building supplies, but it wants to put its vaunted logistics capability to work in managing the supply chain between the manufacturing companies and the distributor network.

In addition to more closely integrating its distributors into its operations, Cemex is also hoping to stake out a pivotal position in the construction materials supply chain and in late-2000 created a new business incubator, CxNetworks, to help it do so. Unlike other incubators born during the Internet boom, CxNetworks' purpose is not to spin out unloved ideas into IPOs, but rather to build new skills and relationships that can multiply the value of existing Cemex competencies and assets. The impetus for the formation of CxNetworks was a realization that the consolidation strategy that was fueling the company's growth would ultimately reach its natural limits—there are only so many cement companies to buy and improve. The goal of CxNetworks is to build new platforms for organic growth. In this sense, CxNetworks is not a sideshow, it is the main show. As Medina described it, "Cx-Networks is the transformation engine for Cemex."

"CxNetworks is a way of helping us develop other business relationships that can create value for Cemex," explains San Agustin, the incubator's leader. "It's not a stand alone attempt to create new businesses." CxNetworks has already spawned several nascent businesses including Arkio (a one-stop shop for professional home builders), Latinexus (a B2B exchange for the kind of maintenance, repair and operating materials bought by facility managers) and Neoris (an IT consultancy which grew out of Cemex's internal IT function). Just as Construrama links Cemex more tightly to its downstream distributors, the B2B exchanges are bringing efficiencies to the construction materials supplier network, while Arkio is bringing supply chain efficiencies to the house-building industry. Tellingly, these businesses are staffed with veteran executives, not 20-something Web-heads. For instance, Iñiguez transferred from his CIO position at Cemex to become the CIO of CxNetworks and Arkio's boss was formerly the CEO of Grainger's Mexican operations. "The new skills, developed in the new business models," says San Agustin, "will help to improve the blood of the company." Clearly, all of these people and ideas are expected, in some form or other, to eventually be pumped back into Cemex. CxNetworks is well funded, with up to 10 percent of free cash flow—about $100 million a year—available to it if necessary (although, in its first two years it tapped into less than half that amount). CxNetworks is, essentially, a business R&D unit seeking to leverage Cemex's distribution, logistics and IT competencies in new ways. But CxNetworks does not have a monopoly on new ideas. Every operating company is free to experiment on its own.

Indeed, Francisco Garza has charged his colleagues with the task of making innovation a deeply embedded and widely distributed capability. Although Garza was pleased with the outcome of the "reverse-PMI" project, which produced a multiyear plan for improving the Mexican operations, he felt that innovation needed to be more than a periodic project; nor could it be confined to a single unit, like CxNetworks. There is an expression in Mexico, "wearing the T-shirt." It is a metaphor for the kind of devotion shown by a football fan who wears a T-shirt emblazoned with the emblem of a favorite team. Garza wanted to make it possible for many people to wear the T-shirt of innovation and transformation—to get involved in the work of revolution and renewal.

In 2000, as an initial step toward this goal, Garza, along with Juan Romero, approved the formation of an innovation staff group within the Mexican operating company. By 2002, this group had grown to include nine full-time employees with responsibility for a $3.5 million annual budget. Carlos Gonzalez, innovation director at Cemex Mexico, and leader of the innovation team, comments on his first priority after taking up his responsibilities as innovation czar:

> We had been very innovative, but most of it had come from the top. We wanted to tap into more minds. So we started with a cultural study to identify the barriers. We were too hierarchical, did not have enough cross-cultural teamwork and we had no real established processes.

Overseeing the work of the innovation group is an "innovation board" comprised of five insiders (three Cemex Mexico VPs and two younger managers) and two outsiders (a supplier and a consultant). Working closely with the innovation board, and other senior executives, the innovation staff periodically commissions multifunctional teams from across the company to generate new ideas around major "platforms" or themes. By mid-year 2002, five platform teams were at work, searching for innovative answers to questions as diverse as how to achieve manufacturing breakthroughs, how to make it easier for customers to do business with Cemex, how to develop alternative uses of concrete, how to serve extremely poor customers and how to bring integrated solutions to builders and contractors.

Each platform team consists of 10 to 12 members who devote at least one day a week, over three or four months, to the challenge of generating new ideas and breakout proposals. Although team assignments "expire" after several months, the platforms may live on. (Platform themes are reviewed each year by the innovation board and may be carried forward for another year or retired.) Thus, over the course of a year or two, a platform theme may be addressed by a succession of teams. When a new platform is launched, or a new team formed, job postings are used to solicit talent from across the company. Most weeks, the team members assemble in Monterrey for a day to share ideas and work up detailed proposals. The innovation staff supports the work of the platform teams in many ways—by providing creativity training, leading brainstorming sessions, arranging field trips, bringing in outside experts and assisting with the design of exploratory projects.

After a period of research, learning and brainstorming, each team is expected to identify several "macro–opportunities" that will help to focus its creative energies. For example, the first "integrated solutions" platform team identified two macro–opportunities: helping contractors accelerate construction times and refocusing Cemex Capital on providing funding to builders in addition to its traditional role of extending trade credit to suppliers. **Like many of Cemex's micro–opportunities, these two grew out of a concerted effort to uncover the unarticulated needs of customers.** Platform team members would undoubtedly agree with the realization expressed by one Cemex officer: "We know we can reduce costs, but in the end, this is not a point of differentiation with customers."

One of the first innovation projects to be launched grew out of a conversation with a contractor who specializes in building low–income housing. Since the low income housing is financed by the Mexican government, the builder had no problem selling the houses. "But," as he told the platform team, "the problem is the time it takes to build the houses." In Mexico, house construction is even more labor intensive than it is in more developed countries. With construction workers flitting from job to job, the builder would lose up to 20 percent of his crew every week. As a result, the builder often missed his production targets.

Listening to such a complaint, most cement companies would say, "Sorry, your labor turnover is not our problem." But not Cemex. Not only did the builder's frustrations help to crystallize the team's thinking around a new micro–problem (speed of construction), but it also engendered a proposal for a practical solution. One way of reducing the labor intensity of construction, the team proposed, would be to use metal molds into which wet cement could be poured to quickly form walls and floors. These molds were already available in the States and Europe, but there were two obstacles to using them in Mexico. The first was that if you poured normal ready–mix sludge into them, air bubbles would form in the walls and make them structurally unsound. The second issue was that the molds were too expensive for most builders in Mexico to purchase. One of the members of the platform team, from the ready–mix business in Mexico, realized that just recently his area had developed a more fluid form of ready–mix that would be perfect for this application since it would fill up the molds more evenly. The second issue was addressed by creating a plan through which Cemex Capital would help builders finance the purchase of the required molds.

The innovation board approved the project and it was soon a successful new Cemex offering. Now, the contractor no longer has to build houses with a large crew and concrete blocks. He can put together a house with a handful of workers in three weeks. "Instead of just providing the ready-mix," says Gonzalez, "we are providing a new way to construct houses." And the best thing for Cemex is that the method requires about 50 percent more cement than before, which helps keep its plants running at full capacity. In the project's first year, Cemex expected 30,000 houses in Mexico to be built this way. Inspired by this success, another group was launched to help speed construction for smaller builders by developing Lego-like concrete blocks that would not require mortar.

Each platform team is expected to develop three specific investment proposals that can be taken to the innovation board for funding. Multiply this by the five platform themes, and the two or three teams that will be on each platform over the course of a year, and you get some sense of the range of experimentation that is being engendered by the new innovation group. The initial funding for the projects can range from a few hundred thousand dollars (when there are substantial uncertainties associated with the proposal) to several million dollars (when the business case seems rock solid). As an example, the metal molds initiative received $5 million in funding, while the Lego-block experiment was awarded a much more modest $250,000. As their experience with the innovation process has grown, the innovation board has become more and more willing to fund proposals that start out as something less than a sure bet. Explains Gonzalez:

> [In the beginning], there was a tendency to straitjacket the project
> by going into too much detail. We realized that if the idea is
> powerful and well thought out, it will grow by itself. If you try to
> specify exactly the number of clients you're going to reach, or the
> number of units you're going to sell, people start trying to meet
> the exact numbers of the plan, instead of being open to wider
> opportunities. Cemex has a tradition of being very aggressive. So
> our people don't always expect to see an iron-clad business case.
> If the project is exciting, our folks will fund it. But when they do
> fund a project, they follow through very carefully—month-by-
> month.

Since most of the ideas that come out of the platform teams fit snugly within Cemex's core business, experimental projects are quickly transferred back into operating units. Gonzalez's innovation staff continues to monitor the projects once they reach the implementation stage, and regular reports go back to the innovation board. This visibility helps to ensure that nascent projects aren't ignored or abandoned by operating executives.

The innovation process within Cemex Mexico is also helping to build a cadre of freethinking, innovation-savvy managers. "It is leaving a genetic imprint on these people," says Gonzalez. When team members go back to their jobs or talk to customers, they take with them a probing mindset that questions conventional wisdom and searches restlessly for new avenues of growth.

Another component of the innovation process is an electronic Idea Bank designed to make it easy for employees to share their ideas, big or small. In rolling out the Idea Bank, members of the innovation staff visited plants, teaching employees about the system and encouraging them to contribute their ideas. In its nine months of operation, 504 ideas were submitted from across Cemex Mexico, and 40 were implemented. Employees who may not be comfortable using a computer can submit their idea on paper to a secretary who will enter the suggestion in the Idea Bank. Although many of the initial ideas were modest in scope (for example, a plan for recycling water), some were of sufficient magnitude to be forwarded to one of the platform teams.

At Cemex, the IT platform, the shared performance scorecard, the PMI process, the cross-company e-groups, the monthly meetings of country managers, the resources devoted to CxNetworks, the innovation board and innovation staff group, the platform teams and the Idea Bank are all components of a well-functioning "renewal engine." The fuel for this engine is a belief that is shared by virtually all of Cemex: Industry is not destiny. Here is a company that has never let itself be defined by the views that others have of its product or its prospects. It is a beacon to companies across the developing world that want to compete and win on the world stage. **Cemex's ability to continually reinvent both its industry and itself is a testament to the fact that at Cemex, nothing is ever set in cement.**

LESSONS FROM A GRAY-HAIRED REVOLUTIONARY:

Not only has Cemex succeeded at both revolution and renewal, it has also made a commitment to make innovation a ubiquitous capability. There are many things that underpin the company's capacity for revolution and renewal:

○ A *burning desire* to prove to the world that a Mexican company can out–compete all comers.
○ A *passion for finding and solving customer problems.*
○ A *dense network of lateral communication* and a *common performance scorecard* that facilitates the rapid transfer of new ideas.
○ Ever–changing *patterns of cross-corporate collaboration* that constantly combine and recombine ideas from a wide cross–section of employees.
○ A *deeply felt humility* that admits to the possibility that there's a better way of doing things.
○ A willingness to *push the boundaries* that constrain the definition of "served market."
○ A continuing investment in *creating the time and the space* for innovative thinking and real–world experimentation.

ROUTES TO RENEWAL

By now it should be apparent that there are many routes to renewal and revolution. Sometimes renewal requires major portfolio changes. Generale des Eaux had a 130–year history as a French water services company before it started diversifying into pay–TV and telecommunications. After a buying spree that included Seagram's Universal Studios, mp3.com and the U.S. publisher Houghton Mifflin, the company rechristened itself as Vivendi. Today it is one of the world's leading media companies. Cable *&* Wireless, Disney and Bombardier are some of the other companies that have attempted a deal–driven metamorphosis. By definition, a major portfolio shift doesn't leverage many of a company's existing competencies or assets, yet it also doesn't require an extended period of organizational therapy—as the goal is not so much to transform the core business, as to escape what are perceived to be its inherent limits. There is, of course, a difference between mega–deals of the sort that created Vivendi and highly targeted acquisitions designed to close specific competence gaps—such as the ones UPS has been making to buttress its logistics business. In general, pinpoint acquisitions have a higher success rate than do big deals aimed at a radical corporate makeover. The smaller deals involve less financial risk and are aimed at leveraging competencies and assets that already exist.

The inverse of the mega–acquisition is the mega–divestment. Hewlett–

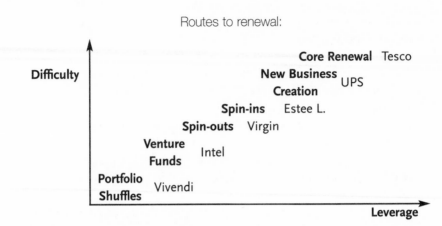

Routes to renewal:

Packard (Agilent), 3M (Imation) and AT&T (Lucent) are some of the companies that have disgorged major businesses in recent years. A company divests a business either because the unit is a perennial underperformer, dragging down the stock performance of the parent, or because it has great growth prospects that are not fully reflected in the valuation of the parent. For its part, Cemex sold off its noncement interests in order to focus its full attention on the task of reinventing its core business. Having reshuffled its portfolio, a company is still left with the challenge of innovating in ways that will lift its remaining or newly acquired businesses above the average.

Corporate venture funds constitute another route to renewal. As we saw with UPS, a venture fund can be a relatively low-cost way of learning about emerging opportunities; a way of taking options on the future. In May 1999, for example, two years before the launch of its Itanium 64-bit processor, Intel created the Intel 64 fund with $250 million earmarked for investing in hardware and software companies developing products that would exploit the new Itanium architecture. Intel, along with Johnson & Johnson and Microsoft, views venture investments as catalysts for renewal. Over the past few years, literally hundreds of companies established venture funds. Unfortunately, few saw these investments as vehicles for bringing new thinking and new technology into the core business. While UPS's Strategic Enterprise Fund won't invest in a business unless an operating executive sees an opportunity to learn something important from the new company, and must also be willing to supply an observer to sit on the young company's board, this tight coupling between venture fund investments and existing businesses is the exception, not the rule. For most companies, the logic of venture investing has been primarily

SUSTAINING THE REVOLUTION

financial—companies hoped to catch a ride on the IPO gravy train. When that train ground to a halt, many of the corporate VC wannabes simply closed up shop. And even for the strategic investors, venture funds can only do so much in revitalizing a core business. While Intel's venture fund has been financially successful (its $3.7 billion gain in 2000 amounted to one-third of Intel's profits in that year), it hasn't prevented the company from losing a significant amount of market share to competitors like Applied Micro Devices (microprocessors for PCs) and Sun (UNIX-based servers).

Closely related to venture funds are spin-outs. Here the goal is not to invest in outside start-ups, but to find and fund underexploited ideas that may be languishing within the hidden corners of a company. Spin-outs make sense when a business idea is clearly outside the company's scope. If venture funds were popular in recent years, corporate incubators were even more so, with more than 600 formed between 1995 and 2000. Yet these incubators haven't made much of a difference as far as shareholders are concerned. Since the ideas that get funded are, by definition, tangential, there is little that the new business can borrow from the core—beyond, perhaps, some cash, a few technical experts and a patent or two. This means the new ventures don't get much of a boost from their parent. As any VC will tell you, building a new business is hard work; there are dozens of failures for every unqualified success. Most companies have neither the patience nor the "mentor capital" necessary to shepherd nascent businesses into fully fledged companies. All too often, incubators were staffed with newbie managers who possessed little or no experience in actually scaling a business.

But again, there are exceptions. Sir Richard Branson's Virgin group is, essentially, a giant incubator which has "spun off" a clutch of successful companies—from Virgin Atlantic Airways to Virgin Money, Virgin Mobile (mobile phones), Virgin Trains and Virgin Cars. While these companies aren't publicly listed, nearly all of them involve outside investors and strategic partners. Virgin sees itself as a branded venture capitalist company. Each new company that Virgin forms has its own management team and its own capital structure. Virgin provides seed financing to the new ventures as well as its eponymous brand. Virgin doesn't have a "core" business. Its corporate function is dedicated to finding new opportunities, lining up an experienced management team, providing guidance and support and ensuring that the brand is well cared for. In short, Virgin is an exception. On average, spin-outs are a very poor substitute for genuine renewal.

I believe venture funds and spin-outs can play no more than a sup-porting role in the hard work of renewal. **For many companies, starting a venture fund or setting up an incubator is a little bit like putting a belly button ring on granny. It's an attention-grabbing ornament, but what granny needs is a liver trans-plant, not a navel ring.** In the end, the work of renewal comes down to two fundamental challenges: inventing new businesses that direct-ly leverage the company's core competencies and strategic assets (I once termed these "white space" businesses because they exist in the white spaces between existing divisions or product offerings); and/or transforming the core business in some profound way. Logistics was a white space opportunity for UPS, as were Neoris and Arkio for Cemex. OneSource and Schwab.com represented radical transformations of Schwab's core business. Creating big new businesses and transforming old ones are organizationally difficult. In the first case, you have to move talent and cash into the new business—that means taking resources away from existing business unit leaders. You don't create a $1-billion-a-year business like UPS Logistics by putting a couple of 20-somethings and a million dollars in an incubator. Consequently, there's no way to build a substantial new business unless everyone in the company understands the new opportunity and is willing to sacrifice some talent and some cash to help make the new business a success. This requires a *shared point of view* about the new opportunity. On the other hand, to transform the core business, one must challenge long-held dogmas and practices. This requires that individuals be willing to write off at least some of the intellectual capital they have built up over the years. That's not an easy thing to do. Though they are organiza-tionally challenging, core business renewal and white space business creation offer the greatest potential rewards, in that they leverage a company's accumulated skills, customer relationships, brands and capabilities.

The continued success of companies like UPS, Charles Schwab, Cemex, Microsoft and other gray-haired revolutionaries suggests it's possible to build substantial new businesses *and* fundamentally trans-form the core. When one digs deep, one finds that gray-haired revo-lutionaries share many qualities in common. These qualities suggest that there is a set of "design rules" for building companies capable of leading the revolution again and again. It is to these design rules that we now turn our attention.

8

DESIGN RULES FOR INNOVATION

WATCH A FLOCK OF GEESE TURNING AND
swooping in flight, undeterred by wind, obstacles and distance. There is no grand vizier goose, no chairman of the gaggle. They can't call ahead for a weather report. They can't predict what obstacles they will meet. They don't know which of their number will expire in flight. Yet their course is true. And they are a flock. Complexity theorists describe this, and the many other examples of spontaneous harmony in the world around us, as order without careful crafting or order for free. The intricate play of the many markets that make up the global economy, the vibrant diversity of the Internet, the behavior of a colony of ants, that winged arrow of geese—these are just a few instances in which order seems to have emerged in the absence of any central authority. All of them have something to teach us about how revolutionary strategies should emerge in a chaotic and ever-changing world. Complexity theorists have demonstrated that by creating the right set of preconditions, one

can provoke the emergence of highly ordered things—maybe even things like rule–breaking, wealth–creating strategies.

Order emerges out of deep but simple rules. Craig Reynolds has shown that with three simple rules, one can simulate the behavior of a flock of birds in flight.[1] Too many executives have been trying to design flight plans for their far–flung flock rather than working to create the conditions that would help their brood get off the ground and on their way to new and distant shores. They have spent too much time working on "the strategy" and not enough time working to create the pre–conditions out of which new wealth–creating strategies are likely to emerge.

Assembling grand strategies in the corporate tower is a futile under–taking in the age of revolution. This doesn't mean that top management is irrelevant. Far from it. But top management's job isn't to build strategies. Its job is to build an organization that is capable of continu–ously spawning cool, new business concepts and reinvigorating old ones. Its contribution is to design the context rather than invent the content. Its role is to operationalize the design rules for creating a deeply innovative organization—the design rules we see at work in our gray–haired revolutionaries.

So what are the rules for building habitually and perpetually inno–vative organizations?

DESIGN RULE #1: UNREASONABLE EXPECTATIONS

Listen to senior executives from a couple of gray–haired revolutionaries:

GE Capital: It is expected that we will grow our earnings 20 per–cent per year or more. When you have objectives that are that outlandish, it forces you to think very differently about your op–portunities. If one guy has a 10 percent target and the other has a 20 percent target, the second guy is going to do different things.

Charles Schwab: We are a growth company. This is our charter. Every year you have to say that last year is over, and we're starting from zero. This creates an incredible desire to innovate.

Here's an experiment. Do a quick poll of 25 people in the middle of your organization. Ask them this question: "What do you believe would be a reasonable expectation for top–line growth this year?" Compute the average answer—is it 20 percent, 30 percent, or some–thing substantially less ambitious? It is tautological but true: *No com-*

pany outperforms its aspirations. If most of your colleagues believe you are in a 5 or 10 percent growth business, you are. Their *beliefs set the upper limit on what's possible.*

I meet few individuals who truly believe their organization should be able to grow two or three times as fast as the industry average. Research across 20 industries over the past ten years shows that only one company out of ten managed to grow at double its industry average. I'm willing to bet that no more than one company out of ten has set itself the goal of growing at twice the industry average. And although a bold aspiration won't by itself produce a multitude of nonconformist strategies, its absence always yields bland, me–too strategies.

Whether the objective is growth in revenue, earnings or efficiency, nonlinear innovation begins with unreasonable goals. Modest aspirations beget incrementalism. Señor Zambrano and his colleagues at Cemex were not content to be a mediocre, mid–size Mexican company. Listen to Juan Pablo San Agustin, president of CxNetworks:

> I am very, very proud that we come from a developing country. If you have everything come easy to you, then you become lazy. But if you have to fight for everything, that becomes part of your competitive advantage.

The point is, Cemex's aspirations were completely unreasonable, given the company's starting point. Indeed, they were completely unreasonable even when judged by the performance standards of Cemex's supposedly world–class global competitors.

Strategy convergence, that pernicious margin killer, is the product of expectations convergence across an industry. I'll bet there aren't many people at American Airlines who believe their company can grow two times faster than United Airlines. In most companies, the majority of individuals believe there is some preordained, and typically uninspiring, "industry" growth rate—typically defined by the underlying growth rate of aggregate demand for what is seen as a more or less standardized product—that sets a cap on the growth rate of their own company. Yet unless one's expectations diverge from industry norms, there is little chance that one's ideas will diverge from industry norms. Only when people subscribe to unreasonable goals will they start searching for breakthrough ideas.

Convincing people in an organization that it is actually reasonable to strive for unreasonable goals is tricky. Mere exhortation is not enough. You have to demonstrate that it's actually possible to dramatically outperform the average—and you have to do this with real examples. Otherwise, the aspiration has no credibility. For example, ask your colleagues what they would do if they were in the lettuce business. You can't put a Pentium chip in a head of lettuce. It's not easy to digitize green leaves and send them zipping over the Internet. Yet thanks to Fresh Express and its imitators, the market for prewashed, precut, prepackaged lettuce (a salad in a bag) grew from nothing in the late 1980s to $1.6 billion by 1999. With a 38 percent market share, Fresh Express produces about 40 million pounds of salad per month. Eighty-one percent of Americans have purchased a prepackaged salad at least once. So send an e-mail to everyone you know in your company: **"Table-ready lettuce. $1.6 billion. If someone can do this with a vegetable, what the hell is our excuse?"** Never, ever believe you are in a mature industry. There are no mature industries, only mature managers who unthinkingly accept someone else's definition of what's possible. Be unreasonable!

One caveat: If you push for unreasonable growth goals, some folks in your organization will search for shortcuts—a mega–acquisition, deep price cuts, rebates. Don't let them get away with it. Only nonlinear innovation will drive long–term wealth creation.

DESIGN RULE #2: ELASTIC BUSINESS DEFINITION

Gray–haired revolutionaries aren't bound by a narrow self-concept. Their opportunity horizon is expansive and forever changing:

UPS: We are a technology company with trucks versus a trucking company with technology.
Charles Schwab: There are very few people here who feel they have a narrow business charter and have to defend their business against new models that will undermine those businesses.
GE Capital: We don't talk about market share because when people talk about market share it means they are defining their business too narrowly.

Who are we? This is, perhaps, the most fundamental question a company's employees and executives can ask themselves. How they answer it determines whether or not the company searches for unconventional opportunities. Too many companies define themselves by what they do, rather than by what they know (their core competencies) and what they own (their strategic assets). Thus they become prisoners of their existing business concept. For years, Xerox has defined itself as "The Document Company." So why, then, does Hewlett-Packard dominate the printer business? Printers handle documents—and are technically very similar to copiers. While "The Document Company" was a catch marketing slogan, it's not how Xerox employees saw their core business.

Here's how Michael Schrage, of MIT's famed Media Lab, views the challenges facing traditional universities as they seek to compete with newcomers like the University of Phoenix.

> Yes, MIT, Harvard and Berkeley are famous brands. But there's every reason to believe that market-oriented entities like [the University of] Phoenix have every incentive to be even more innovative than an MIT in crafting compelling online curricula and content. A decade hence, whose courseware sensibilities will be educating more people faster, better and cheaper around the globe?[2]

MIT certainly deserves credit for pushing the boundaries of its own business model. The school's OpenCourseWare initiative, announced in April 2001, aims to make the materials for all of the school's more than 2,000 courses available online. Yet, significantly, this courseware won't be part of an online degree program; rather, it will merely be a resource for anyone who wants to peruse MIT's course-related materials (readings, syllabus, lecture notes, etc.). If you want an MIT education, you'll still have to buy a plane ticket to Boston. A university that views itself first and foremost as a bricks-and-mortar, degree-granting institution training teenagers and 20-somethings will never take seriously the opportunity to use the Internet for the on-demand education of mid-career adults. But if the august professors define their institution by its competencies (curriculum development and knowledge transfer) and its assets (a respected brand name), rather than by its current business model (in-person instruction), the opportunity seems a bit less eccentric. If poor and under-resourced newcomers grab new markets, it is because incumbents so often imprison themselves within an excessively narrow business concept.

Virgin spans industries as diverse as air travel, packaged holidays, mobile phone retailing, banking and radio broadcasting. Says Virgin's Gordon McCallum, head of business development, "There is no assumption about what business Virgin should be in or shouldn't be in." Yet Virgin will enter an industry only if it believes it can (a) challenge existing rules, (b) give customers a better deal, (c) be more entertaining and more fun, and (d) put a thumb in the eye of complacent incumbents. Says McCallum, "The culture is one of why not, rather than why."

Like Virgin, Disney owns a brand that transcends any particular business. Judson Green, chairman of Disney Attractions, doesn't define his business as "theme parks" but as "three-dimensional entertainment." Disney's success with cruise ships, Broadway shows, mini-theme parks and a host of other ventures evinces an elastic business definition. An elastic business definition helps to reduce the protectionist instincts of executives worried about cannibalization. At GE Capital, the senior executives who run the company's major business spend as much as 50 percent of their time looking for opportunities outside the boundaries of the business they're managing. Every business leader is assumed to be a business development officer for the entire company. Is that how divisional vice presidents feel in your company? Is that how you feel? Parochialism is one of innovation's most deadly enemies. It's not only the CEO who needs an elastic definition of business boundaries—so does every single employee.

To drive this point home, former GE chairman and CEO Jack Welch asked GE's business heads to redefine their markets so that each business has less than a 10 percent share of its market. After spending years driving home the message that a business needs to be number one or two in its industry to survive, GE's famed leader had to remind his divisional executives of the obverse truth that only companies with expansive business boundaries will grow faster than their competitors. In a similar way, Schwab's employees don't see their company as the undisputed leader in discount brokerage, but as having captured only about 1 percent of the accumulated savings of American investors.

An elastic business concept isn't a license for ill-conceived diversification. Entering a business where one's competencies don't count for much is a recipe for a big write-off. Disney's Judson Green notes, "You can look back over time at everything Disney has done and put it into two buckets: the stuff that leverages the Disney brand and the stuff that isn't really related to the Disney franchise. We haven't done very well in the latter stuff." In the absence of a clear plan for leveraging competencies and assets, an elastic business definition is an accident waiting to happen.

In enlarging its mission from package delivery to enabling global commerce, UPS substantially expanded its potential market, yet stayed true to the company's roots and capabilities. UPS demonstrates that it's possible to expand your horizons without forgetting where you come from. So start asking your colleagues, Who are we? Where does our opportunity horizon begin and end? What do we currently regard as "out of scope"? Get a few people together and start redefining your company in terms of what it knows and what it owns, rather than what it does. This will help you stitch some elastic into your company's sense of self.

DESIGN RULE #3: A CAUSE, NOT A BUSINESS

Gray-haired revolutionaries draw much of their strength from their allegiance to a cause that goes beyond growth and profits—a cause that goes beyond themselves, a cause that is truly noble. Listen to what they say:

Charles Schwab: Around here, we think we're curing cancer.
Virgin Atlantic: Our business is about creating memorable moments for our customers.
UPS: We had a sense that we were given something, and we had to make it better.

Without a transcendent purpose, without a deep sense of responsibility, individuals will lack the courage to behave like revolutionaries. Gray-haired revolutionaries must periodically shed their skin. Every time they abandon a decaying strategy or jettison an out-of-date belief, they leave a bit of themselves behind. The most unsettling thing about the process of renewal is the need to write off one's own depreciating intellectual capital. To a great extent, an individual's worth in an organization is determined by what he or she knows. Business concept innovation changes the price tag on every bit of knowledge in the firm. Some knowledge becomes more valuable, and other knowledge less so.

Perhaps even more distressing is that business concept innovation often undercuts the value of an individual's accumulated social capital. Think, for example, of an insurance company exec who's spent years schmoozing with brokers and agents. Countless boozy dinners, boondoggles in Hawaii with star agents, a few hundred rounds of golf—and now you're going to tell this person that, in some brave new world, the traditional insurance broker may be a handicap rather than an asset? Good luck. It's hard enough to write off some of what we know; it's even harder to watch social relationships fray under the strain of a radical new strategy.

Any individual poised between a familiar but tattered business model and a lustrous but untested new idea is bound to ask a few questions: Will my skills and my relationships be as valuable in this new world as they were in the old? How much will I be asked to unlearn? How much effort will it take for me to adapt myself to a new order of things? These are genuine, heartfelt questions. And, for the most part, they can't be answered in advance. As one wag once remarked about his ever-cautious colleagues: Few of them would have sailed with Columbus. The courage to leave some of oneself behind and strike off for parts unknown comes not from some banal assurance that "change is good" but from a devotion to a wholly worthwhile cause.

Where did Schwab get the courage to preemptively migrate its business model to the Web, knowing that the move would force it to slash prices by up to 60 percent and more? Think about how your company would react if it were faced with this kind of decision. (We know how Merrill Lynch reacted. It denied, denied, denied, then debated, debated, debated, and, finally, decided.) In most companies there would be months, perhaps years, of savage debate. Factions would form, positions would harden. The specter of cannibalization would roam the hallways, striking fear into fainthearted executives. All this was avoided at Schwab for a single, simple reason—online trading was the right thing to do for customers.

When asked to describe the cause that imbues his colleagues with their revolutionary fervor, David Pottruck, president and co-CEO of Charles Schwab, says this: "We are the guardians of our customers' financial dreams." Think about that. When was the last time a bank teller looked like the guardian of your financial dreams? It's not surprising that Schwab regularly turns itself inside out on behalf of customers. After all, how many companies do you know that list "empathy" as one of their core values?

Sometimes a "cause" is nothing more than a genuine desire to make a very special difference in the lives of customers. The commitment of Cemex to improve the housing of the world's poor is such a cause. It led a group of Cemex executives to spend a year in one of the poorest regions of Mexico, in order to better understand how they might help impoverished Mexicans improve their housing.

However mundane a company's products or services, they must be infused with a sense of transcendent purpose. This can't be a thin coating of sickly sweet sentiment; instead, it must come from the part of every human being that yearns to make the world a bit better off. Roy Disney, Disney's vice chairman, knows why his company is in business: "You go talk to anyone who works in the parks, and they're all moved by the chance to make a difference in people's lives. We all feel very much the same. You do a good movie and you watch people walk out of the theatre with more hope in their lives. I get letters every once in a while from folks who just say, 'Thanks for what you have done in my life.'" When a company loses this sense of calling, when employees look at their leaders and see unshackled greed or commercial instincts that are not ennobled by any higher purpose, it also loses a good share of the righteous courage which is so essential for innovation.

For most of the industrial age, employees were valued only for their muscle power. Henry Ford is reputed to have once asked, "Why is it that whenever I ask for a pair of hands, a brain comes attached?" Henry wanted robots, but they hadn't yet been invented. Today, we celebrate our enlightenment. We live in the "knowledge" economy. We want employees to bring their brains to work. Yet if we rob them of the chance to feel they are working on something that really matters, are we really so enlightened? Brainpower versus muscle power, neurons versus tendons—is that really such a big leap forward? Is that what distinguishes us from machines—our slightly more advanced cognitive abilities? **What we need is not an economy of hands or heads, but an economy of hearts. Every employee should feel that he or she is contributing to something that will actually make a genuine and positive difference in the lives of customers and colleagues.** For too many employees, the return on emotional equity is close to zero. They have nothing to commit to other than the success of their own career. Why is it that the very essence of our humanity, our desire to reach beyond ourselves, to touch others, to do something that matters, to leave the world just a little bit better, is so often denied at work? After all, most people devote more of their waking hours to work than to home, family, community, and faith combined. To succeed in the age of revolution, a company must give its members a reason to bring all of their humanity to work. Viktor Frankl, the great Austrian psychiatrist, said it well: "For success, like happiness, cannot be pursued; it must ensue ... as the unintended side–effect of one's personal dedication to a cause greater than oneself."[3]

So ask yourself, What are you actually working for? What kind of difference would you like to make? Who will thank you, I mean really thank you, if you succeed? Do you have a calling, or do you just have a job?

DESIGN RULE #4: NEW VOICES

If senior management wants revolutionary strategies, it must learn to listen to revolutionary voices. Ian Schrager and super–chic urban hotels (Ian Schrager Hotels), Julian Metcalfe, Sinclair Beecham and fast food (Pret A Manger), Jeff Bezos and retailing (Amazon.com), Pierre Omidyar and auctions (eBay), Dietrich Mateschitz and energy drinks

(Red Bull), Phil Knight and athletic wear (Nike)—none of these industry revolutionaries started out as industry insiders. More often than not, industries get reinvented by outsiders—by newcomers free from the prejudices of industry veterans. Yet in most companies strategy is the preserve of the old guard. Strategy conversations have the same ten people talking to the same ten people year after year. No wonder the strategies that emerge are dull as dishwater.

What, after all, do the top 20 or 30 executives in a company have to learn from each other? They've been talking at each other for years—their positions are well rehearsed, they can finish each other's sentences. What is required is not a cohort of wise elders or a bevy of planners, but a taproot sunk deep into the organization. The Information Technology Strategy Committee at UPS was comprised of next-generation leaders who ultimately involved 1,000 managers in a cross-company dialogue about potential new opportunities. The postmerger integration (PMI) teams at Cemex paid particular attention to the views of frustrated activists in the middle ranks of acquired companies.

Put simply, without new voices in the strategy conversation, the chance of coming up with a rule-breaking strategy is nil. There are revolutionaries in your company. But all too often there is no process that lets them be heard. They are isolated and impotent, disconnected from others who share their passions. Their voices are muffled by layers of cautious bureaucrats. They are taught to conform rather than to challenge. And too many senior executives secretly long for a more compliant organization rather than a more vociferous one.

Maybe you think I'm being too hard on top management. Consider this: A disaffected employee in one of America's largest companies recently showed me a simple chart that had been distributed throughout the firm as part of a major cultural change program. He pointed out the fact that only "senior executives" were accountable for "creating strategy." Not a word about thinking strategically appeared in the performance criteria for "managers" and "associates." With a single chart, the company managed to disenfranchise 99.9 percent of its employees, relieving them of any responsibility for business concept innovation and of any involvement in their own future. Ironically, the company expects executives to be "open to learning," unless, of course, it involves a suggestion for a new strategy or business concept. You may wince at this example, but don't kid yourself: This is the reality in all too many companies.

For a company to become or remain the author of industry revolution, top management must give a disproportionate share of voice to three constituencies that are typically underrepresented in conversations about destiny and direction.

The first constituency is young people or, more accurately, those with a youthful perspective. There are 30–year–olds who qualify as "old fogies" and 70–year–olds who are still living in the future. On average, though, young people live closer to the future than those who have more history than future. It is ironic that **THE VERY GROUP WITH THE BIGGEST EMOTIONAL STAKE IN THE FUTURE—YOUNG PEOPLE—IS TYPICALLY MOST LIKELY TO BE PREVENTED FROM CONTRIBUTING TO THE PROCESS OF STRATEGY CREATION.**

While at Siemens Nixdorf, Gerhard Schulmeyer instituted a process of "reverse mentoring" where 20–somethings got the chance to teach senior executives a thing or two about the future. A few years ago Anheuser-Busch set up a "shadow" management committee whose members were a couple of decades younger than the executives on the "real" management committee. The youngsters get to second–guess their elders on key decisions—from acquisitions to ad campaigns. What's more, they are given their own reporting channel to the board. If you want to get close to the future, listen to someone who's already living there.

A second constituency that deserves a larger share of voice is those near the geographic edges of the organization. The capacity for radical innovation increases proportionately with each kilometer you move away from HQ. The highly successful reverse–PMI team that unlocked $100 million of wealth within Cemex's Mexican operations brought together 45 employees drawn from Spain, Venezuela, Colombia and other far–flung subsidiaries. Less encumbered by tradition and less respectful of corporate shibboleths, this group found opportunities that were invisible to home country executives.

For an American company, the periphery might be India or Singapore or even the West Coast. For a Japanese company, it might be the UK or the United States. In the late 1990s, pretty much everyone at the top of GM would have pointed to Brazil as the most innovative place in the GM empire. At the periphery, people typically have fewer resources. They are forced to be more creative. They are less easily "controlled." Orthodoxy doesn't hold the same sway it does inside the corporate heartland. Freethinkers on the periphery understand well the rationale traditionally offered by rebels in the Chinese hinterland—the emperor is far away and the hills are high. But again, in many companies, the periphery has a scant share of voice in the strategy-making process.

LET NEWCOMERS HAVE THEIR SAY

The third constituency is the newcomers. Particularly useful are newcomers who have arrived from other industries or who have so far managed to escape the stultifying effect of corporate training. **Again, they deserve a disproportionate share of voice in any conversation about business innovation.** Perhaps your company has looked outside for senior executives with fresh, new perspectives. But how systematically has it sought out the advice of newcomers at all levels who've not yet succumbed to the creeping death of orthodoxy?

It is ironic that companies so often pretend to celebrate "diversity" while systematically stamping it out. The kind of diversity that really counts is not gender diversity or racial diversity or ethnic diversity. It is, instead, a diversity of thinking. An organization that mimics the United Nations in its diversity is of little practical use if corporate training, "best practices," "alignment" and "focus" have destroyed intellectual diversity. In many companies, what could be a rainbow is instead monotonously monochromatic. Here's a benchmark: The next time someone in your organization convenes a meeting on "strategy" or "innovation," make sure that 50 percent of those who attend have never been asked to attend such a meeting before. Load the meeting with young people, newcomers and those from the far-flung edges of the company. Do this, and you'll quadruple the chances of coming up with truly revolutionary business concepts.

DESIGN RULE #5: A MARKET FOR INNOVATION

When it comes to innovation, most companies are more like hierarchies than they are like markets—they are more like the old Soviet Union than they are like the New York Stock Exchange. Yet history has shown again and again that markets almost always outperform hierarchies when it comes to getting the right resources behind the right opportunities at the right times. Oh sure, markets sometimes suffer from the kind of mass hysteria that fueled the Internet boom, but on average the collective intelligence of a market beats the smarts of any single person. If innovation is going to flourish in large companies—if new ideas are going to compete with the old on an equal footing, if resources are going to flow quickly and fluidly to the best new opportunities—then companies are going to have to become more like markets and less like hierarchies.

Despite the collapse of the Internet bubble, Silicon Valley has a unique track record of creating new business models and new wealth—in fact, over the past 50 years, no other region on the planet has done these two things quite as successfully as Silicon Valley. It's not surprising, then, that Silicon Valley is, in essence, three tight-coupled markets: a market for ideas, a market for capital and a market for talent. If, decade after decade, Silicon Valley has managed to create new industries, new companies and new wealth, it's not because the Valley is filled with brilliant visionaries. And if your company has consistently failed to create new billion-dollar businesses it's not because it's filled with witless drones. In Silicon Valley, ideas, capital and talent swirl in a frenetic entrepreneurial dance, melding into whatever combinations are most likely to generate new wealth. In most large companies, by contrast, ideas, capital and talent are inert and indolent. They don't move unless someone orders them to move. Where Silicon Valley is a vibrant market, the average big company is a centrally planned economy. It's no wonder that many Silicon Valley entrepreneurs are corporate exiles. Throughout its history, **Silicon Valley has been a refugee camp for revolutionaries who couldn't get a hearing elsewhere.**

If an established company wants to recreate the same kind of vibrant entrepreneurial spirit that pervades Silicon Valley, it must do more than establish a venture fund or a new business incubator. It must create an innovation marketplace that spans the entire company and is accessible to every potential innovator.

A MARKET FOR IDEAS

An average-sized venture-capital firm in Silicon Valley gets as many as five thousand unsolicited business plans a year. How many unsolicited business plans does a senior vice president in your company get every year? Five? Ten? Zero? There's not much chance of catching the next wave when your corner of the ocean is as placid as a bathtub. So what's the difference between Silicon Valley and your company?

For starters, everyone in Silicon Valley understands that radical new ideas are the only way to create new wealth. Until employees believe that rule-breaking ideas are the surest way to wealth creation, both for their companies and themselves, the market for ideas will remain as barren as a Soviet supermarket in the Brezhnev era.

There's another difference between Silicon Valley and the corporate hierarchy. In most companies, the marketplace for ideas is a monopsony—there's only one buyer. There's only one place to pitch a new idea—up the chain of command—and all it takes is one *nyet* to kill it. In the Valley, there's no one person who can say no to a new idea. It's rare to find a successful start-up whose initial business plan wasn't rejected by several venture capitalists before finding a sponsor.

What's more, in Silicon Valley there's no prejudice about who is capable of giving birth to an innovative idea and who's not. Silicon Valley is a meritocracy. It matters not a whit how old you are, what academic degrees you've earned, where you've worked before, or whether you wear denim or Armani. All that matters is the quality of your thinking and the power of your vision. In the Valley, no one assumes that the next great thing will come from a senior vice president running the last great thing. This is yet another reason the marketplace for ideas is more vibrant in Silicon Valley than in most companies.

Ailsa Petchey was a young flight attendant at Virgin Atlantic Airways. This unlikely entrepreneur got her brain wave when she was helping a friend plan a wedding. Like most brides-to-be, her friend was overwhelmed by a seemingly endless list of to-dos: find the church and a reception hall, arrange the catering, hire the limousine, pick out a dress, outfit the bridesmaids, choose the flowers, plan the honeymoon, send out the invitations and on and on. Suddenly Ailsa was struck by an idea—why not offer brides-to-be a kind of one-stop wedding planning service? Petchey took her idea to Sir Richard Branson, who encouraged her to go for it. The result: a 10,500-square-foot bridal emporium, which is Britain's largest, and an array of bridal coordinators who will help arrange everything for the big day. The name of the new business? Virgin Bride, of course. Could this happen in your company—could a 20-something first-line employee buttonhole the chairman and get permission to start a new business?

A MARKET FOR CAPITAL

Does this sound like the way capital budgeting works in your company?

Virgin: In terms of new projects, we're not in the business of calculating hurdle rates. We don't have hurdle rates. The questions we ask are, Is it sustainable? Is it innovative? Can we make money? If the answer is yes, we'll go into a business. If you think something's off the page as an opportunity, there's no point in saying it's two times off the page.

Cemex: Our people don't always expect to see an iron–clad business case. If the project is exciting, our folks will fund it. But when they do fund a project, they follow through very carefully—month–by–month.

So called "angel" investors often provide seed money to companies with a business concept that is not yet well enough developed to at-tract venture capital funding. Angel funding can range from a few tens of thousands of dollars up to half a million or so. Angel investors are often successful entrepreneurs who are eager to make ground floor in-vestments in companies that just might be the next big thing. Angel in-vestors are not financially stupid people, but they don't think like CFOs. While both may be in the business of funding projects, the mar-ket for capital in Silicon Valley isn't anything like the market for capital in large companies. The first difference is access. How easy is it for someone seven levels down in a large company to get a few hundred thousand dollars to develop a new idea? Whether the sum is $100,000 or $10,000,000, the investment hurdles usually appear insurmountable to someone far removed from top management.

Historically, roughly two–thirds of Silicon Valley start–ups received their initial funding from angels. Angels typically band together to fund new companies. The average angel puts in around $50,000, and the average first–round investment for a start–up is something less than $500,000. That's a rounding error in the annual report of a medium–sized company. Yet how easy would it be for an ardent entrepreneur in your company to find ten angels willing to invest $50,000 each?

Creative ideas seldom make it through traditional financial screens. If financial projections can't be supported with reams of analysis, top management takes a pass. But does it really make sense to set the same hurdles for a small investment in a new experiment as for a large and irreversible investment in an existing business? Why should it be so difficult for someone with an unconventional idea to get the funding needed to build a prototype, design a little market trial or merely flesh out a business case—particularly when the sum involved is peanuts?

The market for capital works differently in Silicon Valley. Talk to

Steve Jurvetson, who funded Hotmail and is one of the Valley's hottest young VCs. Ask him how he evaluates a potential business idea, and this is what he'll tell you:

> The first thing I ask is, Who will care? What kind of difference will this make? Basically, How high is up? I want to fund things that have just about unlimited upside. The second thing I ask is, How will this snowball? How will you scale this thing? What's the mechanism that drives increasing returns? Can it spread like a virus? Finally, I want to know how committed the person is. I never invest in someone who says they're going to do something; I invest in people who say they're already doing something and just want the funding to drive it forward. Passion counts for more than experience.

A VC has a very different notion of what constitutes a business plan than the typical CFO. Again, listen to Jurvetson:

> The business plan is not a contract in the way a budget is. It's a story. It's a story about an opportunity, about the migration path, and how you're going to create and capture value.
>
> I never use Excel at work. I never run the numbers or build financial models. I know the forecast is a delusional view of reality. I basically ignore this. Typically, there are no IRR forecasts or EVA calculations. But I spend a lot of time thinking about how big the thing could be.

The point is this: In most companies the goal of capital budgeting is to make sure the firm never, ever makes a bet-the-business investment that fails to deliver an acceptable return. But in attempting to guarantee that there's never an unexpected downside, the typical capital-budgeting process places an absolute ceiling on the upside.

Venture capitalists start with a very different set of expectations about success and failure. Out of 5,000 ideas, a five-partner VC firm may invest in ten, which it views as a portfolio of options. Out of ten, five are likely to be total write-offs, three will be modest successes, one will double the initial investment and one will return 50 to 100 times the investment. **The goal is to make sure you have a big winner, not to make sure there are no losers.**

In most large companies someone with a vision of a cool new business model, or a dramatically reconfigured business model, has to go to the defenders of the status quo to get funding. All too often the guy running the old thing has veto power over the new thing. To understand the problem this creates, imagine that every innovator in Silicon Valley had to go to Bill Gates for funding. Pretty soon everyone in the Valley would be working to extend the Windows franchise. ICQ instant messaging, Java, the PalmPilot and dozens of other innovations might never have come to market.

A VC doesn't ask how one venture plays off against the success of another. Nobody asks, Is this new venture consistent with our existing strategy? Now, consistency is a virtue, but in a world where the life span of the average business concept is longer than a butterfly's but shorter than a dog's, a company has to be willing to consider a few opportunities that are inconsistent with its current strategy. One of those opportunities might just turn out to be a whole lot more attractive than what you're already working on. But how will you ever know unless you're willing to create a market for capital that puts a bit of cash behind the unorthodox?

A MARKET FOR TALENT

Every Silicon Valley CEO knows that if you don't give your very best people truly exhilarating work—and a potential upside—they'll start turning in their badges.

The market for talent works with a brutal efficiency in Silicon Valley. In the early 1990s, companies such as Apple and Silicon Graphics hemorrhaged talent, while up-and-comers like Cisco and Yahoo! were magnets for the cerebrally gifted. As these companies faltered, they lost talent to a new wave of start-ups. In old economy companies, employees are still viewed as something akin to indentured servants. Divisional vice presidents think they own their key people. And if those people work in South Bend, St. Louis, Des Moines, Nashville or a hundred other cities that don't have the kind of superheated economy that exists in Silicon Valley, they may not find it so easy to jump ship. But that's no reason to chain ambitious and creative employees to the deck of a slowly sinking business model.

In too many companies there's a sense of entitlement among divisional vice presidents and business heads. "Hey, we make all the money; we ought to have the best people," they'll say. But the marginal value a talented employee adds to a business running on autopilot is often a fraction of the value that individual could add to a breakthrough project just getting started. Why not create an internal market for talent where divisional vice presidents, project leaders and others can bid for the best talent? A market for talent is more than a list of job openings. **Employees have to believe that the best way**

to win big is to be part of a team doing something new.
That means providing incentives for employees who are willing to take a "risk" on something out of the ordinary. It means celebrating every courageous employee who abandons the security of a well-defined job for the chance to work on a new project or business.

The last bastion of Soviet-style central planning can be found in Fortune 500 companies—it's called resource allocation. Big companies are not markets, they're hierarchies. The guys at the top decide where the money goes. Unconventional ideas are forced to make a tortuous climb up the corporate pyramid. If an idea manages to survive the gauntlet of skeptical vice presidents, senior vice presidents, and executive vice presidents, some distant CEO finally decides whether or not to invest.

In contrast, Silicon Valley is based on resource attraction. If an idea has merit, it will attract resources in the form of venture capital and talent. If it doesn't, it won't. There's no CEO of Silicon Valley. There's no giant brain making global allocation decisions. Resource allocation is well suited to investments in existing businesses. After all, the guys at the top built the business, and they're well placed to make judgments about investments aimed at perpetuating existing business models. But management veterans are not usually the best ones to judge the merits of investing in entirely new business models or making radical changes to existing models.

It's not that top–down resource allocation has no place in companies. It does. But it can't be the only game in town. If the goal is to create new wealth, something much more spontaneous and less circumscribed is required—something much more like resource attraction. For this reason every company must become an amalgam of disciplined resource allocation and impromptu resource attraction. Can it be done? Yep.

Royal Dutch/Shell, the Anglo–Dutch oil giant headquartered more than 6,000 miles from Silicon Valley, is seldom mistaken for a lithe and nimble upstart. Shell's globe-trotting managers are famously disciplined, diligent and methodical; they don't come across as wild-eyed dreamers. But a band of renegades, led by Tim Warren, the director of research and technical services in Shell's largest division, Exploration and Production, has been intent on changing all this. Warren and his team have been working hard to free up the flow of ideas, capital and talent—to make E&P an innovation-friendly zone. Their initial success suggests that it is possible to imbue a global giant with the kind of damn-the-conventions ethos that permeates Silicon Valley.

By late 1996, it had become apparent to Warren and some of his colleagues that E&P was unlikely to meet its earnings targets without radical new innovation. Looking to stir up some new thinking, Warren had encouraged his people to devote up to 10 percent of their time to "nonlinear" ideas, but the results were less than he'd hoped for. His frustration was the genesis for an entirely new approach to innovation, one both simple and slightly deviant. He gave a small panel of free-thinking employees the authority to allocate $20 million to game-changing ideas submitted by their peers. Anyone could submit an idea, and the panel would decide which deserved funding. Proposals would be accepted from anywhere across Shell.

The GameChanger process, as it came to be known, went live in November 1996. At first, the availability of venture funding failed to yield an avalanche of new ideas. Even bright and creative employees long accustomed to working on well-defined technical problems found it difficult to think revolutionary thoughts. Hoping to kick start the process, the GameChanger panel enlisted the help of a team of consultants from Strategos who designed a three-day "Innovation Lab" to help employees develop rule-busting ideas. Seventy-two enthusiastic would-be entrepreneurs showed up for the initial lab, a much larger group than the panel had anticipated. Many were individuals no one would have suspected of harboring entrepreneurial impulses.

In the Innovation Lab, the budding revolutionaries were encouraged to learn from radical innovations from outside the energy business. They were taught how to identify and challenge industry conventions, how to anticipate and exploit discontinuities of all kinds, and how to leverage Shell's competencies and assets in novel ways. Groups of eight attendees were then seated at round tables in front of networked laptop computers and encouraged to put their new thinking skills to work. Slowly at first, then in a rush, new ideas began to flow through the network. Some ideas attracted a flurry of support from the group; others remained orphans. By the end of the second day, a portfolio of 240 ideas had been generated. Some were for entirely new businesses, and many more were for new approaches within existing businesses.

The attendees then agreed on a set of screening criteria to determine which of the ideas deserved a portion of the seed money. Twelve ideas were nominated for funding, and a volunteer army of supporters coalesced around each one. The nascent venture teams were invited to attend an "Action Lab." Here the teams were taught how to scope out the boundaries of an opportunity, identify potential partnerships, enumerate sources of competitive advantage and identify the broad financial implications. Next, they were coached in developing 100-day action plans: low-cost, low-risk ways of testing the ideas. Finally, each team presented its story to a "venture board" consisting of the GameChanger panel, a sampling of senior managers and representatives from Shell Technology Ventures—a unit that funds projects that don't fall under the purview of Shell's operating units.

Since the completion of the labs, the GameChanger panel has been working hard to institutionalize the internal entrepreneurial process. It meets weekly to discuss new submissions—320 were received in the first two years of the panel's existence, many through Shell's intranet. An employee with a promising idea is invited to give a ten–minute pitch to the GameChanger panel, followed by a 15–minute Q&A session. If the members agree that the idea has real potential, the employee is invited to a second round of discussions with a broader group of company experts whose knowledge or support may be important to the success of the proposed venture. Before rejecting an idea, the panel looks carefully at what Shell would stand to lose if the opportunity turned out to be all its sponsors claim. Ideas that get a green light often receive funding—on average, $100,000, but sometimes as much as $600,000—within eight or ten days. Those that don't pass muster enter a database accessible to anyone who would like to compare a new idea with earlier submissions.

Some months later, each project goes through a proof–of–concept review in which the team has to show that its plan is indeed workable and deserves further funding. This review typically marks the end of the formal GameChanger process, although the panel will often help successful ventures find a permanent home inside Shell. About a quarter of the efforts that get funded ultimately come to reside in an operating unit or in one of Shell's various growth initiatives; others get carried forward as R&D projects, and still others are written off as interesting, but unproductive experiments. Of Shell's five–largest growth initiatives in early 1999, four had their genesis in the GameChanger process. Perhaps even more important, the GameChanger process has helped convince Shell's top management that entrepreneurial passion lurks everywhere and that you really can bring Silicon Valley inside.

In Silicon Valley, ideas, talent and capital are concentrated in a small geographic area. There is seldom more than one or two degrees of separation between any given entrepreneur, VC or brilliant engineer. Given the tightly knit social fabric of Silicon Valley, it's not hard for ideas, capital and talent to find each other. This is much less true for a global company like Shell. Ideas, capital and talent are often separated by geographical and organizational distance. Hence the need for something like the GameChanger process that can serve as a magnet for new ideas, and as a central switching node for capital and talent.

Building a marketplace for innovation may sound a bit daunting, not to mention unconventional. So think of it this way, you've already turned your company inside out for ERP and CRM—projects aimed at only incremental improvements—wouldn't the potential pay-off for creating a marketplace for innovation be at least as big? Shell thinks so—and if Shell can do it, so can your company.

DESIGN RULE #6: LOW-RISK EXPERIMENTATION

Being a revolutionary doesn't mean being a big risk taker:

UPS: We have [new] subsidiaries. They are nimble, entrepreneurial, innovative, quick. We tell them to try new things and fail small and fast. That is what our subsidiaries do.
GE Capital: We go for things where the barriers to entry are small. You won't find us doing many mega-mergers. We do hundreds of acquisitions. But it's very unusual for us to do a big transaction. Big transactions bring you big risks. Have you timed the market right? Are you buying a business because the other guy thinks it's the right time to get out?
Virgin: We're very adept at managing the downside. We usually take someone else's skills and someone else's money.

There is an implicit assumption in many companies that it is less risky to be incremental than to be revolutionary. Many believe that it is best to let a foolhardy competitor take the risk of testing a new business concept, that the safe bet is to be a fast follower. There are others, a minority in most companies, who will argue that to capture new markets a company must be bold. They will argue that if you're not first off the blocks, you will never win the race to tomorrow's riches. "We need more risk takers around here" is an oft-heard plea in companies that have missed exciting new markets.

Yet there is a false dichotomy here. The choice is not between being a cautious follower on one hand and a rash risk taker on the other. Neither of these approaches is likely to pay off in the age of revolution. For example, Motorola got caught behind Nokia in the move to digital phones and paid a heavy price for its ambling pace. The company learned that you can't play catch-up with a competitor that moves at light speed. On the other hand, Motorola took a huge gamble with its participation in Iridium, the satellite-based communication business, and was ultimately forced into a big write-off when expectations about the rate of customer adoption turned out to be wildly overoptimistic. It is possible, though, to find a way between these two extremes. Gray-haired revolutionaries are prudent and bold, careful and quick.

Again, the venture capital community provides a useful analogy. Venture capitalists are risk takers, but they're not big risk takers. AT&T buying into the cable TV industry, Monsanto spending billions on seed companies, Sony betting a billion on a new video game chip—these are big risks. Indeed, in the five years through 2000, companies in the S&P 500 took more than $220 billion in extraordinary charges against earnings. This is nearly four times as much as all the venture capital raised in Silicon Valley over the same time period (which, of course, was the greatest VC spending boom in history). By contrast, extraordinary gains amounted to only about $60 billion. So no one can argue that big companies are unwilling to take big risks—on poorly conceived acquisitions and bold but highly uncertain mega–opportunities.

Historically, venture capitalists have not been big risk takers. (They got a bit carried away by all that dot–com nonsense.) VCs look for opportunities that don't need a lot of cash to get started. The initial investment in Hotmail was $300,000; the company was sold to Microsoft for something north of $400 million. Historically, Silicon Valley was fueled by nifty new ideas, not zillions of greenbacks. VCs worked hard to enforce a culture of frugality in the companies they backed. And because they were intimately involved in those companies—helping to appoint the management team, sitting on the board, plotting strategy with the owners—they were well positioned to know when to double their bets and when to cut and run. Compared to VCs, the average CFO is a spendthrift. Yet VCs also know that speed is everything. They have no tolerance for talking about doing, for getting ready to get ready. They know that the only way you resolve the inevitable uncertainty around new opportunities is to actually dangle something in front of customers and see if they bite.

VCs live by Virgin's motto of "Screw it, let's do it." Indeed, Virgin has shuttered more businesses than most companies have ever created. Virgin has an exit plan for every business it enters—one that minimizes the potential damage to the Virgin brand. This kind of forward planning doesn't evince any lack of commitment to new opportunities, it simply recognizes that what is true for Silicon Valley is also true for Virgin: Most start–ups will fail (though Virgin claims a better track record than the average VC fund).

There is an important mind–set here: Most new ventures will fail. Do people in your company understand this? A VC could have five or six failures in ten starts and still be a hero. Could anyone survive that kind of ratio in your company? What matters less than the success rate is the number of new experiments you get started. It is perverse that in many companies billion-dollar commitments to moribund businesses can be thought of as "safe," while Lilliputian experiments are viewed as risky. Risk is the product of investment multiplied by the probability of failure. A $100,000 experiment with an 80 percent chance of failing is substantially less risky than a $100 million investment with a 1 percent chance of failure. Assuming no residual value for either project in the event of failure, the expected downside for the "risky" venture is $80,000 ($100,000 × 80%) and $1 million ($100 million × 1%) for the "sure thing." Yet which would be quicker to win funding in your company? Most companies fail to grasp this simple arithmetic. If they did, they'd be doing fewer big mergers, for example, and would instead be spawning dozens upon dozens of radical low-cost, low-risk experiments.

It is important to **make a distinction between project risk and portfolio risk.** The risk that any single new experiment fails may be high—say, 80 percent. Yet in a portfolio of ten such experiments, each with a one-in-ten chance of success, the likelihood is that one of them will pay off. And while the best possible rate of return on large, incremental investments is typically modest, the same is not true of small investments in radical new business concepts or in ideas that can reinvigorate an otherwise moribund business concept. VCs look for opportunities with enormous upside potential, on the order of 10:1, 100:1, or even 1,000:1. If most of the ventures in a portfolio have this kind of upside potential, the "expected value" of the portfolio can be substantial, even though each project is far more likely to fail than succeed. A prudent investor would not want to invest in any single project but would be delighted to invest in the entire portfolio. Again, many companies fail to grasp this simple portfolio logic. This is why most companies don't have dozens upon dozens of new-rule experiments bubbling away. But to find a breathtaking breakout opportunity, every company must build a portfolio of business concept experiments.

By the way, if you treat the person who just blew a 20-percent "sure thing" the same way you treat the guy or gal who just blew a 99-percent "sure thing," you're going to end up with a company full of timid little mice. The person who is managing a highly speculative project in a portfolio of such projects is almost expected to fail. But the gal who has an incremental project in a long-established business should never fail. Yet again, this distinction is seldom made. It's a bit like treating the person who fails to get a hole-in-one on a 300-yard, par-4 golf hole the same way you treat the person who just missed a two-foot putt. Do this, and you'll end up with a company full of two-foot putters—nervous souls who will congregate in "safe" businesses. And there's not a chance in the world your company will join the ranks of the wealth creators. Personal risk must be divorced from project risk. Celebrate the individual or the team that leads an expedition into the unknown.

Companies often overestimate the risk of doing something new for the simple reason that top management is too distant to make an informed assessment—too far from the voice of the customer and too far from the voice of the future. There is an important difference between actual risk and perceived risk. Actual risk is a function of irreducible uncertainty: Will the technology work? Will customers value this new service? What will they be willing to pay for it? and so on. Perceived risk is a function of ignorance. The farther you are from a hands-on, first-person understanding of the new opportunity, the greater the perceived risk. For years Detroit designed dependably boring automobiles—cars like the Chevrolet Lumina and Ford Contour. Was this because these were the only kind of cars that Americans wanted to buy or because Detroit's designers weren't in touch with the leading edge of customer demand? Cars like the Dodge Viper and the Chrysler PT Cruiser looked risky only to those who weren't in tune with trendy young buyers and wild-eyed enthusiasts. The point is simple: You can't let people who couldn't see the leading edge with a pair of binoculars make judgments about what is and isn't risky.

In the end, though, **companies don't need more risk takers; they need people who understand how to de-risk big aspirations.** There are several ways to do this. Like Virgin, you can pass off risk to strategic partners. When Virgin launched its financial services business, Virgin Money, it relied on an Australian insurance company for the majority of the initial capital and on a British bank for back-office support. Like GE Capital, you can buy small "popcorn stands," little businesses that will help you learn about bigger opportunities. Once GE understands the basics and the opportunity to reinvent the business, it pours in capital. In the early stages of any new business concept experiment, the goal is to maximize the ratio of learning over investment.

Reconnoitering a broad new opportunity is a bit like trying to shoot a game bird in a fast-flying flock. If you use a rifle, you'll almost certainly miss. A rifle is fine if the target is big and slow. If the target is small and swift, a shotgun is your only hope. Too often a company makes a single, premature bet when confronting a new and underdefined opportunity. The greater the initial uncertainty about which customers will buy, what product configuration is best, what pricing scheme will work and which distribution channels will be most effective, the greater the number of experiments that should be launched.

Many large companies feel that it is virtually a waste of time to pour scarce management talent into pint-sized experiments. After all, the thinking goes, how big would these experiments have to be in order to make an appreciable impact in a company with $10 billion, $20 billion or $50 billion in revenue? This isn't the way they think at GE Capital. To qualify as a "bubble," the name GE Capital gives to its major operating units, a business has to be able to generate $25 million in profits per year. That may sound like a lot, but it's significantly less than 1 percent of what GE Capital earns in a good year. "Popcorn stands" are even smaller. GE Capital's senior managers spend a lot of time searching for popcorn stands and trying to grow them into pre-bubble "ventures." All too often there is a 1:1 ratio between the amount of management attention a project or business receives and its current revenues. This is a misapplication of management attention, and it is a recipe for maintaining the status quo. Small things need to be nourished by top management attention. Without the fertilizer of top management interest, they will remain small things.

Inevitably, the time will come when a fledgling business needs to borrow some critical resource from somewhere else in the organization, to win some argument around channel conflict, or to double up its investments. If top management's attention has been elsewhere, it will lack the confidence to "go for it." GE Capital's ventures and popcorn stands don't languish in some isolated "new ventures division." Instead they are nurtured and guided by line executives who know that the only way to keep growing is to keep starting a lot of small experiments.

Make small bets. Make a lot of small bets. Think of your experiments as a portfolio of options. Pass off risk to your partners. Accelerate learning. Celebrate the pathfinders. This is the ethos of low-risk experimentation. And it is a critical design rule for building organizations that are consistently revolutionary.

DESIGN RULE #7: CELLULAR DIVISION

Gray-haired revolutionaries are not monoliths. They are big companies that have been divided into a large number of revolutionary cells.

A human embryo grows through a process of cell division: a single cell becomes two, then four, then eight, then sixteen and so on. Some cells become lungs, others fingernails, bones, tendons and all the other organs and structures of the body. Division and differentiation—that's the essence of growth. The same is true for organizations. **WHEN COMPANIES STOP DIVIDING AND DIFFERENTIATING, INNOVATION DIES AND GROWTH SLOWS.**

For example, when Virgin Records showed the first signs of lethargy, Sir Richard Branson took the deputy managing director, deputy sales director and deputy marketing director and made them the nucleus of a new company—in a new building. Suddenly, they were no longer deputies, they were in charge. Collectively, Virgin became the largest independent record company in the world, but nowhere, Branson claims, did it feel like a large company. Says one of Virgin's senior executives:

> We don't run an empire, we run a lot of small companies. We call it a big, small company. We want to be a substantial business with a small company feel so people can see the results of their own efforts.

Virgin's not the only believer in cellular division. The last few years have seen a record number of de-mergers, divestitures, and spin-offs. Yet much of this is too little too late. The real champions of cellular division practice a much more radical version of corporate mitosis.

Illinois Tool Works is a $6 billion company you've probably never heard of. Yet between 1994 and 1999, its earnings growth was twice that of the S&P 500. ITW is broken into nearly 400 business units, with average revenues of just $15 million each. Each unit has its own general manager, who has all the authority of a CEO—as long as the unit is outperforming the competition. When a business gets to $50 million in revenue, it is split into two or three units. For example, the company's Deltar business, which sells plastic fasteners to the auto market, took seven years to hit $2 million in sales. After being split off from the Fastex division and getting its own manufacturing facility and dedicated sales force, its revenues grew 700 percent in four years. Since then, Deltar itself has been split again and again. The original business now has 26 "children" with combined sales of $300 million. An $800 million acquisition made in 1998 was soon split up into more than 30 units. Here's what some of ITW's executive team say about the company's penchant for cellular division:

> We love competing against a big company, because their management teams don't have the same feel that our people have. It's not that we're smarter. It's that our people are only

concentrating on one small part of the market. They are like entrepreneurs—it's not an exaggeration.

We develop managers so rapidly that a person can start running a business when he is in his 20s. Some segments start out very small, perhaps $5 million to $8 million. That's a great place to try a young person. If they fail, we just pick up the pieces and move on. If they worked for another company, they would be trapped in some function. Here they get a chance to do everything.[4]

The advantages of cellular division for business concept innovation are many. First, it frees human and financial capital from the tyranny of any single business model. You've heard it said that size is the enemy of innovation. That's wrong. Size is not the issue. Orthodoxy is the issue. A business unit, whether $1 million or $10 billion in size, typically corresponds to a single business model. It is the allegiance to that business model that inhibits innovation, not the size of the business per se. Cellular division creates space for new business models.

Second, cellular division provides opportunities to nurture entrepreneurial talent. It reduces the number of stewards minding someone else's store and increases the number of entrepreneurs running their own businesses. Third, by keeping units small and focused, cellular division keeps general managers close to the voice of the customer. And fourth, by dispersing power, it undermines the ability of strong divisions to kill projects that might cannibalize their revenue streams. For example, Hewlett-Packard's decision to put its ink jet printer unit and its laser jet printer business in separate divisions helped both businesses to sidestep the cannibalization debate that so often cramps the style of new initiatives. The benefit for HP was that it became the world leader in two printing businesses.

Sure, cellular division forces companies to forgo some shared economies, but scale's not quite the advantage it used to be, and fragmentation is not quite as expensive as it used to be. Speed, flexibility, and focus have never been more important. That's why cellular division is a critical design principle for innovation. So does your company have any $1-billion-plus divisions? Give W. James Farrell, the CEO of Illinois Tool Works, a carving knife, and he'll turn it into 66 independent businesses, more or less!

DESIGN RULE #8: CONNECTIVITY

Innovation is not a private act—it is seldom the product of a single individual's intellectual brilliance. Innovation is a product of the connections between individuals and their ideas—the more connections, the greater the number of combinatorial possibilities. It is the constant interplay of ideas, perspectives, experiences and values that spawns innovation. In this sense, innovation is like great cooking—new flavors come from new and imaginative combinations of existing ingredients. For nearly 20 years, Wolfgang Puck's Chinois has been one of LA's trendiest restaurants—a place where moguls and movie stars compete for the best tables. The food at Chinois is a French–Californian–Chinese fusion of flavors that delights the senses but defies categorization. *Fusion*—that's the essence of innovation, and it depends on connections.

This is why boundary–spanning teams and projects are so important— they connect people with diverse backgrounds and skill sets and out of this mélange, new ideas arise. How many opportunities have you had in the last month to interact deeply with colleagues who work outside of your business unit or country? At Cemex, the monthly country manager meetings, the expert groups (e-groups), the PMI teams and the innovation platform teams are just a few of the ways individuals from various backgrounds and geographies get connected. Cemex's senior executives believe this rich tapestry of interaction is central to the company's ability to innovate.

Of course, what is important is not merely the connections that you make internally, but those you make externally, as well. Today, it is important to view the world as a reservoir of interesting skills, assets and ideas—all of which can be combined and recombined to create new and interesting business concepts. In developing a strategy to compete with its tough Japanese rivals, Swatch went to Lego, in Denmark, to learn how to make watches out of brightly colored plastic, and built a design center in Milan to serve as a lightning rod for the artistic talents that would ultimately make Swatch into a fashion icon. More recently, GolfPro International added GPS technology, ultrasound sensing and an LCD screen to an electrically propelled golf cart. The result is a golf cart that will follow you down the course, stop just behind you as you reach your ball, notify you of the distance to a hazard or the green and then find its way to the back of the green as you putt out. Oh, and if you jump across a stream, the InteleCady will roll to the nearest bridge and rejoin you as you walk to the next tee. Innovation is about making unexpected connections—in this case, between technologies that heretofore had never joined forces on a golf course.

Connections are just as important on the "output" side of innovation as they are on the "input" side. The value of any innovation within a company is a product of its inherent value multiplied by the speed and breadth of propagation. Ideas that stay isolated produce little economic value. What's required for propagation is more than some sterile, IT-based knowledge system. An IT system can be helpful in transferring simple, explicit knowledge, but it's not much help in creating the kind of synthetic, cross-boundary interaction that creates *new* knowledge. What is required instead are frequent face-to-face meetings where individuals are given the time and space to question, share and learn. This was the role of the Information Technology Strategy Committee at UPS, and of the innovation platform teams at Cemex. Balkanized companies, where there are few cross-unit teams, projects or working groups are not going to be very good at radical innovation. They will be even worse at propagating new ideas. New voices are important to innovation. Just as important is the ability to connect those voices in new ways.

IS YOUR COMPANY BUILT FOR INNOVATION?

Step back for a moment and reflect on the design rules for innovation—on the qualities that imbue gray-haired revolutionaries with their revolutionary fervor. Your company may pretend to be serious about innovation, but has it fully committed itself to embodying the design rules in every way, every day?

Ask yourself these questions:

○ Is your company ready to pump up its aspirations to the point where anything less than radical innovation won't suffice?
○ Is your company ready to throw out its definition of "served market" and define its opportunity space more broadly?
○ Is your company ready to begin searching for a cause that will be so great, so totally righteous, that it will turn a bunch of apprehensive cubicle dwellers into crusaders?
○ Is top management in your company ready to shut up for a while and start listening—really listening—to the young, the new hires and those at the geographic periphery?
○ Is your company ready to throw open its strategy process to every great idea, no matter where it comes from?
○ Is your company ready to start funding ideas from the fringe even if many of them return precisely zilch?
○ Is your company ready to emancipate some of its best people so they can get to work on the new?

○ Is your company ready to start paying attention to the tiny seeds of innovation that are right now struggling to break through the topsoil?

○ Is your company ready to take on the imperialists who would rather preside over a big but slowly crumbling empire than give self-rule to eager young business builders?

○ Is your company building the cross-boundary connections, both internally and externally, that create the kind of fusion that produces truly cool new ideas?

There are dozens—probably hundreds—of ways to institutionalize the design rules that have been covered in this chapter. My goal has not been to give you a detailed implementation guide, because what works for UPS, Virgin, Cemex, GE Capital or some other gray-haired revolutionary may not work for your company. Instead, what you must do is engage your colleagues in a serious and prolonged discussion about how to put the design rules to work in your company. I don't believe it's possible to systematize innovation—there's no simple three-step process. On the other hand, I believe that you can make innovation systemic—you can bake the values and beliefs that support innovation deeply into an organization. And, with the design rules as a foundation, you can begin to create the metrics, skills and processes that will support innovation whenever and wherever it arises. It is to this capability-building agenda we turn next.

9

THE NEW INNOVATION SOLUTION

FOR ONCE, YOU ARE NOT START-
ing from behind. Yeah, there are companies that embody some of the design rules for innovation, but none of them will claim to have made innovation as ubiquitous as six sigma, cycle time, rapid customer service or any of a dozen less essential capabilities. That's the good news. The bad news is that by the time you read fawning stories in *Business Week* or *Fortune* about companies that have bolstered internal activism, baked the "design rules" into their organizations and declared radical innovation to be a core competence, it's going to be too late.

Just how long will it take your company to embrace the new innovation agenda? Are you willing to start now, long before the principles and practices of business concept innovation have been reduced to the kind of prosaic manuals of "best practice" so beloved by consultants and the bottom-quartile companies on which they feed?

Take a moment before you respond. After all, your share of the future's wealth depends on how you answer.

It took companies such as Ford, Xerox and Caterpillar a decade and more to regain the ground they lost when they fell behind their Japanese competitors in the march toward quality. This time, you're not going to get ten years to catch up. This time you're not even going to see the warning lights come on. **Industry revolutionaries— whether they have acne or gray temples—are like a missile up the tailpipe. Boom! You're irrelevant!**

SHAKING THE FOUNDATIONS

To embrace the new innovation agenda you are going to have to challenge every management tenet you inherited from the age of progress. Belief by belief and brick by brick, you must examine the philosophical foundations that undergird your convictions about leadership, wealth creation and competitiveness. Whenever you find a brick that is old and fractured, kick it out and push a new one in. By now you should have a few ideas on where to start:

Old brick: Top management is responsible for setting strategy.
New brick: Everybody can help build innovative strategies.

Old brick: Getting better, faster is the way to win.
New brick: Rule-busting innovation is the way to win.

Old brick: Information technology creates competitive advantage.
New brick: Unconventional business concepts create competitive advantage.

Old brick: Being revolutionary is high risk.
New brick: More of the same is high risk.

Old brick: We can merge our way to competitiveness.
New brick: There's no correlation between size and profitability.

Old brick: Innovation equals new products and new technology.
New brick: Innovation equals entirely new business concepts.

Old brick: Strategy is the easy part, implementation is the hard part.
New brick: Strategy is easy only if you're content to be an imitator.

Old brick: Change starts at the top.
New brick: Change starts with activists.

Old brick: Our real problem is execution.
New brick: Our real problem is incrementalism.

Old brick: Alignment is always a virtue.
New brick: Diversity and variety are the keys to innovation.

Old brick: Big companies can't innovate.
New brick: Big companies can become gray-haired revolutionaries.

Old brick: You can't make innovation a capability.
New brick: Oh yes, you can, but not without effort.

If you want your company to be revolution-ready, no belief can go unexamined.

GETTING COMMITTED

You have to believe three things in order to commit your organization to building a capability for radical innovation:

○ An investment in making innovation a capability will yield huge dividends.
○ There is a wealth of latent imagination and untapped entrepreneurial zeal in your organization.
○ It's actually possible to make innovation a systemic capability.

THE RETURN ON INNOVATION

If you've ever worked in a company where quality has become a religion, you know how much time and effort were devoted to institutionalizing quality as a capability. Quality may be free, but building quality as an advantage is an expensive undertaking. Yet it is universally deemed worth the effort. Given the potential payoff to industry revolution—a payoff that's reflected in the wealth creation of rule-breaking companies—I believe the case for investing in business concept innovation as a capability is at least as sound as the case for investing in quality.

If you agree, then you must also agree that many companies have been misdirecting their energies: They've been moving heaven and hell to eke out the last bit of wealth from a dying business model while largely ignoring the chance to create new wealth from new business concepts or from a radically reconceived business concepts. Maybe your company has held a few brainstorming sessions. Maybe top management has hosted a two-day conference in a bucolic resort to consider the challenges of innovation and growth. Maybe there's even a corporate incubator or skunk works tucked away in some dark corner. But if you're honest, you're going to have to admit that there is a huge disparity in the amount of energy your company has devoted to getting better and the amount of effort it has expended in getting different—in getting revolution-ready. The implicit belief seems to be that incremental improvement is backbreaking work, while nonlinear innovation is easy. This is, of course, nonsense. Building any woof-and-warp capability is difficult and expensive. But the return on an investment in innovation will beat the return on any other capability one can imagine.

REVOLUTIONARIES EVERYWHERE

Despite the lesson of Silicon Valley, where the most unlikely sorts of people have created (and sometimes lost) fortunes, there's still a prejudice in most companies that first-line employees are unlikely to be sources of wealth-creating innovation. Thirty years ago, few people believed that blue-collar workers with no more than 12 years of formal education could take responsibility for improving quality. In a few years, the notion that "ordinary" employees are the wellspring for business concept innovation will be no more remarkable than the proposition that everyone is responsible for quality. Yet unless you and your colleagues are ready right now to accept the fact that there are revolutionaries everywhere in your company, you will lose. There is no place for elitism in the age of revolution.

MAKING SERENDIPITY HAPPEN

Can something as effervescent as innovation be systemized? Again, the analogy with quality is useful. In times past, quality of the sort offered by Rolls–Royce, Tiffany or Hermès required the unerring eye and skilled hands of an artisan. Who would have believed that a Toyota could be made as reliable as a Bentley or that a Swatch could keep better time than a Rolex? Yet this was the singular contribution of the quality movement: to make what had been unique, ubiquitous. It goes without saying that eureka moments cannot be programmed in advance. Innovation will always be a mixture of serendipity, genius and sheer bloody-mindedness. **WHILE YOU CAN'T BOTTLE LIGHTNING, YOU CAN BUILD LIGHTNING RODS.** Nonlinear innovation can be legitimized, fostered, celebrated and rewarded.

To create a hotbed of business concept innovation, you have to start with the design rules. But you can't stop there. It's not enough to create a climate for radical innovation and it's not enough to venerate the activists. You must create a positive capability for business concept innovation. What follows is an agenda for anyone who would like to get a head start on building the pivotal source of competitive advantage in the age of revolution.

THE NEW INNOVATION SOLUTION

While the eight design rules and the principles of activism are parts of the innovation solution, there are other equally important components:

INNOVATION AS A CAPABILITY

○ Skills
○ Metrics
○ Information technology
○ Management processes

Each of these is a critical component of the new innovation solution. Each has an essential role to play in creating a deep capability for business concept innovation (see the figure "Innovation as a Capability").

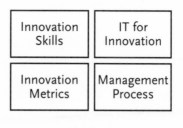

SKILLS

Your company has virtually no chance of leading the revolution if it is populated by industrial-age mind-sets. Every mind in your company must be re-tooled for the age of revolution. Training is tedious, and learning is hard work, but there's no other way to embed capability. Ask yourself these questions:

○ How many people in your company understand the role industry revolution plays in wealth creation?
○ How many know how to calculate the decay rate of current business models?
○ How many know how to identify and deconstruct industry and company orthodoxies?
○ How many are able to distill proprietary foresight out of an ocean of information on "discontinuities"?
○ How many are adept at inventing new business concepts and rein-venting old ones?
○ How many feel personally responsible for business concept innovation?
○ How many understand the principles of activism and would know how to launch a grassroots innovation campaign?
○ How many would know how to build a low-cost experiment to test a radical new idea?
○ How many are working to apply the design rules for innovation to their parts of the company?

If you didn't answer "the majority," your organization isn't yet revolution-ready. If you've read the other eight chapters in this book, you've already taken a substantial step in "re-skilling" yourself for the age of revolution, but that's not enough. To thrive in the age of revolution, companies will need thousands, not tens, of individuals who are revo-lution-ready. It's not enough to have little islands of capability—a few individuals here and there who are sources of nonlinear innovation. In most companies, it took systematic, cross-company training to firm-ly embed quality as a capability. The same will be true for business concept innovation. Forget all that blather in your company's mission statement about creativity and innovation. Unless it's running boot camps for industry insurgents, it's still substituting rhetoric for action. Radical innovation must become the next agenda item for every cor-porate university. So get on the phone to your HR VP or the person who runs corporate training. Tell them you have a few ideas for some curriculum changes.

Did you ever read the classic article "On the Folly of Rewarding A, While Hoping for B"?[1] There's a lesson in there for every company that wants to fuel the fires of innovation and create new wealth. Most companies have dozens of measures focused on cost, efficiency, speed and customer satisfaction—and pay people for making progress against these metrics. Yet in my experience, there are few companies that have any metrics that focus on radical innovation. If you have any doubts about this, take the following quiz:

○ How many measures do you have in your company that focus explicitly on innovation (versus optimization)?
○ How many individuals in your company could say as much about your company's innovation performance as they could say about your company's cost efficiency?
○ How many people in your company have any personal performance metrics related to innovation?
○ Does your company systematically benchmark other companies on innovation?

Most companies use a decidedly unbalanced scorecard—one that is heavily weighted toward optimization rather than innovation. Measures like RONA, ROCE, EVA and ROI often encourage managers to beat a dead horse even harder. How often have you heard an entrepreneur boasting about capital efficiency? The fact that you haven't should tell you something. It's not that industrial-age metrics are anti-innovation; it's just that they're not pro-innovation. And in a world where business concept innovation is the surest route to wealth creation, that's a fatal flaw. Without strong pro-innovation metrics, the default setting in most organizations is "more of the same."

Traditional metrics don't force a company to consider how it is performing against new and unorthodox competitors in the quest for wealth creation. What does it matter to an investor if a company is earning its cost of capital if its rivals are capturing the lion's share of new wealth in an industry? Companies need a way of measuring their relative capacity to invent new business concepts and create new wealth. One such measure is the wealth creation index, or WCI. It is currently being used by a number of companies that are eager to focus attention on the challenge of new wealth creation. The WCI lets a company determine how it has performed against a relevant set of "competitors" in creating new wealth. The process of determining your company's WCI involves two steps: defining the domain and calculating changes in the market value of your company versus the value of the entire domain.

DEFINING THE DOMAIN

The first step in calculating a company's WCI is to specify a competitive domain. I use the word "domain" rather than "industry" because measuring wealth creation within an "industry" often leads to an overly narrow definition of a company's potential opportunity horizon. The domain should include all the companies that are positioned either upstream or downstream from your own company in a vertical "value chain." It should also encompass companies that supply complementary products or services within a broader "value network." For example, an auto manufacturer would need to include the new Internet auto retailers as well as the providers of ancillary services such as body shops and oil change shops.

Further, the definition of domain should include companies that possess similar core competencies or those that satisfy the same deep customer needs. For example, Tower Records must include in its definition of domain all the new Web-based businesses where consumers can download music. An oil company should define its domain as "energy." An insurance company would define its domain as "financial services," and so on. If the definition of domain includes companies with similar competencies or serving the same broad class of needs, there is little chance of being surprised by a "disruptive technology."

CALCULATING CHANGES IN MARKET
VALUE VERSUS DOMAIN VALUE

The next step is to measure changes in a company's market value versus changes in the market value of all the companies within its domain. This lets you answer an important question: Has my company created more or less than its "fair share" of new wealth? To calculate a company's share of wealth creation, simply divide its share of total domain value at the end of a period by its share at the beginning of a period. If a company's market capitalization represented 5 percent of total domain value in Year 1, and 10 percent in Year 5, the company would have a WCI of two.

A company's market value is the net present value of its expected future net earnings—based on the collective assessment of investors. In a world of diminishing returns to incrementalism, it is unlikely that any company can dramatically grow its market capitalization in the absence of business concept innovation. Incremental efficiency programs are seldom capable of producing a step-function change in investor expectations about a company's profit potential. Aside from acquisitions and mergers, it is virtually impossible for a company to dramatically raise its market cap without inventing new profit streams.

Likewise, if a company's market value is stagnant or collapsing, it suggests a decrepit strategy. For all these reasons, changes in market cap are a reasonable proxy for strategic innovation. (Of course one must make adjustments for de-mergers and disposals, as well as for acquisitions and mergers.) Changes in a company's market capitalization relative to other companies in the same domain provide an even better proxy for strategic innovation. If a company is a division of a much larger company or privately held, one must calculate an implied market cap for that particular division using well-known valuation techniques. Don't expect to derive wealth creation measures straight out of the *Wall Street Journal*. Defining the relevant domain and establishing valuation numbers is hard work. But in my experience, the discussion engendered and the insights derived always justify the effort. When the value of the entire domain is increasing, only companies that achieve above-average growth in market cap can claim to be true strategy innovators. It is nearly tautological: In the absence of acquisitions or mergers, any company that achieves a sustained jump in its share of domain value is an industry revolutionary.

Let's take one example. The value of the nonfood retailing domain grew 6.3 times over the last decade (only U.S. companies were included in the calculation). The table "The Nonfood Retailing Domain" summarizes changes in wealth share between 1988 and 1998. Already number one in 1988, Wal-Mart continued to grow its share of wealth over the next decade. The Home Depot was another awesome wealth creator. Sears, Kmart, JCPenney and Toys "R" Us were big WCI losers. They failed to reinvent themselves or their industries.

A WCI score of less than one is a sure sign of nostalgia for an out-of-date business concept. All too often, the bonds of misplaced loyalty are severed only when the company suffers some catastrophic earnings failure. Instead of looking back over a decade and bemoaning a failure to grab new opportunities, track share-of-wealth data on an ongoing basis. A WCI that is edging lower suggests that the company is falling behind in the search for new business concepts.

The percentage of new wealth created by newcomers is a simple way of judging the susceptibility of incumbents to nonlinear innovation. Upstarts captured fully 27 percent of the new wealth in the com-

	Share of Wealth (% in 1988)	Share of Wealth (% in 1998)	Wealth Creation Index (1988–1998)
The Home Depot	1.8	13.9	7.7
Wal-Mart	20.0	28.0	1.4
Gap	1.7	4.9	2.9
Amazon.com	0.0	2.6	∞
Costco	0.0	2.4 A	∞
Walgreens	2.1	4.5	2.1
Sears	17.1	2.5 B	0.15
Kmart	7.9	1.2	0.1
JCPenney	7.3	1.8	0.2
Toys "R" Us	5.4	0.7	0.1

A 0.3 percent of Costco's gain reflects market cap added from Costco's 1993 $1.7 billion all-equity acquisition of Price Co.

B During this period Sears spun off two large holdings with a combined market value of $16.8 billion. Without these disposals, Sears' PSW would have been higher by about 2.6 percent.

Source: Standard and Poor's COMPUSTAT; Strategos calculations.

puter domain over the past ten years. In retailing, companies that didn't even exist in 1988 captured 16 percent of the new wealth created. This means that despite all their advantages, retailing incumbents surrendered $107 billion of new opportunities to agile and innovative upstarts. A caveat here: Occasionally, as we saw with high tech shares in the late 1980s, an entire sector can be overvalued. As ever, one has to be careful not to give too much weight to market values that are not supported by an underlying earnings stream. Yet because WCI is a *relative* measure, it is mostly by such bursts of irrational exuberances (or pessimism). Relatively speaking WCI still differentiates between those who are valued more from those who are valued less.

If new entrants can capture billions of dollars of new wealth in an industry without the resources and accumulated experience of an established player, imagine the possibilities if the energy and resources of an already successful company could be focused on the challenge of inventing new opportunities for new wealth creation.

Calculate your company's WCI over the past year, or two, or five. Get a discussion going over the appropriate definition of "domain." Challenge the definitions of "industry" and "served market" that prevail in your company. Ask yourself: Are these definitions broad enough? Do they blind us to nontraditional competitors? What opportunities have we missed? Then look at the companies that have created a disproportionate share of new wealth and ask, How did they define their opportunity horizon? Why did they see opportunities we didn't? What was their implicit definition of domain? How did they exploit our myopia? Answering these questions will expose the biases and beliefs that have aborted innovation in your own company.

Use the new metrics to challenge complacency. Redefine "acceptable" performance so it includes not only good stewardship but also an above–average WCI score. Look for companies that have excelled in the wealth creation sweepstakes, and use their example to reset aspirations in your own company. The distilled essence of entrepreneurial energy is the quest for new wealth. When widely discussed and understood, metrics like WCI can help you bring that energy inside your own company.

Of course, no single metric, on its own, can endow employees with imagination, make management responsive to new ideas, and bestow the courage needed to abandon comfortable orthodoxies. But be sure of this: If you don't get the metrics right, none of the other needed behaviors are likely to follow.

INFORMATION TECHNOLOGY

Intranets. E-mail. Newsgroups. Instant messaging. The fact is so obvious, it's hardly worth noting: Information technology has been dramatically changing the way organizations work. Digital communication drills through layers of bureaucracy, undermines hierarchy, makes much of middle management redundant, enables globe–spanning collaboration, unites far–flung supplier networks, makes 24/7 tech support available worldwide—and that's just for starters. Odd, then, that IT vendors and professionals have contributed so little to the cause of radical innovation. There are few companies where IT has helped to turbocharge business concept innovation.

Imagine a corporationwide IT system—an innovation network— designed to support radical innovation. Any employee with a germ of an idea, or just an urge to create, could go online and find a wealth of innovation tools—here's how you discover industry orthodoxies, here's how you build a business concept, here's how you develop a 100–day new–rules experiment, and so on. The tyro entrepreneur could toss his or her idea into a corporation–wide "Ideaspace"—essentially an online market for radical ideas. An "innovation editor" would group similar ideas together and post them on the company's intranet. Anyone visiting the site could build on the ideas submitted—"Have you thought about this?" or "Here's another way of going to market."

It would be easy to host real-time online discussions for particularly hot ideas. Ideas that attracted attention and thoughtful inputs would flower and grow, while those that didn't would wither. Individuals across the company could register their interest in working on a particular idea—"Yeah, I'd be willing to spend six months helping you get this launched," or "I'll loan you one of my team members to help you build the prototype." There could also be an internal market for funding. Anyone in the company with a budget could decide to sponsor a radical new idea. Ordinary employees might even be able to buy "options" in the nascent venture—whether in the form of phantom equity or a share of some future profit stream. A divisional vice-president might say, "Okay, I'll put $100,000 in so you can take this idea to the next stage," or an individual might say, "I'll invest $5,000 for a quarter-percent of equity." Conversely, innovators could bid for talent and capital, using phantom options in return. If the new idea is a reinvention of an existing business concept, rather than an entirely new business with its own P&L, the valuation problem gets more difficult, but the providers of talent and capital might be given a share in the profit growth of an existing business. In any case, ideas that attracted talent and money would get implemented; those that didn't, wouldn't. Of course, top management could monitor the innovation marketplace and put big money and top-flight talent behind ideas that showed great promise.

To institutionalize radical innovation, companies will need to build highly efficient electronic markets for ideas, capital and talent. As they do so, it will no longer be the knowledge management function that constitutes the leading edge of corporate IT, but the innovation marketplace. Are you ready for this?

MANAGEMENT PROCESSES

Many companies have spent a decade reinventing their core business processes for efficiency. The goal has been to straighten out the kinks in the supply chain—from suppliers through incoming logistics through work-in-progress through outbound logistics and customer fulfillment. Dell Computer is the poster child for supply chain integration. To a customer, Dell Computer's delivery pipeline appears both short and slick. While supersmooth business processes are great for efficiency—Dell operates with negative working capital—they don't do squat for innovation. **In most large companies, the innovation pipeline is about as efficient as Victorian plumbing lined with Velcro.** Radical ideas get hung up in the

Byzantine complexity of the strategic planning process, the capital budgeting process, the staffing process or the product development process. Companies that have reengineered their core business processes for efficiency are now going to have to reinvent their core management processes for innovation. If supply chain integration was about minimizing the time between an order and delivery, reinventing management processes for innovation is about accelerating the payoff for radical ideas. There are several ways in which management processes are inimical to innovation. First, most of them are calendar-driven—there seems to be an implicit assumption that you can count on new opportunities to wait patiently for the arrival of the October planning round. Budgets are set on a quarterly or annual basis and, once set, are inviolable. Second, **most management processes are biased toward conservation rather than growth.** They tend to put a premium on efficiency and undervalue experimentation aimed at exploring new competitive space. Ideas for trying something new and out-of-bounds are implicitly viewed as dangerous diversions from the central task of driving down costs and building market share in the core business. I have seldom seen a management process that explicitly challenges managers to develop and test a portfolio of unconventional strategic options. In general, management processes are focused on minimizing variances rather than maximizing opportunities.

Third, most management processes take the existing business model as the point of departure. Traditional definitions of market structure, traditional ways of describing the value chain, traditional assumptions about the cost structure, traditional beliefs about where you take your profits—all these are woven into the form and substance of management processes. In ways subtle and not so subtle, management processes perpetuate the status quo. Champions of business concept innovation will, invariably, find themselves working against the grain of key management processes.

Most management processes are focused on existing customers and markets. Again, there is a subtle bias toward serving existing customers better, rather than finding entirely new types of customers. Even worse, it is the articulated needs of customers that get all the attention, rather than their unarticulated needs. Most management processes have a place to plug in the banalities produced by market research, but have no way of accommodating the highly impressionistic but infinitely more profound insights that come from experiential, out-of-bounds learning. And, of course, market share gets a lot more discussion than wealth share.

Most management processes are controlled by the defenders of the past. The senior staff who "own" corporate training, planning and capital budgeting view their role as serving the barons who run today's big businesses. Any redesign of the management process usually begins by polling the executive vice presidents. Seldom is any attention given to the needs of struggling entrepreneurs and would-be activists.

Finally, most management processes are implicitly risk averse. The burden of proof is on those who would like to change the status quo. Seldom is the risk of overinvesting in a decaying business model made explicit. In countless ways, internal revolutionaries are given the message that incrementalism is safe and radicalism is risky, when of course the reverse is more often true.

Interview successful revolutionaries in large companies, and you'll hear a familiar refrain: "I succeeded despite the system." All of them know that "the system" is there to frustrate the new, the unconventional, and the untested. Management systems are designed to enforce conformance, alignment and continuity. We would be horrified if employees said they managed to deliver quality products and services "despite the system." We should be horrified that employees have to produce innovation "in spite of the system."

So here's what you do. Identify the four or five most pervasive and powerful management processes in your company: compensation, succession planning, leadership training, strategic planning, capital budgeting, product development, whatever. For each core process, assemble a review team, comprising a diagonal slice of your company. Make sure you have a senior staff person, a VP, a couple of middle managers and a mix of successful and unsuccessful corporate rebels on each team. Ask a proven revolutionary to chair each team. Give each team one management process to redesign. Have them pull together all of the documentation used to support that process. Have them map the process across time and across the organization by asking, What are the milestones? Who gets to participate? What are the inputs? What are the outputs? What kinds of decisions does the process produce? Have them interview a couple dozen process "users." In what ways does the process hinder business concept innovation and in what ways does it foster it? Have the team go back and review the purpose behind the process—what was it originally designed to do? Is that goal still valid? Is it possible to design a process that will meet that goal without killing innovation? Ask them to review each component of the management process for any evidence that the process is any of the following: inappropriately calendar-driven; biased toward conservation and efficiency rather than experimentation and growth; too tightly intertwined with the existing business model; overfocused on existing customers and markets; controlled by and run for the benefit of those defending large, established businesses; inherently risk averse. Finally, have the team suggest ways in which each component of the process could be redesigned to make it less backward-looking and more innovation-friendly. The team will need to write a new mission statement for the process—one that explicitly includes nonlinear innovation and wealth creation.

THE WHEEL OF INNOVATION

So you're baking the design rules into your organization, you're offering succor to the activists, and you're working to make business concept innovation a systemic capability. But there's still more to do. Innovation is a dynamic process, with the following elements:

○ Heretics and novelty addicts imagine new possibilities.
○ Using the principles of business concept innovation, they design coherent business models around those ideas, or redesign existing business models.
○ They launch small-scale experiments to test the viability of their business concepts and then adapt them.

THE WHEEL OF INNOVATION

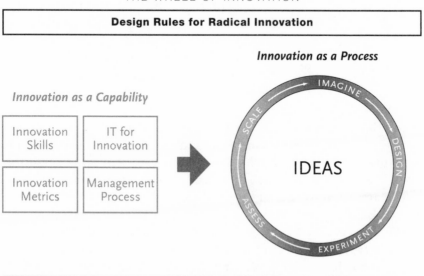

○ Having conducted an experiment or two or three, they assess what has been learned.
○ Depending on what has been learned, they decide whether to scale up or go through another experiment cycle.

Imagine, Design, Experiment, Assess, Scale. (By now you've spotted the helpful mnemonic.) This is the wheel of innovation, and it is the next critical component in the innovation solution (see the figure "The Wheel of Innovation").

MAKING THE WHEEL SPIN FASTER

The speed at which a company gets the wheel of innovation turning determines the amount of new wealth it creates. The first stumbling block is often an inability of potential innovators to go from the fragment of an idea to a reasonably holistic business concept design. Senior executives often tell me, "Our problem isn't a lack of ideas—we have too many ideas." But when I ask them whether they have too many truly compelling and coherent strategic options, the answer is always "no." This is why the skills needed to design a new business concept or reinvent an old one must be widely distributed. Would-be innovators must be able to do some initial quality assessment on their own ideas—is this a brainwave or a brainfart? If you can't imagine a coherent, profitable business concept supporting your idea, or if you can't imagine how your idea can profitably transform an existing business concept, send it aloft with all the other greenhouse gases.

SUCCESSIVE APPROXIMATION

Once there is a potential business concept, it must be tested experimentally, in much the same way an aeronautical engineer tests the flight characteristics of a high-performance fighter on a computer before strapping a pilot into the cockpit. Experiment, assess, adapt. Experiment, assess, adapt. The faster a company can go through this cycle, the faster it can resolve the uncertainty that inevitably surrounds a new and unconventional business concept, and the faster it can get to a viable, cash-generating business concept.

When every little new-rules experiment is scrutinized and reviewed as if it were a $100 million investment, the wheel of innovation comes to a grinding halt. **Companies are going to have to learn to run at more than one speed:** at "all deliberate speed" for big investments in capital-intensive projects where assets last for

20 years and at "light speed" for experiments in imagination–intensive opportunities. *You can't win a Formula 1 race with a John Deere tractor.*

Listen to a couple of speed demons from our cast of gray–haired revolutionaries:

> **Charles Schwab:** We have a learning mentality: It's better to start early and learn more than to wait around and try to get the thing perfect before you start.
> **GE Capital:** We deal with short cycle times. We'll have a dinner, study something, and then do a transaction within weeks.

These companies understand that developing great new business concepts, or reinventing fading business concepts, is often a process of successive approximation—a succession of fast–paced experiments, each designed to test some particular aspect of a novel business concept.

CUSTOMERS AS CO-DEVELOPERS

In the age of revolution, there is simply no way to stay ahead of the innovation curve unless your customers are your co–developers. The larger the community of co–developers, the quicker problems and opportunities for improvement are identified. As Lego demonstrates, sometimes even kids can be co–developers.

The MindStorms Robotics Invention System from Danish toy manufacturer Lego lets children build and bring to life robotic machines. MindStorms kits include a microprocessor brick and an infrared connection between the microprocessor and a PC. This connection allows children to transfer instructions from the PC to the microprocessor brick and hence control the robot. Children write instructions that specify the robot's behavior by using a simplified Lego programming language.

Children have shown remarkable creativity in the design of their robots and in finding innovative uses for their robots. In fact, some of those "children" are actually college and graduate students. Regardless, recognizing that this creativity can suggest new product opportunities for Lego, the company has established several online forums, hosted on the official Lego website.[2] These open source–type communities enable MindStorms enthusiasts to share their ideas and code and help each other to overcome difficulties in programming their robots. This forum provides Lego engineers with insights into new, and unimagined, uses of the MindStorms product line—insights that can be used to generate new products and software.

Ask yourself a question: Is the development team you're using outside your company bigger than the one inside your company? If not, your wheel of innovation isn't going to spin fast enough to get you to the future first.

KILL THE LOSERS FAST

In the absence of bounded experiments with tightly defined learning objectives, it's all too easy for eager innovators to fall in love with a deeply flawed business concept. To kill the losers fast, you must have a short market feedback loop. While the innovation board at Cemex is willing to take a bit of a flyer on new ideas, it also insists on a month-by-month update. The focus of these frequent reviews is more than financial. It is understood that a nascent project may, at times, miss its budget numbers. The real question is whether the project's initial assumptions about customer demand, technical feasibility and business economics are being confirmed or disconfirmed. If the starting assumptions are being challenged by the reality of the market experiment, a second question arises—can we reconfigure this project or is it fatally flawed? Short-cycle feedback and dispassionate diagnosis are critical to making sure that loser projects get killed quick.

Are you getting this?

○ Be honest about what you don't know.
○ Design tight, short experiments.
○ Maximize the ratio of learning over investment.
○ Bring your customers inside the tent.
○ Love your project but kill it quick if you find unfixable flaws.

THE INNOVATION PORTFOLIO

Think of nascent business designs and early-stage experiments as options on the future. Your company's chance of creating new wealth is directly proportional to the number of ideas it fosters and the number of experiments it starts. So ask yourself, **How diverse is your company's portfolio of unconventional strategy options?** What percentage of corporate initiatives are aimed at incremental improvement, and how many are testing opportunities for business concept innovation?

The innovation portfolio is actually three distinct portfolios. First is the portfolio of ideas, of credible, but untested, new business concepts. Second is the portfolio of experiments. Ideas that have particular merit get advanced to the portfolio of experiments, where they are validated through low-cost market incursions. Third is the portfolio of new ventures. (For our purposes, the term "ventures" refers to projects that could significantly change an existing business concept as well as to projects that could spawn an entirely new business concept.) Experiments that look promising advance to venture status. Here the goal is to begin to scale up the original idea. The "imagine" and "design" phases of the innovation process fill up the first portfolio with ideas. Ideas that advance to the "experiment" and "assess" stages populate the second portfolio, and those ready to be taken to "scale" comprise the third (see the figure "The Innovation Portfolio").

While top management often views the company as a portfolio of businesses, it seldom applies the logic of portfolio investing to investments in business concept experiments. This is particularly surprising when more and more companies are setting up venture funds to invest in a portfolio of upstarts outside the company. The logic of portfolio investing is to minimize the risk of the overall portfolio by diversifying your investments. With a diversified portfolio, the risk that the entire portfolio will take a big dive is substantially less than the risk that any single stock will fall through the floor. Yet all too often, exec-

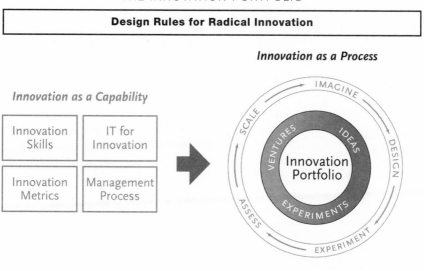

THE INNOVATION PORTFOLIO

Design Rules for Radical Innovation

Innovation as a Process

Innovation as a Capability

Innovation Skills | IT for Innovation

Innovation Metrics | Management Process

IMAGINE · SCALE · VENTURES · Innovation Portfolio · IDEAS · DESIGN · ASSESS · EXPERIMENTS · EXPERIMENT

Activism

utives expect every new idea or experiment to yield a bonanza. Such an expectation will invariably make a company overconservative and will quickly drain the portfolio of ideas and the portfolio of experiments of many interesting strategic options. It is important to distinguish between the risk that a particular idea or experiment doesn't pan out and the risk that the entire innovation portfolio yields a big fat zero. A bias against anything with the slightest hint of downside ensures a company will never find anything with an amazing upside. Spectacular new opportunities seldom start out as 90 percent sure things. That's why it's important to distinguish an "idea" or an "experiment" from a venture or a fully-fledged business. Perhaps the following analogy will help. In the act of procreation, millions of sperm get "wasted." You need a lot of little swimmers to fertilize an egg. Yet we seldom bemoan the lost sperm. One huge win—a new baby—offsets millions of small failures—dead sperm. Although we can hope for a substantially better ratio of wins to losses than a prospective father, the principle is much the same: You have to be willing to tolerate a lot of small losses for the occasional gigantic win. You don't have to risk big, but you have to risk often.

While companies have long recognized the low odds of success in new product development, and have endeavored to build and fill new product pipelines in response, they haven't applied the same principle to strategy development. As a result, most companies have no process for generating a surfeit of fresh strategy ideas, nor for starting and tracking dozens of strategy experiments, and then committing to those that prove most promising. Instead of building an innovation pipeline filled with unconventional strategy options, many companies have created innovation ghettoes—incubators, new venture divisions and venture funds that are largely divorced from innovation in the core business. The assumption seems to be that it is impossible to really innovate in the core business—that the fear of cannibalization is so overpowering and the constraints of orthodoxy so absolute that the only way to innovate is to create a separate organization filled with native-born entrepreneurs. While dedicated innovation units have a purpose, they are no substitute for an innovation pipeline overflowing with ideas for revitalizing the core business.

A PORTFOLIO OF IDEAS

The portfolio of ideas is really a "portfolio of possibilities." There are hundreds of half-baked, ill-formed ideas that bump around in the heads of your colleagues. Most never get articulated. Others exist only as water cooler conversations. Few organizations have attempted to collect and manage nonlinear ideas as part of an explicit portfolio of possibilities. Fewer still actually encourage front-line employees to contribute to an innovation portfolio. So for the dozen or so ideas that actually work their way up through the usual sclerotic approval channels, there are hundreds that never escape the heads of eager but isolated entrepreneurs.

A few years back, a young woman selling sewing machines for Sears noticed a worrying trend—more and more customers were returning recently purchased sewing machines. Perplexed, she began calling her dissatisfied customers and quickly learned that many had been stymied by the sheer complexity of the feature-laden machines. Her solution was to invite these frustrated customers into the store for sewing classes. As the flood of returns began to recede, it occurred to this enterprising employee that hers might not be the only Sears store facing such a challenge. Yet to her frustration, she quickly discovered that Sears, like most companies, had no systematic way of encouraging and propagating grass roots innovation like her own.

In the absence of an explicit process for building and managing an innovation portfolio, local experiments, even when successful, are unlikely to become company-wide programs. Just as bad, small ideas, like teaching customers how to use a sewing machine, that don't get shared and discussed never get the chance to become big ideas, like developing an entire portfolio of training programs focused on everything from kitchen remodeling to assembling a home entertainment system.

This is why companies must create opportunities for the advocates of nonlinear innovation to be heard and a way of cataloging radical, innovative ideas. One can easily imagine a number of things a company might do to help fill out its portfolio of ideas.

○ Appoint several business development officers (BDOs) to serve as advisors to prospective entrepreneurs. Rather than schmoozing with investment bankers, the BDOs would get rewarded for finding and nurturing internal innovation.
○ Ask each member of the executive committee to spend a couple days every month coaching eager, young entrepreneurs drawn from the far reaches of the organization. Each member of the executive committee would be asked to sponsor at least one new idea every quarter.
○ Put an "innovation" button on your company's internal home page. Anyone who clicks on it would find a simple form that

would allow them to post their idea in a corporation-wide, virtual "Ideaspace."

Or, if you're willing to be a bit bolder, you might want to try the following. Create an internal competition for bright new ideas, perhaps offering it to every branch, region or office. Use a peer review panel to determine which projects get an initial dose of funding. Make it easy for volunteer teams to coalesce around nascent experiments by widely publicizing the list of such projects. Set up a 30-day dash where the goal is to flesh out the basic idea and design an experiment that could be used to refine and validate the original idea. At the end of the 30-day period, run the ideas through a second peer review process to decide which get to advance to the experiment stage. In my experience, this is a surer way to transform a hide-bound company than incubators, mega-deals or top-down strategic planning.

Of course, none of this obviates the need to first train people in the basics of radical innovation and successful activism.

A PORTFOLIO OF EXPERIMENTS

Ideas that have great upsides, offer the chance for increasing returns, and are sponsored by truly passionate advocates get moved into the portfolio of experiments. Ideas that fail these tests get kicked out of the portfolio or are held back for further development as ideas. The portfolio of experiments contains ideas that have been worked into reasonably coherent versions of a business concept. They are ideas that have begun to attract a constituency.

Few companies make it easy for the advocates of radical innovation to attract sponsors and team members with complementary skills. Why not, for example, let internal innovators post banner ads on the company's intranet as a way of attracting talent and resources? Moreover, most companies don't have an explicit and legitimate designation for experimental-stage businesses or for radical but underdeveloped ideas that could dramatically transform the core business.

Indeed, many large companies have a bias against small experiments. They believe you have to do something BIG to make a noticeable impact on the top line. A typical objection goes something like this: "Sure, we can start a bunch of small experiments, but you have to understand we're a $20 billion company. It takes something pretty big to make a material difference to our shareholders." This helps explain the preference for mega-mergers and bet-the-company investments. Yet the real problem is that senior management too often can't see an oak tree in an acorn. They need to consider, for a moment, the current market capitalization of eBay, Dell, The Home Depot or Southwest Airlines and then ask themselves, How big were these companies a decade or two ago? Take a walk through a forest strewn with acorns—can you pick out which ones will grow into oak trees? Neither can I. And neither can even the most vaunted CEO. In the age of revolution, the challenge isn't finding that one enormous mega–deal but planting enough acorns to raise the chances of getting an oak tree. Yeah, you can go find an oak tree, uproot it and try to replant it, but this is a difficult and risky proposition, as any CEO who's ever tried to integrate a large acquisition will tell you. It's the innovation portfolio a CEO needs to worry about, not the queue of investment bankers panting outside the door.

For every 1,000 ideas, perhaps one in ten will have enough merit to be turned into an experiment. So after you've asked yourself whether your company has a portfolio of 1,000 ideas, ask yourself if your organization has a portfolio of 100 ongoing experiments. If it doesn't, and it's a sizable organization, its future is at risk.

A portfolio of new–rules experiments should cover the discontinuities most likely to upend current business models as well as those most likely to spawn entirely new opportunities. For example, a maker of mobile phones in the late 1990s would have wanted to have a few experiments focused on the mobile telephone as a replacement for fixed–line services in large corporations. It would have focused other experiments on the cell phone as a chic fashion accessory or as a requisite in every student's backpack. Other experiments would have addressed the convergence of voice and data and the wireless phone as a way to surf the Net. Others might have explored the convergence of the phone with online games. Yet another set of experiments would have focused on using wireless technology to build a communications capability into everything from household appliances to car engines.

Capital One, an enormously successful issuer of credit cards, has taken the idea of experimentation to an extreme. George Overholser, Senior Vice President of New Business Development at Capital One, told *Esquire* magazine, "We run thirty thousand tests a year, and they all compete against each other on the basis of economic results." *Esquire*'s Ted C. Fishman expands on the story:

> All the big players in the credit business run tests, of course, but Capital One's mania for them is unique. The tests take almost limitless forms, each with some rejiggering of components such

as interest rates, quantities of cards, fees and so-called affinity groups—like classic-rock fans. The vast majority of experiments fail, but the ones that hit, hit very big. One of the company's early innovations—allowing customers to transfer balances from one card to another—put Capital One on the map and forced the rest of the industry to play catch-up. The company is in its sixth year of showing 20 percent earnings growth per share and a 20 percent return on equity. Only ten other publicly traded U.S. companies compare.[3]

At Capital One, just about any employee can suggest a new idea. Again, listen to Overholser, "... individuals within Capital One are reporting to an idea they've created, not to their manager ... their job is not necessarily to tell their boss about it, but to find the best host for it at any given time."[4] Now, not every company can afford to conduct 30,000 experiments in a year—it's a bit easier to do a small direct mail test of a new credit card offering than it is to test a new automobile concept. Yet the principle still applies—to survive in a highly discontinuous world, every company must become capable of conducting low-cost, low-risk experiments on a broad front.

MOST EXPERIMENTS WON'T PAY OFF. BUT THIS HARDLY MEANS THEY ARE WORTHLESS. After all, your fire insurance wasn't a bad investment last year, even if your house didn't burn down. A business concept that gets killed rather than scaled up isn't a dead loss. Every experiment produces learning, which, if captured and shared, can help a company increase the odds that the next radical idea finds its mark.

A PORTFOLIO OF VENTURES

At the experimentation stage, the goal is to identify and reduce market and technology risk: Does the business concept generate sufficient customer interest? Is it technically feasible? If there's sufficient upside, and no insurmountable technical hurdles, the idea advances to the venture stage. At the venture stage learning focuses on the feasibility of the profit model and the operating model, as opposed to the business concept itself. The question is not whether the business concept will create new revenue streams, but whether they can be created economically: Can we manage the execution risk? Can we avoid the competitive risk that our innovation will be quickly imitated?

This is also the stage where one begins a serious search for strategic partners who will share risks and contribute complementary skills. There are three primary factors to consider when deciding whether to partner and how many partners to have:

○ Financial commitments: If scaling requires large, irrevocable financial commitments, partners may be needed.
○ Range of skills or assets required: If a company doesn't have all the critical skills in–house, it will need partners.
○ Size of the strategic window: If the risk of preemption is high, partners may be needed to help accelerate market penetration.

At this point, it may well be that the original sponsors have to give way to venture leaders with business–building experience. With the quality of the business concept already validated, it is the quality of the venture team that becomes critical.

This is also the stage where decisions must be made about whether to reintegrate the innovation into a line unit, set it up as a stand–alone business, license the intellectual property to another company or spin the venture off as an independent entity. At least four criteria are key to this decision:

○ The *fit* between the venture and the company's long–term strategic goals. If a venture is clearly tangential to a company's long–term aspirations, it should be spun off in order to conserve management's time for projects that are more congruent with long–term ambitions. If the venture is not spun off, it probably won't get the love and attention it needs to reach its potential.
○ The venture's *dependence on firm assets and competencies*. If a venture could benefit enormously from leveraging existing assets and competencies, it probably should not be spun off. If it is spun off, it should be given preferential access to those competencies and assets.
○ The possibility that the venture will be *a platform for other ventures*. Some ventures are ends in themselves; others are stepping–stones to other ventures. If a venture promises to open up a broad new opportunity arena, that may be a reason to keep it inside.
○ The potential for the venture to *dramatically outperform other businesses* in the portfolio. Increasingly companies are spinning off ventures that might be undervalued by Wall Street were they to be imprisoned inside a company with otherwise mediocre performance.

Clearly, some ventures will lack a tight fit with the company's long-term goals, will be only partly dependent on the company's existing assets and competencies, and won't be a gateway to a vast array of new opportunities. Hence we shouldn't be surprised if some of the ventures end up as spin-offs or licensing deals, rather than as new business units or transformation projects within existing business units.

Spinning a business off is easy—giving it sufficient independence to grow, while at the same time helping it leverage well-honed competencies, is a much more delicate balancing act. Reintegration is more subtle still. A company that embraces the new innovation agenda should expect to create, as Shell has done, dozens of game-changing ventures that need to be reintegrated into existing businesses—a radical new pricing approach here, an unconventional distribution model over there, and so on. At Cemex, most of the projects identified by the innovation platform teams were reintegrated back into the operating units. The fact that the innovation board, staffed by senior executives, continued to review the transformation projects, even once they had been reintegrated, was a powerful incentive for unit managers to make sure the projects received continued funding and access to talent.

So while high-potential ventures based on entirely new business concepts should probably be nurtured in a new business incubator, successful ventures with the power to transform the core business should be "spun up" inside those businesses. Simply, there is no single mechanism for going from a venture to a business. Most of Cemex's innovations have been spin-ups rather than spin-offs, reinforcing and reinventing Cemex's core cement business. In contrast, GE Capital's popcorn stand experiments often end up as new business units.

Let's recap. To go from a possibility to an experiment, an idea must be able to be described as a reasonably coherent business concept—with an attractive value proposition, a credible story around wealth creation potential and a clear sense of how the various components of the business concept will fit together and be mutually reinforcing. For an experiment to become a venture, it must have elicited genuine customer enthusiasm and be technically feasible (at least on a small scale). For a venture to move out of the innovation portfolio and become a business, or be spun up inside an existing business, there must be a sound profit model and evidence that the business concept can be scaled up.

Now take a detailed look at your company's various innovation portfolios. How many ideas does your company have in its innovation bank? Do you have thousands? How many rule-bashing experiments

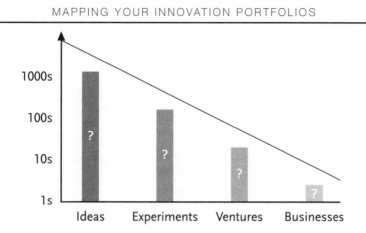

are being conducted across your company right now? Do you have hundreds? How many new ventures are being nurtured right now? Do you have dozens? And how many big new businesses are being built right now? Can you think of even one or two?

Map the size of each portfolio (see the graph "Mapping Your Innovation Portfolios"), and it will be immediately clear whether or not your company is investing in enough options on the future. Turn the diagram 90 degrees to the right, and you have a funnel. If a company hasn't learned how to fill the top of the funnel, it won't get much out the bottom. To return to our earlier analogy, you have to ask yourself, What's my company's sperm count? You don't get a terrific new business without hundreds of dumb ideas, failed experiments and aborted ventures.

GETTING YOUR TIMING RIGHT

Perhaps the most critical issue in scaling up a venture is the issue of timing—this is true whether the venture is focused on an entirely new business, or some major modification (a new channel, a dramatically altered value proposition, etc.) of an existing business. As every student of business knows, too much too soon, or too little too late can destroy an otherwise sterling opportunity.

At the height of dot–com mania, "first mover advantage" was a near-sacred mantra for VCs and entrepreneurs alike. Indeed, e–commerce zealots argued that early success would compound even more quickly on the Web than in the dawdling "old economy"—this due to the multiplicative impact of the "network effect." Being first to build a consumer brand in a new category (Amazon), invent a new business model (eBay) or achieve critical mass (what WebVan was hoping to do) were seen as sure-fire routes to Midas-like profits.

In reality, of course, first-mover advantages proved elusive. For most dot-com start-ups, being first was simply a way to lose more, faster. As a result, many pundits argued that the Net spawned *too much* innovation and that being a "fast follower" was often a better strategy than trying to lead from the front. After all, the argument goes, pioneers often end up with arrows in their backs. Big company CEOs, eager to avoid the hard work of strategic innovation, seized upon this diagnosis as justification for their instinctive fear of novelty. Suddenly, timidity was once again in fashion and incrementalism, a.k.a. "getting back to basics," was heralded as a virtue. Yet the conclusions which seem to justify these reactionary tendencies are every bit as superficial as the simple-minded adage which they challenge. Most Internet companies failed not because they were *first* movers, but because they were *dumb* movers. What companies should learn from the Internet debacle is not that being first is a dangerous form of hubris, but that being dumb seldom succeeds. When it comes to trailblazing, there are at least three ways to be a dumb mover—none of which are unique to Internet start-ups.

DUMB: MISTAKING A MARATHON FOR A SPRINT, OR VICE VERSA

Building a first-mover advantage requires impeccable timing. If a company invests faster than it learns, it will "overdrive" the opportunity and end up with an expensive and embarrassing failure. This is the fate that befell Apple's pioneering handheld computer, the Newton. Was there a potential market out there for "palm" computers? Absolutely. Could investment and marketing hype alone force the market to develop on Apple's time frame? No way. Companies that overdrive an emerging opportunity early on, often "underdrive" it later. The initial performance gap, a product of unrealistic expectations and overinvestment, produces a rapid retrenchment. In this way, overcommitment leads to undercomment. If the original vision was directionally correct, this de-commitment provides an opening for latecomers.

There is an optimally feasible market penetration curve for every emerging opportunity. This curve describes what is possible in terms of market penetration over time. Typically, the curve has an inflection point—a moment in time when all the pieces of the business model finally fall into place, when customer demand explodes, and the market takes off. The curve for videocassette recorders was long, beginning with an abortive effort by Ampex to produce a consumer video tape recorder in the mid–60s. The curve began to slope gently upward with the launch of Matsushita's VHS format in the late '70s, and it would take another seven years for VCRs to find their way into one million American homes. In contrast, the market penetration curve for Hotmail was a near vertical line, with more than 10 million users signing up in the first 18 months. Matsushita, which started working on a VCR in the 1960s, ran a marathon. Hotmail ran a sprint. The Apple Newton might have evolved into something Palm–like, but only if Apple had better paced itself by spending less, learning faster, and iterating more quickly. Apple blew the handheld opportunity not because it was the first mover, but because it was a dumb mover.

Any management team that aspires to be a first mover must ask itself, what race are we running: sprint or marathon. If you try to run a 100–yard sprint like a marathon, you'll get beat. If you try to run a marathon like a 100–yard sprint, you'll quickly keel over from exhaustion. For this reason, it is critically important to correctly estimate the general shape of the market penetration curve. To make this assessment, a number of questions have to be answered: How significant are the remaining technical hurdles? Does market take–off depend on the development of complementary products or services? Will a new infrastructure be required? Will customers need to learn new skills or adopt new behaviors? Are there high switching costs for customers? Will competing standards confuse customers and delay adoption? Does success depend on aligning the interests of diverse constituents? Are there powerful competitors who will seek to delay or derail us? If the answer to any of these questions is "yes," a company must be careful not to pour in too many resources too soon. This is going to be a marathon. (Think the wireless Internet, streaming video or industry–wide B2B hubs.) Other questions to consider include: Are the customer benefits clear and substantial? Are there potential network effects that will accelerate take–off? Are there powerful competitors who will be compelled to follow us? If the answer to these questions is yes, you'll need to sprint out of the starting blocks. (Think eBay in online auctions or BEA Systems, a pioneer in the market for application servers.)

The shape of the market penetration curve for a new product or business is largely determined by factors outside a company's direct control. All the money in the world won't force a market to develop faster if there are structural impediments that stand in the way of a quick take–off. Conversely, if a company gets behind the optimal penetration curve, all the money in the world may not let it catch up— unless, of course, the company is Microsoft and it actually *has* all the money in the world, or unless some technology discontinuity gives latecomers an opening. Staying on the optimal penetration curve is a neat trick, but it's not impossible. Intuit (Quicken), AOL and Sun Microsystems are companies that have demonstrated a great sense of timing, getting out in front on new product and service curves, but not getting *too* far out in front. There are a bunch of things a company can do to ensure it neither overdrives nor underdrives an emerging opportunity: Build an infrastructure that is easily scaleable, constantly review initial assumptions about product and business design, make sure that premium pricing and a narrow market definition doesn't create a pool of pent-up demand that can be easily drained by latecomers, move quickly to collaborate with would-be competitors, shorten the cycle time for product iterations and use outsourcing to improve flexibility. Like first-time tennis players, dumb movers have a hard time getting their swing in synch with a moving target. Smart movers have Venus Williams's perfect pace and timing.

DUMBER: OVER-PAYING
FOR MARKET SHARE

The allure of capturing a first-mover advantage often produces a spending orgy among a gaggle of look-alike competitors each intent on ramping up faster than its rivals. This is exactly what happened in many areas of e-commerce and in the race to encircle the globe with optical fiber. It's hard to be first when a horde of similarly minded competitors are making tit-for-tat investors. In such cases, it's easy to overpay for market share, particularly when investment funds are eager to come buy.

To reap a first-mover advantage, a company must buy market share at a discount, that is, it must be able to buy a big chunk of market share before its competitors figure out just how much that market share will yield in future profits. This is possible only if a company possesses a unique strategic insight—one not shared by less imaginative or more orthodox competitors. To be first, a company must start with a business idea that is truly revolutionary, as did eBay and ICQ (the instant messaging pioneer). Think of it this way. If you're the only one with a treasure map, you can easily justify the cost of the expedition to recover the hidden bounty. But if the map is widely available, and a teeming throng sets out at roughly the same time in search of the same treasure, the odds of grabbing the loot decline precipitously, and the expected value of one's reward quickly sinks below the cost of the journey. Of course this simple arithmetic was no more effective in deterring investors from backing hundreds of me–too Web–based business models than it was in dissuading otherwise sane individuals from joining the California gold rush of 1849.

The fact is, the Internet didn't produce too *much* in the way of authentic business model innovation, but too *little*. The moral is simple: If you want to profit from a first–mover advantage, you better make sure you start with an idea that is truly unique and, at least initially, unattractive to would–be competitors or protected by a wall of patents. Dumb movers swarm, smart movers take the road less traveled.

DUMBEST: BEING FIRST WITH A BUSINESS MODEL THAT'S DEAD-ON-ARRIVAL

Pets.com. Iridium. WebVan. XFL. NorthPoint. Global Crossing. Many business models are brain dead from the get–go. They breathe as long as they are hooked up to the ventilator of investor funds, but expire the moment investors swallow their grief and pull the plug. There are two fundamental flaws that can render a business model DOA: a complete misread of the customer (does she really want to order dog food online), and/or utterly unsound economics (there will never be enough petroleum geologists and arctic explorers to make satellite telephony pay). There's no advantage in being first if the destination ain't worth the trip. Of course, the pioneers will tell you that "the market wasn't ready." But this is usually nothing more than exculpatory baloney. It was the business model that "wasn't ready."

Being first is no substitute for sound business thinking, and a stupid idea that fails is hardly an indictment of the general concept of first–mover advantage. So think twice before you let someone else's idiocy lull you into believing that being first is always a peril–strewn path. Ask Andy Grove if he is glad that Intel got an early lead in microprocessors, or Herb Kelleher at Southwest Airlines (discount air travel), or Pete Kight at CheckFree (online billing and payment).

I don't believe any company should set out to be a follower, fast or otherwise. Sure, in hindsight, first movers often look dumb, but it would be imprudent to bet that they will always screw up. Indeed, when you look beyond the weirdness of the Internet bubble, and consider companies with high–quality management, deep pockets and real competencies, you find that being first pays off a surprisingly high percentage of the time. So before you bet against the first mover, you'd be wise to ask yourself: Is the first mover a slow learner? Is market penetration still in single digits and likely to stay that way for a while?

Is the rate of technology change extremely high, creating opportunities for a leap–frog strategy? Is the product or service still significantly underdeveloped? Are there a number of potential partners who are still unallied? If you can answer yes to all these questions, then you may want to keep your powder dry.

Instead of betting that your competitors are stupid, learn how to be a smart mover! Face up to the fact that a new business idea can be exhilarating and apparently compelling and yet completely wrong-headed. Don't let enthusiasm get in the way of deep thinking. If you're going to invest, make sure you're starting with a unique insight—a truly revolutionary strategy. And then work hard to keep your financial commitments in synch with the underlying pace of market development. Smart movers don't bet the company—they just learn a little bit faster, while spending a little bit less, than their competitors.

In the end, the distinction between first mover and fast follower hides more than it reveals. The goal, after all, is not to be first to market in some absolute sense, but to be first to put together the precise combination of features, value and sound business economics that unlocks a profitable new market. Sometimes this is the first mover, and sometimes it is not. But it's always the *smart* mover.

FROM RADICAL INNOVATION TO CORPORATE STRATEGY

So where does all this leave corporate strategy? Indeed, where does it leave the very concept of a "corporation"? In the age of revolution, will corporate strategy be anything more than the sum of a few dozen, or a few hundred, loosely connected experiments and ventures? Will companies be anything more than a set of bottom–up projects united by shared overhead? Will some combination of internal markets, de-verticalization, value networks, and self-organizing teams reduce the notion of a corporation to disembodied bits of intellectual property floating free in some kind of virtual innovation network? While all these things will undoubtedly make companies less monolithic, they are not going to remove the need for an overarching strategy, nor are they going to entirely do away with the benefits of size and scale.

SIZE STILL MATTERS

A lot of young entrepreneurs learned a painful lesson in the last few years: Size still matters. Sure, incumbency isn't worth as much as it used to be, but it's still worth something. The companies that survive that dot–com shakeout aren't going to be will-o'-the-wisp, thin–as–

gossamer virtual companies. They are going to be companies like Cisco and Amazon.com—companies that have had their share of ups and downs, but have never lost sight of the fact that scale matters. Most Silicon Valley start-ups fail to capture the full benefits of scale and scope. These companies end up as acquisition fodder for companies that have. Mirabilis, Broadcast.com, Netscape and hundreds of other Internet start-ups have already been swallowed up. Hundreds more have simply folded.

Of course it is not size, per se, that counts. Size is the first-order derivative of profit boosters that rely on increasing returns, network effects, learning effects and economies of scale and scope. Exploit these, and a company will inevitably grow, and smaller, me-too competitors will begin disappearing out the rearview window.

A few years ago, many among the digerati were predicting the collapse of large-scale enterprises. They end wrong. **Size will always matter.** Indeed, at the end of 1999, in the midst of the dot-com craze, 32 companies accounted for half the market capitalization of the S&P 500. An oft-used analogy is the movie industry, where teams of writers, producers, directors and actors coalesce around a project and then disband when the film is completed. Yet the most enduring fact of the movie business has been the power of the big studios. They are repositories for an enormous amount of project management wisdom. Despite the occasional "duds," they are skilled story editors, and they have the global reach necessary to market films around the world. Indeed, as every European cultural minister knows, it is the studios that have given Hollywood its global hegemony in the film business. You don't hear Italian or French filmmakers complaining that their colleagues aren't creative enough; you hear them complaining that they can't match the size and scale of American studios. Of course a market of 250 million customers helps, but a market of this size is of no particular advantage unless there are economies of scale in serving such a market.

It is interesting to note that even highly fluid, project-based companies such as Bechtel, Accenture and Schlumberger are far, far more than a collection of individual projects. If that were all they were, they wouldn't be multibillion-dollar enterprises. So, yes, companies may become more like film studios, relying on free agents, raising outside funding for each new venture and creating short-lived project teams. But somewhere in this brave, new model, size and scale will still matter—because if they don't, you're back to frictionless capitalism where no one has an incentive to invest in something new. On average, companies may shrink. After all, scale and scope advantages apply to activities, not companies per se. But size will be far from irrelevant in the age of revolution.

Indeed, without scale and scope advantages, it is difficult to imagine how a company can enjoy the fruits of radical innovation. Of course when a hot start-up is sold, its founders get a big win. But this just shifts the problem of building scale and scope onto the acquirer—and if the acquirer fails at this, it will never recoup its investment (a common enough occurrence, by the way).

CONSISTENCY COUNTS

You can't build economies of scale and scope without consistency, without doing things over and over in a reasonably consistent way. You can't build difficult-to-imitate competencies without cumulative learning. In turn, it is impossible to achieve consistency and cumulativeness without a degree of coordination across projects or businesses. Consistency requires a set of mutually agreed upon rules about what is "in" and what is "out," what a company is and what it isn't. Lacking some overarching strategy, a company will have a vast greenhouse where thousands of shoots are pushing up through the soil but where few grow big enough to yield a substantial harvest. So **innovation is not the whole story, but it is the big story**—because most companies have already figured out the scale and scope thing and now need to start planting new seeds.

In the age of revolution, the challenge will be to marry radical innovation with disciplined execution—to merge the efficiency of a Toyota production line with the radical innovation of Silicon Valley, to blend diligence and curiosity. To be a gray-haired revolutionary, a company must be systematic and spontaneous, highly focused and opportunistic, brutally efficient and wildly imaginative.

Oil and water, chalk and cheese, such amalgams are impossible without a new synthesis. Notice that in making an argument for mass and scale, I haven't used words like hierarchy, control and plan. These are industrial-age words. Instead I talk about consistency, cumulativeness, boundaries and focus. Remember, the goal is "order without careful crafting." So where does this order come from? It must emerge from the stream of radical innovation that begins to flow once you make innovation a corporate-wide capability.

SUSTAINING THE REVOLUTION

In any stream of ideas, some kind of deeper pattern will be evident.

The trick is to look for patterns, for consistency and cumulativeness that will yield advantages of scale and scope across ideas, experiments and ventures. Patterns come in many forms:

○ Allegiance to a standard, such as Microsoft's allegiance to the Windows operating system, which spawned, both within Microsoft and without, hundreds of small innovations built atop the Windows standard.
○ A widely shared core competence, such as UPS's competence in logistics, based on cumulative learning.
○ A set of values around a brand that can be applied broadly, as in the case of Virgin and Disney, and thereby yield economies of scope.
○ A common customer set that is best served in a coordinated way, which is the logic behind Amazon.com's creating a wide variety of "stores within a store" rather than making each store an entirely independent entity.

These patterns provide the logic for the corporation. They provide the connective tissue that makes the company more than a collection of stand-alone projects. While there is nothing new in saying that a company must be more than the sum of its parts, what is new is how the summing up gets done. It can't start with some grand pronouncement from on high about "what business we're in." It can't come from a bunch of senior vice presidents working to craft a common mission statement. It certainly shouldn't come as the panicked reaction to demands from stock analysts for a strategy that will hold water. Instead, it has to be filtered out of the stream of innovation that flows from the fertile minds of individuals throughout the organization.

While senior executives can no longer be the sole source of new business concepts, it is their responsibility to look across the patchwork of radical innovation to find the interesting—and wealth-laden—patterns. One set of opportunities will push the company in one direction, allowing it to build one kind of scope or scale advantage; another set of opportunities will push the company in another direction, with another set of potential synergies. While idea generation should be unbounded, a company is compelled to make choices about where it focuses its energies. Yet it is important that such choices do not rule out the possibility of entirely "unscripted" innovation. That's why every company needs well-functioning markets for innovation that funnel resources to nascent ideas and propel them through the experimentation stage. But at some point the most promising experiments will need big injections of capital. It is here that senior management must begin to make choices about which patterns it wants to emphasize and which it wishes to de-emphasize.

Those choices must be based on an unimpeachable and clearly articulated logic—"We will create more wealth by exploiting this particular dimension of scale and relatedness than we will by exploiting some other dimension." Over time, these choices will begin to bias the innovation process. Again, it's not that top management declares some kinds of innovation to be out of bounds. Nothing is out of bounds. Instead, would-be revolutionaries come to understand that by exploiting shared assets and competencies or getting access to a big customer base, they gain scale and scope advantages that give their ideas added momentum. Of course those who want to go off in different directions can still do so, and there will be mechanisms—licensing, spin-offs and alliances—for capturing wealth out of ideas that don't fit within the emerging corporate strategy. Occasionally those out-of-bounds ideas will be so compelling and valuable that they will force the company to redefine the very essence of its strategy. This has been the case at GE, which no one regards any longer as an "industrial" company. In this sense, top management doesn't so much make strategy as find strategy.

Of course there are already deep patterns that determine what kinds of strategies people create in your company—I've called these patterns orthodoxies. But they are the patterns of precedent, not the patterns of possibility. So don't take any of what I've just said as an excuse to simply lock down your current definition of corporate strategy. Remember, corporate strategy must be distilled from a torrent of innovation. If you don't yet have a torrent of nonlinear business concepts and weird and wonderful experiments, that's where you need to start. Don't build a dam before you have a stream.

ARE YOU REVOLUTION-READY?

Is your organization ready for the age of revolution? Does it have an irrevocable commitment to building the components of the new innovation solution? Is its top management finished "making" strategy and ready to "find" it? To determine this, ask yourself these questions:

○ Have individuals been given the training and the tools they need to become business concept innovators?
○ Do the metrics in your company focus as much on innovation and wealth creation as on optimization and wealth conservation?
○ Does your IT system support a corporation–wide electronic marketplace for innovation?
○ Has your organization committed itself to systematically redesigning its core management processes to make them more innovation–friendly?
○ Does the "wheel of innovation" spin rapidly in your organization, or is it limited by the speed of quarterly and annual processes?
○ Do would–be entrepreneurs know how to design experiments around radical ideas?
○ Are there formal mechanisms for capturing and monitoring the learning from innovation experiments?
○ Does your organization get the very best talent behind the best new ideas, even when those ideas are at an early stage of development?
○ Is your organization explicitly managing a portfolio of ideas, a portfolio of experiments, and a portfolio of ventures?
○ Is your organization flexible enough to design the right kind of institutional home for promising ventures?
○ Are you confident that your company is in charge of the transformation agenda in its industry?

Don't despair if you answered "no" more often than "yes." There's not one company in a hundred that has fully committed itself to building the new innovation solution. What matters is what you're going to do next.
Are you ready to commit yourself to the new innovation agenda?

THE NEW INNOVATION AGENDA

Continuous improvement	*and*	Nonlinear innovation
Product and process innovation	*and*	Business concept innovation
"Releasing" wealth	*and*	Creating wealth
Serendipity	*and*	Capability
Visionaries	*and*	Activists
Hierarchies	*and*	Markets

Are you ready to start working on the new innovation solution? (See the figure "The Innovation Solution.")

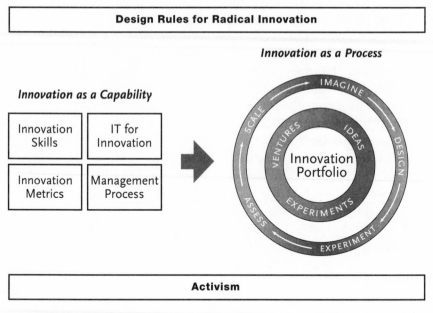

Design Rules for Radical Innovation

Innovation as a Process

Innovation as a Capability

Innovation Skills	IT for Innovation
Innovation Metrics	Management Process

IMAGINE • IDEAS • DESIGN • EXPERIMENT • EXPERIMENTS • ASSESS • VENTURES • SCALE

Innovation Portfolio

Activism

You can start now and get ahead of the curve, or wait and fight a rearguard action. What's it going to be?

ARE *YOU* A REVOLUTIONARY?

It doesn't matter whether you're the big cheese or a cubicle rat. It doesn't matter whether you fly in a Gulfstream V or ride the crosstown bus. It doesn't matter whether you command a legion of minions or only your PalmPilot. All that matters is whether you care enough to start from where you are. So ask yourself, Do you care enough about your integrity to speak the truth and challenge the little lies that jeopardize your company's future? Do you care enough about the future to argue with precedent and stick a thumb in the eye of tradition? Do you care enough about your colleagues to help them get off the treadmill of progress? Do you care so much about the magnificent difference you can make in this world that you're willing to try and change it with your bare heart? Do you care enough about finding meaning and significance in the 80 percent of your life you devote to work that you're ready to start a movement within your company? Do you care enough about the creative impulse that resides in every human breast that you're ready to help everyone be a revolutionary? Do you care enough about doing something so wonderful and unexpected for customers that you're willing to put your comfy job on the line? Go ahead, ask yourself, Do you care enough to lead the revolution?

I began this book with a simple observation—that for the first time in history our heritage is no longer our destiny. Our dreams are no longer fantasies, but possibilities. There isn't a human being who has ever lived who wouldn't want to be alive right now, at this moment so pregnant with promise. Among all your forebears, among the countless generations who had no hope of progress, among all those whose spirits were betrayed by progress, you are the one who now stands on the threshold of a new age—the age of revolution. You are blessed beyond belief. Don't falter. Don't hesitate. You were given this opportunity for a reason. Find it. Lead the revolution.

○ NOTES

1 THE END OF PROGRESS

1 Patricia Sellers, "Who's in Charge Here?" *Fortune*, 24 December 2001, 79.
2 "Competition 2000," an unpublished survey sponsored by MCI and carried out by The Gallup Organization.
3 "P&G to Slash 15,000 Jobs, Shut 10 Plants," *Wall Street Journal*, 10 June 1999.
4 "ConAgra Products," <www.conagra.com/product.html>.
5 Susan Moran, "The Candyman," *Business 2.0*, June 1999, 66–67.

2 FACING UP TO STRATEGY DECAY

1 Nikhil Deogun and Steven Lipin, "When the Big Deal Turns Bad," *Wall Street Journal*, 8 December 1999.
2 "Addicted to Mergers?" *Business Week*, 6 December 1999, 85.
3 Strategos calculations.
4 Tish Williams, "WorldCom's Big Bluffer," *Upside Today*, 14 July 1999, ,www.upside.com/texis/mvm/daily_tish?id37649f420.
5 Richard Waters, "Shape-up for long distance telecoms," *Financial Times*, 7 June 2001, 22.
6 Martin Brookes and Zaki Wahhaj, "Is the Internet Better Than Electricity," Global Economics Paper No. 49, Goldman Sachs.
7 Jolie Solomon, "When Cool Goes Cold," *Newsweek*, 30 March 1998, 37.
8 John Markoff, "Silicon Valley Accelerates to Web Speed," *International Herald Tribune*, 4 June 1996.
9 *Primetime Network Ratings and Shares*, Nielsen Media Research, 2000.
10 Bill Carter, "As Their Dominance Erodes, Networks Plan Big Changes," *New York Times*, 11 May 1978.

3 BUSINESS CONCEPT INNOVATION

1 Marianne Wilson, "Say Chic—C'est Sephora," *Chain Store Age*, July 1998, 134.
2 Neal Templin, "Electronic Kiosk Checks in Guests at More Hotels," *Wall Street Journal*, 16 February 1999.
3 "Interview: Gordon Moore, Intel," *PC Magazine*, 25 March 1997, 236.
4 United Rentals, <www.unitedrentals.com> (23 August 1999).
5 Michael A. Hiltzik, *Dealers of Lightning: Xerox PARC and the Dawn of the Computer Age* (New York: HarperBusiness, 1999).

4 BE YOUR OWN SEER

1 "Garbage In, Garbage Out," *The Economist*, 3 June 1995, 70.
2 Fara Warner and Joseph B. White, "New From Japan: Bar Stools on Wheels," *Wall Street Journal*, 25 October 1999.
3 Michael Kavanagh, "Porn Will Continue to Dominate Web Revenue," *Marketing Week*, 27 May 1999, 43.
4 These distinctions are adapted and reprinted from *European Management Journal*, volume 13, Georg von Krogh and Johan Roos, "Conversation Management," page 393, copyright 1995, with permission from Elsevier Science.

5 CORPORATE REBELS

1 Debra E. Meyerson and Maureen A. Scully, "Tempered Radicalism and the Politics of Ambivalence and Change," *Organizational Science* 6, no. 5 (September–October 1995): 585–600.
2 Robert A. Guth, "Inside Sony's Trojan Horse," *Wall Street Journal*, 25 February 2000.

6 GO AHEAD! REVOLT!

1 Saul D. Alinsky, *Rules for Radicals: A Practical Primer for Realistic Radicals* (New York: Vintage Books, 1989).
2 Mary Beth Rogers, *Cold Anger: A Story of Faith and Power Politics* (Denton, TX: University of North Texas Press, 1990), 88.

8 DESIGN RULES FOR INNOVATION

1 M. Mitchell Waldrop, *Complexity: The Emerging Science at the Edge of Order and Chaos* (New York: Simon & Schuster, 1992), 241, 242.
2 Writing for MIT's *Technology Review*, Michael Schrage was quoted in the University of Phoenix's 2001 Annual Report.
3 Viktor E. Frankl, *Man's Search for Meaning* (New York: Pocket Books, 1984), 17.
4 Tim Stevens, "Breaking Up Is Profitable Too," *Industry Week*, 21 June 1999, 28–34.

9 THE NEW INNOVATION SOLUTION

1 Steve Kerr, "On the Folly of Rewarding A, While Hoping for B," *Academy of Management Journal* 18 (December 1975): 769–783.
2 mindstorms.lego.com/forums/default.asp.
3 Ted C. Fishman, "Disruption, Subversion, Disorder, Yes!" *Esquire*, October 2000.
4 "Simulation and the Venture Capital Business," an unpublished paper by George Overholser, Josh Epstein, and Rob Axtell.

○ INDEX

Boston Scientific Corp., 108
boundaries, 73, 97–99, 221;
    pushing, 247, 257, 318;
    spanning teams, 280
BP, 42
Brady, Sarah, 155
BrainReserve, 134, 137
brand appeal, declining, 8
Branson, Sir Richard, 82, 249, 266, 278
breakeven, 116
British Telecom, 5
"broadband," vii, 109
Broadcast.com, 317
broad recommendations, 193–94
Brookes, Martin, 51, 52
Brown, John Seely, 138, 145
Brown, Linda Carol, 155
building industry, 80–81, 242–45
build-to-order model, 46, 80
Burger King, 15, 93
business concept: blind spots in, 73,
    75;
    network effect and, 104
business concept innovation, x, 59–118,
    286;
    alignment as enemy of, 154;
    becoming innovator and, 117–18;
    competitors and, 72;
    creating space for, 153–58;
    cyber B-school as, 65–69;
    defined, 61–65, 69–73;
    employees and, 288;
    goals of, 64–65, 69–70;
    investing in, 285–87;
    management processes and, 297–99;
    systemizing, 287–88;
    unpacking business model and,
    73–117;
    wheel of innovation and, 299
business definition, elastic, 256–58
business development officers (BDOs),
    305
business mission, 74–75
business model(s), 73–118;
    bridge components, 73, 81–83, 91–93,
    97–99;
    as built-in monopolies, 103;
    core components, 73, 74–81, 83–91,
    93–97;
    creative accounting and, 41;
    dead-on-arrival, 315–16;
    decay of, 154;
    efficiency and, 74, 99;
    fit and, 74, 99, 101–2;
    four distinct, 153;
    increasing returns and, 104–6;
    Internet and, 4;
    learning effects and, 105–6;
    new, 69, 72;
    profit boosters and, 74, 99–117;

pushing boundaries of, 257–58;
    rethinking, 117–18;
    strategy convergence and, 46–47;
    strategy decay and, 36, 37;
    uniqueness and, 74, 99;
    wealth potential and, 74, 99–117
business plan, 268
business process improvement, 24–25
business schools, cyber, 65–69
business-to-business hubs and ex-
    changes, 96
Butterfield & Butterfield, 10
buyback champs, 40
Buy.com, 100
buyers, 53

cable television companies, 47, 56, 109,
    274
Cable & Wireless, 247
call centers, outsourcing, 220
Calloway, 128
Cambridge University, 103
Canadair, 10
Canavino, Jim, 162
cannibalization, 125, 200, 222, 228, 260
Canon, 62
capability, 20–24, 287–88, 290
capital: budgeting, 65, 268, 298;
    market for, 266–69;
    spending, boom in, 33
capitalism, 5
Capital One, 307
Carrefour, 96
Casey, Jim, 220
catalysts, 200
category killers, 8, 52, 127
Caterpillar, 79, 286
cause, business as, 259–61
cellular division, 278–79
cellular telephone business, 6–7, 15, 94,
    170, 212, 307
cement industry, 230–47, 248
Cemex, 26, 58, 125, 211, 212, 230–47,
    250, 255, 260, 262, 263, 267, 280,
    281, 302, 310;
    Capital, 244;
    Dynamic Synchronization of Oper-
    ations (DSO), 238;
    Key Value Creators group, 239
Centex, 35
CEOs, 12, 21, 43, 44
chain of consequences, 133–34
Chambers, John, 45
Champion, 44
change, ix–x, 45, 138, 155, 222, 287;
    abrupt, 5–7, 11–13;
    knowing what's not, 134–35;
    rates of, 126–28
Charles Schwab, 8, 26, 38, 211–12, 222–30,
    250, 254, 256, 258–60, 301

○ ABOUT THE AUTHOR

Gary Hamel is a Founder and Chairman of Strategos, a company dedicated to helping its clients develop revolutionary strategies. He is also Visiting Professor of Strategic and International Management at London Business School.

The Economist calls Hamel "the world's reigning strategy guru." Peter Senge calls him "the most influential thinker on strategy in the Western world." As the author of a multitude of landmark business concepts, he has fundamentally changed the focus and content of strategy in many of the world's most successful companies. The *Journal of Business Strategy* recently ranked Professor Hamel as one of the top 25 business minds of the twentieth century.

His previous book, *Competing for the Future*, has been hailed by *The Economist*, the *Financial Times*, the *Washington Post*, and many other journals as one of the decade's most influential business books, and by *Business Week* as "Best Management Book of the Year." With C. K. Prahalad, Hamel has published seven articles in the *Harvard Business Review*, introducing such breakthrough concepts as strategic intent, core competence, corporate imagination, expeditionary marketing, and strategy as stretch. Hamel's more recent articles, "Strategy as Revolution" and "Bringing Silicon Valley Inside," are already on their way to becoming management classics. His articles have also been published in *Fortune*, the *Wall Street Journal*, MIT's *Sloan Management Review*, and a myriad of other journals. Hamel serves on the board of the Strategic Management Society.

Hamel has led initiatives within many of the world's leading companies. In his work he helps companies to first imagine and then create the new rules, new businesses, and new industries that will define the industrial landscape of the future.

He resides in Woodside, California.